Lecture Notes in Computer Science 4876

Commenced Publication in 1973
Founding and Former Series Editors:
Gerhard Goos, Juris Hartmanis, and Jan van Leeuwen

T0223155

Carlisle Adams Ali Miri Michael Wiener (Eds.)

Selected Areas in Cryptography

14th International Workshop, SAC 2007
Ottawa, Canada, August 16-17, 2007
Revised Selected Papers

 Springer

Volume Editors

Carlisle Adams
University of Ottawa, School of Information Technology and Engineering (SITE)
SITE Building, 800 King Edward Avenue, Ottawa, Ontario K1N 6N5, Canada
E-mail: cadams@site.uottawa.ca

Ali Miri
University of Ottawa, School of Information Technology and Engineering (SITE)
and Department of Mathematics and Statistics
Colonel By Hall (CBY), 161 Louis Pasture Street, Ottawa, Ontario K1N 6N5, Canada
E-mail: samiri@site.uottawa.ca

Michael Wiener
Cryptographic Clarity
20 Hennepin Street, Nepean, Ontario K2J 3Z4, Canada
E-mail: michael.james.wiener@gmail.com

Library of Congress Control Number: 2007941250

CR Subject Classification (1998): E.3, D.4.6, K.6.5, F.2.1-2, C.2, H.4.3

LNCS Sublibrary: SL 4 – Security and Cryptology

ISSN   0302-9743
ISBN-10   3-540-77359-2 Springer Berlin Heidelberg New York
ISBN-13   978-3-540-77359-7 Springer Berlin Heidelberg New York

Springer is a part of Springer Science+Business Media

springer.com

© Springer-Verlag Berlin Heidelberg 2007
Printed in Germany

Typesetting: Camera-ready by author, data conversion by Scientific Publishing Services, Chennai, India
Printed on acid-free paper   SPIN: 12206629   06/3180   5 4 3 2 1 0

Preface

SAC 2007 was the 14th in a series of annual workshops on Selected Areas in Cryptography. This is the first time this workshop was held at the University of Ottawa. Previous workshops were held at Queen's University in Kingston (1994, 1996, 1998, 1999, and 2005), Carleton University in Ottawa (1995, 1997, and 2003), University of Waterloo (2000 and 2004), Fields Institute in Toronto (2001), Memorial University of Newfoundland in St. Johns (2002), and Concordia University in Montreal (2006). The intent of the workshop is to provide a stimulating atmosphere where researchers in cryptology can present and discuss new work on selected areas of current interest. The themes for SAC 2007 were:

- Design and analysis of symmetric key cryptosystems
- Primitives for symmetric key cryptography, including block and stream ciphers, hash functions, and MAC algorithms
- Efficient implementations of symmetric and public key algorithms
- Innovative cryptographic defenses against malicious software

A total of 73 papers were submitted to SAC 2007. Of these, one was withdrawn by the authors, and 25 were accepted by the Program Committee for presentation at the workshop. In addition to these presentations, we were fortunate to have two invited speakers:

- Dan Bernstein: "Edwards Coordinates for Elliptic Curves"
- Moti Yung: "Cryptography and Virology Inter-Relationships." This talk was designated the Stafford Tavares Lecture.

We are grateful to the Program Committee and the many external reviewers for their hard work and expertise in selecting the program. They completed all reviews in time for discussion and final decisions despite events conspiring to compress the review schedule. We apologize if anyone was missed in the list of external reviewers.

We would like to thank the Ontario Research Network for Electronic Commerce (ORNEC) for financial support of the workshop. We would also like to thank Gail Deduk for administrative support and Aleks Essex and Terasan Niyomsataya for technical support.

Finally, we thank all those who submitted papers and the conference participants who made this year's workshop a great success.

October 2007

Carlisle Adams
Ali Miri
Michael Wiener

14th Annual Workshop on Selected Areas in Cryptography

August 16–17, 2007, Ottawa, Ontario, Canada

in cooperation with the
International Association for Cryptologic Research (IACR)

Conference Co-chairs

Carlisle Adams	University of Ottawa, Canada
Ali Miri	University of Ottawa, Canada
Michael Wiener	Cryptographic Clarity, Canada

Program Committee

Roberto Avanzi	Ruhr University Bochum, Germany
Orr Dunkelman	Katholieke Universiteit Leuven, Belgium
Ian Goldberg	University of Waterloo, Canada
Helena Handschuh	Spansion, France
M. Anwar Hasan	University of Waterloo, Canada
Antoine Joux	DGA, Université de Versailles St-Quentin-en-Yvelines, France
Pascal Junod	Nagravision, Switzerland
Tanja Lange	Technische Universiteit, Eindhoven, Netherlands
Arjen Lenstra	EPFL, Switzerland
Christof Paar	Ruhr University Bochum, Germany
Bart Preneel	Katholieke Universiteit Leuven, Belgium
Vincent Rijmen	Graz University of Technology, Austria
Matt Robshaw	France Telecom, France
Greg Rose	QUALCOMM, USA
Doug Stinson	University of Waterloo, Canada
Serge Vaudenay	EPFL, Switzerland
Robert Zuccherato	Entrust Inc., Canada

External Reviewers

Abdulaziz Alkhoraidly	Elena Andreeva	Thomas Baignères
Siavash Bayat-Sarmadi	Anja Becker	Côme Berbain
Daniel J. Bernstein	Eli Biham	Olivier Billet
Toni Bluher	Andrey Bogdanov	Reinier Broker

Christophe De Cannière
Scott Contini
Thomas Eisenbarth
Matthieu Finiasz
Jovan Golić
Arash Hariri
Laurent Imbert
David Jacobson
Alexandre Karlov
Cédric Lauradoux
Reynald Lercier
Marine Minier
Dag Arne Osvik
Souradyuti Paul
Emmanuel Prouff
Kai Schramm
Marc Stevens
Martin Vuagnoux
Huapeng Wu

Yaniv Carmeli
Christophe Doche
Lars Elmegaard-Fessel
Steven Galbraith
Johann Großschädl
Phil Hawkes
Sebastiaan Indesteege
Shaoquan Jiang
Shahram Khazaei
Gregor Leander
Cameron McDonald
Bodo Möller
Elisabeth Oswald
Raphael Phan
Christian Rechberger
Yaniv Shaked
Nicolas Theriault
Johannes Wolkerstorfer
Brecht Wyseur

Jaewook Chung
Nevine Ebeid
Andreas Enge
Henri Gilbert
Tim Guneysu
Rafi Hen
Takanori Isobe
Marcelo Kaihara
Mario Lamberger
Kerstin Lemke
Florian Mendel
Jean Monnerat
Sylvain Pasini
Norbert Pramstaller
Arash Reyhani-Masoleh
Martijn Stam
Frederik Vercauteren
Hongjun Wu
Lu Xiao

Table of Contents

Reduced Complexity Attacks on the Alternating Step Generator

Shahram Khazaei[1], Simon Fischer[2], and Willi Meier[2]

[1] EPFL, Lausanne, Switzerland
[2] FHNW, Windisch, Switzerland

Abstract. In this paper, we present some reduced complexity attacks on the Alternating Step Generator (ASG). The attacks are based on a quite general framework and mostly benefit from the low sampling resistance of the ASG, and of an abnormal behavior related to the distribution of the initial states of the stop/go LFSR's which produce a given segment of the output sequence. Our results compare well with previous results as they show a greater flexibility with regard to known output of the ASG, which amounts in reduced complexity. We will also give a closed form for the complexity of attacks on ASG (and SG) as presented in [13].

Keywords: Stream Cipher, Clock-Controlled Generator, Alternating Step Generator.

1 Introduction

The Alternating Step Generator (ASG), a well-known stream cipher proposed in [11], consists of two stop/go clocked binary LFSR's, $LFSR_X$ and $LFSR_Y$, and a regularly clocked binary LFSR, $LFSR_C$ of which the clock-control sequence is derived. The original description of ASG [11] is as follows. At each time, the clock-control bit determines which of the two stop/go LFSR's is clocked, and the output sequence is obtained as bit-wise sum of the two stop/go clocked LFSR sequences. It is known [13, 8, 12] that instead of working with the original definition of ASG we can consider a slightly different description for which the output is taken from the stop/go LFSR which has been clocked. More precisely, at each step first $LFSR_C$ is clocked; then if the output bit of $LFSR_C$ is one, $LFSR_X$ is clocked and its output bit is considered as the output bit of the generator, otherwise $LFSR_Y$ is clocked and the output bit of the generator is taken from this LFSR. Since in a cryptanalysis point of view these two generators are equivalent, we use the later one all over this paper and for simplicity we still call it ASG.

Several attacks have been proposed on ASG in the literature. Most of these attacks are applied in a divide-and-conquer based procedure targeting one or two of the involved LFSR's. We will focus on a divide-and-conquer attack which targets one of the two stop/go LFSR's.

A correlation attack on individual $LFSR_X$ or $LFSR_Y$ which is based on a specific edit probability has been introduced in [10]. The amount of required keystream is linear in terms of the length of the targeted LFSR and the correct initial state

C. Adams, A. Miri, and M. Wiener (Eds.): SAC 2007, LNCS 4876, pp. 1–16, 2007.

of the targeted LFSR is found through an exhaustive search over all possible initial states. In [13] some reduced complexity attacks on ASG and SG (Shrinking Generator, see [2]) were presented and the effectiveness of the attacks was verified numerically for SG while only few general ideas were proposed for ASG without any numerical or theoretical analysis. These methods avoid exhaustive search over all initial states, however, the amount of needed keystream is exponential in terms of the length of the targeted LFSR. One of our contributions of this paper is to give a closed form for these reduced complexity attacks.

Our major objective of this paper is to investigate a general method which does not perform an exhaustive search over all possible initial states of the targeted LFSR. We will take advantage of the low *sampling resistance* of ASG. The notion of sampling resistance was first introduced in [1] and it was shown that a low sampling resistance has a big impact on the efficiency of time/memory/data trade-off attacks. Sampling is the capability of efficiently producing all the initial states which generate an output sequence starting with a particular m-bit pattern. Recently it was noticed that sampling may be useful along with other attacks in a unified framework [3]. The results of this paper represent a positive attempt to exploit such a connection for a concrete stream cipher.

For ASG, sampling is easy if the output length m is chosen to be about the total length of the two stop/go LFSR's. Another weakness of ASG which enables us to mount our attack is that different initial states of any of the two stop/go LFSR's have far different probabilities to be accepted as a candidate which can produce a given segment of length m of the output sequence. Systematic computer simulations confirm this striking behavior. The highly non-uniform distribution of different initial states of any of the stop/go LFSR's is valid for any segment of length about m, and the effect is more abnormal for some special outputs which we refer to as weak outputs. Thanks to the low sampling resistance of ASG we first try to find a subset of the most probable initial states which contains the correct one, then using the probabilistic edit distance [10] we distinguish the correct initial state. Our general approach can be faster than exhaustive search even if the amount of keystream is linear in terms of the length of the targeted LFSR, improving the results in [10]. With regard to reduced complexity attacks, our approach does assume less restricted output segments than in [13], a fact that has been confirmed by large-scale experiments. This enables attacks with significantly lower data complexity even for large instances of ASG (whereas asymptotical complexity is shown to be comparable over known methods).

The paper is organized as follows. In section 2 we will give a comprehensive list of the known attacks on ASG along with a short overview of them. A closed form for the reduced complexity attacks of [13] on ASG is given in Sect. 3. In Sect. 4 we present our attack in detail. Experimental results are in Sect. 5, and we finally conclude in Sect. 6.

2   Previous Attacks on ASG

Several attacks have been proposed on the ASG in the literature. This section will provide an overview of the different attacks. We will denote the length of registers $\mathsf{LFSR_C}$, $\mathsf{LFSR_X}$ and $\mathsf{LFSR_Y}$ by L_C, L_X and L_Y, respectively. If we only use parameter L, we apply the simplification $L := L_C = L_X = L_Y$.

2.1 Divide-and-Conquer Linear Consistency Attack

It is shown in [11] that the initial state of $\mathsf{LFSR_C}$ can be recovered by targeting its initial state in a divide-and-conquer based attack based on the fact that the output sequence of the ASG can be split into the regularly clocked $\mathsf{LFSR_X}$ and $\mathsf{LFSR_Y}$ sequences, which are then easily tested for low linear complexity. Hence the complexity of this attack is $\mathcal{O}(\min^2(L_X, L_Y)2^{L_C})$ assuming that only the feedback polynomial of $\mathsf{LFSR_C}$ is available. Under the assumption that the feedback polynomial of all LFSR's are available, which is the basic assumption of all other known attacks (including ours in this paper), the complexity of this attack would be $\mathcal{O}(\min(L_X, L_Y)2^{L_C})$ instead, since a parity check test can be used in place of linear complexity test. In this case the attack is a linear consistency attack [17]. We will use the idea of this attack to sample ASG in Sect. 4.1.

2.2 Edit Distance Correlation Attack

A correlation attack on $\mathsf{LFSR_X}$ and $\mathsf{LFSR_Y}$ combined, which is based on a specific edit distance, was proposed in [8]. If the initial states of $\mathsf{LFSR_X}$ and $\mathsf{LFSR_Y}$ are guessed correctly, the edit distance is equal to zero. If the guess is incorrect, the probability of obtaining the zero edit distance was experimentally shown to exponentially decrease in the length of the output string. Later, a theoretical analysis of this attack was developed in [12, 5]. The minimum length of the output string to be successful for an attack is about four times total lengths of $\mathsf{LFSR_X}$ and $\mathsf{LFSR_Y}$. As the complexity of computing the edit distance is quadratic in the length of the output string, the complexity of this attack is $\mathcal{O}((L_X + L_Y)^2 2^{L_X+L_Y})$. In addition, it was shown that the initial state of $\mathsf{LFSR_C}$ can then be reconstructed with complexity $\mathcal{O}(2^{0.27L_C})$.

2.3 Edit Probability Correlation Attack

A correlation attack on individual $\mathsf{LFSR_X}$ or $\mathsf{LFSR_Y}$ which is based on a specific edit probability was developed in [10]. For a similar approach, see [13]. The edit probability is defined for two binary strings: an input string, produced by the regularly clocked targeted LFSR from an assumed initial state, and a given segment of the ASG output sequence. The edit probability is defined as the probability that the given output string is produced from an assumed input string by the ASG in a probabilistic model, where the LFSR sequences are assumed to be independent and purely random. It turns out that the edit probability tends to be larger when the guess about the LFSR initial state is correct. More precisely, by experimental analysis of the underlying statistical hypothesis testing problem, it was shown that the minimum length of the output string to be successful for an attack is about forty lengths of the targeted LFSR. As the complexity of computing the edit probability is quadratic in the length of the output string, the complexity of reconstructing both LFSR initial states is $\mathcal{O}(\max^2(L_X, L_Y)2^{\max(L_X,L_Y)})$. This yields a considerable improvement over the edit distance correlation attack if L_X and L_Y are approximately equal and relatively large, as is typically suggested (for example, see, [15]).

Remark 1. Note that "edit distance correlation attack" means that the initial states of LFSR$_X$ and LFSR$_Y$ can be recovered regardless of the unknown initial state of LFSR$_C$, whereas "edit probability correlation attack" means that the initial state of LFSR$_X$ (LFSR$_Y$) can be recovered regardless of unknown initial states of LFSR$_Y$ (LFSR$_X$) and LFSR$_C$. However, the targeted LFSR initial states should be tested exhaustively. The main motivation for this paper is to investigate if the initial states of LFSR$_X$ (LFSR$_Y$) can be reconstructed faster than exhaustive search regardless of unknown initial states of LFSR$_Y$ (LFSR$_X$) and LFSR$_C$.

2.4   Reduced Complexity Attacks

A first step to faster reconstruction of LFSR's initial states was suggested in [13], in which some reduced complexity attacks on ASG and SG are presented. In the next section, we will give a general expression in the parameter L_X, the length of target register LFSR$_X$ (and in Appendix A, we give general expressions for SG). A second movement to faster reconstruction of LFSR initial states was suggested in [7], using an approach based on computing the posterior probabilities of individual bits of the regularly clocked LFSR$_X$ and LFSR$_Y$ sequences, when conditioned on a given segment of the output sequence. It is shown that these probabilities can be efficiently computed and the deviation of posterior probabilities from one half are theoretically analysed. As these probabilities represent soft-valued estimates of the corresponding bits of the considered LFSR sequences when regularly clocked, it is argued that the initial state reconstruction is thus in principle reduced to fast correlation attacks on regularly clocked LFSR's such as the ones based on iterative probabilistic decoding algorithms. Although this valuable work shows some vulnerability of the ASG towards fast correlation attacks, the practical use of these probabilities has not yet been deeply investigated. Nonetheless, these posterior probabilities can certainly be used to mount a distinguisher on ASG. This can be compared with [4], a similar work on SG for which a distinguisher was later developed in [9].

3   Johansson's Reduced Complexity Attacks

In [13] some reduced complexity attacks on the ASG and SG were presented, and the effectiveness of the attacks was verified numerically for the SG (while only few general ideas were proposed for the ASG without any numerical or theoretical analysis). We give a closed form for the reduced complexity attack on ASG, using the approximation $\binom{n}{w} \approx 2^{nh(w/n)}$ where $h(p)$ is the binary entropy function defined as

$$h(p) := -p\log_2(p) - (1-p)\log_2(1-p) \ . \tag{1}$$

In the first scenario, the attacker waits for a segment of M consecutive zeros (or ones) in the output sequence and assumes that exactly $M/2$ of them are from LFSR$_X$. This is true with probability $\beta = \binom{M}{M/2}2^{-M}$. The remaining $L - M/2$ bits of LFSR$_X$ are then found by exhaustive search. Time and data complexities of this attack are $C_T = L^2 2^{L-M/2}\beta^{-1} = L^2 2^{L+M/2}\binom{M}{M/2}^{-1}$ and $C_D = 2^{M-1}\beta^{-1} = 2^{2M-1}\binom{M}{M/2}^{-1}$ (using overlapping blocks of keystream). Ignoring the polynomial and constant terms and equaling the time and data complexities, we have $L - M/2 = M$, which shows $M = \frac{2}{3}L$. Thus the optimal complexities of this attack are $C_T = \mathcal{O}(L^2 2^{\frac{2}{3}L})$ and $C_D = \mathcal{O}(2^{\frac{2}{3}L})$. These arguments apply to both LFSR$_X$ and LFSR$_Y$.

Remark 2. The total time of the attack is composed of the time to filter the blocks of data with desired properties, and of the time to further process the filtered blocks. Although the unit of examination time of these two phases are not equal, we ignore this difference to simplify the analysis.

In another scenario in [13], it is suggested to wait for a segment of length M containing at most w ones (zeros) and make the assumption that only half of the zeros (ones) come from the LFSR$_X$. All the ones (zeros) and the remaining zeros (ones) are assumed to come from the LFSR$_Y$. This is true with probability $\beta = 2^{-w}\binom{M-w}{(M-w)/2}2^{-(M-w)}$. The time and data complexities of this attack are then $C_T = L^2 2^{L-(M-w)/2}\beta^{-1}$ and $C_D = 2^{M-1}\binom{M}{w}^{-1}\beta^{-1}$, respectively. With $w := \alpha M$, ignoring the constant and polynomial terms, and equaling the time and data complexities, we have $L-(1-\alpha)M/2+\alpha M = M - h(\alpha)M + \alpha M$, which results in $M = L/(3/2-\alpha/2-h(\alpha))$. The minimum value of the exponents $M(1-h(\alpha)+\alpha)$ is $0.6406L$, which is achieved for $\alpha \approx 0.0727$ (and hence $M = 0.9193L$ and $w = 0.0668L$). Therefore, the optimal complexities are $C_T = \mathcal{O}(L^2 2^{0.64L})$ and $C_D = \mathcal{O}(2^{0.64L})$. Note that this complexity is only for reconstruction of the initial state of LFSR$_X$. The complexity for recovering the initial state of LFSR$_Y$ highly depends on the position of ones (zeros) in the block. In the best case, the block starts with w ones (zeros) and the complexity becomes $C_T = L^2 2^{L-(M+w)/2}$. In the worst case, the attacker has to search for the positions of ones (zeros), and the complexity becomes $C_T = \binom{(M+w)/2}{w}L^2 2^{L-(M-w)/2}$. It is difficult to give an average complexity, but we expect that it is close to the worst case complexity. With $M = 0.9193L$ and $w = 0.0668L$, this gives $C_T = \mathcal{O}(L^2 2^{0.69L})$ to recover the initial state of LFSR$_Y$. Consequently, as a distinguishing attack, this scenario operates slightly better than the previous one, but as an initial state recovery it is slightly worse.

4   New Reduced Complexity Attack

Before we describe our attack in detail, let us introduce some notations. Throughout the paper, the symbols Pr and E are respectively used for probability of an event and expectation of a random variable. For simplicity we do not distinguish between random variables and their instances. We use $A := \{a_i\}$ for a general binary sequence, $A_k^m := \{a_i\}_{i=k}^m$ for a segment of it and $A^m := \{a_i\}_{i=1}^m$ for a prefix of length m. The number of 1's in A is denoted by $\text{wt}(A)$. We define the first derivative of A as $\{a_i + a_{i+1}\}$ and denote it by $\dot{A}$. Let C, X, Y and Z denote the regular output sequences of LFSR_C, LFSR_X, LFSR_Y and the output sequence of the ASG itself, respectively. The initial state of the LFSR's can be represented by C^L, X^L and Y^L.

4.1   Sampling Resistance

Any initial state (C^L, X^L, Y^L) of ASG which can produce Z^m, a given prefix of the output sequence of ASG, is called a preimage of Z^m. The sampling resistance is defined as 2^{-m} where m is the maximum value for which we can efficiently produce all preimages of m-bit outputs. As will be shown in this subsection, the low sampling resistance of ASG is an essential ingredient for our attack. Let $\mathcal{A}(Z^m)$ denote the set of all preimages of Z^m. Based on the divide-and-conquer linear consistency attack, introduced in Sect. 2, we can compute $\mathcal{A}(Z^m)$ as in Alg. 1.

Algorithm 1. Sampling of ASG

Input: Output sequence Z^m of m bits.
Output: Find $\mathcal{A}(Z^m)$ with all preimages of Z^m.
1: Initially, set $\mathcal{A}(Z^m) = \emptyset$.
2: **for all** non-zero initial states C^L **do**
3:     Set $\mathcal{X} = \mathcal{Y} = \emptyset$.
4:     Compute C^m, a prefix of length m of the output sequence of LFSR_C.
5:     Based on C^m, split up Z^m into X^w and Y^{m-w}, where $w = \text{wt}(C^m)$.
6:     Add all (non-zero) X^L to $\mathcal{X}$, if LFSR_X can generate X^w.
7:     Add all (non-zero) Y^L to $\mathcal{Y}$, if LFSR_Y can generate Y^{m-w}.
8:     For all $X^L \in \mathcal{X}$ and $Y^L \in \mathcal{Y}$, add (C^L, X^L, Y^L) to the set $\mathcal{A}(Z^m)$.
9: **end for**

Let us discuss the complexity of Alg. 1. If $|\mathcal{A}(Z^m)| \leq 2^L$, then the overall complexity is 2^L, because the complexity of Steps 3 to 8 are $\mathcal{O}(1)$. On the other hand, if $|\mathcal{A}(Z^m)| > 2^L$, then Steps 3 to 8 introduce additional solutions, and overall complexity is about $|\mathcal{A}(Z^m)|$. The following statement is given under the assumption of balancedness, *i.e.* the average number of preimages of ASG for any output Z^m is about 2^{3L-m}, where $m \leq 3L$.

Statement 1. *Time complexity of Alg. 1 is* $C_T = \mathcal{O}(\max(2^L, 2^{3L-m}))$.

With the previous definition of sampling resistance, this algorithm can be considered as an efficient sampling algorithm iff $|\mathcal{A}(Z^m)| \geq \mathcal{O}(2^L)$ or equivalently $m \leq 2L$. That is, the sampling resistance of ASG is about 2^{-k} with $k = 2L$ the total length of the two stop/go LFSR's.

A related problem is how to find a multiset $\mathcal{B}$ with T uniformly random independent elements of $\mathcal{A}(Z^m)$. We suggest to modify Alg. 1 as follows: $\mathcal{A}(Z^m)$ is replaced by $\mathcal{B}$ and T is added as another input parameter. In Step 2, a uniform random (non-zero) initial state C^L is chosen, and Steps 3 to 8 are not modified. The new Steps 2 to 8 are then repeated, until T preimages have been found. This modified algorithm will be referred to as Alg. 1B. We assume correctness of the algorithm, *i.e.* the preimages found with Alg. 1B are uniformly random elements of $\mathcal{A}(Z^m)$ (for which we will give experimental evidence). The following statement is presented under the assumption that the average number of preimages of ASG for any output Z^m, given some fixed initial state of LFSR$_C$, is about 2^{2L-m}, where $m \leq 2L$.

Statement 2. *Time complexity of Alg. 1B is $C_T = \mathcal{O}(T)$ for $m \leq 2L$, and $C_T = \mathcal{O}(\min(2^L, T2^{m-2L}))$ for $m > 2L$, where $1 \leq T \leq \mathcal{O}(2^{3L-m})$.*

4.2   Conditional Distribution of the Initial States

With the sampling algorithm described in Sect. 4.1, we can find T random preimages of an output sequence Z^m. The natural question which arises is *how large should T be so that our subset contains the correct initial state of one of the LFSR's, let say* LFSR$_X$? The answer is related to the conditional distribution of different initial states of LFSR$_X$ which can produce a given segment of length m of the output sequence of the ASG. Consider the following two general propositions (with proofs in Appendix B):

Proposition 1. *Let $X_0, \ldots, X_T$ be a sequence of i.i.d. random variables, defined over the finite set $\{s_1, \ldots, s_N\}$ with probability distribution $p := (p_1, \ldots, p_N)$ and $p_i := \Pr(X_j = s_i)$. Then, the probability $P := \Pr(X_0 \in \{X_1, \ldots, X_T\})$ that a realisation of $X_1, \ldots, X_T$ contains a realisation of X_0 is*

$$P = 1 - \sum_{i=1}^{N}(1 - p_i)^T p_i \ . \tag{2}$$

Proposition 2. *Let $H := -\sum_{i=1}^{N} p_i \log_2(p_i)$ be the entropy of random variable X_j. With about $T = 2^H$, the probability $\Pr(X_0 \in \{X_1, \ldots, X_T\})$ is significant.*

To apply these propositions to the situation of ASG, let $\mathcal{A}_X(x, Z_m)$ be a subset of $\mathcal{A}(Z_m)$, defined by $\{(u, v, w) \in \mathcal{A}(Z_m) \mid v = x\}$. The conditional probability for a fixed initial state x of LFSR$_X$ is then defined by $p_X(x|Z^m) = |\mathcal{A}_X(x, Z_m)|/|\mathcal{A}(Z_m)|$. Consequently, we need to draw about $T = 2^{H_X}$ uniformly random elements of $\mathcal{A}(Z^m)$ to include the correct initial state of LFSR$_X$ where H_X is the conditional entropy of the initial state of the LFSR$_X$ given Z^m, defined by

$$H_X(Z^m) = -\sum_{x} p_X(x|Z^m) \cdot \log_2 p_X(x|Z^m) \ . \tag{3}$$

The same argument applies to LFSR$_Y$, and the symmetry of ASG motivates the simplification $H := H_X = H_Y$ (if not mentioned otherwise). Another natural question is the expected number of different elements Q drawn in this sample of size T. This is related to the Coupon-Collector Problem with non-uniform distribution. However, we can assume that $Tp_i \ll 1$, which results in $Q \approx T$.

Remark 3. Any adversary who *would know* the distribution p_X could try to recover the unknown initial state of $\mathsf{LFSR_X}$ by considering the most probable initial state first, then the second most probable one and so on. Here, to cope with *unknown* distribution p_X, we simulate it by choosing uniformly random elements of $\mathcal{A}(Z^m)$ (where element x is chosen with probability $p_X(x|Z^m)$). This procedure is similar to [14] in which an equivalent description of the underlying cipher was used, for which the initial states were no longer equiprobable.

Remark 4. As mentioned in Sect. 2.4, it has been suggested in [7] to take advantage of the posterior probabilities of the individual bits of the regularly clocked $\mathsf{LFSR_X}$ and $\mathsf{LFSR_Y}$ sequences, when conditioned on a given segment of the output sequence for faster reconstruction of LFSR initial states. Our attack can be considered as a generalization of this attack in which we take advantage of the posterior probabilities of the initial states rather than individual bits, when conditioned on a given segment of the output sequence. Although unlike [7] we are able to give an estimation for the time and data complexities of our attack, a theoretical analysis of the conditional entropy of the initial states remains an open problem, see Sect. 5.1.

4.3 Description of the Attack

In the basic edit probability correlation attack on the ASG [6,10], the edit probability is computed for each of the 2^L possible initial states of $\mathsf{LFSR_X}$ (given a segment of length $n \approx 40L$ of the output sequence of the ASG) to find the correct initial state. This is repeated also for $\mathsf{LFSR_Y}$, and finally the initial state of $\mathsf{LFSR_C}$ can be recovered. In our improved attack, we take the output sequence Z^m into account to compute a smaller multiset $\mathcal{B}$ of candidates of initial states, which is of size T and contains the correct initial state of $\mathsf{LFSR_X}$ (resp. $\mathsf{LFSR_Y}$) with some probability P, see Prop. 1. The multiset $\mathcal{B}$ is constructed with Alg. 1B. In Alg. 2, we give a formalisation of this attack.

Remark 5. One would think that it is better to compute the edit probability between Z^n and only the LFSR output sequence of all *distinct* initial states suggested by multiset $\mathcal{B}$ to avoid processing the same initial state several times. However, this needs memory of $\mathcal{O}(|\mathcal{B}|)$ and extra effort to keep the track of the non-distinct initial states. Since $|\mathcal{B}| \approx T$ the achieved gain is negligible and therefore we alternatively compute the edit probability at the time where a preimage is found.

Algorithm 2. Attack on ASG

Input: Parameters T, m, n, output Z^n.
Output: Recover the initial state of ASG with some success probability δ.
 1: Given the segment Z^m, find T preimages using Alg. 1B.
 2: Compute the edit probability between Z^n and the output sequence for each suggested initial state.
 3: Choose the most probable candidates for $\mathsf{LFSR_X}$ resp. $\mathsf{LFSR_Y}$.
 4: Recover $\mathsf{LFSR_C}$ and verify the validity, see Sect. 2.3.

Parameters for the Entropy. The complexity of the attack is related to the conditional entropy H. However, for large instances of ASG, the conditional probabilities and hence H are unknown. To be able to evaluate our attack and give an explicit expression for the data and time complexities, we need to know the relation between conditional entropies H and all parameters which can possibly affect them. The parameters are LFSR's feedback polynomials and the output prefix Z^m, which implicitly include the lengths of LFSR's and output segment length as well. In our simulations we noticed that feedback polynomials have almost no effect and the only important parameters are LFSR lengths L, the size of the output segment m (as larger values of m reduce uncertainty about the correct preimage), and the weight w of the output segment Z^m or the weight w of the first derivative of the output segment Z^m (as will be shown in our simulations). The entropy is significantly reduced if $|\mathrm{wt}(Z^m)/m - 0.5| \gg 0$ (*i.e.* many zeros or ones) or if $\mathrm{wt}(\dot{Z}^m)/m \ll 0.5$ (*i.e.* many runs of zeros or ones). This can be explained by the fact that a biased output segment results in a biased LFSR segment, and we will refer to such outputs as *weak* outputs. In Sect. 5.1, we will predict the average value of H depending on these parameters using some regression analysis, hence $\mathrm{E}(H) = f(L, m, w)$.

Time Complexity. Let us discuss time complexity of Alg. 2. According to Prop. 2, we set $T = 2^H$. Complexity of Step 1 is described in Statement 2. Computation of the edit probability distance of a single preimage takes about $\mathcal{O}(L^2)$, hence complexity of Step 2 is at most $\mathcal{O}(L^2 T)$. Finally, the complexity of Step 4 is $\mathcal{O}(2^{0.27L})$, which can be neglected here.

Statement 3. *Time complexity of Alg. 2 is about $C_T = \mathcal{O}(L^2 2^H)$ for $m \le 2L$, and $C_T = \mathcal{O}(2^{H+m-2L})$ for $m \gg 2L$.*

This should be compared to the attack by Golic *et al.* of complexity $C_T = \mathcal{O}(L^2 2^L)$ using an output sequence of length about $C_D = 40L$ which was described in Sect. 2.3, and Johansson's attack of complexity $C_T = \mathcal{O}(L^2 2^{\frac{2}{3}L})$ using an output sequence of length $C_D = \mathcal{O}(2^{\frac{2}{3}L})$ as described in Sect. 3.

Data Complexity. The parameter w has some influence on the data complexity of our attack. Once we know that the weight of Z^m is at most w or at least $m-w$, or that the weight of the first derivative of Z^m is at most w, a prefix of length about $n = 40L$ suffices to recover the initial states, see [10]. However, in order to obtain such an output segment Z_{t+1}^{t+m} for some t, the required amount of keystream bits is $C_D = 2^m (3 \sum_{i=0}^{w} \binom{m}{i})^{-1}$. This can be roughly approximated by $C_D = \mathcal{O}(2^{m(1-h(w/m))})$.

Success Probability. The success probability δ of the attack depends on three events: 1) The probability that our multiset $\mathcal{B}$ of size $T = 2^H$ contains the correct initial state. 2) The probability that our prediction of the entropy gives at least H. 3) The success probability of the edit distance correlation attack. The first probability corresponds to P according to Eq. 2. The second probability comes from the fact that we use an estimation of the average value of H instead of the exact value of H.

5 Experimental Results

In this section, we give experimental results on ASG. We estimate the conditional entropy, give a detailed discussion of the complexity for different scenarios and present an example of an attack.

5.1 Distribution of Initial States

For specific instances of ASG, we investigate the distributions of initial states. Here, ASG is small enough such that an exact computation of initial states with Alg. 1 is feasible. We use registers of the same length, but our results do not significantly change if the lengths are pairwise coprime and about the same, as suggested in [15]. The following example has illustrative character: First, we compute the distributions for one fixed output sequence. Second, the block size m is varied for average-weighted output sequences. Third, an output sequences of low weight is investigated.

Example 1. Consider a setup with $L = 20$ and some randomly chosen primitive feedback polynomials. Fix a random output sequence Z^m of $m = 40$ bits according to

$$Z^m = 1110110110100101010000100100101011000110 .$$

The number of preimages is $|\mathcal{A}(Z^m)| = 1\,046\,858 = 2^{20.00}$, and the entropies are $H_C = 17.49$, $H_X = 17.32$, and $H_Y = 17.34$. If this output is padded by the 2 additional bits 01, then the number of preimages becomes $|\mathcal{A}(Z^m)| = 264\,265 = 2^{18.01}$ and the entropies are $H_C = 16.26$, $H_X = 16.46$, and $H_Y = 16.45$. On the other hand, consider the following output sequence for $m = 40$ and with weight $w = 7$,

$$Z^m = 0001010000100000000110000001000100000000 .$$

The number of preimages for this low-weight output sequence is $|\mathcal{A}(Z^m)| = 1\,117\,725 = 2^{20.09}$, with entropies $H_C = 17.39$, $H_X = 12.24$, and $H_Y = 12.63$. □

Let us discuss this example. The number of preimages is about 2^{60-m}, as expected. In all three registers, the entropy is not maximal for the random output sequence of size $m = 40$. This may be explained by the fact that sequences are not fully random, as they satisfy a linear recurrence. In the stop/go LFSR's, the entropy is strongly reduced for outputs of low weight, without any losses in the number of preimages. Notice that H_C does not depend on the weight of the output, which is optimal for efficient sampling.

In the following we will focus on the case $m = 2L$. The entropy H of the stop/go LFSR's is exactly determined for different values of L and w, where $L = 5, \ldots, 21$ and $w = 0, \ldots, m$. More precisely, given some L (and randomly

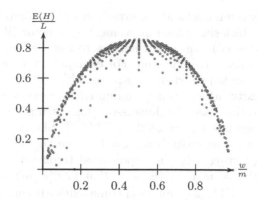

Fig. 1. $E(H)/L$ versus w/m for all $0 \le w \le m$ and $5 \le L \le 21$

chosen primitive feedback polynomials), we determine the average entropy $E(H)$ using 500 randomly chosen outputs of weight w. The values of $E(H)/L$ as a function of w/m are shown in Fig. 1. The inner dots in this figure relate to smaller values of L, and the outer dots relate to larger values of L. A convergence behavior of $E(H)/L$ for increasing L is perceivable from this figure.

It turns out that $E(H)/L$ can be well approximated by a scaled binary entropy function, namely $E(H)/L \approx \gamma \cdot h(w/m)$ with $0 < \gamma \le 1$ depending on L. Notice that $\gamma = \max_w (E(H)/L)$, which can be well approximated by $\gamma \approx 1 - 1/(0.19L + 3.1)$, see Appendix C. Consequently, with this regression analysis, the average value of the entropy is approximated by:

$$E(H) \approx \gamma(L) \cdot L \cdot h\left(\frac{w}{m}\right) \tag{4}$$

$$\gamma(L) \approx 1 - \frac{1}{0.19L + 3.1}. \tag{5}$$

In the case $w = \text{wt}(\dot{Z}^m)$ the shape is not symmetric, however it seems that for $w/m < 0.5$ for a fixed L the figures of $E(H)$ versus w/m are well comparable regardless of what w represents ($w = \text{wt}(\dot{Z}^m)$ or $w = \text{wt}(Z^m)$), see Appendix C. For $m > 2L$, the expected entropy does not correspond to this functional form anymore. The maximum of $H(w/m)$ decreases linearly with m, but the graph of $E(H)/L$ versus w/m is broader compared to $h(w/m)$, which means that a reduction of the entropy requires an output of very low weight. We do not further investigate this scenario.

5.2 Complexity of the Attack

Our attack allows different time/data trade-offs. We describe the complexity of our attack for $m = 2L$ and different values of parameters L and w. According to Statement 3, time complexity of our attack is $C_T = \mathcal{O}(L^2 2^H)$. Including the approximation for H, we obtain $C_T = \mathcal{O}(L^2 2^{\gamma L h(w/m)})$. Given an random output sequence, the complexity of our attack is $C_T = \mathcal{O}(L^2 2^{\gamma L})$. In this case the data complexity is minimal and our attack should be compared to the attack by Golic et al. [10] which shows an improvement by a factor $2^{(1-\gamma)L}$. In the limit $\gamma \to 1$ (hence for $L \to \infty$), our attack reduces to the previous attack. However for moderate values there is some gain. For example, we expect $\gamma = 0.945$ for $L = 80$, which gives an improvement of a factor $2^{4.4}$.

Reduced complexity attacks can be mounted by using weak outputs. This can be compared to the attack by Johansson [13]. Asymptotical data complexity of our attack becomes $C_D = \mathcal{O}(2^{m(1-h(w/m))})$. Similar to what we do in Sect. 3, the optimised complexity is achieved if time and data complexities are almost equal. Considering only the exponential terms and $\gamma = 1$, this happens when $h(w/m)L = m(1 - h(w/m))$, that is $h(w/m) = 2/3$ and hence $w \in \{0.174m, 0.826m\}$. The asymptotical complexities become $C_T = \mathcal{O}(L^2 2^{\frac{2}{3}L})$ and $C_D = \mathcal{O}(2^{\frac{2}{3}L})$, which is identical to the complexities of the attack by Johansson, see Sect. 3. However, compared to the simple attack in [13], it is clear that our attack allows for more flexibility in the structure of the output sequence: the weight can be arbitrary, we can also use outputs of low weight derivative, and we do not need a hypothesis about the origin of the output bits. With a more subtle (non-asymptotical) investigation of the complexities, we show that data (and/or time) complexity can be significantly reduced with our attack. More precisely, we evaluate the exact complexities of our and Johansson's attack for reasonable value of L. Regarding Johansson's attack, consider the special point $M = \frac{2}{3}L$ in the time/data tradeoff curve. For $L = 80$, this gives $C_T = 2^{69.4}$ and $C_D = 2^{55.2}$. If we choose $w = 0.21m$ in our attack, we obtain about the same time complexity and require only $C_D = 2^{42.3}$ data. This is an improvement of a factor $2^{12.9}$ (notice that a significant reduction can be expected even for $\gamma = 1$).

5.3   Example of an Attack

In this section, we present a large-scale example of a partial attack. We fix a random initial state in all three registers, such that the corresponding output sequence has weight $w = 0.174m$. Then, H is computed according to Eq. 4 and 5. Alg. 1B is used to compute the multiset $\mathcal{B}$ of size $T = 2^H$, and we check if the correct initial state of the LFSR$_X$ (resp. LFSR$_Y$) is included in $\mathcal{B}$. This is repeated several times, in order to determine the success probability P. In addition, time complexity of Alg. 1B is measured experimentally: For each choice of C^L, the complexity is increased by the number of preimages found (and by one if no preimage can be found), see Remark 5. For $m = 2L$, this should be compared to $C_T = \mathcal{O}(T)$, see Statement 2. Notice that we do not implement the edit probability correlation attack and rely on the results of [10].

Example 2. Let $L = 42$ and fix a random initial state such that the corresponding output sequence Z^m of $m = 84$ bits has weight $w = 14$. The expected entropy becomes $H = 24.16$, we set $T = 2^H = 18\,782\,717$ and apply Alg. 1B. This is repeated 200 times, and the correct initial state of LFSR$_X$ is found in 84 cases which shows a success probability of $P = 0.42$ for our algorithm. The average time complexity of the sampling algorithm is $2^{25.35}$.   □

6 Conclusions

A reduced complexity attack on the Alternating Step generator (ASG) has been presented, the success of which has been confirmed experimentally. For comparison, the complexity of the best previous attack has been determined and described in closed form. Estimates of the overall complexity of our new attack are shown to improve the complexity of the previous attack. Our attack allows for greater flexibility in known output data constraints, and hence for lower data complexity, for being successful. The attack method demonstrates the usefulness of a quite general attack principle exemplified in the case of ASG: to exploit low sampling resistance and heavily biased inputs for outputs satisfying certain constraints.

Acknowledgments

This work is supported in part by the National Competence Center in Research on Mobile Information and Communication Systems (NCCR-MICS), a center of the Swiss National Science Foundation under grant number 5005-67322. The third author is supported by Hasler Foundation www.haslerfoundation.ch under project number 2005. We would like to thank the anonymous reviewers for their helpful comments.

References

1. Biryukov, A., Shamir, A., Wagner, D.: Real Time Cryptanalysis of A5/1 on a PC. In: Schneier, B. (ed.) FSE 2000. LNCS, vol. 1978, pp. 1–18. Springer, Heidelberg (2001)
2. Coppersmith, D., Krawczyk, H., Mansour, Y.: The Shrinking Generator. In: Stinson, D.R. (ed.) CRYPTO 1993. LNCS, vol. 773, pp. 22–39. Springer, Heidelberg (1994)
3. Fischer, S., Meier, W.: Algebraic Immunity of S-boxes and Augmented Functions. In: Biryukov, A. (ed.) FSE 2007. LNCS, vol. 4593. Springer, Heidelberg (2007)
4. Dj. Golic, J.: Correlation Analysis of the Shrinking Generator. In: Kilian, J. (ed.) CRYPTO 2001. LNCS, vol. 2139, pp. 440–457. Springer, Heidelberg (2001)
5. Dj. Golic, J.: Embedding probabilities for the Alternating Step Generator. IEEE Transactions on Information Theory 51(7), 2543–2553 (2005)
6. Dj. Golic, J., Menicocci, R.: Edit Probability Correlation Attacks on Stop/Go Clocked Keystream Generators. J. Cryptology 16(1), 41–68 (2003)
7. Dj. Golic, J., Menicocci, R.: Correlation Analysis of the Alternating Step Generator. Des. Codes Cryptography 31(1), 51–74 (2004)
8. Dj. Golic, J., Menicocci, R.: Edit Distance Correlation Attack on the Alternating Step Generator. In: Kaliski Jr., B.S. (ed.) CRYPTO 1997. LNCS, vol. 1294, pp. 499–512. Springer, Heidelberg (1997)
9. Dj. Golic, J., Menicocci, R.: Statistical Distinguishers for Irregularly Decimated Linear Recurring Sequences. IEEE Transactions on Information Theory 52(3), 1153–1159 (2006)
10. Dj. Golic, J., Menicocci, R.: Edit Probability Correlation Attack on the Alternating Step Generator. In: Sequences and Their Applications - SETA 1998 (1998)

11. Günther, C.G.: Alternating Step Generators Controlled by De Bruijn Sequences. In: Price, W.L., Chaum, D. (eds.) EUROCRYPT 1987. LNCS, vol. 304, pp. 5–14. Springer, Heidelberg (1988)
12. Jiang, S., Gong, G.: On Edit Distance Attack to Alternating Step Generator. In: Other Combinatorial Structures, pp. 85–92 (2003)
13. Johansson, T.: Reduced Complexity Correlation Attacks on Two Clock-Controlled Generators. In: Ohta, K., Pei, D. (eds.) ASIACRYPT 1998. LNCS, vol. 1514, pp. 342–356. Springer, Heidelberg (1998)
14. Meier, W., Staffelbach, O.: Analysis of Pseudo Random Sequence Generated by Cellular Automata. In: Davies, D.W. (ed.) EUROCRYPT 1991. LNCS, vol. 547, pp. 186–199. Springer, Heidelberg (1991)
15. Menezes, A.J., Van Oorschot, P.C., Vanstone, S.A.: Handbook of Applied Cryptography. CRC Press, Boca Raton, USA (1997)
16. Sundaresan, R.: Guessing Under Source Uncertainty. IEEE Transactions on Information Theory 53(1), 269–287 (2007)
17. Zeng, K., Yang, C.H., Rao, T.R.N.: On the Linear Consistency Test (LCT) in Cryptanalysis with Applications. In: Brassard, G. (ed.) CRYPTO 1989. LNCS, vol. 435, pp. 164–174. Springer, Heidelberg (1990)

A   Johansson's Reduced Complexity Attack on SG

Here, we give a closed form for the reduced complexity attacks on SG in [13]. In the approach B, the attacker waits for an output sequence of length $2M + 1$ of the form $(z_{t-M}, z_{t-M+1}, ..., z_{t-1}, z_t, z_{t+1}, ..., z_{t+M-1}, z_{t+M}) = (0, 0, ..., 0, 1, 0, ..., 0, 0)$. Then, an exhaustive search is performed over all typical initial states $(x_1, x_2, ..., x_L)$ satisfying

$$\Pr(x_i = 0) = \begin{cases} 0 \text{ for } i = \lfloor \frac{L+1}{2} \rfloor \\ 3/4 \text{ for } 1 \leq |i - \lfloor \frac{L+1}{2} \rfloor| \leq 2M \\ 1/2 \text{ for } 1 \leq i < \lfloor \frac{L+1}{2} \rfloor - 2M, \lfloor \frac{L+1}{2} \rfloor + 2M < i \leq L \end{cases} \quad (6)$$

for the LFSR from which the output sequence of the SG is derived. The time and data complexities are $C_T = L^2 2^{L-4M-1} \binom{4M}{M}$ and $C_D = 2^{2M}$, with the restriction $2M + 1 \leq L$. Assuming $2M = \alpha L$ with $\alpha \leq 1$, again ignoring the polynomial and constant terms and equaling the time and data complexities, we have $L - 2\alpha L + 2\alpha L h(0.25) = \alpha L$ which shows $\alpha = 1/(3 - 2h(0.25)) \approx 0.726$. Thus in the best case, the complexities of this attack are $C_T = \mathcal{O}(L^2 2^{0.726L})$ and $C_D = \mathcal{O}(2^{0.726L})$, where $M = 0.363L$. For approach C, the gain is negligible when L is increased.

B   Proofs

B.1   Proof of Prop. 1

The probability P can be expressed as

$$\Pr(X_0 \in \{X_1, ..., X_T\}) = 1 - \Pr(X_0 \neq X_j, 1 \leq j \leq T)$$

$$= 1 - \sum_{i=1}^{N} \Pr(X_0 \neq X_j, 1 \leq j \leq T \mid X_0 = s_i) \cdot \Pr(X_0 = s_i)$$

$$= 1 - \sum_{i=1}^{N} \Pr(s_i \neq X_j,\ 1 \leq j \leq T\ ) \cdot \Pr(X_0 = s_i)$$

$$= 1 - \sum_{i=1}^{N} (1 - p_i)^T p_i\ . \qquad\qquad \square$$

B.2   Proof of Prop. 2

From Prop. 1 we have $\Pr(X_0 \in \{X_1, \ldots, X_T\}) = 1 - \sum_{i=1}^{N}(1 - p_i)^T p_i$. With the assumption $T p_i \ll 1$, we obtain $(1 - p_i)^T \approx 1 - T p_i$, which gives the approximation $\Pr(X_0 \in \{X_1, \ldots, X_T\}) \approx 1 - \sum_{i=1}^{N}(1 - T p_i)p_i = T\sum_{i=1}^{N} p_i^2$. Assuming $\Pr(X_0 \in \{X_1, \ldots, X_T\}) \approx 1$, we have $T \approx 1/\sum_{i=1}^{N} p_i^2$, or equivalently $T \approx 2^G$ with $G := -\log_2 \sum_{i=1}^{N} p_i^2$. This can be compared with the entropy function H. Both H and Q are approximated with a multivariate Taylor series of order 2 at the point p_0, such that $p_i = p_0 + \varepsilon_i$. If T_2 denotes the second order part, this gives

$$T_2(H) = \frac{N p_0}{\ln 2} - \frac{1}{\ln 2} - \log_2 p_0$$

$$T_2(G) = \frac{2}{\ln 2} - \frac{2}{N p_0 \ln 2} - \log_2 N - \log_2 p_0^2\ .$$

Now let $p_0 := 1/N$, then we have $T_2(H) = \log_2 N$ and $T_2(G) = -\log_2 N + 2\log_2 N = \log_2 N$. Consequently, the difference becomes $T_2(H) - T_2(G) = 0$, hence $H = G$ of order 2 on the points $p_i = 1/N$. $\qquad\qquad \square$

Remark 6. The quantity $G := -\log_2 \sum_{i=1}^{N} p_i^2$ is the Rényi entropy of order 2. It is known that guessing a random value, drawn from a *known* nonuniform probability distribution, on average requires the number of steps related to the Rényi entropy of order 2, *e.g.* see [16] or references therein. The Prop. 2 shows that this is still true when the distribution is not directly known but can be simulated. One can directly use this entropy instead of Shannon entropy which is only an approximation in this regard, however, we prefer to use the better known Shannon entropy.

For the case $p_i = 1/N$ we have $G = H = \log_2 N$, hence $T = N$ and $P = 1 - \sum_{i=1}^{N}(1 - 1/N)^N (1/N)$. For $N \gg 1$ we have $(1 - 1/N)^N \approx e^{-1}$ which shows $P \approx 1 - e^{-1} \approx 0.63$. We guess that in general we have $P \geq 1 - e^{-1}$. Our extensive simulations for several distributions verifies this conjecture. $\qquad\qquad \square$

C   Additional Figures

Fig. 2 shows some additional figures of the average entropy, together with our approximations using nonlinear regression. Fig. 3 compares the average value of

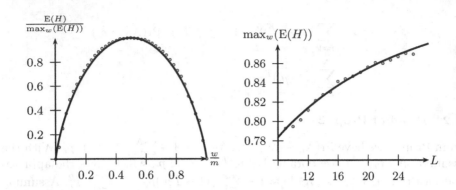

Fig. 2. Left: $E(H)/(\max_w(E(H)))$ versus w/m for $L = 21$, approximated by the entropy function. Right: $\max_w(E(H))$ versus L, approximated by $\gamma(L)$.

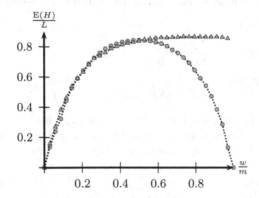

Fig. 3. $\frac{E(H)}{L}$ versus w/m for $L = 17$ in two cases: $w = \mathrm{wt}(\dot{Z}^m)$ and $w = \mathrm{wt}(Z^m)$

the entropy as a function of the weight of the output sequence and as a function of the weight of the derivative of the output sequence.

Extended BDD-Based Cryptanalysis of Keystream Generators

Dirk Stegemann

Theoretical Computer Science, University of Mannheim, Germany

Abstract. The main application of stream ciphers is online-encryption of arbitrarily long data. Many practically used and intensively discussed stream ciphers consist of a small number of linear feedback shift registers (LFSRs) and a compression function that transforms the bitstreams produced by the LFSRs into the output keystream. In 2002, Krause proposed a Binary Decision Diagram (BDD) based attack on this type of ciphers, which ranges among the best generic short-keystream attacks on practically used ciphers such as the A5/1 generator used in GSM and the E_0 generator from the Bluetooth standard. In this paper we show how to extend the BDD-technique to nonlinear feedback shift registers (NFSRs), feedback shift registers with carry (FCSRs), and arbitrary compression functions. We apply our findings to the eSTREAM focus ciphers TRIVIUM, Grain and F-FCSR. In the case of Grain, we obtain the first nontrivial cryptanalytic result besides generic time-memory-data tradeoffs.

Keywords: Stream cipher, cryptanalysis, BDD, TRIVIUM, Grain, F-FCSR.

1 Introduction

The main purpose of LFSR-based keystream generators is online encryption of bitstreams $p \in \{0,1\}^*$ that have to be sent over an insecure channel, e.g., for encrypting speech data to be transmitted from and to a mobile phone over the air interface. In many stream ciphers, the output keystream $z \in \{0,1\}^*$ of the generator is bitwise XORed to the plaintext stream p in order to obtain the ciphertext stream $c \in \{0,1\}^*$, i.e., $c_i = p_i \oplus z_i$ for all i. Based on a secret key, which has to be exchanged between the sender and the authorized receiver prior to the transmission, and a public initialization vector (IV), the receiver can compute the keystream z in the same way as the sender computed it and decrypt the message using the above rule.

We consider the special type of FSR-based keystream generators that consist of an internal bitstream generator with a small number of Feedback Shift Registers (FSRs) and a compression function $\mathcal{C} : \{0,1\}^* \to \{0,1\}^*$. The secret key and the IV determine the initial state of the FSRs, which produce an internal bitstream $w \in \{0,1\}^*$ that is transformed into the output keystream z via

C. Adams, A. Miri, and M. Wiener (Eds.): SAC 2007, LNCS 4876, pp. 17–35, 2007.

$z = \mathcal{C}(w)$. Practical examples for this design include the E_0 generator used in Bluetooth [4], the A5/1 generator from the GSM standard for mobile telephones [5], and the self-shrinking generator [18].

In 2002, Krause proposed a Binary Decision Diagram (BDD) attack [14,15] on stream ciphers that are based on Linear Feedback Shift Registers (LFSRs). The BDD-attack is a generic attack in the sense that it does not depend on specific design properties of the respective cipher. It only relies on the assumptions that the generator's output behaves pseudorandomly and that the test whether a given internal bitstream w produces a sample keystream can be represented in a Free Binary Decision Diagram (FBDD) of size polynomial in the length of w. In addition, the attack reconstructs the secret key from the shortest information-theoretically possible prefix of the keystream (usually a small multiple of the keysize), whereas other generic attack techniques like algebraic attacks [1,6] and correlation attacks [10] in many cases require amounts of known keystream that are unlikely to be available in practice. In the case of E_0, the A5/1 generator and the self-shrinking generator, it has been shown in [16] that the performance of the attack in practice does not deviate significantly from the theoretical figures. The inherently high memory requirements of the attack can be reduced by divide-and-conquer strategies based on guessing bits in the initial state at the expense of slightly increased runtime [16,20].

In the ECRYPT stream cipher project eStream [8], a number of new ciphers have recently been proposed and analyzed. Many new designs partly replace LF-SRs by other feedback shift registers such as nonlinear feedback shift registers (NFSRs) and feedback shift registers with carry (FCSRs) in order to prevent standard cryptanalysis techniques like algebraic attacks and correlation attacks. Moreover, combinations of different types of feedback shift registers permit alternative compression functions. We show that the BDD-based approach remains applicable in the presence of NFSRs and FCSRs combined with arbitrary output functions as long as not too many new internal bits are produced in each clock cycle of the cipher.

Three of the most promising hardware-oriented submissions to the eStream project are the ciphers TRIVIUM [7], Grain [12], and the F-FCSR family [2]. All three ciphers are part of the focus group and are now being considered for the final portfolio that will be announced in the middle of 2008. We show that the BDD-attack is applicable to these ciphers and obtain the first exploitable cryptanalytic result on the current version of Grain besides generic time-memory-data-tradeoff attacks. Our results for the F-FCSR family emphasize already known but differently motivated security requirements for the choice of parameters.

This paper is organized as follows. We discuss some preliminaries on FSR-based keystream generators and BDDs in Sect. 2 and explain the extended BDD-attack in Sect. 3. Section 4 presents generic constructions for the BDDs that are used in the attack, and Sect. 5 applies our observations to the eStream focus ciphers TRIVIUM, Grain and F-FCSR.

2 Preliminaries

2.1 FSR-Based Keystream Generators

A keystream generator consists of an n-bit internal state $s = (s_0, \ldots, s_{n-1})$, a state update function $F : \{0,1\}^n \to \{0,1\}^n$ and an output function $C : \{0,1\}^n \to \{0,1\}^*$. The starting state s^0 of the generator is derived from a secret key K and a public initialization vector IV. At each clock t, output bits are produced according to $C(s^t)$ from the current state s^t, and the internal state is updated to $s^{t+1} = F(s^t)$. Hence, the output of the generator is completely determined by the starting state s^0.

A widely adopted architecture especially for hardware oriented keystream generators is to represent the internal state in a number of Feedback Shift Registers (FSRs) $R^1, \ldots, R^{k-1}$ of lengths $n^{(0)}, \ldots, n^{(k-1)}$. The state s of the generator is the combined state of the FSRs, hence $n = \sum_{i=0}^{k-1} n^{(i)}$. Among the many types of FSRs discussed in the literature, Linear and Nonlinear Feedback Shift Registers as well as Shift Registers with Carry have proved to be particularly suitable building blocks for keystream generators.

Definition 1. *A* Feedback Shift Register (FSR) *consists of an n-bit register $a = (a_0, \ldots, a_{n-1})$ and a state update function $F : \{0,1\}^n \to \{0,1\}$. Starting from an initial configuration a^0, in each clock a_0 is produced as output and the register is updated according to $a := (a_1, \ldots, a_{n-2}, F(a_0, \ldots, a_{n-1}))$. Depending on whether F is a linear function, we call the register a* Linear Feedback Shift Register (LFSR) *or a* Nonlinear Feedback Shift Register (NFSR).

The FSR-construction is illustrated in Fig. 1.

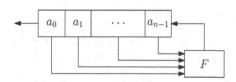

Fig. 1. Feedback Shift Register (FSR) of length n

The definition implies that the output bitstream $(w_t)_{t \geq 0}$ produced from an initial configuration $a^0 = (a_0^0, \ldots, a_{n-1}^0)$ can be expressed as

$$w_t = \begin{cases} a_t^0 & \text{for } t \in \{0, \ldots, n-1\} \\ F(w_{t-n}, \ldots, w_{t-1}) & \text{for } t \geq n \end{cases}.$$

As an alternative to LFSRs and NFSRs, Feedback Shift Registers with Carry were introduced and extensively analyzed in [13].

Definition 2. *A* Feedback Shift Register with Carry *in* Fibonacci architecture *(Fibonacci FCSR) consists of an n-bit feedback shift register $a = (a_0, a_1, \ldots,$*

a_{n-1}) *with feedback taps* $(c_1, \ldots, c_n)$ *and an additional q-bit memory b with* $q \le \lfloor \log_2(n) \rfloor$.

Starting from an initial configuration (a^0, b^0), in each clock a_0 is produced as output, the sum $\sigma := b + \sum_{i=1}^{n} a_{n-i} c_i$ is computed over the integers, and the shift register and memory are updated according to $a := (a_1, \ldots, a_{n-1}, \sigma \bmod 2)$ and $b := \sigma \bmod 2$.

A Fibonacci FCSR of length n is illustrated in Fig. 2.

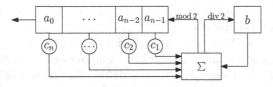

Fig. 2. FCSR of length n in Fibonacci architecture

We call an FCSR state (a, b) *periodic* if, left to run, the FCSR will eventually return to that same state. In case the Fibonacci FCSR is in a periodic state, the memory required to store the integer sum b can be further bounded as follows (cf. [11], Proposition 3.2).

Proposition 1. *If a Fibonacci FCSR is in a periodic state, then the value of the memory b is in the range* $0 \le b < \mathrm{wt}(c)$, *where* $\mathrm{wt}(x)$ *for an* $x \in \{0, 1\}^*$ *denotes the Hamming weight of x.*

Hence, if we know that the initial state (a^0, b^0) is periodic, we can limit the size of the memory to $q := \lfloor \log_2(\mathrm{wt}(c) - 1) \rfloor + 1$ bits.

Based on the initial configuration (a^0, b^0), we can describe the output bit-stream $(w_t)_{t \ge 0}$ of a Fibonacci FCSR by

$$w_t = \begin{cases} a_t^0 & \text{for} \quad t \in \{0, \ldots, n-1\} \\ \sigma_t \bmod 2 & \text{for} \quad t \ge n \end{cases},$$

where $\sigma_t = b^{t-n} + \sum_{i=1}^{n} w_{t-i} c_i$ and $b^{t-n+1} = \sigma_t \bmod 2$ for $t \ge n$, which implies

$$\sigma_t = (\sigma_{t-1} \bmod 2) + \sum_{i=1}^{n} w_{t-i} c_i \quad \text{with} \quad \sigma_{n-1} = 2b^0 . \tag{1}$$

Similarly to the Galois architecture of LFSRs, there exists a Galois architecture for FCSRs, which was first observed in [19] and further analyzed in [11].

Definition 3. *A Feedback Shift Register with Carry in Galois architecture (Galois FCSR) consists of a main register and a carry register. The main register has n register cells* $a_0, \ldots, a_{n-1}$ *and an associated multiplier vector* $(c_1, \ldots, c_n)$ *with* $c_n \ne 0$. *The cells of the carry register are denoted* $b_1, \ldots, b_{n-1}$. *The sign* $\sum$ *represents a full adder. At the j-th adder, the following input bits are received: 1)* a_j *from the preceding cell, 2)* $a_0 c_j$ *from the feedback line and 3)* b_j *from the* *memory cell. These are added to form a sum σ_j (with $1 \leq j \leq n-1$). At the next clock cycle, this sum modulo 2 is passed on to the next cell in the register, and the higher order bit is used to replace the memory, i.e., $a'_{j-1} = \sigma_j \bmod 2$ and $b'_j = \sigma_j \operatorname{div} 2$. At the beginning of the computation, the register is initialzied with a start configuration (a^0, b^0).*

We note that the Galois architecture is generally more efficient than the Fibonacci architecture because the feedback computations can be performed in parallel and each addition involves at most 3 bits. An example Galois FCSR is illustrated in Fig. 3.

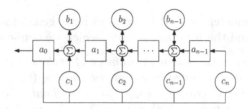

Fig. 3. FCSR of length n in Galois architecture

If memory bits are only present at those positions $i \in \{1, \ldots, n-1\}$ for which $c_i = 1$, which is equivalent to $b_i \leq c_i$ for all i, the Galois-FCSR can be mapped to a Fibonacci-FCSR (cf. Theorem 5.2 and Corollary 5.3 of [11]).

Theorem 1. *For a Galois FCSR with multiplier vector $(c_1, \ldots, c_n)$ and an initial loading (a^0, b^0) where $b_i^0 \leq c_i$ for all $i \in \{1, \ldots, n-1\}$ there exists a Fibonacci FCSR with feedback taps $(c_1, \ldots, c_n)$ and a starting state $(\tilde{a}^0, \tilde{b}^0)$ such that both FCSRs will produce the same output.*

In an FSR-based keystream generator, the FSRs may be interconnected in the sense that the update function F^i of R^i may also depend on the current content of the other registers, i.e., we have $F^i : \{0,1\}^{n_i} \rightarrow \{0,1\}$, $n_i \leq n$, for all $i \in \{0, \ldots, k-1\}$. The output function $C : \{0,1\}^n \rightarrow \{0,1\}^*$, which derives the output of each clock from the current state, usually depends on one or more state bits from each FSR.

Similarly to a single FSR, we can think of an FSR-based keystream generator with k registers as producing an internal bitstream $(w_t)_{t \geq 0}$, where

$$w_t := w_{s(t)}^{r(t)} \text{ with } r(t) = t \bmod k \text{ and } s(t) = s \operatorname{div} k \ ,$$

i.e., the t-th internal bit of the generator corresponds to the $s(t)$-th bit in the bitstream produced by $R^{r(t)}$. Again, the internal bitstream and hence the output of an FSR-based keystream generator are entirely determined by its starting state s^0, and the first m bits of the internal bitstream w can be computed as $(w_0, \ldots, w_{m-1}) = H_{\leq m}(s^0)$, where $H_{\leq m} : \{0,1\}^n \rightarrow \{0,1\}^m$. We denote the prefix of the keystream that is produced from an m-bit internal bitstream w by $C_m(w)$ with $C_m : \{0,1\}^m \rightarrow \{0,1\}^*$.

We call an integer i an *initial position* in an internal bitstream w, if w_i corresponds to a bit from the initial state of some FSR, and a *combined position* otherwise. Correspondingly, we denote by $IP(i)$ the set of initial positions and by $CP(i)$ the set of combined positions in $\{0, \ldots, i-1\}$. For an internal bistream w, let $IB(w)$ denote the bits at the initial positions in w. Let $n_{\min}$ denote the maximum i for which all $i' \leq i$ are initial positions and $n_{\max}$ the minimum i for which all $i' > i$ are combined positions.

Definition 4. *We call an FSR-based keystream generator* regular, *if* $|C_m(w)| = \beta(m)$ *for all* $w \in \{0,1\}^m$, *i.e., an internal bitstream of length m always yields $\beta(m)$ keystream bits.*

Two important parameters of FSR-based keystream generators are the *best-case compression ratio* and the *information rate*, which we define as follows.

Definition 5. *If γm is the maximum number of keybits that the generator produces from internal bitstreams of length m, we call $\gamma \in (0,1]$ the best-case compression ratio of the generator. Moreover, for a randomly chosen and uniformly distributed internal bitstream $W^{(m)} \in \{0,1\}^m$ and a random keystream Z, we define as* information rate α *the average information that Z reveals about $W^{(m)}$, i.e., $\alpha := \frac{1}{m} I\left(W^{(m)}, Z\right) \in (0,1].$*[1]

Assumption 1 (Independence Assumption). *For all $m \geq 1$, a randomly chosen, uniformly distributed internal bitstream $w^{(m)}$, and all keystreams $z \in \{0,1\}^*$, we have $Prob_w[C(w)$ is prefix of $z] = p_C(m)$, i.e., the probability of $C(w)$ being a prefix of z is independent of z.*

As shown in [14], the computation of α can be simplified as follows if the generator fulfills the independence assumption.

Lemma 1. *If the Independence Assumption holds for a keystream generator, we have $\alpha = -\frac{1}{m} \log_2(p_C(m))$.*

Corollary 1. *The information rate α of a regular FSR-based keystream generator fulfilling the Independence Assumption is given by $\alpha = \frac{\beta(m)}{m}$.*

Proof. The Independence Assumption and Definition 4 imply that the $2^{\beta(m)}$ possible keystream blocks of length $\beta(m)$ that can be produced from the m-bit internal bitstream all have probability $p_C(m)$. Hence $p_C(m) = 2^{-\beta(m)}$ and therefore $\alpha = -\frac{1}{m} \log_2(2^{-\beta(m)}) = \frac{\beta(m)}{m}$. □

Finally, we assume the output keystream to behave pseudorandomly, which we formalize as follows.

Assumption 2 (Pseudorandomness Assumption). *For $m \leq \lceil \alpha^{-1} n \rceil$, let $w^{(m)}$ and s^0 denote randomly chosen, uniformly distributed elements of $\{0,1\}^m$ and $\{0,1\}^{|IP(m)|}$, respectively. Then, it holds for all keystreams z that $Prob_w[C(w)$ is prefix of $z] \approx Prob_{s^0}[C(H_{\leq m}(s^0))$ is prefix of $z]$.*

---

[1] Recall that for two random variables A and B, the value $I(A,B) = H(A) - H(A|B)$ defines the information that B reveals about A.

We expect the Pseudorandomness Assumption to hold since a significant violation would imply the vulnerability of the generator to a correlation attack.

2.2 Binary Decision Diagrams (BDDs)

We briefly review the definitions of Binary Decision Diagrams and their most important algorithmic properties.

Definition 6. *A* Binary Decision Diagram *(BDD) over a set of variables $X_n = \{x_1, \ldots, x_n\}$ is a directed, acyclic graph $G = (V, E)$ with $E \subseteq V \times V \times \{0, 1\}$. Each inner node v has exactly two outgoing edges, a 0-edge $(v, v_0, 0)$ and a 1-edge $(v, v_1, 1)$ leading to the 0-successor v_0 and the 1-successor v_1, respectively. A BDD contains exactly two nodes with outdegree 0, the sinks s_0 and s_1. Each inner node v is assigned a label $v.label \in X_n$, whereas the two sinks are labeled $s_0.label = 0$ and $s_1.label = 1$. There is exacly one node with indegree 0, the root of the BDD. We define the size of a BDD to be the number of nodes in G, i.e., $|G| := |V|$. Each node $v \in V$ represents a Boolean Function $f_v \in B_n = \{f | f : \{0, 1\}^n \rightarrow \{0, 1\}\}$ in the following manner: For an input $a = (a_1, \ldots, a_n) \in \{0, 1\}^n$, the computation of $f_v(a)$ starts in v. In a node with label x_i, the outgoing edge with label a_i is chosen, until one of the sinks is reached. The value $f_v(a)$ is then given by the label of this sink.*

Definition 7. *For a BDD G over X_n, let $G^{-1}(1) \subseteq \{0, 1\}^n$ denote the set of inputs accepted by G, i.e., all inputs $a \in \{0, 1\}^n$ such that $f_{\text{root}}(a) = 1$.*

Since general BDDs have many degrees of freedom for representing a particular Boolean function, many important operations and especially those that are needed in our context are NP-hard. We therefore concentrate on the more restricted model of Ordered Binary Decision Diagrams (OBDDs), which are defined as follows.

Definition 8. *A* variable ordering π *for a set of variables $X_n = \{x_1, \ldots, x_n\}$ is a permutation of the index set $I = \{1, \ldots, n\}$, where $\pi(i)$ denotes the position of x_i in the π-ordered variable list $x_{\pi^{-1}(1)}, x_{\pi^{-1}(2)}, \ldots, x_{\pi^{-1}(n)}$.*

Definition 9. *A* π-Ordered Binary Decision Diagram *(π-OBDD) with respect to a variable ordering π is a BDD in which the sequence of tests on a path from the root to a sink is restricted by π, i.e., if an edge leads from an x_i-node to an x_j-node, then $\pi(i) < \pi(j)$. We call a BDD G an OBDD, if there exists a variable ordering π such that G is a π-OBDD. We define the width of an OBDD G as $w(G) := \max_i \{|\{v \in G | v.label = x_i\}|\}$.*

Figure 4 shows a π-OBDD that computes the function $f(z_0, \ldots, z_3) = z_0 z_2 \vee z_0 \bar{z}_2 z_3 \vee \bar{z}_0 z_1 z_3$.

In contrast to BDDs, OBDDs allow for efficient implementations of the operations that we are interested in. Let π denote a variable ordering for $X_n = \{x_1, \ldots, x_n\}$ and let the π-OBDDs G_f, G_g and G_h represent Boolean functions $f, g, h : \{0, 1\}^n \rightarrow \{0, 1\}$. We have $|G_f| \leq m \cdot w(G_f)$, and there exists an algorithm MIN that computes in time $O(|G_f|)$ the uniquely determined minimal

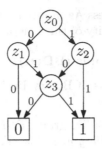

Fig. 4. A π-OBDD over $\{z_0, \ldots, z_3\}$ with $\pi(0) = 0$, $\pi(1) = 2$, $\pi(2) = 1$ and $\pi(3) = 3$

π-OBDD G with $w(G) \leq |G_f^{-1}(1)|$ that represents f. In time $O(|G_f| \cdot |G_g| \cdot |G_h|)$, we can compute a minimal G_0-OBDD G with $w(G) \leq w(G_f) \cdot w(G_g) \cdot w(G_h)$ that represents the function $f \wedge g \wedge h$. Additionally, it is possible to enumerate all elementes in $G_f^{-1}(1)$ in time $O\left(n \cdot |G_f^{-1}(1)|\right)$. We refer the reader to [21] for details on BDDs, OBDDs and the corresponding algorithms.

Note that we can straightforwardly use BDDs as a datastructure for subsets of $\{0, 1\}^n$. In order to represent an $S \subseteq \{0, 1\}^n$, we construct a BDD G_S that computes the characteristic function f_S of S given by $f_S(x) = 1$ if $x \in S$ and $f_S(x) = 0$ otherwise. Hence, G_S will accept exactly the elements of S. Moreover, we can compute a BDD representing the intersection $S \cap T$ of two sets S and T from their BDD-representations G_S and G_T by an AND-synthesis of G_S and G_T.

3   BDD-Based Initial State Recovery

The BDD-based attack on keystream generators, which was first introduced in [14], is a known-plaintext initial state recovery attack, i.e., the attacker tries to reconstruct the unknown initial state s^0 of the keystream generator from a few known plaintext bits $p_1, p_2, \ldots$ and their encryptions $c_1, c_2, \ldots$. Since a ciphertext bit c_i is computed from a plaintext bit p_i and a keystream bit z_i via $c_i = p_i \oplus z_i$, the keystream bit z_i can be reconstructed from (p_i, c_i) by computing $p_i \oplus c_i = z_i$.

We observe that for any internal bitstream $w \in \{0, 1\}^m$ that yields a prefix of the observed keystream, the following two conditions must hold.

Condition 1. w *is an m-extension of the initial state bits in w, i.e., we have* $H_{\leq m}(\mathrm{IB}(w)) = w$.

Condition 2. $C_m(w)$ *is a prefix of the observed keystream z.*

We call any $w \in \{0, 1\}^m$ that satisfies these conditions an m-*candidate*. Our strategy is now to start with $m = n_{\min}$ and to dynamically compute the m-candidates for $m > n_{\min}$, until only one m-candidate is left. The first bits of this m-candidate will contain the initial state s^0 that we are looking for. We can expect to be left with only one m-candidate for $m \geq \lceil \alpha^{-1} n \rceil$, which follows directly from the following Lemma (cf. [14] for a proof).

Lemma 2. *Under Assumption 2, it holds for all keystreams z and all $m \leq \lceil \alpha^{-1} n \rceil$ that $|\{s^0 \in \{0,1\}^n : C_m(H_{\leq m}(s^0))$ is prefix of $y\}| \approx 2^{|\mathrm{IP}(m)| - \alpha m} \leq 2^{n - \alpha m}$. Hence, there exist approximately $2^{n - \alpha m}$ m-candidates.*

In order to compute and represent the intermediate m-candidates efficiently, we use the following BDD-based approach. For a given regular keystream generator we choose a suitable reading order π and represent bitstreams w fulfilling conditions 1 and 2 in the minimal π-OBDDs R_m and Q_m, respectively. Starting from $P_{n_{\min}} = Q_{n_{\min}}$, we compute for $n_{\min} < m \leq \lceil \alpha^{-1} n \rceil$ the π-OBDD $P_m = \mathrm{MIN}(P_{m-1} \wedge Q_m \wedge S_m)$, where the minimum π-OBDD S_m tests whether w_{m-1} is in the m-extension of $\mathrm{IB}(w)$. Note that we have $P_m = \mathrm{MIN}(Q_m \wedge R_m)$ with $R_m = \bigwedge_{i=1}^m S_i$ for all m, and P_m accepts exactly the m-candidates.

The cost of this strategy essentially depends on the sizes of the intermediate results P_m, which can be determined as follows.

Assumption 3 (BDD Assumption). *For all $m \geq n_{min}$, it holds that $w(R_m) \leq 2^{p \cdot |\mathrm{CP}(m)|}$ for an integer $p \geq 1$ and $w(S_m), w(Q_m) \in m^{O(1)}$.*

Lemma 3. *Let $\mathcal{K}$ denote a regular FSR-based keystream generator with k FSRs $R^0, \ldots, R^{k-1}$ of lengths $n^{(0)}, \ldots, n^{(k-1)}$. If $\mathcal{K}$ fulfills the BDD assumption and the Pseudorandomness Assumption, it holds for $n = \sum_{i=0}^{k-1} n^{(i)}$ and all $n_{\min} < m \leq \lceil \alpha^{-1} n \rceil$ that $w(P_m) \leq n^{O(1)} 2^{\frac{p(1-\alpha)}{p+\alpha} n}$.*

The proof of Lemma 3 is analogous to the LFSR-case presented in [14,15] and can be found in Appendix A.

From this bound on $w(P_m)$, we can straightforwardly derive the time, space and data requirements of the BDD-based attack.

Theorem 2. *Let $\mathcal{K}$ denote a regular FSR-based keystream generator with an unknown initial state $s^0 \in \{0,1\}^n$, information rate α and best-case compression ratio γ. If $\mathcal{K}$ fulfills the Independence Assumption, the Pseudorandomness Assumption and the BDD Assumption, an initial state $\tilde{s}^0$ that yields the same keystream as s^0 can be computed in time and with space $n^{O(1)} 2^{\frac{p(1-\alpha)}{p+\alpha} n}$ from the first $\lceil \gamma \alpha^{-1} n \rceil$ consecutive keystream bits of $\mathcal{K}$ under s^0.*

4 Generic BDD Constructions

4.1 Keystream Consistency Check Q_m

In most cases, the BDD Q_m that checks Condition 2 can be straightforwardly derived from the definition of the output function C. If the computation of an output bit z_t depends on $u(j) > 1$ bits from an FSR R^j, a fixed bit in the bitstream produced by R^j will generally appear and have to be read in the computation of up to $u(j)$ output bits. In this case, we compute an output bit z_t from a number of *new bits* which are being considered for the first time, and several *old bits* that were already involved in the computation of previous output bits. This would imply reading a fixed variable more than once on the same path in Q_m, which is prohibited by the OBDD-definition. The less restrictive BDDs permit this construction, but can no longer guarantee the efficiency of the operations that our attack depends on. A similar problem has been considered in [14] in the context of the irregularly clocked A5/1 generator [5], which uses the bits of the internal bitstream both for computing output bits and as input for the clock control mechanism. A possible solution, which was also proposed in [14], is to increase the number of unknowns by working with $u(j)$ synchronized duplicates of the R^j-bitstream at the expense of a reduced information rate α.

We now consider the more general situation that the update function depends on the new bits and some function(s) $g_1, \ldots, g_r$ in the old bits. In this case, it suffices to introduce auxiliary variables for the values of these functions in order to ensure that z_t is computed only from new bits. This construction is illustrated in the following example.

Example 1. Consider the output function $z_t = C(w_{t+5}, w_{t+7}, w_{t+9})$, where C is defined by $C(x_1, x_2, x_3) = x_1 \oplus x_2 \oplus x_3$. Assuming canonical reading order, w_{t+9} would be the new bit and w_{t+5} and w_{t+7} the old bits. With the auxiliary variable $\tilde{w}_t := g_1(w_{t+5}, w_{t+7})$ and $g_1(x_1, x_2) := x_1 \oplus x_2$, we can express z_t as $z_t = \tilde{w}_t \oplus w_{t+9}$.

If we add for each auxiliary variable an FSR to the generator that outputs at clock t the corresponding value of g_j, we can compute z_t without considering the bits from the internal bitstream more than once. Obviously, the resulting equivalent generator is regular, but will have a lower information rate as before, since more bits of the internal bitstream have to be read in order to compute the same number of keystream bits.

4.2   FSR Consistency Check R_m

Recall that each bit w_t of an internal bitstream w is either an initial state bit of some FSR or a combination of other internal bits. In order to decide for a given internal bitstream whether it satisfies Condition 1, we need to check whether the update relations imposed on the bits at the combined positions are fulfilled. Hence, if a combined bit w_t is produced by an update relation $f^i(s_0, \ldots, s_{n-1})$, we need to check whether $f^i(w_{i_1}, \ldots, w_{i_p}) = w_t$, which is equivalent to testing whether

$$\tilde{f}^i(w_{i_1}, \ldots, w_{i_p}, w_t) := f^i(w_{i_1}, \ldots, w_{i_p}) \oplus w_t = 0 \ .$$

The OBDD S_m implements this test for a single combined bit w_{m-1} and represents the constant-one function if w_{m-1} is an initial bit. The OBDD $R_m = \bigwedge_{i=1}^{m} S_i$ performs the consistency tests for the whole internal bitstream.

We first consider the case of FSRs (without additional memory), for which we need the following definition.

Definition 10. *For a polynomial* $f : \{0,1\}^n \to \{0,1\}$ *with*

$$f(w_1, \ldots, w_n) = \bigoplus_{j \in M} m_j \ with \ m_j = \bigwedge_{l \in M^j} w_l \ and \ M^j \subseteq \{1, \ldots, n\} \ ,$$

and a reading order $\pi \in \sigma_n$, *we define the set of* active monomials *at clock t as*

$$\mathrm{AM}_\pi(f,t) := \{m_j : 0 < |\{\pi^{-1}(1),\ldots,\pi^{-1}(t)\} \cap M^j| < |M^j|\} \ .$$

Hence, $\mathrm{AM}(f,t)$ contains all monomials in f for which at least one, but not all factors are known after the first t inputs have been read.

Lemma 4. *For a polynomial $f : \{0,1\}^n \to \{0,1\}$ with $n > 1$ and a reading order π for the inputs, the set of inputs satisfying $f(w_1,\ldots,w_n) = 0$ can be represented in a π-OBDD of width $2^{\max_{1\le t\le n}\{|\mathrm{AM}_\pi(f,t)|\}+1}$.*

Proof. Let $p := \max_{1\le t\le n}\{|\mathrm{AM}_\pi(f,t)|\}$. In order to compute $f(w_1,\ldots,w_n)$, we may proceed in the following way. We define p auxiliary variables $b_1,\ldots,b_p$, which will store the intermediate values of partly evaluated monomials, and an additional variable b_0 for the sum of evaluated monomials. We initialize $b_0 := 0$, $b_t := 1$ for $t > 0$, and read the variables $w_1,\ldots,w_n$ in the order given by π. For each variable w_t, we update all auxiliary variables that are associated with monomials containing w_t. If a monomial becomes active by reading w_t, we allocate an auxiliary variable b_j and define $b_j := w_t$. If a monomial is entirely evaluated after reading w_t, we add its value to b_0 and free the associated auxiliary variable. Since there are at most p active monomials at any time, no more than $p+1$ auxiliary variables will be needed simultaneously.

From this strategy, we construct a π-OBDD G_f as follows. We define the vertex set

$$V(G_f) := \{(t,b_0,\ldots,b_p)\} \subseteq \{1,\ldots,n\} \times \{0,1\}^{p+1}$$

and the root of G_f as $(1,1,\ldots,1)$. For a monomial m_j, let $b_{\delta(j)}$ denote the auxiliary variable associated with m_j. For each $t \in \{1,\ldots,n-1\}$ and $i \in \{0,1\}$, we define the i-successor of $(\pi^{-1}(t),b_0,\ldots,b_p)$ as $(\pi^{-1}(t+1),b_0^i,\ldots,b_p^i)$. If m_j became inactive in $\pi^{-1}(t)$, i.e., m_j is active in $\pi^{-1}(t-1)$ but inactive in $\pi^{-1}(t)$, we set $b_0^i := b_0 \oplus b_{\delta(j)} \cdot i$ and reset $b_{\delta(j)}$ to 1. If m_j is active in t, we set $b_{\delta(j)}^i := b_{\delta(j)} \cdot i$. For all remaining auxiliary variables, we define $b_{\delta(j)}^i := b_{\delta(j)}$. If $t = n$, we compute $b_0^i,\ldots,b_p^i$ as before, and the i-successor of $(\pi^{-1}(t),b_0,\ldots,b_p)$ is defined to be the sink labeled with the value of $b_0^i \oplus 1$. This construction results in a π-OBDD that accepts only those inputs $(w_1,\ldots,w_n)$ that satisfy $f(w_1,\ldots,w_n) = 0$.

For all $i \in \{1,\ldots,n\}$, the OBDD contains at most 2^{p+1} vertices that are labeled with w_i, which implies the claim. $\square$

From Lemma 4, we can directly derive an upper bound for the width of the π-OBDD S_m for an FSR.

Corollary 2. *For a given reading order π, an integer $m > 0$, an FSR R with update relation f, and $p := \max_{0\le t<m}\{|\mathrm{AM}_\pi(\tilde{f},t)|\} + 1$, we can construct a π-OBDD S_m of width at most 2^p that tests for an internal bitstream $w \in \{0,1\}^m$ if w fulfills the update relation imposed on w_{m-1}.*

Note that for $p = 1$, we obtain the LFSR-bound that was proved in [14].

We now turn to the case of Fibonacci FCSRs. Equation (1) implies that we need access to σ_{t-1} in order to check whether the update relation holds for w_t. Therefore, we work with a modified FCSR that outputs the sum σ_t instead of the bit $w_t = \sigma_t$ mod 2 in each clock. More precisely, the modified FCSR outputs for an initial memory state $(b_{q-1}^0, \ldots, b_0^0)$ with $b^0 = \sum_{i=0}^{q-1} b_i^0 2^i$ the values $a_t^0 =: \sigma_t^0$ for $t < n - 1$, $(b_0^{q-1}, \ldots, b_0^0, a_{n-1}^0)$ for $t = n - 1$, and $(\sigma_t^q, \sigma_t^{q-1}, \ldots, \sigma_t^0)$ for $t \geq n$ with $\sigma_t = \sum_{i=0}^q \sigma_t^i 2^i$ and $w_t = \sigma_t^0$.

Lemma 5. *For a Fibonacci FCSR R with q bits of memory, an integer $m > 0$, and π the canonical reading order, we can construct a π-OBDD S_m of width at most 2^{q+1} that tests for the internal bitstream $w \in \{0,1\}^m$ of the modified FCSR with $m = n - 1 + t(q + 1)$ whether the last $q + 1$ bits fulfill the update relation.*

Proof. In order to check whether $\sigma_t = (\sigma_{t-1} \text{ div } 2) + \sum_{i=1}^n w_{t-i} \cdot c_i$, we can equivalently test if

$$\sigma_t = \sum_{i=1}^q \sigma_{t-1}^i + \sum_{i=1}^n \sigma_{t-i}^0 \cdot c_i \ .$$

This test can be performed in a π-OBDD as follows. Define the vertex set V as

$$V := \{0, \ldots, m - 1\} \times \{0,1\}^{q+1} \ ,$$

such that a vertex $v = (k, \sigma)$ with $\sigma = (\sigma^0, \ldots, \sigma^q)$ consists of a variable number k corresponding to some σ_l^j, and $q + 1$ bits for storing the comparison value for $\sigma_t^0, \ldots, \sigma_t^q$. The root of the OBDD is $(0, 0, \ldots, 0)$. For each vertex $v \in V$ and each $i \in \{0,1\}$, the i-successor $v_i = (k + 1, \tilde{\sigma})$, $\tilde{\sigma} = (\tilde{\sigma}^0, \ldots, \tilde{\sigma}^q)$, is defined as follows. If $l \in \{t - n, \ldots, t - 1\}$ and $j = 0$, we compute $\tilde{\sigma} = \sigma + \sigma_{t-j}^0 \cdot c_j$. If $l = t - 1$ and $j \in \{1, \ldots, q\}$, we define $\tilde{\sigma} = \sigma + \sigma_{l-1}^j 2^j$. If $l = t$ and $j \in \{0, \ldots, q\}$ and $\sigma_l^j \neq \sigma^j$, we define v_i to be the 0-sink. If $l = t$, $j = q$ and $\sigma_l^j = \sigma^j$, v_i is the 1-sink.

We can straightforwardly verify that this construction yields a π-OBDD of width at most 2^{q+1} which accepts only those inputs for which σ_t satisfies the update relations. □

In the case of Galois FCSRs with $b_i \leq c_i$ at all times, we denote by $a_i(t)$ and $b_i(t)$ the value of the register cells a_i and b_i at time t. The definition of Galois FCSRs implies $a_{n-1}(t) = a_0(t - 1)$ and for $i \in \{n - 2, \ldots, 0\}$ that $a_i(t) = a_{i+1}(t - 1)$ if $c_i = 0$ and $a_i(t) = a_{i+1}(t-1) \oplus b_{i+1}(t-1) \oplus a_0(t-1)$ if $c_i = 1$. We therefore focus on the nontrivially computed bits and think of the main register as producing the bitstream

$$a_0(0), a_1(0), \ldots, a_{n-1}(0), \ldots, a_{i_1}(t), \ldots, a_{i_l}(t), \ldots \ ,$$

where $\{i_1, \ldots, i_l\} = \{1 \leq i < n | c_{i+1} = 1\}$, $l = \text{wt}(c) - 1$, and $t > 0$. Similarly, we view the bitstream produced by the carry register as $b_{i_1}(t), \ldots, b_{i_l}(t), \ldots$ for $t \geq 0$.

Lemma 6. *For a Galois FCSR R with $b_i \leq c_i$ for all $i \in \{1, \ldots, n - 1\}$, an integer $m > 0$, and π the canonical reading order, we can construct a π-OBDD S_m of width at most 2 that tests whether a bit in the bitstream produced by the main register fulfills the corresponding update relations. For a bit in the bitstream of the carry register, we can perform this consistency test in a π-OBDD of maximum width 8.*

Proof. According to Corollary 2, we can test the linear conditions on the $a_i(t)$ where $c_{i+1} = 1$ in a π-OBDD of width at most 2. Similarly, Corollary 2 yields a maximum width of $2^3 = 8$ in the case of the carry register since $b_{i_j}(t)$ can be computed as

$$b_{i_j}(t) = a_{i_j}(t-1)b_{i_j}(t-1) \oplus b_{i_j}(t-1)a_0(t-1) \oplus a_0(t-1)a_{i_j}(t-1) . \qquad \square$$

From the bounds on $w(S_m)$ for the different types of FSRs, we can now straightforwardly derive a bound for $w(R_m)$ for an FSR-based keystream generator. Let $\mathcal{K}$ denote an FSR-based keystream generator consisting of k FSRs $R^0, \ldots, R^{k-1}$ with π-OBDDs $S_m^0, \ldots, S_m^{k-1}$ with sizes at most $m^{O(1)}2^{p_i}$ for all $i \in \{0, \ldots, k-1\}$. Moreover, let s_i denote the fraction of combined bits that R^i contributes to the internal bitstream.

Corollary 3. *There exists a π-OBDD R_m of width at most $2^{|CP(m)|\sum_{i=0}^{k-1} p_i s_i}$ that tests for a bitstream $w \in \{0,1\}^m$ whether it is an m-extension of the initial bits.*

Proof. The claim follows directly from $R_m = \bigwedge_{i=1}^m S_i$ and the OBDD-properties described in Sect. 2.2. $\qquad \square$

5 Applications

5.1 Trivium

TRIVIUM [7] is a regular keystream generator consisting of three interconnected NFSRs R^0, R^1, R^2 of lengths $n^{(0)} = 93$, $n^{(1)} = 84$, and $n^{(2)} = 111$. The 288-bit initial state of the generator is derived from an 80 bit key and an 80 bit IV. The output function computes a keystream bit z_t by linearly combining six bits of the internal state, with each NFSR contributing two bits (cf. Appendix 6 for details). In order to mount the BDD-attack on TRIVIUM, we write the output function as

$$z_t = g_1(s_1, s_{94}, s_{178}) \oplus s_{28} \oplus s_{109} \oplus s_{223}$$

and proceed as described in Sect. 4.1 by adding an LFSR R^3 which computes g_1 to the generator. For π equal to the canonical reading order, we have $p_i = \max_{1 \le t \le 288}\{|AM_\pi(\tilde{f}^i, t)|\} + 1 = 2$ and $s_i = \frac{1}{4}$ for $i \in \{0,1,2\}$ as well as $p_3 = 1$ and $s_3 = \frac{1}{4}$, which implies $p = \sum_{i=0}^3 p_i s_i = \frac{7}{4}$. Since the modified generator computes one keystream bit from four internal bits, we have $\beta(m) = \frac{1}{4}m$ and $\alpha = \gamma = \frac{1}{4}$. Based on Lemma 4, we can obviously construct a π-OBDD Q_m with $w(Q_m) \le 2$ that performs the consistency test for the observed keystream z such that the generator fulfills the BDD Assumption. Since each keystream bit involves 3 new bits, we can expect the Independence Assumption to hold. By plugging α, γ and p into the statement of Theorem 2, we obtain:

Theorem 3. *The secret initial state of the TRIVIUM automaton can be recovered from the first n keystream bits in time and with space $n^{O(1)}2^{0.65625n} \approx 2^{189}$ for $n = 288$.*

Theorem 3 shows that the BDD-attack is applicable to TRIVIUM, but its performance is not competitive with recently published attacks, which recover the initial state in around 2^{100} operations from $2^{61.5}$ keystream bits [17] or in around 2^{135} operations from $O(1)$ keystream bits [9].

5.2   Grain-128

The regularly clocked stream cipher Grain-128 was proposed in [12] and supports key size of 128 bits and IV size of 96 bits. The design is based on two interconnected shift registers, an LFSR R^0 and an NFSR R^1, both of lengths $n^{(0)} = n^{(1)} = 128$ and a nonlinear output function. The content of the LFSR is denoted by $s_t, s_{t+1}, \ldots, s_{t+127}$ and the content of the NFSR by $b_t, b_{t+1}, \ldots, b_{t+127}$. The corresponding update functions and the output function are given in Appendix C.

We add to the keystream generator an NFSR R^2 which computes the output bits z_t and have the generator output the values produced by R^2 in each clock. Hence, we can compute one keystream bit from 3 internal bits, which implies $\beta(m) = \frac{1}{3}m$ and $\alpha = \gamma = \frac{1}{3}$. For π equal to the canonical reading order, it is $p_0 = 1$, and we have $p_1 = \max_{0 \le i \le 117}\{|\mathrm{AM}_\pi(\tilde{f}^1, t + i)|\} + 1 = 4$, and $p_2 = \max_{0 \le i \le 95}\{|\mathrm{AM}_\pi(\tilde{f}^2, t + i)|\} + 1 = 4$. Hence, $p = \frac{1}{3} + \frac{4}{3} + \frac{4}{3} = 3$. Obviously, the consistency test for an observed keystream can be performed by a π-OBDD Q_m with $w(Q_m) \le 2^3 = 8$ according to Lemma 4. Therefore, the modified generator fulfills the BDD Assumption. Since new bits are utilized in the computation of each keybit, we can expect the Independence Assumption to hold. Hence, the application of Theorem 2 yields

Theorem 4. *The secret initial state of the Grain automaton can be recovered from the first n keystream bits in time and with space $n^{O(1)}2^{0.6n} \approx 2^{154}$ for $n = 256$.*

Theorem 4 is to the best of our knowledge the first exploitable cryptanalytic result besides generic time-memory-data-tradeoff attacks [3], which require time and keystream around 2^{128}.

5.3   The F-FCSR Stream Cipher Family

The F-FCSR stream cipher family in its current version is specified in [2]. It consists of the variants F-FCSR-H and F-FCSR-16.

F-FCSR-H has keylength 80 bits and consists of a single Galois FCSR M of length $n = 160$ and a feedback tap vector c of Hamming weight 83. Memory cells are only present at those 82 positions $i \in \{1, \ldots, n-1\}$, for which $c_i = 1$. At each clock, eight output bits b_j are created by taking the XOR-sum of up to 15 variables of the current internal state (cf. Appendix D for details).

In order to mount the BDD-attack, we split the FCSR into the main register R^0 and the carry register R^1. Since each output bit is computed as the sum of up to 15 internal bits, we are in a similar situation as described in Example 1 and need additional LFSRs $R^2, \ldots, R^9$ to compute the keystream bits b_j, $0 \le j < 8$. The modified output function simply returns these bits in each clock. With $l :=$ wt$(c) - 1$ we obtain eight output bits from $2l + 8$ internal bits, hence $\beta(m) = \frac{8}{2l+8} m$ and $\alpha = \gamma = \frac{8}{2l+8} = \frac{2}{43}$. We have $p_0 = p_1 = l$, $p_i = 1$ for $i \in \{2, \ldots, 9\}$, $s_0 = s_1 = \frac{l}{2l+8}$, and $s_i = \frac{1}{2l+8}$ for $2 \le i \le 9$, which implies $p = \frac{2l^2+1}{2l+1}$. Obviously, the consistency test for the observed keystream z can be performed by an OBDD Q_m with $w(Q_m) \le 2$. Hence, the modified F-FCSR-H fulfills the BDD Assumption. Since the computation of the keybits involves new internal bits in every clock, we can expect the Independence Assumption to hold. Note that we have l additional unknowns from the initial value of the carry register. Plugging the computed values into the statement of Theorem 3 implies the following theorem.

Theorem 5. *The secret initial state of the F-FCSR-H automaton can be recovered from the first $n + l$ keystream bits in time and with space $n^{O(1)} 2^{0.9529(n+l)} \approx 2^{231}$ for $n = 160$ and $l = 82$.*

The F-FCSR-16 generator has the same structure as F-FCSR-H, but larger parameters. More precisely, we have keylength 128 bits, $n = 256$, and the feedback tap vector has Hamming weight 131 (i.e., $l = 130$), where memory cells are only present at nonzero tap positions as before. Since F-FCSR-16 produces 16 output bits per clock, construct 16 additional LFSRs that produce these bits. Hence, we can compute 16 output bits from $2l + 16$ internal bits, which implies $\beta(m) = \frac{16}{2l+16} m$ and $\alpha = \gamma = \frac{16}{2l+16} = \frac{4}{69}$. Analogously to the case of F-FCSR-H, we obtain $p = \frac{2l^2+16}{2l+16}$. The modified generator satisfies the Independence Assumption and the BDD assumption as before, and we have $l = 130$ additional unknowns. We obtain by applying Theorem 3:

Theorem 6. *The secret initial state of the F-FCSR-16 automaton can be recovered from the first $n + l$ keystream bits in time and with space $n^{O(1)} 2^{0.94(n+l)} \approx 2^{363}$ for $n = 256$ and $l = 130$.*

Our analysis supports the security requirement that the Hamming weight of c should not be too small, which was also motivated by completely different arguments in [2]. Although the BDD-attack is to the best of our knowledge the first nontrivial attack on the current version of the F-FCSR family, it is far less efficient than exhaustive key search.

6   Conclusion

In this paper, we have shown that the BDD-attack can be extended to keystream generators based on nonlinear feedback shift registers (NFSRs) and feedback shift registers with carry (FCSRs) as well as arbitrary output functions. We have applied our observations to the three eStream focus candidates TRIVIUM, Grain and F-FCSR. In the case of Grain, we obtain the first exploitable cryptanalytic result besides generic time-memory-data tradeoffs. Our analysis of the F-FCSR family provides additional arguments for already proposed security requirements.

Acknowledgement. I would like to thank Willi Meier, Simon Künzli, and Matthias Krause for their valuable comments helping to improve this article.

References

1. Armknecht, F., Krause, M.: Algebraic attacks on combiners with memory. In: Boneh, D. (ed.) CRYPTO 2003. LNCS, vol. 2729, pp. 162–176. Springer, Heidelberg (2003)
2. Arnault, F., Berger, T.P., Lauradoux, C.: Update on F-FCSR stream cipher. eSTREAM, ECRYPT Stream Cipher Project, Report 2006/025 (2006), http://www.ecrypt.eu.org/stream
3. Biryukov, A., Shamir, A.: Cryptanalytic time/memory/data tradeoffs for stream ciphers. In: Okamoto, T. (ed.) ASIACRYPT 2000. LNCS, vol. 1976, pp. 1–13. Springer, Heidelberg (2000)
4. The Bluetooth SIG. Specification of the Bluetooth System (February 2001)
5. Briceno, M., Goldberg, I., Wagner, D.: A pedagogical implementation of A5/1 (May 1999), http://jya.com/a51-pi.htm
6. Courtois, N.: Fast algebraic attacks on stream ciphers with linear feedback. In: Boneh, D. (ed.) CRYPTO 2003. LNCS, vol. 2729, pp. 177–194. Springer, Heidelberg (2003)
7. de Cannière, C., Preneel, B.: Trivium specifications. eSTREAM, ECRYPT Stream Cipher Project (2005), http://www.ecrypt.eu.org/stream
8. eSTREAM, ECRYPT stream cipher project. http://www.ecrypt.eu.org/stream
9. eSTREAM Discussion Forum. A reformulation of Trivium. eSTREAM, ECRYPT Stream Cipher Project, Discussion Forum (2005), http://www.ecrypt.eu.org/stream/phorum/read.php?1,448
10. Golić, J.: Correlation properties of general binary combiners with memory. Journal of Cryptology 9(2), 111–126 (1996)
11. Goresky, M., Klapper, A.: Fibonacci and galois representations of feedback-with-carry shift registers. IEEE Transactions on Information Theory 48(11), 2826–2836 (2002)
12. Hell, M., Johansson, T., Maximov, A., Meier, W.: A stream cipher proposal: Grain-128. eSTREAM, ECRYPT Stream Cipher Project, Report 2005/010 (2005), http://www.ecrypt.eu.org/stream
13. Klapper, A., Goresky, M.: Feedback shift registers, 2-adic span, and combiners with memory. Journal of Cryptology 10, 111–147 (1997)
14. Krause, M.: BDD-based cryptanalysis of keystream generators. In: Knudsen, L.R. (ed.) EUROCRYPT 2002. LNCS, vol. 2332, pp. 222–237. Springer, Heidelberg (2002)
15. Krause, M.: OBDD-based cryptanalysis of oblivious keystream generators. Theor. Comp. Sys. 40(1), 101–121 (2007)
16. Krause, M., Stegemann, D.: Reducing the space complexity of BDD-based attacks on keystream generators. In: Robshaw, M. (ed.) FSE 2006. LNCS, vol. 4047, pp. 163–178. Springer, Heidelberg (2006)
17. Maximov, A., Biryukov, A.: Two trivial attacks on Trivium. eSTREAM, ECRYPT Stream Cipher Project, Repor 2007/006 (2007), http://www.ecrypt.eu.org/stream
18. Meier, W., Staffelbach, O.: The self-shrinking generator. In: De Santis, A. (ed.) EUROCRYPT 1994. LNCS, vol. 950, pp. 205–214. Springer, Heidelberg (1995)

19. Noras, J.: Fast pseudorandom sequence generators: Linear feedback shift registers, cellular automata, and carry feedback shift registers. Technical Report 94, Univ. Bradford Elec. Eng. Dept., Bradford, U.K (1997)
20. Shaked, Y., Wool, A.: Cryptanalysis of the bluetooth E_0 cipher using OBDDs. Technical report, Cryptology ePrint Archive, Report 2006/072 (2006)
21. Wegener, I.: Branching Programs and Binary Decision Diagrams: Theory and Applications. SIAM Monographs on Discrete Mathematics and Applications (2000)

A   A Proof for Lemma 3

Proof. The definitions of Q_m and R_m imply that $P_m = Q_m \wedge R_m$ for $n_{\min} < m \le \lceil \alpha^{-1} n \rceil$, and therefore $w(P_m) \le w(Q_m) \cdot w(R_m)$. Under the BDD assumption we obtain

$$w(P_m) \le w(Q_m) \cdot 2^{p \cdot |\mathrm{CP}(m)|} \ . \tag{2}$$

On the other hand, Lemma 2 implies that $w(P_m) \le |P_m^{-1}(1)| \approx m \cdot 2^{n^* - \alpha m}$ for $n^* = |\mathrm{IP(m)}|$ and $n_{\min} < m \le \lceil \alpha^{-1} n \rceil$, which means

$$w(P_m) \le 2^{n^* - \alpha m} = 2^{(1-\alpha)n^* - \alpha \cdot |\mathrm{CP}(m)|} \ . \tag{3}$$

Combining eqns. (2) and (3), we obtain for $n_{\min} < m \le \lceil \alpha^{-1} \rceil n$

$$
\begin{aligned}
w(P_m) &\le w(Q_m) \min\{2^{p \cdot |\mathrm{CP}(m)|}, 2^{(1-\alpha)n^* - \alpha \cdot |\mathrm{CP}(m)|}\} \\
&= w(Q_m) \min\{2^{p \cdot r(n^*)}, 2^{(1-\alpha)n^* - \alpha r(n^*)}\} \text{ with } r(n^*) = m - |\mathrm{IP}(m)| \\
&\le w(Q_m) \cdot 2^{p \cdot r^*(n^*)} \ ,
\end{aligned}
$$

where $r^*(n^*)$ denotes the solution of $p \cdot r(n^*) = (1 - \alpha)n^* - \alpha r(n^*)$. We obtain $r^*(n^*) = \frac{1-\alpha}{p+\alpha} n^*$ and hence $w(P_m) \le w(Q_m) 2^{\frac{p(1-\alpha)}{p+\alpha} n^*}$. With $n_{\min} < m \le \lceil \alpha^{-1} n \rceil$ and therefore $w(Q_m) \in m^{O(1)} \subseteq n^{O(1)}$ and $n^* = |\mathrm{IP}(m)| \le n$, we get

$$w(P_m) \le n^{O(1)} 2^{\frac{p(1-\alpha)}{p+\alpha} n} \text{ for all } n_{\min} < m \le \lceil \alpha^{-1} n \rceil \ ,$$

which concludes the proof.   □

B   Trivium Algorithm

From a starting state $(s_1, \ldots, s_{288})$ the algorithm produces keystream bits z_t as follows.

for $t = 0$ **to** $N - 1$ **do**
    $t_1 \leftarrow s_1 \oplus s_{28}$
    $t_2 \leftarrow s_{94} \oplus s_{109}$
    $t_3 \leftarrow s_{178} \oplus s_{223}$
    $z_t \leftarrow t_1 \oplus t_2 \oplus t_3$
    $u_1 \leftarrow t_1 \oplus s_2 s_3 \oplus s_{100}$
    $u_2 \leftarrow t_2 \oplus s_{95} s_{96} \oplus s_{202}$

$$u_3 \leftarrow t_3 \oplus s_{179}s_{180} \oplus s_{25}$$
$$(s_1, \ldots, s_{93}) \leftarrow (s_2, \ldots, s_{93}, u_3)$$
$$(s_{94}, \ldots, s_{177}) \leftarrow (s_{95}, \ldots, s_{177}, u_1)$$
$$(s_{178}, \ldots, s_{288}) \leftarrow (s_{179}, \ldots, s_{288}, u_2)$$
end for

C   Grain Algorithm

$$s_{t+128} = s_t \oplus s_{t+7} \oplus s_{t+38} \oplus s_{t+70} \oplus s_{t+81} \oplus s_{t+96}$$
$$b_{t+128} = s_t \oplus b_t \oplus b_{t+26} \oplus b_{t+56} \oplus b_{t+91} \oplus b_{t+96} \oplus b_{t+3}b_{t+67} \oplus b_{t+11}b_{t+13}$$
$$\oplus b_{t+17}b_{t+18} \oplus b_{t+27}b_{t+59} \oplus b_{t+40}b_{t+48} \oplus b_{t+61}b_{t+65} \oplus b_{t+68}b_{t+84} \ .$$

In each clock, an output bit z_t is derived by

$$z_t = \left(\bigoplus_{j \in A} b_{t+j} \right) \oplus b_{t+12}s_{t+8} \oplus s_{t+13}s_{t+20} \oplus b_{t+95}s_{t+42}$$
$$\oplus s_{t+60}s_{t+79} \oplus b_{t+12}b_{t+95}s_{t+95}$$

with $A = \{2, 15, 36, 45, 64, 73, 89\}$.

D   F-FCSR-H Algorithm

At each clock, the generator uses the following static filter to extract a pseudo-random byte:

$$F = (\text{ae985dff } 26619\text{fc5 } 8623\text{dc8a af46d590 } 3\text{dd4254e})_{16}$$

The filter splits into 8 subfilters (subfilter j is obtained by selecting the bit j in each byte of F)

$$F_0 = (0011\ 0111\ 0100\ 1010\ 1010)_2 \ , \ F_4 = (0111\ 0010\ 0010\ 0011\ 1100)_2$$
$$F_1 = (1001\ 1010\ 1101\ 1100\ 0001)_2 \ , \ F_5 = (1001\ 1100\ 0100\ 1000\ 1010)_2$$
$$F_2 = (1011\ 1011\ 1010\ 1110\ 1111)_2 \ , \ F_6 = (0011\ 0101\ 0010\ 0110\ 0101)_2$$
$$F_3 = (1111\ 0010\ 0011\ 1000\ 1001)_2 \ , \ F_7 = (1101\ 0011\ 1011\ 1011\ 0100)_2$$

The bit b_i (with $0 \le i \le 7$) of each extracted byte is expressed by

$$b_i = \bigoplus_{j=0}^{19} f_i^{(j)} a_{8j+i} \quad \text{where } F_i = \sum_{j=0}^{19} f_i^{(j)} 2^j \ ,$$

and where the a_k are the bits contained in the main register.

The cipher is initialized with an 80-bit key and an IV of length $32 \le v \le 80$ according to the following procedure.

1. The main register a is initialized with the key and the IV:

$$a := K + 2^{80} \cdot \text{IV} = (0^{80-v}||\text{IV}||K)$$

2. All carry cells are initialized to 0.

$$C := 0 = (0^{82}) \ .$$

3. A loop is iterated 20 times. Each iteration of this loop consists in clocking the FCSR and then extracting a pseudorandom byte S_i, $0 \leq i \leq 19$, using the filter F.
4. The main register a is reinitialized with these bytes:

$$a := \sum_{i=0}^{19} S_i = (S_{19}||\cdots||S_1||S_0) \ .$$

5. The FCSR is clocked 162 times (output is discarded in this step).

After the setup phase, the output stream is produced by repeating the following two steps as many times as needed.

1. Clock the FCSR.
2. Extract one pseudorandom byte $(b_0, \ldots, b_7)$ according to the linear filter described above.

Two Trivial Attacks on TRIVIUM

Alexander Maximov and Alex Biryukov

Laboratory of Algorithmics, Cryptology and Security
University of Luxembourg
6, rue Richard Coudenhove-Kalergi, L-1359 Luxembourg
movax@mail.ru, alex.cryptan@gmail.com

Abstract. TRIVIUM is a stream cipher designed in 2005 by C. De Cannière and B. Preneel for the European project eSTREAM. It has an internal state of 288 bits and the key of length 80 bits. Although the design has a simple and elegant structure, no attack on it has been found yet.

In this paper a family of TRIVIUM-like designs is studied. We propose a set of techniques for methodological cryptanalysis of these structures in general, including state recovering and linear distinguishing attacks. In particular, we study the original TRIVIUM and present a state recovering attack with time complexity around $c2^{83.5}$, which is 2^{30} faster than the best previous result. Our attack clearly shows that TRIVIUM has a very thin safety margin and that in its current form it can not be used with longer 128-bit keys.

Finally, we identify interesting open problems and propose a new design TRIVIUM/128, which resists all of our attacks proposed in this paper. It also accepts a 128 bit secret key due to the improved security level.

1 Introduction

Additive stream ciphers are an important class of data encryption primitives, in which the process of encryption simulates the one-time-pad. The core of any stream cipher is its *pseudo-random keystream generator* (PRKG). It is initialized with a *secret key K*, and an *initial value* (IV). Afterwards, it produces a long *pseudo-random sequence* called *keystream* $\mathbf{u}$. In the encryption procedure, the ciphertext $\mathbf{c}$ is then obtained by a bitwise xor of the message $\mathbf{m}$ and the keystream $\mathbf{u}$, i.e., $\mathbf{c} = \mathbf{m} \oplus \mathbf{u}$.

Many stream ciphers are currently used in various aspects of our life. To mention some of them, they are: RC4 [Sma03] (is used on the Internet), E_0 [Blu03] (in Bluetooth), A5/1 [BGW99] (in GSM communication), and others. However, it has been shown that these primitives are susceptible to various kinds of weaknesses and attacks [FM00, MS01, LV04, LMV05, BSW00, MJB04]. In 1999 the European project NESSIE was launched [NES99] and among other encryption and signature primitives it attempted to select stream ciphers for its final portfolio. However after a few rounds of evaluation and cryptanalysis, most of the

C. Adams, A. Miri, and M. Wiener (Eds.): SAC 2007, LNCS 4876, pp. 36–55, 2007.

proposals were broken[1]. As a result the board of the project NESSIE could not select any of the stream cipher proposals for its final portfolio.

The recent European project ECRYPT [ECR05] has started in 2004 within the Sixth Framework Programme (FP6). It announced a new call for stream cipher proposals, for its subproject eSTREAM. In the first phase 34 proposals were received, but only a few of them got the status of "focused" algorithms in the second phase. In the *hardware portfolio* only four new designs are in focus, they are: TRIVIUM [CP05], Grain [HJM05], Mickey [BD05], and Phelix [WSLM05].

In this paper we analyze one of these designs – TRIVIUM. The stream cipher TRIVIUM was proposed in 2005 for the project eSTREAM by C. De Cannière and B. Preneel [CP05]. It has an internal state of 288 bits and the key of 80 bits. Though the cipher was designed for hardware implementation it is also very fast in software, which makes it one of the most attractive candidates of the competition. The structure of the cipher is elegant and simple, and it follows clearly described design principles. After the design was announced many cryptographers tried to analyze it. However, only two results on TRIVIUM are known so far.

The first known result is actually given on the eSTREAM discussion forum [eDF05] where the complexity to recover the internal state from given keystream is argued to be 2^{135}. The second result is a paper from H. Raddum [Rad06], where a new algorithm for solving nonlinear systems of equations is proposed and applied on TRIVIUM. The attack complexity found was 2^{164}. Two reduced versions of this design, BIVIUM -A and -B, were proposed in that paper as well. The first reduced version was broken "in about one day", whereas the second version required time of around 2^{56} *seconds*.

In this paper we consider the design of TRIVIUM in general, and as examples we consider two instances: the original design of TRIVIUM and a reduced version BIVIUM, the one given in [Rad06] under the name BIVIUM-B. We propose a set of techniques to analyse this class of stream ciphers, and show how its internal state can be recovered given the keystream. The complexity of this attack determines the upper bound for the security level of the cipher. Its complexities for TRIVIUM and BIVIUM are found to be $c \cdot 2^{83.5}$ and $c \cdot 2^{36.1}$, respectively, where c is the complexity of solving a sparse system of linear equations (192 for TRIVIUM and 118 for BIVIUM). It means that, for example, the secret key cannot be increased to 128 bits in a straightforward way unless the design in general is changed. This time complexity is much better than in [eDF05] and [Rad06], and is the best known result on TRIVIUM so far.

In the second attack linear statistical methods are applied. We show how a distinguisher can be built, and propose a linear distinguishing attack on BIVIUM with less than 2^{32} operations in total. This attack was implemented and in practice works even slightly better than expected.

We also show how cryptanalysis of TRIVIUM can be related to another general problem. For example, if one would know how to solve a highly structured system

---

[1] There was a discussion at NESSIE on whether a distinguishing attack of very high complexity qualifies as a break of a cipher.

of 576 quadratic equations on 576 unknowns efficiently, he would be able find the full secret state of the cipher. On the other hand, putting a designer hat on, we propose several simple ideas which could help strengthen a TRIVIUM-like design. Following those we propose a tweaked design TRIVIUM/128, which is a slight modification of TRIVIUM, but is believed to have a larger security margin, and thus can be used with a larger 128 bit secret key.

This paper is organized as follows. In Section 2 we define the structures of TRIVIUM and BIVIUM. Afterwards, in Section 3, we give methods for a *state recovering attack*, and propose a set of attack scenarios for both TRIVIUM and BIVIUM. In Section 4 we propose a general attack scenario on the whole family of TRIVIUM-like stream ciphers. A linear distinguishing attack is given in Section 5. We identify a few interesting open problems, and propose an improved design TRIVIUM/128 in Section 6 (and in Appendix A). The paper ends with the summary of our results and conclusions.

1.1   Notation

In this paper we accept the following notation. A single bit will commonly be denoted by $x_i^{(t)}$, where i is an index of a variable, and t is the time instance. Bold symbols $\mathbf{u}$ represent a stream or a vector of bit-oriented data $u_1, u_2, \ldots$. Let us also define *triple-clock* of a cipher as just three consecutive clocks of it.

2   Bivium and Trivium

In Figure 1 two classes of stream ciphers are shown, namely, BIVIUM and TRIVIUM.

The number of basic components is two or three, respectively. Each basic component (a register) consist of *three blocks, each of size divisible by 3*. An instance of this class is a *specification vector* with the blocks' sizes specified, i.e.,

$$\begin{aligned} \text{BIVIUM} &\Rightarrow \text{BI}(A_1, A_2, A_3; B_1, B_2, B_3), \\ \text{TRIVIUM} &\Rightarrow \text{TRI}(A_1, A_2, A_3; B_1, B_2, B_3; C_1, C_2, C_3). \end{aligned} \tag{1}$$

Notation on the registers is summarized in Table 1.

The exact algorithm of TRIVIUM is given in Table 2.

At any time t, the keystream bits of BIVIUM and TRIVIUM are derived as $u_t = x_t + y_t$, and $v_t = x_t + y_t + z_t$, respectively. In this paper two examples from

Table 1. The structure of the internal state's registers

Reg	total length	cells denoted	the AND gate	In:Out	Res
R_A	$A = A_1 + A_2 + A_3$	$a_0^{(t)}, \ldots, a_{A-1}^{(t)}$	$a_{A-3}^{(t)} \cdot a_{A-2}^{(t)}$	$p_t : q_t$	x_t
R_B	$B = B_1 + B_2 + B_3$	$b_0^{(t)}, \ldots, b_{B-1}^{(t)}$	$b_{B-3}^{(t)} \cdot b_{B-2}^{(t)}$	$q_t : p_t/r_t$	y_t
R_C	$C = C_1 + C_2 + C_3$	$c_0^{(t)}, \ldots, c_{C-1}^{(t)}$	$c_{C-3}^{(t)} \cdot c_{C-2}^{(t)}$	$r_t : p_t$	z_t

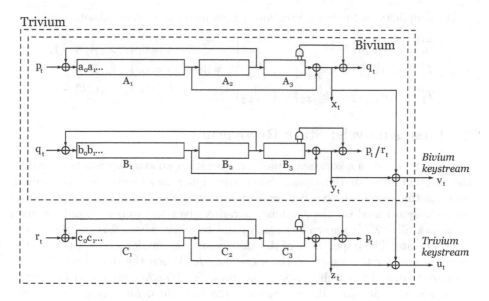

Fig. 1. Bivium and Trivium classes of stream ciphers

Table 2. TRIVIUM stream cipher

Initialisation Procedure(Key, IV)
Repeat until enough of keystream is produced
$a_0^{(t+1)} = a_{A_1+A_2-1}^{(t)} \oplus c_{C-1}^{(t)} \oplus c_{C_1-1}^{(t)} \oplus c_{C-3}^{(t)} \cdot c_{C-2}^{(t)}$
$b_0^{(t+1)} = b_{B_1+B_2-1}^{(t)} \oplus a_{A-1}^{(t)} \oplus a_{A_1-1}^{(t)} \oplus a_{A-3}^{(t)} \cdot a_{A-2}^{(t)}$
$c_0^{(t+1)} = c_{C_1+C_2-1}^{(t)} \oplus b_{B-1}^{(t)} \oplus b_{B_1-1}^{(t)} \oplus b_{B-3}^{(t)} \cdot b_{B-2}^{(t)}$
$a_i^{(t+1)} = a_{i-1}^{(t)}, \quad \forall i \in [1 : A-1]$
$b_j^{(t+1)} = b_{j-1}^{(t)}, \quad \forall j \in [1 : B-1]$
$c_k^{(t+1)} = c_{k-1}^{(t)}, \quad \forall k \in [1 : C-1]$
$u_t = a_{A-1}^{(t)} \oplus a_{A_1-1}^{(t)} \oplus b_{B-1}^{(t)} \oplus b_{B_1-1}^{(t)} \oplus c_{C-1}^{(t)} \oplus c_{C_1-1}^{(t)}$

Table 3. Two instances' specifications, TRIVIUM and BIVIUM

Description	Specification	$A : B : C$	Size, θ
TRIVIUM [CP05]	TRI$(66, 3, 24; 69, 9, 6; 66, 21, 24)$	$93 : 84 : 111$	288
BIVIUM [Rad06]	BI$(66, 3, 24; 69, 9, 6)$	$93 : 84 : -$	177

this class of stream ciphers are considered in detail, the specification of which is given in Table 3. These correspond to TRIVIUM and BIVIUM as described in [CP05, Rad06].

For simplicity in further derivations let us introduce three subsets:

$$
\begin{aligned}
\mathcal{T}_0^{(t)} &= \{a_{3i+0}^{(t)}\} \cup \{b_{3j+0}^{(t)}\} \cup \{c_{3k+0}^{(t)}\} & & i = 0, 1, \ldots, A/3 - 1, \\
\mathcal{T}_1^{(t)} &= \{a_{3i+1}^{(t)}\} \cup \{b_{3j+1}^{(t)}\} \cup \{c_{3k+1}^{(t)}\} & \text{where} \quad & j = 0, 1, \ldots, B/3 - 1, \quad (2) \\
\mathcal{T}_2^{(t)} &= \{a_{3i+2}^{(t)}\} \cup \{b_{3j+2}^{(t)}\} \cup \{c_{3k+2}^{(t)}\} & & k = 0, 1, \ldots, C/3 - 1.
\end{aligned}
$$

3   First Analysis: State Recovering

In this attack, given a keystream $\mathbf{u}$ of some length n an attacker wants to recover the internal state of the cipher. Since the cipher has invertible state-update function this also leads to a *key recovery attack*. A classical time-memory trade-off technique based on the birthday paradox gives the upper bound for such an attack of $O(2^{\theta/2})$ known keystream, and memory, where θ is the size of the internal state. The importance of the *state recovering analysis* is that it gives the upper bound for the length of the secret key K. When the design of TRIVIUM appeared, several researchers raised the question: *Whether the secret key can be increased from 80 bits till, for example, 128 bits, thus, improving the security level?* In this section we will give the precise answer.

3.1   Guessing $\mathcal{T}_0^{(t)}$ at Some Time t

One of the main observations is that all blocks of the cipher are divisible by 3. Moreover, the transition of the internal state at time t to time $t + 1$ is a linear transformation of the subset $\mathcal{T}_{t \bmod 3}^{(t)}$, plus a minor one bit disturbance from the adjacent two subsets. Therefore, the attack scenario can consist of the following phases.

PHASE I: Guess the state $\mathcal{T}_0^{(t)}$ at some time t,
PHASE II: Having the state $\mathcal{T}_0^{(t)}$ guessed correctly, recover the rest of the bits.

Since the second phase depends on the first phase, the total complexity of the attack C_{tot} is

$$
C_{\text{tot}} = C_{\text{PHASE I}} \cdot C_{\text{PHASE II}}. \tag{3}
$$

Phase I could be done by an exhaustive search of the true state $\mathcal{T}_0^{(t)}$ at some time t. The time complexity of this search is $O(2^{\theta/3})$, and the keystream length required is $O(1)$. However, this complexity can be reduced if we note that the first $d = \min\{A_1, B_1, C_1\}/3$ forward triple-clocks we receive d linear equations on the bits of $\mathcal{T}_0^{(t)}$. By this way the total time complexity is reduced down to

$$
O(2^{(\theta - \min\{A_1, B_1, C_1\})/3}).
$$

For TRIVIUM and BIVIUM these complexities are 2^{74} and 2^{37}, respectively. In the following subsections we discuss other ideas on what can be done to make the total complexity of an attack smaller.

3.2   Guessing Outcomes for Specific AND Gates

To receive more linear equations for the two phases, one can consider a set of specific AND gates:

$$a_{A-3}^{(t+3i)} \cdot a_{A-2}^{(t+3i)}, \quad i = 0, 1, \ldots, g_a - 1,$$
$$b_{B-3}^{(t+3j)} \cdot b_{B-2}^{(t+3j)}, \quad j = 0, 1, \ldots, g_b - 1, \qquad (4)$$
$$c_{C-3}^{(t+3k)} \cdot c_{C-2}^{(t+3k)}, \quad k = 0, 1, \ldots, g_c - 1,$$

where g_a, g_b, g_c are some chosen parameters. Whenever the outcomes of these gates are guessed, the number of linear equations that one can derive for the first phase is

$$d' = \min\{g_a + \frac{B_1}{3}, g_b + \frac{C_1}{3}, g_c + \frac{A_1}{3}\}.$$

The most probable guess would be that all these gates produce zeros, since $\Pr\{x \& y = 0\} = 0.75$, and we simply search in the keystream for the place where this is satisfied. The expected length of the keystream in this case is around $(0.75)^{-(g_a + g_b + g_c)}$. However, if we allow some of the gates to produce ones, the length of the keystream can be reduced significantly.

Let G gates out of $g_a + g_b + g_c$ AND gates produce zeros, and the remaining H gates produce ones. The total probability of this event is

$$p_g = 0.75^G 0.25^H.$$

Note that we can allocate H ones among $G + H$ positions in $\binom{G+H}{H}$ ways. Therefore, the keystream is needed to be of length approximately $O\left(1 / \left[p_g \cdot \binom{G+H}{H}\right]\right)$.

3.3   Guessing Sums of Specific AND Gates

The right guess of the specific AND gates from the previous subsection allowed us to increase the number of linear equations for the first phase till d'. However, the remaining bits of $T_0^{(t)}$ should be guessed with probability $1/2$. The total probability of the remaining guess could, however, be reduced if the available keystream can be increased. Below we show another trade-off between the keystream and the complexity of the remaining guessing part.

After d' triple-clocks, we start receiving nonlinear equations, where the linear part consists of the bits from $T_0^{(t)}$, and the nonlinear part is the sum of w AND gates, for some small w. Since the outcome of each of them is biased, then their sum is biased as well. Let p_w be the probability that the sum of w gates is zero, which is derived as

$$p_w = \sum_{i=0}^{\lfloor w/2 \rfloor} \binom{w}{2i} 0.75^{w-2i} 0.25^{2i} \quad (> 0.5), \qquad (5)$$

or, via its recursive formula as $p_{w+1} = 0.75 p_w + 0.25(1 - p_w)$, with $p_0 = 1$. Let l_w be the number of nonlinear equations with the sum of w AND gates. The time complexity to recover l_w bits is $p_w^{l_w}$, instead of 0.5^{l_w}, but, however, it requires to increase the length of the keystream by the ratio $p_w^{-l_w}$. The total probability of such an event is

$$q = \sum_{w=1}^{\infty} p_w^{l_w}.$$

This approach is reasonable to use for small ws, say for $w \in \{1, 2, 3, 4\}$, since for large ws the probability p_w is close to 0.5 and, therefore, it does not give a big gain versus a truly random guess, but rather increases the length of the keystream rapidly.

3.4   Collecting System of Equations for Remaining Unknowns

Assume that the state of $T_0^{(t)}$ and the outcomes of specific $G + H$ AND gates are guessed and derived correctly. To recover the remaining $2/3$ of the state we need to collect a number of equations on $T_1^{(t)}$ and $T_2^{(t)}$, enough to derive the exact solution.

At any time t, if the values $a_{A-3}^{(t)}, b_{B-3}^{(t)}, c_{C-3}^{(t)}$ are known, then two consecutive clocks of the cipher are linear. Because of our specific guess, we know that d' triple-clocks the system is linear. In one triple-clock two linear equations on the remaining unknowns of the internal state are received. The first nonlinearity will not affect on the degree of receiving equations immediately, but rather with some delay. The first nonlinear equations will be of degree 2, and then of degree 3, and so on. Also note that each of H guesses also give us two equations of degree 1 of the form $x_i = 1$ and $x_{i+1} = 1$, and each of the G guesses give us another equation of degree 2 of the form $x_i x_j = 0$. The structure of this cipher is such that backward clocks increase the degree of equations rapidly[2]. Therefore, only a few equations of low degree can be collected by backward clocking.

Let the number of equations of degrees 1 and 2 that can be collected be n_1 and n_2, respectively. Whenever all the parameters are fixed, a particular scenario can be described.

3.5   Attack Scenarios for TRIVIUM and BIVIUM

In this subsection we accumulate techniques given in the previous subsections, and propose a set of attack scenarios for TRIVIUM and BIVIUM in Table 4[3]. Moreover, a brief algorithm of the scenario T1 is presented in Table 5.

In all scenarios above the constant c is the time required for the second phase, where the remaining bits are recovered, and it is different for different scenarios.

T0 and B0 are trivial scenarios for TRIVIUM and BIVIUM, where no outcomes of any AND gates are guessed. However, the number of linear equations

---

[2] TRIVIUM is designed to maximize parallelism in forward direction. This allows hardware designers to choose trade-off between speed and chip-size.

[3] The keystream length given in the table is an average number of positions at the keystream from where we need to study a window of around $A + B + C$ consecutive bits.

Table 4. Attack scenarios

SCENARIO T0	Descr. = TRI	$l_1:l_2:l_3:l_4 = 0:0:0:0$						Ph.II unknowns=192	
$g_a:g_b:g_c$	$G:H$	r	d'	q	p_g	n_1	n_2	time	keystream
0:0:0	0:0	1	22	1	1	100	61	$c \cdot 2^{74.0}$	$O(1)$
SCENARIO T1	Descr. = TRI	$l_1:l_2:l_3:l_4 = 5:5:4:1$						Ph.II unknowns=192	
$g_a:g_b:g_c$	$G:H$	r	d'	q	p_g	n_1	n_2	time	keystream
46:37:42	125:0	1	59	$2^{-9.7}$	$2^{-51.9}$	192	178	$c \cdot 2^{83.5}$	$2^{61.5}$
SCENARIO T2									
42:33:38	113:4	$2^{22.6}$	55	$2^{-9.7}$	$2^{-53.2}$	192	162	$c \cdot 2^{88.9}$	$2^{40.3}$
SCENARIO T3	Descr. = TRI	$l_1:l_2:l_3:l_4 = 0:0:5:4$						Ph.II unknowns=192	
$g_a:g_b:g_c$	$G:H$	r	d'	q	p_g	n_1	n_2	time	keystream
29:30:30	89:0	1	52	$2^{-7.8}$	$2^{-36.9}$	158	152	$c \cdot 2^{79.7}$	$2^{44.7}$
SCENARIO B0	Descr. = BI	$l_1:l_2:l_3:l_4 = 0:0:0:0$						Ph.II unknowns=118	
$g_a:g_b:g_c$	$G:H$	r	d'	q	p_g	n_1	n_2	time	keystream
0:0:—	0:0	1	22	1	1	100	61	$c \cdot 2^{37.0}$	$O(1)$
SCENARIO B1									
9:5:—	14:0	1	27	1	$2^{-5.8}$	118	67	$c \cdot 2^{37.8}$	$2^{5.8}$

is not enough to recover the remaining bits using simple Gaussian elimination. Therefore, equations of a higher degree need to be collected and used. These scenarios have the least possible time and keystream complexities, and are the lower bounds.

In T1 and B1 we show optimal, on our view, choice of parameters such that the second phase has enough linear equations and the time complexity is minimal. However, along with linear equations we also have many equations of degree 2, which we are not using at all. Note that the attack complexities presented here are much lower than those given in [Rad06].

In T2 we show how the trade-off between the length of the keystream and time works. For a small increase of time we can reduce keystream significantly.

In T3 we receive a system of equations of degree ≤ 2 on 192 variables. This system is quite over-defined (more than 50%), and it might be possible to have an efficient algorithm for solving such a system.

However, the results given in these scenarios can be improved significantly if a *pre-* or/and a *post-* statistical tests can be applied efficiently. The goal of such a test is to reduce the constant c. For these approaches see Appendices A and B.

Another possibility to reduce the constant c can be achieved via efficient solving a system of sparse linear equations (in cases of T1, T2, B1), or through the use of high degree equations (in cases of T3, B0). Finding such an algorithm is a hard problem, and we leave it as an open problem, identified in a more general form in Section 6.

3.6   Our Results vs. Exhaustive Search

We have shown that BIVIUM can be broken in time around $c \cdot 2^{37}$, which determines a really low bound for the security level. This example was taken into

Table 5. Attack scenario T1 for TRIVIUM in brief

Given: $\mathbf{u} = u_1, u_2$ – the keystream of TRIVIUM of length $2^{61.5}$
Attack Scenario T1:
1. For every $t = 0, 1, 2, \ldots, \lceil 2^{61.5} \rceil$ assume that $a_{90}^{(t+3i)} a_{91}^{(t+3i)} = 0, b_{81}^{(t+3j)} b_{82}^{(t+3j)} = 0, c_{108}^{(t+3k)} c_{109}^{(t+3k)} = 0$, for $i = [0:45], j = [0:36], k = [0:41]$.
2. Collect 59 linear equations on T_0 with probability 1, and 15 more linear equations with the total probability $2^{-9.7}$, see Subsection 3.3.
3. For every guess of the remaining 22 bits from T_0, derive the state of T_0 using the linear equations collected in step 2.
4. Collect 192 linear equations on T_1 and T_2, clocking the cipher forward, under the assumption that the guess above was correct.
5. Recover the state of T_1 and T_2 by any linear technique (e.g., Gaussian elimination) in fixed time, and verify the solution in time $O(1)$.
6. Repeat the loops in steps 1 and 3 until the right internal state is found.

account in order to make a comparison of the techniques versus the ones used in the paper [Rad06], where the best attack on this design has been found to be of the complexity around $c \cdot 2^{56}$ *seconds*.

Although the security level of TRIVIUM is 2^{80}, we believe that an exhaustive search will require much more time, $\gamma 2^{80}$, where γ is the initialization time of the cipher that includes 1152 clocks to be done before the first keystream bits are produced. Because of different implementation issues can be applied, including parallelism, an average time required for one clock of the cipher can vary. However, we believe that a conservative value for the coefficient γ is around 2^{10}, and an exhaustive search would require around 2^{10+80} operations. This means that such scenarios, such as T1, T3, are competitive in terms of the time complexity, and at least are very close to the exhaustive search, if not faster.

Obviously, in this particular design the security level cannot be improved by simply increasing the size of the key – our attack will definitely be faster than an exhaustive search in that case. Therefore, in order to increase the security level the design of TRIVIUM should be changed, for example, the size of the state could be increased. This would result in a longer initialization time and a larger hardware footprint.

4   General Attack Scenario

Let us investigate a general structure of TRIVIUM-like stream ciphers with the following properties[4].

– It has k nonlinear shift registers $S = (S_1, S_2, \ldots, S_k)$, with the corresponding lengths $L = (L_1, L_2, \ldots, L_k)$. The bits of each register S_i are $S_i[1], \ldots, S_i[L_i]$;

---

[4] In this section a slightly changed manner of the indexation for the vectors is used, starting to count the indices from 1, instead of 0.

– Each register is divided into blocks, all divisible by d;
– There are k AND gates, and they are placed as $\text{AND}(S_i[L_i - 2], S_i[L_i - 1])$ like in TRIVIUM.

Let us denote this structure as $\text{TRIVGEN}(k, d, L)$. For simplicity, Let the vector of the lengths L be sorted such that $L_i \leq L_{i+1}, \forall i$. In this section we study a scenario of a *general state recovering attack* on the whole class of the TRIVIUM-like family of stream ciphers. The total size of the internal state S is

$$l = \sum_{i=1}^{k} L_i. \tag{6}$$

The d subsets of the total state S are defined as

$$\mathcal{T}_i = \left\{ \begin{cases} \forall j = 1, \ldots, k \\ \forall t = 0, \ldots, \frac{L_j}{d} - 1 \end{cases} : S_j[td + i] \right\}, \quad \forall i = 1, \ldots, d. \tag{7}$$

4.1 Phase I: Deriving $\mathcal{T}_1$ and $\mathcal{T}_2$

Let us first explain how $|\mathcal{T}_1|$ bits of the first subset $\mathcal{T}_1$ can be derived. We simply assume (or guess) that during consecutive $d \cdot |\mathcal{T}_1|$ clocks of TRIVGEN enough linear equations on $\mathcal{T}_1$ are collected. One observes every d's output bit at the keystream and writes up equations one by one, where every new AND term is approximated by zero.

Assume Δ is the number of linear equations that can be received from the keystream without any approximations. Let for the remaining $|\mathcal{T}_1| - \Delta$ equations the number of G AND terms have to be approximated. The values of Δ and G are easy to calculate once an exact instance of the design is given. The number of such guesses G is upper bounded as

$$G \leq k \left(\frac{l}{d} - \Delta \right). \tag{8}$$

The same procedure can be done for $\mathcal{T}_2$. Note that these two parts share the same values of Δ and G.

Instead of approximating $2G$ AND gates with probability 0.75 each, when deriving linear equations on $\mathcal{T}_1$ and $\mathcal{T}_2$, one can use the fact that these gates are not independent. At some time i two gates, one for the equation on $\mathcal{T}_1$ and one on $\mathcal{T}_2$, share one variable, i.e., if the first gate is $\text{AND}(a, b)$, then the second is $\text{AND}(b, c)$. The probability that both gates produce zeros is $5/8$. Therefore, the total probability of the required guess is

$$p_I = (5/8)^G. \tag{9}$$

4.2 Phase II: Calculating $\mathcal{T}_3 \ldots \mathcal{T}_d$

In the first phase two subsets $\mathcal{T}_1$ and $\mathcal{T}_2$ are received. Additionally, by guessing every AND term we also guaranteed that during the first l clocks only linear transformations over the two subsets are applied. It means that an outcome of every AND gate that is connected to T_3 is known. Thus, required number of linear equations on T_3 can be collected, and then Gaussian elimination is applied.

After T_3 is determined, we can start with a similar procedure to derive T_4, and so on. When the final subset T_d is derived, one can use the guesses from the first phase to check if they are in a conflict with the recovered state or not.

The total complexity of this part is

$$c_{II} \approx O(d \cdot (l/d)^{2.808}), \tag{10}$$

if the *Strassen's algorithm* for computing solution of a linear system is used. In this complexity we also included time for similar computation of the first phase. This attack scenario requires around p_I^{-1} of the keystream, and c_{II}/p_I of time.

4.3   Example: Trivium-6

Let us consider the following construction

$$\text{TRIVIUM-6} \Rightarrow \text{TRI}(66, 6, 24; \ 72, 12, 6; \ 66, 24, 24). \tag{11}$$

This is a slightly modified Trivium stream cipher with the internal state of size 300 bits, and all building blocks are divisible by 6 (still divisible by 3, but also by 2). The design of Trivium-6 belongs to the class $\text{TRIVGEN}(3, 6, (90, 96, 114))$.

I.e., we have $k = 3$, $d = 6$, $l = 300$, and $T_1, \ldots, T_6$ are defined as in (7), each of size $|T_i| = 50 \ (= l/d)$. One can easily check that

$$\Delta = \min\{66, 72, 66\}/6 + 1 = 12,$$

$$G = \left[(|T_1| - \Delta) - (\frac{66}{6} - 11) \right] + \left[(|T_1| - \Delta) - (\frac{72}{6} - 11) \right]$$

$$+ \left[(|T_1| - \Delta) - (\frac{66}{6} - 11) \right] = 38 + 37 + 38 = 113, \tag{12}$$

where 11 equations of Δ are received from $11 \cdot 6$ forward clocking, and one from backward clockings. Thus,

$$p_I \approx 2^{-76.6}, \quad c_{II} \approx 2^{18.4}. \tag{13}$$

It means that the total time complexity is 2^{95} for this example, which is smaller than for Trivium, although the internal state is larger. Note also that the keystream complexity can significantly be reduces in a similar manner as in Section 3.2 for a small penalty in time.

5   Second Analysis: Statistical Tests

Linear cryptanalysis is one of the most powerful tools for analysis of stream ciphers. In this section we find a way of sampling from the keystream such that their distribution is biased. By this mean we build a linear distinguisher for the cipher.

5.1   Standard Approximation Technique

Let the variables of $\mathcal{T}_0$ be denoted as $\{w_0, w_1, \ldots, w_{95}\}$. Then, *assuming that all* AND *terms are zeros*, we receive a system of linear equations of rank 93 (instead of 96). It means that we can sample from the stream as follows

$$\sum_{i \in \mathcal{I}_k} w_i = N_k, \quad \forall k \in \{93, 94, 95, 96\}, \tag{14}$$

where

$\mathcal{I}_{93} = \{0, 1, 4, 6, 8, 9, 12, 13, 14, 17, 19, 20, 23, 25, 27, 30, 31, 34, 35, 38, 39, 41, 43, 44,$
$\qquad 67, 68, 70, 72, 73, 76, 77, 80, 81, 84, 85, 88, 89, 92, 93\};$

$\mathcal{I}_{94} = \{0, 2, 4, 5, 6, 7, 8, 10, 12, 15, 17, 18, 19, 21, 23, 24, 25, 26, 27, 28, 30, 32, 34, 36,$
$\qquad 38, 40, 41, 42, 43, 45, 67, 69, 70, 71, 72, 74, 76, 78, 80, 82, 84, 86, 88, 90, 92, 94\};$

$\mathcal{I}_{95} = \{0, 3, 4, 5, 7, 11, 12, 14, 16, 17, 18, 22, 23, 24, 26, 28, 29, 30, 33, 34, 37, 38, 42,$
$\qquad 46, 67, 71, 75, 76, 79, 80, 83, 84, 87, 88, 91, 92, 95\};$

$\mathcal{I}_{96} = \{0, 5, 9, 14, 15, 18, 20, 24, 29, 41, 44, 47, 67, 70, 73, 96\}.$

$$\tag{15}$$

The noise variable N_k is a sum of a set of random AND gates. Therefore, the bias and the complexity of a distinguisher can be summarized in Table 6.

Table 6. Linear distinguishers for TRIVIUM and its attack complexities

k	# of AND gates in N_k	bias ϵ	attack complexity
93	108	2^{-108}	2^{216}
94	126	2^{-126}	2^{252}
95	112	2^{-112}	2^{224}
96	72	2^{-72}	2^{144}

Table 7. Linear distinguishers for BIVIUM and their attack complexities

k	# ANDs	time	$\mathcal{I}_k$
57	49	2^{98}	$\{0, 2, 4, 5, 6, 7, 8, 14, 16, 18, 20, 22, 24, 26, 28, 30, 32, 33, 34,$ $35, 37, 39, 41, 43, 45, 47, 49, 51, 53, 55, 57\}$
58	49	2^{98}	$\{1, 3, 5, 6, 7, 8, 9, 15, 17, 19, 21, 23, 25, 27, 29, 31, 33, 34, 35,$ $36, 38, 40, 42, 44, 46, 48, 50, 52, 54, 56, 58\}$
59	16	2^{32}	$\{0, 5, 9, 10, 14, 33, 36, 59\}$

Obviously, we could also mix these four equations to receive other 8 linear combinations that are different in principal from the found four. However, we could not achieve complexity lower than 2^{144}.

For BIVIUM, the rank appeared to be 57 (instead of 59), and similar resulting Table 7 is as follows.

Table 8. A linear distinguishing attack on BIVIUM in detail

Given: $\mathbf{v} = v_1, v_2$ – the keystream of BIVIUM of length 2^{32}
  Init: $P[2] = \mathbf{0}$ – a binary distribution, not normalized
A *linear distinguishing attack on* BIVIUM:
1. For every $t = 1, 2, \ldots, 2^{32}$ calculate

$$s = v_t + v_{t+15} + v_{t+27} + v_{t+30} + v_{t+42} + v_{t+99} + v_{t+108} + v_{t+177},$$

   and attune the distribution as $P[s] + +$.
2. After the loop is finished, calculate the distance

$$\xi = P[0]/2^{32} - 0.5.$$

3. Make the final decision

$$\delta(\xi) = \begin{cases} \mathbf{v} \text{ is from BIVIUM,} & \text{if } \xi > 2^{-16}/2, \\ \mathbf{v} \text{ is Random,} & \text{if } \xi \leq 2^{-16}/2. \end{cases}$$

I.e., BIVIUM can be distinguished from random in time complexity 2^{32}, which is much faster than all previously known attacks on it. Since the complexity of the attack is feasible, we could run the simulation of the attack on BIVIUM, which confirmed the found theoretical bias. This attack is shown in brief in Table 8.

5.2   Another Way of Approximation

In the previous section all AND terms were approximated as zero. However, another sort of approximation is possible, such as

$$\text{AND}(x, y) = \tau_x x + \tau_y y + n,$$

where τ_x, τ_y are chosen coefficients, and n is the noise variable with the bias $\epsilon = 2^{-1}$. Whenever approximations for every AND gate are appropriately chosen, there must exist a biased linear equation on a shorter window of the keystream than that in the previous subsection. Our goal is to reduce the number of noise variables in the final expression for sampling. Unfortunately, the search for appropriate coefficients, which give us a strongly biased expression for sampling, is a hard task. Moreover, the probability that we can find an expression with the number of gates less than 72 is low. In our simulations we could find several biased equations on a shorter window, but the number of approximations were larger than 72. This issue is an interesting open problem.

5.3   Multidimensional Approximation

In Subsection 5.1 we gave a set of linear relations for a biased sampling from the keystream. The best equations for TRIVIUM and BIVIUM require 72 and 16 approximations of AND gates, respectively. However, these samples are not independent, and some of the noises appear in several samples at different time instances. Therefore, the attack complexity can be improved by considering several samples jointly. I.e., we suggest to test a multidimensional approximation where one sample comes from a joint distribution.

Unfortunately, this did not give us a significant improvement. We considered three samples jointly, and the bias of that noise was $2^{-15.4}$, which is larger than 2^{-16}, but does not differ significantly.

6 Open Problems

Below we would like to identify several interesting open problems that we found while working on TRIVIUM.

OP-1 Let the complete internal state of TRIVIUM be 288 unknowns. When clocking forward, we receive several equations on these unknowns. Every time when a new AND gate appears, we will make a substitution, introducing a new variable into the system. After exactly $k = 288$ clocking, we will receive k linear equations on $3k$ unknowns, and also $2k$ equations of degree 2 (substitutions). All terms of degree 2 will look like $a_0a_1, a_1a_2, a_2a_3, \ldots$, and the same for b's and c's. After partial Gaussian elimination we can remain with $2k$ nonlinear equations on $2k$ unknowns[5].

Let X be a variable, an integer number of length $2k$ bits ($=576$), representing the solution. Then, the problem of breaking TRIVIUM can, after a slight modification, be interpreted as solving the following equation in $\mathbb{Z}_{2^{2k}}$.

$$X \& (X \ll 1) \oplus M \cdot X = V, \tag{16}$$

where M is a known and fixed Boolean matrix, and V is a known vector, constructed from the keystream. Our task is to find at lest one solution of the equation (guaranteed to exist).

OP-2 The set T_0 is a set of 96 unknowns. We know that each guess of T_0 allows us to construct a system of linear equations on the remaining sets T_1 and T_2. However, we believe that after a partial Gaussian elimination that matrix will look similar to

$$\begin{pmatrix} T_1 \\ T_2 \end{pmatrix} \cdot \begin{pmatrix} I & W_1 \\ W_2 & I \end{pmatrix} = V, \tag{17}$$

where W_1 and W_2 are sub-matrices dependent on the guess of T_0, and V is a known vector. Since we made a set of guesses that particular AND(T_1, T_2) gates are zeros, we would like then to "extract" somehow only one pair of bits from this system. Afterwards, we can make a test whether their

---

[5] The idea of writing up equations with specific substitutions was first proposed by Steve Babbage at SASC-06.

product is zero or not, and then in a case of a wrong result, skip the calculations of the remaining bits.

If it would be possible, then this technique would allow to reduce the constant c in the time complexity of the attack significantly.

OP-3 Finally an interesting open problem is how to strengthen Trivium, while keeping its elegance, simplicity and degree of parallelism. We propose one possible solution to this problem in Appendix A.

7   Results and Conclusions

In this paper we have studied various methods for analysis of Trivium-like stream ciphers. Below we give a comparison Table 9 of the known attacks on two instances, original Trivium and a reduced version called Bivium.

Table 9. Resulting comparison of various attacks

Case	State	Complexity	Exhaustive search	State Recovering Attack		Distinguishing Attack	
				previous	new attack	previous	new attack
Trivium	288 bits	time	$\gamma 2^{80}$ $\gamma \approx 2^{10}$	$\delta \cdot 2^{135}$ [eDF05] 2^{164} [Rad06]	$c \cdot 2^{83.5}$ $c \approx 2^{16}$	2^{144} [CP05]	—
		keystream	$O(1)$	$O(1)$	$2^{61.5}$	2^{144}	$\perp$
Bivium	177 bits	time	$\gamma 2^{80}$	2^{56} sec. [Rad06]	$c \cdot 2^{36.1}$ $c \approx 2^{14}$	—	2^{32} verified
		keystream	$O(1)$	$O(1)$	$2^{11.7}$	—	2^{32}
Triv-6	300 bits	time	—	—	$c \cdot 2^{76.6}$ $c \approx 2^{18.4}$	—	—
		keystream	—	—	$2^{76.6}$	—	—

A brief summary for the algorithm of the state recovering attack on Trivium is given in Table 5, and a distinguishing attack on Bivium is presented in Table 8.

With the key of 80 bits Trivium seems to be secure. However, contrary to what one could expect from its almost 300 bit state, there is no security margin. This also means that one cannot use 128 bit keys and IVs with the current design. For this purpose, either the internal state has to be increased or some other re-design should take place. Moreover, we have clearly shown on the example of Trivium-6 that one has to be very carefully when introducing the property of d-divisibility of the construction blocks' lengths.

In this paper we have proposed a modified design Trivium/128, which we believe is more secure than the original Trivium. In hardware, its speed of encryption is the same as in Trivium, but the footprint is slightly larger due to the 3 additional AND terms. For the same reason, in software it is also slightly slower. However, its security level seems to be much better.

References

[BD05]   Babbage, S., Dodd, M.: Mickey-128 (2005),
            http://www.ecrypt.eu.org/stream/ciphers/mickey128/mickey128.pdf
[BGW99]   Briceno, M., Goldberg, I., Wagner, D.: A pedagogical implementation of
            A5/1 (1999) (accessed August 18, 2003), available at
            http://jya.com/a51-pi.htm
[Blu03]   SIG Bluetooth. Bluetooth specification (2003) (accessed August 18, 2003),
            available at http://www.bluetooth.com
[BSW00]   Biryukov, A., Shamir, A., Wagner, D.: Real time cryptanalysis of A5/1
            on a PC. In: Schneier, B. (ed.) FSE 2000. LNCS, vol. 1978, pp. 1–13.
            Springer, Heidelberg (2001)
[CP05]   De Canniére, C., Preneel, B.: Trivium – a stream cipher construction
            inspired by block cipher design principles. eSTREAM, ECRYPT Stream
            Cipher Project, Report 2005/030 (2005-04-29) (2005),
            http://www.ecrypt.eu.org/stream
[ECR05]   eSTREAM: ECRYPT Stream Cipher Project, IST-2002-507932 (2005)
            (accessed September 29, 2005), available at
            http://www.ecrypt.eu.org/stream/
[eDF05]   eSTREAM Discussion Forum. A reformulation of TRIVIUM created on
            02/24/06 12:52PM (2005),
            http://www.ecrypt.eu.org/stream/phorum/read.php?1,448
[FM00]   Fluhrer, S.R., McGrew, D.A.: Statistical analysis of the alleged RC4
            keystream generator. In: Schneier, B. (ed.) FSE 2000. LNCS, vol. 1978,
            pp. 19–30. Springer, Heidelberg (2001)
[HJM05]   Hell, M., Johansson, T., Meier, W.: Grain V.1. — a stream cipher for
            constrained environments (2005),
            http://www.it.lth.se/grain/grainV1.pdf
[LMV05]   Lu, Y., Meier, W., Vaudenay, S.: The conditional correlation attack: A
            practical attack on Bluetooth encryption. In: Shoup, V. (ed.) CRYPTO
            2005. LNCS, vol. 3621, pp. 97–117. Springer, Heidelberg (2005)
[LV04]   Lu, Y., Vaudenay, S.: Cryptanalysis of Bluetooth keystream generator
            two-level E_0. In: Lee, P.J. (ed.) ASIACRYPT 2004. LNCS, vol. 3329,
            Springer, Heidelberg (2004)
[MJB04]   Maximov, A., Johansson, T., Babbage, S.: An improved correlation at-
            tack on A5/1. In: Handschuh, H., Hasan, M.A. (eds.) SAC 2004. LNCS,
            vol. 3357, pp. 1–18. Springer, Heidelberg (2004)
[MS01]   Mantin, I., Shamir, A.: Practical attack on broadcast RC4. In: Matsui,
            M. (ed.) FSE 2001. LNCS, vol. 2355, pp. 152–164. Springer, Heidelberg
            (2002)
[NES99]   NESSIE: New European Schemes for Signatures, Integrity, and Encryption
            (1999) (accessed August 18, 2003), available at
            http://www.cryptonessie.org
[Rad06]   Raddum, H.: Cryptanalytic results on TRIVIUM. eSTREAM, ECRYPT
            Stream Cipher Project, Report 2006/039 (2006),
            http://www.ecrypt.eu.org/stream
[Sma03]   Smart, N.: Cryptography: An Introduction. McGraw-Hill Education, New
            York (2003)

[WSLM05] Whiting, D., Schneier, B., Lucks, S., Muller, F.: Phelix - fast encryption and authentication in a single cryptographic primitive. eSTREAM, ECRYPT Stream Cipher Project, Report 2005/020 (2005-04-29) (2005), http://www.ecrypt.eu.org/stream

Appendix A: Modification of Trivium: Trivium/128

In this section we present several modifications of the original Trivium design which improve its security against our attacks and which allow to use Trivium with 128-bit keys.

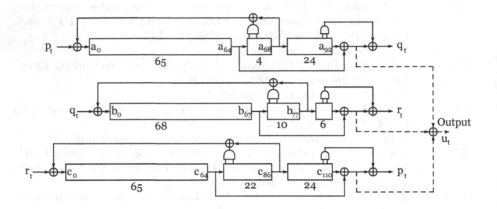

Fig. 2. A 128-bit improved design TRIVIUM/128

Suggestions for possible improvements of TRIVIUM are as follows.

I-1 Although clocking forward allows us to receive many linear or low degree equations, the backward clocking does not. The backward evaluation of TRIVIUM seem to be "well-protected", since the outcome of the AND gates are connected *forward*, thus, supporting a huge avalanche effect of noise propagation when clocking backward. We suggest to introduce 3 additional gates, but connected *backward*, in order to support a similar effect when clocking forward. To keep the parallelism property (64 clocks at once), the distance between the taps and the outcome pins of the new gates should be not less than 64;

I-2 In all our attacks we used the property that the building blocks of TRIVIUM are divisible by 3. We think that if one can remove this property, the attack could be more complex. However, this could create a risk of an existence of a good distinguisher.

According to the suggestions above we propose a modification TRIVIUM/128, which is similar to TRIVIUM, but possibly more secure. TRIVIUM/128 is presented in Figure 2. We keep the size of the internal state to be 288 bits, as well as the sizes of the nonlinear registers, 94, 84, and 111 bits, respectively. In each register the size of the first block is decreased by 1 bit, and the second block is increased by 1 bit. This would destroy the "3-divisibility" property. Moreover, in each register we introduce an additional AND gate, the inputs of which are the *first* and the *third* taps of the second block. For example, in the register A the tap positions are a_{65} and a_{67}. The new gate will make the complexity of equations to grow faster than in the original TRIVIUM, keeping the parallelism property of the cipher (ideally we should jump just a few bits back, but this would destroy parallelism). If only 32-bit parallelism suffices, then the new AND gates could jump in the middle of the first blocks in the registers. The propagation of the noise would be twice faster then. Yet another option which would have very fast growth of non-linearity would be to move the AND gates to the beginning of the long register (ex. tap positions a_1, a_2). We keep the same initialization procedure as in TRIVIUM, but with a 128 bit secret key to be loaded instead.

We believe that this tweak of the original design would resist our attacks and, possibly stay resistant against distinguishing attacks as well. We are currently checking Trivium-like designs in order to find one with best security/performance tradeoff.

Appendix B: Statistical Pre-Test for the Phase I

In the scenarios above the constant c within time complexity denotes the time needed for solving a system of equations in the second phase. Although the equations are sparse, this constant can still be large. When the number of variables is 192, we assume that this constant is approximately lower bounded as $c \approx 2^{16}$.

One idea to reduce the total time complexity is to consider only those "windows" in the stream where the probability for the guess of the AND gates is larger than in a random case.

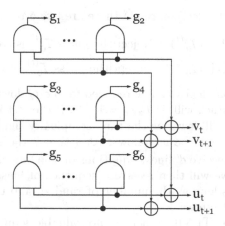

Fig. 3. Statistical pre-test

Table 10. Keystream influence for the pre-test technique

(u_t, u_{t+1})	Pr{the sum of AND gates is zero}	
(v_t, v_{t+1})	in TRIVIUM	in BIVIUM
$(0,0)$	0.53125	0.625
$(0,1)$	0.5	0.5
$(1,0)$	0.5	0.5
$(1,1)$	0.5	0.5

Let us observe an output pair (u_t, u_{t+1}) (or (v_t, v_{t+1})) at some time t and $t+1$, each component of which is the sum of 6 (respectively, 4) bits of the state from $T_1^{(t)}$ and $T_2^{(t)}$, as shown in Figure 3. The question here is: What is the probability that the sum of six (four) AND gates is zero, given the observed pair? We can use this criteria to cut undesired cases, since the sum of the gates must be zero when all of them are zeros as well. Below, in Table 10, we give these probabilities in accordance.

I.e., when the keystream in a specified "window" is a zero sequence, then the probability of our guess, a set of specific AND gates is zero, is larger than otherwise. However, this approach would require a much longer keystream, and the gain in time complexity is not significant. More complicated tests can also be developed.

Appendix C: Statistical Post-test of the Phase I

Another approach is to make a test after the first 1/3rd of the state is guessed and derived. Let us introduce a decision rule for the test

$$\delta(T_0^{(t)}) = \begin{cases} \text{Accept}, & T_0^{(t)} \text{ passes the test}, \\ \text{Reject}, & \text{otherwise}. \end{cases} \tag{18}$$

Associated with the decision rule δ there are two error probabilities.

$$\alpha = \Pr\{\delta(T_0^{(t)}) = \text{Reject}|\text{the guess } T_0^{(t)} \text{ is correct}\},$$
$$\beta = \Pr\{\delta(T_0^{(t)}) = \text{Accept}|\text{the guess } T_0^{(t)} \text{ is wrong}\}. \tag{19}$$

Thus, the time complexity can be reduced from $c \cdot Q$ down to $\beta \cdot c \cdot Q$. However, the success of the attack will be $P_{\text{succ}} = 1 - \alpha$. If the test is statistically strong, then α and β are small, lowering the time complexity significantly.

One such a test could be as follows. At a time t the sequence of d' triple-clocks allows us to receive d' linear equations on the bits of $T_0^{(t)}$. However, if we continue clocking, we will then receive a sequence of biased samples. The bias decreases rapidly as long as the number of random AND terms in the equation for the noise variable grows.

Unfortunately, for TRIVIUM there is no valuable gain, but for BIVIUM the gain is more visible. Consider the scenario B1. After the first phase the following triple-clocks give us the following samples.

AND gates in the noise, $i =$	1 2 3 4	...
Number of samples, $l_i =$	5 4 1 13	∞

Let us denote the first 23 samples (24=5+4+1+13) as $\mathbf{s}^{23} = s_0, s_1, \ldots, s_{22}$, and the decision rule for our test be

$$\delta(\mathbf{s}^{23}) = \begin{cases} \text{Accept,} & \text{if } H_w(\mathbf{s}^{23}) \geq \sigma_0, \\ \text{Reject,} & \text{otherwise,} \end{cases}$$

where $0 \leq \sigma_0 \leq 23$ is some appropriately chosen *decision threshold*. The error probabilities are then as follows.

$$\alpha = \sum_{\left\{ \substack{\forall t_w : 0 \leq t_w \leq l_w, w = 1 \ldots 4 \\ t_1 + t_2 + t_3 + t_4 < \sigma_0} \right\}} \prod_{w=1}^{4} \binom{l_w}{t_1} p_w^{t_w} (1 - p_w)^{l_w - t_w},$$

$$\beta = 2^{-23} \sum_{t=\sigma_0}^{23} \binom{23}{t}, \tag{20}$$

where the probabilities p_w are calculated via (5). Additional information is extracted from the fact that the distribution of α is "shifted" with regard to the distribution of β, and, therefore, the gain can be achieved. In Table 11 these probabilities are given for several values of the threshold σ_0.

Table 11. Error probabilities for the post-test technique

σ_0	0	7	11	12	14	18	23
α	~ 0	0.0038	0.1585	0.2964	0.6275	0.9839	~ 1
β	~ 1	0.9826	0.6612	0.5000	0.2024	0.0053	~ 0

I.e., if we choose $\sigma_0 = 18$ in B1, then the time complexity will be $c \cdot 2^{30.2}$, instead of $2^{37.8}$. The length of the keystream remains the same. However, the success probability of this attack is $P_{\text{succ}} = 0.0161$, which is low.

The situation with the success rate can be improved if the attack will be repeated $1/P_{\text{succ}}$ times. Thus, we have the overall time complexity around $2^{5.9} \cdot 2^{30.2} = 2^{36.1}$, but the keystream is also increased till $2^{11.7}$. We could trade-off a better time complexity with the length of the keystream, and the overall success probability is around 1.

Searching for a proper statistical test is a challenge and is not an easy task.

Collisions for 70-Step SHA-1:
On the Full Cost of Collision Search

Christophe De Cannière[1], Florian Mendel[2,*], and Christian Rechberger[2]

[1] Katholieke Universiteit Leuven, Dept. ESAT/SCD-COSIC,
Kasteelpark Arenberg 10, B–3001 Heverlee, Belgium
[2] Graz University of Technology
Institute for Applied Information Processing and Communications
Inffeldgasse 16a, A–8010 Graz, Austria

Abstract. The diversity of methods for fast collision search in SHA-1 and similar hash functions makes a comparison of them difficult. The literature is at times very vague on this issue, which makes comparison even harder. In situations where differences in estimates of attack complexity of a small factor might influence short-term recommendations of standardization bodies, uncertainties and ambiguities in the literature amounting to a similar order of magnitude are unhelpful. We survey different techniques and propose a simple but effective method to facilitate comparison. In a case study, we consider a newly developed attack on 70-step SHA-1, and give complexity estimates and performance measurements of this new and improved collision search method.

1 Introduction

Recently, claims for small improvements of collision search attacks attract the attention of the cryptographic community. Examples are a 2^3-fold speed-up for collision search in SHA-1 reduced to 58 steps [14] and full SHA [10] (the predecessor of SHA-1). Apart from the interest in new techniques, reports on new improvements (especially in the case of SHA-1) might also influence short-term recommendations of standardization bodies.

Motivated by the growing importance of estimating the complexity of newly developed or improved collision search attacks on members of the SHA family, we point out a number of technical issues which are, if at all, only very vaguely addressed in the literature.

- Computational cost of message modification (and similar methods)
- Influence of early-stop technique
- Impact of the last conditions of both blocks in a 2-block attack

All these issues contribute to the total cost of a differential collision search. Once devised, these methods require very little memory, are trivially parallelizable with negligible communication cost. Note that this contrasts the situation

---

* This author is supported by the Austrian Science Fund (FWF), project P18138.

C. Adams, A. Miri, and M. Wiener (Eds.): SAC 2007, LNCS 4876, pp. 56–73, 2007.

in many other types of cryptanalytic attacks, where *e. g.* the need for memory access significantly contributes to the full cost of an attack [21].

As an example of our findings we show that a very new and promising speed-up method named Boomerang-method is less efficient than expected in an collision search. Additionally, we are describing the technical details of a fast collision search method for SHA-1 reduced to 70 steps and for the first time give an example of a colliding message pair.

2 Short Description of SHA-1

SHA-1 is an iterative hash function that processes 512-bit input message blocks and produces a 160-bit hash value. Like all dedicated hash functions used today, it is based on the design principle of MD4, pioneered by Rivest. In the following we briefly describe the SHA-1 hash function. It basically consists of two parts: the message expansion and the state update transformation. A detailed description of the hash function is given in [11]. For the remainder of this article we follow the notation of [3] and restate it whenever needed.

Table 1. Notation

notation	description
$X \oplus Y$	bit-wise XOR of X and Y
$X + Y$	addition of X and Y modulo 2^{32}
X	arbitrary 32-bit word
X^2	pair of words, shortcut for (X, X^*)
M_i	input message word i (32 bits)
W_i	expanded input message word t (32 bits)
$X \lll n$	bit-rotation of X by n positions to the left, $0 \le n \le 31$
$X \ggg n$	bit-rotation of X by n positions to the right, $0 \le n \le 31$
N	number of steps of the compression function

2.1 Message Expansion

The message expansion of SHA-1 is a linear expansion of the 16 message words (denoted by M_i) to 80 expanded message words W_i.

$$W_i = \begin{cases} M_i, & \text{for } 0 \le i \le 15, \\ (W_{i-3} \oplus W_{i-8} \oplus W_{i-14} \oplus W_{i-16}) \lll 1 & \text{for } 16 \le i \le 79 . \end{cases} \tag{1}$$

2.2 State Update Transformation

The state update transformation of SHA-1 consists of 4 rounds of 20 steps each. In each step the expanded message word W_i is used to update the 5 chaining variables A_i, B_i, C_i, D_i, E_i as follows:

$$A_{i+1} = E_i + A_i \lll 5 + f(B_i, C_i, D_i) + K_j + W_i$$
$$B_{i+1} = A_i$$
$$C_{i+1} = B_i \ggg 2$$
$$D_{i+1} = C_i$$
$$E_{i+1} = D_i$$

Note that the function f depends on the actual round: round 1 (steps 0 to 19) use f_{IF} and round 3 (steps 40 to 59) use f_{MAJ}. The function f_{XOR} is applied in round 2 (steps 20 to 39) and round 4 (steps 60 to 79). The functions are defined as follows:

$$f_{IF}(B, C, D) = B \wedge C \oplus \overline{B} \wedge D \qquad (2)$$
$$f_{MAJ}(B, C, D) = B \wedge C \oplus B \wedge D \oplus C \wedge D \qquad (3)$$
$$f_{XOR}(B, C, D) = B \oplus C \oplus D . \qquad (4)$$

Note that $B_i = A_{i-1}$, $C_i = A_{i-2} \ggg 2$, $D_i = A_{i-3} \ggg 2$, $E_i = A_{i-4} \ggg 2$. This also implies that the chaining inputs fill all A_j for $-4 \leq j \leq 0$. Thus it suffices to consider the state variable A, which we will for the remainder of this paper.

After the last step of the state update transformation, the chaining variables A_0, B_0, C_0, D_0, E_0 and the output values of the last step $A_{80}, B_{80}, C_{80}, D_{80}, E_{80}$ are combined using word-wise modular addition, resulting in the final value of one iteration (feed forward). The result is the final hash value or the initial value for the next message block.

3   Collision Search Strategies

In order to construct efficient attacks, differentials with high probability are used. Since no secret key is involved, in addition to the message difference, also the actual values of bits in certain positions in the message influence the probability of such a differential. Exploitation of this additional degree of freedom led to remarkable progress in the cryptanalysis of hash function in recent years. For hash functions like SHA-1, most (complex) differentials through the earlier parts of the compression function can have for various reasons a very low probability. More recently, the impact of this fact was systematically studied in detail in [3]. It is shown that the degrees of freedom from the message largely neutralize the disadvantages of this low probability. This shifts the goal to optimizing the probability of a differential through the later part of the compression function. Additionally, this allows to remove all restrictions on the input differences of such high probability differentials. By using a second message block as an additional degree of freedom also all restrictions on the output differences of such a high probability differential can be removed.

Methods for searching high probability characteristics through (parts of) the compression function suitable for such an optimization were already discussed in [5,7,12,13,18]. In Section 5.1, we describe an improved variant of such an optimization we used for our case study of 70-step SHA-1.

Optimality of 2-block approach. It turns out that by removing the constraint to have a collision already after a single message block, differentials with significantly better probabilities can be found. On the other hand, more than two blocks do not give any additional exploitable degrees of freedom anymore. Hence, aiming for a differential spanning two message blocks is preferable, since the workloads to find the right message pairs for each block add up. Note that due to less effective methods, the first collision for SHA (the predecessor of SHA-1) was built using a differential spanning four message blocks [2].

4   Computational Cost of Differential Collision Search

By fixing a difference and having random trials we expect to have to try around 2^n times. With appropriate choices for differences and part of the actual messages, the aim is to reduce the work to find a colliding pair below the work of a birthday search of order $2^{n/2}$ trials.

We divide the involved computational costs into three categories.

- Determining a suitable message difference
- Determining a suitable characteristic
- Searching for a message pair that roughly follows this characteristic

For complexity estimates in the literature, usually only the last step is considered. We note that the first two steps used to have manual steps. With the possibility to fully automate also these parts (as shown in [3]) it becomes possible to also estimate this computational effort and consider trade-offs with other parts of an collision search attack.

4.1   General Method to Estimate Work Factor of a Chosen Characteristic

We briefly recall some methods and definitions given in [3] needed for the subsequent discussion.

Generalized conditions and generalized characteristics. Generalized conditions for hash functions were first defined in [3]. The generalized conditions on a particular pair of words X^2 will be denoted by ∇X. ∇X represents as a set, containing the values for which the conditions are satisfied. In order to write this in a more compact way, we will use the notation listed in Table 2.

Total work factor for generalized characteristic. Let us assume that we have given a complete generalized characteristic for SHA-1, specified by $\nabla A_{-4}, \ldots, \nabla A_N$ and $\nabla W_0, \ldots, \nabla W_{N-1}$. Our goal is to estimate how much effort it would take to find a pair of messages which follows this characteristic, assuming a simple depth-first search algorithm which tries to determine the pairs of message words M_i^2 one by one starting from M_0^2.

In order to estimate the work factor of this algorithm, we will compute the expected number of visited nodes in the search tree. But first some more definitions, which are all needed to estimate the work factor.

Table 2. Notation for generalized conditions, possible conditions on a pair of bits

$(x_i, x_i{}^*)$	(0,0)	(1,0)	(0,1)	(1,1)	(x_i, x_i^*)	(0,0)	(1,0)	(0,1)	(1,1)
?	✓	✓	✓	✓	3	✓	✓	-	-
-	✓	-	-	✓	5	✓	-	✓	-
x	-	✓	✓	-	7	✓	✓	✓	-
0	✓	-	-	-	A	-	✓	-	✓
u	-	✓	-	-	B	✓	✓	-	✓
n	-	-	✓	-	C	-	-	✓	✓
1	-	-	-	✓	D	✓	-	✓	✓
#	-	-	-	-	E	-	✓	✓	✓

Definition 1. *The* message freedom $F_W(i)$ *of a characteristic at step i is the number of ways to choose W_i^2 without violating any (linear) condition imposed on the expanded message, given fixed values W_j^2 for $0 \le j < i$.*

We note that since the expanded message in SHA-1 is completely determined by the first 16 words, we always have $F_W(i) = 1$ for $i \ge 16$.

Definition 2. *The* uncontrolled probability $P_u(i)$ *of a characteristic at step i is the probability that the output A_{i+1}^2 of step i follows the characteristic, given that all input pairs do as well, i.e.,*

$$P_u(i) = P\left(A_{i+1}^2 \in \nabla A_{i+1} \mid A_{i-j}^2 \in \nabla A_{i-j} \text{ for } 0 \le j < 5, \text{ and } W_i^2 \in \nabla W_i\right).$$

Definition 3. *The* controlled probability $P_c(i)$ *of a characteristic at step i is the probability that there exists at least one pair of message words W_i^2 following the characteristic, such that the output A_{i+1}^2 of step i follows the characteristic, given that all other input pairs do as well, i.e.,*

$$P_c(i) = P\left(\exists W_i^2 \in \nabla W_i : A_{i+1}^2 \in \nabla A_{i+1} \mid A_{i-j}^2 \in \nabla A_{i-j} \text{ for } 0 \le j < 5\right).$$

With the definitions above, we can now easily express the number of nodes $N_s(i)$ visited at each step of the compression function during the collision search. Taking into account that the average number of children of a node at step i is $F_W(i) \cdot P_u(i)$, that only a fraction $P_c(i)$ of the nodes at step i have any children at all, and that the search stops as soon as step N is reached, we can derive the following recursive relation:

$$N_s(i) = \begin{cases} 1 & \text{if } i = N, \\ \max\left\{ N_s(i+1) \cdot F_W(i)^{-1} \cdot P_u^{-1}(i), \, P_c^{-1}(i) \right\} & \text{if } i < N. \end{cases}$$

The total work factor is then given by

$$N_w = \sum_{i=1}^{N} N_s(i).$$

Once a characteristic has been fixed, we have to find a message pair that follows the characteristic. By using a simple greedy approach or techniques such as message modification or neutral bits the probability of the characteristic after step 16 can be improved. In the following we will describe these techniques in more detail.

4.2   Corrective Factors for Speed-Up Methods

In order to include methods that speed-up collision search into the very useful general method to estimate the work factor of a chosen characteristic as described above, we introduce corrective factors. It is easy to see that if a method aims for higher speed, less steps need to be computed and hence less nodes in the search tree are visited.

We now briefly describe how corrective factors can be derived for the different methods that can be found in the literature. Because of its actuality, we chose the so-called Boomerang-method as an example for our model in Section 4.8. The adaption of our model to other methods works similarly.

Before that, we discuss how to incorporate also less probable characteristics and the impact of conditions at the end of a block into this general model by the use of corrective factors $C_{1...n}(i)$ where $i < N$ and n enumerates all considered corrective factors. The corrected probability for each step is hence

$$P_{corr}(i) = P_u(i) \prod C_n(i) .$$

The corrected number of nodes N_{corr} and total work factor is then based on P_{corr} instead of P_u.

4.3   Effect of Additionally Considering Related Characteristics

We give here two methods to consider additional characteristics that are related to the originally chosen main characteristic.

Less probable characteristics. Even if all message conditions for the main characteristic are already in place, there exist a number of less probable characteristics. For the case of high probability characteristics through the compression function of SHA/SHA-1, these have been systematically studied in [9]. We propose to model the impact of them by setting a $C(i) > 1$ for each disturbance in step i where there exist also less probable characteristics. Examples will be given in Section 5.4.

Conditions at the end of each block. By using a 2-block approach, characteristics with a better probability can be found. Furthermore, the conditions at the end of each block can be partially ignored (without further explanation already observed in [18]). This improves the probability of the characteristic significantly. For the first message block all the conditions in the last 2 steps can be ignored. For the second block this is not the case, since for every difference in the initial value a correcting difference is needed to cancel it out. However, if we can guarantee that the sign of the disturbances in the last 2 steps is opposite to the sign of the according differences in the initial value, then we can ignore the carry conditions for these disturbances. This also improves the probability of the characteristic in the second block. In general the attack complexity is dominated by the complexity of the second block, since only the carry conditions in the last 2 steps can be ignored. We propose to model the impact of them by setting a $C(i) > 1$ for each case. An example will be given in Section 5.4.

4.4   Greedy Approach

The simple greedy approach was introduced in [3]. The idea is to run through all bit positions of every state variable and every expanded message word, check which conditions can be added to improve the total work factor, and finally pick the position and corresponding condition which yields the largest gain. By repeating this many times, the work factor can be gradually improved. No corrective factor is needed.

4.5   Message Modification

Message Modification was introduced by Wang *et al.* in the cryptanalysis of MD4 [15], MD5 [19] and the SHA-family [18,20]. The main idea of message modification is to use the degrees of freedom one has in the choice of the message words to fulfill conditions on the state variables. Since every message word is only used once in the first 16 steps, all the conditions on the state variables can be easily fulfilled for these steps. This method is referred to as simple message modification. After step 16 each message word depends on at least 4 previous message words. Hence, a more sophisticated method (referred to as advanced message modification) is needed to fulfill conditions after step 16. It can be described as follows:

1. Check if one of the conditions on the state variables is not satisfied. (starting at the LSB)
2. If one condition does not hold then flip the according bit in message word W_i. This causes a change in a previous W_t for some $t < 16$ due to the message expansion. Hence, a change in A_{t+1}. This can be compared to introducing a new difference (disturbance) in step t.
3. Correct the differences in $A_{t+1}, \ldots, A_{t+6}$ by adjusting the according message words $W_{t+1}, \ldots, W_{t+5}$.

In detail this correction is equal to constructing a *new* local collision with a disturbance in step t. Note that this method does not work if the correction in the message words affects one of the conditions on the state variables or message words themselves. Thus, the degree of freedom for advanced message modification is determined by the characteristic in the first 16 steps.

As shown in unpublished but informally presented results by Wang [16,17] the attack complexity of 2^{69} can be improved to 2^{63} by doing message modification up to step 25. Wang *et al.* estimated the cost for message modification of about 2^2 SHA-1 compression function evaluations. Note that a new characteristic for the first 16 steps was needed to do message modification up to step 25.

4.6 Equation Solving

At FSE 2007, Sugita *et al.* presented a new method for message modification in SHA-1 using symbolic computation [14]. Their method reduces the number of trials (needed message pairs) significantly at the cost of increased message modification costs. With their method a collision in 58-step SHA-1 can be constructed with complexity close to 2^8 message modification (symbolic computation) steps which they claim is approximately 2^{31} SHA-1 computations (experimentally). Note that the complexity of Wang's attack on 58-step SHA-1 is about 2^{34} hash computations. Unfortunately, Sugita *et al.* do not give any information how this comparison to SHA-1 was done. This makes it very difficult to compare their approach to others. Furthermore, the description of their method is vague and they do not give any estimations for the attack complexity on the full SHA-1 hash function. At the current state it is not clear if this method can lead to any improvements in the attack complexity of SHA-1.

4.7 Neutral Bits

This technique was invented by Biham and Chen in the analysis of SHA [1]. The main idea of this approach is to start the collision search from some intermediate step r and hence improving the complexity of the attack. Therefore, Biham and Chen invented the notion of neutral bits. For a given message pair (m, m^*) that follows the characteristic up to step r the jth-bit is called neutral if the message pair $(m \oplus 2^j, m^* \oplus 2^j)$ also follows the characteristic up to step r. Every set of neutral bits can be used to generate 2^t new message pairs, where t denote the number of neutral bits. The attack is based on the observation that a fraction $(1/8)$ of these message pairs again follow the characteristic up to step r. Hence, one get 2^{t-3} message pairs following the characteristic up to step r. It is easy to see that this reduces the complexity of the collision search in SHA.

4.8 Boomerangs/Tunnels

At CRYPTO 2007, Joux and Peyrin presented a new idea on how to improve the attack complexity of SHA-1 [6]. It uses a variant of the boomerang attack, known from analysis of block ciphers. The method is similar to the idea of tunneling as introduced by Klima [8]. Each message pair that follows the characteristic in the first steps is related to another message pair by a high probability auxiliary differential. This auxiliary differential ensure that the characteristic also holds in the first steps for the other message pair. Hence, each auxiliary differential doubles the number of message pairs that follow the characteristic in the first steps, which improves the complexity of the attack. An easy method to construct these auxiliary differentials is to combine several local collisions. With this method auxiliary differentials can be constructed up to step 29. However, to guarantee that the auxiliary differential holds a set of additional conditions have to be fulfilled in the steps before. This on the one hand reduces the degrees of freedom needed in the final collision search and on the other hand a characteristic is needed for the first 16 steps that is compatible with the auxiliary differential. It is an interesting research problem to maximize the number of auxiliary differentials that fit into a suitable characteristic for collision search. However, issues like available message freedom and implementation aspects can *hugely* influence the resulting work factor for collision search.

We propose to model the impact of auxiliary differentials as follows. Each auxiliary differentials allows to increase a single $C(i)$ by $2 \cdot p_{aux}$, where i is the first step where $P_{corr}(i) < 1$, and p_{aux} is the probability for the auxiliary differential to hold up to step i which is often 1 or close to 1. The details depend on the characteristic being used and the auxiliary differentials. The consequences are interesting: even in favorable settings, the resulting corrected work factor can not be improved by a factor of 2 per auxiliary differential, but noticeably less. As an example, consider a setting where 6 auxiliary differentials are used. Instead of a 64-fold improvement, the improvement is less than 45-fold. This has several reasons, *i. e.* the precise way our model takes the early-stop strategy into account.

4.9 Comparison of Methods

Comparison of different approaches to speed-up collision search for SHA and SHA-1 is difficult because usually not enough information is provided in the respective descriptions.

Chabaud and Joux count in their attack on SHA [4] the number of needed message pairs for constructing a collision to estimate the attack complexity. Furthermore, they provide some measurements to confirm their estimates. This makes it easy to compare their results with other implementations. Unfortunately, this is not the case for most of the recent published attacks on SHA and SHA-1.

In their recent attacks on SHA and SHA-1 Wang *et al.* count the number of conditions that have to be fulfilled such that the message follows the characteristic to estimate the complexity of attack. Furthermore, they consider improvements achieved by message modification techniques as well as early stop. This lead to an estimated attack complexity for SHA and SHA-1 of about 2^{39} and 2^{63} hash computations, respectively. However, since the description message modification is vague, it is difficult to compare it to other methods.

In [14], Sugita *et al.* count the number of symbolic computations (message modification steps) needed for their message modification technique. Unfortunately, they do not give any timing information for the algorithm, which makes it difficult to compare the method to others.

In [3], De Cannière and Rechberger count the number of nodes in a search tree that have to be visited to find a collision in the hash function to estimate the complexity of the attack. This estimation already includes improvement of message modification and early stop. With their approach a collision for 64-step SHA-1 can be found with a complexity of about 2^{35} hash computations.

An other notable example is the SHA collision by Naito *et al.* given in [10]. They improved the collision attack of Wang *et al.* on SHA by a factor of 2^3. To estimate the complexity of the attack, they build upon the work of Wang *et al.* in the original attack. In addition to counting conditions for the characteristic and considering the improvement of early stop and the cost for message modification, they also provide measurements. Their finding is that a collision in SHA has a complexity of about 2^{36} hash computations and takes on average about 100 hours (on a Pentium4 3.4GHZ CPU). This shows an interesting gap between claimed complexity and measurement. In fact one can expect more than 2^{20} SHA compression function calls per second on such a machine and hence would expect a runtime of less than 20 hours.

4.10 Proposal

In order to avoid misinterpretation and allow fair comparison of different methods, we propose to directly compare every fast collision search method with a standard implementation of SHA-1 (*e. g.* OpenSSL) on the same platform. This would make comparison of different approaches easier in the future. In cases where collision search can not be implemented it is still possible to give measurement results for parts of the characteristic. We refer to our case study for an example.

5   Case Study: Collision Search for 70-Step SHA-1

5.1   Message Difference

We developed efficient search algorithms to find suitable message differences. They are based on methods developed in [12], with the improvement that exact probabilities as described in [3,9] instead of Hamming weights are used to prune and rank them.

As described in Section 3, the effort to find colliding message pairs for SHA-1 mainly depends on the number of conditions between state and/or message bits where no method to fulfill them better than random trials is known. For evaluating and comparing candidate message differences, it will be useful to have the following definition:

Definition 4. *The* truncated total work from step i $N_t(i)$ *of a characteristic is the product of all corrected probabilities down to step i, i.e.,*

$$N_t(i) = \prod P_{corr(j)},$$

where j runs from R downto i.

Assuming that the controlled probability $P_c(i)$ can be ignored (which is perfectly reasonable for $i > 16$), $N_t(i)$ for $i > 16$ can be used as an estimate of the total work without fully specifying the generalized characteristic from step 0 on. The argument i in $N_t(i)$ can be interpreted as the threshold up to which methods more efficient than random trials are known to look for right message pairs.

For the attack we used the message difference MD 2, since it has the best truncated total work after step 18 and 20. This perfectly matches to the greedy method we use to speed-up collision search.

Table 3. Disturbance vectors for 70-step SHA-1

message	steps 18-70 Hamming weight	$N_t(18)$	steps 20-70 Hamming weight	$N_t(20)$
MD 1	19	$2^{51.66}$	17	$2^{47.40}$
MD 2	19	$2^{48.66}$	17	$2^{47.23}$
MD 3	19	$2^{50.36}$	16	$2^{47.37}$
MD 4	19	$2^{50.22}$	17	$2^{49.87}$
MD 5	19	$2^{49.09}$	17	$2^{47.32}$
MD 6	19	$2^{50.14}$	18	$2^{48.50}$

5.2   Detailed Characteristic

Table 4 shows the used message difference, which is the same for both blocks. The characteristics found for the two blocks are given in Tables 5 and 6 respectively. For improved collision search efficiency the probability of them was further improved by fixing the actual values of certain bits in the message and the internal state using available degrees of freedom. Table 7 and 8 show the respective results.

The total expected work for both blocks amounts to about 2^{44} compression function equivalents. In contrast to other figures given in the literature this includes the impact of a less than ideal implementation (which is in our case about a factor 10).

We run experiments for parts of the used characteristic to give this estimate. Our experiment which produced an actual 70-step collision confirms this estimates. Note that this includes the impact of a less than optimal implementation of the collision search and compares to a fast implementation of SHA-1 (OpenSSL) on the same platform. For that, we used as a means of comparison the SHA-1 implementation of OpenSSL, which can do about 2^{20} compression functions per second on our PC.

A straightforward extension of the method used for the 64-step collision as presented in [3] to 70 steps would have required more than 2^{50} compression function equivalents. The gain in speed is partly due to the choice of a different disturbance vector, and partly due to an improvement of the greedy-approach.

5.3   The Employed Improved Greedy-Approach

In our case study, we employ the greedy approach as described in Section 4.4. We improve upon [3] in the following way. Instead of picking only single bit positions, we pick several of them at once. This results in a larger search space but also in better results. We always pick a set of 7 bits (a local collision) and test for each bit which condition would yield to the largest gain in the work factor. This is an easy way to estimate the improvement of the work factor for one local collision. Note that checking all 2^7 possibilities to add conditions for a local collision would be inefficient. After testing all local collisions we pick the one with the largest improvement and set the corresponding conditions. By repeating this method the work factor can be gradually improved.

Table 4. Example of a 70-step SHA-1 collision using the standard IV

i	Message 1 (m_0), first block				Message 1 (m_1), second block			
1–4	3BB33AAE	85AECBBB	57A88417	8137CB9C	ABDDBEE2	42A20AC7	A915E04D	5063B027
5–8	4DE99220	5B6F12C7	726BD948	E3F6E9B8	4DDF989A	E0020CF7	7FFDC0F4	EFEFE0A7
9–12	23607799	239B2F1D	AAC76B94	E8009A1E	0FFBC2F0	C8DE16BF	81BBE675	254429CB
13–16	C24DE871	5B7C30D8	000359F5	90F9ED31	5F37A2C6	CD1963D3	FFCA1CB9	9642CB56

i	Message 2 (m_0^*), first block				Message 2 (m_1^*), second block			
1–4	ABB33ADE	35AECBE8	67A8841F	8137CBDF	3BDDBE92	F2A20A94	9915E045	5063B064
5–8	9DE99252	EB6F12D7	826BD92A	23F6E9FA	9DDF98E8	50020CE7	8FFDC096	2FEFE0E5
9–12	236077A9	C39B2F5F	8AC76BF4	08009A5F	0FFBC2C0	28DE16FD	A1BBE615	C544298A
13–16	E24DE821	9B7C3099	E0035987	30F9ED32	7F37A296	0D196392	1FCA1CCB	3642CB55

i	XOR-difference are the same for both blocks							
1–4	90000070	B0000053	30000008	00000043	90000070	B0000053	30000008	00000043
5–8	D0000072	B0000010	F0000062	C0000042	D0000072	B0000010	F0000062	C0000042
9–12	00000030	E0000042	20000060	E0000041	00000030	E0000042	20000060	E0000041
13–16	20000050	C0000041	E0000072	A0000003	20000050	C0000041	E0000072	A0000003

i	The colliding hash values				
1–5	151866D5	F7940D84	28E73685	C4D97E18	97DA712B

5.4   Some Corrective Factors

Conditions at the end of each block. Applying the rules described in Section 4.3 to the characteristic in both blocks (Tables 7 and 8) we can remove all 6 conditions in the last two steps of the first block and 2 conditions in the second block. In terms of corrective factors as introduced in Section 4.2, we arrive at a $C(69) = 2^3$ and $C(70) = 2^3$ for the first block and $C(69) = 2^1$ and $C(70) = 2^1$ for the second block.

Impact of additional less probable characteristics. We achieve some more speedup if also less probable characteristics are allowed. Once at bit position 0 in step 34, we would get a speed-up by 25%. The three disturbances in step 62, 65 and 66 would each allow a speedup of about 6.25%. By avoiding strict checking of conditions/differences in the implementation, we can hence expect to visit only about 66% nodes in order to find a suitable message pair. In terms of corrective factors as introduced in Section 4.2, we arrive at a $C(34) = 1.25$, and $C(62) = C(65) = C(66) = 1.0625$. Note that this speed-up applies to both blocks in the same way.

6   Conclusions

Currently known differential collision search attacks on hash functions like SHA-1 need little memory and are trivially parallizable. Still, theoretical analysis (counting conditions, calculate probabilities for successful message modification) often leads to optimistic conclusions about actual collision search implementation costs.

Measurement results and comparison with standard hash implementations on the same platform are needed to compare different collision search strategies. As a case study, a collision search method and an example of a colliding message pair for 70-step SHA-1 was used. The highest number of steps for which a SHA-1 collision was published so far was 64.

References

1. Biham, E., Chen, R.: Near-Collisions of SHA-0. In: Franklin, M.K. (ed.) CRYPTO 2004. LNCS, vol. 3152, pp. 290–305. Springer, Heidelberg (2004)
2. Biham, E., Chen, R., Joux, A., Carribault, P., Lemuet, C., Jalby, W.: Collisions of SHA-0 and Reduced SHA-1. In: Cramer, R.J.F. (ed.) EUROCRYPT 2005. LNCS, vol. 3494, pp. 36–57. Springer, Heidelberg (2005)
3. De Cannière, C., Rechberger, C.: Finding SHA-1 Characteristics: General Results and Applications. In: Lai, X., Chen, K. (eds.) ASIACRYPT 2006. LNCS, vol. 4284, pp. 1–20. Springer, Heidelberg (2006)
4. Chabaud, F., Joux, A.: Differential Collisions in SHA-0. In: Krawczyk, H. (ed.) CRYPTO 1998. LNCS, vol. 1462, pp. 56–71. Springer, Heidelberg (1998)
5. Iwasaki, T., Yajima, J., Sasaki, Y., Naito, Y., Shimoyama, T., Kunihiro, N., Ohta, K.: On the complexity of collision attack against SHA-1 and new disturbance vectors. In: Presented at rump session of CRYPTO 2006 (August 2006)
6. Joux, A., Peyrin, T.: Hash Functions and the (Amplified) Boomerang Attack. In: Menezes, A. (ed.) CRYPTO 2007. LNCS, vol. 4622, pp. 244–263. Springer, Heidelberg (2007)
7. Jutla, C.S., Patthak, A.C.: Provably Good Codes for Hash Function Design. In: Biham, E., Youssef, A.M. (eds.) SAC 2006. LNCS, vol. 4356. Springer, Heidelberg (2006)
8. Klima, V.: Tunnels in Hash Functions: MD5 Collisions Within a Minute. Cryptology ePrint Archive, Report 2006/105 (2006), http://eprint.iacr.org/
9. Mendel, F., Pramstaller, N., Rechberger, C., Rijmen, V.: The Impact of Carries on the Complexity of Collision Attacks on SHA-1. In: Robshaw, M.J.B. (ed.) FSE 2006. LNCS, vol. 4047, pp. 278–292. Springer, Heidelberg (2006)
10. Naito, Y., Sasaki, Y., Shimoyama, T., Yajima, J., Kunihiro, N., Ohta, K.: Improved Collision Search for SHA-0. In: Lai, X., Chen, K. (eds.) ASIACRYPT 2006. LNCS, vol. 4284, pp. 21–36. Springer, Heidelberg (2006)
11. National Institute of Standards and Technology (NIST). FIPS-180-2: Secure Hash Standard (August 2002), available online at http://www.itl.nist.gov/fipspubs/
12. Pramstaller, N., Rechberger, C., Rijmen, V.: Exploiting Coding Theory for Collision Attacks on SHA-1. In: Smart, N.P. (ed.) Cryptography and Coding. LNCS, vol. 3796, pp. 78–95. Springer, Heidelberg (2005)
13. Rijmen, V., Oswald, E.: Update on sha-1. In: Menezes, A.J. (ed.) CT-RSA 2005. LNCS, vol. 3376, pp. 58–71. Springer, Heidelberg (2005)
14. Sugita, M., Kawazoe, M., Perret, L., Imai, H.: Algebraic Cryptanalysis of 58-round SHA-1. In: Biryukov, A. (ed.) FSE 2007. LNCS, vol. 4593, pp. 349–365. Springer, Heidelberg (2007)
15. Wang, X., Lai, X., Feng, D., Chen, H., Yu, X.: Cryptanalysis of the Hash Functions MD4 and RIPEMD. In: Cramer, R.J.F. (ed.) EUROCRYPT 2005. LNCS, vol. 3494, pp. 1–18. Springer, Heidelberg (2005)
16. Wang, X., Yao, A., Yao, F.: Cryptanalysis of SHA-1. In: Cryptographic Hash Workshop hosted by NIST (October 2005)
17. Wang, X., Yao, A., Yao, F.: New Collision Search for SHA-1. In: Presented at rump session of CRYPTO 2005 (August 2005)
18. Wang, X., Yin, Y.L., Yu, H.: Finding Collisions in the Full SHA-1. In: Shoup, V. (ed.) CRYPTO 2005. LNCS, vol. 3621, pp. 17–36. Springer, Heidelberg (2005)

19. Wang, X., Yu, H.: How to Break MD5 and Other Hash Functions. In: Cramer, R.J.F. (ed.) EUROCRYPT 2005. LNCS, vol. 3494, pp. 19–35. Springer, Heidelberg (2005)
20. Wang, X., Yu, H., Yin, Y.L.: Efficient Collision Search Attacks on SHA-0. In: Shoup, V. (ed.) CRYPTO 2005. LNCS, vol. 3621, pp. 1–16. Springer, Heidelberg (2005)
21. Wiener, M.J.: The Full Cost of Cryptanalytic Attacks. J. Cryptology 17(2), 105–124 (2004)

Table 5. Characteristic for the first block of the 70-step collision before optimization

i	∇A_i	∇W_i	F_W	$P_u(i)$	$P_c(i)$	$N_s(i)$
-4:	0000111101001011100001111000011					
-3:	0100000011001001010100001111011000					
-2:	0110001011101101101110011111111010					
-1:	1110111111001101101010111110001001					
0:	0110011101000101001000110000001	n--u1011--1-------111---1nun1110	14	-4.42	0.00	0.00
1:	u1-u1011--10---1--010-1-nuun0001	u0nn----------1----01----n1u--uu	20	-13.00	-0.79	0.79
2:	0u0u10--0-01--100--0nun1-00nnn1u	--nu----------0-----0-----01n111	22	-17.09	-1.00	1.00
3:	111n111---1-nuuu1u-00n11u-0110u1	100------------11----01-1n0111nn	17	-16.00	-1.00	1.83
4:	101001111--nn011n1u11n000101n10n	nu0n--------10------0010-nun00n0	15	-14.83	-2.83	2.83
5:	1100100u0--010101u110unn-100u10u	n1nu--11--------------------n011-	21	-19.09	-1.00	1.00
6:	n10--0unnnnnnnnnnnnn0--0n10-0un-	nuuu00-----------------1-un---n-	22	-18.27	-2.00	2.00
7:	000111----11101u001u10-1100nn-00	uu------------1---1------n--10n0	23	-18.16	-2.75	2.75
8:	u-0-----10111111--1010u-0-0uu0u1	0-1-----------------------nu---1	26	-11.00	-1.42	1.42
9:	1-0-------------0-111u-1----01-	nnu--------------------n0---n-	25	-11.00	-3.42	3.42
10:	0-0-----------------1nu--nn001-	1-u-----------------------nn----0	23	-6.00	-1.00	1.00
11:	----------------------n1----100n	uuu----------------------n-1---n	25	-7.00	-3.42	3.42
12:	u1--------------------------00nn	-1n-----------------------u-u----	22	-7.00	-0.61	13.00
13:	u-1-0--------------1--0-1n-	nu------------------------u----n	13	-3.00	-1.00	28.00
14:	-0------------------------1---u	nnn----------------------uuu--n-	11	-6.00	-2.19	38.00
15:	110-0-----------------------0u--	u0n-----------------------------nu	14	-4.00	-2.42	43.00
16:	n0--------------------1-01-	nn------------------------u-n-	0	-3.00	-1.00	53.00
17:	---0------------------------u1	0un--------------------1n---1-n	0	-3.00	-2.00	50.00
18:	n-0------------------------	nu-----------------------un--n-	0	0.00	-0.00	47.00
19:	--------------------------	0-u-----------------------1---1n	0	-0.00	-0.00	47.00
20:	nu------------------------	nu-----------------------0-----u-	0	-2.00	-1.42	47.00
21:	---------------------u-	nun----------------------n----u1	0	-2.00	-2.00	45.00
22:	---------------------u-	1un----------------------n----n0	0	-1.00	-1.00	43.00
23:	-------------------------n-	n------------------------1u0	0	-1.00	-1.00	42.00
24:	--------------------------	------------------------1	0	-0.00	0.00	41.00
25:	--------------------------	10------------------------0-----0	0	0.00	-0.00	41.00
26:	--------------------------	u0-------------------------0----	0	0.00	0.00	41.00
27:	--------------------------	100-----------------------u-	0	-1.00	-0.42	41.00
28:	----------------------u-	0-------------------------n-----	0	0.00	0.00	40.00
29:	--------------------------	0-------------------------0	0	-2.00	-1.00	40.00
30:	-----------------------n-	u-------------------------u--1-0	0	-0.00	-0.00	38.00
31:	--------------------------	u-0-----------------------1	0	-2.00	-1.00	38.00
32:	-----------------------n-	0-0-----------------------u--1-	0	-0.00	-0.00	36.00
33:	--------------------------	n0------------------------0n	0	-2.00	-2.00	36.00
34:	------------------------u	------------------------nu---0	0	0.00	-0.00	34.00
35:	--------------------------	n1------------------------0nu	0	-1.00	-1.00	34.00
36:	--------------------------	-n------------------------u1	0	-2.00	-2.00	33.00
37:	----------------------u-	nu------------------------n---1-	0	-1.00	-1.00	31.00
38:	--------------------------	nu------------------------0-----n-	0	-1.00	-1.00	30.00
39:	--------------------------	u-------------------------00-	0	0.00	-0.00	29.00
40:	--------------------------	u--------------------------	0	-1.00	-1.00	29.00
41:	--------------------------	u-0-----------------------u0	0	-1.00	-1.00	28.00
42:	------------------------u-	0-------------------------n-----	0	0.00	0.00	27.00
43:	--------------------------	-1------------------------n0	0	-1.00	-1.00	27.00
44:	--------------------------	u-------------------------10	0	-1.00	-1.00	26.00
45:	--------------------------	n-------------------------10	0	-1.00	-1.00	25.00
46:	--------------------------	n-------------------------0-	0	-0.00	0.00	24.00
47:	--------------------------	11------------------------0u1	0	-1.00	-1.00	24.00
48:	------------------------u-	-------------------------n---0-	0	0.00	0.00	23.00
49:	--------------------------	-------------------------1-1	0	-2.00	-1.00	23.00
50:	------------------------u-	u-------------------------n----0	0	-1.00	-1.00	21.00
51:	--------------------------	x-------------------------11n-	0	-2.00	-2.00	20.00
52:	--------------------------	0--------------------------	0	-1.00	-1.00	18.00
53:	--------------------------	x0------------------------11	0	-1.00	-1.00	17.00
54:	--------------------------	x-------------------------	0	-0.00	0.00	16.00
55:	--------------------------	-------------------------1	0	0.00	0.00	16.00
56:	--------------------------	--------------------------	0	0.00	0.00	16.00
57:	--------------------------	-------------------------0--	0	0.00	0.00	16.00
58:	--------------------------	-------------------------1-0-	0	0.00	0.00	16.00
59:	--------------------------	--------------------------	0	-0.00	0.00	16.00
60:	--------------------------	--------------------------	0	0.00	-0.00	16.00
61:	--------------------------	-------------------------u-1	0	-1.00	-0.42	16.00
62:	------------------------u--	-------------------------n--0----	0	0.00	0.00	15.00
63:	--------------------------	-------------------------x--	0	-1.00	0.00	15.00
64:	--------------------------	-------------------------n--x	0	-2.00	-0.19	14.00
65:	----------------------n--	-------------------------u-0--n-x	0	-2.00	-0.42	12.00
66:	----------------------n--	-------------------------u--x-n	0	-1.00	0.00	10.00
67:	--------------------------	-------------------------n-xx-	0	-3.00	-0.36	9.00
68:	----------------------n---	-------------------------u---u-xx	0	-3.00	-0.42	6.00
69:	----------------------u---	-------------------------n---xx-ux	0	-3.00	-0.42	3.00
70:	----------------------x---					

Table 6. Characteristic for the second block of the 70-step collision before optimization

i	∇A_i	∇W_i	F_W	$P_u(i)$	$P_c(i)$	$N_s(i)$
-4:	010100110101010101001011011110n00					
-3:	011001101011000101000111111001010					
-2:	0000001111010101011011000000nu1011					
-1:	0100010101011010000011001101u010					
0:	0101001110100011001110111000n101	u01n1011------------111101uun0010	11	-2.52	0.00	0.00
1:	n11n1000-------1-1-11001nnun0nuu	n1nn-----------------0101u0n01uu	17	-8.00	-0.96	0.96
2:	1u0u10100------0---n-nn11100010u	10un-----------------0000100u101	17	-9.38	-0.35	0.35
3:	u1un00001-----nn-u-0-00nu1011u0n	010----------------1-0000n1001uu	17	-14.00	0.00	3.79
4:	n0101110n1u-u-101-n1011011uu0010	nu0n11------------1-0001nnu10u0	14	-14.62	-2.61	6.79
5:	010n011u11010n1-nu-10u01u0101nnu	u1un000000------------0111u0111	13	-16.19	-5.17	6.18
6:	1n000111100uu001-0100-n00011001u	nuuu1111111------------01uu--1n0	14	-12.44	-2.99	2.99
7:	1nnnnnnnnnnnnnnnn-111--01nn1--u00	uu1-111111--------------1n10-1u1	16	-6.00	0.00	0.00
8:	100-11000-----1100-u---1un11-101	000---------------------1uu---0	25	-19.68	0.00	0.00
9:	010011111111100111--01-0-100--0n	uun---------------------n111-u1	23	-10.00	-4.00	4.00
10:	u1--01---------------11--nu0u0un0	10n---------------------uu10--1	22	-6.42	-1.61	1.61
11:	111-1------------------n--0000011	nnu---------------------x00---u	25	-7.83	-2.61	2.61
12:	0-1-0-----------------1n-1n1	01n---------------------u-n---0	22	-2.42	-0.68	9.51
13:	u---------------------0-0-u	uu0---------------------x0----u	14	-7.00	-3.00	29.09
14:	101--------------------1-1-u	uuu---------------------xuu--n1	13	-5.09	-2.83	36.09
15:	--1-0------------------11u--	u0n---------------------10-un	13	-4.00	-2.83	44.00
16:	n1----------------------0-11	un0----------------------0-u--n1	0	-3.00	-2.00	53.00
17:	--0------------------------n1	0un----------------------u0--10n	0	-3.00	-2.00	50.00
18:	n-0-------------------------	uu1----------------------un--n1	0	0.00	0.00	47.00
19:	----------------------------	00u-----------------------0---0n	0	-0.00	0.00	47.00
20:	----------------------------	nu0-----------------------1-----n0	0	-2.00	-2.00	47.00
21:	-----------------------n-	nun-----------------------u----n0	0	-2.00	-2.00	45.00
22:	-----------------------n-	0un-----------------------u----u1	0	-1.00	-1.00	43.00
23:	----------------------------	u11-----------------------------1n1	0	-1.00	-1.00	42.00
24:	----------------------------	100----------------------10----00	0	0.00	0.00	41.00
25:	----------------------------	110-----------------------------11	0	-0.00	-0.00	41.00
26:	----------------------------	u00-----------------------0---11	0	0.00	0.00	41.00
27:	----------------------------	100-----------------------------n0	0	-1.00	-1.00	41.00
28:	-----------------------n-	011-----------------------u----00	0	0.00	0.00	40.00
29:	----------------------------	001-----------------------------01	0	-2.00	-2.00	40.00
30:	----------------------u-	n10-----------------------n---111	0	0.00	-0.00	38.00
31:	----------------------------	u00-----------------------------110	0	-2.00	-2.00	38.00
32:	----------------------u-	100-----------------------n--1011	0	0.00	0.00	36.00
33:	----------------------------	u10----------------------------000u	0	-2.00	-2.00	36.00
34:	-----------------------n	011-----------------------un-0001	0	0.00	-0.00	34.00
35:	----------------------------	u10----------------------------01un	0	-1.00	-1.00	34.00
36:	----------------------------	0u0-----------------------------1-1n1	0	-2.00	-2.00	33.00
37:	-----------------------n	uu-----------------------------u--1011	0	-1.00	-1.00	31.00
38:	----------------------------	un-----------------------1-----1n0	0	-1.00	-1.00	30.00
39:	----------------------------	u10----------------------------011	0	-0.00	-0.00	29.00
40:	----------------------u-	u-0-----------------------1----110	0	-1.00	-1.00	29.00
41:	----------------------------	n-0-----------------------------1n0	0	-1.00	-1.00	28.00
42:	-----------------------n-	10----------------------------u---010	0	0.00	-0.00	27.00
43:	----------------------------	-1------------------------------0u1	0	-1.00	-1.00	27.00
44:	----------------------------	x11----------------------------100	0	-1.00	-1.00	26.00
45:	----------------------------	u-------------------------------101	0	-1.00	-1.00	25.00
46:	----------------------------	n-1-----------------------------011-	0	0.00	0.00	24.00
47:	----------------------------	11------------------------------00n-	0	-1.00	-0.42	24.00
48:	-----------------------n-	-------------------------------u--0011	0	0.00	-0.00	23.00
49:	----------------------------	-1------------------------1---10-0	0	-2.00	-1.00	23.00
50:	-----------------------n	u-1-----------------------u--11-0	0	-1.00	-1.00	21.00
51:	----------------------------	x-1-----------------------------10u-	0	-2.00	-2.00	20.00
52:	----------------------------	1-------------------------------1-1-	0	-1.00	-1.00	18.00
53:	----------------------------	x0-----------------------------0-10	0	-1.00	-1.00	17.00
54:	----------------------------	x-------------------------------11--	0	0.00	0.00	16.00
55:	----------------------------	-------------------------------0-1	0	0.00	0.00	16.00
56:	----------------------------	0------------------------------01-	0	0.00	0.00	16.00
57:	----------------------------	0-------------------------------0---	0	0.00	0.00	16.00
58:	----------------------------	-------------------------------0-1-	0	0.00	0.00	16.00
59:	----------------------------	-------------------------------11-1	0	-0.00	0.00	16.00
60:	----------------------------	-------------------------------n-0	0	0.00	-0.00	16.00
61:	----------------------------	-------------------------------n-0	0	-1.00	-0.42	16.00
62:	-----------------------n--	-------------------------------u--01-0-	0	0.00	0.00	15.00
63:	----------------------------	-------------------------------x1-	0	-1.00	0.00	15.00
64:	----------------------------	-------------------------------u--x	0	-2.00	-0.19	14.00
65:	-----------------------u--	-------------------------------n1-11-u-x	0	-2.00	-2.00	12.00
66:	-----------------------u--	-------------------------------n---x--u	0	-1.00	0.00	10.00
67:	----------------------------	-------------------------------1---u-xx-	0	-3.00	-0.36	9.00
68:	-----------------------u--	-------------------------------n-xx	0	-3.00	-0.42	6.00
69:	-----------------------n--	-------------------------------u---xu-nx	0	-3.00	-0.42	3.00
70:	-----------------------u--					

Table 7. Characteristic for the first block of the 70-step collision after applying the greedy approach. Bold numbers in column $P_{corr}(i)$ highlight impact of new corrective factors.

i	∇A_i	∇W_i	F_W	$P_u(i)$	$P_{corr}(i)$	$N_s(i)$	$N_{corr}(i)$
-4:	0101001101010101010100101101110n00						
-3:	0110011010110001010001111001010						
-2:	0000001111010101011011000000nu1011						
-1:	01000101011010000011001101u010						
0:	011001110100010100010001100000001	n01u10111011001100110--1nun1110	2	-1.00	0.00	1.02	0.00
1:	u10u101101100111110100-nuun0001	u0nn01011010111011-010111n1u10uu	1	-1.00	0.00	2.02	0.00
2:	0u0u100101011010000nun1000nnn1u	01nu0111101010001000010000001n111	0	0.00	0.00	2.02	0.00
3:	111n11111111nuuu1u100n11u10110u1	10000001001101111100101111n0111nn	0	0.00	0.00	2.02	0.00
4:	10100111100nn011n1u11n000101n10n	nu0n11011110100110010010 0nnun00n0	0	0.00	0.00	2.02	0.00
5:	1100100u000010101u110unn0100u10u	n1nu101101101111110001001---0n0111	3	-3.00	0.00	2.02	0.00
6:	n10000unnnnnnnnnnnnnnn0100n1000un1	nuuu0010011010110110-10un010n0	1	0.00	-3.00	2.02	0.00
7:	000111110011101u001u10-1100nn000	uu100011111101101-1010--1n1110n0	3	-2.00	-1.00	3.02	0.00
8:	u0001101101111110110010u-010uu0u1	00100110110000001-1011-10nu1001	2	-1.00	-5.00	4.02	0.00
9:	110011111111100011001111u-11001011	nnu0001110011011--------0n0111n1	8	-4.00	-2.00	5.02	0.00
10:	01000100001000101---1nu-10nn0010	10u0101011000-110--------nn10100	9	-6.00	-4.00	9.02	2.88
11:	10011101100011-1000--n1--10100n	uuu010000-00000----------n01111n	11	-3.00	-7.42	12.02	5.88
12:	u101111110100001----------0000nn	11n000100100-1----------u1u0001	12	-8.00	-7.00	20.02	13.88
13:	u11001111111100111111------1-1011n1	nu011011011111-00--------u01100n	9	-4.00	-2.00	24.02	17.88
14:	1010111000100000----------11111u	nnn000000000001----------uuu01n1	10	-1.00	-8.00	29.02	22.88
15:	110101110111----------------0u01	u0n10000111-1---1----------100nu	14	-5.00	-6.00	38.02	31.88
16:	n0111011--0011-------------1001	nn10100000001-11--------111u00n0	0	-0.02	-0.55	47.02	40.88
17:	000--1111----------------11u1	0un01110000000----------1n01111n	0	0.00	0.00	47.00	40.86
18:	n00-------------------------	nu00000011-1---1----------un01n0	0	-1.00	-1.00	47.00	40.86
19:	--0-------------------------	00u10100-010-1----------110101n	0	0.00	0.00	46.00	39.86
20:	---------------------------	nu100111100-1----------000011u1	0	-1.00	-1.00	46.00	39.86
21:	-----------------------u-	nun001100-1---0----------n0001u1	0	-2.00	-2.00	45.00	38.86
22:	-----------------------u-	1un0101-010-1----------1n0111n0	0	-1.00	-1.00	43.00	36.86
23:	---------------------------	n110111000-1--------------1101u0	0	-1.00	-1.00	42.00	35.86
24:	---------------------------	11001111-0---0----------11110101	0	0.00	0.00	41.00	34.86
25:	---------------------------	100111-1-0-0----------00000010	0	-0.00	0.00	41.00	34.86
26:	---------------------------	u00011001-0----------11101110	0	0.00	0.00	41.00	34.86
27:	---------------------------	1001000-----0----------101100u0	0	-1.00	-1.00	41.00	34.86
28:	-----------------------u	01110-0-1----------0n010010	0	0.00	0.00	40.00	33.86
29:	---------------------------	00000010-1----------000000	0	-2.00	-2.00	40.00	33.86
30:	-----------------------n-	u11001-----0----------0u010110	0	-0.00	0.00	38.00	31.86
31:	---------------------------	u000-0-0----------010111	0	-2.00	-2.00	38.00	31.86
32:	-----------------------n-	0100101-0----------100u000011	0	-0.00	0.00	36.00	29.86
33:	---------------------------	n0000-----0----------0100000n	0	-2.00	**-1.91**	36.00	29.86
34:	------------------------u	010-0-1----------1nu00100	0	0.00	0.00	34.00	27.94
35:	---------------------------	n10100-0----------001110nu	0	-1.00	-1.00	34.00	27.94
36:	---------------------------	1n11----------------11100000u1	0	-2.00	-2.00	33.00	26.94
37:	-----------------------u-	uu-1-0-1----------0n101010	0	-1.00	-1.00	31.00	24.94
38:	---------------------------	nu100-1----------0000011n1	0	-1.00	-1.00	30.00	23.94
39:	---------------------------	u00----------------01000001	0	0.00	0.00	29.00	22.94
40:	---------------------------	u-1-0----------011100101	0	-1.00	-1.00	29.00	22.94
41:	---------------------------	u101-1----------1111110u0	0	-1.00	-1.00	28.00	21.94
42:	------------------------u	01-----1----------00n110010	0	0.00	0.00	27.00	20.94
43:	---------------------------	-1-0----------10111n0	0	-1.00	-1.00	27.00	20.94
44:	---------------------------	u11-0----------001111011	0	-1.00	-1.00	26.00	19.94
45:	---------------------------	n----0----------00011110	0	-1.00	-1.00	25.00	18.94
46:	---------------------------	n-0----------1000100-	0	-0.00	0.00	24.00	17.94
47:	---------------------------	11-0----------10110u1	0	-1.00	-1.00	24.00	17.94
48:	------------------------u	100n111001	0	0.00	0.00	23.00	16.94
49:	---------------------------	-0-1----------0000101-1	0	-2.00	-2.00	23.00	16.94
50:	------------------------u	u-1----------1n011100	0	-1.00	-1.00	21.00	14.94
51:	---------------------------	x----------------111011n-	0	-2.00	-2.00	20.00	13.94
52:	---------------------------	0----------------1111000-0-	0	-1.00	-1.00	18.00	11.94
53:	---------------------------	x0----------111101011	0	-1.00	-1.00	17.00	10.94
54:	---------------------------	x----------01000110-	0	-0.00	0.00	16.00	9.94
55:	---------------------------	----------0100-0-1	0	0.00	0.00	16.00	9.94
56:	---------------------------	1----------100111101-	0	-0.00	0.00	16.00	9.94
57:	---------------------------	----------01010---	0	0.00	0.00	16.00	9.94
58:	---------------------------	----------01001-1-0-	0	0.00	0.00	16.00	9.94
59:	---------------------------	----------101010-1	0	0.00	0.00	16.00	9.94
60:	---------------------------	----------001100----	0	0.00	0.00	16.00	9.94
61:	---------------------------	----------01-1-u-1	0	-1.00	**-0.99**	16.00	9.94
62:	-----------------------u-	----------00n0000-0-	0	0.00	0.00	15.00	8.96
63:	---------------------------	----------100--x--	0	-1.00	-1.00	15.00	8.96
64:	---------------------------	----------10110-0-n--x	0	-2.00	**-1.98**	14.00	7.96
65:	------------------------n--	----------001u0101-n-x	0	-2.00	**-1.98**	12.00	5.98
66:	------------------------n--	----------011u1--x--n	0	-1.00	-1.00	10.00	4.00
67:	---------------------------	----------111-0-n-xx-	0	-3.00	-3.00	9.00	3.00
68:	------------------------n---	----------0u0100-u-xx	0	-3.00	**0.00**	6.00	0.00
69:	------------------------u---	----------1n0--xx-ux	0	-3.00	**0.00**	3.00	0.00
70:	------------------------x---						

Table 8. Characteristic for the second block of the 70-step collision after applying the greedy approach. Bold numbers in column $P_{corr}(i)$ highlight impact of new corrective factors.

i	∇A_i	∇W_i	F_W	$P_u(i)$	$P_{corr}(i)$	$N_s(i)$	$N_{corr}(i)$
-4:	010100110101010101001011011110n00						
-3:	011001101011000101000111111001010						
-2:	00000011110101011011000000nu1011						
-1:	0100010101011010000011001101u010						
0:	0101001101000110011101110n101	u01n10111101110110111111101uun0010	0	0.00	0.00	0.97	0.00
1:	n11n100010010000101011001nnun0nuu	n1nn00101010001000010101u0n01uu	0	0.00	0.00	0.97	0.00
2:	1u0u101001010010n0nn11100010u	10un100100010101111000000100u101	0	0.00	0.00	0.97	0.00
3:	u1un0000100111nn1u00100nu1011u0n	01010000011000110110000n1001uu	0	0.00	0.00	0.97	0.00
4:	n0101110n1u1u11010n1011011uu0010	nu0n11011101111110011000110nnu10u0	0	0.00	0.00	0.97	0.00
5:	010n011u11010n10nu010u01u0101nnu	u1un00000000001000001-00111u0111	1	0.00	0.00	0.97	0.00
6:	1n000111100uu00110100-n00011001u	nuuu1111111111---1000-001uu101n0	4	-3.00	-3.00	1.97	0.00
7:	1nnnnnnnnnnnnnnnn01111-01nn101u00	uu10111111101111-1100--01n1001u1	3	-1.00	-1.00	2.97	0.24
8:	10001100001111110010---1un110101	00001111111111011--000---11uu0000	5	-5.00	-5.00	4.97	2.24
9:	010011111111001110001-00100010n	uun0100011011110--------1n1111u1	8	-2.00	-2.00	4.97	2.24
10:	u10101100100011------11--nu0u0un0	10n0000110111-1-1--------uu10101	10	-4.00	-4.00	10.97	8.24
11:	111010101111----------n--0000011	nnu001010--00010----------x00101u	12	-7.42	-7.42	16.97	14.24
12:	0011001000011-------------1n01n1	01n111110011-1-----------u0n0110	12	-7.00	-7.00	21.55	18.82
13:	u00100011111000----------000001u	uu0011010001-0-1----------x01001u	12	-2.00	-2.00	26.55	23.82
14:	10110001010----------------1111u	uuu1111111-0101----------xuu10n1	12	-8.00	-8.00	36.55	33.82
15:	0010010001111--------------11u10	u0n10110010-0-1-1----------101un	13	-6.00	-6.00	40.55	37.82
16:	n1100111111000-------------10011	un000000010-0-0----------00u10n1	0	-0.55	-0.55	47.55	44.82
17:	000001111---------------------1n1	0un010111-1010-----------u00110n	0	0.00	0.00	47.00	44.27
18:	n00------------------------100	uu10011001-0-1-0----------un10n1	0	-1.00	-1.00	47.00	44.27
19:	--0-------------------------	00u01010-1-0-0----------000010n	0	0.00	0.00	46.00	43.27
20:	----------------------------	nu001101-11-1-----------110010n0	0	-1.00	-1.00	46.00	43.27
21:	--------------------------n-	nun010010-1-0-0-----------u0101n0	0	-2.00	-2.00	45.00	42.27
22:	--------------------------n-	0un0101-0-0-1-----------u1100u1	0	-1.00	-1.00	43.00	40.27
23:	----------------------------	u111100-00-1------------0011n1	0	-1.00	-1.00	42.00	39.27
24:	----------------------------	10001110-1-0-0-----------10010000	0	0.00	0.00	41.00	38.27
25:	----------------------------	110110-0-1-1------------0010111	0	-0.00	0.00	41.00	38.27
26:	----------------------------	u00000-11-1-------------10101111	0	0.00	0.00	41.00	38.27
27:	----------------------------	1001100---1-1-----------00110n0	0	-1.00	-1.00	41.00	38.27
28:	--------------------------n-	01101-1-1----------------u000000	0	-0.00	0.00	40.00	37.27
29:	----------------------------	00100-11-0-----------------111101	0	-2.00	-2.00	40.00	37.27
30:	-------------------------u-	n10110-----1------------n010111	0	0.00	0.00	38.00	35.27
31:	----------------------------	u001-1-0------------------101110	0	-2.00	-2.00	38.00	35.27
32:	-------------------------u-	1001-11-1------------10n111011	0	0.00	0.00	36.00	33.27
33:	----------------------------	u1000---1-0-----------1001000u	0	-2.00	**-1.91**	36.00	33.27
34:	--------------------------n	011-1-0-----------------0un00001	0	0.00	0.00	34.00	31.36
35:	----------------------------	u10-10-1------------111001un	0	-1.00	-1.00	34.00	31.36
36:	----------------------------	0u01------------------0110101n1	0	-2.00	-2.00	33.00	30.36
37:	--------------------------n-	uu-1-1-1----------------1u001011	0	-1.00	-1.00	31.00	28.36
38:	----------------------------	un-01-1-----------------1001001n0	0	-1.00	-1.00	30.00	27.36
39:	----------------------------	u10---0-----------------11000011	0	0.00	0.00	29.00	26.36
40:	----------------------------	u-0-1-------------------110011110	0	-1.00	-1.00	29.00	26.36
41:	----------------------------	n-01-0-----------------011101n0	0	-1.00	-1.00	28.00	25.36
42:	--------------------------n-	10----0-----------------1u011010	0	0.00	0.00	27.00	24.36
43:	----------------------------	-1-1------------------01110u1	0	-1.00	-1.00	27.00	24.36
44:	----------------------------	x11-1------------------011101100	0	-1.00	-1.00	26.00	23.36
45:	----------------------------	u---0-0-----------------10000101	0	-1.00	-1.00	25.00	22.36
46:	----------------------------	n-1--------------------0110011-	0	0.00	0.00	24.00	21.36
47:	----------------------------	11-0-------------------01000n-	0	-1.00	-1.00	24.00	21.36
48:	--------------------------n-	----------------------01u000011	0	0.00	0.00	23.00	20.36
49:	----------------------------	-1-1-------------------0110010-0	0	-2.00	-2.00	23.00	20.36
50:	--------------------------n-	u-1--------------------1u0111-0	0	-1.00	-1.00	21.00	18.36
51:	----------------------------	x-1--------------------101010u-	0	-2.00	-2.00	20.00	17.36
52:	----------------------------	1----------------------1110101-1-	0	-1.00	-1.00	18.00	15.36
53:	----------------------------	x0---------------------010100-10	0	-1.00	-1.00	17.00	14.36
54:	----------------------------	x----------------------0111011--	0	0.00	0.00	16.00	13.36
55:	----------------------------	--------------------0111-0-1	0	0.00	0.00	16.00	13.36
56:	----------------------------	0----------------------00100-01-	0	0.00	0.00	16.00	13.36
57:	----------------------------	0----------------------11010---	0	0.00	0.00	16.00	13.36
58:	----------------------------	---------------------1001-0-1-	0	0.00	0.00	16.00	13.36
59:	----------------------------	---------------------101-11-1	0	-0.00	0.00	16.00	13.36
60:	----------------------------	---------------------11110----	0	-0.00	0.00	16.00	13.36
61:	----------------------------	---------------------01-0-n-0	0	-1.00	**-0.99**	16.00	13.36
62:	--------------------------n--	---------------------1u1-01-0-	0	0.00	0.00	15.00	12.37
63:	----------------------------	---------------------111--x1-	0	-1.00	-1.00	15.00	12.37
64:	----------------------------	---------------------10000-1-u--x	0	-2.00	**-1.98**	14.00	11.37
65:	-------------------------u---	---------------------010n1-11-u-x	0	-2.00	**-1.98**	12.00	9.39
66:	-------------------------u--	---------------------001n1--x--u	0	-1.00	-1.00	10.00	7.42
67:	----------------------------	---------------------11-0-u-xx-	0	-3.00	**-2.42**	9.00	6.42
68:	-------------------------u---	---------------------1n0-01-n-xx	0	-3.00	**-2.00**	6.00	4.00
69:	--------------------------n---	---------------------1u1--xu-nx	0	-3.00	**-2.00**	3.00	2.00
70:	-------------------------u---						

Cryptanalysis of the CRUSH Hash Function

Matt Henricksen[1] and Lars R. Knudsen[2]

[1] Institute for Infocomm Research,
A*STAR, Singapore
mhenricksen@i2r.a-star.edu.sg
[2] Department of Mathematics,
Technical University of Denmark,
DK-2800 Kgs. Lyngby, Denmark
Lars.R.Knudsen@mat.dtu.dk

Abstract. Iterated Halving has been suggested as a replacement to the Merkle-Damgård construction following attacks on the MDx family of hash functions. The core of the scheme is an iterated block cipher that provides keying and input material for future rounds. The CRUSH hash function provides a specific instantiation of the block cipher for Iterated Halving. In this paper, we identify structural problems with the scheme, and show that by using a bijective function, such as the block cipher used in CRUSH or the AES, we can trivially identify collisions and second preimages on many equal-length messages of length ten blocks or more. The cost is ten decryptions of the block cipher, this being less than the generation of a single digest. We show that even if Iterated Halving is repaired, the construction has practical issues that means it is not suitable for general deployment. We conclude this paper with the somewhat obvious statement that CRUSH, and more generally Iterated Halving, should not be used.

Keywords: CRUSH, Iterated Halving, Hash Functions, Cryptanalysis, Collisions, Second preimages.

1 Introduction

The CRUSH hash function was proposed by Gauravaram, Millan and May [3][5] as an example of a new hash-function design paradigm called Iterated Halving, also described in the same paper. Iterated Halving was based on the designers' almost prescient observation that the repeated use of the Merkle-Damgård (MD) construction within hash function design constituted a single point of failure, and that a forthcoming attack on one member of that family may also apply to others. Of course, this view was vindicated by the quick succession of multi-block collision attacks by Wang, *et al.* on MD4, MD5, SHA-1, etc. [6][7][8]. Following this, Gauravaram *et al.* promoted Iterated Halving, specifically CRUSH, as a viable alternative to MD-type hash functions [3][4]. However CRUSH had until now not received significant analysis. In this paper, we demonstrate severe security and implementation problems with the technique of Iterated Halving, and the CRUSH hash function instantiation.

C. Adams, A. Miri, and M. Wiener (Eds.): SAC 2007, LNCS 4876, pp. 74–83, 2007.

Good hash functions possess at least three primary security properties, including collision resistance, preimage resistance and second preimage resistance. Collision resistance refers to the property whereby it is hard to find two messages x and y, such that for $x \neq y, H(x) = H(y)$ for hash function H. Second preimage resistance refers to the difficulty, given message x and its hash $H(x)$, to find y such that $H(y) = H(x)$. A hash function that is not a collision resistant hash function, meaning that it does not offer both collision resistance and second preimage resistance, has limited application. We show that collisions and second-preimages can be found within CRUSH in ten operations. In fact, the same attack applies even if we substitute the Advanced Encryption Standard (AES) [1] with 192-bit or 256-bit keys for CRUSH.

In Section 2, we describe the CRUSH hash function in the context of Iterated Halving. In Section 3, we show how to use the bijective properties of Iterated Halving to find collisions and second preimages on provided messages for CRUSH or instantiations of Iterated Halving using other block ciphers. In Section 4, we show a persistent weakness in the structure of Iterated Halving with relaxed assumptions about the nature of its block cipher core. In Section 5, we indicate a practical issue that shows Iterated Halving to be inferior to Merkle-Damgård construction from an implementation viewpoint. This issue is likely to prevent the uptake on many platforms, of any hash function implemented in the context of Iterated Halving, even assuming that the security issues could be repaired. Finally, in Section 6, we offer closing remarks.

2   The CRUSH Hash Function

The structure of CRUSH is shown in Figure 1. CRUSH consists of a data buffer, a Bijection Selection Component (BSC), boolean functions $f_i, 1 \leq i \leq 3$, and a bijective function B. B is effectively a block cipher, where the plaintext comes from the data buffer, and the key material from the boolean functions. The function B contains a repeated sub-function F, the details of which do not affect our attack.

The authors of CRUSH suggest that another hash function within the Iterated Halving paradigm can be constructed by replacing B with another block cipher. For example, this could be the AES with 192-bit or 256-bit keys.

2.1   Compressing a Message Using CRUSH

Initially the data buffer contains the entire message to be processed – that is, n 64-bit blocks. The value of n is at least 17, and padding must be applied to short messages to accomplish this. The padding includes length encoding, which means that in this paper, we consider only attacks on messages of equal length.

In each round, a pair of blocks, M_a and M_b, are removed from the head of the buffer for processing by the B function. B also accepts three "keying" elements k_1, k_2 and k_3. The output of B is a pair of blocks y_a and y_b. B is a bijective function. Aside from that, its details are unimportant to our attack.

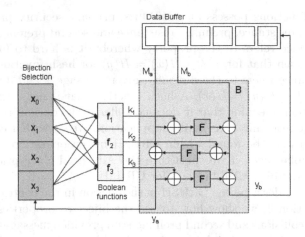

Fig. 1. The CRUSH hash function

Block y_b is appended to the buffer. Thus with each round, the buffer shrinks by one block. After $\frac{n}{2}$ iterations of the B function, there will be $\frac{n}{2}$ blocks in the buffer. After another $\frac{n}{4}$ iterations, the buffer will contain $\frac{n}{4}$ blocks and so on[1]. This is the "halving" aspect of iterated halving. The process is iterated until the point when there are only d blocks remaining in the buffer, where d is the desired digest size in 64-bit blocks. The algorithm terminates, and its output, the digest, is taken as the remaining contents of the buffer. The CRUSH paper suggests a value of $d = 4$, and we analyze CRUSH according to this recommendation. However, the attacks in this paper apply no matter what the value of d.

The BSC holds four 64-bit blocks in its state. In each round, the states in the BSC are shifted such that at time i, block $S_t^i = S_{t+1}^{i-1}$ for $0 \leq t < 3$. State S_0^{i-1} is discarded. The block S_3^i is populated with y_a^i.

Table 1. A toy example of Iterated Halving

Round	Buffer	BSC State	B Function
0	a b c d e f g h	c_0 c_1 c_2 c_3	$(a,b) \rightarrow (y_a^1, y_b^1)$
1	c d e f g h y_b^1 –	y_a^1 c_0 c_1 c_2	$(c,d) \rightarrow (y_a^2, y_b^2)$
2	e f g h y_b^1 y_b^2 – –	y_a^2 y_a^1 c_0 c_1	$(e,f) \rightarrow (y_a^3, y_b^3)$
3	g h y_b^1 y_b^2 y_b^3 – – –	y_a^3 y_a^2 y_a^1 c_0	$(g,h) \rightarrow (y_a^4, y_b^4)$
4	y_b^1 y_b^2 y_b^3 y_b^4 – – – –	y_a^4 y_a^3 y_a^2 y_a^1	—

A toy example of a message compression illustrates the principle of Iterated Halving below. This example (ignoring padding and message length constraints) compresses an eight-block message $abcdefgh$ into the four-block digest $y_b^1 y_b^2 y_b^3 y_b^4$.

---

[1] This description does not quite apply if the number of initial blocks is not a power of two. When the number of blocks on the buffer is odd, a dummy block is taken from the BSC to maintain pairing of message blocks. For expediency we do not consider this case in detail.

3   Finding Collisions and Second Preimages

CRUSH implements iterated halving by taking a pair of blocks from the data buffer, processing them concurrently within the B function, returning one element of the pair to the data buffer, and moving the other into the BSC. The BSC and associated boolean functions implement an analog to Key Feedback Mode, whereby one half of the output of one B function round becomes the key for the next. This appears to makes differential cryptanalysis of the function more difficult since the attacker does not have direct control over the key material, which is a highly non-linear function of the input. However, the BSC contains a flaw which allows differential cryptanalysis to be simply applied. Furthermore, the F sub-function within the B block cipher is designed to be bijective so that for x_0, x_1 when $F(x_0) = F(x_1)$, then by necessity $x_0 = x_1$. This is intended to complicate the identification of collisions on the B structure.

However we can easily find collisions and second-preimages by making use of the fact that B is a bijection and reversible. In addition to the bijection property, we use the fact that any difference entering into the BSC endures for only four rounds before it is discarded. By ensuring that differences enter into the BSC rather than the buffer, we need only be concerned with message words for five rounds (ie. ten pairs of words), including the words that introduce the difference.

Recall that at round i, the B block cipher function takes two message words M_a^i and M_b^i as inputs, and produces y_a^i and y_b^i as outputs. Then for the ten pairs of message words $(M_a^i, M_a'^i), (M_b^i, M_b'^i), \ldots, (M_a^{i+4}, M_a'^{i+4})$ and $(M_b^{i+4}, M'i + 4_b)$, we want to use a differential $D1 : (\Delta x_0, \Delta x_1) \rightarrow (\Delta y_0, \Delta 0)$ at all times. This ensures that the difference never goes into the buffer. Without loss of generality, we assume that $i = 0$. However, it can be any value less than $\frac{L}{2} - 5$, where L is the length of the message in 64-bit blocks.

3.1   Identifying Collisions

Because the block cipher B is reversible, it is possible to work backwards through the function by starting with the desired outputs and crafting the message words to satisfy them. To generate a collision, set the outputs of the first call to the block cipher in each message such that $y_a^0 \neq y_a'^0$ and $y_b^0 = y_b'^0$. In the example below, we set $y_a^0 = 0$, $y_a'^0 = 1$, and $y_b^0 = y_b'^0 = 0$. Since the keying material to the block cipher is readily known – the initial state of the BSC is public – it is trivial to calculate M_a^0, M_b^0, $M_a'^0$, $M_b'^0$ (respectively $C51F7BC286ECFA2B$, $877C26794DC08412$ and $BF24001D4DF6E8E5$ and $2DA41C2E7C0DBBCD$ in the example below).

For the following three output words, set $y_a^i = y_a'^i$ and $y_b^i = y_b'^i, 1 \leq i \leq 4$. The only input differences occur in the BSC. In the example below, we set all words equal to 0, but any other value is equally legitimate. Calculate the message words that act as input to B as before. After four rounds, the difference introduced by $y_a^0 \neq y_a'^0$ disappears from the BSC. An internal collision results (ie. the states of both instances of CRUSH are now the same). Of the course, the collision is maintained by appending identical words to each message, and the resulting digests are identical.

The complexity for finding a collision on any two messages that differ in ten words is just ten decryptions of B (five per message instance). Since all digests, even including a null message, involve the processing of at least seventeen blocks, the collision complexity is at most $\frac{10}{17}$ of generating a single digest.

An example collision on two length-ten messages is shown below.

Message 1 (before padding):

```
C51F7BC286ECFA2B 877C26794DC08412 36E90FCF9B55342D 5CA8F7C75E0DDC9D
64955AF928952224 05C8EFFDC93A2C3B 1009BAE571FC033B 3F9716020BD2918D
AA727095411A8B26 81B4ED776F2ADA41
```

Message 2 (before padding):

```
BF24001D4DF6E8E5 2DA41C2E7C0DBBCD E125E4AFB770AAC9 5C3BEE7C15F27ED0
64955AF928952224 05C8EFFDC93A2C3B  B07155E6E33D428E EAAC9F125F2CF906
BA6A889D411A9B26 2E5A2980EC439EBB
```

Colliding 256-bit digest:

```
AF1E98C1CAFD0CC8 FC0421CCE65C9902 E7478613CD9C2867 D5EAFE307674B3AF
```

3.2 Identifying Second Preimages

The technique for finding second preimages is very similar to that for identifying collisions. It too deals with five rounds and has a complexity of only ten operations.

Generate a digest for message M, taking note of the output of B for rounds $i \ldots i + 4$. For the second preimage M', set $y_b'^i = y_b^i$ and $y_a'^i = x, x \neq y_a^i$. Then for the following four rounds for M', set $y_b'^j = y_b^j$ and $y_a'^k = y_a^k$ for $i < j \leq i + 4$. Decrypt over B for each $y_a'^i, y_b^i$ to obtain $M_a'^i, M_b^i$.

An example second preimage is shown for the ten-block message containing all zeroes prior to padding. It is easy to find any of the 2^{64} ten-block preimages for this message. The second state word of the BSC is not used as an input to the boolean functions - hence the all zero values in the fifth and sixth words of the preimage.

Message (before padding):

```
0000000000000000 0000000000000000 0000000000000000 0000000000000000
0000000000000000 0000000000000000 0000000000000000 0000000000000000
0000000000000000 0000000000000000
```

256-bit Digest of Message:

```
0923D64E00506F55 FB0B37D9841B5B23 12DEE7CAB0C369B8 1D5F834530C72B22
```

Second preimage (before padding):

B0D922EE3E5BF143 D32F46652DA2CEEA 51FE1E43AF1B4800 78F085DFDD4ADC23
0000000000000000 0000000000000000 1136516598C9E675 183DA3ED247AC07D
1030627ADD029C59 C9E9BA651935AE16

Digest of Second preimage:

0923D64E00506F55 FB0B37D9841B5B23 12DEE7CAB0C369B8 1D5F834530C72B22

3.3   Constraints on Messages

These attacks apply to all messages of equal length which are at least ten blocks in length, and differ only in four consecutive words, provided that differences in the BSC are not transferred as dummy blocks to the buffer. This occurs only for the last word of a message with an odd number of blocks, hence is not a major concern to the applicability of our attack. In the majority of cases in which the attack applies, there are 2^{32} choices for the paired values of each word with a difference. These conditions are much less restrictive than the attacks on MD4 [6], etc, which must adhere to specially prescribed bit-conditions. It is very unusual to find such an low complexity attack on a hash function that also has such a large degree of freedom in choice of message words.

4   Corner-Then-Pass: An Observation on Iterated Halving

Our best attack on CRUSH, presented in the previous section, relies on the fact that the B function is bijective and reversible, as is the case whenever B is a block cipher. Here we relax that assumption to make an observation about Iterated Halving that shows that its problems are more deeply ingrained than in the selection of the B function.

In the case where B is not bijective (that is, we replace it with an ideal compression function, using for example, a block cipher with a feed-forward), we are able to generate a collision on a single round by a (standard) birthday attack on B, which is of complexity 2^{64}. For example, find different message words $(M_a^1, M_a'^1)$ and $(M_b^1, M_b'^1)$, such that the outputs $y_a^1 = y_a'^1$ and $y_b^1 = y_b'^1$. Subsequently the internal states for the two messages are equal and a collision is easily found. This attack is far better than a generic birthday collision attack on CRUSH which is of complexity 2^{128} for a 256 bit construction.

Note that in the above collision attack, the inputs to BSC were kept equal in the collision on B. In the defense of CRUSH one may argue that it is possible to find constructions for B such that the complexity of finding these collisions is larger than a standard birthday attack when some of the input is kept constant. However in the following it is demonstrated that iterated halving method contains a fundamental flaw which allows collisions faster than the generic ones for any constructions of B.

We augment differential $D1 : (\Delta x_0, \Delta x_1) \rightarrow (\Delta y_0, \Delta 0)$ from the previous section with $D2 : (\Delta x_2, \Delta x_3) \rightarrow (\Delta 0, \Delta y_1)$. The values of $\Delta x_0, \Delta x_1, \Delta x_2, \Delta x_3, \Delta y_0$

and Δy_1 are immaterial - we are interested in the half collisions $\Delta 0$. Nor do we need to concern ourselves with the internal structure of either B or F to find these half collisions. By the birthday paradox, we can find inputs and outputs that match each differential with an effort[2] of around 2^{32}.

Using differential $D1$ we can keep non-zero (active) differences flowing into the BSC, and using differential $D2$ we can direct active differences into the buffer. In the latter case, the active difference either becomes part of the digest or is processed by B at a later time. If it becomes part of the digest, then no collision is possible. Therefore we want to avoid this outcome in our attack.

On the other hand, using differential $D1$ directs active differences to the BSC, where it will be used in three of the following four rounds as input into the boolean functions. This will affect the subsequent differences into B in a non-linear way, and make them harder to control. We also want to avoid this in our attack.

So it seems that in either case, an active difference hinders our attack. But this is not so. We place message differences very carefully. We then use $D2$ to direct active differences to the buffer until just before the digest is formed, and in the very last round, use the $D1$ differential to route the sole remaining difference to the BSC, removing it from the buffer and creating a collision. The active element is retired to the BSC at just the moment the digest is formed. The algorithm terminates before the boolean functions propagate the difference in the BSC. Therefore the differences coming from the BSC into the B function are zero at all times.

This kind of 'corner-then-pass' technique is possible due to another flaw in Iterated Halving - that the BSC is a sink for differences in message input which may be delayed so that they have no effect on the digest. The technique does not apply to the Merkle-Damgård construction, as it does not have this delay component.

The shortest message pair from which this collision can be generated has a length of twenty 64-bit blocks, due to padding requirements, the need to use both differentials, and on the limitation that the $D1$ differential can only be used to produce the last block of the digest. In this message pair, differences must be introduced only in words 5, 6, 7 and 8.

This can be seen in the diagram below, which shows the differences in the message words within the buffer. For clarity, the message difference $\Delta 0$ is represented by '–', and padding by P. At round 17, the requisite amount of material in the buffer is available and the algorithm terminates.

$D2_a$ and $D2_b$ can be generated independently at a cost of 2^{32} operations each. The success of finding a collision on $D2_c$ depends upon the choice of message values made for $D2_a$ and $D2_b$, and $D1_a$ on all three prior message choices. If the

---

[2] In practice, at the time of publication, the complexity will become slightly higher as storing $2^{32} \times 8$ bytes of material in order to find a match is beyond the capability of most modern hardware. Virtual memory could be used, but this will add a large coefficient to the cost of each operation. In the near future, sufficient volatile memory will be available on commodity machines to avoid this penalty.

Round	Buffer	B
0	$----\ \Delta A\ \Delta B\ \Delta C\ \Delta D -------------$ P P	
1	$\Delta A\ \Delta B\ \Delta C\ \Delta D ------------$ P P $--$	
2	$\Delta C\ \Delta D -------------$ P P $-- \Delta E$	$D2_a$: $(\Delta A, \Delta B) \rightarrow (\Delta 0, \Delta E)$
3	$------------$ P P $-- \Delta E\ \Delta F$	$D2_b$: $(\Delta C, \Delta D) \rightarrow (\Delta 0, \Delta F)$
9	P P $-- \Delta E\ \Delta F ------$	
11	$\Delta E\ \Delta F --------$	
12	$-------- \Delta G$	$D2_c$: $(\Delta E, \Delta F) \rightarrow (\Delta 0, \Delta G)$
16	$\Delta G ----$	
17	$----$	$D1_a$: $(\Delta G, \Delta 0) \rightarrow (\Delta H, \Delta 0)$

values do not successfully chain, then backtracking is required. Therefore the complexity of the attack is $2^{33+32+32} = 2^{97}$. This is well below the complexity of finding collisions on the whole hash function by the birthday paradox (ie. 2^{128} for a 256-bit digest), and is an attack that does not depend upon the bijective nature of the embedded block cipher.

5   Iterated Halving Is Not Implementation-Friendly

In [3], it is noted that dedicated hash functions are generally more efficient than hash functions based upon block ciphers. This may be the case in terms of raw throughput, but efficiency is multi-dimensional and Iterated Halving (also [3]), which defines CRUSH as a new dedicated hash function, is an interesting case study in why this statement may not be true in other dimensions, specifically storage costs.

Iterated Halving is embodied by the behaviour of CRUSH's data buffer in accepting one data block for every two that it releases. The buffer is a First-in First-out (FIFO) queue, and blocks must be processed in order. All blocks of the original message must be processed before any blocks produced as output from the B function are reprocessed by B and appended to the buffer. This impacts another dimension of efficiency, since after r rounds, the number of blocks in the buffer will be $min(n - r, d)$. Therefore, assuming streaming of the original message, the buffer must be allocated to contain $\frac{n}{2}$ blocks.

This imposes limits on the length of a message that can be hashed using Iterated Halving. A hardware chip that implements Iterated Halving using x bytes of memory cannot process a $(2 \times x + 1)$-length message. For very large messages, this even applies to general purpose processors aided by virtual memory. The limit imposed by Iterated Halving is far short of the $2^{64} - 1$-bit message limit imposed by the length-encoding of SHA-1.

Consider the performance of SHA-1 on a hardware accelerator. It requires approximately 80 bytes of memory (five 32-bit states, and 512 bits for the current message block), and can handle all real-world messages. It can also be implemented very cheaply, in contrast to a flexible implementation of Iterated Halving, in which the cost is linearly related to the amount of on-board memory and maximum message size. The SHA-1 accelerator does not obsolete faster than its algorithm: it can process a High-Density (HD)-DVD equally as well as a standard DVD. This is in contrast to an Iterated Halving accelerator carrying 2.5 Gb of onboard memory, which is already substantial and expensive, but incapable of processing in one pass the data on a HD-DVD.

This dimension of efficiency was signposted early on in the history of hash functions. Quoting from Damgård [2],

> ...things seem to get more complex as the length of the messages hashed increase. On the other hand, a hash function is of no use, if we are not allowed to hash messages of arbitrary lengths.

It is important for hash function designers to consider the efficiency of their designs in multiple dimensions, rather than just in terms of raw throughput. Iterated Halving, irrespective of its security flaws, is not suitable for practical deployment.

6 Conclusion

In this paper, we have shown that CRUSH, and more generally Iterated Halving, which mandates a bijective B function, do not satisfy the requirements of good hash functions from either implementation or security viewpoints.

We have shown how to generate collisions and second preimages for Iterated Halving using a block cipher, for messages of equal length in which four words differ. The freedom in choosing those words is very large. The ability to create these collisions and second preimages relies upon the B function of CRUSH being bijective, and upon the BSC rapidly discarding differences. The complexity of these attacks is extremely small, amounting to only ten decryptions of the B function irrespective of the digest size. The attacks apply when any block cipher is used, including the AES with 192-bit or 256-bit keys. It is rare to see practical attacks on symmetric ciphers or hash functions with such a low complexity.

We have also shown that irrespective of the properties of the B function, the structure of Iterated Halving is flawed, because it introduces a delay into the effect of its state upon the message digest. Careful positioning of differences in the message words may result in a collision through the 'corner-and-pass' technique.

Iterated Halving has shown itself to be inefficient relative to the Merkle-Damgård construction, which has a small, fixed memory requirement irrespective of the message length to be hashed. This will almost certainly inhibit the real-life usage of CRUSH and/or Iterated Halving.

CRUSH is not by itself an especially significant hash function. However, the cryptographic community, following the attacks on the MDx family, now has a particular interest in finding alternative constructions to the long established Merkle-Damgård construction. To be useful to industry, such a replacement must meet the efficiency benchmarks set by Merkle-Damgård, and must surpass its level of security. Iterated Halving has been suggested by its designers as such a replacement. As it stands, Iterated Halving as an abstract construction, with CRUSH as a concrete instantiation, is far from the desirable replacement for which the community is searching. We do not recommend the use of CRUSH.

References

1. Daemen, J., Rijmen, V.: The Design of Rijndael: AES—the Advanced Encryption Standard. Springer, Heidelberg (2002)
2. Damgård, I.: A Design Principle for Hash Functions. In: Brassard, G. (ed.) CRYPTO 1989. LNCS, vol. 435, pp. 416–427. Springer, Heidelberg (1990)
3. Gauravaram, P.: Cryptographic Hash Functions: Cryptanlaysis, Design and Applications. PhD Thesis, Information Security Institute, Faculty of Information Technology, Queensland Unversity of Technology (2007)
4. Gauravaram, P., Millan, W., Dawson, E.P., Viswanathan, K.: Constructing Secure Hash Functions by Enhancing Merkle-Damgård Construction. In: Batten, L.M., Safavi-Naini, R. (eds.) ACISP 2006. LNCS, vol. 4058, pp. 407–420. Springer, Heidelberg (2006)
5. Gauravaram, P., Millan, W., May, L.: CRUSH: A New Cryptographic Hash Function Using Iterated Halving Technique. In: Cryptographic Algorithms and Their Uses, QUT, pp. 28–39 (July 2004)
6. Wang, X., Lai, X., Feng, D., Chen, H., Yu, X.: Cryptanalysis of the Hash Functions MD4 and RIPEMD. In: Cramer, R.J.F. (ed.) EUROCRYPT 2005. LNCS, vol. 3494, pp. 1–18. Springer, Heidelberg (2005)
7. Wang, X., Yin, Y.L., Yu, H.: Finding Collisions in the Full SHA-1. In: Shoup, V. (ed.) CRYPTO 2005. LNCS, vol. 3621, pp. 17–36. Springer, Heidelberg (2005)
8. Wang, X., Yu, H.: How to Break MD5 and Other Hash Functions. In: Cramer, R.J.F. (ed.) EUROCRYPT 2005. LNCS, vol. 3494, pp. 19–35. Springer, Heidelberg (2005)

Improved Side-Channel Collision Attacks
on AES

Andrey Bogdanov

Chair for Communication Security
Ruhr University Bochum, Germany
abogdanov@crypto.rub.de
www.crypto.rub.de

Abstract. Side-channel collision attacks were proposed in [1] and applied to AES in [2]. These are based on detecting collisions in certain positions of the internal state after the first AES round for different executions of the algorithm. The attack needs about 40 measurements and 512 MB precomputed values as well as requires the chosen-plaintext possibility.

In this paper we show how to mount a collision attack on AES using only 6 measurements and about $2^{37.15}$ offline computational steps working with a probability of about 0.85. Another attack uses only 7 measurements and finds the full encryption key with an offline complexity of about $2^{34.74}$ with a probability of 0.99. All our attacks require a negligible amount of memory only and work in the known-plaintext model. This becomes possible by considering collisions in the S-box layers both for different AES executions and within the same AES run. All the attacks work under the assumption that one-byte collisions are detectable.

Keywords: AES, collision attacks, side-channel attacks, generalized collisions, connected components, random graphs.

1 Introduction

An internal collision, as defined in [1] and [2], occurs, if a function f within a cryptographic algorithm processes different input arguments, but returns an equal output argument. As applied to AES, Schramm et al. [2] consider the byte transforms of the MIXCOLUMN operation of the first AES round as the colliding function f. To detect collisions, power consumption curves bytewise corresponding to separate S-box operations in the second round at a certain internal state position after the key addition are compared.

The key idea of our improved collision attacks on AES is that one can detect equal inputs to various S-boxes by comparing the corresponding power consumption curves. This turns out to be possible not only for the outputs of the same function f: Using this technique, it can be possible to detect whether two inputs to the AES S-box are equal within the same AES execution as well as for different AES runs.

C. Adams, A. Miri, and M. Wiener (Eds.): SAC 2007, LNCS 4876, pp. 84–95, 2007.

We introduce the notion of *a generalized internal collision* for AES that occurs within one or several AES runs, if there are two equal input bytes to the S-box operation in some (possibly different) rounds at some (possibly different) byte positions for one or several measurements. In other words, we take all applications of the S-box transform within a number of AES executions and compare them pairwise to each other. As the S-box operation is applied 16 times in each of the 10 rounds (160 varied S-box operations), this gives us about 40 generalized collisions within a single AES run or about 710 generalized collisions within just 6 AES executions.

Each of such collisions can be considered as a (generally) non-linear equation over $GF(2^8)$. The set of all detected collisions corresponds to a system of non-linear equations with respect to the key bytes. In this paper we explore the question of how to solve this large number of equations *linearly*. To be able to linearize, we restrict our consideration to the first two rounds. There are three most efficient attacks in this class we found. The first one requires 7 measurements and $2^{34.74}$ offline operations on average with a probability of 0.99. The second attack needs about 6 measurements and about $2^{37.15}$ offline operations with probability 0.854 or about $2^{44.3}$ operations with probability 0.927. The third one recovers the key with just 5 measurements and about $2^{37.34}$ simple offline operations with probability 0.372 or about $2^{45.5}$ operations with probability 0.548. This is to be compared to about 40 measurements required in the basic collision attack [2] on AES with some non-negligible post-processing, 29 measurements required for the AES-based Apha-MAC internal state recovery in [3] with about 2^{34} offline operations with a success probability > 0.5, and typically several hundred measurements for a DPA (differential power analysis) attack.

Our attacks work, as DPA and the collision attacks on Alpha-MAC in [3], in the *known-plaintext model*, while the attack in [2] is applicable in the *chosen-plaintext scenario* only. Moreover, as in [3], we do not need to know the output of the cryptographic transformation for the side-channel attack itself. However, our attacks mentioned above do need one plaintext-ciphertext pair for choosing the correct key from a set of key candidates in the offline post-processing stage. Note that this input-output pair does not have to be one of the those for which the measurements have been performed.

We use both theoretical and experimental tools for estimating the efficiency of our attacks. Linear systems of equations are rewritten in terms of associated undirected graphs. As the resulting equation systems never possess the full rank, combinatorial methods are applied to solve these systems. The complexity of these methods can be analyzed through connected components of those graphs. The expected number of edges in such a graph is computed theoretically. The number of connected components, which defines the overall complexity of the offline attack stage, is estimated using thorough computer simulations for the numbers of edges obtained theoretically.

The remainder of the paper is organized as follows. Section 2 outlines the basic collision attack on AES. Section 3 rigorously introduces the notion of a generalized internal collision for AES as well as specifies and analyzes our enhanced collision attacks. In Section 4 we discuss the technical framework and practical feasibility of our attacks. We conclude in Section 5.

2   Basic Collision Attack on AES

Side-channel collision attacks were proposed for the case of the DES in [1] and enhanced in [4]. AES was attacked using collision techniques in [2]. This side-channel collision attack on AES is based on detecting internal one-byte collisions in the MixColumns transformation in the first AES round. The basic idea is to identify pairs of plaintexts leading to the same byte value in an output byte after the MixColumns transformation of the first round and to use these pairs to deduce information about some key bytes involved into the transformation.

Let $A = (a_{ij})$ with $i, j = \overline{0, 3}$ and $a_{ij} \in GF(2^8)$ be the internal state in the first AES round after key addition, byte substitution and the ShiftRows operation. Let $B = (b_{ij})$ with $i, j = \overline{0, 3}$ and $b_{ij} \in GF(2^8)$ be the internal state after the MixColumns transformation, $B = \mathrm{MixColumns}(A)$, where the MixColumns transformation is defined for each column j as follows:

$$\begin{pmatrix} b_{0j} \\ b_{1j} \\ b_{2j} \\ b_{3j} \end{pmatrix} = \begin{pmatrix} 02\ 03\ 01\ 01 \\ 01\ 02\ 03\ 01 \\ 01\ 01\ 02\ 03 \\ 03\ 01\ 01\ 02 \end{pmatrix} \times \begin{pmatrix} a_{0j} \\ a_{1j} \\ a_{2j} \\ a_{3j} \end{pmatrix}. \tag{1}$$

Here all operations are performed over $GF(2^8)$. Let $P = (p_{ij})$ with $i, j = \overline{0, 3}$, $p_{ij} \in GF(2^8)$, and $K = (k_{ij})$ with $i, j = \overline{0, 3}$, $k_{ij} \in GF(2^8)$, denote the plaintext block and the first subkey, respectively. Then b_{00} can be represented as:

$$\begin{aligned} b_{00} &= 02 \cdot a_{00} \oplus 03 \cdot a_{10} \oplus 01 \cdot a_{20} \oplus 01 \cdot a_{30} = \\ &= 02 \cdot S(p_{00} \oplus k_{00}) \oplus 03 \cdot S(p_{11} \oplus k_{11}) \\ &\quad \oplus 01 \cdot S(p_{22} \oplus k_{22}) \oplus 01 \cdot S(p_{33} \oplus k_{33}). \end{aligned} \tag{2}$$

For two plaintexts P and P' with $p_{00} = p_{11} = p_{22} = p_{33} = \delta$ and $p'_{00} = p'_{11} = p'_{22} = p'_{33} = \epsilon$, $\delta \neq \epsilon$, one obtains the following, provided $b_{00} = b'_{00}$:

$$\begin{aligned} &02 \cdot S(k_{00} \oplus \delta) \oplus 03 \cdot S(k_{11} \oplus \delta) \oplus 01 \cdot S(k_{22} \oplus \delta) \oplus 01 \cdot S(k_{33} \oplus \delta) \\ &= 02 \cdot S(k_{00} \oplus \epsilon) \oplus 03 \cdot S(k_{11} \oplus \epsilon) \oplus 01 \cdot S(k_{22} \oplus \epsilon) \oplus 01 \cdot S(k_{33} \oplus \epsilon) \end{aligned} \tag{3}$$

Let $C_{\delta, \epsilon}$ be the set of all key bytes $k_{00}, k_{11}, k_{22}, k_{33}$ that lead to a collision (3) with plaintexts (δ, ϵ). Such sets are pre-computed and stored for all 2^{16} pairs (δ, ϵ). Each set contains on average 2^{24} candidates for the four key bytes. Actually, every set $C_{\epsilon, \delta}$ can be computed from the set $C_{\epsilon \oplus \delta, 0}$ using some relations between the sets. Due to certain dependencies within the sets, this optimization reduces the required disk space to about 540 megabytes.

The attack on the single internal state byte b_{00} works as follows. The attacker generates random values (ϵ, δ) and inputs them to the AES module as described above. The power consumption curve for the time period, where b_{00} is processed, is stored. Then the attacker proceeds with other random values (ϵ', δ'), measures the power profile, stores it and correlates it with all stored power curves. And so on. One needs about 4 collisions (one in each output byte of a column) to recover the four bytes involved into the MixColumns transformation. The probability that after N operations at least one collision $b_{00} = b'_{00}$ occurs in a single byte is:

$$p_N = 1 - \prod_{l=0}^{N-1} (1 - l/2^8). \tag{4}$$

Actually, the attack can be parallelized to search for collisions in all four columns of B in parallel. In this case the attacker needs at least 16 collisions, 4 for each column of B, so $p_N^{16} \geq 1/2$ and $N \approx 40$. Once the required number of collisions was detected, he uses the pre-computed tables $C_{\epsilon \oplus \delta, 0}$ to recover all four key bytes for each column by intersecting the pre-computed key sets corresponding to the collisions (ϵ, δ) detected. Thus, on average one has to perform about 40 measurements to obtain all 16 collisions needed and to determine all 16 key bytes. Note that since the cardinality of the intersections for the sets $C_{\epsilon, \delta}$ is not always 1, there are a number of key candidates to be tested using a known plaintext-ciphertext pair.

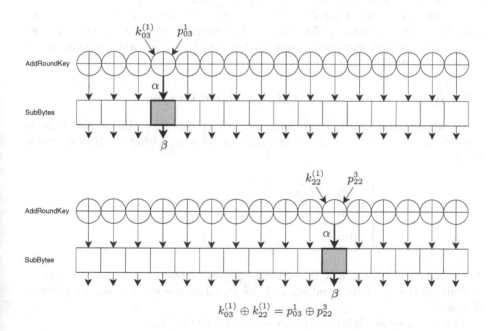

Fig. 1. Generalized internal collision within the first round of two AES runs

3   Our Improved Collision Attacks on AES

3.1   Generalized Internal Collisions

In round $i = \overline{1,10}$, AES performs the SUBSYTES operation (16 parallel S-box applications) on the output bytes of the previous round XORed with the i-th round subkey $K^{(i)}$. A generalized internal AES collision occurs, if there are two S-boxes within the same AES execution or within several AES runs accepting the same byte value as their input.

In Figure 1 a collision within the first round of two different AES executions (number 1 and 3) is illustrated. $p_{v,u}^j$, $v, u = \overline{0,3}$, are plaintext bytes for the jth measurement. $k_{v,u}^{(1)}$, $v, u = \overline{0,3}$, are the first subkey bytes remaining constant for the both executions. In the example of Figure 1, byte 03 in the first execution and byte 22 in the third execution collide.

A detected collision in the S-box layer of the first round in bytes (i_1, j_1) and (i_2, j_2) with $i_1, j_1, i_2, j_2 = \overline{0,3}$ corresponds to the following linear equation:

$$S(k_{i_1,j_1}^{(1)} \oplus p_{i_1,j_1}^x) = S(k_{i_2,j_2}^{(1)} \oplus p_{i_2,j_2}^y), \tag{5}$$

$$k_{i_1,j_1}^{(1)} \oplus k_{i_2,j_2}^{(1)} = \Delta_{(i_1,j_1),(i_2,j_2)}^{(1)} = p_{i_1,j_1}^x \oplus p_{i_2,j_2}^y \tag{6}$$

for some known plaintext bytes p_{i_1,j_1}^x and p_{i_2,j_2}^y with some positive integers x, y indicating measurement numbers. In the same way, one can rewrite equations resulting from collisions within some other round $i = \overline{2,10}$. In this case we have some unknown key- and plaintext-dependent byte variables instead of the plaintext bytes p_{i_1,j_1}^x and p_{i_2,j_2}^y.

3.2   Systems of Equations and Associated Graphs

First, we consider the structure of a random system of m linear equations of type (6) resulting from a number of collisions detected within the S-box layer in the first round:

$$S_m : \begin{cases} k_{i_1,j_1}^{(1)} \oplus k_{i_2,j_2}^{(1)} = \Delta_{(i_1,j_1),(i_2,j_2)}^{(1)} \\ k_{i_3,j_3}^{(1)} \oplus k_{i_4,j_4}^{(1)} = \Delta_{(i_3,j_3),(i_4,j_4)}^{(1)} \\ \dots \\ k_{i_{2m-1},j_{2m-1}}^{(1)} \oplus k_{i_{2m},j_{2m}}^{(1)} = \Delta_{(i_{2m-1},j_{2m-1}),(i_{2m},j_{2m})}^{(1)}. \end{cases} \tag{7}$$

Note that this system has 16 variables (bytes of the first round subkey). In system (7) the key byte numbers and the variables are not necessarily pairwise distinct.

The following straightforward proposition holds for S_m:

Proposition 1. *The maximal rank of S_m is 15, $rank(S_m) \le 15$.*

Proof. The maximal rank of 15 is attained, for instance, for

$$
\begin{cases}
k_{0,0}^{(1)} \oplus k_{0,1}^{(1)} = \Delta_{(0,0),(0,1)}^{(1)} \\
k_{0,1}^{(1)} \oplus k_{0,2}^{(1)} = \Delta_{(0,1),(0,2)}^{(1)} \\
\cdots \\
k_{3,1}^{(1)} \oplus k_{3,2}^{(1)} = \Delta_{(3,1),(3,2)}^{(1)} \\
k_{3,2}^{(1)} \oplus k_{3,3}^{(1)} = \Delta_{(3,2),(3,3)}^{(1)}.
\end{cases}
\tag{8}
$$

It is easy to see that the XOR of any other pair of variables can be obtained as a sum of two of the 15 equations in (8). Thus, 15 is the maximal rank for S_m □

We use the graph representation of S_m for our analysis.

Definition 1. *A random graph* $G_m = \langle V, E \rangle$ *is associated with the random system* S_m *of linear equations, where* $V = \{k_{0,0}^{(1)}, k_{0,1}^{(1)}, \ldots, k_{3,3}^{(1)}\}$ *is the set of 16 vertices of* G_m *and the edge* $(k_{i_1,j_1}^{(1)}, k_{i_2,j_2}^{(1)})$ *belongs to the edge set* E *iff the binomial equation*

$$
k_{i_1,j_1}^{(1)} \oplus k_{i_2,j_2}^{(1)} = \Delta_{(i_1,j_1),(i_2,j_2)}
$$

belongs to the system S_m, $|E| = m$.

Among others, the associated graph possesses the following obvious properties:

Proposition 2. *The system* S_m *is of the maximal rank 15 iff its associated graph* G_m *is connected.*

Proposition 3. *Let* $G = \langle V, E \rangle$ *be a non-directed graph with* n *vertices,* $|V| = n$. *If*

$$
|E| > \binom{n-1}{2},
$$

the graph G *is connected.*

For G_m Proposition 3 implies that if $|E| > 105$, G_m is necessarily connected and, thus, S_m has the maximal rank of 15. A system of type (7) having the maximal rank can be solved by assigning a byte value to some variable $k_{i,j}^{(1)}$ (which is equivalent to adding a further, linearly non-dependent equation $k_{i,j}^{(1)} = \Delta_{i,j}^{(1)}$ to the system) and uniquely solving the system

$$
S_m \cup \left\{ k_{i,j}^{(1)} = \Delta_{i,j}^{(1)} \right\}
$$

of rank 16. Then another byte value is assigned to that variable. The correct key is identified on the basis of a known plaintext-ciphertext pair.

Generally speaking, it is not necessary for S_m to have the maximal rank. If there are several isolated subsystems within S_m, then each of them can be solved independently as described above. If there are q independent subsystems $SS_m^1, \ldots, SS_m^q$ in S_m, then S_m can be represented as a union of these subsystems:

$$
S_m = SS_m^1 \cup \cdots \cup SS_m^q, \quad SS_m^i \cap SS_m^j = \varnothing, \; i \neq j.
$$

To solve S_m in this case, one has to assign q byte values to some q variables in the subsystems $\{SS_m^i\}_{i=1}^q$. At the end there are 2^{8q} key candidates. The correct key is identified using a known plaintext-ciphertext pair as outlined above.

It is clear that the independent subsystems $\{SS_m^i\}_{i=1}^q$ of S_m correspond to the q connected components of the associated graph G_m.

The number of connected components of a random graph has the following asymptotic behaviour:

Proposition 4. *Let G be a random graph with n labeled vertices and $N = \lfloor \frac{1}{2}n \log n + cn \rfloor$ for some constant c. Let $q = q_{n,N}$ be the number of connected components in G. Then:*

$$\lim_{n \to \infty} \Pr\{q = i + 1\} = \frac{(e^{-2c})^i}{i!} \exp\{-e^{-2c}\}.$$

Proof. See Theorem 2.3 in [5]   □

Unfortunately, the estimate of Proposition 4 for the number of connected components cannot be directly applied for S_m, since its associated graph has only 16 vertices.

3.3   Expected Number of Random Binomial Equations

The number of edges in the associated graph G_m can be estimated using the following

Proposition 5. *If generalized byte collision in AES are always detectable, the expected number $E(m)$ of edges in G_m (equivalently, the expected number of binomial equations in S_m) for the first round of AES after $t \geq 1$ measurements is*

$$E(m) = 120 \cdot \left(1 - \left(\frac{119}{120}\right)^{16t - 256 + 256 \cdot \exp\left\{16t \cdot \ln \frac{255}{256}\right\}}\right).$$

Proof. The expected number of generalized collisions within the first round after t measurements can be estimated as:

$$N_{1R} = 16t - 256 + 256 \cdot \left(\frac{255}{256}\right)^{16t}, \tag{9}$$

where $16t$ is the number of S-box operations in one AES round within t measurements. This equation is a reformulation of the birthday paradox.

The expected number of edges in a random graph with n labeled vertices after N_{1R} random selections of edges (after N_{1R} generalized collisions) can be interpreted as the expected number of filled boxes after N_{1R} random shots in the classical shot problem, which was studied e.g. in Chapter 1 of [6]. In the case of a graph, one deals with $\binom{n}{2}$ boxes (possible graph edges) and the expected number of edges after N_{1R} collisions is

Table 1. Number of collisions and edges in G_m according to Proposition 5

Measurements, t	4	5	6	7	8	9	11	29
1R collisions, N_{1R}	7.27	11.18	15.82	21.14	28.12	33.70	48.55	249.64
Edges, $E(m)$		7.09	10.72	14.88	19.46	24.36	29.49	40.07	105.14

$$E(m) = \binom{n}{2}\left(1 - \left(1 - \frac{1}{\binom{n}{2}}\right)^{N_{1R}}\right). \tag{10}$$

As $n = 16$ for the case of AES, one obtains the claim of the proposition by combining (9) and (10)   □

Table 1 contains theoretical estimations for the numbers of 1R-collisions N_{1R} and edges $E(m)$ depending on the number of measurements t for some interesting t's.

Note that according to Proposition 3, it is expected that after 29 measurements one obtains 105 edges which provide the maximal rank of S_m. However, on average a lower number of edges are sufficient for the G_m to be connected with a high probability (see Section 3.4).

3.4   Number of Connected Components in Associated Graphs

In order to estimate the number q of connected components for G_m accounting for the offline complexity, statistical simulation was applied consisting of generating a random graph on 16 vertices corresponding to t measurements as well as counting the number of connected components q using a variation of Karp and Tarjan's algorithm [7] for finding connected components of a graph. Note that the expected complexity of this algorithm in $O(n)$, that is, linear in the number of vertices. For each number of measurement we performed 2^{16} simulations with random graphs.

The results of our simulations are shown in Table 2. The first and second rows of the table represent measurement numbers and average numbers of edges in G_m according to Proposition 5 (see also Table 1), respectively. The offline

Table 2. Offline complexity and success probabilities

Measurements, t	4	5	6	7	8	9	11	29
Number of edges in G_m, m	7.09	10.72	14.88	19.46	24.36	29.49	40.07	105.14
Connected components of G_m, q	8.81	5.88	3.74	2.20	1.43	1.15	1.04	1.00
Offline complexity $\leq$ 40 bit	34.70	37.34	37.15	34.74	30.32	21.36	12.11	8
Success probability $\leq$ 40 bit	0.037	0.372	0.854	0.991	0.999	1.000	1.000	1.000
Offline complexity $\leq$ 48 bit	43.90	45.50	44.30	41.14	30.32	21.36	12.11	8
Success probability $\leq$ 48 bit	0.092	0.548	0.927	0.997	0.999	1.000	1.000	1.000

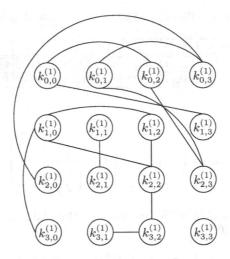

Fig. 2. Typical random graph with 13 edges and 4 components

complexity is given for two cases: ≤ 40 bit and ≤ 48 bit. In the first case, only offline complexities $\leq 2^{40}$ are considered in the computation of the average offline complexity value. For each number of measurements the probability is provided that the overall offline complexity is $\leq 2^{40}$. In the second case, the upper bound for the offline complexities taken into account is 2^{48}. The corresponding success probabilities are also provided in the table.

A low-complexity offline stage of the attack becomes probable after 5 measurements ($2^{45.5}$ simple steps with a probability of 0.548). Practically all instances of linear systems resulting from 7 measurements are easily solvable with an average complexity of $2^{34.74}$ steps (with a probability of 0.99). After 11 measurements the expected offline attack complexity is about $2^{12.11}$.

Figure 2 shows a typical random graph G_m associated with a random system S_m of linear equations with $m = 13$ and 4 independent subsystems (4 connected components): $\{k_{0,0}^{(1)}, k_{2,3}^{(1)}, k_{0,1}^{(1)}, k_{0,2}^{(1)}, k_{0,3}^{(1)}, k_{1,3}^{(1)}, k_{2,0}^{(1)}\}$, $\{k_{2,2}^{(1)}, k_{3,0}^{(1)}, k_{3,1}^{(1)}, k_{3,2}^{(1)}, k_{1,0}^{(1)}, k_{1,2}^{(1)}\}$, $\{k_{1,1}^{(1)}, k_{2,1}^{(1)}\}$, $\{k_{3,3}^{(1)}\}$.

3.5   Optimization of the Attack

In this subsection we propose an optimization of the attack described in the previous subsections. It consists in generating additional collisions for the first round by considering the second round and key schedule.

The basis of this optimization is the fact that there are also generalized byte collisions within the second AES round as well as between the first and the second AES rounds. However, as opposed to those in the first round, the values of inputs to the second round are not known and depend on the key and plaintext bytes in a non-linear way.

Suppose after N_{1R} collisions have been detected, the graph G_m consists of q connected components, but their number is too high to allow for an efficient solution of the corresponding system (e.g. $q = 7$). Let 2 or 3 connected components of this graph contain at least two diagonals of the first subkey $K^{(1)}$. Then we can test all 2^{16} or 2^{24}, respectively, possible candidates for these diagonals. Each subkey diagonal in the first round corresponds to a column in the second round. Thus, at least two columns of the input to the second round can be considered as known. Now we assume that a number of other bytes of the first round subkey also lie in the same 2 or 3 connected components of G_m. This can allow for the recovery of some of the second round subkey bytes corresponding to the known input columns. Thus, the corresponding inputs to the S-box layer of the second round can be assumed as known.

Now we have a number of variables in the second round virtually belonging to the 2 or 3 connected components of G_m. Note that adding the vertices corresponding to the second round subkey bytes described above does not increase the number of connected components. These can be seen as further reference points for the recovery of the remainder of the first subkey bytes by reducing the number of connected components in the new, larger graph.

Our thorough simulations show that such methods do increase the expected number of edges in the original graph G_m. Note that this improvement of our attack is not enough to decrease the number of measurements needed, though it increases the success probability of all our attacks for a fixed number of measurements.

4   Practical Feasibility

To make the detection of byte collisions during the S-box applications within AES possible, the AES implementation has to satisfy the property that all instances of the AES S-box are implemented in a similar way. The requirement is not necessary for [2] or [3]. This is the only difference of our technical framework with respect to that in [2] or [3]. Note that this requirement is very likely to be fulfilled in low-end real-world embedded systems, which are the main target of such attacks, since AES implementations in these systems are deliberately simplified by reducing diversity in order to save code size in software and area in hardware. On constrained 8-bit microcontrollers, the implementation of the AES S-box transform is likely to be a separate routine, thus, being exactly the same for all S-box applications.

As in standard collision attacks on AES, the attacker has to precisely know the times when the S-boxes leak. Note that this is not the case for DPA or similar differential techniques. Another advantage of the DPA method is that it works for the absolute majority of AES implementations including software and hardware ones. At the same time, the collision attacks on AES are mainly constrained to 8-bit software implementations on simple controllers.

However, the practical feasibility of collision attacks for AES was shown in [3] for a PIC16F687 microcontroller and in [2] for an i8051-type controller. To detect a collision, the attacker compares the corresponding power curves using such basic techniques as correlation functions or more advanced wavelet methods [2].

Measurements of high accuracy are required to detect byte collisions. The usage of averaging techniques can improve the probability of correct collision detection in the cases where the implementation and the measurement setup do not allow for a reliable byte collision detection using a single power curve for each input. In this case, one cannot speak of a known-plaintext model any more, since the same plaintexts have to be input several times to increase the signal-to-noise ratio.

Note that our collision attack, as any other power analysis attack, can be significantly hampered or even made impossible by minimizing the signal-to-noise ratio, using sound masking techniques [8], [9] or advanced clock randomizing methods [10]. However, the collision attack is likely to break through basic time randomization countermeasures such as simple random wait states, which can be detected using SPA or alignment techniques.

5   Conclusions

In this paper we proposed and analyzed several improved side-channel collision attacks on AES. The first one requires 7 measurements and $2^{34.74}$ offline operations on average with a probability of 0.99. The second attack needs about 6 measurements and about $2^{37.15}$ offline operations with probability 0.854 or about $2^{44.3}$ operations with probability 0.927. The third one recovers the key with just 5 measurements and about $2^{37.34}$ simple offline operations with probability 0.372 or about $2^{45.5}$ operations with probability 0.548. This is to be compared to about 40 measurements required in the basic collision attack [2] on AES with some non-negligible post-processing, 29 measurements required for the AES-based Apha-MAC internal state recovery in [3] with about 2^{34} offline operations with a success probability > 0.5, and typically several hundred measurements for a classical DPA attack.

Acknowledgements. The author would like to thank Oxana Radetskaya for fruitful discussions during the work on this paper, Timo Kasper for providing some technical background about collision detection while working on another paper about collision attacks, the Horst-Görtz Institute for IT Security at the Ruhr-University of Bochum for financial support, and the anonymous referees for their comments that helped him to improve the paper.

References

1. Schramm, K., Wollinger, T.J., Paar, C.: A new class of collision attacks and its application to DES. In: Johansson, T. (ed.) FSE 2003. LNCS, vol. 2887, pp. 206–222. Springer, Heidelberg (2003)
2. Schramm, K., Leander, G., Felke, P., Paar, C.: A collision-attack on AES: combining side channel- and differential-attack. In: Joye, M., Quisquater, J.-J. (eds.) CHES 2004. LNCS, vol. 3156, pp. 163–175. Springer, Heidelberg (2004)

3. Biryukov, A., Bogdanov, A., Khovratovich, D., Kasper, T.: Collision Attacks on Alpha-MAC and Other AES-based MACs. In: Paillier, P., Verbauwhede, I. (eds.) CHES 2007. LNCS, vol. 4727. Springer, Heidelberg (2007)
4. Ledig, H., Muller, F., Valette, F.: Enhancing collision attacks. In: Joye, M., Quisquater, J.-J. (eds.) CHES 2004. LNCS, vol. 3156, pp. 176–190. Springer, Heidelberg (2004)
5. Sachkov, V.N.: Probabilistic Methods in Combinatorial Analysis. Encyclopedia of Mathematics and Its Applications, vol. 56. Cambridge University Press, Cambridge (1997)
6. Kolchin, V.F., Sevastyanov, B., Chistyakov, V.P.: Random Allocations. V. H. Winston & Sons (1978)
7. Karp, R.M., Tarjan, R.E.: Linear extected-time algorithms for connectivity problems. J. Algorithms 1 (1980)
8. Oswald, E., Mangard, S., Pramstaller, N., Rijmen, V.: A side-channel analysis resistant description of the AES S-box. In: Gilbert, H., Handschuh, H. (eds.) FSE 2005. LNCS, vol. 3557, Springer, Heidelberg (2005)
9. Oswald, E., Schramm, K.: An Efficient Masking Scheme for AES Software Implementations. In: Song, J., Kwon, T., Yung, M. (eds.) WISA 2005. LNCS, vol. 3786, Springer, Heidelberg (2006)
10. Herbst, C., Oswald, E., Mangard, S.: An AES implementation resistant to power analysis attacks. In: Zhou, J., Yung, M., Bao, F. (eds.) ACNS 2006. LNCS, vol. 3989, Springer, Heidelberg (2006)

Analysis of Countermeasures Against Access Driven Cache Attacks on AES

Johannes Blömer and Volker Krummel*

Faculty of Computer Science, Electrical Engineering and Mathematics
University of Paderborn, Germany
{bloemer,krummel}@uni-paderborn.de

Abstract. Cache based attacks (CBA) exploit the different access times of main memory and cache memory to determine information about internal states of cryptographic algorithms. CBAs turn out to be very powerful attacks even in practice. In this paper we present a general and strong model to analyze the security against CBAs. We introduce the notions of *information leakage* and *resistance* to analyze the security of several implementations of AES. Furthermore, we analyze how to use random permutations to protect against CBAs. By providing a successful attack on an AES implementation protected by random permutations we show that random permutations used in a straightforward manner are not enough to protect against CBAs. Hence, to improve upon the security provided by random permutations, we describe the property a permutation must have in order to prevent the leakage of some key bits through CBAs.

Keywords: cache attacks, AES, threat model, countermeasures, random permutations.

1 Introduction

Modern computers use a hierarchical organization of different types of memories among them fast but small cache memory and slow but large main memory. In 2002 Page [14] presented a theoretical attack on DES that exploited timing information to deduce information about cache accesses, which in turn reveal information about secret keys being used. In the sequel we call attacks that exploit information about the cache behavior *cache based attacks* or CBAs. In particular, it turned out that large tables such as sboxes render an encryption algorithm susceptible to CBAs. Tsunoo et al. [17] published a practical CBA against DES. Further publications of Page [15], Percival [16], Bernstein [3], Osvik et al. [13] and Brickell et al. [7] disclosed the full power of CBAs. See [4,10,12,1,2] for further improvements of CBAs. In particular, the fast AES implementation [8] is susceptible to CBAs. Note that the fast implementation is used in virtually all crypto libraries. It is susceptible to CBAs since it depends heavily on the usage of 5 large sboxes $\mathbf{T}_0, \dots, \mathbf{T}_4$ each of the size of 1024 bytes.

---

* This work was partially supported by grants from Intel Corporation, Portland.

C. Adams, A. Miri, and M. Wiener (Eds.): SAC 2007, LNCS 4876, pp. 96–109, 2007.
© Springer-Verlag Berlin Heidelberg 2007

In this paper we present a strong model for CBAs. Within this model we propose and analyze countermeasures that although they are quite general we describe in detail only for AES. As was pointed out by Bernstein in [3], the threat model that is often implicitly used for CBAs may not be strong enough. In particular, often it is assumed that the adversary $\mathcal{A}$ only can extract information from the cache before and after the encryption. This assumption is wrong from the theoretical point of view due to the process switching of the operating system. Moreover, it also has been practically disproved in [11]. Hence, several of the countermeasures proposed in the literature so far may not be effective. In this paper, we take into account powerful adversaries that are able to obtain cache information even during the encryption. Within this model we show that using random permutations to mitigate the leakage of information as proposed in [7] is not an effective countermeasure for CBAs against AES. On one hand, we present a CBA that shows that random permutations do not increase the complexity of CBAs as much as one might expect. On the other hand, the same attack shows that a random permutation does not prevent the leakage of the complete secret key. We also consider a modified countermeasure based on so called *distinguished permutations* that hedge a certain number of bits of the last round key in AES. By this we mean, that using our countermeasure a CBA on the last round of AES, say, will only reveal about half the bits of the last round key. As one can see, this is the least amount of leaking information that can be provably protected by permutations. To determine the remaining bits, an attacker has to combine the CBA with another attack, for example a CBA on the next to last round. We give a mathematical precise description and analysis of the property of permutations that we need for our countermeasure. This analysis also sheds some light on the difference between the CBA by Osvik et al. on the first two rounds of AES [13] and the attack of Brickell et al. on the tenth round of AES [7]. We give a more detailed comparison of these two attacks in [6]. Finally, we analyze the security of several implementations of AES against CBAs. One of these implementations is provably secure within our model and can also be used to protect the applications of permutations that are realized as table lookups. How to apply permutations securely has not been considered before.

The paper is organized as follows. In Section 2 we introduce our threat model. After that we introduce our main security measures, information leakage and resistance in Section 3. We use our security measures to analyze the security of several different implementations of AES in Section 4. In Section 5, first we consider random permutations as a countermeasure and describe a CBA on this countermeasure. Then, we present and discuss an improved countermeasure using so called distinguished permutations.

2   Threat Model

We consider computers with a single processor, fast but small cache memory and large but slow main memory. Every time a process wants to read a word from the main memory a portion of data in the size of a cache line is transferred to the cache. An AES encryption or decryption process is running on that computer that takes as input a plaintext (or ciphertext) and computes the corresponding AES ciphertext (or plaintext) with a fixed secret key k. To define our threat model we make the following assumptions about an adversary $\mathcal{A}$.

1. $\mathcal{A}$ knows all technical details about the underlying cryptographic algorithm and its implementation, i.e., the position of sbox tables in memory.
2. $\mathcal{A}$ can feed the AES process with chosen plaintexts (or ciphertexts) and gets the corresponding ciphertexts (or plaintexts).
3. $\mathcal{A}$ can determine the indices of the cache lines that were accessed during the encryption (decryption). To do so $\mathcal{A}$ could use a similar method as described in [9]. In the sequel, we call the set of indices of accessed cache lines *cache information*. The plaintext or ciphertext together with the cache information is called a *measurement*.
4. $\mathcal{A}$ can restrict the cache information to certain rounds of the encryption. As mentioned in [3] that this assumption might be realistic and the authors of [7] practically proved its correctness.
5. $\mathcal{A}$ cannot distinguish between the elements of a single cache line.

A more detailed description of our threat model, i.e., further explanations and justifications of our assumptions, can be found in [6].

3   Information Leakage and Resistance

The threat model described above is stronger than the threat models published so far. The adversary is more powerful because $\mathcal{A}$ can restrict the cache information to a smaller interval of encryption operations. This reduces the number of accessed cache lines per measurement and increases the efficiency of CBAs. The main questions when analyzing the security against CBAs are information leakage and complexity of a CBA. After giving a formal definition of information leakage we introduce the notion of the so called *resistance* of an implementation as a measure that allows to estimate the complexity of a CBA.

Information leakage. The most important aspect of an implementation regarding the security against access driven CBAs is to determine the maximal amount of information that leaks via access driven CBAs. As we will see, the amount of leaking information about the secret key varies depending on the details of the CBA and the implementation of the cryptographic algorithm. We make the following definition:

Definition 1 (information leakage). *We consider an adversary who can mount a CBA using an arbitrary number of measurements as described in Assumption 3. Let $\widehat{\mathcal{K}}_i$ be the set of remaining key candidates for a key byte k_i^{10} at the end of the attack on AES. Then the leaking information is $8 - \log_2\left(|\widehat{\mathcal{K}}_i|\right)$ bits.*

The amount of leaking information allows to estimate the uncertainty of an attacker about the secret key that remains after an access driven CBA. To quantify the maximal amount of information $\mathcal{A}$ can obtain about the secret key by access driven CBAs, we define $|CL|$ to be the size of a cache line in bits, $|S|$ the number of entries of the sbox and s the size of a single sbox element in bits. Hence, the number of elements that fits into a cache line is $\frac{|CL|}{s}$ and the cache information of a single measurement leaks at most $\log_2(|S|) - \log_2\left(\frac{|CL|}{s}\right) = \log_2\left(\frac{|S|}{|CL|} \cdot s\right)$ bits. Depending on the exact nature of an attack, the sets of measurements let the attacker reduce the number of remaining key candidates after the attack. The information leakage varies between 0 and 8 bits of information per byte. For example, the attack on the first round of [13] mounted on the fast implementation can determine at most 4 bits of every key byte regardless of the number of measurements. In contrast, the attack of [7] based on the last round allows an adversary to determine all key bits. In Section 4 we present an implementation that does not leak any information in our model.

Complexity of a CBA. The information leakage as defined above measures the maximal amount of information a CBA can provide using an arbitrary number of measurements. Determining the expected number of measurements an attacker needs to obtain the complete leaking information depends on the details of the implementation and on details of the CBA. For simplification we introduce the notion of so called resistance. It is a general measure to estimate the complexity of CBAs on different implementations.

Definition 2 (resistance). *The resistance of an implementation is the expected number E_r of key candidates that are proven to be wrong during a single measurement that is based on r rounds of the encryption.*

The larger E_r the more susceptible is the implementation to access driven CBAs. In particular, if an implementation does not leak any information, then an adversary cannot rule out key candidates and hence the resistance is 0. To compute E_r we always assume that all sbox lookups are independently and uniformly distributed. This assumption is justified because an attacker $\mathcal{A}$ usually does not have any information about the distribution of the sbox lookups. Hence, the best he can do in an attack is to choose the parts of the plaintexts/ciphertexts that are not relevant for the attack uniformly at random.

Let m be the number of cache lines needed to store the complete sbox. Each cache line can store v elements of an sbox. Furthermore, let w be the number of sbox lookups per round and let r be the number of rounds the attack focuses on. In an access driven CBA a key candidate is proven to be incorrect if it causes an access of a cache line that was not accessed during a measurement. Assuming that all sbox lookups are uniformly distributed the expected number of key candidates that can be sorted out after a single measurement is

$$E_r := \left(\frac{m-1}{m}\right)^{r \cdot w} \cdot m \cdot v \qquad (1)$$

However, the maximal amount of information an arbitrary number of measurements can reveal is limited by the information leakage. Further measurements will not reveal additional information. We verified by experiments that the number of measurements needed to achieve the full information leakage only depends on E_r.

In the sequel, we focus on methods to counteract CBAs. In general, there are two approaches to counteract such a side channel. The first approach is to use some kind of randomization to ensure that the leaking information does not reveal information about the secret key. Using randomization is a general strategy that protects against several kinds of side channel attacks, see for example [5]. In Section 5 we analyze a more efficient method based on random permutations. Before that, we consider the second approach, that is methods to reduce the bandwith of the side channel. We present several implementations of AES and examine their information leakage and their resistance.

4   Countermeasure 1: Modify Implementation

As Bernstein pointed out in [3] to thwart CBAs it is not sufficient to load all sbox entries into the cache before accessing the sbox in order to compute an intermediate result because $\mathcal{A}$ can get cache information at all times. Hence, loading the complete sbox into the cache does not suffice to hide all cache information. Therefore, he advises to avoid the usage of table lookups in cryptographic algorithms. Computing the AES SubBytes operation according to its definition $f : \{0,1\}^8 \to \{0,1\}^8$, $x \mapsto a \cdot \mathrm{INV}(x) \oplus b$ would virtually cause no cache accesses and hence seems to be secure against CBAs. However, implementing SubBytes like this would result in a very inefficient implementation on a PC. To achieve a high level of efficiency people prefer to use precomputed tables. In the sequel, we analyze the security of some well known and some novel variations of implementations of AES. First, we explain the different implementations of AES. See [8] for a detailed description of AES. After that we examine the information leakage and the resistance as defined in (1) against CBAs:

the standard implementation as described in Section 3 of [8].

the fast implementation as described in Section 4.2 of [8].

fastV1 is based on the fast implementation. The only difference is that the sbox $\mathbf{T}_4$ of round 10 is replaced by the standard sbox as proposed in [7].

fastV2 is also based on the fast implementation but uses only sbox $\mathbf{T}_0$. The description of the fast implementation of AES shows that the ith entry of the sboxes $\mathbf{T}_1, \ldots, \mathbf{T}_3$ is equal to the ith entry of the sbox $\mathbf{T}_0$ cyclically shifted by $1, 2$ and 3 bytes to the right respectively (see [8]). Hence, we propose to use only sbox $\mathbf{T}_0$ in the encryption and shift the result as needed to compute the correct AES encryption. E.g., to compute the sbox lookup $\mathbf{T}_1[i]$ using the sbox $\mathbf{T}_0$ we simply cyclically shift the value $\mathbf{T}_0[i]$ by 1 byte to the right.

small-n: A simple but effective countermeasure to counteract CBAs is to split the sbox $\mathbf{S}$ into n smaller sboxes $\mathbf{S}_0, \ldots, \mathbf{S}_{n-1}$ such that every small sbox $\mathbf{S}_i$ fits completely into a single cache line. An application $\mathbf{S}_i[x]$ of sbox $\mathbf{S}_i$ yields d_i bits of the desired result $\mathbf{S}[x]$. Hence, the correct result can be calculated by computing all bits separately and shift them into the correct position. We construct the small sboxes $\mathbf{S}_i$ for $0 \leq i \leq n-1$ as follows:

$$\mathbf{S}_i : \{0,1\}^8 \to \{0,1\}^{d_i}, \ x \mapsto \lfloor \mathbf{S}[x] \rfloor_{(\sum_{j=0}^{i-1} d_j, (\sum_{j=0}^{i} d_j)-1)}$$

where $\lfloor y \rfloor_{(b,e)}$ are the bits $y_b \ldots y_e$ of the binary representation of $y = (y_0, \ldots, y_7)$. Instead of applying the sbox $\mathbf{S}$ to x directly each $\mathbf{S}_i$ is applied. The result is computed as $\mathbf{S}[x] = \sum_{i=0}^{n-1} \mathbf{S}_i[x] \cdot 2^{\sum_{j=0}^{i-1} d_j}$. In the sequel, we assume that the size of the sbox is a multiple of the size of a cache line and that all d_j are equal. Depending on the number n of required sboxes we call this implementation small-n. E.g., let $|CL| = 512$ and for $0 \le i \le 3$ let each $\mathbf{S}_i$ store the bits $\langle \mathbf{S}[x] \rangle_{2i,2i+1}$. The result $\mathbf{S}[x]$ is then computed as $\mathbf{S}[x] = \mathbf{S}_0[x] \oplus \mathbf{S}_1[x] \cdot 4 \oplus \mathbf{S}_2[x] \cdot 16 \oplus \mathbf{S}_3[x] \cdot 64$. We call this implementation *small*-4. Obviously, the performance depends on the number of involved sboxes and shifts to move bits into the right position. To estimate the efficiency we used the small-n variants in the last round of the fast implementation. Due to the inefficient bit manipulations on 32 bit processors our ad hoc implementation of using small-4 only in the last round shows that the penalty is about 60%. We expect that a more sophisticated implementation reduces this penalty significantly. Table 1 in the appendix shows a summary of timing measurements of the implementations described above. The measurements were done on a Pentium M (1400MHz) running linux kernel 2.6.18, gcc 4.1.1.

Next, we consider CBAs based on different sboxes and examine the information leakage and the resistance of each of the implementations described above. The standard implementation uses only a single sbox. Hence, a CBA as described above is based on that sbox. We verified by experiments that measurements taken over ≤ 3 rounds of the standard implementation leak all key bits. Experiments with a larger number of rounds are too complex due to the rapidly decreasing resistance E_r. We assume that even more rounds will leak all key bits. The resistance for all numbers of rounds is listed in column 1 of Table 2 in the appendix.

The second implementation is the fast implementation. The CBA on the first round of [13] on one of the sboxes $\mathbf{T}_0, \ldots, \mathbf{T}_3$ shows that in this case the fast implementation will reveal half of the key bits, even with an arbitrary number of measurements. The resistance of the fast implementation against such an attack is shown in column 2 of Table 2. The CBA on the last round of [7] based on the sbox $\mathbf{T}_4$ shows that in this case the fast implementation leaks all key bits. Since this sbox is only used in the last round the resistance as shown in column 3 of Table 2 does not change for a different number of rounds.

The implementation called fastV1 also leaks all key bits. The resistance against CBAs based on sboxes $\mathbf{T}_0, \ldots, \mathbf{T}_3$ remains the same as listed in column 2 of Table 2. The resistance against CBAs based on the standard sbox is shown in column 4 of Table 2. It remains constant over the number of rounds because the standard sbox is only used in the last round.

Like the fast implementation, the variation called fastV2 also leaks all key bits. It uses only the large sbox $\mathbf{T}_0$ in every round. The resistance for all possible numbers of rounds is listed in column 5 of Table 2.

Last, we consider the variants small-2, small-4 and small-8 that use smaller sboxes than the standard sboxes. Computing $\mathbf{S}[x]$ using variant small-4 or small-8 leaks 0 bits of information having cache lines of size 512 bits because of two reasons:

1. Every S_i fits completely into a single cache line.
2. For every x each S_i is used exactly once to compute $S[x]$.

Hence, the cache information remains constant for all inputs. The only assumption that is involved is that $\mathcal{A}$ cannot distinguish between the accesses on different elements within the same cache line (Assumption 5). We expect that the variant small-2 leaks all key bits in our setting. As we have shown above, the variants small-4 and small-8 leak no key bit and hence have resistance 0 (see column 7 and 8 of Table 2). The resistance of small-2 is listed in column 6 of Table 2.

Comparison of implementations. As Table 2 shows, the standard implementation provides rather good resistance against CBAs but only has low efficiency. The fast implementation provides the lowest resistance against CBAs but is very efficient. Its variants fastV1 and fastV2 are almost as efficient on 32 bit platforms but provide better resistance against CBAs. The variants using small sboxes provide the best resistance. Especially small-4 and small-8 prevent the leakage of information. For high security applications we propose to use one of the variants using small sboxes and adapt the number of sboxes to the actual size of cache lines of the system.

5   Countermeasure 2: Random Permutation

Another class of countermeasure that was already proposed but not analyzed in [7] is to use secret random permutations to randomize the accesses to the sbox. In this section we present a CBA against an implementation of AES secured by a random permutation that needs roughly 2300 measurements to reveal the complete key. This shows that the increase of the complexity of CBAs induced by random permutations is not as high as one would expect. In particular, the uncertainty of the permutation is not a good measure to estimate the gain of security. A random permutation has uncertainty of $\log_2(256!) \approx 1684$ bits and the uncertainty of the induced partition on the cache lines is $\log_2(256!/(16!)^{16}) \approx 976$ bits.

On the other hand, we present a subset of permutations, so called distinguished permutations, that reduce the information leakage from 8 bits to 4 bits per key byte. Hence, the remaining bits must be determined by an additional attack thereby increasing the complexity. In our standard scenario this is the best one can achieve.

We focus only on the protection of the last round of AES and we assume that the output x of the 9th round is randomized using some secret random permutation π. To be more precise, each byte x_i of the state $x = x_0, \ldots, x_{15}$ is substituted by $\pi(x_i)$. To execute the last round of AES a modified sbox T_4' that depends on π fulfilling $T_4'[\pi(x_i)] = T_4[x_i]$ is applied to every byte x_i. This ensures that the resulting ciphertext $c = c_0, \ldots, c_{15}$ is correct. We denote the ℓ-th cache line used for the table lookups for $\mathbf{T}'_4$ by $CL_\ell, \ell = 0, \ldots, 15$. Hence, CL_ℓ contains the values $\{\mathbf{S}[\pi^{-1}(x)] | x = 16\ell, \ldots, 16\ell + 15\}$. Using a permutation π, information leaking through accessed cache lines does not depend directly on x_i but only on the permuted value $\pi(x_i)$. Since π is unknown to $\mathcal{A}$ the application of π prevents him to deduce information about the secret key $k^{10} = k_0^{10}, \ldots, k_{15}^{10}$ directly. However, in the sequel we will show how to bypass random permutations by using CBAs.

5.1   An Access Driven CBA on a Permuted Sbox

We assume that we have a fast implementation of AES that is protected by a random permutation π as described above. We also assume that the adversary $\mathcal{A}$ has access to the AES decryption algorithm. This assumption can be avoided. However, the exposition becomes easier if we allow $\mathcal{A}$ access to the decryption. We show how $\mathcal{A}$ can compute the bytes $k_0^{10}, \ldots, k_{15}^{10}$ of the last round key. Let $\widehat{k}_0$ denote a candidate for byte k_0^{10} of the last round key. In a first step for each possible value $\widehat{k}_0$ the adversary $\mathcal{A}$ determines the assignment $P_{\widehat{k}_0}$ of bytes to cache lines induced by π under the assumption that $\widehat{k}_0 = k_0^{10}$. To be more precise $\mathcal{A}$ computes a function

$$P_{\widehat{k}_0} : \{0,1\}^8 \to \{0, \ldots, 15\}$$

such that if $\widehat{k}_0$ is correct then for all x:

$$\pi(x) \in \{16 P_{\widehat{k}_0}(x), \ldots, 16 P_{\widehat{k}_0}(x) + 15\}.$$

I.e., if $\widehat{k}_0$ is correct then $P_{\widehat{k}_0}$ is the correct partition of values $\pi(x)$ into cache lines. Let us fix some x and a candidate $\widehat{k}_0$ for k_0^{10}. We set $c_0 = \mathbf{S}[x] \oplus \widehat{k}_0$ and $\widehat{M}_0 = \{0, \ldots, 15\}$. The adversary repeats the following steps for $j = 1, 2, \ldots$, until $\widehat{M}_0$ contains a single element.

1. $\mathcal{A}$ chooses a ciphertext c^j, whose first byte is c_0, while the remaining bytes of c^j are chosen independently and uniformly at random.
2. Using his access to the decryption algorithm, $\mathcal{A}$ computes the plaintext p^j corresponding to the c^j.
3. By encrypting p^j, the adversary $\mathcal{A}$ determines the set D_0^j of indices of cache lines accessed for the table lookups for T'_4 during the encryption of p^j.
4. $\mathcal{A}$ sets $\widehat{M}_0 := \widehat{M}_0 \cap D_0^i$.

If $\widehat{M}_0 = \{y\}$, then $\mathcal{A}$ sets $P_{\widehat{k}_0}(x) = y$. Repeating this process for all x yields the function $P_{\widehat{k}_0}$ which has the desired property.

Under the assumption that the guess $\widehat{k}_0$ was correct, the function $P_{\widehat{k}_0}$ is the correct partition of values $\pi(x)$ into cache lines. Moreover, it is not difficult to see that the information provided by $P_{\widehat{k}_0}$ enables the adversary to mount an attack similar to the CBA on the last round of [7]. This attack can be used to determine for each possible $\widehat{k}_0$ a set of vectors $\widehat{k}_1, \ldots, \widehat{k}_{15}$ of hypotheses for the other key bytes. For the time being, we assume that π has the property that for each $\widehat{k}_0$ there remains only a single vector of hypotheses for the other key bytes. In general, a random permutation has this property (for a mathematical precise definition and analysis of that property see Section 5.2). Hence, based on this property in the end there are only 256 AES keys left and a simple brute force attack reveals the correct one.

Cost Analysis. Experiments show that in the first step of the attack $\mathcal{A}$ needs on average 9 measurements consisting of a pair (p^i, c^i) and the corresponding cache information D_0^i such that the intersection $\widehat{M}_0 := \bigcap D_0^i$ contains only a single element $y = P_{\widehat{k}_0}(x)$. We need to determine the mapping $P_{\widehat{k}_0}(x)$ for every key candidate $\widehat{k}_0$ and every argument $x \in \{0,1\}^8$. Hence, a straightforward implementation of the attack needs roughly $256 \cdot 256 \cdot 9$ measurements to determine the function $P_{\widehat{k}_0}(x)$ for all arguments $x \in \{0,1\}^8$ and all key candidates $\widehat{k}_0 \in \{0,1\}^8$. However, one can reuse measurements for different key candidates $\widehat{k}_0, \widehat{k}_0'$ to reduce the number of measurements to roughly $256 \cdot 9 = 2304$. To determine the vector of hypothesis based on the candidate $\widehat{k}_0$ we can reuse the measurements obtained by determining the function $P_{\widehat{k}_0}$. Hence, the expected number of measurements of this attack is 2304.

5.2   Separability and Distinguished Permutations

From a security point of view, it is desirable to reduce the information leakage. E.g., a CBA alone should reveal as little information as possible, in particular it should not reveal the complete key. Then the adversary is forced to either mount a refined and more complex CBA based on other intermediate results or combine the CBA with some other method to determine the key bytes uniquely. In this case, the situation is similar to the attack of [13], where a CBA on the first round only reveals 4 bits of each key byte. Hence Osvik et al. combine CBAs on the first and second round of AES.

First, we present the property a permutation applied to the result of the 9-th round should have such that $\mathcal{A}$ cannot determine the key bytes uniquely using only a CBA on the last round. We denote the ℓth cache line by CL_ℓ and the elements of CL_ℓ by $a_0^{(\ell)}, \ldots, a_{15}^{(\ell)}$. Hence, the underlying permutation used to define this cache line is given by

$$\pi^{-1}(16\ell + j) = \mathbf{S}^{-1}[a_j^{(\ell)}]. \tag{2}$$

We say that a key candidate $\widehat{k}_0$ is *separable* from the first key byte k_0 of the last round if there exists a measurement that proves $\widehat{k}_0$ to be wrong. Conversely, a key candidate $\widehat{k}_0$ is *inseparable* from the key k_0 if there does not exist a measurement that proves $\widehat{k}_0$ to be wrong. More precisely, writing $\widehat{k}_0 = k_0 \oplus \delta$ the bytes $\widehat{k}_0$ and k_0 are inseparable if and only if

$$\forall \ell \in \{0, \ldots, 15\} \forall a \in CL_\ell : a \oplus \delta \in CL_\ell. \tag{3}$$

Notice that this property only depends on the difference δ and not on the value of k_0. Since there are 16 elements of the sbox in every cache line property (3) can only be satisfied by at most 16 differences. It turns out that for $|\Delta| = 16$ the set

$$\Delta := \{\delta \mid \text{for all } k_0 \in \{0,1\}^8 \text{ the bytes } k_0 \text{ and } k_0 \oplus \delta \text{ are inseparable}\}$$

forms a 4 dimensional subspace of $\mathbb{F}_{2^8}$ viewed as a 8 dimensional vector space over $\mathbb{F}_2$. It is obvious that the neutral element 0 is an element of Δ and that every $\delta \in \Delta$ is its own inverse. It remains to show that Δ is closed with respect to addition. Consider $\delta, \delta' \in \Delta$ and an arbitrary $a \in CL_\ell$. Then $a' = a \oplus \delta \in CL_\ell$ implies that $a' \oplus \delta' = a \oplus \delta \oplus \delta' \in CL_\ell$ because of (3) and $\delta \oplus \delta' \in \Delta$ holds.

Hence, any partition that has the maximal number of inseparable key candidates must generate a subspace of dimension 4. Using this observation we describe how to efficiently construct permutations such that the set Δ of inseparable differences has size 16. In the sequel, we will call any such permutation a *distinguished permutation*. Next, we describe how to construct the subspace.

Construction of the subspace. We first construct a set Δ of 16 differences that is closed with respect to addition over $\mathbb{F}_{256}$. We can do this in the following way

1. set $\Delta := \{\delta_0 := 0\}$, choose δ_1 uniformly at random from the set $\{1, \ldots, 255\}$, set $\Delta := \Delta \cup \{\delta_1\}$
2. choose δ_2 uniformly at random from $\{1, \ldots, 255\} \setminus \Delta$, set $\Delta := \Delta \cup \{\delta_2, \delta_3 := \delta_1 \oplus \delta_2\}$
3. choose δ_4 uniformly at random from $\{1, \ldots, 255\} \setminus \Delta$, set $\Delta := \Delta \cup \{\delta_4, \delta_5 := \delta_4 \oplus \delta_1, \delta_6 := \delta_4 \oplus \delta_2, \delta_7 := \delta_4 \oplus \delta_3\}$
4. choose δ_8 uniformly at random from $\{1, \ldots, 255\} \setminus \Delta$, set $\Delta := \Delta \cup \{\delta_8, \delta_9 := \delta_8 \oplus \delta_1, \delta_{10} := \delta_8 \oplus \delta_2, \delta_{11} := \delta_8 \oplus \delta_3, \delta_{12} := \delta_8 \oplus \delta_4, \delta_{13} := \delta_8 \oplus \delta_5, \delta_{14} := \delta_8 \oplus \delta_6, \delta_{15} := \delta_8 \oplus \delta_7\}$

This construction ensures that Δ is closed with respect to addition and hence Δ forms a subspace as desired.

Construction of the permutation. Now we can compute the function P that maps $\mathbf{S}[x] \in \mathbb{F}_2^8$ to a cache line. We use the fact that 16 proper translations of a 4 dimensional subspace form a partition of a 8 dimensional vector space $\mathbb{F}_2^8$. A basis $\{b_0, \ldots b_3\}$ of the subspace Δ can be expanded by 4 vectors $b_4, \ldots b_7$ to a basis of $\mathbb{F}_2^8$. The 16 translations of Δ generated by linear combinations of $b_4, \ldots, b_7$ form the quotient space $\mathbb{F}_2^8 / \Delta$ that is a partition of $\mathbb{F}_2^8$. To construct the function P we do the following:

1. for every cache line CL_ℓ do
2. choose $a^{(\ell)}$ uniformly at random from $\mathbb{F}_{256} / \{a^{(j)} \oplus \delta \mid j < \ell, \delta \in \Delta\}$
3. fill CL_ℓ with the values of the set $\{a^{(\ell)} \oplus \delta \mid \delta \in \Delta\}$

Using (2) this partition into cache lines defines the corresponding permutation.

Analysis of the countermeasure. The security using a distinguished permutation as defined above rests on two facts.

1. Using a distinguished permutation where the set Δ of inseparable differences has size 16, a CBA on the last round of AES will reveal only four bits of each key byte k_i^{10}. Overall 64 of the 128 bits of the last round key remain unknown. Therefore, the adversary has to combine his CBA on the last round with some other method to determine the remaining 64 unknown bits. For example, he could try a modified CBA on the 9-th round exploiting his partial knowledge of the last round key. Or he could use a brute force search to determine the last round key completely.

2. There are several distinguished permutations and each of these permutations leads to 16! different functions mapping elements to 16 lines. If we choose randomly one of these functions, before an adversary can mount a CBA on the last round of [7], he first has to use some method like the one described in Section 5.1 to determine the function P that is actually used.

We stress that we consider the first fact to be the more important security feature. We saw already in Section 5.1 that determining a random permutation used for mapping elements to cache lines is not as secure as one might expect. Since we are using permutations of a special form the attack described in Section 5.1 can be improved somewhat. In the remainder of this section we briefly describe this improvement. To do so, first we have to determine the number of subspaces leading to distinguished permutations. As before view $\mathbb{F}_2^n := \{0,1\}^n$ as an n-dimensional $\mathbb{F}_2$ vector space. For $0 \leq k \leq n$ we define $D_{n,k}$ to be the number of k-dimensional subspaces of $\mathbb{F}_2^n$. To determine $D_{n,k}$ for V an arbitrary m-dimensional subspace of $\mathbb{F}_2^n$ we define

$$N_{m,k} := |\{(v_1, \ldots, v_k)|v_i \in V, v_1, \ldots v_k \text{ are linearly independent}\}|.$$

The number $N_{m,k}$ is independent of the particular m-dimensional subspace V, it only depends on the two parameters m and k. Then $D_{n,k} = \frac{N_{n,k}}{N_{k,k}}$. Next we observe that $N_{m,k} = \prod_{j=0}^{k-1}(2^m - 2^j) = 2^{k(k-1)/2} \prod_{j=0}^{k-1}(2^{m-j} - 1)$. Hence, we obtain that

$$D_{n,k} = \frac{\prod_{j=0}^{k-1}(2^{n-j} - 1)}{\prod_{j=0}^{k-1}(2^{k-j} - 1)}.$$

In our special case we have $n = 8$ and $k = 4$ and hence the number of 4 dimensional subspaces is $D_{8,4} = \frac{255 \cdot 127 \cdot 63 \cdot 31}{15 \cdot 7 \cdot 3 \cdot 1} = 200787$.

As mentioned above, each subspace leads to 16! different distinguished permutations. Hence, overall we have $200787 \cdot 16! \approx 2^{60}$ distinguished permutations. On the other hand, because of the special structure of our permutations, to determine the function P by CBAs can be done more efficiently than determining an arbitrary function mapping elements to cache lines (see Section 5.1). In particular, $\mathcal{A}$ only needs to observe about 7 accesses of a single but arbitrary cache line. With high probability this will be enough to determine a basis of the subspace being used. In addition, $\mathcal{A}$ needs at least one access for every other cache line in order to determine the function P. The corresponding probability experiment follows the multinomial distribution. We did not calculate the expected number of tries exactly. Experiments show that if we can determine the accessed cache line exactly, on average 62 measurements suffice to compute the function P exactly. However, a single measurement only yields a set of accessed cache lines. But arguments similar to the ones used for the first part of the attack in Section 5.1 show that we need on average 9 measurements to uniquely determine an accessed cache line. Therefore, on average we need $62 \cdot 9 = 558$ experiments to determine the function P.

Hence, compared to the results of Section 5.1 we have reduced the number of measurements used to determine the function P by a factor of 3. However, we want to stress again, that the main security enhancement of using distinguished permutations instead of arbitrary permutations is the fact, that distinguished permutations have a lower information leakage. To improve the security, one can choose larger key sizes such as 192 bits or 256 bits. Since distinguished permutations protect half of the key bits, the remaining uncertainty about the secret key after CBAs can be provably increased from 64 bits to 96 bits or 128 bits, respectively. In the full version of the paper [6] we describe an efficient and secure realization of random and distinguished permutations using small sboxes as described in Section 4.

Separability and random permutations. In our CBA on an implementation protected by a random permutation (Section 5.1) we assumed that fixing a candidate $\widehat{k}_0$ determines the candidates for all other key bytes. With sufficiently many measurements for a fixed $\widehat{k}_0$ we can determine the function $P_{\widehat{k}_0}$ as defined in Section 5.1. Furthermore, we saw that the separability of candidates $\widehat{k}, \widehat{k}'$ depends only on their difference $\delta = \widehat{k} \oplus \widehat{k}'$. Hence, to be able to rule out all but one candidate $\widehat{k}_i$ at position i for a fixed $\widehat{k}_0$ the permutation π must have the following property:

$$\forall \delta \neq 0 \exists j \in \{0, \ldots, 15\} \exists a \in CL_j : a \oplus \delta \notin CL_j.$$

There are less than 2^{844} of the $256! \approx 2^{1684}$ permutations that do not have this property. Hence, a random permutation satisfies this condition with probability $1 - \frac{2^{844}}{2^{1684}}$.

6 Summary of Countermeasures and Open Problems

In this paper we presented and analyzed the security of several different implementations of AES. Moreover, we analyzed countermeasures based on permutations: random permutations and distinguished permutations. We give a short overview over the advantages and disadvantages of selected countermeasures:

countermeasure	# measurements	information in bits /security	efficiency
small-4	∞	0 / high	slow
random permutation	2300	128 / low	fast
distinguished permutations	560	64 / medium	fast

The second column shows the expected number of measurements an attacker has to perform in order to get the amount of information shown in the third column.

References

1. Aciiçmez, O., Koç, Ç.K.: Trace-driven cache attacks on AES (short paper). In: Ning, P., Qing, S., Li, N. (eds,) ICICS 2006. LNCS, vol. 4307, pp. 112–121. Springer, Heidelberg (2006)
2. Aciiçmez, O., Schindler, W., Koç, Ç.K.: Cache based remote timing attack on the AES. In: Abe, M. (ed.) CT-RSA 2007. LNCS, vol. 4377, pp. 271–286. Springer, Heidelberg (2006)
3. Bernstein, D.J.: Cache-timing attacks on AES (2005), http://cr.yp.to/papers.html, Document ID: cd9faae9bd5308c440df50fc26a517b4
4. Bertoni, G., Zaccaria, V., Breveglieri, L., Monchiero, M., Palermo, G.: AES power attack based on induced cache miss and countermeasure. In: ITCC (1), pp. 586–591. IEEE Computer Society, Los Alamitos (2005)
5. Blömer, J., Guajardo, J., Krummel, V.: Provably secure masking of AES. In: Handschuh, H., Hasan, M.A. (eds.) SAC 2004. LNCS, vol. 3357, pp. 69–83. Springer, Heidelberg (2004)
6. Blömer, J., Krummel, V.: Analysis of countermeasures against access driven cache attacks on AES (full version). Cryptology ePrint Archive, Report 2007/282 (2007)
7. Brickell, E., Graunke, G., Neve, M., Seifert, J.-P.: Software mitigations to hedge AES against cache-based software side channel vulnerabilities. Cryptology ePrint Archive, Report 2006/052 (2006), http://eprint.iacr.org/
8. Daemen, J., Rijmen, V.: The Design of Rijndael: AES - The Advanced Encryption Standard. Information Security and Cryptography. Springer, Heidelberg (2002)
9. Hu, W.-M.: Lattice scheduling and covert channels. In: IEEE Symposium on Security and Privacy, pp. 52–61. IEEE Computer Society Press, Los Alamitos (1992)
10. Lauradoux, C.: Collision attacks on processors with cache and countermeasures. In: Wolf, C., Lucks, S., Yau, P.-W. (eds.) WEWoRC. LNI, vol. 74, pp. 76–85 (2005)
11. Neve, M., Seifert, J.-P.: Advances on access-driven cache attacks on AES. In: Proceedings of Selected Areas in Cryptography 2006 (2006)
12. Neve, M., Seifert, J.-P., Wang, Z.: A refined look at Bernstein's AES side-channel analysis. In: Lin, F.-C., Lee, D.-T., Lin, B.-S., Shieh, S., Jajodia, S. (eds.) ASIACCS, p. 369. ACM, New York (2006)
13. Osvik, D.A., Shamir, A., Tromer, E.: Cache attacks and countermeasures: The case of AES. In: Pointcheval, D. (ed.) CT-RSA 2006. LNCS, vol. 3860, pp. 1–20. Springer, Heidelberg (2006)
14. Page, D.: Theoretical use of cache memory as a cryptanalytic side-channel. Cryptology ePrint Archive, Report 2002/169 (2002), http://eprint.iacr.org/
15. Page, D.: Partitioned cache architecture as a side-channel defence mechanism. Cryptology ePrint Archive, Report 2005/280 (2005), http://eprint.iacr.org/
16. Percival, C.: Cache missing for fun and profit. In: BSDCan 2005 (2005)
17. Tsunoo, Y., Saito, T., Suzaki, T., Shigeri, M., Miyauchi, H.: Cryptanalysis of DES implemented on computers with cache. In: Walter, C.D., Koç, Ç.K., Paar, C. (eds.) CHES 2003. LNCS, vol. 2779, pp. 62–76. Springer, Heidelberg (2003)

A   Appendix

Table 1. Timings for different implementations of AES

# sboxes	fast	standard	fastV1	fastV2	small-2	small-4	small-8
time factor	1	~ 3	~ 1	~ 1	1.32	1.6	1.95

Table 2. The resistance E_r of AES implementations as defined in (1)

	1	2	3	4	5	6	7	8
	standard	fast	fast T_4	fastV1	fastV2	small-2	small-4	small-8
	$\mathbf{S}$	$\mathbf{T_0, \ldots, T_3}$	$\mathbf{T_4}$	$\mathbf{S}$	$\mathbf{T_0}$	$\mathbf{S_0, S_1}$	$\mathbf{S_0, \ldots, S_3}$	$\mathbf{S_0, \ldots, S_7}$
E_1	2.57	198.0	91.2	2.57	91.2	$3.91 \cdot 10^{-3}$	0	0
E_2	$2.57 \cdot 10^{-2}$	153.0	91.2	2.57	32.5	$5.96 \cdot 10^{-8}$	0	0
E_3	$2.58 \cdot 10^{-4}$	118.0	91.2	2.57	11.6	$9.09 \cdot 10^{-13}$	0	0
E_4	$2.58 \cdot 10^{-6}$	91.2	91.2	2.57	4.12	$1.39 \cdot 10^{-17}$	0	0
E_5	$2.59 \cdot 10^{-8}$	70.4	91.2	2.57	1.47	$2.12 \cdot 10^{-22}$	0	0
E_6	$2.59 \cdot 10^{-10}$	54.4	91.2	2.57	$5.22 \cdot 10^{-1}$	$3.23 \cdot 10^{-27}$	0	0
E_7	$2.60 \cdot 10^{-12}$	42.0	91.2	2.57	$1.86 \cdot 10^{-1}$	$4.93 \cdot 10^{-32}$	0	0
E_8	$2.61 \cdot 10^{-14}$	32.5	91.2	2.57	$6.62 \cdot 10^{-2}$	$7.52 \cdot 10^{-37}$	0	0
E_9	$2.61 \cdot 10^{-16}$	25.1	91.2	2.57	$2.36 \cdot 10^{-2}$	$1.15 \cdot 10^{-41}$	0	0
E_{10}	$2.62 \cdot 10^{-18}$	25.1	91.2	2.57	$8.39 \cdot 10^{-3}$	$1.75 \cdot 10^{-46}$	0	0

Power Analysis for Secret Recovering and Reverse Engineering of Public Key Algorithms

Frederic Amiel[1,*], Benoit Feix[2,**], and Karine Villegas[1]

[1] GEMALTO, Security Labs,
La Vigie, Avenue du Jujubier, ZI Athélia IV,
F-13705 La Ciotat Cedex, France
firstname.familyname@gemalto.com
[2] INSIDE CONTACTLESS
41 Parc Club du Golf
13856 Aix-en-Provence, Cedex 3, France
bfeix@insidefr.com

Abstract. Power Analysis has been deeply studied since 1998 in order to improve the security of tamper resistant products such as Trusted Platform Module (TPM). The study has evolved from initial basic techniques like simple and differential power analysis to more complex models such as correlation. However, works on correlation techniques have essentially been focused on symmetric cryptography. We analyze here the interests of this technique when applied to different smartcard coprocessors dedicated to asymmetric cryptography implementations. This study leads us to discover and realize new attacks on RSA and ECC type algorithms with fewer curves than classical attacks. We also present how correlation analysis is a powerful tool to reverse engineer asymmetric implementations.

Keywords: Public key cryptography, arithmetic coprocessors, exponentiation, side-channel analysis, reverse engineering.

1 Introduction

Public key cryptography has been widely used since its introduction by Diffie and Hellman [DH76] in 1976. Nowadays most famous applications are RSA [RSA78], invented in 1978 by Rivest, Shamir, and Adleman, and elliptic curves cryptosystems independly introduced by Koblitz [Kob87] and Miller [Mil86].Both kinds of asymmetric schemes require arithmetic operations in finite fields. For instance the use of modular arithmetic is necessary for exponentiation primitive in RSA or DSA [NIS00], as well as for point multiplication in elliptic curves. Therefore to obtain efficient computations, dedicated arithmetic coprocessors have been introduced in embedded devices.

For years tamper resistant devices have been considered as secure until 1996 when Kocher introduced the first side-channel attack (SCA) based on execution

---

* This author has recently left Gemalto.
** Part of this work has been done when this author was with Gemalto.

C. Adams, A. Miri, and M. Wiener (Eds.): SAC 2007, LNCS 4876, pp. 110–125, 2007.
© Springer-Verlag Berlin Heidelberg 2007

time measurements [Koc96]. A few years later power analysis was introduced by Kocher, Jaffe and Jun [KJJ99]. Their techniques, named simple power analysis (SPA) and differential power analysis (DPA), threaten any naive cryptographic algorithm implementation. Because an electronic device is composed of thousands of logical gates that switch differently depending on the executed operations, the power consumption depends on the executed instructions and the manipulated data. Thus by analyzing the power consumption of the device on an oscilloscope it is possible to observe its behavior and then to deduce from this power curve some secret data. Later, in 1999, Messerges, Dabbish and Sloan [MDS99] applied DPA to modular exponentiation which is the heart of several public key algorithms. In 2004, Brier, Clavier and Olivier [BCO04] introduced correlation power analysis (CPA) with a leakage model. This method has proven its efficiency on symmetric key algorithms, and needs very few curves to recover a secret key compared to classical DPA.

In this paper, we focus on this technique for which application to asymmetric algorithms has not been yet publicly reported. We introduce new attacks, illustrated by concrete experiments, to apply CPA on these algorithms. Indeed any arithmetic operation can be threatened by correlation analysis. For instance, we show how to reveal on a single correlation curve the whole private exponent during RSA exponentiation, and even during RSA CRT exponentiations. In addition we introduce a new case for CPA: the ability to realize precise reverse engineering. Once secret implementation and component hardware design have been recovered more powerful attacks can be envisaged.

The paper is organized as follows. Section 2 gives an overview of asymmetric algorithms embedded implementations. Section 3 describes well-known SCA techniques related to this article. New applications of correlation analysis on public key algorithms are discussed in Section 4. Practical results on different smartcard coprocessors are presented, they validate our attacks and their efficiency compared to classical differential power analysis. In Section 5 we present another application domain of correlation analysis by describing how it can be used to realize reverse engineering. We conclude our research in Section 6.

2 Public Key Embedded Implementations

We introduce here principles used later in this paper: modular multiplication and exponentiation, especially the ones designed by Montgomery that are particularly suitable for embedded implementations, and the RSA public key cryptosystem.

2.1 Modular Multiplication

Chip manufacturers usually embed arithmetic coprocessors to compute modular multiplications $x \times y \mod n$ for long integers x, y and n.

Montgomery introduced in [Mon85] an efficient algorithm named Montgomery Modular Multiplication. Other techniques exist: interleaved multiplication-reduction with Knuth, Barrett, Sedlack or Quisquater methods [Dhe98].

Montgomery modular multiplication

Given a modulus n and two integers x and y, of size v in base b, with $\gcd(n, b) = 1$ and $r = b^{\lceil \log_b(n) \rceil}$, MontMul algorithm computes:

$$\text{MontMul}(x, y, n) = x \times y \times r^{-1} \mod n$$

Algorithm 2.1. MontMul: Montgomery modular multiplication algorithm

INPUT: n, $0 \leq x = (x_{v-1} x_{v-2} \ldots x_1 x_0)_b, y = (y_{v-1} y_{v-2} \ldots y_1 y_0)_b \leq n - 1$,
$n' = -n^{-1} \mod b$
OUTPUT: $x \times y \times r^{-1} \mod n$

Step 1. $a = (a_{v-1} a_{v-2} \ldots a_1 a_0) \leftarrow 0$
Step 2. for i from 0 to $v - 1$ do
$\quad u_i \leftarrow (a_0 + x_i \times y_0) \times n' \mod b$
$\quad a \leftarrow (a + x_i \times y + u_i \times n)/b$
Step 3. if $a \geq n$ then $a \leftarrow a - n$
Step 4. Return(a)

Refer to papers [Mon85] and [KAK96] for details of MontMul implementation.

2.2   RSA

RSA signature of a message m consists in computing the value $s = m^d \mod n$. Signature s is then verified by computing $m = s^e \mod n$. Integers e and d are named the *public exponent* and the *private exponent*, n is called the *modulus*.

Some of the attacks introduced in this paper aim at recovering this private exponent d during decryption. Many implementations of the RSA algorithm rely on the Chinese Remainder Theorem (CRT) as it greatly improves performance in terms of execution speed, theoretically up to four times faster, cf. Alg. 2.2..

Algorithm 2.2. RSA CRT

INPUT: $p, q, d_p, d_q, i_q = q^{-1} \mod p$: the private elements, m: the message
OUTPUT: s: the signature

Step 1. Compute $m_p = m \mod p$ and $m_q = m \mod q$
Step 2. Compute $s_p = m_p^{d_p} \mod p$ and $s_q = m_q^{d_q} \mod q$
Step 3. Compute $s = s_q + ((s_p - s_q) \times i_q \mod p) \times q$
Step 4. Return(s)

In this case SCA is applied either to exponentiations to recover d_p and d_q, or to the recombination step to find q or to the initial reductions to recover p and q.

Modular exponentiation is the most time-consuming operation of RSA primitives. It is then essential to use an efficient method for exponentiation. Alg. 2.3.

below, based on MontMul, gives the Montgomery exponentiation algorithm and is particularly suited for embedded RSA implementations.

For a given modulus $n = (n_{v-1}n_{v-2}\ldots n_1 n_0)_b$, we define $r = b^{\lceil \log_b(n) \rceil}$ and the following function f_n:

$$f_n : [0, n-1] \longrightarrow [0, n-1]$$
$$x \longrightarrow x \times r \mod n$$

Let x and y be integers such that $0 \leq x, y < n$, we denote $\overline{x} = f_n(x)$ and $\overline{y} = f_n(y)$. We have the following property: $\mathsf{MontMul}(\overline{x}, \overline{y}, n) = x \times y \times r \mod n = f_n(x \times y)$ which is very useful to define the Montgomery modular exponentiation, cf. Alg. 2.3..

Algorithm 2.3. MontExp: Montgomery Square and Multiply from left to right

INPUT: integers m and n such that $m < n$, k-bit exponent $d = (d_{k-1}d_{k-2}\ldots d_1 d_0)_2$
OUTPUT: $\mathsf{MontExp}(m,d,n) = m^d \mod n$

Step 1. $a = r$
Step 2. $\overline{m} = f_n(m)$
Step 3. for i from $k-1$ to 0 **do**
  $a = \mathsf{MontMul}(a,a,n)$
  if $d_i = 1$ **then** $a = \mathsf{MontMul}(a,\overline{m},n)$
Step 4. $a = a \times r^{-1} \mod n = \mathsf{MontMul}(a,1,n)$
Step 5. Return(a)

---

3 Power Analysis

Among the different side-channel analysis techniques, we present in this section DPA applied to modular exponentiation and recall the principles of CPA based on a Hamming distance linear model.

3.1 Differential Power Analysis on Exponentiation

We want to recover the secret exponent d during Alg. 2.3.. We explain here the Zero-Exponent Multiple-Data (ZEMD) attack from Messerges, Dabbish and Sloan [MDS99]. Suppose we know the u most significant bits of d; i.e. $d_{k-1}\ldots d_{k-u}$, and we want to recover the $(u+1)^{st}$ bit of d. We make the guess $d_{k-u-1} = g$ with $g = 0$ or 1, and we want to confirm this guess. We execute on the device to attack t executions of the algorithm with input messages $m_1 \ldots m_t$ and collect the curves $C_1 \ldots C_t$ corresponding to the power consumption of these executions.

Let S_ϵ be the integer $S_\epsilon = \sum_{j=0}^{\epsilon-1} d_{k-1-j}.2^{\epsilon-j-1}$. A selection function $D(m_j, d_{k-u-1})$ is defined and used to split the set of curves into two subgroups such as: $G_{0,u+1} = \{C_j$ such that $D(m_j, d_{k-u-1}) = 0\}$ and $G_{1,u+1} = \{C_j$ such that $D(m_j, d_{k-u-1}) = 1\}$. For instance $D(m_j, d_{k-u-1})$ could be equal to the least significant bit of $f_n(m_j^{S_{u+1}}) = f_n(m_j^{2S_u+g})$ (if the guess of g is correct). Then compute the differential trace T_{u+1}:

$$T_{u+1} = \frac{\sum_{C_j \in G_{1,u+1}} C_j}{|G_{1,u+1}|} - \frac{\sum_{C_j \in G_{0,u+1}} C_j}{|G_{0,u+1}|}$$

Finally if the guess of d_{k-u-1} is correct, the trace T_{u+1} will have DPA peaks in the part of the curve corresponding to the manipulation of data associated to $D(m_j, d_{k-u-1})$, for instance in the next square. If the guess of d_{k-u-1} is wrong, no peak should be visible on trace T_{u+1}. Once d_{k-u-1} is recovered, the same analysis can be applied successively to the following secret bits of exponent d with $T_{u+2}, T_{u+3} \ldots$ This attack can be improved by multi-bit selection. In that case, the function $D(m_j, d_{k-u-1})$ takes into consideration several bits of the value $f_n(m_j^{2S_u+d_{k-u-1}})$ [Mes00].

We refer the reader to Appendix C where differential trace results are presented.

3.2   Correlation Power Analysis

As published by Brier, Clavier and Olivier [BCO04], it is known that CPA can be applied to obtain successful attacks on symmetric algorithms, for instance DES and AES, with fewer messages than classical DPA. The power consumption of the device is supposed to be linear in $H(D \oplus R)$, the Hamming distance of the data manipulated D, with respect to a *reference state* R. The linear correlation factor is used to correlate the power curves with this value $H(D \oplus R)$. The maximum correlation factor is obtained for the right guess of secret key bits.

Let W be the power consumption of the chip, its consumption model is:

$$W = \mu H(D \oplus R) + \nu.$$

The correlation factor $\rho_{C,H}$ between the set of power curves C and values $H(D \oplus R)$ is defined as: $\rho_{C,H} = \frac{cov(C,H)}{\sigma_C \sigma_H}$.

The principle of the attack is then the following:

- Perform t executions on the chip with input data $m_1 \ldots m_t$ and collect the corresponding power curves $C_1 \ldots C_t$.
- Predict some intermediate data D_i as a function of m_i and key hypothesis g.
- Produce the set of the t predicted Hamming distances: $\{H_{i,R} = H(D_i \oplus R), i = 1 \ldots t\}$.
- Calculate the estimated correlation factor:

$$\hat{\rho}_{C,H} = \frac{cov(C,H)}{\sigma_C \sigma_H} = \frac{t \sum (C_i H_{i,R}) - \sum C_i \sum H_{i,R}}{\sqrt{t \sum C_i^2 - (\sum C_i)^2} \sqrt{t \sum H_{i,R}^2 - (\sum H_{i,R})^2}}, i = 1 \ldots t$$

When the attacker makes the right guesses for values of the reference state R and secret leading to data D, the correlation factor ρ is maximum. It can also be seen graphically by tracing the correlation curve $C_{\rho,g}$. Of course, peak(s) of correlation is (are) visible on $C_{\rho,g}$ when the guess is correct. The attacker has recovered a part of the secret value and a reference state during the execution. R can be an *opcode* value or a *look-up-table* address for instance.

4 Correlation Power Analysis of Asymmetric Implementations

Previous CPA publications were mainly focused on symmetric algorithms such as DES and AES. The use of CPA against public key implementations has never been publicly investigated, except for Joye who theoretically introduced its application to a second order attack in ECC [Joy04]. This is the subject of this section where we present new attacks based on CPA.

4.1 Correlation on Intermediate Value in Modular Exponentiation

When computing an RSA exponentiation, if a guess g (0 or 1) is made for a bit d_{k-u-1} of the secret exponent, for a message m_j you can aim to correlate the power curve with the full data $R \oplus m_j^{2S_u+g} \mod n$. A more realistic choice is to select, depending on the size b of the chip multiplier, only a part of the intermediate data :

$$(R \oplus (m_j^{2S_u+g} \mod n)) \wedge \omega_{b,s}$$

where $\omega_{b,s} = b^s(b-1)$ and $s \in [0, v-1]$, for instance choose $s = 0$. Thus from ZEMD DPA we derive a ZEMD CPA (Alg. 4.4. with MontExp).

Algorithm 4.4. ZEMD CPA on Montgomery exponentiation

INPUT: n the modulus, $m_1, \ldots, m_t$ t messages
OUTPUT: the secret exponent $d = (d_{k-1}d_{k-2} \ldots d_1 d_0)_2$

Step 1. Choose $s \in \{0, .., v\text{-}1\}$
Step 2. for u from 0 to $k-1$ **do**
    Guess $d_{k-1-u} = 1$
    $$A_1 = \left\{ H((R \oplus f_n(m_i^{2S_u+d_{k-u-1}})) \wedge \omega_{b,s}), \quad i = 1, \ldots, t \right\}$$
    $\rho_1 = \hat{\rho}_{C,A_1}$
    Conclude $d_{k-1-u} = 1$ if C_{ρ_1} has correlation peaks **else** $d_{k-1-u} = 0$
Step 3. Return(d**)**

This attack can be optimized by simultaneously searching for many bits (α) of d, kind of α-ary CPA. In that case you have to compare $2^\alpha - 1$ correlation values, the maximum correlation value corresponding to the right guess of the α bits of d.

Reference state value: The difficulty in correlation analysis is the knowledge of the reference state value R, which must be known or at least guessed by the attacker. The natural choice is to take $R = 0$. In that case the correlation

Fig. 1. ZEMD CPA on MontExp: correct guess

Fig. 2. ZEMD CPA on MontExp: wrong guess

model is reduced from the Hamming distance model to the Hamming weight one. Indeed we can expect to have either a hardware erase operation on initial register(s) of the multiplication algorithm, or the combinatorial part of the hardware modular multiplier to be in a stall state. If not, suppose $b = 2^8$ and $s = 0$: if R is a constant value then try the whole 256 different possible values for R. The correlation analysis will be successful only for right guess of d_{k-1-u} and R. A more complex case can be envisaged to evaluate $H(R \oplus D)$: it consists in choosing for R previous intermediate data, for instance $R = u_i$, and for the newly obtained data D the value $D = u_{i+1}$ at step 2 in Alg. 2.1. (Practical results are shown in Fig. 1 and Fig. 2.)

The correlation peaks can appear either during the data handling of the guessed intermediate value leading to the output result of the current operation, or caused by setting this value as input operand of the next operation (for instance, in the next square). Therefore, there are two different possible sources of correlation.

4.2   Correlation on Multiplicand Data

The drawback of ZEMD CPA is that the attack must be iterated for each guessed bit of d (or even l-bit per l-bit), we need then to compute k (or k/l) correlation curves. A more efficient attack can be considered when the correlation peaks are caused by the handling of the input operand. Indeed, during an exponentiation, for each multiplication (as opposed to squarings), one of the multiplicands is constant and equal to m (or $f_n(m)$ for Montgomery). Therefore, by computing correlation on this multiplicand value we can expect to obtain CPA peaks each

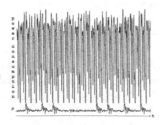

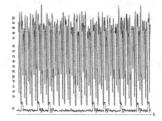

Fig. 3. CPA on multiplicand partial size during exponentiation, $R = 0$

Fig. 4. CPA on multiplicand full size during exponentiation, $R = 0$

time it is manipulated. Thus all the multiplications by m (or $f_n(m)$) could be seen on this single correlation curve. The full secret d is thus recovered with a single correlation computation on all the curves. This attack has been realized with success on different chips. Practical results for a partial and a full correlation on the multiplicand value during an exponentiation are shown in Fig. 3 and Fig. 4. Indeed in Fig. 4 each multiplication can be seen on the correlation curve and as result d can be easily deduced as it would be done in SPA.

Algorithm 4.5. CPA on Multiplicand Data in Montgomery exponentiation

INPUT: n the modulus, $m_1, \ldots, m_t$ t messages
OUTPUT: secret exponent $d = (d_{k-1} d_{k-2} \ldots d_1 d_0)_2$

Step 1. Choose $s \in \{0, .., v - 1\}$
Step 2. Compute $A = \{H((R \oplus f_n(m_i)) \wedge \omega_{b,s}), \quad i = 1, \ldots, t\}$
Step 3. Compute $\rho = \hat{\rho}_{C,A}$ and its related correlation curve C_ρ
Step 4. Detect on C_ρ the peaks to identify all the multiplications and deduce d
Step 5. **Return**(d)

4.3 Correlation on RSA CRT

This section introduces new CPA attacks to recover the private key elements for each step of the Algorithm 2.2..

Correlation during CRT modular exponentiations

During modular exponentiations of message m_j; $s_p = m_j^{d_p} \mod p$ and $s_q = m_j^{d_q} \mod q$, it is not possible to apply ZEMD because p and q are unknown to the attacker.

However it is possible to do correlation on the multiplicand's value to recover d_p when $m_j < p$ and d_q when $m_j < q$. Choose $m_j < \min(p, q)$ to recover simultaneously d_p and d_q. For instance if p and q are both k-bit primes, select messages m_j in $[2, 2^{k-1}]$.

Note that this attack is not applicable to RSA CRT using Montgomery exponentiation as $f_p(m_j)$ and $f_q(m_j)$ are unpredictable. However it can be done on other exponentiations, using different modular arithmetic such as Barrett.

Correlation during the CRT recombination

The recombination (Step 3 of Alg. 2.2.) gives the ability to guess bits of the value of q by CPA as s is known. Indeed, one can observe that for the upper half bits of s we have:

$$\left\lfloor \frac{s}{q} \right\rfloor = ((s_p - s_q) \times i_q \mod p) + \left\lfloor \frac{s_q}{q} \right\rfloor = (s_p - s_q) \times i_q \mod p$$

As $(s_p - s_q) \times i_q \mod p$ is an operand of the recombination step, it is then obvious that for the right guess of q we should be able to obtain the best correlation factor by estimating this operand value. In practice, the attack realization needs to guess the value of q by groups of b bits starting from the most significant words. For instance take $b = 2^8$ and the right guess of b bits of q corresponds to the highest correlation value obtained among the 256 guesses. For more details please refer to Alg. 4.6..

Algorithm 4.6. CPA on RSA CRT recombination

INPUT: $s_1, \ldots, s_t$ t signatures
OUTPUT: the secret element $q = (q_{v-1} q_{v-2} \ldots q_1 q_0)_b$

Step 1. $q = 0$

Step 2.

  for i from $v - 1$ to 0 **do**
  　$g_{max} = 0,\ \rho_{max} = 0$
  　for g from 0 to $b - 1$ **do**
  　　$\hat{q} = q + (g + 0.5) \times b^i$
  　　$A = \left\{ H((R \oplus \left\lfloor \frac{s_j}{\hat{q}} \right\rfloor) \wedge \omega_{b,i}),\ \ j = 1 \ldots t \right\}$
  　　$\rho_g = \hat{\rho}_{C,A}$
  　　if $|\rho_g| > |\rho_{max}|$ **then** $g_{max} = g,\ \rho_{max} = \rho$
  　$q = q + g_{max} \times b^i$

Step 3. Return(q)

Choosing $\hat{q} = q + (g + 0.5) \times b^i$ instead of $\hat{q} = q + g \times b^i$ as estimator gives the correct decision when the correct value belongs to $\left[g \times b^i, (g + 1) \times b^i \right] + q$.

On our implementation based on a Montgomery multiplier, one should take into account that the estimation of A will depend on f_n (see Paragraph 2.2).

Correlation during the initial reductions

Attacks on the initial reductions $m \mod p$ and $m \mod q$ would aim at recovering p and q. Previous studies have been presented by Boer, Lemke and Wicke [BLW02] and Akkar [Akk04]. Contrary to those previous attacks, CPA works with any messages and fewer curves on any arithmetic operation such as addition or subtraction. Indeed, for message reduction and no matter what the algorithm is, the first steps always require a subtraction and/or an addition between a part of the message and the secret modulus p or q. Note that even if the implementation is supposed to be protected against SPA, like the secure shift and reduce division algorithm [JV02], it is possible to perform CPA. For example, if p has k bits and the messages used for CPA, $m_1, \ldots m_t$, have $2k$ bits, the guesses will be performed on operands $\left\lfloor \frac{m_i - m_i \mod 2^k}{2^k} \right\rfloor - p$, for $i = 1, \ldots, t$. All the bytes of p or q from the least significant bytes to the most significant ones can be retrivied using this technique.

4.4   Application to Elliptic Curves Cryptosystems

ECDSA and El Gamal are two of the most widely known elliptic curves schemes. For details we suggest the reader refer to Appendix A and [ACD+06].

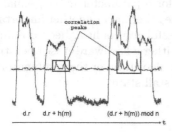
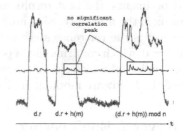

Fig. 5. CPA on ECDSA, correct guess   **Fig. 6.** CPA on ECDSA, wrong guess

CPA on El Gamal Decryption: This primitive can be vulnerable to CPA during the scalar multiplication $P_k = [d]Q_k$ where d is the private key. Q_k is a point of the curve returned in the ciphertext. CPA targets d. If the scalar multiplication is performed with the Double and Add algorithm (cf. Appendix A), different processes are done whether a given bit of d is equal to 0 or 1. An attacker could identify the addition part by correlating consumption curves with $g(x_Q)$ a function of coordinate(s) of the point added according to the targeted implementation. For instance $g(x_Q)$ can be $x_Q \wedge \omega_{b,0}$.

CPA on ECDSA signature: here, $d \times r \mod n$ operation, with d the private key and r known as part of the signature, could be sensitive to CPA. On a modular multiplier based on Montgomery implementation (see Alg. 2.1 for further details) such leakage could occur during $x_i \times y_0$ or $x_i \times y$ operations. Fig. 5 illustrates a successful attack, the most significant byte of d is recovered among 256 guesses. The attack algorithm is described in Appendix B.

4.5 Practical Results and Remarks

All the attacks presented have been tested with success on several smartcard coprocessors using different modular arithmetic implementations, cf. Fig. 7. In

Chip	Algorithm	Attack	Curves for DPA	Curves for CPA
Coprocessor 1	RSA Exponentiation	Intermediate value	1500	150
	RSA Exponentiation	Multiplicand value	2500	300
Coprocessor 2	RSA Exponentiation	Intermediate value	500	100
	RSA Exponentiation	Multiplicand value	1500	250
	RSA CRT	Recombination step	No success	150
Coprocessor 3	RSA CRT	Recombination step	No success	4000
	ECDSA	$d \times r \mod n$	No success	4000
	RSA Exponentiation	Intermediate value	No success	1000
	RSA Exponentiation	Multiplicand value	No success	3000

Fig. 7. Practical results

our experiments, the best results are obtained for b parameter in $\omega_{b,s}$ equal to the radix of the multi-precision multiplier. On the other hand, another important parameter is the reference state value R. Successful results have been obtained with $R = 0$, which confirms the hypothesis that either a hardware erase operation is done on initial register(s) of the multiplication algorithm, or the combinatorial part of the hardware modular multiplier is in a stall state.

5   Reverse Engineering

Side channel analysis has already been used by Novak [Nov03] and Clavier [Cla04] to reverse engineer secret GSM A3/A8 algorithms. Later Daudigny, Ledig, Muller and Valette processed similarly on a DES implementation [DLMV].

Previously we showed that each data manipulation by the coprocessor could be observed by CPA. It has been used to recover secret keys and data in the previous analysis. We now show how CPA can also be used to recover the design of the coprocessor embedded in the chip.

In most software implementations, encryption and signature verification primitives do not implement any countermeasure as they do not manipulate secret data. Such primitives could then be used by an attacker to increase knowledge about the hardware multiplier. It could be useful as in software implementations, unsecure and secure primitives share the same hardware resources.

Fig. 8 gives the details of the leakage of a hardware multiplier during a square operation in RSA exponentiation.

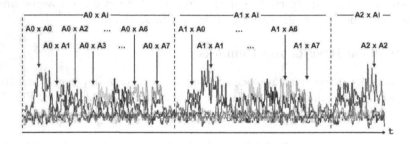

Fig. 8. Reverse engineering by CPA on Montgomery multiplication

By CPA, we are able to determine the precise implementation of the b-bit words multiplications in the modular multiplication algorithm: the size b of the hardware multiplier and the order in which the operands are used can be determined. We can precisely localize the instant when each data x_i, y_i, $x_i \times y$, $u_i \times n$, etc. in Alg. 2.1. is manipulated. The order of use of such intermediate values depends on the algorithm supposed to be implemented (for instance FIOS, CIOS in [KAK96]). Thus, for each guessed implementation, we can observe if the expected intermediate values appear and their exact position on the correlation curves. If not, the guess of the implementation is incorrect. Else, by combining many correlation curves for the different consecutives intermediate values, the exact implementation of the multiplication can be deduced. Fig. 8 illustrates part of the analysis we made on a chip using a Montgomery multiplier. We successfully recovered the size b of the hardware multiplier, the sequence and the kind of operations processed and thus the algorithm implemented for MontMul.

With such a precise knowledge, more complex attacks can be considered and achieved to defeat the classical DPA countermeasures. Indeed higher order power analysis attacks can also be envisaged with more precision on the cycles to combine together. In [Wal01] Walter introduced the *Big Mac Attack* to recover a secret exponent d only with the single power curve of the executed exponentiation. Such a reverse engineering by CPA gives the necessary knowledge required to realize this attack in the best conditions.

Such information can also be used to recover secret variables in asymmetric algorithms based on private specifications when the basic structure of the algorithm is known. Of course this implies that the attacker also needs to learn about the implementation done: the kind of coordinates that are used for elliptic curves (projective, Jacobian), kind of modular arithmetic, etc.

Furthermore in a fault attack scenario, the benefit of such information cannot be neglected as the effect of each fault injection during hardware multiplier execution could become predictable and with a really precise effect.

To avoid risks of reverse engineering we advise randomizing public elements during the computations using techniques such as described in [Cor99], [Koc96].

6   Conclusion

Several new attacks based on CPA have been presented in this paper. These attack schemes threaten most of public key algorithms such as RSA, RSA CRT or Elliptic Curves ones (ECES, ECDSA) if efficient countermeasures, such as blinding technics, are not implemented. Through experiments, we have demonstrated that CPA can detect and characterize leakages of arithmetic coprocessors. Therefore it gave us the ability to successfully implement the attacks we present by using the power consumption model based on the Hamming distance between the handled data and a constant reference state. As results of these experiments, we have proven also that the use of CPA is an improvement compared to classical attacks such as DPA. The efficiency of CPA has led us to proceed to reverse engineering of the design of coprocessors and then it has given the knowledge of the type of algorithm implemented (Montgomery, Barrett, ...), the size of hardware multiplier, the way to interleave operations and words in the multiplication algorithm etc. Furthermore, we have stressed that such precise knowledge of an arithmetic coprocessors can make realistic high-order side channel attacks or even fault attack scenarios and improves their efficiency. Therefore, in order to avoid any potential attacker gaining experience on a secure device, we suggest using randomization techniques even for encryption or signature verification primitives usually considered as not sensitive.

Acknowledgements

The authors would like to thank Benoit Chevallier-Mames and Christophe Clavier for their fruitful comments and advices on this paper.

References

[ACD⁺06]   Avanzi, R.-M., Cohen, H., Doche, C., Frey, G., Lange, T., Nguyen, K., Verkauteren, F.: Handbook of elliptic and hyperelliptic curve cryptography (2006)

[Akk04]   Akkar, M.-L.: Attaques et méthodes de protections de protections de systèmes de cryptographie embarquée. PhD thesis, Université de Versailles (2004)

[BCO04]   Brier, E., Clavier, C., Olivier, F.: Correlation power analysis with a leakage model. In: Joye, M., Quisquater, J.-J. (eds.) CHES 2004. LNCS, vol. 3156, pp. 16–29. Springer, Heidelberg (2004)

[BLW02]   den Boer, B., Lemke, K., Wicke, G.: A DPA attack against the modular reduction within a CRT implementation of RSA. In: Kaliski Jr., B.S., Koç, Ç.K., Paar, C. (eds.) CHES 2002. LNCS, vol. 2523, pp. 228–243. Springer, Heidelberg (2003)

[Cla04]   Clavier, C.: Side channel analysis for reverse engineering (SCARE), an improved attack against a secret A3/A8 GSM algorithm. IACR Cryptology eprint archive (049) (2004)

[Cor99]   Coron, J.-S.: Resistance against differential power analysis for elliptic curve cryptosystems. In: Koç, Ç.K., Paar, C. (eds.) CHES 1999. LNCS, vol. 1717, pp. 292–302. Springer, Heidelberg (1999)

[DH76]   Diffie, W., Hellman, M.E.: New directions in cryptography. IEEE Transactions on Information Theory 22(6), 644–654 (1976)

[Dhe98]   Dhem, J.-F.: Design of an efficient public-key cryptographic library for RISC-based smart cards. PhD thesis, Université catholique de Louvain, Louvain (1998)

[DLMV]   Daudigny, R., Ledig, H., Muller, F., Valette, F.: Scare of the DES. In: Ioannidis, J., Keromytis, A.D., Yung, M. (eds.) ACNS 2005. LNCS, vol. 3531, pp. 393–406. Springer, Heidelberg (2005)

[Joy04]   Joye, M.: Smart-card implementation of elliptic curve cryptography and DPA-type attacks. In: Quisquater, J.-J., Paradinas, P., Deswarte, Y., El Kalam, A.A. (eds.) CARDIS, pp. 115–126. Kluwer, Dordrecht (2004)

[JV02]   Joye, M., Villegas, K.: A protected division algorithm. In: CARDIS 2002. Proceedings of the Fifth Smart Card Research and Advanced Application Conference (2002)

[KAK96]   Koç, Ç.K., Acar, T., Kaliski, B.-S.: Analysing and comparing Montgomery multiplication algorithms. IEEE Micro 16(3), 26–33 (1996)

[KJJ99]   Kocher, P.C., Jaffe, J., Jun, B.: Differential power analysis. In: Wiener, M.J. (ed.) CRYPTO 1999. LNCS, vol. 1666, pp. 388–397. Springer, Heidelberg (1999)

[Kob87]   Koblitz, N.: Elliptic curve cryptosystems. Math. of Comp. 48(177), 203–209 (1987)

[Koc96]   Kocher, P.C.: Timing attacks on implementations of Diffie-Hellman, RSA, DSS, and other systems. In: Koblitz, N. (ed.) CRYPTO 1996. LNCS, vol. 1109, pp. 104–113. Springer, Heidelberg (1996)

[MDS99]   Messerges, T.S., Dabbish, E.A., Sloan, R.H.: Power analysis attacks of modular exponentiation in smartcards. In: Koç, Ç.K., Paar, C. (eds.) CHES 1999. LNCS, vol. 1717, pp. 144–157. Springer, Heidelberg (1999)

[Mes00]   Messerges, T.S.: Power analysis attacks and countermeasures for cryptographic algorithms. PhD thesis, University of Illinois at Chicago (2000)

[Mil86]   Miller, V.S.: Use of elliptic curves in cryptography. In: Odlyzko, A.M. (ed.) CRYPTO 1986. LNCS, vol. 263, pp. 489–502. Springer, Heidelberg (1987)

[Mon85]   Montgomery, P.L.: Modular multiplication without trial division. Mathematics of Computation 44(170), 519–521 (1985)

[NIS00]   NIST. Digital signature standard (DSS). Federal Information Processing Standards Publication 186-2 (January 2000)

[Nov03]   Novak, R.: Side-channel attack on substitution blocks. In: Zhou, J., Yung, M., Han, Y. (eds.) ACNS 2003. LNCS, vol. 2846, pp. 307–318. Springer, Heidelberg (2003)

[RSA78]   Rivest, R.L., Shamir, A., Adleman, L.: A method for obtaining digital signatures and public-key cryptosystems. Communications of the ACM 21, 120–126 (1978)

[Wal01]   Walter, C.D.: Sliding windows succumbs to big mac attack. In: Koç, Ç.K., Naccache, D., Paar, C. (eds.) CHES 2001. LNCS, vol. 2162, pp. 286–299. Springer, Heidelberg (2001)

A Elliptic Curves

A.1 Double and Add Algorithm

Algorithm A.7. Double and Add

INPUT: E the curve, $Q = (x_Q, y_Q)$ a point of E, $d = (d_{k-1}d_{k-2}\ldots d_1 d_0)$ a scalar of k bits

OUTPUT: value $P = [d]Q$

Step 1. $P = Q$

Step 2. for i from $k - 2$ to 0 **do**

$\quad P = 2P$

$\quad$ **if** $d_i = 1$ **then** $P = P + Q$

Step 3. Return(P)

A.2   ECDSA Signature

Let the knowledge of the domain parameters be $D = (p, a, b, G, n, h)$, the key pair be (d, Q) with $Q = [d]G$ and the required hash function be $h(.)$.

Algorithm A.8. ECDSA signature

INPUT: D, private key $d = (d_{k-1}d_{k-2}\ldots d_1 d_0)_2$, message m, $h(.)$.
OUTPUT: m signature= (s, r).

Step 1. Select a random u, $1 \leq u \leq n - 1$

Step 2. Compute $R = [u]G = (x_R, y_R)$

Step 3. Compute $r = x_R \mod n$, if $r = 0$ go to Step1

Step 4. Compute $s = u^{-1}(h(m) + d \times r) \mod n$, if $s = 0$ go to Step1

Step 5. Return(r, s)

B   Algorithm for CPA on ECDSA

Algorithm B.9. CPA on ECDSA signature

INPUT: $(s_1, r_1), \ldots, (s_t, r_t)$ t signatures
OUTPUT: the secret element $d = (d_{k-1}d_{k-2}\ldots d_1 d_0)_b$

Step 1. $d = 0$

Step 2.

> for i from $k - 1$ to 0 **do**
>> $g_{max} = 0$, $\rho_{max} = 0$
>> for g from 0 to $b - 1$ **do**
>>> $\hat{d} = d + (g + 0.5) \times d^i$
>>> $A = \left\{ H((R \oplus f(\hat{d} \times r_j)) \wedge \omega_{b,i}), \quad j = 1 \ldots t \right\}$
>>> $\rho_g = \hat{\rho}_{C,A}$
>>> **if** $|\rho_g| > |\rho_{max}|$ **then** $g_{max} = g$, $\rho_{max} = \rho$
>> $d = d + g_{max} \times b^i$

Step 3. Return(d)

C   ZEMD DPA Practical Result

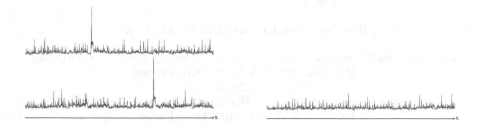

Fig. 9. ZEMD DPA: right guesses for d_{n-2} and d_{n-4}, single bit selection

Fig. 10. ZEMD DPA: wrong guess for d_{n-2}, single bit selection

Koblitz Curves and Integer Equivalents of Frobenius Expansions[*]

Billy Bob Brumley[1] and Kimmo Järvinen[2]

[1] Laboratory for Theoretical Computer Science, Helsinki University of Technology,
P.O. Box 5400, FIN-02015 TKK, Finland
billy.brumley@tkk.fi
[2] Signal Processing Laboratory, Helsinki University of Technology,
P.O. Box 3000, FIN-02015 TKK, Finland
kimmo.jarvinen@tkk.fi

Abstract. Scalar multiplication on Koblitz curves can be very efficient due to the elimination of point doublings. Modular reduction of scalars is commonly performed to reduce the length of expansions, and τ-adic Non-Adjacent Form (NAF) can be used to reduce the density. However, such modular reduction can be costly. An alternative to this approach is to use a random τ-adic NAF, but some cryptosystems (e.g. ECDSA) require both the integer and the scalar multiple. This paper presents an efficient method for computing integer equivalents of random τ-adic expansions. The hardware implications are explored, and an efficient hardware implementation is presented. The results suggest significant computational efficiency gains over previously documented methods.

Keywords: Koblitz curves, elliptic curve cryptography, digital signatures.

1 Introduction

While compact keys and signatures occur naturally when using elliptic curves, the computational efficiency of elliptic curve cryptosystems is the subject of much research. Koblitz [1] showed that scalar multiplication can be done very fast on a certain family of binary curves now commonly referred to as Koblitz curves. In the same paper, Koblitz credited Hendrik Lenstra for first suggesting random base-τ expansions for key agreement protocols using Koblitz curves.

Meier and Staffelbach [2] showed how to significantly reduce the length of τ-adic expansions by performing modular reduction on scalars. Solinas [3,4] later built on this idea and additionally reduced the weight by designing a τ-adic analogue of Non-Adjacent Form (NAF).

Unfortunately, performing such modular reduction can be costly. As future work, Solinas suggested a study of the distribution of random τ-adic NAFs. Lange and Shparlinski [5,6] have studied the distribution of such expansions in depth.

---

[*] This work was supported by the project "Packet Level Authentication" funded by TEKES.

C. Adams, A. Miri, and M. Wiener (Eds.): SAC 2007, LNCS 4876, pp. 126–137, 2007.
© Springer-Verlag Berlin Heidelberg 2007

For key agreement protocols like Diffie-Hellman [7], the integer equivalent of such a random τ-adic expansion is not needed. However, for ElGamal [8] type digital signatures like ECDSA [9], both the integer and the scalar multiple are needed to generate a signature. Lange [10] discussed many of the details of this approach, as well a straightforward method for recovering the integer equivalent using a number of multiplications.

In this paper, we present a new method for recovering integer equivalents of random τ-adic expansions using only additions and one field multiplication. This method is shown to be very efficient and has significant hardware implications. A hardware implementation is also presented and studied in depth. The results are then compared to current similar methods in hardware.

Sec. 2 reviews background information on Koblitz curves and τ-adic expansions. Sec. 3 covers more recent research on random τ-adic expansions, as well as our new method for efficiently computing integer equivalents of such expansions. Sec. 4 presents an efficient hardware implementation of our new method on a field programmable gate array (FPGA), as well as a comparison to current methods. We conclude in Sec. 5.

2   Koblitz Curves

Koblitz curves [1] are non-supersingular elliptic curves defined over $\mathbb{F}_2$, i.e.

$$E_a(\mathbb{F}_{2^m}) : y^2 + xy = x^3 + ax^2 + 1 \text{ where } a \in \{0,1\} . \tag{1}$$

These curves have the nice property that if a point $P = (x,y)$ is on the curve, so is the point (x^2, y^2). The map $\sigma : E_a(F_{2^m}) \to E_a(F_{2^m})$; $(x,y) \mapsto (x^2, y^2)$ is called the Frobenius endomorphism. From the point addition formula, it can be shown that for all $(x, y) \in E_a$

$$(x^4, y^4) + 2(x, y) = \mu(x^2, y^2), \text{ where } \mu = (-1)^{1-a}, \text{ equivalently}$$
$$(\sigma^2 + 2)P = \mu\sigma P, \text{ and hence}$$
$$\sigma^2 + 2 = \mu\sigma \text{ as curve endomorphisms.} \tag{2}$$

The last equation also allows us to look at σ as a complex number τ and we can extend scalar multiplication to scalars $d_0 + d_1\tau$ from $\mathbb{Z}[\tau]$. Higher powers of τ make sense as repeated applications of the endomorphisms.

Koblitz showed how to use use the Frobenius endomorphism very efficiently in scalar multiplication: A scalar $n = d_0 + d_1\tau$ is expanded using (2) repeatedly, i.e. put $\epsilon_0 = d_0 \pmod{2}$ and replace n by $(d_0 - \epsilon_0)/2\mu + d_1 - (d_0 - \epsilon_0)/2\tau$ to compute ϵ_1 etc. This iteration leads to a so called τ-adic expansion with coefficients $\epsilon \in \{0, 1\}$ such that $nP = \sum_{i=0} \epsilon_i \tau^i(P)$.

As a result of representing integers as the sum of powers of τ, scalar multiplication can be accomplished with no point doublings by combining point additions and applications of σ. Koblitz noted in [1] that such base-τ expansions unfortunately have twice the length when compared to binary expansions. This leads to twice the number of point additions on average.

2.1   Integer Equivalents

To overcome this drawback, Meier and Staffelbach [2] made the following observation. Given any point $P \in E_a(\mathbb{F}_{2^m})$, it follows that

$$P = (x, y) = (x^{2^m}, y^{2^m}) = \tau^m P$$
$$\mathcal{O} = (\tau^m - 1)P.$$

Two elements $\gamma, \rho \in \mathbb{Z}[\tau]$ such that $\gamma \equiv \rho \pmod{\tau^m - 1}$ are said to be *equivalent* with respect to P as γ multiples of P can also be obtained using the element ρ since for some κ

$$\gamma P = \rho P + \kappa(\tau^m - 1)P = \rho P + \kappa \mathcal{O} = \rho P .$$

While this relation holds for all points on the curve, cryptographic operations are often limited to the main subgroup; that is, the points of large prime order. Solinas [4] further improved on this. The small subgroup can be excluded since $(\tau - 1)$ divides $(\tau^m - 1)$, and for multiples of points in the main subgroup scalars can be reduced modulo $\delta = (\tau^m - 1)/(\tau - 1)$ to further reduce the length to a maximum of $m + a$. For computational reasons, it is often convenient to have the form $\delta = c_0 + c_1\tau$ as well. For reference, the procedure for performing such modular reduction is presented as Algorithm 1, which calculates ρ' such that the probability that $\rho' \neq \rho$ holds is less than $2^{-(C-5)}$. This probabilistic approach is used to avoid costly rational divisions, trading them for a number of multiplications.

Algorithm 1. Partial reduction modulo $\delta = (\tau^m - 1)/(\tau - 1)$.

Input: Integer n, constants $C > 5$, $s_0 = c_0 + \mu c_1$, $s_1 = -c_1$,
$\qquad V_m = 2^m + 1 - \#E_a(\mathbb{F}_{2^m})$.
Output: n partmod δ.
$n' \leftarrow \lfloor n/2^{a-C+(m-9)/2} \rfloor$
for $i \leftarrow 0$ **to** 1 **do**
$\qquad g' \leftarrow s_i n'$
$\qquad j' \leftarrow V_m \lfloor g'/2^m \rfloor$
$\qquad \lambda_i \leftarrow \lfloor (g' + j')/2^{(m+5)/2} + \frac{1}{2} \rfloor / 2^C$
end
$(q_0, q_1) \leftarrow \text{Round}(\lambda_0, \lambda_1)$ /* Using Algorithm 2 */
$d_0 \leftarrow k - (s_0 + \mu s_1)q_0 - 2s_1 q_1$, $d_1 \leftarrow s_1 q_0 - s_0 q_1$
return $d_0 + d_1\tau$

Solinas [4] also developed a τ-adic analogue of Non-Adjacent Form (NAF). Signed representations are used as point subtraction has roughly the same cost as point addition; NAF guarantees that no two adjacent coefficients are non-zero. By reducing elements of $\mathbb{Z}[\tau]$ modulo δ and using τ-adic NAF, such expansions have roughly the same length and average density (1/3 when $\epsilon_i \in \{0, 1, -1\}$) as normal NAFs of the same integers.

Algorithm 2. Rounding off in $\mathbb{Z}[\tau]$.

Input: Rational numbers λ_0 and λ_1.
Output: Integers q_0, q_1 such that $q_0 + q_1\tau$ is close to $\lambda_0 + \lambda_1\tau$.
for $i \leftarrow 0$ **to** 1 **do**
    $f_i \leftarrow \lfloor \lambda_i + \frac{1}{2} \rfloor$
    $\eta_i \leftarrow \lambda_i - f_i,\, h_i \leftarrow 0$
end
$\eta \leftarrow 2\eta_0 + \mu\eta_1$
if $\eta \geq 1$ **then**
    if $\eta_0 - 3\mu\eta_1 < -1$ **then** $h_1 \leftarrow \mu$
    else $h_0 \leftarrow 1$
end
else
    if $\eta_0 + 4\mu\eta_1 \geq 2$ **then** $h_1 \leftarrow \mu$
if $\eta < -1$ **then**
    if $\eta_0 - 3\mu\eta_1 \geq 1$ **then** $h_1 \leftarrow -\mu$
    else $h_0 \leftarrow -1$
end
else
    if $\eta_0 + 4\mu\eta_1 < -2$ **then** $h_1 \leftarrow -\mu$
$q_0 \leftarrow f_0 + h_0,\, q_1 \leftarrow f_1 + h_1$
return q_0, q_1

---

3 Random τ-adic Expansions

Instead of performing such non-trivial modular reduction, Solinas [4] suggested (an adaptation of an idea credited to Hendrik Lenstra in Koblitz's paper [1]) producing a *random* τ-adic NAF; that is, to build an expansion by generating digits with $\Pr(-1) = 1/4$, $\Pr(1) = 1/4$, $\Pr(0) = 1/2$, and following each non-zero digit with a zero. Lange and Shparlinski [5] proved that such expansions with length $\ell = m - 1$ are well-distributed and virtually collision-free.

This gives an efficient way of obtaining random multiples of a point (for example, a generator). For some cryptosystems (e.g. Diffie-Hellman [7]), the integer equivalent of the random τ-adic NAF is not needed. The expansion is simply applied to the generator, then to the other party's public point. However, for generating digital signatures (e.g. ECDSA [9]), the equivalent integer is needed.

Lange [10] covered much of the theory of this approach, as well as a method for recovering the integer. Given a generator G of prime order r and a group automorphism σ, there is a unique integer s modulo r which satisfies $\sigma(G) = sG$, and s (fixed per-curve) is obtained using $(T - s) = \gcd((T^m - 1)/(T - 1), T^2 - \mu T + 2)$ in $\mathbb{F}_r[T]$. We note that s also satisfies $s = (-c_0)(c_1)^{-1} \pmod{r}$. Values of s for standard Koblitz curves are listed in Table 1 for convenience.

Given some τ-adic expansion $\sum_{i=0}^{\ell-1} \epsilon_i \tau^i$ with $\epsilon_i \in \{0, 1, -1\}$, it follows that the equivalent integer can be recovered deterministically as $\sum_{i=0}^{\ell-1} \epsilon_i s^i$ using at most $\ell - 2$ multiplications and some additions for non-zero coefficient values, all modulo r [10]. Our approach improves on these computation requirements

Table 1. Integer s such that $\sigma P = sP$ modulo r on $E_a(\mathbb{F}_{2^m})$

Curve a				s		
K-163 1 00000003	81afd9e3	493dccbf	c2faf1d2	84e6d34e	bd67a6da	
K-233 0				00000060	6590ef0a	
0a0abf8d	755a2be3	1f5449df	ff5b4307	33472d49	10444625	
K-283 0				00d5d05a	1b6c5ace	e76b8ee3
f925a572	19bcb952	12945154	588d0415	a5b4bb50	57f69216	
K-409 0						0024ef90
54eb3a6c	f4bdc6ed	021f6e5c	b8da0c79	5f913c52	ebaa9239	
8d1b7d3d	0adb8a34	add81800	acf7e302	a7d25095	1701d7a4	
K-571 0 01cc6c27	e62f3e0d	df5ea7eb	1ab1cc4d	0da631c0	d70a969a	
a14b0350	85b31511	f5a97455	20cba528	e2d1e647	f4f708d3	
9fba0c3b	e4e35543	821344d1	662727bd	2d59dbc0	5e6853b1	

to recover the integer equivalent. Solinas [4] showed that given the recurrence relation

$$U_{i+1} = \mu U_i - 2U_{i-1} \text{ where } U_0 = 0, U_1 = 1 ,$$

it is true that

$$\tau^i = \tau U_i - 2U_{i-1} \text{ for all } i > 0 .$$

Solinas noted that this equation can be used for computing the order of the curve. In addition to the aforementioned application, it is clear that this equation can also be directly applied to compute the equivalent element $d_0 + d_1\tau \in \mathbb{Z}[\tau]$ of a τ-adic expansion. Once $d_0 + d_1\tau$ is computed, the equivalent integer n modulo r is easily obtained using $n = d_0 + d_1 s \pmod{r}$.

We present an efficient algorithm to compute d_0 and d_1 as Algorithm 3. Note that the values d_0 and d_1 are built up in a right-to-left fashion. Clearly it makes sense to generate the fixed U sequence right-to-left. So if the coefficients are generated left-to-right and are not stored then U should be precomputed and stored and given as input to Algorithm 3, which is then modified to run

---

Algorithm 3. Integer equivalents of τ-adic expansions.

Input: ℓ-bit τ-adic expansion ϵ, curve constants r, s, μ
Output: Integer equivalent n
$d_0 \leftarrow \epsilon_0, d_1 \leftarrow \epsilon_1$ /* accumulators */
$j \leftarrow 1, k \leftarrow 0$ /* $j = U_{i-1}$, $k = U_{i-2}$ */
for $i \leftarrow 2$ **to** $\ell - 1$ **do**
      $u \leftarrow \mu j - 2k$ /* $u = U_i$ */
      $d_0 \leftarrow d_0 - 2j\epsilon_i$
      $d_1 \leftarrow d_1 + u\epsilon_i$
      $k \leftarrow j, j \leftarrow u$ /* setup for next round */
end
$n \leftarrow d_0 + d_1 s \mod r$ /* integer equivalent */
return n

left-to-right. The storage of ϵ is small; indeed it can be stored in ℓ-bits if zeros inserted to preserve non-adjacency are omitted. Either way, the choice of which direction to implement Algorithm 3 is dependent on many factors, including storage capacity and direction of the scalar multiplication algorithm. In any case, the main advantage we are concerned with in this paper is the ability to compute the integer equivalent in parallel to the scalar multiple, and hence in our implementations ϵ is assumed to be stored. Thus, we omit any analysis of generating coefficients of ϵ one at a time, and concentrate on the scenario of having two separate devices, each with access to the coefficients of ϵ: one for computing the integer equivalent, and one for computing the scalar multiple.

As s is a per-curve constant, it is clear that the integer equivalent n can be computed using one field multiplication and one field addition. This excludes the cost of building up $d_0 + d_1\tau$ from the τ-adic expansion, done as shown in Algorithm 3 using the U sequence with only additions.

For the sake of simplicity, only width-2 τ-adic NAFs are considered here (all $\epsilon_i \in \{0, 1, -1\}$). Since generators are fixed and precomputation can be done offline, it is natural to consider arbitrary window width as well; we defer this to future work.

Following this reasoning, our method can be summarized as follows.

1. Generate a random τ-adic NAF of length $m - 1$. (After this, the scalar multiple can be computed in parallel to the remaining steps.)
2. Build up $d_0 + d_1\tau$ from the expansion using the U sequence as shown in Algorithm 3.
3. Calculate the integer equivalent $n = d_0 + d_1 s \pmod{r}$.

4   Hardware Implementation

If scalar multiplication is computed with a random integer, the integer is typically first reduced modulo δ. The τ-adic NAF then usually needs to be computed *before* scalar multiplication because algorithms for producing the τ-adic NAF presented in [4] produce them from right-to-left[1], whereas scalar multiplication is typically more efficient when computed from left-to-right. In either case, the end-to-end computation time is $T_\tau + T_{sm}$ where T_τ is the conversion time (including reducing modulo δ and generating the τ-adic NAF) and T_{sm} is the scalar multiplication time. However, when scalar multiplication is computed on hardware with a random τ-adic NAF of length ℓ, the calculation of an integer equivalent can be performed *simultaneously* with scalar multiplication (assuming separate dedicated hardware) thus resulting in an end-to-end time of only $\max(T_\tau, T_{sm}) = T_{sm}$ with the reasonable assumption that $T_{sm} > T_\tau$. In this case, T_τ denotes the time needed to generate a random τ-adic NAF and calculate the integer equivalent. We assume storage for the coefficients ϵ_i exists. This parallelization implies that our method is especially well-suited for hardware implementations.

---

[1] There are alternatives which produce an expansion with similar weight from right-to-left, but this does not change the arguments that follow.

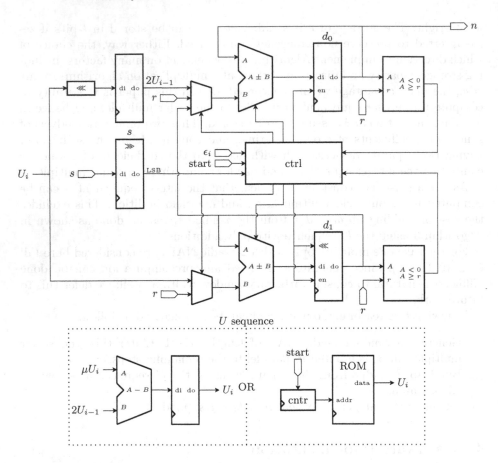

Fig. 1. Block diagram of the design. All registers are reset to zero at the beginning of a conversion, except the $2U_{i-1}$ register which is initialized to -1. Shifts to the left and to the right are denoted as $\lll$ and $\ggg$, respectively.

An FPGA design was implemented in order to investigate the practical feasibility of our method on hardware. The implementation consists of two adders, two comparators, a U sequence block and certain control logic. The structure of the implementation is shown in Fig. 1. An integer equivalent is computed so that, first, d_0 and d_1 are built up using the U sequence and, second, $n = d_0 + d_1 s$ is calculated as shown in Sec. 3. The design operates in two modes.

The first mode computes d_0 and d_1 in parallel using the adders. A τ-adic expansion is input into the design in serial starting from ϵ_0 and the U sequence is either read from ROM or computed on-the-fly. As shown in Sec. 3, U_i can be directly applied in computing d_1 by simply adding or subtracting U_i to d_1 according to ϵ_i. In d_0 calculation, $2U_{i-1}$ is received by shifting U_i to the left and delaying it by one clock cycle. Because the least significant bit (LSB) ϵ_0 is handled similarly, an additional value $U_{-1} = -0.5$ is introduced into the U sequence in order to get $d_0 = \epsilon_0$.

Table 2. ROM sizes for the NIST curves

Curve	m	Depth	Width	Bits
K-163	163	163	83	13,529
K-233	233	233	118	27,494
K-283	283	283	143	40,469
K-409	409	409	204	83,436
K-571	571	571	287	163,877

If the U sequence is precomputed and stored in ROM, the required size of the ROM depends on m. The depth of the ROM is m and the width is determined by the longest U_i in the sequence. ROM sizes for the NIST curves [9] are listed in Table 2. It makes sense not to reduce the sequence U modulo r, as $r > 1 + 2\sum_{i=0}^{m-3}|U_i|$ and hence U modulo r requires significantly more storage space than U alone.

If the amount of memory is an issue, the U sequence can be computed on-the-fly by using an adder as shown in Algorithm 3. This implies that extra storage for the coefficients ϵ_i is also needed for performing the scalar multiplication simultaneously. The width of the adder is also determined by the longest U_i. As shown in Table 2, the size of the ROM grows rapidly with m and in practice ROMs can be used only when m is small. However, the on-the-fly computation is also a viable approach for large m.

The second mode computes $n = d_0 + d_1 s$ in two phases which are repeated for all bits of s. In the first phase, the first adder accumulates d_0 with d_1 according to the LSB of s and, at the same time, d_1 is shifted to the left resulting in $2d_1$ and s is shifted to the right. In the second phase, r is either added to $d_{0,1}$ if $d_{0,1} < 0$ or subtracted from $d_{0,1}$ if $d_{0,1} \geq r$. This ensures that both d_0 and d_1 are in the interval $[0, r[$. When all bits of s have been processed, the register d_0 holds n. In order to guarantee that the procedure results in $n \in [0, r[$, r must fulfill $r > 1 + 2\sum_{i=0}^{m-3}|U_i|$ which is the maximum value of d_0 after the first mode. This ensures that $d_{0,1} \in]-r, r[$ in the end of the first mode for all τ-adic expansions with $\ell \leq m - 1$ and $\epsilon_i \in \{0, 1, -1\}$. It is easy to check that all r listed in [9] fulfill this condition.

The first mode requires $\ell + 1$ clock cycles. Because both phases in the second mode require one clock cycle and the length of s is m bits, the latency of the second phase is $2m$ clock cycles. Thus, the latency of a conversion is exactly $\ell + 2m + 1$ clock cycles where ℓ is the length of the τ-adic expansion. As $\ell = m - 1$, the conversion requires $3m$ clock cycles. The design is inherently resistant against side-channel attacks based on timing because its latency is constant.

If the U sequence is stored in ROM, it would be possible to reduce the latency by on average $\frac{2}{3}m$ clock cycles by skipping all zeros in random τ-adic NAFs in the first mode. This could also be helpful in thwarting side-channel attacks based on power or electromagnetic measurements. Unfortunately, latency would not be constant anymore making the design potentially insecure against timing attacks. Reductions based on zero skippings are not possible if the U sequence is computed on-the-fly because that computation always requires m clock cycles.

4.1   Results

The design presented in Sec. 4 was written in VHDL and simulated in ModelSim SE 6.1b. To the best of our knowledge, the only published hardware implementation of the integer to τ-adic NAF conversion was presented in [11] where the converter was implemented on an Altera Stratix II EP2S60F1020C4 FPGA. In order to ensure fair comparison, we synthesized our design for the same device using Altera Quartus II 6.0 SP1 design software. Two curve-specific variations of the design were implemented for the NIST curves K-163 and K-233.

The K-163 design with ROM requires 929 ALUTs (Adaptive Look-Up Tables) and 599 registers in 507 ALMs (Adaptive Logic Modules) and 13,529 bits of ROM which were implemented by using 6 M4K memory blocks. The maximum clock frequency is 56.14 MHz which yields the conversion time of 8.7 µs. The K-233 design with ROM has the following characteristics: 1,311 ALUTs and 838 registers in 713 ALMs, 27,612 memory bits in 7 M4Ks and 42.67 MHz resulting in 16.4 µs. Implementations where the U sequence is computed on-the-fly require 1,057 and 1,637 ALUTs and 654 and 934 registers in 592 and 894 ALMs for K-163 or K-233, respectively. They operate at the maximum clock frequencies of 55.17 and 43.94 MHz resulting in the computation times of 8.9 µs and 15.9 µs. The differences in computation times compared to the ROM-based implementations are caused by small variations in place&route results which yield slightly different maximum clock frequencies. The latencies in clock cycles are the same for both ROM-based and memory-free implementations, i.e. 489 for K-163 and 699 for K-233. As the required resources are small and the conversion times are much shorter than any reported scalar multiplication time, our method is clearly suitable for hardware implementations.

4.2   Comparisons

The implementation presented in [11] computes τ-adic NAF mod $(\tau^m - 1)$ so that it first converts the integer to τ-adic NAF with an algorithm from [3], then reduces it modulo $(\tau^m - 1)$ and finally reconstructs the NAF which was lost in the reduction. This was claimed to be more efficient in terms of required resources than reductions modulo δ presented in [3] because their implementation is problematic on hardware as they require computations of several multiplications, and hence either a lot of resources or computation time.

Table 3 summarizes the implementations presented here and in [11]. Comparing the implementations is straightforward because FPGAs are the same. It should be noted that the converter in [11] has a wider scope of possible applications since our approach is only for taking random multiples of a point (this is not useful in signature verifications, for example). Obviously, the computation of an integer equivalent can be performed with fewer resources. The reductions are 35 % in ALUTs and 39 % in registers for K-163 and 27 % and 30 % for K-233 when the U sequence is stored in the ROM. However, it should be noted that the implementations presented in [11] do not require such additional memory. When the U sequence is computed with logic and no ROM is needed, the reductions in

Table 3. Comparison of the published designs on Stratix II FPGA

Design	m	ALUTs	Regs.	M4Ks	Clock (MHz)	T_τ (μs)	Total time
[11][a]	163	1,433	988	0	80.44	6.1	$T_{sm} + T_\tau$
	233	1,800	1,198	0	58.89	11.9	$T_{sm} + T_\tau$
This work[b]	163	929 (-35 %)	599 (-39 %)	6	56.14	8.7	T_{sm}
	163	1,057 (-26 %)	654 (-34 %)	0	55.17	8.9	T_{sm}
	233	1,311 (-27 %)	838 (-30 %)	7	42.67	16.4	T_{sm}
	233	1,637 (-9 %)	934 (-22 %)	0	43.94	15.9	T_{sm}

[a] Integer to τ-adic NAF conversion.
[b] τ-adic expansion to integer conversion.

ALUTs and registers are 26 % and 34 % for K-163 and 9 % and 22 % for K-233 and so it is obvious that our converter is more compact.

The average latencies of both converters are approximately the same. The difference is that the latency of our converter is always exactly 489 or 699 clock cycles whereas the converter in [11] has an average latency of 491 or 701 clock cycles for K-163 and K-233, respectively. The maximum clock frequencies of our converters are lower and, thus, the implementations of [11] can compute conversions faster. However, an integer equivalent can be computed in parallel with scalar multiplication and, thus, it can be claimed that the effective conversion time is $0\,\mu$s.

To support the argument that the effective elimination of the conversion time T_τ is significant, there are several implementations existing in the literature computing scalar multiplications on K-163 in less than $100\,\mu$s. For example, [12] reports a time of $44.8\,\mu$s, and [13] a time of $75\,\mu$s. Hence conversions requiring several μs are obviously significant when considering the overall time.

To summarize, computing the integer equivalent of a random τ-adic expansion offers the following two major advantages from the hardware implementation point-of-view compared to computing the τ-adic NAF of a random integer:

- Conversions can be computed in parallel with scalar multiplications.
- Computing the integer equivalent can be implemented with fewer resources.

As a downside, the calculation of an integer equivalent has a longer latency; however, this is insignificant since the conversion is not on the critical path.

5   Conclusion

As shown, our new method for computing integer equivalents of random τ-adic expansions is very computationally efficient. This has been demonstrated with an implementation in hardware, where the parallelization of computing the integer equivalent and the scalar multiple yields significant efficiency gains. It seems unlikely that such gains are possible with this approach in software.

Future Work

Side-channel attacks based on timing, power, or electromagnetic measurements are a serious threat to many implementations; not only on smart cards, but on FPGAs [14] as well. Our converter provides inherent resistance against timing attacks because its latency is constant. Side-channel countermeasures against other attacks are beyond the scope of this paper. However, before the suggested implementation can be introduced in any practical application where these attacks are viable, it must be protected against such attacks. This will be an important research topic in the future.

As mentioned, only width-2 τ-adic NAFs have been considered here (all $\epsilon_i \in \{0, 1, -1\}$). Arbitrary window width would clearly be more efficient for the scalar multiplication. We are currently researching efficient methods for scanning ϵ multiple bits at once, as well as simple alternatives to using the U sequence.

Acknowledgements

We thank Tanja Lange for useful discussions and comments during the preparation of this paper. We also thank the anonymous reviewers for comments on the manuscript.

References

1. Koblitz, N.: CM-curves with good cryptographic properties. In: Feigenbaum, J. (ed.) CRYPTO 1991. LNCS, vol. 576, pp. 279–287. Springer, Heidelberg (1992)
2. Meier, W., Staffelbach, O.: Efficient multiplication on certain nonsupersingular elliptic curves. In: Brickell, E.F. (ed.) CRYPTO 1992. LNCS, vol. 740, pp. 333–344. Springer, Heidelberg (1993)
3. Solinas, J.A.: An improved algorithm for arithmetic on a family of elliptic curves. In: Kaliski Jr., B.S. (ed.) CRYPTO 1997. LNCS, vol. 1294, pp. 357–371. Springer, Heidelberg (1997)
4. Solinas, J.A.: Efficient arithmetic on Koblitz curves. Des. Codes Cryptogr. 19(2-3), 195–249 (2000)
5. Lange, T., Shparlinski, I.: Collisions in fast generation of ideal classes and points on hyperelliptic and elliptic curves. Appl. Algebra Engrg. Comm. Comput. 15(5), 329–337 (2005)
6. Lange, T., Shparlinski, I.E.: Certain exponential sums and random walks on elliptic curves. Canad. J. Math. 57(2), 338–350 (2005)
7. Diffie, W., Hellman, M.E.: New directions in cryptography. IEEE Trans. Information Theory IT-22(6), 644–654 (1976)
8. ElGamal, T.: A public key cryptosystem and a signature scheme based on discrete logarithms. In: Blakely, G.R., Chaum, D. (eds.) CRYPTO 1984. LNCS, vol. 196, pp. 10–18. Springer, Heidelberg (1985)
9. National Institute of Standards and Technology (NIST): Digital signature standard (DSS). Federal Information Processing Standard, FIPS PUB 186-2 (2000)
10. Lange, T.: Koblitz curve cryptosystems. Finite Fields Appl. 11(2), 200–229 (2005)

11. Järvinen, K., Forsten, J., Skyttä, J.: Efficient circuitry for computing τ-adic non-adjacent form. In: ICECS 2006. Proc. of the IEEE Int'l. Conf. on Electronics, Circuits and Systems, Nice, France, pp. 232–235 (2006)
12. Dimitrov, V.S., Järvinen, K.U., Jacobson, J.M.J., Chan, W.F., Huang, Z.: FPGA implementation of point multiplication on Koblitz curves using Kleinian integers. In: Goubin, L., Matsui, M. (eds.) CHES 2006. LNCS, vol. 4249, pp. 445–459. Springer, Heidelberg (2006)
13. Lutz, J., Hasan, M.A.: High performance FPGA based elliptic curve cryptographic co-processor. In: Goubin, L., Matsui, M. (eds.) ITCC 2004. International Conference on Information Technology: Coding and Computing, vol. 02, pp. 486–492. IEEE Computer Society Press, Los Alamitos (2004)
14. Standaert, F.X., Peeters, E., Rouvroy, G., Quisquater, J.J.: An overview of power analysis attacks against field programmable gate arrays. Proc. IEEE 94(2), 383–394 (2006)

Another Look at Square Roots
(and Other Less Common Operations)
in Fields of Even Characteristic

Roberto Maria Avanzi

Faculty of Mathematics and Horst Görtz Institute for IT-Security
Ruhr University Bochum, Germany
Roberto.Avanzi@ruhr-uni-bochum.de

Abstract. We discuss a family of irreducible polynomials that can be used to speed up square root extraction in fields of characteristic two. They generalize trinomials discussed by Fong et al. [20]. We call such polynomials *square root friendly*.

The main application is to point halving methods for elliptic curves (and to a lesser extent also divisor halving methods for hyperelliptic curves and pairing computations).

We note the existence of square root friendly trinomials of a given degree when we already know that an irreducible trinomial of the same degree exists, and formulate a conjecture on the degrees of the terms of square root friendly polynomials. Following similar results by Bluher, we also give a partial result that goes in the direction of the conjecture.

We also discuss how to improve the speed of solving quadratic equations. The increase in the time required to perform modular reduction is marginal and does not affect performance adversely. Estimates confirm that the new polynomials mantain their promises. Point halving gets a speed-up of 20% and scalar multiplication is improved by at least 11%.

Keywords: Binary fields, Polynomial basis, Square root extraction, Trace computation, Quadratic equations, Point halving.

1   Introduction

The main topic of this paper is square root extraction in binary fields, even though also other operations are considered.

In [20] it is shown that the extraction of square roots can be accelerated if a suitable irreducible trinomial is used to define the field.

Let $p(X)$ be the irreducible polynomial of degree d used to define the extension field $\mathbb{F}_{2^d}/\mathbb{F}_2$. If the polynomial in X representing the square root of the image x of X in $\mathbb{F}_{2^d}$ has low weight and/or degree, then general square roots can be extracted in $\mathbb{F}_{2^d}$ efficiently. In this case we call $p(X)$ *square root friendly*. (This definition will be made more precise later.)

We give here sufficient conditions for an irreducible polynomial of odd degree d to yield a low weight $\sqrt{x}$. In particular, we give examples of pentanomials

C. Adams, A. Miri, and M. Wiener (Eds.): SAC 2007, LNCS 4876, pp. 138–154, 2007.

and heptanomials, but in at least one case, that of $\mathbb{F}_{2^{233}}$, that can be defined by trinomials, we show how one can perform square root computations even faster than in [20][1].

As the motivation comes from elliptic curve cryptography, in particular from point halving based methods for scalar multiplication, in Section 2 we recall point and divisor halving. In Section 3 we introduce square root computations and our new sufficient conditions. Polynomials for several useful (and used in practice) binary fields are presented in Section 4, together with a result about the existence of square root friendly trinomials, a conjecture about the degrees of the non-leading terms of square root friendly polynomials, and a theorem that supports the conjecture itself.

Finally, we move to implementation issues in Section 5. Not only square root extraction is implemented (§ 5.1), but also the computation of traces over $\mathbb{F}_2$ (§ 5.2) and solving quadratic equations in $\mathbb{F}_{2^d}$ (§ 5.3). These routines are benchmarked showing gains, whereas multiplication and squaring either experience a negligible slowdown or even a minimal speedup. The costs of various elliptic curve group operations and scalar multiplication algorithms using different reduction polynomials for the definition field are also given. The discussion of these results (§ 5.4) also provides the conclusion to the paper. In particular, we prove that a performance gain of around 20% can be expected for the point halving alone, with a speed increase in excess of 11% for scalar multiplication.

Space constraints forced us to omit most proofs. These, as well as further results, will be given in the full version of the paper.

2   Point and Divisor Halving

Let E be an elliptic curve defined over $\mathbb{F}_{2^d}$ by a *Weierstrass equation*

$$E \ : \ Y^2 + XY = X^3 + aX^2 + b$$

with $a, b \in \mathbb{F}_{2^d}$ and having a subgroup $G \leq E(\mathbb{F}_{2^d})$ of large prime order.

Since computing the double of any given point P is the most common operation in a scalar multiplication performed by double-and-add methods, an important direction of research consists in optimizing doubling formulæ (for surveys on scalar multiplication methods and elliptic curve operations see, for example [8, Chs. 9 and 13] or [21, Ch. 3]).

Point halving [22,27], on the other hand, consists in computing a point R whose double is P, i.e. such that $2R = P$. Being the inverse operation of the doubling, it is an automorphism of G. Therefore, given a point $P \in G$, there is a unique $R \in G$ such that $2R = P$.

In order to perform this operation one needs to solve a quadratic equation of the form $\lambda^2 + \lambda + \alpha = 0$ for λ, extract a square root, perform two multiplications

---

[1] Scott [28] considers searching the polynomials until the one giving the optimal reduction and square root routines is found in terms of the amount of logic and shift operations.

and some additions. We refer the reader to [22,26,27,20] for details, including the usage of halving in place of doubling in scalar multiplication algorithms. Furthermore, there are two points R_1 and R_2 on the curve with $2R_1 = 2R_2 = P$, such that $R_1 - R_2$ is the unique point of order 2 of the curve. To determine which one is in G, an additional check involving a trace computation is required. Knudsen [22] and Schroeppel [26,27] show how to perform all these operations. According to the analysis in [20], halving is about two times faster than doubling.

Birkner [14] has devised a divisor halving formula for genus two curves based on the doubling formulae by Lange and Stevens [24]. Birkner and Thériault [15] have dealt with genus three divisors. The performance of all known halving formulæ depends (to a variable degree) on the performance of square root extraction. Further uses of point halving to speed up scalar multiplication on elliptic Koblitz Curves [23] are found in [7,9] and [10].

3   Square Root Extraction and Defining Polynomials

3.1   Background

Let $p(X)$ be an irreducible polynomial of *odd* degree d, and the field $\mathbb{F}_{2^d}$ be constructed as the quotient ring $\mathbb{F}_2[X]/(p(X))$. Let us call x the image of X in $\mathbb{F}_{2^d}$. We consider here polynomial basis representation because we are solely concerned with software applications.

Whereas with a normal basis [4] a square root computation is just a shift of the bits internal representation of the field element by one position, matters are more complicated with polynomial bases. In fact, even the cost of a squaring becomes no longer negligible. If $\alpha = \sum_{i=0}^{d-1} a_i x^i$ then $\alpha^2 = \sum_{i=0}^{d-1} a_i x^{2i}$ which, as a polynomial in x, has degree no longer necessarily bounded by d, and modular reduction (modulo $p(X)$) is necessary. Its cost is very low, but cannot be completely ignored.

Things are more complicated for square roots. Even though squaring just consists in "spacing" the bits of the original element with zeros, the bits of a generic field element cannot be just "compressed". The classic method for computing $\sqrt{\alpha}$ is based on Fermat's little theorem $\alpha^{2^d} = \alpha$, hence $\sqrt{\alpha} = \alpha^{2^{d-1}}$. This requires $d - 1$ squarings. In general, the cost of this operation is that of several field multiplications.

A more efficient method stems from the observation that $\sqrt{\alpha}$ can be expressed in terms of $\zeta := \sqrt{x}$. If

$$\alpha = \sum_{i=0}^{d-1} a_i x^i$$

we separate the even exponents from the odd exponents

$$\alpha = \sum_{i=0}^{\frac{d-1}{2}} a_{2i} x^{2i} + \sum_{i=0}^{\frac{d-3}{2}} a_{2i+1} x^{2i+1} = (\alpha_{\text{even}})^2 + x \cdot (\alpha_{\text{odd}})^2$$

where

$$\alpha_{\text{even}} = \sum_{i=0}^{\frac{d-1}{2}} a_{2i}x^i \quad \text{and} \quad \alpha_{\text{odd}} = \sum_{i=0}^{\frac{d-3}{2}} a_{2i+1}x^i$$

and, since square root in a field of even characteristic is a linear operation:

$$\sqrt{\alpha} = \alpha_{\text{even}} + \zeta \cdot \alpha_{\text{odd}} \tag{1}$$

Therefore, once ζ has been computed on a per-field basis, the computation of a generic square root is reduced to "bits extraction and packing", a "rectangular" multiplication of a degree $\leq d-1$ polynomial ζ with a polynomial $\sum_{i=0}^{(d-3)/2} a_{2i+1}x^i$ of degree $\leq (d-3)/2$ in x, and a modular reduction. Intuitively, the cost should approach a half of the cost of a field multiplication and this is confirmed by the analysis in [20,22].

3.2   Square-Root Friendly Polynomials

The speed of square root computation depends on the efficiency of the multiplication of a generic polynomial of degree $\leq (d-1)/2$ by $\zeta = \sqrt{x}$. If ζ is very sparse, for example of weight two or four (i.e. it has just two or four nonzero terms), then this product can be computed by a few shift and XOR operations. In [20] two types of trinomials have been shown that allow this. The kind that interests us is

$$p(X) = X^d + X^m + 1$$

with m odd. Then $x = x^{d+1} + x^{m+1}$ with $d+1$ and $m+1$ even, and

$$\zeta = x^{(d+1)/2} + x^{(m+1)/2} \; ,$$

and $p(X)$ is square root friendly. In fact, this idea is much more general.

Assume the irreducible polynomial $p(X)$ defining $\mathbb{F}_{2^d}$ over $\mathbb{F}_2$ has form

$$p(X) = X \cdot \mathcal{U}(X)^2 + 1 \tag{2}$$

where $\mathcal{U}$ is a polynomial of degree $(d-1)/2$ and even weight w (hence $p(X)$ has weight $w+1$). Then, ζ has a very simple form in $\mathbb{F}_{2^d}$: from $x^2 \cdot \mathcal{U}(x)^2 + x = 0$ we obtain

$$\zeta = x \cdot \mathcal{U}(x) \; ,$$

and ζ is represented by a polynomial of degree $1 + \frac{d-1}{2} = \frac{d+1}{2}$ and weight w. Furthermore, note that the *polynomial* product

$$\zeta \cdot \sum_{i=0}^{\frac{d-3}{2}} a_{2i+1}x^i$$

has degree bounded by $\frac{d+1}{2} + \frac{d-3}{2} = d-1$, therefore *no polynomial reduction is required if a square root is computed by formula* (1).

Hence, irreducible polynomials of form (2) are square root friendly.

Note that the low degree of ζ not only guarantees that no modular reduction is necessary, but puts also a bound on the complexity of the multiplication by ζ (even though its sparseness has an even bigger influence). It is therefore interesting to ask whether there are irreducible polynomials $P(X)$ that lead to a ζ of even lower degree. This cannot happen, and requiring the degree of the polynomial representing ζ to be at most $(d+1)/2$ in fact *almost* characterizes the polynomials (2).

Theorem 1. *Let the field extension $\mathbb{F}_{2^d}/\mathbb{F}_2$ be defined by an irreducible polynomial $P(X)$ of odd degree d, and let x be a zero of $P(X)$ in $\mathbb{F}_{2^d}$. Suppose that $\zeta := \sqrt{x}$ is a polynomial of degree at most $(d+1)/2$ in x.*
   Then the degree of ζ is exactly $(d+1)/2$ and either

(i) *$P(X) = 1 + X \cdot \mathcal{U}(X)^2$ and $\zeta = x \cdot \mathcal{U}(x)$ for some $\mathcal{U}(X) \in \mathbb{F}_2[X]$ of degree exactly $(d-1)/2$; or*
(ii) *$P(X) = 1 + (X+1) \cdot X^2 \cdot \mathcal{W}(X)^2$ and $\zeta = 1 + (x+1) \cdot x \cdot \mathcal{W}(x)$ for some $\mathcal{W}(X) \in \mathbb{F}_2[X]$ of degree exactly $(d-3)/2$.*

Definition 1. *An irreducible polynomial of form (2) is called a* special square root friendly (SSRF) *polynomial of type I.*
   An irreducible polynomial

$$P(X) = 1 + (X+1) \cdot X^2 \cdot \mathcal{W}(X)^2 \tag{3}$$

for some $\mathcal{W}(X) \in \mathbb{F}_2[X]$ of degree exactly $(d-3)/2$ is called a special square root friendly *polynomial of type II.*

We do not know whether there are irreducible polynomials which are not trinomials, not of the forms listed in Theorem 1, and for which $\sqrt{x}$ has small weight. Even for trinomials $X^d + X^m + 1$ with even m one has to check on a case by case basis, but examples are known [20].

   Still, square root friendly polynomials abound. For example $X^{163} + X^{57} + X^{49} + X^{29} + 1$ is irreducible, and the corresponding ζ has weight 4. On the other hand, the standard NIST polynomial [25] $X^{163} + X^7 + X^6 + X^3 + 1$ defines a ζ of weight 79.

Remark 1. Changing polynomial is easy without introducing incompatibilities in cryptographic applications: we just change the base used for representation of the field elements before and after the bulk of the computation. The cost is comparable to a polynomial basis multiplication, and the conversion routines require each a matrix that occupies $O(d^2)$ bits of storage (cf. [19] where the particular base change is to and from a normal basis representation, but the results are the same). Therefore this overhead is essentially negligible with respect to the full cost of a scalar multiplication, that is in the order of magnitude of hundreds to thousands of field multiplications (see for example § 5.3 of [5]).

Remark 2. The cost of a square root extraction implemented by using the sparse version of ζ offered by the above polynomials can be roughly estimated using, for example, already published results. For example in [20], Example 3.12, the NIST-recommended trinomial

$$p(X) = X^{233} + X^{74} + 1 \tag{4}$$

for the finite field $\mathbb{F}_{2^{233}}$ is used. Even though the term X^{74} does not have an odd exponent, ζ has a sparse representation

$$\zeta = (x^{32} + x^{117} + x^{191})(x^{37} + 1) \ .$$

By this, finding a root via equation (1) requires roughly $1/8$ of the time of a field multiplication. As we shall show in the next section we can choose

$$p(X) = X^{233} + X^{159} + 1$$

and in this case

$$\zeta = x^{117} + x^{80} \ .$$

It is clear that an even smaller amount of shift operations and XOR operations are required to multiply by ζ. Furthermore, as already remarked, there is no need to perform a reduction modulo $p(X)$ while with non-SSRF polynomials this is almost always necessary, even with the polynomial (4). Implementation results show the cost of a square root to be less than 9% of that of a multiplication. See § 5.4 for precise results.

Remark 3. Similar formulæ for cube root computations are found in [1] – their results are easily partially generalised to any odd characteristic.

Remark 4. Type I SSRF polynomials enjoy another very useful property. In [2] it is proved that the only trace-one element in the polynomial basis defined by these polynomials is 1. Therefore the trace of an element $\sum_{i=0}^{d-1} a_i x^i$ is just a_0. This is very important, for instance, for point halving. It is especially fortunate that the same family of polynomials makes both square roots *and* trace computations faster.

Type II SSRF polynomials do not enjoy this property, however they are not relevant anyway for most applications: They were also investigated in [2], because all element of the polynomial basis, except at most for 1, have trace one, but the connection to the minimality of the degree of $\sqrt{x}$ is new and surprising.

4   Existence and Degrees of the Terms

Square root friendly polynomials are easy to find. For example, a simple MAGMA [17] script determines all 713 (special) square root friendly pentanomials of degree 163 in less than one minute.

In Table 1 we list square root friendly polynomials of several degrees. The degrees have been taken from the NIST list of recommended binary curves and from the extension degrees used in [12]. All these extension degrees are interesting

Table 1. Some special square root friendly trinomials and pentanomials

Degree	Irreducible tri/pentanomial	$\zeta = \sqrt{x}$	Standard?
47	$X^{47} + X^5 + 1$	$x^{24} + x^3$	Yes
53	$X^{53} + X^{19} + X^{17} + X^{15} + 1$	$x^{27} + x^{10} + x^9 + x^8$	No
59	$X^{59} + X^{21} + X^{17} + X^{15} + 1$	$x^{30} + x^{11} + x^9 + x^8$	No
67	$X^{67} + X^{25} + X^{17} + X^5 + 1$	$x^{34} + x^{13} + x^9 + x^3$	No
71	$X^{71} + X^9 + 1$	$x^{36} + x^5$	No
73	$X^{73} + X^{25} + 1$	$x^{37} + x^{13}$	Yes
79	$X^{79} + X^9 + 1$	$x^{40} + x^5$	Yes
83	$X^{83} + X^{29} + X^{25} + X^3 + 1$	$x^{42} + x^{15} + x^{13} + x^2$	No
89	$X^{89} + X^{51} + 1$	$x^{45} + x^{26}$	No
97	$X^{97} + X^{33} + 1$	$x^{49} + x^{17}$	No
101	$X^{101} + X^{35} + X^{31} + X^3 + 1$	$x^{51} + x^{18} + x^{16} + x^2$	No
107	$X^{107} + X^{37} + X^{33} + X^{23} + 1$	$x^{54} + x^{19} + x^{17} + x^{12}$	No
109	$X^{109} + X^{43} + X^{41} + X^{23} + 1$	$x^{55} + x^{22} + x^{21} + x^{12}$	No
127	$X^{127} + X + 1$	$x^{64} + x$	Yes
131	$X^{131} + X^{45} + X^{41} + X^9 + 1$	$x^{66} + x^{23} + x^{21} + x^5$	No
137	$X^{137} + X^{21} + 1$	$x^{69} + x^{11}$	Yes
139	$X^{139} + X^{53} + X^{33} + X^{25} + 1$	$x^{70} + x^{27} + x^{17} + x^{13}$	No
149	$X^{149} + X^{51} + X^{47} + X^9 + 1$	$x^{75} + x^{26} + x^{24} + x^5$	No
157	$X^{157} + X^{55} + X^{47} + X^{11} + 1$	$x^{79} + x^{28} + x^{24} + x^6$	No
163	$X^{163} + X^{57} + X^{49} + X^{29} + 1$	$x^{82} + x^{29} + x^{25} + x^{15}$	No
179	$X^{179} + X^{61} + X^{57} + X^{41} + 1$	$x^{90} + x^{31} + x^{29} + x^{21}$	No
199	$X^{199} + X^{67} + 1$	$x^{100} + x^{34}$	No
211	$X^{211} + X^{73} + X^{69} + X^{35} + 1$	$x^{106} + x^{37} + x^{35} + x^{18}$	No
233	$X^{233} + X^{159} + 1$	$x^{117} + x^{80}$	No
239	$X^{239} + X^{81} + 1$	$x^{120} + x^{41}$	No
251	$X^{251} + X^{89} + X^{81} + X^3 + 1$	$x^{126} + x^{45} + x^{41} + x^2$	No
269	$X^{269} + X^{91} + X^{87} + X^{61} + 1$	$x^{135} + x^{46} + x^{44} + x^{31}$	No
283	$X^{283} + X^{97} + X^{89} + X^{87} + 1$	$x^{142} + x^{49} + x^{45} + x^{44}$	No
409	$X^{409} + X^{87} + 1$	$x^{205} + x^{44}$	Yes
571	$X^{571} + X^{193} + X^{185} + X^5 + 1$	$x^{286} + x^{97} + x^{93} + x^3$	No

because they are either used in standards for elliptic curve cryptography or they represent good choices for extension degrees for defining hyperelliptic curve for cryptographic applications.

When no trinomial is available, a pentanomial is listed. We always report the polynomial with least degree sediment (the sediment of an univariate is obtained by removing the leading term). Only in a handful of cases is the square root friendly polynomial with least degree sediment the same as the standard one, i.e. the irreducible polynomial with least degree sediment but without the restriction on being square root friendly.

We first note that if an irreducible trinomial of a given degree exists, then we can always find one which is square root friendly. The following result is in fact well known, and we state it only for completeness' sake.

Theorem 2. *Let d be an odd positive integer. If an irreducible trinomial $p(X) = X^d + X^m + 1$ over $\mathbb{F}_2$ of degree d exists, then $p(X)$ can be chosen of form (2), i.e. where the exponent m of the middle term is odd.*

Existence results for pentanomial-defined fields are still an open question. On the basis of Table 1 and further experimental results, we found further evidence for an observation of Ahmadi and Menezes [2]: if the degree $d \equiv \pm 3 \pmod 8$, the degree of the sediment is at least $d/3$, whereas if $d \equiv \pm 1 \pmod 8$, then the degree of the sediment is usually quite small.

For the extension degrees for which there are no trinomials we computed not only the square root friendly pentanomials but also the *heptanomials* with smallest degree sediment – the idea was, that perhaps one can find good heptanomials with a lower degree sediment than the best pentanomials, to improve modular reduction[2] : they are given in Table 2. Similar searches for polynomials with nine and eleven terms have been performed. We immediately observe here that sediment degree differences are very limited, so the heptanomials do not bring advantages. The same observation applies to polynomials with nine or eleven terms. A pattern in the distribution of degrees of the second term of the sediment of square root friendly polynomials up to degree 3000 and with up to eleven terms prompts us to formulate the following conjecture:

Conjecture 1. Let d be an odd positive integer, and let c, resp. c' be the exponents of the second, resp. third largest exponent in the lexicographically minimal square root friendly polynomial of degree d. Then

$$3c - d = c - c' = \begin{cases} 8 & \text{if } d \equiv 1 \pmod 3 \\ 4 & \text{if } d \equiv 2 \pmod 3 \end{cases}.$$

A first result in this direction has already been proved by Bluher [16] using a result of Swan [29] (that in fact goes back to Stickelberger). Her result is: *The odd degree polynomial* $p(X) = X^d + \sum_{i \in \mathcal{S}} X^i + 1$ *in* $\mathbb{F}_2[X]$, *where* $\mathcal{S} \subset \{i : i \text{ odd}, 0 < i < d/3\} \cup \{i : i \equiv d \pmod 4, 0 < i < d\}$ *has no repeated roots; if* $d = \pm 1 \pmod 8$, *then* f *has an odd number of irreducible factors; and if* $d = \pm 3 \pmod 8$, *then* f *has an even number of irreducible factors.* In fact, by adapting the proof given in [3] of Bluher's result, it is possible to prove the following theorem:

Theorem 3. *Let d be an odd positive integer and the polynomial $p(X) \in \mathbb{F}_2[x]$ have degree d and satisfy one of the following conditions:*

1. *If $d \equiv 1 \pmod 3$, then $p(X)$ is either of the form*

   $$- \ X^d + X^{\frac{d+8}{3}} + \sum_{j \in J} X^j + 1 \ \text{where } J = \left\{j : j \text{ odd}, 1 \le j < \tfrac{d-19}{3}\right\}$$

   $$- \ \text{or } X^d + \sum_{j \in J'} X^j + 1 \ \text{where } J' = \left\{j : j \text{ odd}, 1 \le j \le \tfrac{d+5}{3}\right\};$$

2. *If $d \equiv 2 \pmod 3$, then $p(X)$ is either of the form*

---

[2] This quite common assumption is heuristic and not necessarily always true [28]. The search for polynomials with minimal degree sediment among those with given properties is however an interesting mathematical endeavor per se.

Table 2. Some special square root friendly heptanomials

Degree	Irreducible heptanomial	$\zeta = \sqrt{x}$
53	$X^{53} + X^{19} + X^{15} + X^5 + X^3 + X + 1$	$x^{27} + x^{10} + x^8 + x^3 + x^2 + x$
59	$X^{59} + X^{21} + X^{17} + X^{13} + X^3 + X + 1$	$x^{30} + x^{11} + x^9 + x^7 + x^2 + x$
67	$X^{67} + X^{25} + X^{17} + X^7 + X^3 + X + 1$	$x^{34} + x^{13} + x^9 + x^4 + x^2 + x$
83	$X^{83} + X^{29} + X^{25} + X^7 + X^5 + X^3 + 1$	$x^{42} + x^{15} + x^{13} + x^4 + x^3 + x^2$
101	$X^{101} + X^{35} + X^{31} + X^9 + X^7 + X + 1$	$x^{51} + x^{18} + x^{16} + x^5 + x^4 + x$
107	$X^{107} + X^{37} + X^{33} + X^{15} + X^9 + X^7 + 1$	$x^{54} + x^{19} + x^{17} + x^8 + x^5 + x^4$
109	$X^{109} + X^{39} + X^{31} + X^9 + X^5 + X^3 + 1$	$x^{55} + x^{20} + x^{16} + x^5 + x^3 + x^2$
131	$X^{131} + X^{45} + X^{41} + X^{13} + X^9 + X + 1$	$x^{66} + x^{23} + x^{21} + x^7 + x^5 + x$
139	$X^{139} + X^{49} + X^{41} + X^7 + X^5 + X^3 + 1$	$x^{70} + x^{25} + x^{21} + x^4 + x^3 + x^2$
149	$X^{149} + X^{51} + X^{47} + X^9 + X^7 + X + 1$	$x^{75} + x^{26} + x^{24} + x^5 + x^4 + x$
157	$X^{157} + X^{55} + X^{47} + X^{15} + X^9 + X^3 + 1$	$x^{79} + x^{28} + x^{24} + x^8 + x^5 + x^2$
163	$X^{163} + X^{57} + X^{49} + X^{15} + X^9 + X + 1$	$x^{82} + x^{29} + x^{25} + x^8 + x^5 + x$
179	$X^{179} + X^{61} + X^{57} + X^{13} + X^9 + X^5 + 1$	$x^{90} + x^{31} + x^{29} + x^7 + x^5 + x^3$
211	$X^{211} + X^{73} + X^{65} + X^{13} + X^{11} + X^3 + 1$	$x^{106} + x^{37} + x^{33} + x^7 + x^6 + x^2$
251	$X^{251} + X^{85} + X^{81} + X^7 + X^5 + X^3 + 1$	$x^{126} + x^{43} + x^{41} + x^4 + x^3 + x^2$
269	$X^{269} + X^{91} + X^{87} + X^{15} + X^{13} + X^{11} + 1$	$x^{135} + x^{46} + x^{44} + x^8 + x^7 + x^6$
283	$X^{283} + X^{97} + X^{89} + X^{13} + X^9 + X + 1$	$x^{142} + x^{49} + x^{45} + x^7 + x^5 + x$
571	$X^{571} + X^{193} + X^{185} + X^{15} + X^{11} + X^3 + 1$	$x^{286} + x^{97} + x^{93} + x^8 + x^6 + x^2$

$$- X^d + X^{\frac{d+4}{3}} + \sum_{j \in J} X^j + 1 \ \text{where} \ J = \left\{ j \, : \, j \ \text{odd}, \ 1 \le j \le \frac{d-11}{3} \right\}$$

$$- \ \text{or} \ X^d + \sum_{j \in J'} X^j + 1 \ \text{where} \ J' = \left\{ j \, : \, j \ \text{odd}, \ 1 \le j \le \frac{d+1}{3} \right\}.$$

Then $p(X)$ is square-free. Furthermore, if $d \equiv \pm 1 \bmod 8$ then $p(X)$ has an odd number of irreducible factors, whereas $d \equiv \pm 3 \bmod 8$ then $p(X)$ has an even number of irreducible factors and therefore must be reducible.

Remark 5. We already mentioned in Remark 4 that in [2] the polynomials we study are proven to permit efficient computation of traces. In Conjecture 9 of [2] it is also speculated that if an irreducible pentanomial of degree d exists, then an irreducible pentanomial of the same degree defining a polynomial basis with only one trace-one element also exists. In the similar vein we could try to restrict our Conjecture 1 to pentanomials, but we have the following example for degree 1987:

$$X^{1987} + X^{665} + X^{661} + X^{549} + 1 \ .$$

This polynomial has minimal degree sediment, and the sediment has minimal degree second term among all irreducible pentanomials with minimal degree sediment. We have $d \equiv 1 \pmod 3$ and $3c - d = 8$, but the second term of the sediment has degree 661, not 657. On the other hand, with heptanomials we find following irreducible

$$X^{1987} + X^{665} + X^{657} + X^{25} + X^{21} + X^9 + 1 \ ,$$

and we know of no other irreducibles of the form

$$X^{1987} + X^c + X^{c'} + \text{ other lower odd degree terms } + 1$$

with c smaller than 665 or with $c = 665$ and c' smaller than 657.

5   Implementation

For several binary fields $\mathbb{F}_{2^d}$ we implemented a few operations, including (but not only) multiplication, squaring, square roots, and also trace and half-trace computations (the latter is used for solving quadratic equations). The current implementation is an extension of the implementation described in [11], that is also used in [12] and [6], (some performance discrepancies are due to the fact that some other routines have been improved in the meantime) and as such in the current version processes the operands with a 32-bit granularity.

Depending on the nature of the chosen reduction polynomial we implemented some routines such as modular reduction and square root extraction in different ways. In a few cases we implement the same field twice using two different reduction polynomials in order to compare the different situations.

5.1   Extracting a Square Root

To implement square root extraction of a field element α we use formula (1): the only part that changes between different implementations is how the multiplication $\zeta \cdot \alpha_{\mathrm{odd}}$ is realized.

To compute α_{even} and α_{odd} from α we use a 16-bit to 8-bit look-up table to compress the bits. Using a trick due to Robert Harley, this table is stored in 256 consecutive bytes by mapping the *input* i to $(\mathtt{i} + \mathtt{i} \gg 7) \,\&\, \mathtt{0xff}$.

If the reduction polynomial $p(X)$ is not square root friendly, then the Hamming weight of the square root is counted at the time of initialization of the library - hence only once. If this weight is low enough then a simple routine that XORs together shifted copies of α_{odd} according to which bits in ζ are set is used. If the weight is higher than a certain threshold, then a comb binary polynomial multiplication method is used, where the precomputations relative to ζ are performed only once, at initialization time. A reduction modulo $p(X)$ is then performed, if necessary.

By means of this we can always keep the time of the multiplication $\zeta \cdot \alpha_{\mathrm{odd}}$ to just under a half of the time of a *generic* field multiplication: Note, however, that this time can be substantially higher than the time required for the per-field, ad-hoc optimized implementation of multiplication, as our experimental results in § 5.4 show.

In the case where the degree d reduction polynomial $p(X)$ is square root friendly, we also have a simple routine that XORs together shifted copies of α_{odd} according to which bits in ζ are set, but since the weight is very low and known, the routine can be unrolled completely. Furthermore, as already mentioned, in this case no modular reduction is necessary. This routine is the one that delivers the best performance.

5.2   Trace Computation

We follow here [20] and [2]. For generic binary fields, to compute the trace from $\mathbb{F}_{2^d}$ to $\mathbb{F}_2$ we use the fact that it is linear. In other words, once we have computed $\mathrm{Tr}(x^i)$ for all i with $0 \leq i < d$, in order to compute the trace of an element $\alpha \in \mathbb{F}_{2^d}$, $\alpha = \sum_{i=0}^{d-1} a_i x^i$ where the $a_i \in \mathbb{F}_2$, we have

$$\mathrm{Tr}\,(\alpha) = \sum_{i=0}^{d-1} a_i \,\mathrm{Tr}(x^i)\;.$$

The latter sum can be implemented by a componentwise multiplication (hence, a logical AND operation) of the bit vector representing the element α with a bit vector whose i-th component (starting with the zeroth component!) is the trace of x^i, called the *trace vector*, followed by a bit count modulo 2. Both operations can be performed very efficiently. The trace vector is of course computed once for each field.

However, when a square root friendly polynomial is used to represent the field $\mathbb{F}_d$ with d odd, the trace vector contains just one bit set, namely the least significant bit, and $\mathrm{Tr}\,(\alpha) = a_0$.

We therefore implemented two different routines: the first one uses a trace vector and the second one just polls the value of a single bit.

5.3   Solving Quadratic Equations (Half-Traces)

In order to solve quadratic equations of the form

$$\lambda^2 + \lambda = \alpha \tag{5}$$

for $\lambda \in \mathbb{F}_{2^d}$ where $\alpha \in \mathbb{F}_{2^d}$ we implement just one generic routine, that takes the element α as an input.

The *half-trace* operator on $\mathbb{F}_{2^d}$ (d odd) is defined as

$$H(\alpha) = \sum_{i=0}^{(d-1)/2} \alpha^{2^{2i}}\;.$$

It is easily verified that it is $\mathbb{F}_2$-linear, and that it satisfies $H(\alpha)^2 + H(\alpha) = \alpha + \mathrm{Tr}(\alpha)$. Therefore, in order to solve equation (5) we first have to check whether $\mathrm{Tr}(\alpha) = 0$. Only in that case (5) solvable: Then we compute the half-trace $H(\alpha)$ of α by adding together precomputed half-traces of elements of the polynomial base, i.e. $H(x^i)$, and $H(\alpha)$, $H(\alpha) + 1$ are the solutions.

One optimization in [20] consists in removing the coefficients of even powers of x: We write $H(\alpha) = H(\alpha') + \beta$ where α' has fewer nonzero coefficients than α. This can be done by observing that $H(x^{2i}) = H(x^i) + x^{2i} + \mathrm{Tr}(x^{2i})$. Therefore each coefficient of an even power of x can be set to zero. This halves the amount of stored half-traces of powers of x.

Our approach differs from the one in [20] in that we do not make ad-hoc attempts to minimize memory requirements. Instead, we reduce the number of half-traces to be accumulated by increasing the amount of precomputations. We compute and store $H(\ell_0 x^{8i+1} + \ell_1 x^{8i+3} + \ell_2 x^{8i+5} + \ell_3 x^{8i+7})$ for all $i \geq 0$ such that $8i + 1 \leq d - 2$ and all $(\ell_0, \ell_1, \ell_2, \ell_3) \in \mathbb{F}_2^4 \setminus \{(0,0,0,0)\}$ such that the degree of the argument of H is at most $d - 2$. By means of this we reduce by a factor $32/15$ the expected number of table lookups and additions of half-traces.

5.4 Results, Conclusions

We benchmarked our implementation. Table 3 collects the timings of our routines on a PowerPC G4 running at 1.5 Ghz. (Table 5 shows the timings on an Intel Core 2 Duo CPU running at 1.83 Ghz.) Several field operations are timed, and the costs relative to a field multiplication are provided. The reduction polynomials are given (as decreasing lists of exponents) as well as whether the considered polynomial is square root friendly or not.

We have chosen degrees in various more or less evenly spaced ranges to fulfil the following requirements: the "classical" extension degrees 163, 191, and 233 must be included, fields around integer submultiples of these sizes should also be taken into account (that's the reason for degrees in the ranges 40-50 and 80-100, and 127), and we should provide examples of fields where the "standard" polynomial (either in the sense that it comes from standard documents, or that it is the most common one used for computations in computer algebra systems) already is square root friendly as well as cases where it is not – in the latter scenario we also choose a second defining polynomial that is square root friendly. Furthermore, all these combination of cases should happen with trinomial defined fields as well as when pentanomials are used. The "submultiples" ranges are relevant because of Trace Zero Varieties coming from elliptic curves [18], and

Table 3. Operations in some Binary Fields on a PowerPC G4 running at 1.5 Ghz. Mul, Sqr, Inv, Sqrt, Tr and Eq denote multiplication, squaring, field inversion, square root extraction, trace and half-trace computation respectively

Field	Reduction	Sqrt	Operation Timings (μsec)						Costs relative to one Mul				
(Bits)	Polynomial	Frnd	Mul	Sqr	Inv	Sqrt	Trace	Eq	Sqr	Inv	Sqrt	Trace	Eq
41	41,3,0	Yes	.084	.013	.448	.015	.007	.129	.160	5.340	.178	.078	1.536
43	43,6,4,3,0	No	.090	.016	.453	.327	.020	.128	.179	5.010	3.619	.227	1.422
43	43,17,9,5,0	Yes	.090	.017	.454	.018	.007	.126	.186	5.029	.196	.072	1.400
47	47,5,0	Yes	.089	.013	.478	.015	.007	.128	.150	5.344	.167	.083	1.438
83	83,7,4,2,0	No	.212	.030	.915	.383	.023	.191	.141	4.313	1.806	.107	.901
83	83,29,25,3,0	Yes	.214	.045	.925	.054	.007	.192	.209	4.316	.254	.034	.897
89	89,38,0	No	.253	.023	.958	.354	.023	.200	.089	3.782	1.398	.092	.791
89	89,51,0	Yes	.253	.024	.958	.025	.007	.201	.093	3.782	.098	.027	.794
97	97,6,0	No	.311	.028	1.598	.401	.025	.256	.091	5.139	1.289	.081	.823
97	97,33,0	Yes	.304	.024	1.576	.028	.006	.252	.080	5.191	.091	.020	.829
127	127,1,0	Yes	.418	.053	1.814	.062	.007	.288	.127	4.345	.149	.016	.689
163	163,7,6,3,0	No	.819	.086	5.317	.679	.033	.388	.105	6.491	.829	.040	.474
163	163,57,49,29,0	Yes	.821	.090	5.327	.095	.007	.391	.110	6.491	.116	.009	.476
191	191,9,0	Yes	.896	.083	5.804	.093	.008	.429	.093	6.474	.104	.009	.479
223	223,33,0	Yes	1.198	.098	12.865	.113	.006	.501	.082	10.737	.094	.005	.418
233	233,74,0	No	1.336	.101	14.599	.918	.037	.582	.076	10.925	.687	.028	.436
233	233,159,0	Yes	1.330	.090	14.593	.117	.006	.584	.068	10.971	.088	.005	.439

future investigation will consider the use of point and divisor halving for these algebraic groups.

Our implementation shows some interesting results.

1. The claims made in [20] about the speed of optimized square root extraction for fields defined by suitable trinomials are extended to pentanomials. Our results show for fields of 163, 191, and 233 bits an even further reduced Sqrt/Mul ratio. The gain w.r.t. generic implementations of square roots ranges from 8 to 20, and it is higher for smaller fields.

2. Multiplication and squaring may get marginally slower because the square root friendly polynomials usually do not have minimal degree sediments, and thus the reduction routine has to be a bit longer. The differences are minimal, field squaring paying a slightly higher toll than field multiplication. Sometimes a negligible performance improvement (presumably due to randomness) is observed. Field inversion and half-trace computation are unaffected by the choice of polynomial.

3. Computing traces with square root friendly polynomials takes nearly negligible time.

4. In [20] computing an half-trace requires approximately 2/3 the time of a field multiplication, but for fields of the same sizes our ratios are lower than 1/2, because we use a lot of precomputations.

In Table 4 we give estimates of the costs relative to one field multiplication of elliptic curve group addition, doubling, halving and scalar multiplication using various algorithms. We have used the operations counts from [5, §5.2], but the ratios between field operations come from our Table 3. We can see that the use square root friendly polynomials has a noticeable impact on scalar multiplication performance based on point halving. Point halving alone is sped up by about 20%, and the whole scalar multiplication by about 14% for curves defined over $\mathbb{F}_{2^{163}}$ and by 11% if the base field is $\mathbb{F}_{2^{233}}$. These improvements are much larger than the difference in field multiplication performance (a 2.5 ‰ loss for $\mathbb{F}_{2^{163}}$,

Table 4. Estimated costs of elliptic curve group operations and scalar multiplication relative to those of a field multiplication. Add, resp. Dbl, Hlv mean Addition, resp. Doubling, Halving, and D & A, resp. H & A means windowed scalar multiplication based on Double-and-Add, resp. Halve-and-Add. Scalar multiplications methods use affine coordinates as well as mixed affine-Lopez-Dahab coordinates.

Field		Group Operations				Scalar Multiplication		
Degree	Sqrt Frnd	Affine Coords.		Mixed $\mathcal{A} + \mathcal{LD}$		Affine Coords.		Mixed
		Add,Dbl	Hlv	mixed A	Dbl	D & A	H & A	D & A
163	N	8.596	3.343	8.525	5.175	1550.3	834.5	1137.2
163	Y	8.601	2.601	8.550	5.200	1551.4	715.0	1141.1
191	Y	8.567	2.592	8.465	5.115	1801.3	825.0	1310.7
233	N	13.001	3.151	8.380	5.030	3369.4	1291.0	1588.6
233	Y	13.039	2.532	8.340	4.990	3379.2	1149.4	1579.8

Table 5. Operations in some Binary Fields on an Intel Core 2 Duo running at 1.83 Ghz

Field (Bits)	Reduction Polynomial	Sqrt Frnd	Operation Timings (μsec)						Costs relative to one Mul				
			Mul	Sqr	Inv	Sqrt	Trace	Eq	Sqr	Inv	Sqrt	Trace	Eq
41	41,3,0	Yes	.065	.019	1.343	.023	.012	.057	.292	20.662	.358	.184	.883
43	43,6,4,3,0	No	.067	.017	1.381	.141	.023	.057	.253	20.611	2.099	.337	.837
43	43,17,9,5,0	Yes	.069	.021	1.368	.021	.012	.057	.304	19.826	.326	.174	.829
47	47,5,0	Yes	.074	.015	1.452	.025	.012	.063	.203	19.621	.335	.162	.853
83	83,7,4,2,0	No	.184	.041	2.727	.245	.022	.094	.223	14.821	1.333	.120	.512
83	83,29,25,3,0	Yes	.172	.035	2.727	.049	.012	.092	.203	15.855	.285	.070	.537
89	89,38,0	No	.207	.028	2.813	.203	.018	.083	.135	13.589	.982	.089	.402
89	89,51,0	Yes	.201	.036	2.837	.044	.012	.080	.179	14.114	.217	.060	.394
97	97,6,0	No	.223	.032	3.677	.200	.021	.118	.144	16.523	.898	.093	.530
97	97,33,0	Yes	.220	.031	3.670	.046	.012	.118	.141	16.489	.201	.054	.536
127	127,1,0	Yes	.305	.038	4.375	.050	.012	.122	.125	14.344	.164	.039	.400
163	163,7,6,3,0	No	.495	.069	6.855	.314	.028	.160	.139	13.855	.635	.056	.324
163	163,57,49,29,0	Yes	.445	.078	7.055	.066	.012	.158	.175	13.848	.148	.027	.355
191	191,9,0	Yes	.648	.051	8.873	.052	.012	.243	.079	13.692	.081	.018	.375
223	223,33,0	Yes	.775	.072	9.413	.073	.012	.313	.093	12.415	.094	.015	.404
233	233,74,0	No	.945	.086	12.246	.358	.019	.321	.091	12.959	.379	.020	.340
233	233,159,0	Yes	.951	.094	12.225	.070	.012	.320	.099	12.854	.074	.013	.336

a 4.5 ‰ gain for $\mathbb{F}_{2^{233}}$). It is safe to assume that similar improvements can be achieved on the Yao-like scalar multiplication algorithms from [5].

We already mentioned that square root extractions are used in some pairing computation algorithms. For instance, the main loop of Algorithm 2 from [13] requires 7 multiplication, two squarings and two square root extractions in fields of even characteristic. In this context, the overall gain obtained by faster square root extraction is going to be less important than with point halving, but still noticeable.

Square root friendly polynomials should be used when implementing formulæ that make heavy use of square root extraction in fields of characteristic two. For solving quadratic equations then we advise to increase the amount of precomputed half-traces to improve performance. In particular, the improvements in scalar multiplication performance based on point halving obtained in [20] by using special trinomial can be carried over to fields defined by pentanomials. Around 20% can be expected for the point halving alone, with an impact of 11% to 14% on the entire scalar multiplication.

Acknowledgement. The author acknowledges interesting discussions on the subject with Peter Birkner, Toni Bluher, Darrel Hankerson, Alfred Menezes, Mike Scott, and Nicolas Thériault.

References

1. Ahmadi, O., Hankerson, D., Menezes, A.: Formulas for cube roots in $\mathbb{F}_{3^m}$. Discrete Applied Math. 155(3), 260–270 (2007)
2. Ahmadi, O., Menezes, A.: On the number of trace-one elements in polynomial bases for $\mathbb{F}_{2^n}$. Designs, Codes and Cryptography 37, 493–507 (2005)

3. Ahmadi, O., Menezes, A.: Irreducible polynomials of maximum weight. Utilitas Mathematica 72, 111–123 (2007)
4. Ash, D.W., Blake, I.F., Vanstone, S.: Low complexity normal bases. Discrete Applied Math. 25, 191–210 (1989)
5. Avanzi, R.M.: Delaying and Merging Operations in Scalar Multiplication: Applications to Curve-Based Cryptosystems. In: Proceedings of SAC 2006 (to appear)
6. Avanzi, R.M., Cesena, E.: Trace Zero Varieties over Fields of Characteristic 2: Cryptographic Applications. In: SAGA 2007. The first Symposium on Algebraic Geometry and its Applications, May 7-11, 2007,Tahiti (2007)
7. Avanzi, R.M., Ciet, M., Sica, F.: Faster Scalar Multiplication on Koblitz Curves combining Point Halving with the Frobenius Endomorphism. In: Bao, F., Deng, R., Zhou, J. (eds.) PKC 2004. LNCS, vol. 2947, pp. 28–40. Springer, Heidelberg (2004)
8. Avanzi, R., Cohen, H., Doche, C., Frey, G., Lange, T., Nguyen, K., Vercauteren, F.: The Handbook of Elliptic and Hyperelliptic Curve Cryptography. CRC Press, Boca Raton, USA (2005)
9. Avanzi, R.M., Heuberger, C., Prodinger, H.: Scalar Multiplication on Koblitz Curves Using the Frobenius Endomorphism and its Combination with Point Halving: Extensions and Mathematical Analysis. Algorithmica 46, 249–270 (2006)
10. Avanzi, R.M., Heuberger, C., Prodinger, H.: On Redundant τ-adic Expansions and Non-Adjacent Digit Sets. In: Biham, E., Youssef, A.M. (eds.) SAC 2006. LNCS, vol. 4356, Springer, Heidelberg (2006)
11. Avanzi, R.M., Thériault, N.: Effects of Optimizations for Software Implementations of Small Binary Field Arithmetic. In: Proceedings of WAIFI 2007. International Workshop on the Arithmetic of Finite Fields, June 21-22, 2007, Madrid, Spain, p. 18 (2007)
12. Avanzi, R.M., Thériault, N., Wang, Z.: Rethinking Low Genus Hyperelliptic Jacobian Arithmetic over Binary Fields: Interplay of Field Arithmetic and Explicit Formulæ. CACR Technical Report 2006-07
13. Barreto, P.S.L.M., Galbraith, S., OhEigeartaigh, C., Scott, M.: Efficient pairing computation on supersingular abelian varieties. Designs, Codes and Cryptography 42, 239–271 (2007), http://eprint.iacr.org/2004/375
14. Birkner, P.: Efficient Divisor Class Halving on Genus Two Curves. In: Proceedings of Selected Areas in Cryptography – SAC 2006. LNCS, Springer, Heidelberg (to appear)
15. Birkner, P., Thériault, N.: Efficient Divisor Class Doubling and Halving on Genus Three Curves (in preparation)
16. Bluher, A.W.: A Swan-like Theorem. Finite Fields and Their Applications 12, 128–138 (2006)
17. Bosma, W., Cannon, J., Playoust, C.: The MAGMA Algebra System I: The User Language. J. Symbolic Comput. 24, 235–265 (1997)
18. Cesena, E.: Varietá a Traccia Zero su Campi Binari: Applicazioni Crittografiche (Trace Zero Varieties over Binary Fields: Cryptographic Applications.) Master's Thesis. Universitá degli Studi di Milano (in Italian) (2005)
19. Coron, J.-S., M'Raïhi, D., Tymen, C.: Fast generation of pairs $(k, [k]P)$ for Koblitz elliptic curves. In: Vaudenay, S., Youssef, A.M. (eds.) SAC 2001. LNCS, vol. 2259, pp. 151–164. Springer, Heidelberg (2001)
20. Fong, K., Hankerson, D., López, J., Menezes, A.: Field Inversion and Point Halving Revisited. IEEE Trans. Computers 53(8), 1047–1059 (2004)
21. Hankerson, D., Menezes, A.J., Vanstone, S.A.: Guide to elliptic curve cryptography. Springer, Heidelberg (2003)

22. Knudsen, E.W.: Elliptic Scalar Multiplication Using Point Halving. In: Lam, K.-Y., Okamoto, E., Xing, C. (eds.) ASIACRYPT 1999. LNCS, vol. 1716, pp. 135–149. Springer, Heidelberg (1999)
23. Koblitz, N.: CM-curves with good cryptographic properties. In: Feigenbaum, J. (ed.) CRYPTO 1991. LNCS, vol. 576, pp. 279–287. Springer, Heidelberg (1992)
24. Lange, T., Stevens, M.: Efficient doubling for genus two curves over binary fields. In: Handschuh, H., Hasan, M.A. (eds.) SAC 2004. LNCS, vol. 3357, pp. 170–181. Springer, Heidelberg (2004)
25. National Institute of Standards and Technology. Recommended Elliptic Curves for Federal Government Use. NIST Special Publication (July 1999), available from: http://csrc.nist.gov/csrc/fedstandards.html
26. Schroeppel, R.: Point halving wins big. In: (i) Midwest Arithmetical Geometry in Cryptography Workshop, November 17–19, 2000, University of Illinois at Urbana-Champaign (2000), ECC 2001 Workshop, October 29–31, 2001, University of Waterloo, Ontario, Canada (2001)
27. Schroeppel, R.: Elliptic curve point ambiguity resolution apparatus and method. International Application Number PCT/US00/31014, filed (November 9, 2000)
28. Scott, M.: Optimal Irreducible Polynomials for $GF(2^m)$ Arithmetic. IACR ePrint 2007/192. http://eprint.iacr.org/2007/192
29. Swan, R.G.: Factorization of Polynomials over Finite Fields. Pac. J. Math. 19, 1099–1106 (1962)

A   Comparing Some Modular Reduction Routines

The use of a square root friendly polynomial can slow down modular reduction, but we already observed that this performance loss is minimal. This is explained by the fact that even though reduction does become more expensive, the amount of additional operations is rather small.

As an example, we report here the reduction code for the two degree 163 polynomials which we used. The input is given as eleven 32-bit words rA,r9,r8,..., r1,r0 and the reduced output is computed in place in the six least significant words r5,r4,r3,r2,r1,r0.

To reduce modulo $X^{163} + X^7 + X^6 + X^3 + 1$, the number of necessary logical operations between CPU registers is 74. Reduction modulo $X^{163} + X^{57} + X^{49} + X^{29} + 1$ takes 89 logical operations. This example is the one with the largest complexity increase in all the comparisons we worked out.

```
#define bf_mod_163_7_6_3_0(rA,r9,r8,r7,r6,r5,r4,r3,r2,r1,r0) do { \
    /* reduce rA */                                              \
    r5 ^= (rA) ^ ((rA) <<  3) ^ ((rA) <<  4) ^ ((rA) >>  3);     \
    r4 ^=                                       ((rA) << 29);    \
    /* reduce r9 */                                              \
    r5 ^=            ((r9) >> 29) ^ ((r9) >> 28);                \
    r4 ^= (r9) ^ ((r9) <<  3) ^ ((r9) <<  4) ^ ((r9) >>  3);     \
    r3 ^=                                       ((r9) << 29);    \
    /* reduce r8 */                                              \
    r4 ^=            ((r8) >> 29) ^ ((r8) >> 28);                \
    r3 ^= (r8) ^ ((r8) <<  3) ^ ((r8) <<  4) ^ ((r8) >>  3);     \
    r2 ^=                                       ((r8) << 29);    \
    /* reduce r7 */                                              \
```

```
    r3 ^=                 ((r7) >> 29) ^ ((r7) >> 28);               \
    r2 ^= (r7) ^ ((r7) << 3) ^ ((r7) << 4) ^ ((r7) >> 3);           \
    r1 ^=                                    ((r7) << 29);           \
    /* reduce r6 */                                                  \
    r2 ^=                 ((r6) >> 29) ^ ((r6) >> 28);               \
    r1 ^= (r6) ^ ((r6) << 3) ^ ((r6) << 4) ^ ((r6) >> 3);           \
    r0 ^=                                    ((r6) << 29);           \
    /* reduce the 29 most significant bits of r5 */                 \
    r6 = (r5) >> 3; r5 &= 0x00000007;                               \
    r0 ^= (r6) ^ ((r6) << 3) ^ ((r6) << 6) ^ ((r6) << 7);          \
    r1 ^= ((r6) >> 26) ^ ((r6) >> 25);                             \
} while (0)


#define bf_mod_163_57_49_29_0(rA,r9,r8,r7,r6,r5,r4,r3,r2,r1,r0) do { \
    /* reduce rA */                                                  \
    r6 ^= ((rA) << 22) ^ ((rA) << 14);                             \
    r5 ^=                         ((rA) << 26) ^ ((rA) >> 3);      \
    r4 ^=                                         ((rA) << 29);    \
    /* reduce r9 */                                                 \
    r6 ^= ((r9) >> 10) ^ ((r9) >> 18);                            \
    r5 ^= ((r9) << 22) ^ ((r9) << 14) ^ ((r9) >> 6);             \
    r4 ^=                         ((r9) << 26) ^ ((r9) >> 3);     \
    r3 ^=                                         ((r9) << 29);   \
    /* reduce r8 */                                                \
    r5 ^= ((r8) >> 10) ^ ((r8) >> 18);                           \
    r4 ^= ((r8) << 22) ^ ((r8) << 14) ^ ((r8) >> 6);            \
    r3 ^=                         ((r8) << 26) ^ ((r8) >> 3);    \
    r2 ^=                                         ((r8) << 29);  \
    /* reduce r7 */                                               \
    r4 ^= ((r7) >> 10) ^ ((r7) >> 18);                          \
    r3 ^= ((r7) << 22) ^ ((r7) << 14) ^ ((r7) >> 6);           \
    r2 ^=                         ((r7) << 26) ^ ((r7) >> 3);   \
    r1 ^=                                         ((r7) << 29); \
    /* reduce r6 */                                              \
    r3 ^= ((r6) >> 10) ^ ((r6) >> 18);                         \
    r2 ^= ((r6) << 22) ^ ((r6) << 14) ^ ((r6) >> 6);          \
    r1 ^=                         ((r6) << 26) ^ ((r6) >> 3);  \
    r0 ^=                                         ((r6) << 29);\
    /* reduce the 29 most significant bits of r5 */            \
    r6 = (r5) >> 3; r5 &= 0x00000007;                         \
    r2 ^= ((r6) >> 7) ^ ((r6) >> 15);                         \
    r1 ^= ((r6) << 25) ^ ((r6) << 17) ^ ((r6) >> 3);          \
    r0 ^=                         ((r6) << 29) ^ (r6);        \
} while(0)
```

Efficient Explicit Formulae for Genus 2 Hyperelliptic Curves over Prime Fields and Their Implementations

Xinxin Fan and Guang Gong

Department of Electrical and Computer Engineering
University of Waterloo
Waterloo, Ontario, N2L 3G1, Canada
x5fan@engmail.uwaterloo.ca, G.Gong@ece.uwaterloo.ca

Abstract. We analyze all the cases and propose the corresponding explicit formulae for computing $2D_1 + D_2$ in one step from given divisor classes D_1 and D_2 on genus 2 hyperelliptic curves defined over prime fields. Compared with naive method, the improved formula can save two field multiplications and one field squaring each time when the arithmetic is performed in the most frequent case. Furthermore, we present a variant which trades one field inversion for fourteen field multiplications and two field squarings by using Montgomery's trick to combine the two inversions. Experimental results show that our algorithms can save up to 13% of the time to perform a scalar multiplication on a general genus 2 hyperelliptic curve over a prime field, when compared with the best known general methods.

Keywords: Genus 2 hyperelliptic curves, explicit formulae, Cantor's algorithm, Harley's variant, efficient implementation.

1 Introduction

In 1988, Koblitz proposed for the first time to use the Jacobian of a hyperelliptic curve (HEC) defined over a finite field to implement cryptographic protocols based on the difficulty of the discrete logarithm problem [14]. During the past few years, hyperelliptic curve cryptosystems (HECC) have become increasing popular for use in practice to provide an alternative to the widely used elliptic curve cryptosystems (ECC) because of much shorter operand length than that of ECC. Moreover, recent research has also shown that HECC are well suited for various software and hardware platforms and their performance is compatible to that of ECC [1,4,21,22].

The most important and expensive operation in ECC and HECC is the scalar multiplication by an integer k, i.e., computing a scalar multiple kP of a point P on the points group or kD of a divisor class D on the Jacobian, where k might be 160 bits or more. Various techniques for efficiently computing the scalar multiplication have been proposed [2,13]. For general elliptic curves, Eisenträger *et al.* proposed a very elegant method for accelerating the scalar multiplication [10].

C. Adams, A. Miri, and M. Wiener (Eds.): SAC 2007, LNCS 4876, pp. 155–172, 2007.

Their improvements are based on the efficient computation of $2P + Q$ in one step from given points P and Q on an elliptic curve. Since the point doubling is slightly more expensive than the point addition in the group operations of ECC, it is more efficient to calculate $2P + Q$ as $P + (P + Q)$ than first doubling P and then adding Q. This trick can save one field multiplication each time the certain sequence of operations occurs. Furthermore, their method finds applications to simultaneous multiple scalar multiplication, the Elliptic Curve Method of factorization, as well as the computation of the Weil and Tate pairings [10]. In the rest of this paper I represents a field inversion, M a field multiplication, and S a field squaring.

This work generalizes Eisenträger et $al.$'s idea to genus 2 HECs over prime fields where the group doubling costs two more field squarings than the group addition [16]. We analyze all the possible cases during the computation procedure of $2D_1 + D_2$ from given divisor classes D_1 and D_2 on a genus 2 HEC over $\mathbb{F}_p$. For the most frequent case, we propose a basic algorithm and its variant which cost $2I + 42M + 5S$ and $1I + 56M + 7S$, respectively, to compute $2D_1 + D_2$ in one step. Compared to the naive method using two separate group additions, our basic algorithm can save $2M + 1S$. In the variant, which is faster whenever one inversion is more expensive than about sixteen field multiplications, Montgomery's trick [8] is employed to combine the two inversions in the basic algorithm. Furthermore, we implement the proposed algorithms on a Pentium processor to verify the correctness and test the performance of our new explicit formulae. For genus 2 HECs over binary fields, the fastest doubling formula, which requires only half the time of an addition, has been obtained by Lange and Stevens for a special family of curves [17]. We note that the Eisenträger et $al.$'s trick can not be applied to optimize the computation of $2D_1 + D_2$ for the special family of genus 2 curves over binary fields when the group doubling is more efficient than the group addition.

The rest of this paper is organized as follows: Section 2 gives a short introduction to the mathematical background of genus 2 HECs over prime fields. Section 3 makes a thorough case study for the computation of $2D_1 + D_2$, presents the corresponding explicit formulae and analyzes the cost of the NAF scalar multiplication. Section 4 gives the experimental results of our newly derived explicit formulae. Finally, Section 5 ends this contribution.

2   Mathematical Background on Genus 2 Hyperelliptic Curves over Prime Fields

In this section, we present a brief introduction to the theory of genus 2 hyperelliptic curves over prime fields, restricting attention to the material which is relevant to this work. For more details, the reader is referred to [3,6,15,18].

Let $\mathbb{F}_q$ be a finite field of characteristic $p \neq 2$, $q = p^n$, and let $\overline{\mathbb{F}}_q$ denote the algebraic closure of $\mathbb{F}_q$. Let $\mathbb{F}_q(C)/\mathbb{F}_q$ be a quadratic function field defined via an equation

$$C : Y^2 = F(X) \tag{1}$$

where $F(X) = X^5 + f_4X^4 + f_3X^3 + f_2X^2 + f_1X + f_0 \in \mathbb{F}_q[X]$ is a monic and square-free polynomial of degree 5. The curve $C/\mathbb{F}_q$ associated with this function field is called a *hyperelliptic curve of genus 2 defined over* $\mathbb{F}_q$. For our purpose it is enough to consider a point P as an ordered pair $P = (x, y) \in \overline{\mathbb{F}}_q^2$ which satisfies $y^2 = F(x)$. Besides these tuples there is one point P_∞ at infinity. The inverse of P is defined as $-P = (x, -y)$. We call a point P that satisfies $P = -P$ a *ramification point*. Note that for $p \neq 5$ the transform $X \to X - f_4/5$ makes the coefficient of X^4 in $F(X)$ zero.

The divisor class group $\mathcal{J}_C(\mathbb{F}_q)$ of C forms a finite Abelian group and therefore we can construct cryptosystems whose security is based on the difficulty of the discrete logarithm problem on the Jacobian of C. Each element of the Jacobian can be represented uniquely by a so-called reduced divisor [6]. Mumford [19] showed that a reduced divisor can be represented by means of two polynomials $U(X), V(X) \in \mathbb{F}_q[X]$, where $U(X)$ and $V(X)$ satisfy the following three conditions: (i) $U(X)$ is monic, (ii) $\deg V(X) < \deg U(X) \leq 2$, and (iii) $U(X) \mid V(X)^2 - F(X)$. In the remainder of this paper, we will use the notation $[U, V]$ for the divisor class represented by $U(X)$ and $V(X)$. For a genus 2 HEC, we have commonly $[U, V] = [X^2 + u_1X + u_0, v_1X + v_0]$.

Cantor's algorithm [6] describes how to perform the group addition of two divisor classes in Mumford's representation. We review Cantor's algorithm for genus 2 HECs over prime fields in the following Algorithm 1. Cantor's algorithm only involves polynomial arithmetic over the finite field in which the divisor class group is defined. However, there are some redundant computations of the polynomial's coefficients in this classical algorithm. In order to simplify Cantor's algorithm, Harley proposed the first explicit formulae for a group addition and a group doubling of divisor classes on $\mathcal{J}_C(\mathbb{F}_q)$ in 2000. In [11], Gaudry and Harley significantly reduced the computational complexity of the group operations by distinguishing different cases according to the properties of the input divisor classes. They presented a very efficient algorithm, which uses many modern polynomial computation techniques such as Chinese remainder theorem, Newton's iteration, and Karatsuba's multiplication. Algorithm 2 gives a high level description of Harley's variant for adding two reduced divisor classes in the most frequent case for genus 2 HECs over prime fields. The most frequent cases mean that for the addition the inputs are two co-prime polynomials of degree 2, which occur with the overwhelming probability [20], and the remainder cases are called exceptional cases. For more details about Cantor's algorithm and Harley's variant, the reader is referred to [3,16,22].

3   Efficient Algorithms for Computing $2D_1 + D_2$

In this section we adapt the idea of [10] to genus 2 HECs over prime fields. We obtain $D_3 = 2D_1 + D_2$ by the following two steps: we first compute $D' = [U', V'] = D_1 + D_2$ and omit the computation of the coefficients of V' because V' will not be used in the next phase. And then, we find $D_3 = D' + D_1$. Hence, we use two group additions to form $2D_1 + D_2$ instead of a group addition and

---

Algorithm 1. Cantor's Algorithm for Group Addition $(g = 2, \mathbb{F}_p)$

Input: $D_1 = [U_1, V_1], D_2 = [U_2, V_2], C : Y^2 = F(X)$

Output: $D_3 = [U_3, V_3]$ reduced with $D_3 \equiv D_1 + D_2$

1. Compute $d_1 = \gcd(U_1, U_2) = e_1 U_1 + e_2 U_2$
2. Compute $d = \gcd(d_1, V_1 + V_2) = c_1 d_1 + c_2(V_1 + V_2)$
3. Let $s_1 = c_1 e_1, s_2 = c_1 e_2, s_3 = c_2$
4. $U' = \frac{U_1 U_2}{d^2}$
5. $V' = \frac{s_1 U_1 V_2 + s_2 U_2 V_1 + s_3(V_1 V_2 + F)}{d} \mod U'$
6. $U_3 = \frac{F - V^2}{U'}, V_3 = -V' \mod U_3$
7. make U_3 monic

Algorithm 2. Harley's Variant for Group Addition $(g = 2, \mathbb{F}_p)$

Input: $D_1 = [U_1, V_1], D_2 = [U_2, V_2], C : Y^2 = F(X)$

Output: $D_3 = [U_3, V_3]$ reduced with $D_3 \equiv D_1 + D_2$

1. $K = \frac{F - V_1^2}{U_1}$ (exact division)
2. $S \equiv \frac{V_2 - V_1}{U_1} \mod U_2$
3. $L = SU_1$
4. $U_3 = \frac{K - S(L + 2V_1)}{U_2}$ (exact division)
5. make U_3 monic
6. $V_3 \equiv -(L + V_1) \mod U_3$

---

a group doubling. To derive explicit formulae, we first study all the exceptional cases during the computation $2D_1 + D_2$ based on the properties of the input divisor classes and the immediate result D'. We then determine how many field operations are required to calculate $2D_1 + D_2$ in one step in the most frequent case. Furthermore, we also propose a variant of our basic algorithm by using Montgomery's trick to compute the two inversions simultaneously at cost of some multiplications, which will be more efficient whenever a field inversion is more expensive than about sixteen field multiplications.

3.1   Explicit Formulae in Exceptional Cases

In this subsection we discuss all the exceptional cases appearing in the procedure of calculating $2D_1 + D_2$. Suppose that $D_1 = [U_1, V_1]$ and $D_2 = [U_2, V_2]$ are two reduced divisor classes as the inputs of the composition step of the Cantor's algorithm. The final output is $D_3 = 2D_1 + D_2 = [U_3, V_3]$. We need to distinguish the following cases:

1. U_1 is of degree zero, this is only possible in the case $[U_1, V_1] = [1, 0]$, i.e. D_1 is the zero element of the divisor class group. The result of $2D_1 + D_2$ is the second class $D_2 = [U_2, V_2]$.

2. U_1 is of degree one and U_2 has degree zero, one or full degree. Let $U_1 = X + u_{10}$ and $V_1 = v_{10} \neq 0$ is a constant.

A. Assume deg $U_2 = 0$, i.e., D_2 is the zero element of the divisor class group. Therefore, the result of $2D_1 + D_2$ is $2D_1$ and we double the divisor D_1 with $1I + 4M + 1S$ to obtain

$$U_3 = U_1^2 = (X + u_{10})^2, \tag{2}$$
$$V_3 = \frac{F'(-u_{10})(X + u_{10})}{2v_{10}} + v_{10}.$$

B. Assume deg $U_2 = 1$, i.e., $U_2 = X + u_{20}$ and $V_2 = v_{20} \neq 0$ is a constant.
   i. If $U_1 = U_2$ and $V_1 = -V_2$, the result of $D_1 + D_2$ is the zero element $[1, 0]$. Hence, we get $2D_1 + D_2 = [1, 0] + D_1 = D_1$;
   ii. If $U_1 = U_2$ and $V_1 = V_2$, the result of $2D_1 + D_2$ is $3D_1$, which can be computed with $1I + 12M + 4S$ (See Table 5 in the appendix).
   iii. Otherwise the result of $D_1 + D_2$ is $[U', V']$ where

$$U' = U_1 U_2 = (X + u_{10})(X + u_{20}), \tag{3}$$
$$V' = \frac{(v_{20} - v_{10})X + v_{20}u_{10} - v_{10}u_{20}}{u_{10} - u_{20}}.$$

   And then we use Table 6 (see the appendix) to obtain $2D_1 + D_2$ in an additional $1I + 18M + 4S$.

C. Assume deg $U_2 = 2$, i.e. $U_2 = X^2 + u_{21}X + u_{20}$ and $V_2 = v_{21}X + v_{20}$. Then the corresponding divisors are given by $D_1 = (P_1) - (P_\infty)$ and $D_2 = (P_2) + (P_3) - 2(P_\infty)$, with $P_i \neq P_\infty$ ($i = 1, 2, 3$).
   i. If $U_2(-u_{10}) \neq 0$ then P_1 and $-P_1$ do not occur in D_2. This case is dealt with Table 7 (see the appendix). We can obtain $2D_1 + D_2$ at the cost of $I + 28M + 4S$.
   ii. Otherwise if $V_2(-u_{10}) = -v_{10}$ the $-P_1$ occurs in D_2 and the result of $D_1 + D_2$ is $D' = [U', V'] = [X + u_{21} - u_{10}, v_{21}(-u_{21} + u_{10}) + v_{20}]$ because $-u_{21}$ equals the sum of the x-coordinates of the points. And then we compute D_3 using (2), unless $D_2 = 2(-P_1) - 2(P_\infty)$ where we can obtain $D_3 = 2D_1 + D_2 = [1, 0]$.
   iii. The remaining case is that P_1 occurs in D_2. If $D_2 = 2(P_1) - 2(P_\infty) = 2D_1$, which holds if $u_{21} = 2u_{10}$ and $u_{20} = u_{10}^2$, then we have $2D_1 + D_2 = 2D_2$. Therefore, we obtain D_3 by doubling a class D_2 of order different from 2 and with first polynomial of full degree as in 3.A. Otherwise we first use Table 6 (see the appendix) to compute $D' = [U', V'] = [X + u_1'X + u_0', v_1'X + v_0'] = D_1 + D_2$ with $1I + 18M + 4S$ and then differentiate the following three cases to obtain $D_3 = D' + D_1$:
      a. If $U'(-u_{10}) \neq 0$ then P_1 and $-P_1$ do not occur in the support set of D'. In this case, D_3 can be calculated with the explicit addition formula of the case of deg $U_1 = 1$ and deg $U_2 = 2$ in [16] at the cost of $1I + 10M + S$.

b. Otherwise If $V'(-u_{10}) = -v_{10}$ then the $-P_1$ occurs in the support set of D'. In this case, $D_3 = [X + u'_1 - u_{10}, v'_1(-u'_1 + u_{10}) + v'_0]$.

c. The remaining case is that P_1 occurs in D'. This case can be handled with steps 2~7 of Table 6 (see the appendix) at the cost of $1I + 11M + 4S$.

3. U_1 is of degree two and U_2 has degree zero, one or two. Let $U_1 = X^2 + u_{11}X + u_{10}$ and $V_1 = v_{11}X + v_{10}$. The corresponding divisor is given by $D_1 = (P_1) + (P_2) - 2(P_\infty)$ with $P_i \neq P_\infty$ ($i = 1, 2$).

A. Assume deg $U_2 = 0$, i.e. D_2 is the zero element of the divisor class group. Therefore, the result of $2D_1 + D_2$ is $2D_1$ and we are in the case of doubling a divisor of order different from 2 and with first polynomial of full degree. Again we need to consider two subcases depending on wether a point P_i in the support has order 2. The point $P_i = (x_i, y_i)$ is equal to its opposite if and only if $y_i = 0$. To check for this case we compute the resultant of U_1 and V_1.

i. If $\text{res}(U_1, V_1) \neq 0$ then we are in the usual case where both points are not equal to their opposite. This can be computed with the doubling explicit formula of the most frequent case in [16].

ii. Otherwise we compute the $\gcd(U_1, V_1) = (X - x_i)$ to get the coordinate of P_i and double the divisor $[X + u_{11} + x_i, v_{11}(-u_{11} - x_i) + v_{10}]$ to obtain $2D_1 = 2(P_j) - 2(P_\infty)$ ($j \neq i$) with (1).

B. Assume deg $U_2 = 1$, i.e. $U_2 = X + u_{20}$ and $V_2 = v_{20} \neq 0$ is a constant. The corresponding divisor is given by $D_2 = (P_3) - (P_\infty)$ with $P_3 \neq P_\infty$.

i. If $U_1(-u_{20}) \neq 0$ then P_3 and $-P_3$ do not occur in D_1. This case is dealt with Table 8 (see the appendix). We can obtain $2D_1 + D_2$ at the cost of $I + 46M + 7S$.

ii. Otherwise if $V_1(-u_{20}) = -v_{10}$ then $-P_3$ occurs in D_1 and the result of $D_1 + D_2$ is $D' = [U', V'] = [X + u_{11} - u_{20}, v_{11}(-u_{11} + u_{20}) + v_{10}]$ because $-u_{11}$ equals the sum of the x-coordinates of the points. And then we compute $D_3 = D_1 + D'$ using steps 2~7 of Table 6 (see the appendix) in an additional $1I + 11M + 4S$.

iii. The remaining case is that P_3 occurs in D_1. If $D_1 = 2D_2 = 2(P_3) - 2(P_\infty)$, which holds if $u_{11} = 2u_{20}$ and $u_{10} = u_{20}^2$, then we first use Table 5 (see the appendix) to compute $D' = 3D_2$ with $1I + 12M + 4S$. Otherwise we first obtain $D' = D_1 + D_2$ using Table 6 (see the appendix) with $1I + 18M + 4S$. And then we consider the following two cases:

a. If $\text{res}(U_1, U') \neq 0$ then there is no point in the support of D_1 which is equal to a point or its opposite in the support of D'. We deal with this case with the addition explicit formula of the most frequent case in [16].

b. If the above resultant is zero, then $D' = (P_1) + (P_3) - 2(P_\infty)$ or $D' = (-P_1) + (P_3) - 2(P_\infty)$. We first obtain $\gcd(U_1, U') = (X - u_{p1})$. And then we calculate $D_3 = D_1 + D'$ at cost of $1I + 32M + 3S$ and $1I + 7M$ with Table 9 (see the appendix) for these two subcases, respectively.

C. Assume deg $U_2 = 2$, i.e. $U_2 = X^2 + u_{21}X + u_{20}$ and $V_2 = v_{21}X + v_{20}$. The corresponding divisor is given by $D_2 = (P_3) + (P_4) - 2(P_\infty)$ with $P_i \neq P_\infty$ $(i = 3, 4)$.

  i. Let $U_1 = U_2$. This means that the x–coordinates of P_i and P_{i+2} $(i = 1, 2)$ are equal for an appropriate ordering.
   a. If $V_1 \equiv -V_2 \bmod U_1$ then we obtain $2D_1 + D_2 = D_1 + [1, 0] = D_1$.
   b. If $V_1 = V_2$ then we have $2D_1 + D_2 = 3D_1$. We first double D_1 to get D' based on the two cases in 3.A. If the degree of U' is one, then we need to consider three subcases in 2.C.iii. Otherwise, we differentiate two subcases in 3.B.iii to compute D_3.
   c. The remaining case is that $P_i = P_{i+2}$ and $P_j \neq P_{j+2}$ $(i, j \in \{1, 2\}$ and $i \neq j)$ is the opposite of P_{j+2}. Without loss of generality, we assume $P_1 = P_3$ and $P_2 \neq P_4$ is the opposite of P_4. We first calculate $D' = D_1 + D_2 = 2(P_1) - 2(P_\infty)$ by using (1) to double the divisor class $[X - (v_{10} - v_{20})/(v_{21} - v_{11}), V_1((v_{10} - v_{20})/(v_{21} - v_{11}))]$. And then we calculate $D_3 = D' + D_1$ by considering two subcases in 3.B.iii.

  ii. For the remainder cases $U_1 \neq U_2$, the following possibilities may appear:
   a. If $\operatorname{res}(U_1, U_2) \neq 0$ then there is no point in the support of D_1 which is equal to a point or its opposite in the support of D_2. We first only compute the first part U' of D' with the addition explicit formula of the most frequent case in [16]. And then we require to consider the following three subcases:
    1. If the degree of U' is one, which appears when $s'_1 = 0$ (see Table 1), we first calculate the second part V' of D' with the addition explicit formula of the special case in [16]. And then we need to consider three subcases in 2.C.iii to compute D_3.
    2. If $\deg U' = 2$ and $\operatorname{res}(U_1, U') = 0$, we first calculate the second part V' of D' with the addition explicit formula of the most frequent case in [16]. And then we compute D_3 with Table 9 (see the appendix).
    3. The remainder case is $\deg U' = 2$ and $\operatorname{res}(U_1, U') \neq 0$. This is the most frequent case and we will deal with this case in the next subsection.
   b. If $\operatorname{res}(U_1, U_2) = 0$ then we first compute D' with Table 9 (see the appendix). If the degree of U' is one, then we need to consider three subcases in 2.C.iii. Otherwise, we differentiate two subcases in 3.B.iii to compute D_3.

Although there are many exceptional cases during the computation of $2D_1 + D_2$, most frequently we are in the case of $\gcd(U_1, U_2) = \gcd(U_1, U') = 1$ and U' being quadratic. Therefore, if we can reduce the computational complexity of explicit formulae in the most frequent case, the performance of the whole cyptosystem will be improved on average.

3.2   Explicit Formulae in the Most Frequent Case

In this subsection, we present efficient explicit formulae for computing $2D_1 + D_2$ in the most frequent case where U_1, U_2 and U' are quadratic and $\gcd(U_1, U_2) = \gcd(U_1, U') = 1$. Studying Harley's variant carefully, we note that the polynomial V' in the intermediate result D' only is used to obtain S in the second group addition (see Step 2 in Algorithm 2). Therefore, when we substitute the expression of V' into S, we find the following important lemma which results in a significant speedup for calculating $2D_1 + D_2$.

Lemma 1. *Let C be a genus 2 HEC over $\mathbb{F}_q$ given by the equation (1). Assume that $D_1 = [U_1, V_1]$, $D_2 = [U_2, V_2]$ and $D' = [U', V'] = D_1 + D_2$ are reduced divisor classes in the Jacobian $\mathcal{J}_C(\mathbb{F}_q)$ of C and satisfy that U_1, U_2 and U' are quadratic, and $\gcd(U_1, U_2) = \gcd(U_1, U') = 1$. Let S and S' satisfy the congruent relations: $S \equiv \frac{V_2 - V_1}{U_1} \bmod U_2$ and $S' \equiv \frac{V' - V_1}{U_1} \bmod U'$, then we have*

$$S' \equiv -S - \frac{2V_1}{U_1} \bmod U'.$$

Proof. From Harley's variant (see Algorithm 2), we know that

$$V' \equiv -(SU_1 + V_1) \bmod U'.$$

Substitute V' into S', we obtain

$$S' \equiv \frac{V' - V_1}{U_1} \equiv \frac{-SU_1 - 2V_1}{U_1} \equiv -S - \frac{2V_1}{U_1} \bmod U'.$$

Lemma 1 suggests that we can eliminate the computation of V' during the procedure of calculating $2D_1 + D_2$. Table 1 presents our new explicit formula (Basic Algorithm) for computing $2D_1 + D_2$ on a genus 2 HEC over $\mathbb{F}_p$ in the most frequent case.

Table 1. Explicit Formula for $2D_1 + D_2$ on a HEC of Genus 2 over $\mathbb{F}_p$ – Basic Version

Input	Genus 2 HEC $C : Y^2 = F(X), F = X^5 + f_3 X^3 + f_2 X^2 + f_1 X + f_0$;	
	Reduced Divisors $D_1 = (U_1, V_1)$ and $D_2 = (U_2, V_2)$,	
	$U_1 = X^2 + u_{11} X + u_{10}, V_1 = v_{11} X + v_{10}$;	
	$U_2 = X^2 + u_{21} X + u_{20}, V_2 = v_{21} X + v_{20}$;	
Output	Reduced Divisor $D_3 = (U_3, V_3) = 2D_1 + D_2$;	
	$U_3 = X^2 + u_{31} X + u_{30}, V_3 = v_{31} X + v_{30}$;	
Step	**Expression**	**Cost**
1	**Compute the resultant r of U_1 and U_2:**	$3M, 1S$
	$i_1 = u_{21} - u_{11}, w = u_{10} - u_{20}, i_0 = i_1 u_{21} + w, r = i_0 w + i_1^2 u_{20}$;	
2	**Compute the pseudo-inverse $I = i_1 X + i_0 \equiv r/U_1 \bmod U_2$:**	–

Table 1. (*continued*)

3	**Compute $S' = s_1'X + s_0' = rS \equiv (V_2 - V_1)I \bmod U_2$:**	$5M$
	$w_0 = v_{20} - v_{10}, w_1 = v_{21} - v_{11}, w_2 = i_0 w_0, w_3 = i_1 w_1, s_0' = w_2 - u_{20} w_3;$	
	$s_1' = (i_0 + i_1)(w_0 + w_1) - w_2 - w_3(1 + u_{21});$ If $s_1' = 0$, see 3.C.ii.a.1.	
4	**Compute $S'' = X + s_0/s_1 = X + s_0'/s_1'$ and s_1:**	$1I, 5M, 1S$
	$w_1 = (rs_1')^{-1}(= 1/r^2 s_1), w_2 = rw_1(= 1/s_1'), w_3 = rw_2(= 1/s_1);$	
	$w_4 = w_3^2, w_5 = s_1'w_1, s_0'' = s_0'w_2;$	
5	**Compute $U' = (s(l + 2V_1) - k)/U_2 = X^2 + u_1'X + u_0'$:**	$4M$
	$u_0' = (s_0'' - u_{21})(s_0'' - i_1) + u_{11}s_0'' + w + 2v_{11}w_3 + (u_{11} + u_{21})w_4;$	
	$u_1' = 2s_0'' - i_1 - w_4;$	
6	**Compute the resultant $\tilde{r}$ of U_1 and U':**	$4M, 1S$
	$\tilde{i}_1 = u_1' - u_{11}, \tilde{w} = u_{10} - u_0', \tilde{i}_0 = \tilde{i}_1 u_1' + \tilde{w}, \tilde{r} = \tilde{i}_0 \tilde{w} + \tilde{i}_1^2 u_0';$	
7	**Compute the pseudo-inverse $\tilde{I} = \tilde{i}_1 X + \tilde{i}_0 \equiv \tilde{r}/U_1 \bmod U'$:**	$-$
8	**Compute $\tilde{S}' = \tilde{s}_1'X + \tilde{s}_0' = \tilde{r}\tilde{S} \equiv -\tilde{r}S'/r - 2V_1\tilde{I} \bmod U'$:**	$7M$
	$\tilde{r}' = \tilde{r}w_5, \tilde{w}_0 = \tilde{i}_0 v_{10}, \tilde{w}_1 = \tilde{i}_1 v_{11}, \tilde{s}_0' = -[\tilde{r}'s_0' + 2(\tilde{w}_0 - u_0'\tilde{w}_1)];$	
	$\tilde{s}_1' = -[\tilde{r}'s_1' + 2((\tilde{i}_0 + \tilde{i}_1)(v_{10} + v_{11}) - \tilde{w}_0 - \tilde{w}_1(1 + u_1'))];$ If $\tilde{s}_1' = 0$, see below	
9	**Compute $\tilde{S}'' = X + \tilde{s}_0/\tilde{s}_1 = X + \tilde{s}_0'/\tilde{s}_1'$ and $\tilde{s}_1$:**	$1I, 5M, 2S$
	$\tilde{w}_1 = (\tilde{r}\tilde{s}_1')^{-1}(= 1/\tilde{r}^2 \tilde{s}_1), \tilde{w}_2 = \tilde{r}\tilde{w}_1(= 1/\tilde{s}_1'), \tilde{w}_3 = \tilde{s}_1'^2\tilde{w}_1(= \tilde{s}_1);$	
	$\tilde{w}_4 = \tilde{r}\tilde{w}_2(= 1/\tilde{s}_1), \tilde{w}_5 = \tilde{w}_4^2, \tilde{s}_0'' = \tilde{s}_0'\tilde{w}_2;$	
10	**Compute $\tilde{l}' = \tilde{S}''u_1 = X^3 + \tilde{l}_2'X^2 + \tilde{l}_1'X + \tilde{l}_0'$:**	$2M$
	$\tilde{l}_2' = u_{11} + \tilde{s}_0'', \tilde{l}_1' = u_{11}\tilde{s}_0'' + u_{10}, \tilde{l}_0' = u_{10}\tilde{s}_0'';$	
11	**Compute $U_3 = (\tilde{s}(\tilde{l}' + 2V_1) - k)/U' = X^2 + u_{31}X + u_{30}$:**	$3M$
	$u_{30} = (\tilde{s}_0'' - u_1')(\tilde{s}_0'' - \tilde{i}_1) - u_0' + \tilde{l}_1' + 2v_{11}\tilde{w}_4 + (u_1' + u_{11})\tilde{w}_5;$	
	$u_{31} = 2\tilde{s}_0'' - \tilde{i}_1 - \tilde{w}_5;$	
12	**Compute $V_3 = -(\tilde{l}' + V_1) \bmod U_3 = v_{31}X + v_{30}$:**	$4M$
	$w_1 = \tilde{l}_2' - u_{31}, w_2 = u_{31}w_1 + u_{30} - \tilde{l}_1', v_{31} = w_2\tilde{w}_3 - v_{11};$	
	$w_2 = u_{30}w_1 - \tilde{l}_0', v_{30} = w_2\tilde{w}_3 - v_{10};$	
Sum	$\tilde{s}_1' \neq 0$	$2I, 42M, 5S$
9'	**Compute $\tilde{s}_0$:**	$1I, 1M$
	$\tilde{w}_1 = \tilde{r}^{-1}, \tilde{s}_0 = \tilde{s}_0'\tilde{w}_1;$	
10'	**Compute $U_3 = (k - \tilde{s}(\tilde{l} + 2V_1))/U' = X + u_{30}$:**	$1S$
	$u_{30} = -(u_1' + u_{11} + \tilde{s}_0^2);$	
11'	**Compute $V_3 = -(\tilde{l} + V_1) \bmod U_3 = v_{30}$:**	$2M$
	$w_1 = \tilde{s}_0(u_1' + u_{30}) + v_{11}, w_2 = \tilde{s}_0 + v_{10}, v_{30} = u_0'w_1 - w_2;$	
Sum	$\tilde{s}_1' = 0$	$2I, 31M, 4S$

Our explicit formula of the basic version requires $2I + 42M + 5S$ to calculate $2D_1 + D_2$ for genus 2 HECs over $\mathbb{F}_p$. However, the naive method which separately computes the two divisor class additions will cost $2I + 44M + 6S$ [16]. Therefore, our improvements can save $2M + 1S$ each time the operation $2D_1 + D_2$ is performed.

We note that there exist two inversions in the above explicit formula of the basic version. Therefore, we propose a variant of the basic algorithm where we delay the inversion in Step 4 of Table 1 and combine it with the inversion in Step 6 of Table 1 using Montgomery's trick of simultaneous inversions [8]. Table 2 presents the explicit formula for this variant of the basic algorithm.

Table 2. Explicit Formula for $2D_1 + D_2$ on a HEC of Genus 2 over $\mathbb{F}_p$ – Variant

Input	Genus 2 HEC $C : Y^2 = F(X), F = X^5 + f_3 X^3 + f_2 X^2 + f_1 X + f_0$; Reduced Divisors $D_1 = (U_1, V_1)$ and $D_2 = (U_2, V_2)$, $U_1 = X^2 + u_{11}X + u_{10}, V_1 = v_{11}X + v_{10}$; $U_2 = X^2 + u_{21}X + u_{20}, V_2 = v_{21}X + v_{20}$;	
Output	Reduced Divisor $D_3 = (U_3, V_3) = 2D_1 + D_2$, $U_3 = X^2 + u_{31}X + u_{30}, V_3 = v_{31}X + v_{30}$;	
Step	Expression	Cost
1	**Compute the resultant r of U_1 and U_2:** $i_1 = u_{21} - u_{11}, w = u_{10} - u_{20}, i_0 = i_1 u_{21} + w, r = i_0 w + i_1^2 u_{20}$;	$3M, 1S$
2	**Compute the pseudo-inverse $I = i_1 X + i_0 \equiv r/U_1 \bmod U_2$:**	$-$
3	**Compute $S' = s_1' X + s_0' = rS \equiv (V_2 - V_1)I \bmod U_2$:** $w_0 = v_{20} - v_{10}, w_1 = v_{21} - v_{11}, w_2 = i_0 w_0, w_3 = i_1 w_1, s_0' = w_2 - u_{20} w_3$; $s_1' = (i_0 + i_1)(w_0 + w_1) - w_2 - w_3(1 + u_{21})$; If $s_1' = 0$, see 3.C.ii.a.1.	$5M$
4	**Monic $S'' = X + s_0/s_1 = X + s_0'/s_1'$:**	$-$
5	**Compute $U' = (s(l + 2V_1) - k)/U_2 = X^2 + u_1' X + u_0'$:** $s_q = s_1'^2, w_1 = i_1 s_1', w_2 = s_0' - w_1, R = r^2, u_1' = s_1'(s_0' + w_2) - R$; $u_0' = s_0'(w_2 - w_1) + i_0 s_q + 2r v_{11} s_1' + R(u_{11} + u_{21})$;	$7M, 2S$
6	**Compute the resultant $\tilde{r}$ of U_1 and U':** $\tilde{i}_1 = u_1' - u_{11} s_q, \tilde{w} = u_{10} s_q - u_0', \tilde{i}_0 = u_1' \tilde{i}_1 + \tilde{w} s_q, \tilde{r} = \tilde{i}_0 \tilde{w} + \tilde{i}_1^2 u_0'$;	$6M, 1S$
7	**Compute the pseudo-inverse $\tilde{I} = \tilde{i}_1 X + \tilde{i}_0 \equiv \tilde{r}/U_1 \bmod U'$:**	$-$
8	**Compute $\tilde{S}' = \tilde{s}_1' X + \tilde{s}_0' = \tilde{r}\tilde{S} \equiv -\tilde{r}S'/r - 2V_1 \tilde{I} \bmod U'$:** $\tilde{w}_0 = \tilde{i}_0 v_{10}, \tilde{w}_1 = \tilde{i}_1 v_{11}, \tilde{w}_2 = r s_q, \tilde{s}_0' = -[\tilde{r}s_0' + 2\tilde{w}_2(\tilde{w}_0 - u_0' \tilde{w}_1)]$; $\tilde{s}_1' = -[\tilde{r}s_1' + 2\tilde{w}_2((\tilde{i}_0 + \tilde{i}_1 s_q)(v_{10} + v_{11}) - \tilde{w}_0 - \tilde{w}_1(s_q + u_1'))]$; If $\tilde{s}_1' = 0$, see below	$11M$
9	**Compute $\tilde{S}'' = X + \tilde{s}_0/\tilde{s}_1 = X + \tilde{s}_0'/\tilde{s}_1'$ and $\tilde{s}_1$:** $t_1 = \tilde{r}\tilde{s}_1', t_2 = (t_1 \tilde{w}_2)^{-1}, t_3 = \tilde{w}_2 t_2, t_4 = t_1 t_2, t_5 = rt_4, t_6 = s_q t_4$; $\tilde{w}_1 = rt_3, t_7 = (t_6 \tilde{s}_1')^2, \tilde{w}_3 = t_7 \tilde{w}_1, \tilde{w}_4 = \tilde{r}^2 \tilde{w}_1, \tilde{w}_5 = \tilde{w}_4^2, \tilde{s}_0'' = \tilde{r}\tilde{s}_0' t_3$;	$1I, 12M, 3S$
10	**Adjust:** $u_1' = u_1' t_5, u_0' = u_0' t_5, \tilde{i}_1 = \tilde{i}_1 t_5$;	$3M$
11	**Compute $\tilde{l} = \tilde{S}'' u_1 = X^3 + \tilde{l}_2 X^2 + \tilde{l}_1 X + \tilde{l}_0$:** $\tilde{l}_2 = u_{11} + \tilde{s}_0'', \tilde{l}_1 = u_{11} \tilde{s}_0'' + u_{10}, \tilde{l}_0 = u_{10} \tilde{s}_0''$;	$2M$
12	**Compute $U_3 = (\tilde{s}(\tilde{l} + 2V_1) - k)/U' = X^2 + u_{31}X + u_{30}$:** $u_{30} = (\tilde{s}_0'' - u_1')(\tilde{s}_0'' - \tilde{i}_1) - u_0' + \tilde{l}_1 + 2v_{11}\tilde{w}_4 + (u_1' + u_{11})\tilde{w}_5$; $u_{31} = 2\tilde{s}_0'' - \tilde{i}_1 - \tilde{w}_5$;	$3M$
13	**Compute $V_3 = -(\tilde{l} + V_1) \bmod U_3 = v_{31}X + v_{30}$:** $w_1 = \tilde{l}_2 - u_{31}, w_2 = u_{31} w_1 + u_{30} - \tilde{l}_1, v_{31} = w_2 \tilde{w}_3 - v_{11}$; $w_2 = u_{30} w_1 - \tilde{l}_0, v_{30} = w_2 \tilde{w}_3 - v_{10}$;	$4M$
Sum	$\tilde{s}_1' \neq 0$	$I, 56M, 7S$
9'	**Compute $\tilde{s}_0$ and Adjust:** $\tilde{w}_1 = (\tilde{r}s_q)^{-1}, t_1 = s_q \tilde{w}_1, t_2 = \tilde{r}\tilde{w}_1, \tilde{s}_0 = \tilde{s}_0' t_1 s_q, u_1' = u_1' t_2, u_0' = u_0' t_2$;	$1I, 7M$
10'	**Compute $U_3 = (k - \tilde{s}(\tilde{l} + 2V_1))/U' = X + u_{30}$:** $u_{30} = -(u_1' + u_{11} + \tilde{s}_0^2)$;	$1S$
11'	**Compute $V_3 = -(\tilde{l} + V_1) \bmod U_3 = v_{30}$:** $w_1 = \tilde{s}_0(u_1' + u_{30}) + v_{11}, w_2 = \tilde{s}_0 + v_{10}, v_{30} = u_0' w_1 - w_2$;	$2M$
Sum	$\tilde{s}_1' = 0$	$I, 38M, 6S$

In Table 2, the variant of the basic algorithm needs $I + 56M + 7S$ to calculate $2D_1 + D_2$ for genus 2 HECs over $\mathbb{F}_p$. Compared to our explicit formula of the basic version, we trade $1I$ for $14M + 2S$. Therefore, when we implement genus 2 HECC on some application environments where a field inversion is more expensive than fourteen field multiplications and two field squarings, the variant in Table 2 will be faster than the basic algorithm in Table 1.

3.3   Cost of the NAF Scalar Multiplication

The above trick of efficiently computing $2D_1 + D_2$ has found important applications in some scalar multiplication algorithms such as NAF, JSF and so on [7]. In this subsection, we only compare the average cost per bit scalar when implementing NAF scalar multiplication algorithm with the naive method and our newly derived formulae, respectively, because the NAF scalar multiplication algorithm will be used in our implementation in the next section. The results of comparisons are listed in the following Table 3 (The pre- and post-computations are neglected as in [7]).

Table 3. Average Cost Per Bit for NAF on Genus 2 HECs over $\mathbb{F}_p$

Method	Cost of $2D_1 + D_2$	Cost per bit scalar	$S = 0.8M$
Naive	$2I + 44M + 6S$	$\frac{4}{3}I + \frac{88}{3}M + \frac{16}{3}S$	$1.33I + 33.6M$
Basic Algorithm (Table 1)	$2I + 42M + 5S$	$\frac{4}{3}I + \frac{86}{3}M + 5S$	$1.33I + 32.67M$
Variant (Table 2)	$1I + 56M + 7S$	$1I + \frac{100}{3}M + \frac{17}{3}S$	$1I + 37.87M$

From Table 3, we can see clearly that our basic algorithm saves about 2.8% cost for per bit scalar compared to the naive method and the break-even point of the performance between the basic algorithm and the variant is still when one inversion is equivalent to about sixteen field multiplications.

4   Implementation Results

We implement the proposed algorithms on a Pentium-4 @2.8GHz processor and with C programming language in order to check the correctness and test the performance of our explicit formulae. *Microsoft Developer Studio 6* is used for compilation and debugging. For genus 2 HECC over $\mathbb{F}_q$, the most efficient attack is Pollard's Rho algorithm which takes $O(\sqrt{\#\mathcal{J}_C(\mathbb{F}_q)})$ group operations. This means that for genus 2 HECC a 80-bit finite field is enough to achieve the same security level as 160-bit ECC. Considering the security and efficiency of the implementation, we choose a Mersenne prime $p = 2^{89} - 1$ as the characteristic of the prime field $\mathbb{F}_p$ and develop a fast library for the required field and group operations. The implementation of $\mathbb{F}_p$-arithmetic is basically due to [5,9] and further optimized by using the idea in [12] to yield a fast modular reduction

Table 4. Timings of Group Operation on Genus 2 HECs over $\mathbb{F}_{2^{89}-1}$

Method	$2D_1 + D_2$ in μs	Scalar Multiplication in ms	Performance Improvement
Naive	23.1	2.85	–
Basic Algorithm (Table 1)	21.7	2.78	2.46%
Variant (Table 2)	16.4	2.48	12.98%

procedure. Table 4 summarizes our implementation results and comparisons for the group operation $2D_1 + D_2$ and the NAF scalar multiplication algorithm.

The experimental results of Table 4 show that when compared to the implementation with the naive method the performance of genus 2 HECC can be improved by 2.46% and 12.98% with our basic algorithm and the variant, respectively. Furthermore, due to the high MI-ratio (the ratio of the timing of one inversion to one multiplication) in the target processor, the variant is about 10% faster than the basic algorithm.

5   Conclusion

In this paper, we propose the efficient algorithms for computing $2D_1 + D_2$ in one step for genus 2 HECs over prime fields. Our basic algorithm is the direct generalization of Eisenträger *et al.*s' idea, which can save $2M + 1S$ compared with the naive method in the most frequent case. The performance of the variant will be better than that of the basic algorithm whenever a field inversion is more expensive than about sixteen field multiplications. Based our new explicit formulae, we analyze the average cost of per bit scalar in the NAF scalar multiplication algorithm and implement fast genus 2 HECC over $\mathbb{F}_{2^{89}-1}$. The experimental results show that we can obtain up to 13% performance gain when implementing genus 2 HECC with our newly derived explicit formulae.

References

1. Avanzi, R.M.: Aspects of Hyperelliptic Curves over Large Prime Fields in Software Implementations. In: Joye, M., Quisquater, J.-J. (eds.) CHES 2004. LNCS, vol. 3156, pp. 148–162. Springer, Heidelberg (2004)
2. Avanzi, R.M.: The Complexity of Certain Multi-Exponentiation Techniques in Cryptography. Journal of Cryptology 18(4), 357–373 (2005)
3. Avanzi, R.M., Cohen, H., Doche, C., Frey, G., Lange, T., Nguyen, K., Vercauteren, F.: Handbook of Elliptic and Hyperelliptic Curve Cryptography. Chapman & Hall/CRC, Boca Raton, Florida, USA (2006)
4. Avanzi, R.M., Thériault, N., Wang, Z.: Rethinking Low Genus Hyperelliptic Jacobian Arithmetic over Binary Fields: Interplay of Field Arithmetic and Explicit Formulae, Centre for Applied Cryptographic Research (CACR) Technical Reports, CACR 2006-07, available at http://www.cacr.math.uwaterloo.ca/

5. Bailey, D.V., Paar, C.: Optimal Extension Fields for Fast Arithmetic in Public-Key Algorithms. In: Krawczyk, H. (ed.) CRYPTO 1998. LNCS, vol. 1462, pp. 472–485. Springer, Heidelberg (1998)

6. Cantor, D.: Computing in Jacobian of a Hyperelliptic Curve. Mathematics of Computation 48(177), 95–101 (1987)

7. Ciet, M., Joye, M., Lauter, K., Montgomery, L.: Trading Inversions for Multiplications in Elliptic Curve Cryptography. Design, Codes and Cryptography 39, 189–206 (2006)

8. Cohen, H.: A Course in Computational Algebraic Number Theory. Graduate Texts in Math., vol. 138. Springer, Berlin (1993) (fourth corrected printing, 2000)

9. Hankerson, D., Menezes, A., Vanstone, S.: Guide to Elliptic Curve Cryptography. Springer, New York (2004)

10. Eisenträger, K., Lauter, K., Montgomery, P.L.: Fast Elliptic Arithmetic and Improved Weil Pairing Evaluation. In: Joye, M. (ed.) CT-RSA 2003. LNCS, vol. 2612, pp. 343–354. Springer, Heidelberg (2003)

11. Gaudry, P., Harley, R.: Counting Points on Hyperelliptic Curves over Finite Fields. In: Bosma, W. (ed.) Algorithmic Number Theory. LNCS, vol. 1838, pp. 297–312. Springer, Heidelberg (2000)

12. Gonda, M., Matsuo, K., Aoki, K., Chao, J., Tsujii, S.: Improvements of Addition Algorithm on Genus 3 Hyperelliptic Curves and Their Implementation. IEICE Transactions on Fundamentals of Electronics, Communications and Computer Science E88-A(1), 89–96 (2005)

13. Gordon, D.M.: A Survey of Fast Exponentiation Methods. Journal of Algorithms 27(1), 129–146 (1998)

14. Koblitz, N.: A Family of Jacobian Suitable for Discrete Log Cryptosystems. In: Goldwasser, S. (ed.) CRYPTO 1988. LNCS, vol. 403, pp. 94–99. Springer, Heidelberg (1990)

15. Koblitz, N.: Hyperelliptic Cryptosystems. Journal of Cryptology 1(3), 129–150 (1989)

16. Lange, T.: Formulae for Arithmetic on Genus 2 Hyperelliptic Curves. Applicable Algebra in Engineering, Communication and Computing 15(5), 295–328 (2005)

17. Lange, T., Stevens, M.: Efficient Doubling for Genus Two Curves over Binary Fields. In: Handschuh, H., Hasan, M.A. (eds.) SAC 2004. LNCS, vol. 3357, pp. 170–181. Springer, Heidelberg (2004)

18. Menezes, A., Wu, Y., Zuccherato, R.: An Elementary Introduction to Hyperelliptic Curve, Centre for Applied Cryptographic Research (CACR) Technical Reports, CORR 1996-19, available at http://www.cacr.math.uwaterloo.ca/

19. Mumford, D.: Tata Lectures on Theta II. Prog. Math. 43, Birkhäuser (1984)

20. Nagao, K.: Improving Group Law Algorithms for Jacobians of Hyperelliptic Curves. In: Bosma, W. (ed.) Algorithmic Number Theory. LNCS, vol. 1838, pp. 439–448. Springer, Heidelberg (2000)

21. Wollinger, T.: Software and Harware Implementation of Hyperelliptic Curve Cryptosystems, PhD. thesis, Department of Electrical Engineering and Information Sciences, Ruhr-Universitäet Bochum, Bochum, Germany (2004)

22. Wollinger, T., Pelzl, J., Paar, C.: Cantor versus Harley: Optimization and Analysis of Explicit Formulae for Hyperelliptic Curve Cryptosystems. IEEE Transactions on Computers 54(7), 861–872 (2005)

Appendix: Explicit Formulae in Exceptional Cases

In this appendix, we give the explicit addition formulae for the exceptional cases during the computation procedure of $2D_1 + D_2$, which have been discussed in detail in subsection 3.1. These cases usually appear with a very low probability and therefore have not important influence on the performance of genus 2 HECC. Tables 5 to 9 list the detailed steps and the corresponding cost of the group addition in the exceptional cases. In Tables 5 to 9, $\text{ADD}^{i+j \to k}$ denotes the divisor class addition $D_3 = [U_3, V_3] = D_1 + D_2 = [U_1, V_1] + [U_2, V_2]$, and $\text{TRI}^{i \to k}$ denotes the divisor class tripling $D_3 = [U_3, V_3] = 3D_1 = 3[U_1, V_1]$, where i, j and k are the degrees of U_1, U_2 and U_3, respectively.

Table 5. Explicit Formula for $3D_1$ on a HEC of Genus 2 over $\mathbb{F}_p$: $\text{TRI}^{1 \to 2}$

Input	Genus 2 HEC $C : Y^2 = F(X), F = X^5 + f_3 X^3 + f_2 X^2 + f_1 X + f_0$;	
	Reduced Divisors $D_1 = (U_1, V_1), U_1 = X + u_{10}, V_1 = v_{10}$,	
Output	Reduced Divisor $D_3 = (U_3, V_3) = 3D_1$,	
	$U_3 = X^2 + u_{31} X + u_{30}, V_3 = v_{31} X + v_{30}$;	
Step	**Expression**	**Cost**
1	**Compute $V_2 = v_{21} X + v_{20}$ (See Equation (1)):**	$1I, 4M, 2S$
	$\tilde{u}_{10} = u_{10}^2, \tilde{v}_{10} = v_{10}^2, t_1 = 5\tilde{u}_{10}, t_2 = t_1 + 3f_3, t_3 = u_{10}t_2$;	
	$t_4 = t_3 - 2f_2, t_5 = u_{10}t_4, t_6 = t_5 + f_1, t_7 = (2v_{10})^{-1}$;	
	$v_{21} = t_6 t_7, v_{20} = u_{10}v_{21} + v_{10}$;	
2	**Compute $d_1 = \gcd(U_1, U_2) = X + u_{10} = e_1 U_1 + e_2 U_2$:**	$-$
	$e_1 = 1, e_2 = 0$;	
3	**Compute $d = \gcd(d_1, V_1 + V_2) = 1 = c_1 d_1 + c_2 (V_1 + V_2)$:**	$-$
	$s_1 = c_1 e_1 = c_1, s_2 = c_2 e_2 = 0, s_3 = c_2 = t_7$;	
4	**Compute $U' = U_1^3 d^{-2} = (X + u_{10})^3$:**	$-$
5	**Compute $v' = v_2' X^2 + v_1' X + v_0' \equiv [s_1 U_1 V_2 + s_3(V_1 V_2 + F)]d^{-1} \bmod U'$:**	$4M, 1S$
	$\tilde{v}_{21} = v_{21}^2, v_2' = t_7(f_2 - \tilde{v}_{21} - u_{10}(t_1 + t_2))$;	
	$v_1' = v_{21} + 2u_{10}v_2', v_0' = v_{20} + \tilde{u}_{10}v_2'$;	
6	**Compute $U_3 = X^2 + u_{31} X + u_{30} = (F - V'^2)/U'$:**	$2M, 1S$
	$u_{31} = -(v_2'^2 + 3u_{10}), u_{30} = f_3 + t_1 + \tilde{u}_{10} + v_2'(3u_{10}v_2' - 2v_1')$;	
7	**Compute $V_3 = v_{31} X + v_{30} = -V' \bmod U_3$:**	$2M$
	$v_{31} = u_{31}v_2' - v_1', v_{30} = u_{30}v_2' - v_0'$;	
Sum		$1I, 12M, 4S$

Table 6. Explicit Formula for $D_1 + D_2$ on a HEC of Genus 2 over $\mathbb{F}_p$: $\mathrm{ADD}^{1+2\to 2}$

Input	Genus 2 HEC $C : Y^2 = F(X), F = X^5 + f_3 X^3 + f_2 X^2 + f_1 X + f_0$;	
	Reduced Divisors $D_1 = (U_1, V_1)$ and $D_2 = (U_2, V_2)$,	
	$U_1 = X + u_{10}, V_1 = v_{10}, U_2 = (X + u_{10})(X + u_{20}), V_2 = v_{21}X + v_{20}$	
Output	Reduced Divisor $D_3 = (U_3, V_3) = D_1 + D_2$,	
	$U_3 = X^2 + u_{31}X + u_{30}, V_3 = v_{31}X + v_{30}$;	

Step	Expression	Cost
1	**Compute $V_2 = v_{21}X + v_{20}$ (See Equation (2)):**	$1I, 7M$
	$t_1 = u_{10} - u_{20}, t_2 = v_{20} - v_{10}, t_3 = 2v_{10}, t_4 = v_{20}u_{10}, t_5 = v_{10}u_{20}$;	
	$t_6 = (t_1 t_3)^{-1}, t_7 = t_3 t_6, t_8 = t_1 t_6, v_{21} = t_2 t_7, v_{20} = (t_4 - t_5)t_7$;	
2	**Compute $d_1 = \gcd(U_1, U_2) = X + u_{10} = e_1 U_1 + e_2 U_2$:**	–
	$e_1 = 1, e_2 = 0$;	
3	**Compute $d = \gcd(d_1, V_1 + V_2) = 1 = c_1 d_1 + c_2(V_1 + V_2)$:**	–
	$s_1 = c_1 e_1 = c_1, s_2 = c_2 e_2 = 0, s_3 = c_2 = t_8$;	
4	**Compute $U' = U_1 U_2 d^{-2} = (X + u_{10})^2(X + u_{20})$:**	–
5	**Compute $v' = v_2' X^2 + v_1' X + v_0' \equiv [s_1 U_1 V_2 + s_3(V_1 V_2 + F)]d^{-1} \bmod U'$:**	$6M, 3S$
	$\tilde{u}_{10} = u_{10}^2, \tilde{u}_{20} = u_{20}^2, \tilde{v}_{21} = v_{21}^2, w_1 = u_{10} + u_{20}, w_2 = u_{10} + w_1$;	
	$w_3 = f_2 - \tilde{v}_{21} - w_2(f_3 + \tilde{u}_{10} + \tilde{u}_{20}) - 2\tilde{u}_{10}w_1, v_2' = w_3 t_8$;	
	$v_1' = v_2' w_1 + v_{21}, w_4 = u_{10}u_{20}, v_0' = v_2' w_4 + v_{20}$;	
6	**Compute $U_3 = X^2 + u_{31}X + u_{30} = (F - V'^2)/U'$:**	$3M, 1S$
	$u_{31} = -(v_2'^2 + w_2), w_5 = u_{10}(w_1 + u_{20}), u_{30} = f_3 - 2v_1' v_2' - w_5(u_{31} + 1)$;	
7	**Compute $V_3 = v_{31}X + v_{30} = -V' \bmod U_3$:**	$2M$
	$v_{31} = u_{31}v_2' - v_1', v_{30} = u_{30}v_2' - v_0'$;	
Sum		$1I, 18M, 4S$

Table 7. Explicit Formula for $2D_1 + D_2$ on a HEC of Genus 2 over $\mathbb{F}_p$: $\text{ADD}^{1+2\to 2}$

Input	Genus 2 HEC $C: Y^2 = F(X), F = X^5 + f_3X^3 + f_2X^2 + f_1X + f_0$;	
	Reduced Divisors $D_1 = (U_1, V_1)$ and $D_2 = (U_2, V_2)$,	
	$U_1 = X + u_{10}, V_1 = v_{10}, U_2 = X^2 + u_{21}X + u_{20}, V_2 = v_{21}X + v_{20}$	
Output	Reduced Divisor $D_3 = (U_3, V_3) = 2D_1 + D_2$,	
	$U_3 = X^2 + u_{31}X + u_{30}, V_3 = v_{31}X + v_{30}$;	
Step	**Expression**	**Cost**
1	**Compute the resultant r of U_1 and U_2:**	$1M$
	$i_0 = u_{10} - u_{21}, r = i_0u_{10} + u_{20}$;	
2	**Compute the pseudo-inverse $I = -X + i_0 \equiv r/U_1 \bmod U_2$:**	–
3	**Compute $S' = s_1'X + s_0' = rS \equiv (V_2 - V_1)I \bmod U_2$:**	$3M$
	$w_0 = v_{20} - v_{10}, s_1' = u_{10}v_{21} - w_0, s_0' = i_0w_0 + u_{20}v_{21}$;	
4	**Compute $S = s_1X + s_0 = (s_1'/r)X + (s_0'/r)$:**	–
5	**Compute $U' = (k - S(l + 2V_1))/U_2 = X^2 + u_1'X + u_0'$:**	$5M, 3S$
	$R = r^2, w_0 = u_{10} + u_{21}, w_1 = f_3 + u_{10}^2, u_1' = -(s_1'^2 + Rw_0)$;	
	$u_0' = R(w_1 - u_{20} + u_{21}w_0) - s_1(s_1i_0 + 2s_0)$;	
6	**Compute the resultant $\tilde{r}$ of U_1 and U':**	$2M$
	$\tilde{i}_0 = Ru_{10} - u_1', \tilde{r} = \tilde{i}_0u_{10} + u_0'$;	
	If $\tilde{r} = 0$ then factor $U' = (X + u_{10})(X + u_{20}')$ and see Table 6	
7	**Compute the pseudo-inverse $\tilde{I} = -X + \tilde{i}_0 \equiv \tilde{r}/U_1 \bmod U'$:**	–
8	**Compute $\tilde{S}' = \tilde{s}_1'X + \tilde{s}_0' = \tilde{r}\tilde{S} \equiv -S' - 2V_1\tilde{I} \bmod U'$:**	$2M$
	$\tilde{s}_1' = 2v_{10} - s_1', \tilde{s}_0' = -(Rs_0' + 2v_{10}\tilde{i}_0)$;	
9	**Compute $\tilde{S} = \tilde{s}_1X + \tilde{s}_0$:**	$1I, 6M$
	$\tilde{w} = (\tilde{r}R)^{-1}, t_1 = R\tilde{w}, t_2 = \tilde{r}\tilde{w}, \tilde{s}_1 = R\tilde{s}_1't_1, \tilde{s}_0 = \tilde{s}_0't_1$;	
10	**Adjust:**	$3M$
	$u_1' = u_1't_2, u_0' = u_0't_2, \tilde{i}_0 = \tilde{i}_0t_2$;	
11	**Compute $U_3 = (k - \tilde{S}(\tilde{l} + 2V_1))/U' = X^2 + u_{31}X + u_{30}$:**	$3M, 1S$
	$\tilde{w}_0 = u_{10} + u_1', u_{31} = -(\tilde{s}_1^2 + \tilde{w}_0), u_{30} = w_1 - u_0' + u_1'\tilde{w}_0 - \tilde{s}_1(\tilde{s}_1\tilde{i}_0 + 2\tilde{s}_0)$;	
12	**Compute $V_3 = -(\tilde{l} + V_1) \bmod U_3 = v_{31}X + v_{30}$:**	$3M$
	$v_{31} = \tilde{s}_1(u_{31} - u_{10}) - \tilde{s}_0, v_{30} = \tilde{s}_1u_{30} - \tilde{s}_0u_{10} - v_{10}$;	
Sum		$I, 28M, 4S$

Table 8. Explicit Formula for $2D_1 + D_2$ on a HEC of Genus 2 over $\mathbb{F}_p$: ADD$^{2+1\rightarrow2}$

Input	Genus 2 HEC $C : Y^2 = F(X), F = X^5 + f_3X^3 + f_2X^2 + f_1X + f_0$; Reduced Divisors $D_1 = (U_1, V_1)$ and $D_2 = (U_2, V_2)$, $U_1 = X^2 + u_{11}X + u_{10}, V_1 = v_{11}X + v_{10}, U_2 = X + u_{20}, V_2 = v_{20}$	
Output	Reduced Divisor $D_3 = (U_3, V_3) = 2D_1 + D_2$, $U_3 = X^2 + u_{31}X + u_{30}, V_3 = v_{31}X + v_{30}$;	
Step	Expression	Cost
1	**Compute the resultant $r = U_1 \bmod U_2$:** $r = u_{10} - (u_{11} - u_{20})u_{20}$;	$1M$
2	**Compute the inverse $i \equiv 1/U_1 \bmod U_2$:**	–
3	**Compute $S = s_0 \equiv (V_2 - V_1)i \bmod U_2$:** $s_0 = v_{20} - v_{10} - v_{11}u_{20}$;	$1M$
4	**Compute $K = (F - V_1^2)/U_1 = X^3 + k_2X^2 + k_1X + k_0$:** $k_1 = f_3 + u_{11}^2 - u_{10}$;	$1S$
5	**Compute $U' = (k - S(l + 2V_1))/U_2 = X^2 + u'_1X + u'_0$:** $R = r^2, u'_1 = -(s_0^2 + R(u_{11} + u_{20})), u'_0 = Rk_1 - s_0(s_0u_{11} + 2rv_{11}) - u_{20}u'_1$;	$6M, 2S$
6	**Compute the resultant $\tilde{r}$ of U_1 and U':** $\tilde{i}_1 = u'_1 - Ru_{11}, \tilde{w} = Ru_{10} - u'_0, \tilde{i}_0 = \tilde{i}_1u'_1 + R\tilde{w}, \tilde{r} = \tilde{i}_0\tilde{w} + \tilde{i}_1^2u'_0$; **If $\tilde{r} = 0$ then see Table**	$6M, 1S$
7	**Compute the pseudo-inverse $\tilde{I} = \tilde{i}_1X + \tilde{i}_0 \equiv \tilde{r}/U_1 \bmod U'$:**	–
8	**Compute $\tilde{S}' = \tilde{s}'_1X + \tilde{s}'_0 \equiv \tilde{r}\tilde{S} \equiv -S - 2V_1\tilde{I} \bmod U'$:** $\tilde{w}_0 = \tilde{i}_0v_{10}, \tilde{w}_1 = \tilde{i}_1v_{11}, \tilde{s}'_0 = -(Rrs_0 + 2(\tilde{w}_0 - u'_0\tilde{w}_1))$; $\tilde{s}'_1 = -2((\tilde{i}_0 + R\tilde{i}_1)(v_{10} + v_{11}) - \tilde{w}_0 - \tilde{w}_1(R + u'_1))$; **If $\tilde{s}'_1 = 0$ See Below**	$8M$
9	**Compute $\tilde{S}'' = X + \tilde{s}_0/\tilde{s}_1 = X + \tilde{s}'_0/\tilde{s}'_1$ and $\tilde{s}_1$:** $\tilde{w}_0 = \tilde{r}\tilde{s}'_1, \tilde{w}_1 = (R\tilde{w}_0)^{-1}, R_1 = \tilde{w}_0\tilde{w}_1, R_2 = R_1^2, \tilde{w}_2 = \tilde{r}\tilde{w}_1R_2$; $\tilde{w}_3 = \tilde{s}'^2_1\tilde{w}_1R_3, \tilde{w}_4 = \tilde{r}\tilde{w}_2R_3, \tilde{w}_5 = \tilde{w}_4^2, \tilde{s}''_0 = \tilde{s}'_0\tilde{w}_2R_2$;	$1I, 12M, 3S$
10	**Adjust:** $u'_1 = u'_1R_1, u'_0 = u'_0R_1, \tilde{i}_1 = \tilde{i}_1R_1$;	$3M$
11	**Compute $\tilde{l}' = \tilde{S}''u_1 = X^3 + \tilde{l}'_2X^2 + \tilde{l}'_1X + \tilde{l}'_0$:** $\tilde{l}'_2 = u_{11} + \tilde{s}''_0, \tilde{l}'_1 = u_{11}\tilde{s}''_0 + u_{10}, \tilde{l}'_0 = u_{10}\tilde{s}''_0$;	$2M$
12	**Compute $U_3 = (\tilde{s}(\tilde{l} + 2V_1) - k)/U' = X^2 + u_{31}X + u_{30}$:** $u_{30} = (\tilde{s}''_0 - u'_1)(\tilde{s}''_0 - \tilde{i}_1) - u'_0 + \tilde{l}'_1 + 2v_{11}\tilde{w}_4 + (u'_1 + u_{11})\tilde{w}_5$; $u_{31} = 2\tilde{s}''_0 - \tilde{i}_1 - \tilde{w}_5$;	$3M$
13	**Compute $V_3 = -(\tilde{l} + V_1) \bmod U_3 = v_{31}X + v_{30}$:** $w_1 = \tilde{l}'_2 - u_{31}, w_2 = u_{31}w_1 + u_{30} - \tilde{l}'_1, v_{31} = w_2\tilde{w}_3 - v_{11}$; $w_2 = u_{30}w_1 - \tilde{l}'_0, v_{30} = w_2\tilde{w}_3 - v_{10}$;	$4M$
Sum	$\tilde{s}'_1 \neq 0$	$I, 46M, 7S$
9'	**Compute $\tilde{s}_0$:** $\tilde{w}_1 = (\tilde{r}R)^{-1}, t_1 = \tilde{r}\tilde{w}_1, t_2 = R\tilde{w}_1, \tilde{s}_0 = R\tilde{s}'_0t_2$;	$1I, 5M$
10'	**Adjust:** $u'_1 = u'_1t_1, u'_0 = u'_0t_1$;	$2M$
11'	**Compute $U_3 = (k - \tilde{s}(\tilde{l} + 2V_1))/U' = X + u_{30}$:** $u_{30} = -(u'_1 + u_{11} + \tilde{s}_0^2)$;	$1S$
12'	**Compute $V_3 = -(\tilde{l} + V_1) \bmod U_3 = v_{30}$:** $w_1 = \tilde{s}_0(u'_1 + u_{30}) + v_{11}, w_2 = \tilde{s}_0 + v_{10}, v_{30} = u'_0w_1 - w_2$;	$2M$
Sum	$\tilde{s}'_1 = 0$	$I, 31M, 5S$

Table 9. Explicit Formula for $D_1 + D_2$ on a HEC of Genus 2 over $\mathbb{F}_p$: $\text{ADD}^{2+2\to 2}$

Input	Genus 2 HEC $C: Y^2 = F(X), F = X^5 + f_3 X^3 + f_2 X^2 + f_1 X + f_0$;	
	Reduced Divisors $D_1 = (U_1, V_1)$ and $D_2 = (U_2, V_2)$,	
	$U_1 = X^2 + u_{11}X + u_{10} = (X + u_{p1})(X + u_{p2}), V_1 = v_{11}X + v_{10}$,	
	$U_2 = X^2 + u_{21}X + u_{20} = (X + u_{p1})(X + u_{p3}), V_2 = v_{21}X + v_{20}$;	
Output	Reduced Divisor $D_3 = (U_3, V_3) = D_1 + D_2$,	
	$U_3 = X^2 + u_{31}X + u_{30}, V_3 = v_{31}X + v_{30}$;	
Step	Expression	Cost
1	**Compute $d_1 = \gcd(U_1, U_2) = X + u_{p1} = e_1 U_1 + e_2 U_2$:**	–
	$e_1 = 1, e_2 = 0$;	
2	**Compute $d = \gcd(d_1, V_1 + V_2) = c_1 d_1 + c_2(V_1 + V_2)$:**	–
	If $d = X + u_{10}$ then see below, else $d = 1$ and we have	
	$s_1 = c_1 e_1 = c_1, s_2 = c_2 e_2 = 0, s_3 = c_2$;	
3	**Compute $U' = U_1 U_2 d^{-2} = X^4 + u_3' X^3 + u_2' X^2 + u_1' X + u_0'$:**	$3M$
	$u_3' = u_{11} + u_{21}, t_0 = u_{11}u_{21}, u_2' = u_{10} + u_{20} + t_0, u_0' = u_{10}u_{20}$;	
	$u_1' = (u_{11} + u_{10})(u_{20} + u_{21}) - t_0 - u_0'$;	
4	**Compute $v' = v_3' X^3 + v_2' X^2 + v_1' X + v_0' \equiv [s_1 U_1 V_2 + s_3(V_1 V_2 + F)]d^{-1} \bmod U'$:**	$1I, 20M, 1S$
	$t_1 = v_{11} + v_{21}, t_2 = u_{11}v_{21}, t_3 = u_{21}v_{20}, t_4 = v_{11}v_{21}, t_5 = v_{10}v_{20}$;	
	$t_6 = (v_{10} + v_{11})(v_{20} + v_{21}) - t_4 - t_5, t_7 = (u_{11} + u_{21})(v_{20} + v_{21}) - t_2 - t_3$;	
	$t_8 = v_{10} + v_{20} - t_1 u_{p1}, t_9 = f_3 - t_1 v_{21} - u_2' + u_3'^2, t_{10} = (t_8 t_9)^{-1}$;	
	$c_2 = t_9 t_{10}, v_3' = c_2 t_9, v_2' = c_2(f_2 + t_4 - t_1(t_2 + v_{20}) - u_1' + u_2' u_3')$;	
	$v_1' = c_2(f_1 + t_6 - t_1 t_7 - u_0' + u_1' u_3'), v_0' = c_2(f_0 + t_5 - t_1 t_3 + u_0' u_3')$;	
5	**Compute $U_3 = X^2 + u_{31}X + u_{30} = (V'^2 - F)/U'$:**	$5M, 2S$
	$t_1 = t_8^2 t_{10}, u_{31} = t_1(2v_2' - t_1) - u_3', u_{30} = (v_2' t_1)^2 + 2v_1' t_1 - u_2' - u_3' u_{31}$;	
6	**Compute $V_3 = v_{31}X + v_{30} = -V' \bmod U_3$:**	$4M$
	$t_2 = u_{31}v_3' - v_2', v_{31} = u_{30}v_3' - v_1' - u_{31}t_2, v_{30} = -(u_{30}t_2 + v_0')$;	
Sum	$d = 1$	$1I, 32M, 3S$
3'	**Compute $U_3 = U_1 U_2 d^{-2} = (X + u_{p2})(X + u_{p3})$:**	$1M$
	$u_{31} = u_{p2} + u_{p3}, u_{30} = u_{p2}u_{p3}$;	
4'	**Compute $V' = v_{31}X + v_{30}$:**	$1I, 6M$
	$t_0 = (u_{p2} - u_{p3})^{-1}, t_1 = v_{11}u_{p2} + v_{10}, t_2 = v_{21}u_{p3} + v_{20}$;	
	$t_3 = t_2 - t_1, v_{31} = t_0 t_3, t_4 = t_2 u_{p2} - t_1 u_{p3}, v_{30} = t_0 t_4$;	
Sum	$d = X + u_{10}$	$I, 7M$

Explicit Formulas for Efficient Multiplication in $\mathbb{F}_{3^{6m}}$

Elisa Gorla[1], Christoph Puttmann[2], and Jamshid Shokrollahi[3]

[1] University of Zurich, Switzerland
elisa.gorla@math.unizh.ch
[2] Heinz Nixdorf Institute, University of Paderborn, Germany
puttmann@hni.upb.de
[3] B-IT, Dahlmannstr. 2, Universität Bonn, 53113 Bonn, Germany
current address: System Security Group, Ruhr-Universiy Bochum, D-44780
Bochum, Germany
jamshid@crypto.rub.de

Abstract. Efficient computation of the Tate pairing is an important part of pairing-based cryptography. Recently with the introduction of the Duursma-Lee method special attention has been given to the fields of characteristic 3. Especially multiplication in $\mathbb{F}_{3^{6m}}$, where m is prime, is an important operation in the above method. In this paper we propose a new method to reduce the number of $\mathbb{F}_{3^m}$-multiplications for multiplication in $\mathbb{F}_{3^{6m}}$ from 18 in recent implementations to 15. The method is based on the fast Fourier transform and its explicit formulas are given. The execution times of our software implementations for $\mathbb{F}_{3^{6m}}$ show the efficiency of our results.

Keywords: Finite field arithmetic, fast Fourier transform, Lagrange interpolation, Tate pairing computation.

1 Introduction

Efficient multiplication in finite fields is a central task in the implementation of most public key cryptosystems. A great amount of work has been devoted to this topic (see [1] or [2] for a comprehensive list). The two types of finite fields which are mostly used in cryptographic standards are binary finite fields of type $\mathbb{F}_{2^m}$ and prime fields of type $\mathbb{F}_p$, where p is a prime (cf. [3]). Efforts to efficiently fit finite field arithmetic into commercial processors resulted into applications of medium characteristic finite fields like those reported in [4] and [5]. Medium characteristic finite fields are fields of type $\mathbb{F}_{p^m}$, where p is a prime slightly smaller than the word size of the processor, and has a special form that simplifies the modular reduction. Mersenne prime numbers constitute an example of primes which are used in this context. The security parameter is given by the length of the binary representations of the field elements, and the extension degree m is selected appropriately. Due to security considerations, the extension degree for fields of characteristic 2 or medium characteristic is usually chosen to be prime.

C. Adams, A. Miri, and M. Wiener (Eds.): SAC 2007, LNCS 4876, pp. 173–183, 2007.

With the introduction of the method of Duursma and Lee for the computation of the Tate pairing (see [6]), fields of type $\mathbb{F}_{3^m}$ for m prime have attracted special attention. Computing the Tate pairing on elliptic curves defined over $\mathbb{F}_{3^m}$ requires computations both in $\mathbb{F}_{3^m}$ and in $\mathbb{F}_{3^{6m}}$. In [7] calculations are implemented using the tower of extensions

$$\mathbb{F}_{3^m} \subset \mathbb{F}_{3^{2m}} \subset \mathbb{F}_{3^{6m}}.$$

Multiplications in $\mathbb{F}_{3^{2m}}$ and $\mathbb{F}_{3^{6m}}$ are done using 3 and 6 multiplications, respectively. This requires a total 18 multiplications in $\mathbb{F}_{3^m}$. In this paper we make use of the same extension tower, using 3 multiplications in $\mathbb{F}_{3^m}$ to multiply elements in $\mathbb{F}_{3^{2m}}$. Since we represent the elements of $\mathbb{F}_{3^{6m}}$ as polynomials with coefficients in $\mathbb{F}_{3^{2m}}$, we can use Lagrange interpolation to perform the multiplication. This requires only 5 multiplications in $\mathbb{F}_{3^{2m}}$, thus reducing the total number of $\mathbb{F}_{3^m}$ multiplications from 18 to 15. The method that we propose has a slightly increased number of additions in comparison to the Karatsuba method. Notice however that for $m > 90$ (which is the range used in the cryptographic applications) a multiplication in $\mathbb{F}_{3^m}$ requires many more resources than an addition, therefore the overall resource consumption is reduced, as also shown by the results of our software experiments shown in Sect. 4.

In comparison to the classical multiplication method, the Karatsuba method (see [8], [9], and [7]) reduces the number of multiplications while introducing extra additions. Since the cost of addition grows linearly in the length of the polynomials, when the degree of the field extension gets larger multiplication will be more expensive than addition. Hence the above tradeoff makes sense. The negligibility of the cost of addition compared to that of multiplication has gone so far that the theory of multiplicative complexity of bilinear maps, especially polynomial multiplication, takes into account only the number of variable multiplications (see e.g. [10] and [11]). Obviously this theoretical model is of practical interest only when the number of additions and the costs of scalar multiplications can be kept small. A famous result in the theory of multiplicative complexity establishes a lower bound of $2n + 1$ for the number of variable multiplications needed for the computation of the product of two polynomials of degree at most n. This lower bound can be achieved only when the field contains enough elements (see [12] or [13]). The proof of the theorem uses Lagrange evaluation-interpolation, which is also at the core of our approach. This is similar to the short polynomial multiplication (convolution) methods for complex or real numbers in [14]. In order for this method to be especially efficient, the points at which evaluation and interpolations are done are selected as primitive $(2n + 1)$st roots of unity. In a field of type $\mathbb{F}_{3^{2m}}$, fifth roots of unity do not exist for odd m. We overcome this problem by using fourth roots of unity instead. Notice that a primitive fourth root of unity always exists in a field of type $\mathbb{F}_{3^{2m}}$. We use an extra point to compute the fifth coefficient of the product. An advantage of using a primitive fourth root of unity is that the corresponding interpolation matrix will be a 4×4 DFT matrix, and the evaluations and interpolations can be computed using radix-2 FFT techniques (see [15] or [16]) to save some further number of additions and scalar multiplications. The current work can be considered as the continuation of that in [17] for combination of the linear-time multiplication methods with the classical or Karatsuba ones to achieve efficient polynomial multiplication formulas.

Our work is organized as follows. Section 2 is devoted to explaining how evaluation-interpolation can be used in general to produce short polynomial multiplication methods. In Sect. 3 we show how to apply this method to our special case, and produce explicit formulas for multiplication of polynomials of degree at most 2 over $\mathbb{F}_{3^{2m}}$. In Sect. 4 we fine-tune our method using FFT techniques, and give timing results of software implementations and also explicit multiplication formulas. Section 5 shows how our results can be used in conjunction with the method of Duursma-Lee for computing the Tate pairing on some elliptic and hyperelliptic curves. Section 6 contains some final remarks and conclusions.

2 Multiplication Using Evaluation and Interpolation

We now explain the Lagrange evaluation-interpolation for polynomials with co-efficients in $\mathbb{F}_{p^m}$. Throughout this section m is not assumed to be prime (in the next section we will replace m by $2m$). Let

$$a(z) = a_0 + a_1 z + \cdots + a_n z^n \in \mathbb{F}_{p^m}[z]$$
$$b(z) = a_0 + a_1 z + \cdots + a_n z^n \in \mathbb{F}_{p^m}[z]$$

be given such that

$$p^m > 2n. \tag{1}$$

We represent the product of the two polynomials by

$$c(z) = a(z)b(z) = c_0 + c_1 z + \cdots + c_{2n} z^{2n}$$

and let $e = (e_0, \cdots, e_{2n}) \in \mathbb{F}_{p^m}^{2n+1}$ be a vector with $2n + 1$ distinct entries. Evaluation at these points is given by the map ϕ_e

$$\phi_e : \mathbb{F}_{p^m}[z] \to \mathbb{F}_{p^m}^{2n+1}$$
$$\phi_e(f) = (f(e_0), \cdots, f(e_{2n})).$$

Let $A, B, C \in \mathbb{F}_{p^m}^{2n+1}$ denote the vectors $(a_0, \cdots, a_n, 0, \cdots, 0)$, $(b_0, \cdots, b_n, 0, \cdots, 0)$, and $(c_0, \cdots, c_{2n})$, respectively. Using the above notation we have

$$\phi_e(a) = V_e A^T, \quad \phi_e(b) = V_e B^T, \quad \text{and} \quad \phi_e(c) = V_e C^T,$$

where V_e is the Vandermonde matrix

$$V_e = \begin{pmatrix} 1 & e_0 & \cdots & e_0^{2n} \\ 1 & e_1 & \cdots & e_1^{2n} \\ \vdots & \vdots & \ddots & \vdots \\ 1 & e_{2n} & \cdots & e_{2n}^{2n} \end{pmatrix}.$$

The $2n + 1$ coefficients of the product $c(z) = a(z) \cdot b(z)$ can be computed using interpolation applied to the evaluations of $c(z)$ at the chosen $2n + 1$ (distinct) points of $\mathbb{F}_{p^m}$. These evaluations can be computed by multiplying the evaluations of $a(z)$ and $b(z)$ at these points. This can be formally written as

$$\phi_e(c) = \phi_e(a) * \phi_e(b)$$

where we denote componentwise multiplication of vectors by $*$. Equivalently, if we let W_e be the inverse of the matrix V_e, we have that

$$C^T = W_e(\phi_e(a) * \phi_e(b))$$

which allows us to compute the vector C, whose entries are the coefficients of the polynomial $c(z)$.

When condition (1) is satisfied, the polynomial multiplication methods constructed in this way have the smallest multiplicative complexity, i.e. the number of variable multiplications in $\mathbb{F}_{p^m}$ achieves the lower bound $2n + 1$ (see [12]). Indeed (1) can be relaxed to hold even for $p^m = 2n$. In this case, a virtual element ∞ is added to the finite field. This corresponds to the fact that the leading coefficient of the product is the product of the leading coefficients of the factors.

Application of this method to practical situations is not straightforward, since the number of additions increases and eventually dominates the reduction in the number of multiplications. In order for this method to be efficient, n must be much smaller than p^m. An instance of this occurs when computing in extensions of medium size primes (see e.g. [13]). The case of small values of p is more complicated, even for small values of n. We recall that in this case the entries of the matrix V_e are in $\mathbb{F}_{p^m}$ and are generally represented as polynomials of length $m - 1$ over $\mathbb{F}_p$. For multiplication of V_e by vectors to be efficient, the entries of this matrix must be chosen to be sparse. However, this gives no control on the sparsity of the entries of W_e. Indeed one requirement for the entries of W_e, in the basis $\mathcal{B}$, to be sparse is that the inverse of the determinant of V_e, namely

$$\prod_{0 \le i, j \le 2n, i \ne j} (e_i - e_j)$$

has a sparse representation in $\mathcal{B}$. We are not aware of any method which can be used here. On the other hand, it is known that if the e_i's are the elements of the geometric progression ω^i, $0 \le i \le 2n$, and ω is a $(2n + 1)$st primitive root of unity, then the inverse W_e equals $1/(2n + 1)$ times the Vandermonde matrix whose e_i's are the elements of the geometric progression of ω^{-1} (see [2]). We denote these two matrices by V_ω and $V_{\omega^{-1}}$, respectively. The above fact suggests that choosing powers of roots of unity as interpolation points should enable us to control the sparsity of the entries of the corresponding Vandermonde matrix. Roots of unity are used in different contexts for multiplication of polynomials, e.g. in the FFT (see [2]) or for the construction of short multiplication methods in [14]. In the next section we discuss how to use fourth roots of unity to compute multiplication in $\mathbb{F}_{p^{6m}}$, using only 5 multiplications in $\mathbb{F}_{3^{2m}}$.

3   Multiplication Using Roots of Unity

Elements of $\mathbb{F}_{3^{6m}}$ can be represented as polynomials of degree at most 2 over $\mathbb{F}_{3^{2m}}$. Therefore, their product is given by a polynomial of degree at most 4 with coefficients in $\mathbb{F}_{3^{2m}}$. In order to use the classical evaluation-interpolation method we would need a primitive fifth root of unity. This would require $3^{2m} - 1$ to be a multiple of 5, and this is never the case unless m is even (recall that cryptographic applications require m to be prime). However using the relation

$$c_4 = a_2 b_2 \tag{2}$$

we can compute the coefficients of $c(x)$ via

$$\begin{pmatrix} 1 & 1 & 1 & 1 \\ 1 & \omega & \omega^2 & \omega^3 \\ 1 & \omega^2 & 1 & \omega^2 \\ 1 & \omega^3 & \omega^2 & \omega \end{pmatrix} \begin{pmatrix} c_0 \\ c_1 \\ c_2 \\ c_3 \end{pmatrix} = \begin{pmatrix} a(1)b(1) - c_4 \\ a(\omega)b(\omega) - c_4 \\ a(\omega^2)b(\omega^2) - c_4 \\ a(\omega^3)b(\omega^3) - c_4 \end{pmatrix} \tag{3}$$

where ω is a fourth root of unity. Now we apply (2) and (3) to find explicit formulas for multiplying two polynomials of degree at most 2 over $\mathbb{F}_{3^{2m}}$, where $m > 2$ is a prime.

We follow the tower representation of [7], i.e.

$$\begin{aligned} \mathbb{F}_{3^m} &\cong \mathbb{F}_3[x]/(f(x)) \\ \mathbb{F}_{3^{2m}} &\cong \mathbb{F}_{3^m}[y]/(y^2 + 1) \end{aligned} \tag{4}$$

where $f(x) \in \mathbb{F}_3[x]$ is an irreducible polynomial of degree m. Denote by s the equivalence class of y. Note that for odd $m > 2$, $4 \nmid 3^m - 1$ and hence $y^2 + 1$ is irreducible over $\mathbb{F}_{3^m}$ since the roots of $y^2 + 1$ are fourth roots of unity and are not in $\mathbb{F}_{3^m}$. Let

$$a(z) = a_0 + a_1 z + a_2 z^2, \quad b(z) = b_0 + b_1 z + b_2 z^2 \tag{5}$$

be polynomials in $\mathbb{F}_{p^{3^{2m}}}[z]^{\leq 2}$. Our goal is computing the coefficients of the polynomial

$$c(z) = a(z)b(z) = c_0 + c_1 z + \cdots c_4 z^4.$$

Evaluation of $a(z)$ and $b(z)$ at $(1, s, s^2, s^3) = (1, s, -1, -s)$ can be done by multiplying the Vandermonde matrix of powers of s

$$V_s = \begin{pmatrix} 1 & 1 & 1 & 1 \\ 1 & s & -1 & -s \\ 1 & -1 & 1 & -1 \\ 1 & -s & -1 & s \end{pmatrix} \tag{6}$$

by the vectors $(a_0, a_1, a_2, 0)^T$ and $(b_0, b_1, b_2, 0)^T$, respectively. This yields the vectors

$$\phi_e(a) = \begin{pmatrix} a_0 + a_1 + a_2 \\ a_0 + sa_1 - a_2 \\ a_0 - a_1 + a_2 \\ a_0 - sa_1 - a_2 \end{pmatrix} \quad \text{and} \quad \phi_e(b) = \begin{pmatrix} b_0 + b_1 + b_2 \\ b_0 + sb_1 - b_2 \\ b_0 - b_1 + b_2 \\ b_0 - sb_1 - b_2 \end{pmatrix}.$$

Let $\phi_e(c) = \phi_e(a) * \phi_e(b)$ be the componentwise product of $\phi_e(a)$ and $\phi_e(b)$

$$\phi_e(c) = \begin{pmatrix} P_0 \\ P_1 \\ P_2 \\ P_3 \end{pmatrix} = \begin{pmatrix} (a_0 + a_1 + a_2)(b_0 + b_1 + b_2) \\ (a_0 + sa_1 - a_2)(b_0 + sb_1 - b_2) \\ (a_0 - a_1 + a_2)(b_0 - b_1 + b_2) \\ (a_0 - sa_1 - a_2)(b_0 - sb_1 - b_2) \end{pmatrix}.$$

Using (2) and (3) we get

$$\begin{pmatrix} c_0 \\ c_1 \\ c_2 \\ c_3 \end{pmatrix} = W_s \begin{pmatrix} P_0 - P_4 \\ P_1 - P_4 \\ P_2 - P_4 \\ P_3 - P_4 \end{pmatrix},$$

where $P_4 = a_2 b_2$ and

$$W_s = V_s^{-1} = \begin{pmatrix} 1 & 1 & 1 & 1 \\ 1 & -s & -1 & s \\ 1 & -1 & 1 & -1 \\ 1 & s & -1 & -s \end{pmatrix} \tag{7}$$

Thus the explicit formulas for the coefficients of the product are

$$\begin{aligned} c_0 &= P_0 + P_1 + P_2 + P_3 - P_4 \\ c_1 &= P_0 - sP_1 - P_2 + sP_3 \\ c_2 &= P_0 - P_1 + P_2 - P_3 \\ c_3 &= P_0 + sP_1 - P_2 - sP_3 \\ c_4 &= P_4. \end{aligned} \tag{8}$$

4   Efficient Implementation

We owe the efficiency of our method to the Cooley-Tukey factorization of the DFT matrix ([15]). The matrices V_s and W_s in (6) and (7) are not sparse, but they are the DFT matrices of the fourth roots of unity s and s^3, respectively. Hence they can be factored as a product of two sparse matrices as shown in (9) and (10).

$$V_s = \begin{pmatrix} 1 & 1 & 1 & 1 \\ 1 & s & -1 & -s \\ 1 & -1 & 1 & -1 \\ 1 & -s & -1 & s \end{pmatrix} = \begin{pmatrix} 1 & 1 & 0 & 0 \\ 0 & 0 & 1 & s \\ 1 & -1 & 0 & 0 \\ 0 & 0 & 1 & -s \end{pmatrix} \begin{pmatrix} 1 & 0 & 1 & 0 \\ 0 & 1 & 0 & 1 \\ 1 & 0 & -1 & 0 \\ 0 & 1 & 0 & -1 \end{pmatrix}, \tag{9}$$

$$W_s = \begin{pmatrix} 1 & 1 & 1 & 1 \\ 1 & -s & -1 & s \\ 1 & -1 & 1 & -1 \\ 1 & s & -1 & -s \end{pmatrix} = \begin{pmatrix} 1 & 1 & 0 & 0 \\ 0 & 0 & 1 & -s \\ 1 & -1 & 0 & 0 \\ 0 & 0 & 1 & s \end{pmatrix} \begin{pmatrix} 1 & 0 & 1 & 0 \\ 0 & 1 & 0 & 1 \\ 1 & 0 & -1 & 0 \\ 0 & 1 & 0 & -1 \end{pmatrix}. \tag{10}$$

The factorizations in (9) and (10) allow us to efficiently compute the product of the matrices V_s and W_s with vectors. Notice also that the product of an element

$\omega = us + v \in \mathbb{F}_{3^m}[s]^{\leq 1} \cong \mathbb{F}_{3^{2m}}$ with s equals $vs - u$. Hence multiplying by s an element of $\mathbb{F}_{3^{2m}}$ is not more expensive than a change of sign.

Notice that in alternative to the Vandermonde matrix corresponding to s we could use the matrix

$$\begin{pmatrix} 1 & 0 & 0 & 0 \\ 1 & 1 & 1 & 1 \\ 1 & -1 & 1 & -1 \\ 1 & s & -1 & -s \end{pmatrix}$$

whose inverse is

$$\begin{pmatrix} 1 & 0 & 0 & 0 \\ s & 1-s & -1-s & s \\ -1 & -1 & -1 & 0 \\ -s & 1+s & -1+s & -s \end{pmatrix}.$$

Obviously the latter matrices are sparse but since they do not possess any special structure up to our knowledge, multiplying them by vectors is more expensive than multiplying V_s and W_s.

Multiplying elements in the field $\mathbb{F}_{3^{6 \cdot 97}}$ is required in the Tate pairing computation on the group of $\mathbb{F}_{3^{97}}$-rational points of the elliptic curves

$$E_d : y^2 = x^3 - x + d \quad d \in \{-1, 1\}$$

defined over $\mathbb{F}_3$. An efficient algorithm for the computation of the Tate pairings on these curves is discussed in [6].

We have implemented the multiplication over $\mathbb{F}_{3^{6 \cdot 97}}$ using the Karatsuba method, the Montgomery method from [18], and our proposed method on a PC with an AMD Athlon 64 processor 3500+. The processor was running at 2.20 GHz and we have used the NTL library (see [19]) for multiplication in $\mathbb{F}_{3^{97}}$. Please note that although we have chosen $m = 97$ for benchmarking purposes, these methods can be applied to any odd $m > 2$ as mentioned in Sect. 3.

Table 1. Comparison of the execution times of the Karatsuba and Montgomery multipliers with the proposed method for $\mathbb{F}_{3^{6m}}$

Multiplication method	Elapsed time (ms)
Karatsuba method	1.698
Montgomery method	1.605
Proposed method	1.451

The execution times are shown in Table 1. For the Karatsuba and the proposed methods we have used the tower of extensions

$$\mathbb{F}_{3^{97}} \subset \mathbb{F}_{3^{2 \cdot 97}} \subset \mathbb{F}_{3^{6 \cdot 97}},$$

where

$$\mathbb{F}_{3^{97}} \cong \mathbb{F}_3[x]/(x^{97} + x^{16} + 2)$$
$$\mathbb{F}_{3^{2\cdot97}} \cong \mathbb{F}_{3^{97}}[y]/(y^2 + 1)$$
$$\mathbb{F}_{3^{6\cdot97}} \cong \mathbb{F}_{3^{2\cdot97}}[z]/(z^3 - z - 1),$$

whereas for the Montgomery method the representation

$$\mathbb{F}_{3^{6\cdot97}} \cong \mathbb{F}_{3^{97}}[y]/(y^6 + y - 1)$$

has been used. Our implementations show that the new method is almost 14% faster than the Karatsuba and 10% faster than the Montgomery method, which is almost the ratio of saved multiplications. This provides further evidence for the fact that the number of multiplications in $\mathbb{F}_{3^{97}}$ is a good indicator of the performance of the method for $\mathbb{F}_{3^{6\cdot97}}$.

Our multiplications are based on the following formulas. Let $\alpha, \beta \in \mathbb{F}_{3^{6\cdot m}}$ be given as:

$$\alpha = a_0 + a_1 s + a_2 r + a_3 rs + a_4 r^2 + a_5 r^2 s,$$
$$\beta = b_0 + b_1 s + b_2 r + b_3 rs + b_4 r^2 + b_5 r^2 s,$$

where $a_0, \cdots, b_5 \in \mathbb{F}_{3^m}$ and $s \in F_3^{2\cdot m}$, $r \in \mathbb{F}_3^{6\cdot m}$ are roots of $y^2 + 1$ and $z^3 - z - 1$, respectively. Let their product $\gamma = \alpha\beta \in \mathbb{F}_{3^{6\cdot m}}$ be

$$\gamma = c_0 + c_1 s + c_2 r + c_3 rs + c_4 r^2 + c_5 r^2 s.$$

The coefficients c_i, for $0 \le i \le 5$ are computed using:

$$P_0 = (a_0 + a_2 + a_4)(b_0 + b_2 + b_4)$$
$$P_1 = (a_0 + a_1 + a_2 + a_3 + a_4 + a_5)(b_0 + b_1 + b_2 + b_3 + b_4 + b_5)$$
$$P_2 = (a_1 + a_3 + a_5)(b_1 + b_3 + b_5)$$
$$P_3 = (a_0 - a_3 - a_4)(b_0 - b_3 - b_4)$$
$$P_4 = (a_0 + a_1 + a_2 - a_3 - a_4 - a_5)(b_0 + b_1 + b_2 - b_3 - b_4 - b_5)$$
$$P_5 = (a_1 + a_2 - a_5)(b_1 + b_2 - b_5)$$
$$P_6 = (a_0 - a_2 + a_4)(b_0 - b_2 + b_4)$$
$$P_7 = (a_0 + a_1 - a_2 - a_3 + a_4 + a_5)(b_0 + b_1 - b_2 - b_3 + b_4 + b_5)$$
$$P_8 = (a_1 - a_3 + a_5)(b_1 - b_3 + b_5)$$
$$P_9 = (a_0 - a_3 - a_4)(b_0 + b_3 - b_4)$$
$$P_{10} = (a_0 + a_1 - a_2 + a_3 - a_4 - a_5)(b_0 + b_1 - b_2 + b_3 - b_4 - b_5)$$
$$P_{11} = (a_1 - a_2 - a_5)(b_1 - b_2 - b_5)$$
$$P_{12} = a_4 b_4$$
$$P_{13} = (a_4 + a_5)(b_4 + b_5)$$
$$P_{14} = a_5 b_5$$
$$c_0 = -P_0 + P_2 - P_3 - P_4 + P_{10} + P_{11} - P_{12} + P_{14};$$
$$c_1 = P_0 - P_1 + P_2 + P_4 + P_5 + P_9 + P_{10} + P_{12} - P_{13} + P_{14}$$
$$c_2 = -P_0 + P_2 + P_6 - P_8 + P_{12} - P_{14}$$
$$c_3 = P_0 - P_1 + P_2 - P_6 + P_7 - P_8 - P_{12} + P_{13} - P_{14}$$
$$c_4 = P_0 - P_2 - P_3 + P_5 + P_6 - P_8 - P_9 + P_{11} + P_{12} - P_{14}$$
$$c_5 = -P_0 + P_1 - P_2 + P_3 - P_4 + P_5 - P_6 + P_7 - P_8 + P_9 - P_{10} +$$
$$P_{11} - P_{12} + P_{13} - P_{14}$$

5   Other Applications of the Proposed Method

Consider the family of hyperelliptic curves

$$C_d : y^2 = x^p - x + d \quad d \in \{-1, 1\} \tag{11}$$

defined over $\mathbb{F}_p$, for $p = 3$ mod. 4. Let m be such that $(2p, m) = 1$ (in practice m will often be prime), and consider the $\mathbb{F}_{p^m}$-rational points of the Jacobian of C_d. An efficient implementation of the Tate pairing on these groups is given by Duursma and Lee in [6] and [20], where they extend analogous results of Barreto et. al. and of Galbraith et. al. for the case $p = 3$. Notice that this family of curves includes the elliptic curves E_d that we mentioned in the last section. In the aforementioned papers it is also shown that the curve C_d has embedding degree $2p$. In order to compute the Tate pairing on this curve, one works with the tower of field extensions

$$\mathbb{F}_{p^m} \subset \mathbb{F}_{p^{2m}} \subset \mathbb{F}_{p^{2pm}}$$

where the fields are represented as

$$\mathbb{F}_{p^{2m}} \cong \mathbb{F}_{p^m}[y]/(y^2 + 1) \quad \text{and} \quad \mathbb{F}_{p^{2pm}} \cong \mathbb{F}_{p^{2m}}[z]/(z^p - z + 2d).$$

Let $a(z), b(z) \in \mathbb{F}_{p^{2pm}}[z]^{\leq p-1}$,

$$a(z) = a_0 + a_1 z + \ldots + a_{p-1} z^{p-1},$$

$$b(z) = b_0 + b_1 z + \ldots + b_{p-1} z^{p-1}.$$

Then $c(z) = a(z)b(z)$ has $2p - 1$ coefficients, two of which can be computed as

$$c_0 = a_0 b_0 \quad \text{and} \quad c_{2(p-1)} = a_{2(p-1)} b_{2(p-1)}.$$

In order to determine the remaining $2p - 3$ coefficients, we can write a Vandermonde matrix with entries in $\mathbb{F}_{p^{2m}}^*$ using, e.g., the elements

$$1, 2, \ldots, p - 1, \pm s, \ldots, \pm \frac{p-3}{2} s, \frac{p-1}{2} s.$$

Another option is writing a Vandermonde matrix using a primitive $2(p - 1)$-st root of unity combined with the relation:

$$c_{2(p-1)} = a_{2(p-1)} b_{2(p-1)}.$$

Notice that there is an element of order $2(p - 1)$ in $\mathbb{F}_{p^2}$, since $2(p - 1) | p^2 - 1$. If a is a primitive element in $\mathbb{F}_{p^2}$, then $\omega = a^{(p+1)/2}$ is a primitive $2(p - 1)$st root of unity.

6   Conclusion

In this paper we derived new formulas for multiplication in $\mathbb{F}_{3^{6m}}$, which use only 15 multiplications in $\mathbb{F}_{3^m}$. Being able to efficiently multiply elements in $\mathbb{F}_{3^{6m}}$ is a central task for the computation of the Tate pairing on elliptic and hyperelliptic curves. Our method is based on the fast Fourier transform, slightly modified to be adapted to the finite fields that we work on. Our software experiments show that this method is at least 10% faster than other proposed methods in the literature. We have also discussed use of these ideas in conjunction with the general methods of Duursma-Lee for Tate pairing computations on elliptic and hyperelliptic curves.

Acknowledgement

The research described in this paper was funded in part by the Swiss National Science Foundation, registered there under grant number 107887, and by the German Research Foundation (Deutsche Forschungsgemeinschaft DFG) under project RU 477/8. We thank also the reviewers for their precise comments.

References

1. Knuth, D.E.: The Art of Computer Programming. In: Seminumerical Algorithms, 3rd edn., vol. 2, Addison-Wesley, Reading MA (1998), First edition (1969)
2. von zur Gathen, J., Gerhard, J.: Modern Computer Algebra, 2nd edn. Cambridge University Press, Cambridge (2003), First edition (1999)
3. Department, U.S.: of Commerce / National Institute of Standards and Technology: Digital Signature Standard (DSS), Federal Information Processings Standards Publication 186-2 (January 2000)
4. Bailey, D.V., Paar, C.: Optimal Extension Fields for Fast Arithmetic in Public-Key Algorithms. In: Krawczyk, H. (ed.) CRYPTO 1998. LNCS, vol. 1462, pp. 472–485. Springer, Heidelberg (1998)
5. Avanzi, R.M., Mihăilescu, P.: Generic Efficient Arithmetic Algorithms for PAFFs (Processor Adequate Finite Fields) and Related Algebraic Structures (Extended Abstract). In: Matsui, M., Zuccherato, R.J. (eds.) SAC 2003. LNCS, vol. 3006, pp. 320–334. Springer, Heidelberg (2004)
6. Duursma, I., Lee, H.: Tate-Pairing Implementations for Tripartite Key Agreement. In: Laih, C.-S. (ed.) ASIACRYPT 2003. LNCS, vol. 2894, pp. 111–123. Springer, Heidelberg (2003)
7. Kerins, T., Marnane, W.P., Popovici, E.M., Barreto, P.S.L.M.: Efficient Hardware for the Tate Pairing Calculation in Characteristic Three. In: Rao, J.R., Sunar, B. (eds.) CHES 2005. LNCS, vol. 3659, pp. 412–426. Springer, Heidelberg (2005)
8. Karatsuba, A., Ofman, Y.: Multiplication of Multidigit Numbers on Automata. Soviet Physics–Doklady 7(7), 595–596 (1963) Translated from Doklady Akademii Nauk SSSR 145(2), 293–294 (July 1962)
9. Paar, C.: Efficient VLSI Architectures for Bit-Parallel Computation in Galois Fields. PhD thesis, Institute for Experimental Mathematics, University of Essen, Essen, Germany (June 1994)

10. Lempel, A., Winograd, S.: A New Approach to Error-Correcting Codes. IEEE Transactions on Information Theory IT-23, 503–508 (1977)
11. Winograd, S.: Arithmetic Complexity of Computations, vol. 33. SIAM, Philadelphia (1980)
12. Bürgisser, P., Clausen, M., Shokrollahi, M.A.: Algebraic Complexity Theory. Grundlehren der mathematischen Wissenschaften, vol. 315. Springer, Heidelberg (1997)
13. Bajard, J.C., Imbert, L., Negre, C.: Arithmetic Operations in Finite Fields of Medium Prime Characteristic Using the Lagrange Representation. IEEE Transactions on Computers 55(9), 1167–1177 (2006)
14. Blahut, R.E.: Fast Algorithms for Digital Signal Processing. Addison-Wesley, Reading MA (1985)
15. Cooley, J.W., Tukey, J.W.: An Algorithm for the Machine Computation of the Complex Fourier Series. Mathematics of Computation 19, 297–331 (1965)
16. Loan, C.V.: Computational Frameworks for the Fast Fourier Transform. Society for Industrial and Applied Mathematics (SIAM), Philadelphia (1992)
17. von zur Gathen, J., Shokrollahi, J.: Efficient FPGA-based Karatsuba Multipliers for Polynomials over $\mathbb{F}_2$. In: Preneel, B., Tavares, S. (eds.) SAC 2005. LNCS, vol. 3897, pp. 359–369. Springer, Heidelberg (2006)
18. Montgomery, P.L.: Five, Six, and Seven-Term Karatsuba-Like Formulae. IEEE Transactions on Computers 54(3), 362–369 (2005)
19. Shoup, V.: NTL: A library for doing number theory, http://www.shoup.net/ntl
20. Duursma, I., Lee, H.S.: Tate Pairing Implementation for Hyperelliptic Curves $y^2 = x^p - x + d$. In: Laih, C.-S. (ed.) ASIACRYPT 2003. LNCS, vol. 2894, pp. 111–123. Springer, Heidelberg (2003)

Linear Cryptanalysis of Non Binary Ciphers
(With an Application to **SAFER**)

Thomas Baignères[1,*], Jacques Stern[2], and Serge Vaudenay[1]

[1] EPFL
CH-1015 Lausanne – Switzerland
thomas.baigneres@epfl.ch, serge.vaudenay@epfl.ch
[2] École normale supérieure
Département d'Informatique 45, rue d'Ulm
75230 Paris Cedex 05, France
jacques.stern@ens.fr

Abstract. In this paper we re-visit distinguishing attacks. We show how to generalize the notion of linear distinguisher to arbitrary sets. Our thesis is that our generalization is the most natural one. We compare it with the one by Granboulan et al. from FSE'06 by showing that we can get sharp estimates of the data complexity and cumulate characteristics in linear hulls. As a proof of concept, we propose a better attack on their toy cipher **TOY100** than the one that was originally suggested and we propose the best known plaintext attack on **SAFER K/SK** so far. This provides new directions to block cipher cryptanalysis even in the binary case. On the constructive side, we introduce **DEAN18**, a toy cipher which encrypts blocks of 18 decimal digits and we study its security.

1 Introduction and Mathematical Background

In the digital age, information is always seen as a sequence of bits and, naturally, most practical block ciphers and cryptanalytic tools assume that the text space is made of binary strings. In the literature, a block cipher over a finite set M is commonly defined as a set of permutations $C_k : M \to M$ indexed by a key $k \in \mathcal{K}$, with $M = \{0,1\}^\ell$ [36]. This restriction is quite questionable though, as it is easy to think of specific settings in which it could be desirable to adapt the block size to the data being encrypted. For example, when considering credit card numbers, social security numbers, payment orders, schedules, telegrams, calendars, string of alphabetical characters,... it seems that there is no reason what so ever to restrict to binary strings. Whereas an apparently straightforward solution would be to encode the data prior encryption, the loss in terms of simplicity (inevitably affecting the security analysis) and of efficiency would be unfortunate.

Although most modern block ciphers (e.g., [9, 1, 48, 21, 2]) are defined on a binary set, practical and efficient examples of block ciphers defined on a set of arbitrary size exist (see for example Schroeppel's "omnicipher" Hasty Pudding [45]). Some others, although still defined on binary sets, use a mixture of

---

* Supported by the Swiss National Science Foundation, 200021-107982/1.

C. Adams, A. Miri, and M. Wiener (Eds.): SAC 2007, LNCS 4876, pp. 184–211, 2007.

group laws over the same set. For example, IDEA [30] combines three group structures: exclusive bit or, addition modulo 2^{16} and a tweaked multiplication modulo $2^{16} + 1$. Designing a block cipher with an arbitrary block space can be particularly challenging since the state of the art concerning alternate group structures is very limited. Although differential cryptanalysis [5] (through the theory of Markov ciphers [29]) can be specified over an arbitrary group, linear cryptanalysis [34] is based on a metric (the linear probability) that sticks to bit strings. Applying it to a non-binary block cipher would at least require to generalize this notion. Although several generalizations of linear cryptanalysis exist [23, 50, 15, 28, 46, 16, 18, 17, 37, 20, 19, 42, 47, 24], to the best of our knowledge, none easily applies to, say, modulo 10-based block ciphers. So far, only Granboulan et al. [13] provide a sound treatment on non-binary cipher but mostly address differential cryptanalysis. We show that, for linear cryptanalysis, their data complexity cannot be precisely estimated. Furthermore, no cumulating effect of "linear hull" seems possible. We propose another notion of nonlinearity which fixes all those drawbacks and makes us believe that it is the most natural one.

Outline. In the three first sections of this paper, we re-visit distinguishing attacks on random sources (like stream ciphers or pseudo-random generators) and on random permutations (like block ciphers), in the spirit of Baignères et al. [3], but without assuming that domains are vector spaces. Consequently, the only structure we can consider on these sets is that of finite Abelian groups. In particular, we reconsider linear, optimal, and statistical distinguishers against random sources and linear distinguishers against block ciphers.

The following sections apply this theory to TOY100 and SAFER K/SK (on which we devise the best known plaintext attack so far, showing that our generalization can be useful even in the binary case). On the constructive side, we introduce DEAN18, a toy cipher which encrypts blocks of 18 decimal digits.

Notations. Throughout this paper, random variables $X, Y, \ldots$ are denoted by capital letters, whilst their realizations $x \in \mathcal{X}, y \in \mathcal{Y}, \ldots$ are denoted by small letters. The cardinal of a set $\mathcal{X}$ is denoted $|\mathcal{X}|$. The probability function of a random variable X following a distribution D is denoted $\Pr_{X \in_D \mathcal{X}}[x]$, $P_D(x)$, or abusively $\Pr_X[x]$, when the distribution is clear from the context. A sequence $X_1, X_2, \ldots, X_n$ of n random variables is denoted $\mathbf{X}^n$. Similarly, a sequence $x_1, x_2, \ldots, x_n$ of realizations is denoted $\mathbf{x}^n$. We call *support* of a distribution D the set of all $x \in \mathcal{X}$ such that $P_D(x) \neq 0$. As usual, "iid" means "independent and identically distributed". $\mathbf{1}_A$ is 1 if the predicate A is true, 0 otherwise. The distribution function of the standard normal distribution is denoted

$$\Phi(t) = \frac{1}{\sqrt{2\pi}} \int_{-\infty}^{t} e^{-\frac{1}{2}u^2} du \ .$$

Mathematical Background. Let G be a finite group of order n. We let $L^2(G)$ denote the n-dimensional vector space of complex-valued functions f on G. The conjugate $\overline{f}$ of f is defined by $\overline{f}(a) = \overline{f(a)}$ for all $a \in$ G. We define an *inner* *product* on $L^2(G)$ by $(f_1, f_2) = \sum_{a \in G} f_1(a)\overline{f_2}(a)$. The Euclidean norm of $f \in L^2(G)$ is simply $\|f\|_2 = (f, f)^{1/2} = (\sum_a |f(a)|^2)^{1/2}$. Consequently, $L^2(G)$ is a Hilbert Space. A *character* of G is a homomorphism $\chi : G \to \mathbf{C}^\times$, where $\mathbf{C}^\times$ is the multiplicative group of nonzero complex numbers. Then $\chi(1) = 1$ and $\chi(a_1 a_2) = \chi(a_1)\chi(a_2)$ for all $a_1, a_2 \in G$. Clearly, $\chi(a)$ is a nth root of unity, hence $\overline{\chi}(a) = \chi(a)^{-1}$. The *product* of two characters χ_1 and χ_2 is defined as $\chi_1 \chi_2(a) = \chi_1(a)\chi_2(a)$ for all $a \in G$. The character $\mathbf{1}$ defined by $\mathbf{1}(a) = 1$ for all $a \in G$ is the neutral element for this operation. Clearly, $\chi^{-1} = \overline{\chi}$. The set $\widehat{G}$ of all characters of G is the *dual group* of G and is isomorphic to G.

Lemma 1 (Theorems 4.6 and 4.7 in [40]). *Let G be a finite Abelian group of order n, and let $\widehat{G}$ be its dual group. If $\chi \in \widehat{G}$ (resp. $a \in G$) then*

$$\sum_{a \in G} \chi(a) = \begin{cases} n & \text{if } \chi = \mathbf{1}, \\ 0 & \text{otherwise,} \end{cases} \quad resp. \quad \sum_{\chi \in \widehat{G}} \chi(a) = \begin{cases} n & \text{if } a = 1, \\ 0 & \text{otherwise.} \end{cases}$$

If $\chi_1, \chi_2 \in \widehat{G}$ (resp. $a, b \in G$) then

$$\sum_{a \in G} \chi_1(a)\overline{\chi_2}(a) = \begin{cases} n & \text{if } \chi_1 = \chi_2, \\ 0 & \text{otherwise,} \end{cases} \quad resp. \quad \sum_{\chi \in \widehat{G}} \chi(a)\overline{\chi}(b) = \begin{cases} n & \text{if } a = b, \\ 0 & \text{otherwise.} \end{cases}$$

If $\chi_1, \chi_2 \in \widehat{G}$, we deduce $(\chi_1, \chi_2) = n$ if $\chi_1 = \chi_2$ and 0 otherwise. Therefore, the n characters of $\widehat{G}$ is an orthogonal basis of the vector space $L^2(G)$.

Definition 2 (Fourier transform). *The Fourier transform of $f \in L^2(G)$ is the function $\widehat{f} \in L^2(\widehat{G})$ such that $\widehat{f}(\chi) = (f, \chi)$ for all $\chi \in \widehat{G}$.*

If $\widehat{f} \in L^2(\widehat{G})$ is the Fourier transform of $f \in L^2(G)$, the Fourier inversion is

$$f = \frac{1}{n}\sum_{\chi \in \widehat{G}} \widehat{f}(\chi)\chi.$$

Theorem 3 (Plancherel's formula). *If $\widehat{f} \in L^2(\widehat{G})$ is the Fourier transform of $f \in L^2(G)$, then $\|\widehat{f}\|_2 = \sqrt{n}\|f\|_2$.*

Consider the particular case where $G = \{0, 1\}^k$, $\chi_u(a) = (-1)^{u \bullet a}$ for all $u, a \in G$, and where $\bullet$ denotes the inner dot product in G. The mapping $u \mapsto \chi_u$ is an isomorphism between G and $\widehat{G}$. Consequently, when $G = \{0, 1\}^k$ any character χ of G can be expressed as $\chi(a) = (-1)^{u \bullet a}$ for some $u \in G$. In linear cryptanalysis, u is called a mask and there is a one-to-one mapping between masks and characters. So, it seems reasonable to generalize linear cryptanalysis on any finite Abelian group by using characters instead of masks.

2   Distinguishing a Biased Source of Finite Support

We consider a source generating a sequence of d iid random variables Z^d following a distribution D_s of finite support $\mathcal{Z}$. We wonder whether $D_s = U$ or

$D_s = D$ (where U is the uniform distribution over $\mathcal{Z}$) knowing that these two events are equiprobable and that one of them is eventually true. An algorithm which takes a sequence of d realizations z^d as input and outputs either 0 or 1 is a *distinguisher* $\mathcal{D}$ limited to d samples. The ability to distinguish a distribution from another is the *advantage* of the distinguisher and is defined by

$$\mathrm{Adv}_{\mathcal{D}}^d = \Big| \Pr{}_{U^d} [\mathcal{D} \text{ outputs } 1] - \Pr{}_{D^d} [\mathcal{D} \text{ outputs } 1] \Big|, \tag{1}$$

which is a quantity an adversary would like to maximize. If the set $\mathcal{Z}$ has the structure of an Abelian group, we denote it G and denote by n its cardinality.

2.1 Optimal Distinguishers

Due to the Neyman-Pearson lemma, the best distinguisher is based on the maximum likelihood strategy. It consists in comparing $\Pr_{U^d}[z^d]$ and $\Pr_{D^d}[z^d]$.

Definition 4 (Baignères et al. [3]). *The* Squared Euclidean Imbalance *(SEI)* *of a distribution* D *of finite support* $\mathcal{Z}$ *is defined by*

$$\Delta(D) = |\mathcal{Z}| \sum_{z \in \mathcal{Z}} \left(P_D(z) - \frac{1}{|\mathcal{Z}|} \right)^2 = |\mathcal{Z}| \sum_{z \in \mathcal{Z}} P_D(z)^2 - 1 = |\mathcal{Z}| \, 2^{-H_2(D)} - 1$$

where $H_2(D)$ *is the Rényi entropy of order 2.*

It was shown in [3] that when using d samples $Z_1, \ldots, Z_d \in \mathcal{Z}$ the advantage of the best distinguisher $\mathcal{A}$ is such that

$$\mathrm{Adv}_{\mathcal{D}}^d \approx 1 - 2\Phi(-\sqrt{\lambda}/2), \tag{2}$$

where $\lambda = d \cdot \Delta(D)$. When $\lambda = 1$ we obtain $\mathrm{Adv}_{\mathcal{D}}^d \approx 0.38$. Note also that when $\lambda \ll 1$, the previous equation simplifies to $\mathrm{Adv}_{\mathcal{D}}^d \approx \sqrt{\frac{\lambda}{2\pi}}$, whereas, when $\lambda \gg 1$, it simplifies to $\mathrm{Adv}_{\mathcal{D}}^d \approx 1 - \frac{4e^{-\lambda/8}}{\sqrt{2\pi\lambda}}$. This motivates the rule of thumb that the data complexity for the best distinguisher should be $d \approx 1/\Delta(D)$.

Using Theorem 3, we obtain the following expression for the SEI.

Lemma 5. *Given a distribution* D *whose support is a finite Abelian group* G *of order* n, *we have* $\Delta(D) = n\|P_D - P_U\|_2^2 = \|\widehat{P_D} - \widehat{P_U}\|_2^2 = \sum_{\chi \in \widehat{G} \setminus \{1\}} \big|\widehat{P_D}(\chi)\big|^2.$

2.2 Linear Probabilities

Typically, performing a linear cryptanalysis [34] against a source of bit-strings of length ℓ consists in analyzing one bit of information about each sample z_i, by means of a scalar product between a (fixed) *mask* $u \in \{0,1\}^\ell$. By measuring the statistical bias of this bit, it is sometimes possible to infer whether $D_s = U$ (in which case, the bias should be close to 0) or $D_s = D$ (in which case, the bias may be large). Chabaud and Vaudenay [8] adopted the *linear probability* (LP) [35] defined by $\mathrm{LP}_D(u) = (2\Pr_{X \in_D \{0,1\}^\ell}[u \bullet X = 0] - 1)^2 = (\mathbb{E}_{X \in_D \{0,1\}^\ell}((-1)^{u \bullet X}))^2$ as a fundamental measure for linear cryptanalysis. Given the fact that the source is not necessarily binary, it seems natural to generalize the LP as follows.

Definition 6. *For all group character* $\chi : G \to \mathbf{C}^\times$, *the* linear probability *of a distribution* D *over* G *with respect to* χ *is defined by*

$$\mathrm{LP_D}(\chi) = |\mathrm{E}_{A \in_D G}(\chi(A))|^2 = \left|\sum_{a \in G} \chi(a) P_D(a)\right|^2 = |\widehat{P_D}(\chi)|^2.$$

The LP of χ is simply the square of *magnitude* of the discrete Fourier transform of the probability distribution. In the particular case where $G = \{0,1\}^\ell$, we can see that for any u we have $\mathrm{LP_D}(u) = \mathrm{LP_D}(\chi_u)$, so that Definition 6 indeed generalizes the notion of linear probability.

Granboulan et al. [13] adopted a different metric which can be expressed by $\mathrm{LP_D^{alt}}(\chi) = \max_z \left(\mathrm{Pr}_{A \in_D G}[\chi(A) = z] - \frac{1}{m}\right)^2$ where m is the order of χ. When $m = 2$, we easily obtain $\mathrm{LP_D^{alt}}(\chi) = 4 \cdot \mathrm{LP_D}(\chi)$ but when $m > 2$, there is no simple relation. Nevertheless, we have $\mathrm{LP_D}(\chi) \leq \frac{m^2}{2} \mathrm{LP_D^{alt}}(\chi)$ for $m > 2$. This bound is fairly tight since the following distribution reaches $\mathrm{LP_D}(\chi) = \frac{m^2}{4} \mathrm{LP_D^{alt}}(\chi)$: we let $G = \mathbf{Z}_m$ for $m > 2$, $\chi(x) = e^{\frac{2i\pi}{m} x}$, and $P_D(x) = \frac{1}{m} + \varepsilon \times \cos \frac{2\pi x}{m}$. We have $\mathrm{LP_D^{alt}}(\chi) = \varepsilon^2$ and we can easily compute $\mathrm{LP_D}(\chi) = \frac{m^2}{4} \varepsilon^2$. This shows that our $\mathrm{LP_D}(\chi)$ maybe quite larger than $\mathrm{LP_D^{alt}}(\chi)$.

2.3   Linear Distinguisher

We construct a linear distinguisher as follows. Let

$$\mathrm{sa}(\boldsymbol{z}^d; \chi) = \frac{1}{d} \sum_{j=1}^{d} \chi(z_j) \qquad \text{and} \qquad \mathrm{lp}(\boldsymbol{z}^d; \chi) = |\mathrm{sa}(\boldsymbol{z}^d; \chi)|^2.$$

The statistical average $\mathrm{sa}(\boldsymbol{z}^d; \chi)$ over the sample vector $\boldsymbol{z}^d$ can serve for distinguishing U from D. We define the *order* of the linear distinguisher as the order m of χ in $\widehat{G}$. For example, linear distinguishers of order 2 correspond to classical linear distinguishers. Note that this order must be reasonable so that the implementations can compute the complex number $\mathrm{sa}(\boldsymbol{z}^d; \chi)$.

The law of large numbers tells us that $\mathrm{lp}(\boldsymbol{z}^d; \chi) \xrightarrow[d \to \infty]{} |\mathrm{E}_{Z \in_D G}(\chi(Z))|^2 = \mathrm{LP_D}(\chi)$. Informally, when lp is large, it is likely that $D_s = D$, whereas when it is close to 0, it is likely that $D_s = U$. Consequently, the advantage of a linear distinguisher $\mathcal{D}$ can be defined by optimizing a decision threshold τ, i.e., we have

$$\mathrm{Adv}_{\mathcal{D}}^d(\chi) = \max_{0 < \tau < 1} \left| \mathrm{Pr}_{U^d}[\mathrm{lp}(\boldsymbol{Z}^d; \chi) < \tau] - \mathrm{Pr}_{D^d}[\mathrm{lp}(\boldsymbol{Z}^d; \chi) < \tau] \right|.$$

When the exact distribution of $\chi(Z)$ (for $Z \in_D G$) on the unit circle is known, one can build a more powerful distinguisher. However, we will later show that the best improvement factor that is achievable is not particularly large, due to the fact that the order of χ must be small. Besides, one only knows in practice that the distribution of $\chi(Z)$ belongs to a set of m possible distributions. For instance, considering (regular) linear cryptanalysis (that is, using characters of order 2), the expected value of the statistical average is $\pm \varepsilon$ and thus lies on circle of radius ε. The sign is unknown as it depends on an unknown key. This generalizes to characters of higher order, for which the *exact* value of the mean of the statistical average might allow to know which of the m possible distributions we are dealing with and thus give more information about the key. As for the distinguishing issue, we rather stick to the simpler statistical test based on $\text{lp}(\boldsymbol{Z}^d; \chi)$ only.

The following theorem allows to lower bound the advantage of a linear distinguisher in terms of the linear probability of the source with respect to D.

Theorem 7. *Let* G *be a finite Abelian group and let* $\chi \in \widehat{\mathsf{G}}$. *Using heuristic approximations, the advantage* $\text{Adv}_{\mathcal{D}}^d$ *of a d-limited linear distinguisher* $\mathcal{D}$ *trying to distinguish the uniform distribution* U *from* D *is such that* $\text{Adv}_{\mathcal{D}}^d(\chi) \succeq 1 - 2 \cdot e^{-\frac{d}{4}\text{LP}_{\text{D}}(\chi)}$ *(resp.* $\text{Adv}_{\mathcal{D}}^d(\chi) \succeq 1 - 4 \cdot \Phi\left(-\frac{1}{2}\sqrt{d \cdot \text{LP}_{\text{D}}(\chi)}\right)$*) for* χ *of order at least 3 (resp. of order 2), when d is large enough and under the heuristic assumption that the covariance matrix of* $\text{lp}(\boldsymbol{Z}^d; \chi)$ *is the same for both distributions.*[1]

Proof. Let m be the order of χ. We denote $\chi(Z_j) = e^{\frac{2i\pi}{m}\theta_j}$ for all $j = 1, \ldots, d$ and let $X_j = \cos(\frac{2\pi}{m}\theta_j)$ and $Y_j = \sin(\frac{2\pi}{m}\theta_j)$, so that

$$\text{lp}(\boldsymbol{Z}^d; \chi) = \left|\tfrac{1}{d}\textstyle\sum_{j=1}^{d} X_j + i \cdot \tfrac{1}{d}\sum_{j=1}^{d} Y_j\right|^2 = \left(\tfrac{1}{d}\textstyle\sum_{j=1}^{d} X_j\right)^2 + \left(\tfrac{1}{d}\sum_{j=1}^{d} Y_j\right)^2.$$

The law of large numbers gives $\frac{1}{d}\sum_{j=1}^{d} X_j + i \cdot \frac{1}{d}\sum_{j=1}^{d} Y_j \to \text{E}_{Z \in_{\text{D}} \mathsf{G}}(\chi(Z))$ when $d \to \infty$. Considering complex numbers as bidimensional vectors, we obtain from the multivariate central limit theorem [11] that the distribution of $\sqrt{d}(\frac{1}{d}\sum_{j=1}^{d}(X_j + iY_j) - \text{E}_Z(\chi(Z)))$ tends to the bivariate normal distribution with zero expectation and appropriate covariance matrix Σ. We can show that

$$\Sigma = \begin{pmatrix} \frac{1}{2} & 0 \\ 0 & \frac{1}{2} \end{pmatrix} \text{ for } m \geq 3 \text{ and } \Sigma = \begin{pmatrix} 1 & 0 \\ 0 & 0 \end{pmatrix} \text{ for } m = 2.$$

We conclude that, when $\mathsf{D_s} = \mathsf{U}$ and $m \geq 3$, the sums $\frac{1}{\sqrt{d}}\sum X_j$ and $\frac{1}{\sqrt{d}}\sum Y_j$ are asymptotically independent and follow a normal distribution with zero expectation and standard deviation equal to $1/\sqrt{2}$. Consequently, $(\frac{\sqrt{2}}{\sqrt{d}}\sum X_j)^2$ and $(\frac{\sqrt{2}}{\sqrt{d}}\sum Y_j)^2$ both follow a chi-square distribution with 1 degree of freedom and $2 \cdot d \cdot \text{lp}(\boldsymbol{Z}^d; \chi) = (\frac{\sqrt{2}}{\sqrt{d}}\sum X_j)^2 + (\frac{\sqrt{2}}{\sqrt{d}}\sum Y_j)^2$ follows a chi-square distribution with 2 degrees of freedom [44]. Hence,

$$\text{Pr}_{\mathsf{U}^d}[2 \cdot d \cdot \text{lp}(\boldsymbol{Z}^d; \chi) < \alpha] \xrightarrow[d \to \infty]{} \frac{1}{2}\int_0^\alpha e^{-u/2}du = 1 - e^{-\frac{\alpha}{2}}. \qquad (3)$$

On the other hand, by making the heuristic approximation that the covariance matrix is the same in the case where $\mathsf{D_s} = \mathsf{D}$, we similarly obtain that

$$\text{Pr}_{\mathsf{D}^d}\left[2 \cdot d \cdot \left|\tfrac{1}{d}\textstyle\sum_{j=1}^{d}(X_j + iY_j) - \text{E}_Z(\chi(Z))\right|^2 < \beta\right] \approx \frac{1}{2}\int_0^\beta e^{-u/2}du = 1 - e^{-\frac{\beta}{2}}. \qquad (4)$$

---

[1] We use the $\succeq$ symbol instead of $\geq$ to emphasize the heuristic assumptions.

Moreover, assuming that $\tau < \mathrm{LP_D}(\chi)$,

$$\mathrm{Pr}_{\mathsf{D}^d}\left[\mathrm{lp}(\boldsymbol{Z}^d;\chi) < \tau\right] \leq \mathrm{Pr}_{\mathsf{D}^d}\left[\left|\tfrac{1}{d}\textstyle\sum_{j=1}^{d}(X_j+iY_j) - \mathrm{E_D}(\chi(Z))\right|^2 \geq (\sqrt{\mathrm{LP_D}(\chi)} - \sqrt{\tau})^2\right]$$

so that for $\alpha \leq 2d\tau$ and $\beta \leq 2d(\sqrt{\mathrm{LP_D}(\chi)} - \sqrt{\tau})^2$,

$$\mathrm{Adv}_{\mathcal{D}}^d(\chi) \geq \mathrm{Pr}_{\mathsf{U}^d}\left[2 \cdot d \cdot \mathrm{lp}(\boldsymbol{Z}^d;\chi) < \alpha\right] - \mathrm{Pr}_{\mathsf{D}^d}\left[2d \cdot \left|\tfrac{1}{d}\textstyle\sum(X_j+iY_j) - \mathrm{E}_Z(\chi(Z))\right|^2 \geq \beta\right].$$

Using Approximation (4) with $\tau = \tfrac{1}{4}\mathrm{LP_D}(\chi)$ we obtain for $\alpha \leq \tfrac{d}{2}\mathrm{LP_D}(\chi)$

$$\mathrm{Adv}_{\mathcal{D}}^d(\chi) \geq 2 \cdot \mathrm{Pr}_{\mathsf{U}}\left[2 \cdot d \cdot \mathrm{lp}(\boldsymbol{Z}^d;\chi) \leq \alpha\right] - 1.$$

Taking (3) as a heuristic approximation with $\alpha = \tfrac{d}{2}\mathrm{LP_D}(\chi)$ leads to the announced result for $m \geq 3$.

For $m = 2$ and $\mathsf{D_s} = \mathsf{U}$, we have that $\tfrac{1}{\sqrt{d}}\sum_{j=1}^{d}X_j$ tends towards a standard normal distribution, so that $\left(\tfrac{1}{\sqrt{d}}\sum_{j=1}^{d}X_j\right)^2$ tends towards a chi-square distribution. Consequently,

$$\mathrm{Pr}_{\mathsf{U}^d}\left[d \cdot \mathrm{lp}(\boldsymbol{Z}^d;\chi) < \alpha\right] \xrightarrow[d \to \infty]{} \frac{1}{\sqrt{2\pi}}\int_0^\alpha \frac{e^{-x/2}}{\sqrt{x}}\,dx = 1 - 2\Phi(-\sqrt{\alpha}).$$

Similar techniques than in the $m \geq 3$ case lead to the announced result.   □

Note that these lower bounds are only useful (otherwise too low) if the number of samples exceeds $\frac{4\ln 2}{\mathrm{LP_D}(\chi)}$ in the large order case and $\frac{2}{\mathrm{LP_D}(\chi)}$ in the order 2 case. For example, when $d = 4/\mathrm{LP_D}(\chi)$ the advantage is greater than 0.26 in the first case and greater than 0.36 in the second. They validate the rule of thumb that the distinguisher works with data complexity $d \approx 1/\mathrm{LP_D}(\chi)$. In contrast, [13] claims without further justification that $1/\mathrm{LP_D^{alt}}(\chi)$ samples are sufficient to reach a large advantage. It appears that this approximation overestimates the data complexity, actually equal to $1/\Delta(\chi(Z))$, which lies in between $\frac{1}{m^2}(\mathrm{LP_D^{alt}}(\chi))^{-1}$ (when all values of $\chi(z)$ are biased, like for the distribution example in Section 2.2 for which we have $\mathrm{LP_D}(\chi) = \frac{m^2}{4}\mathrm{LP_D^{alt}}(\chi)$) and $\frac{1}{2m}(\mathrm{LP_D^{alt}}(\chi))^{-1}$ (like when only two output values u_1 and u_2 of χ are biased and the others are uniformly distributed, and for which $\mathrm{LP_D}(\chi) = |u_1 - u_2|^2\mathrm{LP_D^{alt}}(\chi)$). The correct estimate of the data complexity requires more than just the $\mathrm{LP_D^{alt}}(\chi)$ quantity.

2.4   Case Study: $\mathbf{Z}_m^r$-Based Linear Cryptanalysis

We illustrate the theory with a concrete example, that is, linear cryptanalysis over the additive group $\mathbf{Z}_m^r$. The m^r characters of this group are called *additive characters modulo m* and are the φ_a^m's for $a = (a_1, \ldots, a_r)$ where $a_\ell \in [0, m-1]$ for $\ell = 1, \ldots, r$ defined by $\varphi_a^m(x) = e^{\frac{2\pi i}{m}\sum_{\ell=1}^r a_\ell x_\ell}$ for $x \in \mathbf{Z}_m^r$ (see [40]).

We revisit an example proposed in [3] where a source generating a random variable $X = (X_1, \ldots, X_{n+1}) \in \mathbf{Z}_4^{n+1}$ is considered (n being any large odd integer). When the source follows distribution U, X is uniformly distributed. When the source follows distribution D, $X_1, \ldots, X_n$ are uniformly distributed mutually independent random variables in $\mathbf{Z}_4$ and $X_{n+1} = B + \sum_{\ell=1}^{n} X_\ell$, where B is either 0 or 1 with equal probability and where the addition is performed modulo 4. Considering X as a bitstring of length $2n + 2$, it was shown in [3] that $\max_\alpha \mathrm{LP}_\mathsf{D}(\varphi_\alpha^2) = 2^{-(n+1)}$ (the max being taken over classical linear masks), which means that the source cannot be distinguished from a perfectly random one using a classical linear distinguisher. On the other hand, let $a = (-1, \ldots, -1, 1) \in \mathbf{Z}_4^{n+1}$ and consider the character φ_a^4 over $\mathbf{Z}_4^{n+1}$. In this case we have $\mathrm{LP}_\mathsf{D}(\varphi_a^4) = \left| \mathrm{E}\left(e^{\frac{\pi i}{2}(X_{n+1} - \sum_{\ell=1}^n X_\ell)}\right) \right|^2 = \left| \mathrm{E}\left(e^{\frac{\pi i}{2} B}\right) \right|^2 = \frac{1}{2}$. Note that $\mathrm{LP}_\mathsf{D}^{\mathrm{alt}}(\varphi_a^4) = \frac{1}{16}$. Theorem 7 suggests that $d = 8$ would be enough for an advantage greater than 0.26. More specifically, the distinguisher can eventually decide that $\mathsf{D}_s = \mathsf{U}$ as soon as $\varphi_a^4(X) \notin \{1, i\}$ (since 1 and i are the only possible values for $\mathsf{D}_s = \mathsf{D}$) for some sample X and that $\mathsf{D}_s = \mathsf{D}$ if all samples X return $\varphi_a^4(X) \in \{1, i\}$. For this distinguisher, $\mathrm{Adv}_\mathcal{D}^d = 1 - \frac{1}{2^d}$, so that $d = 1$ is enough to reach an advantage equal to $\frac{1}{2}$. We notice that there can be a huge gap between linear distinguishers of order 2 and linear distinguishers of order 4.

2.5 A Dash of Differential Cryptanalysis

We can consider a natural (see [13]) generalization of the differential probability (DP) and show the link between the LP and the DP (as in [8]). Let $u \in G$ be an arbitrary group element. The *differential probability* of distribution D over G is defined by $\mathrm{DP}_\mathsf{D}(u) = \Pr[A^{-1} \cdot B = u] = \Pr[A \cdot u = B]$, where A and B are independent random variables following the distribution D. We have $\widehat{\mathrm{DP}}_\mathsf{D}(\chi) = \mathrm{LP}_\mathsf{D}(\chi)$ for any $\chi \in \widehat{G}$. Indeed, by definition, $\mathrm{LP}_\mathsf{D}(\chi) = \mathrm{E}_\mathsf{D}(\chi(A))\mathrm{E}_\mathsf{D}(\overline{\chi}(B))$, where A and B are independent random variable following distribution D. Successively using the facts that A and B are independent, that the mean is linear, and that χ is a homomorphism, we have for all $u \in G$

$$\widehat{\mathrm{LP}}_\mathsf{D}(u) = \sum_{\chi \in \widehat{G}} \mathrm{E}_\mathsf{D}(\chi(A)\overline{\chi}(B))\chi(u) = \mathrm{E}_\mathsf{D}\left(\sum_{\chi \in \widehat{G}} \chi(A \cdot u)\overline{\chi}(B)\right),$$

which is an expression that can be further simplified using Lemma 1, finally leading to $\widehat{\mathrm{LP}}_\mathsf{D}(u) = n\mathrm{E}_\mathsf{D}(1_{A \cdot u = B}) = n\Pr_\mathsf{D}[A \cdot u = B] = n\mathrm{DP}_\mathsf{D}(u)$. Generalizing the LP as we do in Definition 6 naturally leads to a real duality between linear and differential cryptanalysis. We note that this is not the case when considering the $\mathrm{LP}_\mathsf{D}^{\mathrm{alt}}$ measurement suggested in [13].

2.6 Links Between Linear and Optimal Distinguishers

Given Lemma 5 and the definition of LP we obtain the following result.

Theorem 8 (Generalization of Proposition 11 in [3]). *Let* D *be a probability distribution of support* G. *The SEI of* D *and the linear probability of* D *are related by*

$$\Delta(\mathsf{D}) = \sum_{\chi \in \widehat{G} \setminus \{1\}} \mathrm{LP}_\mathsf{D}(\chi).$$

This equation is pretty insightful when trying to improve linear distinguishers by using the rule of thumb. If there is a character χ such that $LP_D(\chi)$ overwhelms all other linear probabilities in the previous equation, a single characteristic χ can be used to approximate the linear hull (that is, the cumulative effect of all the characteristics). In that case, one linear distinguisher becomes nearly optimal in term of required number of samples. As another example we can look at the problem of cumulating linear characteristics. In linear cryptanalysis, if we use k independent characteristics of same bias we can best hope to decrease the data complexity by a factor within the order of magnitude of k. This generalizes results by Kaliski and Robshaw [23] and by Biryukov et al. [6].

We can easily deduce useful results for computing the SEI of combinations of independent sources. Namely, for two independent random variables A and B, $\Delta(A + B) \leq \Delta(A)\Delta(B)$ (Piling-up Lemma) and $\Delta(A||B) + 1 \leq (\Delta(A) + 1)(\Delta(B) + 1)$ so $\Delta(A||B)$ is roughly less than $\Delta(A) + \Delta(B)$ (cumulating effect).

Definition 9. *Let D be a probability distribution over a group G and let LP_D^{max} be the maximum value of $LP_D(\chi)$ over $\chi \in \widehat{G} \setminus \{1\}$ of order dividing m, i.e.,*

$$LP_D^{max}(m) = \max_{\substack{\chi \in \widehat{G} \setminus \{1\} \\ \chi^m = 1}} LP_D(\chi).$$

We note that $\Delta(D)$ does not depend on the group structure whereas LP_D^{max} does. We define a metric LP_D^{MAX} which does not.

Definition 10. *Let D be a probability distribution of support G and $\Diamond$ denote an arbitrary group operation on G. We define*

$$LP_D^{MAX}(m) = \max_{\Diamond} LP_D^{max}(m).$$

Corollary 11. *Let D be a probability distribution whose support is the finite group G of order n. For the exponent m of G, we have*

$$\Delta(D) \leq (n - 1) \cdot LP_D^{max}(m) \quad and \quad \Delta(D) \leq (n - 1) \cdot LP_D^{MAX}(m).$$

This result says that the best distinguisher for D has a data complexity at least $n - 1$ times less than the one of the best linear distinguisher.

Going back to the distinguisher based on $\chi(Z)$ for a given χ of order m, we assume that the support of distribution D of $\chi(Z)$ matches the range of χ which is a group G of order $n = m$. Assuming that χ is such that $LP_D(\chi) = LP_D^{max}(m)$ we deduce that the best distinguisher between $\chi(Z)$ and a uniformly distributed random variable on its support needs at most m times less data than the linear distinguisher that we proposed.

2.7 Optimal Distinguisher Made Practical Using Compression

From a computational point of view, the best distinguisher of Section 2.1 cannot be implemented if the order of the group is too large. We consider this situation by denoting H a finite set of large cardinality N and compress the samples using a *projection*

$$h : \mathsf{H} \longrightarrow \mathsf{G},$$

where G is a set of cardinality $n \ll N$. We assume that h is *balanced*. This implies that $n \mid N$. This projection defines, for a random variable $H \in \mathsf{H}$ of distribution $\widetilde{\mathsf{D}_s}$ (either equal to the uniform distribution $\widetilde{\mathsf{U}}$ or to $\widetilde{\mathsf{D}}$), a random variable $h(H) = Z \in \mathsf{G}$ of distribution $\mathsf{D_s}$ (either equal to U or to D). We can easily prove state the following (intuitive) result by using Cauchy's inequality.

Lemma 12 (Projections reduce the imbalance). *Let H and G be two finite Abelian groups of order N and n respectively, such that $n \mid N$. Let $h : \mathsf{H} \to \mathsf{G}$ be a balanced function. Let $\widetilde{\mathsf{D}}$ be a probability distribution of support H and let $H \in \mathsf{H}$ be a random variable following $\widetilde{\mathsf{D}}$. Let D denote the distribution of $h(H) \in \mathsf{G}$. Then $\Delta(\mathsf{D}) \leq \Delta(\widetilde{\mathsf{D}})$.*

The following theorem shows that, in the particular case where the projection is homomorphic, bounding the linear probability of the source is sufficient to bound the advantage of the best distinguisher on the reduced sample space.

Lemma 13 (Generalization of Theorem 13 in [3]). *Let H and G be two finite Abelian groups of order N and n respectively, such that $n \mid N$. Let $h : \mathsf{H} \to \mathsf{G}$ be a surjective group homomorphism. Let $\widetilde{\mathsf{D}}$ be a probability distribution of support H and let $H \in \mathsf{H}$ be a random variable following $\widetilde{\mathsf{D}}$. Let D denote the distribution of $h(H) \in \mathsf{G}$. Then $\Delta(\mathsf{D}) \leq (n-1)\mathrm{LP}_{\widetilde{\mathsf{D}}}^{\max}(n)$.*

Proof. From Theorem 8, we have

$$\Delta(\mathsf{D}) = \sum_{\chi \in \widehat{\mathsf{G}} \backslash \{1\}} \mathrm{LP}_{\mathsf{D}}(\chi) = \sum_{\chi \in \widehat{\mathsf{G}} \backslash \{1\}} \mathrm{LP}_{\widetilde{\mathsf{D}}}(\chi \circ h) \leq (n-1) \max_{\chi \in \widehat{\mathsf{G}} \backslash \{1\}} \mathrm{LP}_{\widetilde{\mathsf{D}}}(\chi \circ h).$$

We note that $\kappa = \chi \circ h$ is a group character of H such that $\kappa^n = 1$. Consequently, $\max_{\chi \in \widehat{\mathsf{G}} \backslash \{1\}} \mathrm{LP}_{\widetilde{\mathsf{D}}}(\chi \circ h) \leq \max_{\substack{\kappa \in \widehat{\mathsf{H}} \backslash \{1\} \\ \kappa^n = 1}} \mathrm{LP}_{\widetilde{\mathsf{D}}}(\kappa).$ □

We stress that the previous theorem only applies when the adversary reduces the text space through a group homomorphism, i.e., in a *linear* way. Indeed, there exists practical examples of random sources with a small $\mathrm{LP}_{\widetilde{\mathsf{D}_s}}^{\max}$ that are significantly broken when the source space is reduced by a (well chosen) non-homomorphic projection (see the example of Section 2.4 with $h(x) = \mathrm{msb}(\varphi_a^4(x))$ and $\mathsf{G} = \mathbf{Z}_2$). Consequently, the previous result tells us nothing about the advantage of an adversary using an arbitrary projection. In what follows we show a security criterion which is *sufficient* to obtain provable security against *any* distinguisher using a balanced projection.

Theorem 14. *Let H and G be two finite sets of cardinality N and n respectively, such that $n \mid N$. Let $h : \mathsf{H} \to \mathsf{G}$ be a balanced projection. Let $\widetilde{\mathsf{D}}$ be a probability distribution of support H and let $H \in \mathsf{H}$ be a random variable following $\widetilde{\mathsf{D}}$. Let D denote the distribution of $h(H) \in \mathsf{G}$. Then*

$$\Delta(\mathsf{D}) \leq (n-1)\mathrm{LP}_{\widetilde{\mathsf{D}}}^{\mathrm{MAX}}(n).$$

Proof. We first define an arbitrary group structure on G. Given h, we can easily construct a group structure on H such that h is a homomorphism. The final result then follows from Lemma 13. □

Consequently, assuming there exists an "efficient" projective distinguisher on $\widetilde{D}$ using a balanced h on a "small" set G, $\Delta(D)$ must be large and n must be small, therefore, $LP_{\widetilde{D}_s}^{MAX}(n)$ is large. Thus, there exists a group structure on H and a character of small order on this group that define an effective linear cryptanalysis: *if we can efficiently distinguish by compressing the samples, we can also do it linearly.* To the best of our knowledge, all widespread block ciphers provably secure against linear cryptanalysis consider in the proof a *specific* group or field structure on the text space. Usually, the more convenient is the one used to actually define the block cipher. Obviously, a potential adversary is not limited to the description considered by the designers. The previous theorem shows that, provided that a known plaintext attack on the block cipher exists, then some *change* to the group structure of the text space is sufficient to perform a successful linear cryptanalysis of the cipher (note that finding the correct group structure might be a non-trivial task). In other words, although the cipher is stated to be provably secure against linear cryptanalysis, it might not be the case when generalizing linear cryptanalysis to other group structures. This is mainly due to the fact that the SEI does not depend on the group structure given to the text space (only the distance of D from the uniform distribution is relevant) whereas the linear probability is a measure that *depends* on the group structure. Consequently, when proving the resistance against linear cryptanalysis, one should ideally bound the value of $LP_{D}^{MAX}(m)$ and not of $LP_{D}^{max}(m)$ (as it is currently the case for most block ciphers).

3   Linear Cryptanalysis of Block Ciphers

The theory developed in the previous section can be applied as-is to study the indistinguishability of a pseudo-random sequence (e.g., the output of a stream cipher) from a perfectly random one. We show in this section how it can be adapted to study the security of block ciphers.

3.1   Generalized Linear Cryptanalysis of Block Ciphers

We consider a block cipher defined on a finite group M and an adversary who is given access to a generator $\mathcal{G}$ generating iid random variables $(M, C(M)) \in M \times M$, where M is a uniformly distributed random variable, and where C is a random permutation of M either equal to C_K (a random instance of a block cipher, the randomness coming from the secret key $K \in K$) or to C^* (the perfect cipher, that is, a uniformly distributed random permutation defined on M). The objective of the adversary is to guess whether $C = C_K$ or $C = C^*$ (i.e., if the permutation implemented by $\mathcal{G}$ was drawn uniformly at random among the set of permutations defined by the block cipher or among the entire set of permutations of M) after a limited number d of samples $S_i = (M_i, C(M_i))$

for $i = 1, \ldots, d$. In a classical linear cryptanalysis (i.e., when $\mathsf{M} = \{0,1\}^n$), the adversary would typically run over all plaintext/ciphertext pairs and add the value of $a \bullet M_i \oplus b \bullet \mathsf{C}(M_i)$ to a counter, where a and b are input/output masks defined on the text space. The adversary eventually guesses whether the generator is implementing an instance of the block cipher or not by measuring the bias of the counter with respect to $d/2$. By choosing the masks with care, the bias may be large when $\mathsf{C} = \mathsf{C}_k$ for some key k. In this situation, the linear probability $\mathrm{LP}^{\mathsf{C}_k}(a,b) = (2 \cdot \Pr_M(a \bullet M \oplus b \bullet \mathsf{C}_k(M) = 0) - 1)^2 = \left| \mathrm{E}((-1)^{a \bullet M \oplus b \bullet \mathsf{C}_k(M)}) \right|^2$ estimates the efficiency of the attack against C_k. The following definition extends this notion to non-binary linear cryptanalysis.

Definition 15. *Let* $\mathsf{C} : \mathsf{M} \to \mathsf{M}$ *be a permutation over a finite set* M. *Let* G_1 *and* G_2 *be two group structures over the same set* M. *For all group characters* $\chi \in \widehat{\mathsf{G}}_1$ *and* $\rho \in \widehat{\mathsf{G}}_2$ *the linear probability of* C *over* M *with respect to* χ *and* ρ *is defined by*

$$\mathrm{LP}^{\mathsf{C}}(\chi, \rho) = \left| \mathrm{E}_{M \in_U \mathsf{M}} \left(\overline{\chi}(M) \rho(\mathsf{C}(M)) \right) \right|^2.$$

If C *is a random permutation, we denote the expected linear probability by* $\mathrm{ELP}^{\mathsf{C}}(\chi, \rho) = \mathrm{E}_{\mathsf{C}}(\mathrm{LP}^{\mathsf{C}}(\chi, \rho))$.

As direct computation of the linear probability on a realistic instance of a block cipher is not practical, the cryptanalyst typically follows a bottom-up approach, in which he first computes the linear probability of small building blocks of the cipher and then extends the result to the whole construction. In the following section, we study several typical building blocks on which block ciphers are often based. We illustrate our results on a toy cipher in Appendix 6.

3.2   A Toolbox for Linear Cryptanalysis

We can look at a block cipher as a circuit made of building blocks and in which every edge is attached to a specific group. From this point of view, a linear characteristic is a family mapping every edge to one character of the attached group. The building blocks we consider are represented on Figure 1. If χ_1 and χ_2 are characters on G_1 and G_2 respectively, we denote by $\chi_1 \| \chi_2 : \mathsf{G}_1 \times \mathsf{G}_2 \to \mathbf{C}^{\times}$ the character mapping $(a, b) \in \mathsf{G}_1 \times \mathsf{G}_2$ on $\chi_1(a)\chi_2(b)$. We assume that the cryptanalyst constructs a linear characteristic in a reversed way [4] (i.e., starting from the end of the block cipher towards the beginning), his objective being to

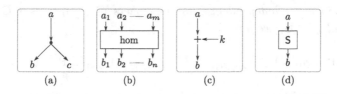

Fig. 1. Typical Building Blocks of Block Ciphers

carefully choose the characters in order to maximize the linear probability on each individual building block.

Building Block (a): We consider a *duplicate gate* such that $a, b, c \in G$ and $a = b = c$. Let χ_1, χ_2 be two characters defined over G, we have (by definition) $\chi_1(b)\chi_2(c) = \chi_1(a)\chi_2(a) = \chi_1\chi_2(a)$. Simply denoting (a) the duplicate gate, we have $\mathrm{LP}^{(a)}(\chi_1\chi_2, \chi_1\|\chi_2) = 1$, so that $\chi_1\|\chi_2$ is an appropriate character on the input of the gate.

Building Block (b): We consider a layer that applies a *group homomorphism* from $G = G_1 \times \cdots \times G_m$ to $H = H_1 \times \cdots \times H_n$. We denote the homomorphism by hom, the m inputs as $a_1, a_2, \ldots, a_m$ and the n outputs $b_1, b_2, \ldots, b_n$, so that $\mathrm{hom}(a_1, a_2, \ldots, a_m) = (b_1, b_2, \ldots, b_n)$. Given n characters χ_i on H_i, $i = 1, \ldots, n$, we have $\chi(b_1, \ldots, b_n) = (\chi \circ \mathrm{hom})(a_1, \ldots, a_m)$ for $\chi = \chi_1\|\cdots\|\chi_n$. As $\chi \circ \mathrm{hom}$ is still a homomorphism from G to $\mathbf{C}^\times$ we obtain $\mathrm{LP}^{(b)}(\chi \circ \mathrm{hom}, \chi) = 1$. Note that we do have $\chi \circ \mathrm{hom} = \chi_1'\|\cdots\|\chi_m'$ for some $(\chi_1', \ldots, \chi_m') \in \widehat{G}_1 \times \cdots \times \widehat{G}_m$, so that χ_i' is an appropriate character for a_i.

Building Block (c): Given $\mathrm{hom}(a) = a + k$ on a given group G (adopting a more traditional additive notation), we have $\chi(b) = \chi(a)\chi(k)$. Since k is constant, $\mathrm{LP}^{(c)}(\chi, \chi) = 1$, so that χ is an appropriate character on the input.

Building Block (d): When considering a (non-homomorphic) permutation S, $\mathrm{LP}^S(\chi, \rho)$ should be computed by considering the substitution table of S.

By piling all relations up on a typical substitution-permutation network C, we obtain a relation of the form $\overline{\chi}(M)\rho(C(M)) = \left(\prod_i \overline{\chi_i}(X_i)\rho(S_i(X_i))\right) \times \left(\prod_j \chi_j(k_j)\right)$ where the first product runs over all building blocks of type (d) and the second over building blocks of type (c). Hence, by making the heuristic approximation of independence of all X_i's (which is commonly done in classical linear cryptanalysis), we obtain that

$$\mathrm{LP}^C(\chi, \rho) \approx \prod_i \mathrm{LP}^{S_i}(\chi_i, \rho_i).$$

This is the classical single-path linear characteristic. Provided that we can lower bound (e.g. using branch numbers) the number of active substitution boxes S to b and that we have $\mathrm{LP}_{\max}^{S_i} \leq \lambda$ for all boxes we obtain that $\mathrm{LP}_{\max}^C$ is heuristically bounded by λ^b for single-path characteristics.

For multipath characteristics, we easily obtain the linear hull effect [41].

Theorem 16. *Given finite Abelian groups $G_0 \ldots, G_r$, let $C = C_r \circ \cdots \circ C_1$ be a product cipher of independent Markov ciphers $C_i : G_{i-1} \longrightarrow G_i$. For any $\chi_0 \in \widehat{G}_0$ and $\chi_r \in \widehat{G}_r$ we have*

$$\mathrm{ELP}^C(\chi_0, \chi_r) = \sum_{\chi_1 \in \widehat{G}_1} \cdots \sum_{\chi_{r-1} \in \widehat{G}_{r-1}} \prod_{i=1}^r \mathrm{ELP}^{C_i}(\chi_{i-1}, \chi_i).$$

It is a common mistake to mix up this result with the hypothesis of stochastic independence. This is a *real* equality which depends on *no* heuristic assumptions.

Proof (Sketch). Recall that a Markov cipher $C : G \longrightarrow G'$ between two groups G and G' is a random mapping such that for any $\delta \in G$ and $\delta' \in G'$ the probability $\Pr[C(x + \delta) = C(x) + \delta']$ does not depend on x.

A straightforward proof is provided in [51] for the binary case. We only have to rephrase it using characters. As a classical result (see e.g. [29]) we easily obtain

$$\mathrm{EDP}^C(\delta_0, \delta_r) = \sum_{\delta_1 \in G_1} \cdots \sum_{\delta_{r-1} \in G_{r-1}} \prod_{i=1}^r \mathrm{EDP}^{C_i}(\delta_{i-1}, \delta_i).$$

Then we simply apply r Fourier transforms.   □

Given d plaintext/ciphertext pairs $z_i = (M_i, C(M_i))$, this geometrically means that the expected value of $\mathrm{sa}(\mathbf{z}^d; (\overline{\chi}, \rho))$ lies on a circle of squared radius equal to $\mathrm{LP}^C(\chi, \rho)$, its exact position on the circle depending on $\prod_j \chi_j(k_j)$.

4   A Z_{100}^{16} Linear Cryptanalysis of TOY100

In [13], Granboulan et al. introduce TOY100, a block cipher that encrypts blocks of 32 decimal digits. The structure of TOY100 is similar to that of the AES. An r rounds version of TOY100 is made of $r - 1$ identical rounds followed by a slightly different final round. Each block is represented as a 4×4 matrix $A = (a_{i,j})_{i,j \in \{0,\ldots,3\}}$, the $a_{i,j}$'s being called subblocks. Round i (for $i = 1, \ldots, r - 1$) first adds modulo 100 a subkey to each subblocks (we do not describe the key schedule here as we assume that the round keys are mutually independent), then applies a fixed substitution box to each resulting subblocks, and finally mixes the subblocks together by applying a linear transformation. The last round replaces the diffusion layer by a modulo 100 subkey addition. The round key addition, confusion and diffusion layers are respectively denoted $\sigma[K]$, γ, and θ. The diffusion layer can be represented as a matrix product $M \times A \times M$ where

$$M = \begin{pmatrix} 1 & 1 & 0 & 1 \\ 1 & 1 & 1 & 0 \\ 0 & 1 & 1 & 1 \\ 1 & 0 & 1 & 1 \end{pmatrix}$$

and where all computations are performed modulo 100. The best attack against TOY100 is based on the generalization of linear cryptanalysis suggested in [13]. It breaks TOY100 reduced to 7 rounds with a data/time complexity of $0.66 \cdot 10^{31}$. We

Table 1. Complexities of the best linear cryptanalysis we obtained on reduced round versions of TOY100

r	Lower bound on $\max_{\alpha_0, \alpha_{r-2}} \mathrm{ELP}^{(\theta \circ \gamma \circ \sigma[K])^{r-2} \circ \theta}(\alpha_0, \alpha_{r-2})$	Data/Time Complexity of the attack against r rounds
4	$0.37 \cdot 10^{-9}$	$0.27 \cdot 10^{10}$
5	$0.47 \cdot 10^{-14}$	$0.21 \cdot 10^{15}$
6	$0.66 \cdot 10^{-19}$	$0.15 \cdot 10^{20}$
7	$0.10 \cdot 10^{-23}$	$0.97 \cdot 10^{24}$
8	$0.18 \cdot 10^{-28}$	$0.55 \cdot 10^{29}$
9	$0.34 \cdot 10^{-33}$	$0.30 \cdot 10^{34}$

propose here a linear cryptanalysis that breaks up to 8 rounds. We first observe that any block

$$A(\delta) = \begin{pmatrix} \delta & 0 & 100 - \delta & 0 \\ 0 & 0 & 0 & 0 \\ 100 - \delta & 0 & \delta & 0 \\ 0 & 0 & 0 & 0 \end{pmatrix}$$

where $\delta \in \{1, \ldots, 99\}$ is such that $M \times A(\delta) \times M = A(\delta)$, i.e., is not changed by the diffusion layer. We let $\mathcal{I} = \{A(\delta), \delta = 1, \ldots, 99\}$ be the set of these 99 blocks. Our attack against TOY100 reduced to r rounds first guesses 4 subblocks of the first round key and 4 subblocks of the last (the positions of which exactly correspond to the non-zero subblocks of $A(\delta)$). This allows to peel-off the first and last layers of substitution boxes, so that we now consider the transformation $(\theta \circ \gamma \circ \sigma[K])^{r-2} \circ \theta$ (where it is understood that the round keys are mutually independent). For any 4×4 input/output masks (i.e., blocks) $\alpha = (\alpha_{i,j})_{i,j \in \{1,\ldots,4\}}$ and $\beta = (\beta_{i,j})_{i,j \in \{1,\ldots,4\}}$ we let, for any transformation C on $\mathbf{Z}_{100}^{16}$,

$$\mathrm{ELP}^{\mathsf{C}}(\alpha, \beta) = \left| \mathrm{E}_M \left(\overline{\varphi_\alpha}(M) \varphi_\beta(\mathsf{C}(M)) \right) \right|^2 \quad \text{where} \quad \varphi_\alpha(M) = e^{\frac{2\pi i}{100} \sum_{i,j=1}^{4} \alpha_{i,j} m_{i,j}}.$$

Applying Theorem 16 and the observation on the diffusion layer of TOY100 we obtain that the linear probability on $(\theta \circ \gamma)^{r-2} \circ \theta$ with input (resp. output) masks $\alpha_0 \in \mathcal{I}$ (resp. $\alpha_{r-2} \in \mathcal{I}$) is such that

$$\mathrm{ELP}^{(\theta \circ \gamma \circ \sigma[K])^{r-2} \circ \theta}(\alpha_0, \alpha_{r-2}) = \mathrm{ELP}^{(\theta \circ \gamma \circ \sigma[K])^{r-2}}(\alpha_0, \alpha_{r-2})$$

$$= \sum_{\alpha_1 \in \mathbf{Z}_{100}^4} \cdots \sum_{\alpha_{r-3} \in \mathbf{Z}_{100}^4} \prod_{i=1}^{r-2} \mathrm{ELP}^{\theta \circ \gamma \circ \sigma[K]}(\alpha_{i-1}, \alpha_i)$$

$$\geq \sum_{\alpha_1 \in \mathcal{I}} \cdots \sum_{\alpha_{r-3} \in \mathcal{I}} \prod_{i=1}^{r-2} \mathrm{ELP}^{\theta \circ \gamma \circ \sigma[K]}(\alpha_{i-1}, \alpha_i)$$

$$= \sum_{\alpha_1 \in \mathcal{I}} \cdots \sum_{\alpha_{r-3} \in \mathcal{I}} \prod_{i=1}^{r-2} \mathrm{LP}^{\gamma}(\alpha_{i-1}, \alpha_i).$$

Practical computations of the previous equations are given in Table 1. Using an 8-round linear hull and guessing the necessary keys on an extra round, we can thus break 9 rounds of TOY100 with data complexity $0.55 \cdot 10^{29}$. We can prove that the time complexity is similar by using classical algorithmic tricks from linear cryptanalysis techniques.

5   A Generalized Cryptanalysis of SAFER K/SK

5.1   A Short Description of SAFER K/SK and Previous Cryptanalysis

The encryption procedures of SAFER K-64, SAFER K-128, SAFER SK-64, and SAFER SK-128 are almost identical. They all iterate the exact same round function, the only difference being that the recommended number of iteration of this round function is 6 for SAFER K-64 [31], 8 for SAFER SK-64 [33], and 10 for

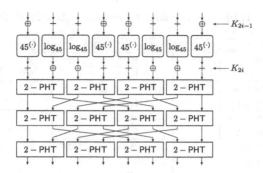

Fig. 2. The ith encryption round function of SAFER

both 128-bit versions of SAFER [31, 33]. The round function is represented on Figure 2. An r-round version of SAFER encrypts 8 bytes of text by applying the round function r times followed by a final mixed key addition (whose structure is identical to the first mixed key addition layer of the round function). Each round is parameterized by two 8-byte round keys so that a $2r + 1$ round keys must be derived from the secret key.

The round function first applies a byte-wise key addition, mixing xor's and additions modulo 256. Then, each byte goes through a substitution box. Two kinds of boxes are used on SAFER: $x \mapsto (45^x \bmod 257) \bmod 256$ and its inverse. The output of the substitution box layer goes through another byte-wise key addition before being processed by a diffusion layer made of boxes called 2-PHT and defined by 2-PHT$(a, b) = (2a+b, a+b)$, the addition being performed modulo 256. Denoting $x \in \mathbf{Z}_{256}^8$ the input of the linear layer, the output $y \in \mathbf{Z}_{256}^8$ can be written as $y = M \times x$ where

$$M = \begin{pmatrix} 8 & 4 & 4 & 2 & 4 & 2 & 2 & 1 \\ 4 & 2 & 2 & 1 & 4 & 2 & 2 & 1 \\ 4 & 4 & 2 & 2 & 2 & 2 & 1 & 1 \\ 2 & 2 & 1 & 1 & 2 & 2 & 1 & 1 \\ 4 & 2 & 4 & 2 & 2 & 1 & 2 & 1 \\ 2 & 1 & 2 & 1 & 2 & 1 & 2 & 1 \\ 2 & 2 & 2 & 2 & 1 & 1 & 1 & 1 \\ 1 & 1 & 1 & 1 & 1 & 1 & 1 & 1 \end{pmatrix}.$$

Finally, we adopt a special notation to denote *reduced-round* versions of SAFER. We consider each of the four round layers as one fourth of a complete round. Consequently, a 2.5 reduced-round version of SAFER corresponds to two full rounds followed by the first mixed key addition and substitution layer of the third round. With these notations, the encryption procedure of SAFER K-64 is actually made of 6.25 rounds. To be consistent with the notations of the original publications, when we refer to a r-round version of SAFER, we actually mean a $r + 0.25$ reduced-round version of SAFER.

For the sake of simplicity, we restrict to give the dependencies of each round key bytes with respect to the main secret key instead of describing the key schedules of the various versions of SAFER.

Table 2. Cryptanalytic results on SAFER K/SK

Type	# rounds	Type of the Attack	Time	Plaintexts	Reference
SAFER K	2	KPA	2^{29}	2^{13}	This paper
SAFER SK	2	KPA	2^{37}	2^{13}	This paper
SAFER K-64	3	KPA/Weak keys	2^{12}	2^{12}	[39]
SAFER K/SK	3	KPA	2^{36}	2^{36}	This paper
SAFER K-64	4	KPA/Weak keys	2^{28}	2^{28}	[39]
SAFER K/SK	4	KPA	2^{47}	2^{47}	This paper
SAFER K-64	5	KPA/Weak keys	2^{58}	2^{58}	[39]
SAFER K	5	CPA	2^{61}	2^{39}	[27, 26]
SAFER K-64	5	CPA	2^{49}	2^{44}	[27, 26]
SAFER K/SK-64	5	CPA	2^{46}	2^{38}	[52]
SAFER K/SK	5	KPA	2^{59}	2^{59}	This paper
SAFER K/SK-64	6	CPA	2^{61}	2^{53}	[52]

- **SAFER K-64:** The jth round key byte $(1 \leq j \leq 8)$ only depends on the jth main secret key byte. For example, guessing the third byte of the main secret key allows to derive the third byte of each round key.
- **SAFER SK-64:** The jth byte $(1 \leq j \leq 8)$ of round key number i $(1 \leq i \leq 2r + 1)$, depends on the ℓth byte of the secret key, where $\ell = (i + j - 2) \bmod 9 + 1$ and where the 9th byte of the secret key is simply the xor of its previous 8 bytes.

In our analysis we assume that the key is a full vector of subkeys. When studying the average complexity of our attack, we further assume that these subkeys are randomly picked with uniform distribution.

Previous Cryptanalysis (see Table 2). Known attacks against SAFER are summarized in Table 2. The resistance of SAFER against differential cryptanalysis [5] was extensively studied by Massey in [32], where it is argued that 5 rounds are sufficient to resist to this attack. It is shown by Knudsen and Berson [27, 26] that 5 rounds can actually be broken using truncated differentials [25], a result which is extended to 6 rounds by Wu et al. in [52]. In [15], Harpes et al. apply a generalization of linear cryptanalysis [34] to SAFER K-64 but do not manage to find an effective homomorphic threefold sum for 1.5 rounds or more. Nakahara et al. showed in [39] that for certain weak key classes, one can find a 3.75-round non-homomorphic linear relation with bias $\epsilon = 2^{-29}$ (which leads to a time/plaintext complexity of $1/\epsilon^2 = 2^{58}$ known plaintexts on five rounds).

The diffusion properties of the linear layer of SAFER have also been widely studied and, compared to the confusion layer, seem to be its major weakness. In [38], Murphy proposes an algebraic analysis of the 2-PHT layer, showing in particular that by considering the message space as a **Z**-module, one can find a particular submodule which is an *invariant* of the 2-PHT transformation. In [49], Vaudenay shows that by replacing the original substitution boxes in a 4 round version of SAFER by random permutations, one obtains in 6.1% of the cases a construction that can be broken by linear cryptanalysis. This also lead Brincat and Meijer to explore potential alternatives of the 2-PHT layer [7]. The other major weakness of SAFER K is indubitably its key schedule. The analysis proposed in [38,26] lead Massey to choose the one proposed by Knudsen in [26] for SAFER SK.

5.2 Linear Cryptanalysis of SAFER: from $\mathbf{Z}_2^8$ to $\mathbf{Z}_{2^8}$

A possible reason why linear cryptanalysis does not seem to be a threat for SAFER is that Matsui's linear characteristics (that fits so well the operations made in DES) are in fact *not* linear when it comes to the diffusion layer of SAFER except when they only focus on the least significant bit of the bytes. Yet, those bits are not biased through the substitution boxes [49]. Indeed, whereas a classical linear cryptanalysis combines text and key bits by performing xor's (i.e., additions in $\mathbf{Z}_2$), SAFER mostly relies on additions in $\mathbf{Z}_{2^8}$. In other words, the group structure that is classically assumed in linear cryptanalysis does not fit when it comes to study SAFER. We will thus focus on the additive group $(\mathbf{Z}_{256}^r, +)$. As noted already in Section 2.4, the 256^r characters of this group are called *additive character modulo* 256 and are the χ_a's for $a = (a_1, \ldots, a_r) \in [0, 255]^r$ defined by $\chi_a(x) = e^{\frac{2\pi i}{256} \sum_{\ell=1}^r a_\ell x_\ell}$ for all $x = (x_1, \ldots, x_r) \in \mathbf{Z}_{256}^r$. The attack on SAFER will only involve additive characters modulo 256. To simplify the notation (and to somehow stick to the vocabulary we are used to in classical linear cryptanalysis), we denote in this section the linear probability of C with respect to χ_a and χ_b by $\mathrm{LP}^C(a, b)$ instead of $\mathrm{LP}^C(\chi_a, \chi_b)$. We call it the linear probability of C with input mask a and output mask b.

Hiding the $\mathbf{Z}_2^8$ Group. As the encryption procedure uses additions modulo 256 together with bit-wise exclusive or, we have to deal with two types of characters. Nevertheless, one can notice that the mixture of group operations only occurs within the *confusion* layer. To simplify the analysis we can think of the succession of a round key xor and a fixed substitution box as a *keyed substitution box* (see Figure 3). Using this point of view, we represent one round of SAFER in Figure 4.

Studying SAFER's Building Blocks. Most of the building of blocks of SAFER were already considered in Section 3.2. With the notations used in this section, the study of the building block (c) can be written as $\mathrm{LP}^{\cdot+k}(a, a) = 1$, where a and k are arbitrary values of $\mathbf{Z}_{256}$. If the key K is random, the previous equation implies that $\mathrm{E}_K(\mathrm{LP}^{\cdot+K}(a, a)) = 1$. Building block (b) allows to deal with the 2-PHT

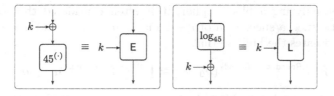

Fig. 3. Viewing key xor and fixed substitution boxes as keyed substitution boxes

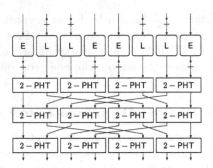

Fig. 4. Another view of SAFER

transformation (which is a homomorphism of $\mathbf{Z}_{256}^2$): denoting by $\boldsymbol{a} = (a_1, a_2) \in \mathbf{Z}_{256}^2$ and $\boldsymbol{b} = (b_1, b_2) \in \mathbf{Z}_{256}^2$ the input and output masks on this transformation, and noting that the 2-PHT transformation is a *symmetric* linear operator (in the sense that 2-PHT^T = 2-PHT), LP$^{\text{2-PHT}}(\boldsymbol{a}, \boldsymbol{b}) = 1 \Leftrightarrow \boldsymbol{a} = $ 2-PHT$(\boldsymbol{b})$. Using the same notations, it is easy to show that when considering the parallel computation of two fixed substitution boxes S_1 and S_2 over $\mathbf{Z}_{256}$, LP$^{\mathsf{S}_1 \| \mathsf{S}_2}(\boldsymbol{a}, \boldsymbol{b}) =$ LP$^{\mathsf{S}_1}(a_1, b_1) \cdot $ LP$^{\mathsf{S}_2}(a_2, b_2)$. When the boxes are random and independent, this leads to $E_{\mathsf{S}_1, \mathsf{S}_2}(\text{LP}^{\mathsf{S}_1 \| \mathsf{S}_2}(\boldsymbol{a}, \boldsymbol{b})) = E_{\mathsf{S}_1}(\text{LP}^{\mathsf{S}_1}(a_1, b_1)) \cdot E_{\mathsf{S}_2}(\text{LP}^{\mathsf{S}_2}(a_2, b_2))$.

Assuming that the key bits are mutually independent, we can now compute the linear probability of *one* full round of SAFER. Indeed if an input/output pair of masks $\boldsymbol{a} = (a_1, \ldots, a_8), \boldsymbol{b} = (b_1, \ldots, b_8)$ are given, and letting $\boldsymbol{b}' = M^T \times \boldsymbol{b} = (b_1', \ldots, b_8')$ (where M is the matrix defined in Section 5.1), then the linear probability on one full round, simply denoted Round, is given by

$$\text{ELP}^{\text{Round}}(\boldsymbol{a}, \boldsymbol{b}) = \prod_{i=1}^{8} \text{ELP}^{\mathsf{S}_i}(a_i, b_i')$$

where S_i corresponds to a keyed E box for $i = 1, 4, 5, 8$ and to a keyed L otherwise.

5.3 Considering Several Rounds of SAFER: the Reduced Hull Effect

When several rounds are considered, Nyberg's linear hull effect [41] applies just as for classical linear cryptanalysis of Markov ciphers (see Theorem 16). Considering a succession of $r > 1$ rounds with independent round keys, and denoting $\boldsymbol{a}_0$ and $\boldsymbol{a}_r$ the input and the output masks respectively, this leads to

$$\text{ELP}^{\text{Round}_r \circ \cdots \circ \text{Round}_1}(\boldsymbol{a}_0, \boldsymbol{a}_r) = \sum_{\boldsymbol{a}_1, \ldots, \boldsymbol{a}_{r-1}} \prod_{i=1}^{r} \text{ELP}^{\text{Round}_i}(\boldsymbol{a}_{i-1}, \boldsymbol{a}_i).$$

When cryptanalyzing a block cipher, it is often considered that one specific characteristic (i.e., a succession of $r + 1$ masks $\boldsymbol{a}_0, \boldsymbol{a}_1, \ldots, \boldsymbol{a}_r$) is overwhelming (i.e., approximates the hull) so that

$$\text{ELP}^{\text{Round}_r \circ \cdots \circ \text{Round}_1}(\boldsymbol{a}_0, \boldsymbol{a}_r) \approx \prod_{i=1}^{r} \text{ELP}^{\text{Round}_i}(\boldsymbol{a}_{i-1}, \boldsymbol{a}_i).$$

This approach was taken by Matsui when cryptanalyzing DES. In that particular case, the correctness of this approximation could be experimentally verified [34].

In this paper we do not consider the full linear hull effect nor restrict ourselves to one specific characteristics. Instead, we consider the characteristics among the hull following a specific *pattern*.

Definition 17. *Let* $a \in \mathbf{Z}_{256}^8$ *be an arbitrary mask. The* pattern *corresponding to the mask* a *is the binary vector of length eight, with zeroes at the zero position of* a *and* $*$ *at the non-zero positions of* a. *The weight* $w(\mathsf{p})$ *of a pattern* p *is the number of* $*$ *in this pattern. We denote the fact that a mask* a *corresponds to pattern* p *by* $a \in \mathsf{p}$. *We denote by* and *the byte-wise masking operation, i.e., given an element* $m \in \mathbf{Z}_{256}^8$ *and a pattern* p, $m' = m$ and p *is such that* $m'_i = 0$ *if* $\mathsf{p}_i = 0$ *and* $m'_i = m_i$ *otherwise, for* $i = 1, \ldots, 8$. *We denote by* $\mathtt{int}_{\mathsf{p}}(m)$ *the integer representation of the concatenation of the bytes of* m and p *corresponding to the non-zero positions of* p, *and by* $\mathcal{I}(\mathsf{p}) = \{\mathtt{int}_{\mathsf{p}}(m) : m \in \mathbf{Z}_{256}^8\}$. *Finally, for an arbitrary integer* $i \in \mathcal{I}(\mathsf{p})$, *we denote* $\mathtt{int}_{\mathsf{p}}^{-1}(i)$ *the element* $m \in \mathsf{p}$ *such that* $\mathtt{int}_{\mathsf{p}}(m) = i$.

For example, the pattern corresponding to $a = [0, 128, 0, 0, 0, 255, 7, 1]$ is $\mathsf{p} = [\mathtt{0*000***}]$ (of weight 4). If $m = [3, 128, 128, 255, 0, 255, 7, 1]$, then m and $\mathsf{p} = a$, and $\mathtt{int}_{\mathsf{p}}(m) = 10000000\,11111111\,00000111\,00000001_2$. Note that for an arbitrary element $m \in \mathbf{Z}_{256}^8$ and any pattern p, $\mathtt{int}_{\mathsf{p}}^{-1}(\mathtt{int}_{\mathsf{p}}(m)) = m$ and p.

The fact that we only consider, among the hull, the characteristics following a given sequence of pattern $\mathsf{p}_0, \mathsf{p}_1, \ldots, \mathsf{p}_r$ can be written as

$$\mathrm{ELP}^{\mathrm{Round}_r \circ \cdots \circ \mathrm{Round}_1}(a_0, a_r) \approx \sum_{\substack{a_1 \in \mathsf{p}_1 \\ \vdots \\ a_{r-1} \in \mathsf{p}_{r-1}}} \prod_{i=1}^r \mathrm{ELP}^{\mathrm{Round}_i}(a_{i-1}, a_i). \tag{5}$$

where $a_0 \in \mathsf{p}_0$ and $a_r \in \mathsf{p}_r$. We call this approximation the *reduced hull effect*. Note that in any case, (5) actually underestimates the true linear hull.

5.4 Sketching the Construction of Reduced Hulls on Two Rounds

In order to construct such *reduced* hulls on SAFER, we start by enumerating the *possible* sequences of patterns $\mathsf{p}_1 \xrightarrow{n} \mathsf{p}_2$ on the linear diffusion layer, where n denotes the number of *distinct* pairs of input/output masks following the pattern $\mathsf{p}_1/\mathsf{p}_2$.[2] We store these sequences in tables (that we do not report here due to space constraints) that we order according to the input/output weights $w_1 \to w_2$ ($1 \leq w_1, w_2 \leq 8$) of the sequence $\mathsf{p}_1 \to \mathsf{p}_2$. To reduce the size of the list, we restrict it to patterns of weight sum 7 or less.

---

[2] For example, on the linear layer, the output mask $[128, 0, 0, 0, 0, 0, 0, 0]$ corresponds to the input mask $[0, 0, 0, 0, 0, 0, 0, 128]$. Moreover, there is no other possible mask with the same input/output patterns, which is denoted $[\mathtt{0000000*}] \xrightarrow{1} [\mathtt{*0000000}]$. Two distinct pairs of masks on the linear layer following the input pattern input pattern $[\mathtt{0000000*}]$ and the output pattern $[\mathtt{***0*000}]$ can be found (namely, $[0, \ldots, 0, 64]$ corresponds to $[192, 128, 128, 0, 128, 0, 0, 0]$ and $[0, \ldots, 0, 192]$ to $[64, 128, 128, 0, 128, 0, 0, 0]$). This is denoted $[\mathtt{0000000*}] \xrightarrow{2} [\mathtt{***0*000}]$.

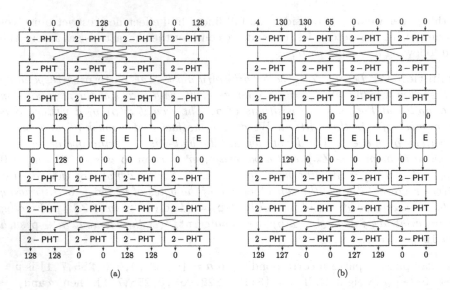

Fig. 5. The characteristics on two successive linear layers of examples 1 and 2

Next, we build characteristics on several rounds based on the lists of possible succession of patterns on the linear layer. We proceed step-by-step, starting with characteristics on two rounds. Two characteristics *on full rounds* can only be concatenated if the output mask of the first one is equal to the input mask of the second one. This translates for patterns as follows: two successions of patterns on the linear layer can only be concatenated if the output pattern of the first succession is equal to the input pattern of the second succession.

Example 1. We can concatenate $[000*000*] \xrightarrow{1} [0*000000]$ and $[0*000000] \xrightarrow{1}$ $[**00**00]$. We denote this by $[000*000*] \xrightarrow{1} [0*000000] \xrightarrow{1} [**00**00]$. This means that succession of patterns of weights $2 \to 1 \to 4$ on two rounds exist. In this particular example, there is only one characteristic corresponding to this succession of masks, which is represented on Figure 5(a).

Example 2. Similarly, we can obtain the succession $[****0000] \xrightarrow{252} [**000000]$ $\xrightarrow{254} [**00**00]$ which is a succession of pattern of weights $4 \to 2 \to 4$ on two rounds. In this case, $252 \times 254 = 64008$ distinct characteristics correspond to this succession (one of which is represented on Figure 5(b)).

Finally, it should be noted that the characteristic of Example 1 actually leads to an ELP equal to 0, as both input and output masks on the substitution box are equal to 128, which is equivalent to computing the traditional linear probability by only considering the least significant bit. In the second example, the computation of the reduced hull leads to a non-zero linear probability.

Table 3. Key Recovery Attack against a r reduced-round version of SAFER

Input: A reduced hull on r rounds with input mask $a_0 \in p_0$ and output mask $a_r \in p_r$.

Output: A set of counters $\text{lp}_{\kappa_1, \kappa_2, \kappa_{2r+1}}$ with $\kappa_1, \kappa_2 = 0, \ldots, 2^{8w(p_0)} - 1$ and $\kappa_{2r+1} = 0, \ldots, 2^{8w(p_r)} - 1$.

Memory: A set of counters $N_{i,j}$ initialized to 0, with $i = 0, \ldots, 2^{8 \cdot w(p_0)} - 1$ and $j = 0, \ldots, 2^{8 \cdot w(p_r)} - 1$.

```
 0: foreach of the d plaintext/ciphertext pair (m, c) do
 1:     i ← int_{p_0}(m) and j ← int_{p_r}(c)
 2:     N_{i,j} ← N_{i,j} + 1
 3: done
 4: foreach (κ_1, κ_2, κ_{2r+1}) ∈ I(p_0) × I(p_0) × I(p_r) do
 5:     k_1 ← int_{p_0}^{-1}(κ_1), k_2 ← int_{p_0}^{-1}(κ_2), and k_{2r+1} ← int_{p_r}^{-1}(κ_{2r+1})
 6:     /* compute the lp corresponding to the round keys guess */
 7:     L ← 0
 8:     foreach (i, j) ∈ [0, ..., 2^{8w(p_0)} - 1] × [0, ..., 2^{8w(p_r)} - 1] such that N_{i,j} > 0 do
 9:         m ← int_{p_0}^{-1}(i) and c ← int_{p_r}^{-1}(j)
10:         Add/xor k_1 to m, apply the subst. box layer, add/xor k_2, call the result m'.
11:         Subtract k_{2r+1} to c, call the result c'
12:         L ← L + N_{i,j} · \overline{χ_{a_0}}(m') χ_{a_r}(c')
13:     done
14:     lp_{κ_1, κ_2, κ_{2r+1}} ← |L|^2.
15: done
```

5.5 Attacks on Reduced-Round Versions of SAFER

From Distinguishing Attacks to Key Recovery. In this section, a *reduced hull on r diffusion layers of* SAFER corresponds to a succession patterns on r successive linear layers separated by confusion layers. The *weight* of a reduced hull is the number of active substitution boxes (i.e., the number of boxes with non-zero input/output masks) for any characteristic of the hull. For example, the succession $[****0000] \xrightarrow{252} [**000000] \xrightarrow{254} [**00**00]$ (of Example 2) is a reduced hull of weight 2 on two diffusion layers. A reduced hull easily leads to a distinguishing attack on a reduced-round version of SAFER that would start and end by a diffusion layer.

Table 3 describes a key recovery attack on a SAFER reduced to r rounds by use of a reduced hull on r diffusion layers. Each of the counters obtained with this algorithm measures the probability that the corresponding subset of round key bits (for round keys 1,2, and $2r+1$) is the correct one. We expect the correct guess to be near the top of a list sorted according to these counters when the number of plaintexts/ciphertext pairs is close to $d = 1/\text{ELP}^C(a_0, a_r)$.

In the worst case, line 4 loops $2^{8 \cdot (2w(p_0) + w(p_r))}$ times. In practice, the complexity is much lower (by considering key dependence due to the key schedule) and depends on the number of bits n_k that we need to guess in our attacks. When considering SAFER K-64 for example, a guess for the meaningful bytes of k_1 uniquely determines the bytes of k_2 (for the reasons given in Section 5.1). Similarly, the meaningful bytes of k_{2r+1} that are at the same positions than those of k_1 are also uniquely determined. When considering SAFER SK-64, similar techniques may apply, depending on the specific shapes of the input/output masks and the number of rounds. In all cases, if the meaningful bytes of k_2 and k_{2r+1} are actually added modulo 256, then they don't need to be guessed (as they don't

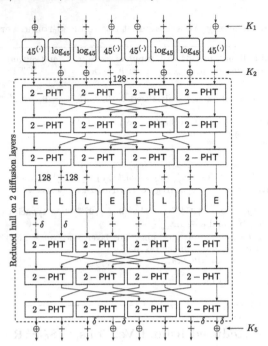

Fig. 6. Reduced hull on two diffusion layers used to attack two rounds of SAFER K

alter the linear probability). If we only consider SAFER SK, this observation also applies to k_2. Finally, line 8 loops 2^{n_p} times where $n_p = \min(8 \cdot (w(\mathsf{p}_0) + w(\mathsf{p}_r)), \log_2 d)$ (as $\sum_{i,j} N_{i,j} = d$). Consequently, given any input/output masks $a_0 \in \mathsf{p}_0$ and $a_r \in \mathsf{p}_r$, the time complexity of the attack is given by

$$T = \frac{1}{\mathrm{ELP}^\mathsf{C}(a_0, a_r)} + 2^{n_k + n_p}. \tag{6}$$

An attack on 2 Rounds. The best attacks we could find on two rounds are based on reduced hull of weight 2 and are listed in Table 4. The best attack on SAFER K exploits the reduced hull represented on Figure 6. To perform the attack, one needs to guess 8 bits of K_1, no bits of K_2 (as those that could be meaningful are added modulo 256 and thus do not influence the linear probability), and 8 bits of K_5 (as those in position 4 are uniquely determined by the guess made on K_1). We thus obtain $n_k = 24$. The algorithm then loops through the $d = 1/\max_{a_0, a_2} \left(\mathrm{ELP}^{\mathsf{H}^{(2)}}(a_0, a_2) \right)$ pairs, where $\mathsf{H}^{(2)}$ here denotes the reduced hull and where a_0 (resp. a_2) denote the input (resp. output) mask on $\mathsf{H}^{(2)}$. The final complexity is computed according to (6) and given in Table 4.

For SAFER SK, the previous reduced hull leads to a higher complexity as 8 more bits of K_5 must be guessed. It appears that the best attack on two rounds of SAFER SK makes use of the first characteristics given in Table 4.

Attacks on 3, 4, and 5 Rounds. To attack three rounds of SAFER K/SK, we make use of reduced hulls on two diffusion layers of weight 6. We restricted

Table 4. Selected reduced hulls on r diffusion layers and attack complexities against r rounds of SAFER K/SK (with $\mathrm{ELP}_{\max}$ denoting $\max_{a_0,a_r} \mathrm{ELP}^{H^{(r)}}(a_0, a_r)$)

r	Reduced hull	$\mathrm{ELP}_{\max}$	n_p	n_k	Complexity
2	$[000*0000] \xrightarrow{1} [**000000] \xrightarrow{254} [**00**00]$	2^{-13}	13	24/24	$2^{37}/2^{37}$
2	$[000*0000] \xrightarrow{1} [**000000] \xrightarrow{255} [00**00**]$	2^{-13}	13	16/24	$2^{29}/2^{37}$
3	$[0*000000]\xrightarrow{1}[**00**00]\xrightarrow{255}[000*000*]\xrightarrow{1}[0*000000]$	2^{-36}	16	8/16	$2^{36}/2^{36}$
4	$[000*0000]\xrightarrow{1}[**000000]\xrightarrow{254}[**00**00]\xrightarrow{255}[000*000*]\xrightarrow{1}[0*000000]$	2^{-47}	16	16/24	$2^{47}/2^{47}$
5	$[000*0000]\xrightarrow{1}[**000000]\xrightarrow{254}[**00**00]\xrightarrow{254}[0*000000]\xrightarrow{1}[0*000*00]\xrightarrow{254}[0*0*0*0*]$	2^{-59}	40	16/24	$2^{59}/2^{59}$

our search to input/output patterns of weight 1 to limit the number of key bits guess. Using similar techniques as for the two rounds case, we manage to mount an attack against both versions of SAFER reduced to three rounds within a complexity of 2^{37} (see Table 4).

To attack four rounds, we use the reduced hull on four diffusion layers listed in Table 4. It appears that SAFER K/SK reduced to four rounds can be attacked within a complexity of 2^{47}. Whereas our generalization of linear cryptanalysis seems necessary to derive this reduced hull on four rounds, the attack itself (which only involves the input and output masks, not the intermediate ones) actually *exactly* corresponds to the original version of linear cryptanalysis: as the non-zero bytes of both input/output masks maximizing the expected linear probability are equal to 128, they only focus on one single bit. The last reduced hull of Table 4 shows that 5 rounds of SAFER K can be broken within a complexity of 2^{59}. Finally, we noted that among the output masks that maximize the expected linear probability, several end by an even byte. For example the best reduced hull is obtained when the last output masks ends by a 2. This remarks applies to the fourth byte of the output mask. Consequently, strictly less than 16 key bits need to be guessed in the last round key, so that the same reduced hull can also be used break 5 rounds of SAFER SK.

6   DEAN: A Toy Example

We introduce DEAN18 (as for Digital Encryption Algorithm for Numbers) a toy cipher that encrypts blocks of 18 decimal digits (which approximatively corresponds to a block size of 60 bits). This could be used to encrypt a credit-card number for example. The structure of the toy cipher we suggest is inspired from that of the AES [9]. We consider an R-round substitution-permutation network, each round being based on the same structure. Blocks are represented as 3×3 arrays of elements of the additive group $\mathbf{Z}_{10} \times \mathbf{Z}_{10}$. Each round successively applies to the plaintext the following operations:

- AddRoundKeys, that performs a digit-wise addition of a round key to the input (the addition being taken modulo 10),
- SubBytes, that applies a fixed bijective substitution box S (defined in Table 5, where an element $(a, b) \in \mathbf{Z}_{10}^2$ are represented as an integer $10 \cdot a + b \in [0, 99]$) on each 2-digit element of the array,

- ShiftRows, that shift to the left each row of the input over a given offset (equal to the row number, starting from 0 at the top),
- MixColumns, that multiplies each column of the input by the matrix

$$M = \begin{pmatrix} \alpha & 1 & 1 \\ 1 & \alpha & 1 \\ 1 & 1 & \alpha \end{pmatrix}$$

where the multiplication of an arbitrary element $(a, b) \in \mathbf{Z}_{10}^2$ by α (resp. 1) is defined by $\alpha \cdot (a, b) = (a + b, -a)$ (resp. $1 \cdot (a, b) = (a, b)$).[3] One can easily see that this defines a structure on $\mathbf{Z}_{10}^2$ or $\mathbf{Z}_{10}^3$ that is isomorphic to $GF(4) \times GF(25)$ or $GF(8) \times GF(125)$ on which the matrix is an MDS matrix [49, 22].

The branch number of the matrix multiplication is 4, i.e., the total number of non-zero elements of the input and output columns is either 0 or 4 or more. Consequently, given a non-trivial character $\rho = (\rho_1, \rho_2, \rho_3)$ on the output of the transformation we obtain (given that we are considering a building block of type (b)) that the appropriate character $\chi = (\chi_1, \chi_2, \chi_3)$ on the input is non-trivial and that among the 6 characters $\chi_1, \ldots, \rho_3$, at least 4 are non-trivial. When at least one of the six characters is non-trivial, we say that the column is active.

Extending this result to the whole MixColumns transformation and applying similar arguments than those used on the AES [9], one can obtain that any two rounds characteristic (i.e., succession of three characters on the text space) has a weight lower bounded by $4Q$, where the weight is simply the number of non-trivial characters on $\mathbf{Z}_{10}^2$ among the 27 components of the three characters and Q is the number of active columns at the output of the first round. Similar arguments also lead to the fact that the sum of the number of active columns at the output of the first and of the third round of a 4-round characteristic is at least 4. Consequently, the weight of a 4-round characteristic is at least 16.

Denoting by LP_{max}^S the maximum value of $LP^S(\chi, \rho)$ over pairs of non-trivial characters, we conclude (under standard heuristic assumptions on the independence of the output of the characters at each round) that the linear probability of a $4r$-rounds characteristic is upper-bounded by $(LP_{max}^S)^{16r}$. Assuming that one characteristic among the linear hull [41] is overwhelming and that the bound given by Theorem 7 is tight, this suggest that in the best case (from an adversary point of view), a distinguishing attack against a $4r$-round version of our toy cipher needs at least $d \approx (LP_{max}^S)^{-16r}$ samples. For the substitution box of our toy cipher, we obtain $LP_{max}^S \approx 0.069$, so that the number of samples that is necessary to attack four rounds with linear cryptanalysis is close to $3.8 \times 10^{18} \approx 2^{61}$. We conclude that $R = 8$ rounds are enough for DEAN18 to keep a high security margin (as far as linear cryptanalysis is concerned).

TOY100 [13] is a similar construction using 11 rounds and blocks of 32 digits, but where a block is a 4×4 array of $\mathbf{Z}_{100}$ elements. One problem with the algebraic structure of $\mathbf{Z}_{100}$ is that its 2-Sylow subgroup is cyclic so there are no MDS matrices. This is not the case of $\mathbf{Z}_{10}^2$.

---

[3] Considering the elements of $\mathbf{Z}_{10}^2$ as elements of $\mathbf{Z}_{10}[\alpha]/(\alpha^2 - \alpha + 1)$ naturally leads to this definition. One could also try to encrypt blocks of 27 digits by using $\mathbf{Z}_{10}^3$ considered as $\mathbf{Z}_{10}[\alpha]/(\alpha^3 - \alpha^2 - 1)$.

Table 5. A fixed substitution box on $\mathbf{Z}_{10}^2$

0	1	2	3	4	5	6	7	8	9	10	11	12	13	14	15	16	17	18	19
27	48	46	31	63	30	91	56	47	26	10	34	8	23	78	77	80	65	71	43
20	21	22	23	24	25	26	27	28	29	30	31	32	33	34	35	36	37	38	39
36	72	29	79	83	7	58	95	69	74	67	35	32	59	82	14	75	99	24	87
40	41	42	43	44	45	46	47	48	49	50	51	52	53	54	55	56	57	58	59
16	90	76	51	28	93	50	38	25	3	13	97	55	60	49	86	57	89	62	45
60	61	62	63	64	65	66	67	68	69	70	71	72	73	74	75	76	77	78	79
18	37	1	6	98	68	39	17	19	20	64	44	33	40	96	2	12	41	52	85
80	81	82	83	84	85	86	87	88	89	90	91	92	93	94	95	96	97	98	99
81	5	0	15	54	88	92	21	84	22	53	11	4	94	42	66	70	9	61	73

7 Conclusion

The theory developed in this paper makes it possible to generalize linear cryptanalysis to random sources and random permutations defined over sets of any cardinality. This generalization appears to be very natural as it encompasses the original one in the binary case, always preserves cumulative effects of linear hulls, and keeps the intrinsic link with differential cryptanalysis. We also showed that there always exists a group law allowing to express the best distinguisher in a linear way (yet, finding this law certainly is a hard task in general). The theory proves to be useful not only in the non binary case but also in the binary case, e.g. when a mixture of group laws is used in the block cipher design.

Acknowledgments. The authors would like to thank anonymous referees for their valuable comments, Jean Monnerat for a quite useful pointer to [40] and Matthieu Finiasz for a priceless help regarding the attack on SAFER.

References

1. Adams, C., Heys, H.M., Tavares, S.E., Wiener, M.: CAST256: a submission for the advanced encryption standard. In: First AES Candidate Conference (AES1) (1998)
2. Baignères, T., Finiasz, M.: Dial C for Cipher. In: Selected Areas in Cryptography 2006. LNCS, Springer, Heidelberg (2006)
3. Baignères, T., Junod, P., Vaudenay, S.: How far can we go beyond linear cryptanalysis? In: Lee, P.J. (ed.) ASIACRYPT 2004. LNCS, vol. 3329, pp. 432–450. Springer, Heidelberg (2004)
4. Biham, E.: On Matsui's linear cryptanalysis. In [10], pp. 341–355
5. Biham, E., Shamir, A.: Differential cryptanalysis of DES-like cryptosystems. Journal of Cryptology 4, 3–72 (1991)
6. Biryukov, A., De Cannière, C., Quisquater, M.: On multiple linear approximations. In: Franklin, M. (ed.) CRYPTO 2004. LNCS, vol. 3152, pp. 1–22. Springer, Heidelberg (2004)
7. Brincat, K., Meijer, H.: On the SAFER cryptosystem. In: Darnell, M. (ed.) Cryptography and Coding. LNCS, vol. 1355, pp. 59–68. Springer, Heidelberg (1997)
8. Chabaud, F., Vaudenay, S.: Links between differential and linear cryptanalysis. In: [10], pp. 356–365

9. Daemen, J., Rijmen, V.: AES proposal: Rijndael. NIST AES Proposal (1998)
10. De Santis, A. (ed.): EUROCRYPT 1994. LNCS, vol. 950. Springer, Heidelberg (1995)
11. Feller, W.: An Introduction to Probability Theory and Its Applications, 2nd edn. Wiley Series in Probability and Mathematical Statistics, vol. 2. John Wiley & Sons, Chichester (1971)
12. Gollmann, D. (ed.): Fast Software Encryption. LNCS, vol. 1039. Springer, Heidelberg (1996)
13. Granboulan, L., Levieil, E., Piret, G.: Pseudorandom permutation families over Abelian groups. In: Robshaw, M. (ed.) FSE 2006. LNCS, vol. 4047, pp. 57–77. Springer, Heidelberg (2006)
14. Handschuh, H., Hasan, M.A. (eds.): SAC 2004. LNCS, vol. 3357. Springer, Heidelberg (2004)
15. Harpes, C., Kramer, G.G., Massey, J.: A generalization of linear cryptanalysis and the applicability of Matsui's piling-up lemma. In: Guillou, L.C., Quisquater, J.-J. (eds.) EUROCRYPT 1995. LNCS, vol. 921, pp. 24–38. Springer, Heidelberg (1995)
16. Harpes, C., Massey, J.: Partitioning cryptanalysis. In: Biham, E. (ed.) FSE 1997. LNCS, vol. 1267, pp. 13–27. Springer, Heidelberg (1997)
17. Jakobsen, T.: Higher-order cryptanalysis of block ciphers. PhD thesis, Department of Mathematics, Technical University of Denmark (1999)
18. Jakobsen, T., Harpes, C.: Non-uniformity measures for generalized linear cryptanalysis and partitioning cryptanalysis. In: Pragocrypt 1996, CTU Publishing House (1996)
19. Junod, P.: On the optimality of linear, differential and sequential distinguishers. In: Biham, E. (ed.) EUROCRPYT 2003. LNCS, vol. 2656, pp. 17–32. Springer, Heidelberg (2003)
20. Junod, P., Vaudenay, S.: Optimal key ranking procedures in a statistical cryptanalysis. In: Johansson, T. (ed.) FSE 2003. LNCS, vol. 2887, pp. 235–246. Springer, Heidelberg (2003)
21. Junod, P., Vaudenay, S.: FOX: a new family of block ciphers. In: [14], pp. 114–129
22. Junod, P., Vaudenay, S.: Perfect diffusion primitives for block ciphers. In [14], pp. 84–99
23. Kaliski, B., Robshaw, M.: Linear cryptanalysis using multiple approximations. In: Desmedt, Y.G. (ed.) CRYPTO 1994. LNCS, vol. 839, pp. 26–39. Springer, Heidelberg (1994)
24. Kelsey, J., Schneier, B., Wagner, D.: mod n cryptanalysis, with applications against RC5P and M6. In: Knudsen, L.R. (ed.) FSE 1999. LNCS, vol. 1636, pp. 139–155. Springer, Heidelberg (1999)
25. Knudsen, L.: Truncated and higher order differentials. In [43], pp. 196–211
26. Knudsen, L.: A detailed analysis of SAFER K. Journal of Cryptology 13(4), 417–436 (2000)
27. Knudsen, L., Berson, T.: Truncated differentials of SAFER. In [12], pp. 15–26
28. Knudsen, L., Robshaw, M.: Non-linear approximations in linear cryptanalysis. In: Maurer, U.M. (ed.) EUROCRYPT 1996. LNCS, vol. 1070, pp. 224–236. Springer, Heidelberg (1996)
29. Lai, X., Massey, J., Murphy, S.: Markov ciphers and differential cryptanalysis. In: Davies, D.W. (ed.) EUROCRYPT 1991. LNCS, vol. 547, pp. 17–38. Springer, Heidelberg (1991)
30. Lai, X., Massey, J.L.: A proposal for a new block encryption standard. In: Damgård, I.B. (ed.) EUROCRYPT 1990. LNCS, vol. 473, pp. 389–404. Springer, Heidelberg (1991)

31. Massey, J.: SAFER-K64: a byte-oriented block-ciphering algorithm. In: Anderson, R. (ed.) Fast Software Encryption. LNCS, vol. 809, pp. 1–17. Springer, Heidelberg (1994)
32. Massey, J.: SAFER-K64: one year later. In [43], pp. 212–241
33. Massey, J.: Strengthened key schedule for the cipher SAFER. Posted on USENET newsgroup sci.crypt (September 9, 1995)
34. Matsui, M.: The first experimental cryptanalysis of the Data Encryption Standard. In: Desmedt, Y.G. (ed.) CRYPTO 1994. LNCS, vol. 839, pp. 1–11. Springer, Heidelberg (1994)
35. Matsui, M.: New structure of block ciphers with provable security against differential and linear cryptanalysis. In [12], pp. 205–218
36. Menezes, A., Van Oorschot, P., Vanstone, S.: Handbook of applied cryptography. The CRC Press series on discrete mathematics and its applications. CRC-Press, Boca Raton, USA (1997)
37. Minier, M., Gilbert, H.: Stochastic cryptanalysis of Crypton. In: Schneier, B. (ed.) FSE 2000. LNCS, vol. 1978, pp. 121–133. Springer, Heidelberg (2001)
38. Murphy, S.: An analysis of SAFER. Journal of Cryptology 11(4), 235–251 (1998)
39. Nakahara, J., Preneel, B., Vandewalle, J.: Linear cryptanalysis of reduced-round versions of the SAFER block cipher family. In: Schneier, B. (ed.) FSE 2000. LNCS, vol. 1978, pp. 244–261. Springer, Heidelberg (2001)
40. Nathanson, M.B.: Elementary Methods in Number Theory. Graduate Texts in Mathematics. Springer, Heidelberg (2000)
41. Nyberg, K.: Linear approximation of block ciphers. In [10], pp. 439–444
42. Parker, M.: Generalized S-Box linearity. Technical report, NESSIE Project (2003), https://www.cryptonessie.org
43. Preneel, B. (ed.): Fast Software Encryption. LNCS, vol. 1008. Springer, Heidelberg (1995)
44. Rice, J.A.: Mathematical Statistics and Data Analysis, 2nd edn. Duxbury Press, Boston, MA (1995)
45. Schroeppel, R.: Hasty pudding cipher specification (June 1998), available on http://www.cs.arizona.edu/~rcs/hpc/hpc-spec
46. Shimoyama, T., Kaneko, T.: Quadratic relation of S-Box and its application to the linear attack of full round DES. In: Krawczyk, H. (ed.) CRYPTO 1998. LNCS, vol. 1462, pp. 200–211. Springer, Heidelberg (1998)
47. Standaert, F.-X., Rouvroy, G., Piret, G., Quisquater, J.-J., Legat, J.-D.: Key-dependent approximations in cryptanalysis: an application of multiple Z4 and non-linear approximations. In: 24th Symposium on Information Theory in the Benelux (2003)
48. Stern, J., Vaudenay, S.: CS-Cipher. In: Vaudenay, S. (ed.) FSE 1998. LNCS, vol. 1372, pp. 189–204. Springer, Heidelberg (1998)
49. Vaudenay, S.: On the need for multipermutations: Cryptanalysis of MD4 and SAFER. In [43], pp. 286–297
50. Vaudenay, S.: An experiment on DES statistical cryptanalysis. In: 3rd ACM Conference on Computer and Communications Security, pp. 139–147. ACM Press, New York (1996)
51. Vaudenay, S.: On the security of CS-cipher. In: Knudsen, L.R. (ed.) FSE 1999. LNCS, vol. 1636, pp. 260–274. Springer, Heidelberg (1999)
52. Wu, H., Bao, F., Deng, R., Ye, Q.-Z.: Improved truncated differential attacks on SAFER. In: Ohta, K., Pei, D. (eds.) ASIACRYPT 1998. LNCS, vol. 1514, pp. 133–147. Springer, Heidelberg (1998)

The Delicate Issues of Addition with Respect to XOR Differences

Gaoli Wang[1,*], Nathan Keller[2,**], and Orr Dunkelman[3,***]

[1] School of Mathematics and System Sciences, Shandong University
Jinan 250100, China
wanggaoli@mail.sdu.edu.cn
[2] Einstein Institute of Mathematics, Hebrew University
Jerusalem 91904, Israel
nkeller@math.huji.ac.il
[3] Katholieke Universiteit Leuven
Dept. of Electrical Engineering ESAT/SCD-COSIC
Kasteelpark Arenberg 10, B-3001 Leuven-Heverlee, Belgium
orr.dunkelman@esat.kuleuven.be

Abstract. In this paper we analyze the previous attacks on the block cipher SHACAL-1 and show that all the differential-based attacks fail due to mistreatment of XOR differences through addition. We show that the previously published differential and rectangle attacks on SHACAL-1 fail as some of the underlying differentials are impossible. The related-key rectangle attacks on the cipher generally fail, but if some conditions are imposed on the key (i.e., for a weak key class) they work. After identifying the flaws in previous attacks, we present possible fixes to these attacks. We then present some modified differentials which lead to a related-key rectangle attack which can be applied to 2^{504} weak keys. Our observations are then used to improve a related-key rectangle attack on IDEA by a factor of 2.

Keywords: Related-Key Rectangle attack, Block cipher, SHACAL-1, IDEA.

1 Introduction

Differential cryptanalysis [5] was introduced by Biham and Shamir in 1990, and it is one of the most powerful known attacks on block ciphers. The related-key attack [1] was introduced by Biham in 1993. The attack considers the encryption under two unknown but related keys. The attack's applicability depends on the

* Supported by National Natural Science Foundation of China Key Project No.90604036 and 973 Program No.2007CB807902.
** The research presented in this paper was supported by the Adams fellowship.
*** This work was supported in part by the Concerted Research Action (GOA) Ambiorics 2005/11 of the Flemish Government and by the IAP Programme P6/26 BCRYPT of the Belgian State (Belgian Science Policy).

C. Adams, A. Miri, and M. Wiener (Eds.): SAC 2007, LNCS 4876, pp. 212–231, 2007.
© Springer-Verlag Berlin Heidelberg 2007

key schedule algorithm and shows that a block cipher with a weak key schedule algorithm may be vulnerable to this kind of attack. Many cryptanalytic results of this attack model were presented in [6, 10, 11, 12, 15].

Illuminated by the complex local collisions of the analysis of SHA-0 which were pointed in the earlier papers in 1997 by X.Y.Wang [25], SHA-0 [24], and SHA-1 [22], we show that in the case of SHACAL-1 [8], all previous differential attacks [2, 7, 10, 13, 14, 17] fail due to this fact. For example, we show that the attack of [10] uses a differential that can never be satisfied. For other attacks, e.g., the related-key rectangle attack on the full SHACAL-1 in [7], we show that the attack is applicable only to a weak key class (of 2^{496} keys). We show that the combination of XOR differentials (or related-key XOR differentials) when the addition operation is used should be done in a very delicate manner.

After pointing out the problems in the various attacks on SHACAL-1, we try to salvage them. Some of the attacks are fully salvaged, while some others are either shortened (due to lower probabilities of the differentials), or are applicable only in a weak key class (which is larger than previously known).

We then present a related-key rectangle attack on the full SHACAL-1. We use two related-key differentials, where the first one of 33 rounds is built using the technique of modular differences, achieving high probability and correctness. The new attack has a data complexity of 2^{146} related-key chosen plaintexts and time complexity of 2^{465} encryptions. The attack is successful against one out of 256 keys (or more precisely one quartet of keys out of 256 quartets). We summarize the results on SHACAL-1 and our findings in Table 1.

The attack is applicable against the largest set of weak keys (one out of 256). Finally, we show how to improve the 6.5-round rectangle attack on IDEA from [4] by using the additive properties of the differentials. We succeed in reducing the time complexity of the attack by a factor of two.

The rest of the paper is organized as follows: in Section 2, we give the notations used in the paper, present SHACAL-1 and introduce some useful properties of the nonlinear functions in SHACAL-1. Section 3 describes the flaws in previous attacks against SHACAL-1. We present fixes to the various problems in Section 4. In Section 5 we give a related-key rectangle attack on the full SHACAL-1 which can be applied to one out of 2^8 keys (quartets of keys). We improve the 6.5-round related-key rectangle attack on IDEA in Section 6. Finally, we summarize the paper in Section 7.

2   Background

2.1   Notations

Throughout the paper we shall use the following notations which are partially based on these of [21, 23]:

- We shall address the words in a little endian manner, where x_0 is the least significant bit of x, and x_{31} is the most significant bit of 32-bit words.

Table 1. Comparison of our results with the previous attacks on SHACAL-1

Attack	Rounds	Complexity		Observation
		Data	Time	
Differential [14]	30 (0–29)	2^{110} CP	$2^{75.1}$	AF
Differential [14]	41 (0–40)	2^{141} CP	2^{491}	AF
Differential [17]	49 (0–48)	2^{141} CP	$2^{496.5}$	AF
Differential [17]	55 (15–69)	2^{154} CP	$2^{507.3}$	AF
Amplified Boomerang [14]	47 (0–46)	$2^{158.5}$ CP	$2^{508.4}$	AF
Rectangle [2]	47 (0–46)	$2^{151.9}$ CP	$2^{482.6}$	AF
Rectangle [2]	49 (29–77)	$2^{151.9}$ CC	$2^{508.5}$	AF
Rectangle [17]	51 (0–50)	$2^{153.7}$ CP	$2^{503.7}$	AF
Rectangle [17]	52 (28–79)	2^{160} CP	$2^{510.0}$	AF
Related-Key Rectangle [13]	57 (0–56)	$2^{154.8}$ RK-CP	$2^{503.4}$	AF
Related-Key Rectangle [13]	59 (0–58)	$2^{149.7}$ RK-CP	$2^{503.4}$	AF
Related-Key Rectangle [10]	70 (0–69)	$2^{151.8}$ RK-CP	$2^{500.1}$	AF
Related-Key Rectangle [7]	80 (0–79)	$2^{159.8}$ RK-CP	$2^{420.0}$	WK (2^{496})
Related-Key Rectangle [7]	80 (0–79)	$2^{153.8}$ RK-CP	$2^{501.2}$	WK (2^{498})
Related-Key Rectangle (*New*)	70 (0–69)	2^{146} RK-CP	2^{145}	WK (2^{504})
Related-Key Rectangle (*New*)	80 (0–79)	2^{146} RK-CP	2^{465}	WK (2^{504})
Related-Key Rectangle (*New*)	70 (0–69)	2^{144} RK-CP	2^{174}	WK (2^{504})
Related-Key Rectangle (*New*)	80 (0–79)	2^{144} RK-CP	2^{494}	WK (2^{504})
Differential (*New*)	39 (30–68)	2^{144} CC	2^{176}	
Differential (*New*)	49 (20–68)	2^{144} CC	2^{496}	
Rectangle (*New*)	41 (0–40)	$2^{150.3}$ CP	$2^{176.9}$	
Rectangle (*New*)	51 (0–50)	$2^{150.3}$ CP	$2^{496.9}$	

CP: Chosen Plaintexts, CC: Chosen Ciphertexts.
RK-CP: Relate-Key Chosen Plaintexts.
AF: The Attack is Flawed, WK: Weak Key Class (with size).

- $x_i[j]$ and $x_i[-j]$ denote the resulting values by only changing the jth bit of the word x_i. In case the change of the bit is from 0 to 1, then $x_i[j]$ is used and the sign is considered to be positive. Otherwise, $x_i[-j]$ is used and the sign of the difference is negative.
- $x_i[\pm j_1, \pm j_2, \ldots, \pm j_l]$ is the value obtained by changing j_1th, j_2th, ..., j_lth bits of x_i. The "+" sign (which may be omitted) means that the bit is changed from 0 to 1, where the "−" denotes the opposite change.
- $[j]$ denotes a difference in bit j such that the pair (x, x^*) satisfies $x_i^* - x_i = 2^j$ (i.e., $x_i^* = x_i[j]$). $[-j]$ denotes a difference in bit j such that the pair (x, x^*) satisfies $x_i^* - x_i = -2^j$ (i.e., $x_i^* = x_i[-j]$). Similarly, $[j_1, j_2]$ denotes $x_i^* - x_i = 2^{j_1} + 2^{j_2}$ and $[j_1, -j_2]$ denotes $x_i^* - x_i = 2^{j_1} - 2^{j_2}$, etc.
- e_j represents the 32-bit word composed of 31 0's and 1 in the jth place, $e_{j,k} = e_j \oplus e_k$ and $e_{j,k,l} = e_j \oplus e_k \oplus e_l$, etc.
- $\Delta(A, A^*)$ denotes $A^* - A$ or $A^* \oplus A$ according the the value attached to it. $\Delta(A, A^*) = e_j$ stands for XOR difference, i.e., $A^* \oplus A = e_j$. Otherwise $\Delta(A, A^*) = [j]$ stands for an modular difference, i.e., $A^* - A = 2^j$ and $A^* \oplus A = e_j$.

2.2   Description of SHACAL-1

SHACAL-1 [8] is a 160-bit block cipher supporting variable key lengths $(0,\ldots,512$ bits). It is based on the compression function of the hash function SHA-1 [20] introduced by NIST. The 160-bit plaintext P is divided into five 32-bit words A_0, B_0, C_0, D_0 and E_0. The encryption process iterates the following round function for 80 rounds:

$$A_{i+1} = K_i + ROTL_5(A_i) + F_i(B_i, C_i, D_i) + E_i + Con_i$$
$$B_{i+1} = A_i$$
$$C_{i+1} = ROTL_{30}(B_i)$$
$$D_{i+1} = C_i$$
$$E_{i+1} = D_i$$

for $i = 0, \ldots, 79$, where $ROTL_j(X)$ represents rotation of the 32-bit word X to the left by j bits, K_i is the round subkey, Con_i is the round constant, and

$$F_i(X,Y,Z) = IF(X,Y,Z) = (X \wedge Y) \vee (\neg X \wedge Z), \qquad (0 \le i \le 19)$$
$$F_i(X,Y,Z) = XOR(X,Y,Z) = X \oplus Y \oplus Z, \qquad (20 \le i \le 39, 60 \le i \le 79)$$
$$F_i(X,Y,Z) = MAJ(X,Y,Z) = (X \wedge Y) \vee (X \wedge Z) \vee (Y \wedge Z), \quad (40 \le i \le 59)$$

The ciphertext is composed of A_{80}, B_{80}, C_{80}, D_{80} and E_{80}.

The key schedule of SHACAL-1 supports a variable key length of 0–512 bits. Keys shorter than 512 bits are first padded with as many zeroes as needed to obtain 512 bits. Let the 512-bit (padded) key be $K = K_0 K_1 \ldots K_{15}$, where K_i is a 32-bit word. The key expansion of 512-bit K to 2560 bits is as follows:

$$K_i = ROTL_1(K_{i-3} \oplus K_{i-8} \oplus K_{i-14} \oplus K_{i-16}), \quad (16 \le i \le 79)$$

We note that in [8] a minimal key length of 128-bit is required.

2.3   Several Propositions on the Differential Behavior of Addition and IF

In this section we present some properties of additive differences and XOR differences, as well as some properties of the nonlinear function $IF(X,Y,Z)$ which were summarized in [22].

Proposition 1. *Let A_1, A_2 and B be n-bit words, and let $C_i = A_i + B$ (mod 2^n) for $i = 1, 2$. If $A_1 \oplus A_2 = e_j$ for $0 \le j \le n - 2$, then $C_1 \oplus C_2 = e_j$ if and only if $C_{i,j} = A_{i,j}$ for $i = 1, 2$ and $0 \le j \le n - 2$.*

Proof. Assume without loss of generality that $A_{1,j} = 0$. Thus, $A_{2,j} = 1$, and $A_1 + 2^j = A_2$. It follows that $C_2 = C_1 + 2^j$. Hence, if $C_{1,j} = 0$ then $C_{2,j} = 1$ and there is no carry due to the difference, i.e., $C_1 \oplus C_2 = e_j$. In the other way, if $C_1 \oplus C_2 = e_j$, there was no carry by the addition of 2^j to C_1, which means that $C_{1,j} = 0$. Q.E.D.

Proposition 2. *Let A_1, A_2, B_1 and B_2 be n-bit words, and let $C_i = A_i + B_i$ (mod 2^n) for $i = 1, 2$. If $A_1 \oplus A_2 = B_1 \oplus B_2 = e_j$ for some bit $0 \leq j \leq n - 2$, then $C_1 = C_2$ if and only if $A_{i,j} = \neg B_{i,j}$ for $i = 1, 2$.*

Proof. Without loss of generality assume that $A_{1,j} = 0$ and that $A_{2,j} = 1$, thus, $A_2 = A_1 + 2^j$. If $B_{1,j} = 1$, then it follows that $B_2 = B_1 - 2^j$, and thus $C_1 = C_2$. To prove the other direction we note that $C_1 = C_2$ requires that $B_2 = B_1 - 2^j$ (mod 2^n). As B_1 and B_2 differ only in one bit, i.e., bit j, it follows that $B_{1,j} = 1$ and $B_{2,j} = 0$. Q.E.D.

Proposition 3. *For the nonlinear function $IF(X, Y, Z) = (X \wedge Y) \vee (\neg X \wedge Z)$, the following properties hold [21, 23]:*

1. *$IF(x, y, z) = IF(\neg x, y, z)$ if and only if $y = z$.*
   $IF(0, y, z) = 0$ and $IF(1, y, z) = 1$ if and only if $y = 1$ and $z = 0$.
   $IF(0, y, z) = 1$ and $IF(1, y, z) = 0$ if and only if $y = 0$ and $z = 1$.
2. *$IF(x, y, z) = IF(x, \neg y, z)$ if and only if $x = 0$.*
   $IF(x, 0, z) = 0$ and $IF(x, 1, z) = 1$ if and only if $x = 1$.
3. *$IF(x, y, z) = IF(x, y, \neg z)$ if and only if $x = 1$.*
   $IF(x, y, 0) = 0$ and $IF(x, y, 1) = 1$ if and only if $x = 0$.

3   Flaws in Previously Published Attacks

We find all previous differential attacks on SHACAL-1 have some flaws illuminated by Wang's modular difference. In some cases, these flaws prevent the attacks from being applicable to all keys. The first flaw, which affects the attacks in [2, 10, 13, 14, 17] is an impossibility flaw, i.e., the differentials which are used in these attacks can not hold. The second flaw, which affects the related-key attacks in [7, 10, 13] is the fact that the related-key differential holds only if the key satisfies some conditions. The third flaw is wrong keys which suggest the same number of "right" pairs/quartets as the right key. We show that the same pairs suggest even wrong keys.

3.1   The Use of Differentials with Probability 0

In the attacks of [2, 10, 13, 14, 17] there is a part of the differentials (or the related-key differentials) which cannot hold. We present the problem with the related-key differential of [10], but note that the key difference has no affect on the problem, and thus it exists in all the attacks mentioned earlier.

The related-key rectangle attack on 70-round SHACAL-1 [10] uses a 33-round related-key differential characteristic for rounds 0–32 with probability 2^{-45}. The differential characteristic in [10] from round 6 to round 12 is shown in Table 2.

We shall now prove that this differential characteristic can never hold, i.e., the actual probability is 0. Let A, B, C, D, E and A^*, B^*, C^*, D^*, E^* be the intermediate encryption values corresponding to a pair which allegedly satisfies this differential.

Table 2. The differential Characteristic in [10] from Round 6 to Round 12

i	ΔA_i	ΔB_i	ΔC_i	ΔD_i	ΔE_i	ΔK_i	$Prob.$
6	e_3	0	0	$e_{13,31}$	0	0	2^{-3}
7	e_8	e_3	0	0	$e_{13,31}$	e_{31}	2^{-3}
8	0	e_8	e_1	0	0	0	2^{-2}
9	0	0	e_6	e_1	0	0	2^{-2}
10	0	0	0	e_6	e_1	0	2^{-2}
11	e_1	0	0	0	e_6	0	2^{-2}
12	0	e_1	0	0	0	0	2^{-1}

1. According to $A_{i+1} = K_i + ROTL_5(A_i) + F_i(B_i, C_i, D_i) + E_i + Con_i$ and proposition 1, we get that $A_{7,8} = A_{6,3}$ and $A_{7,8}^* = A_{6,3}^*$.
2. From the encryption algorithm and proposition 1, we get that $A_{11,1} = E_{10,1} = A_{6,3}$, $A_{11,1}^* = E_{10,1}^* = A_{6,3}^*$, $E_{11,6} = A_{7,8}$ and $E_{11,6}^* = A_{7,8}^*$.
3. From 1 and 2, we obtain that $A_{11,1} = E_{11,6}$ and $A_{11,1}^* = E_{11,6}^*$. By $A_{i+1} = K_i + ROTL_5(A_i) + F_i(B_i, C_i, D_i) + E_i + Con_i$ and proposition 2, we obtain that $A_{12} \neq A_{12}^*$, i.e., $\Delta A_{12} \neq 0$, which is a contradiction with $\Delta A_{12} = 0$ in the differential characteristic.

To summarize the above, as there is no carry from the addition of the differences in round 6, the sign of $A_{7,8}$ is the same as the sign of $A_{6,3}$. The sign of $A_{6,3}$ is then copied to $A_{11,1}$ (as there is no carry). Thus, when these two differences enter the addition in round 12 they have the same sign, and thus, cannot cancel each other. Therefore the attack on 70-round SHACAL-1 [10] is infeasible (as well as other attacks which use this transition).

We note that when considering only XOR differences (as was done in [10]), the probabilities of the differential is larger than 0. However, only when we consider modular difference, this problem is found.

3.2 Conditions on the Keys

The related-key differential attacks [7, 10, 13] have to deal with another issue which follows from the addition operation. Some of the XOR differences of the differentials can hold only if some key conditions are applied. We show that the related-key attacks in [7, 10, 13] imposes conditions on the keys, so they can actually be used only for weak key classes. The attack in [13] has one such condition, the attack in [10] has 2 conditions, and the attack in [7] has 16 conditions. Thus, the attack of [7] is applicable only for a weak key class with the size of 2^{496} keys (rather than all the keys as implicitly assumed in [7]).

Consider rounds 26–34 of the first related-key differential used in [7] which are depicted in Table 3. Consider for example the difference e_2 in A_{27}, we know the the sign of this difference is as the sign of key difference that caused it. In order for this difference to be canceled during the addition of round 27 (with the key difference of K_{27}), by proposition 2 it must hold that the sign of the key difference is opposite to that of $A_{27,2}$. This imposes a condition on the keys

Table 3. The Related-Key Differential Characteristic in [7] (Steps 26–34)

i	ΔA_i	ΔB_i	ΔC_i	ΔD_i	ΔE_i	ΔK_i	Prob.
26	0	0	0	0	0	e_2	2^{-1}
27	e_2	0	0	0	0	e_7	2^{-1}
28	0	e_2	0	0	0	e_2	2^{-1}
29	0	0	e_0	0	0	$e_{0,3}$	2^{-2}
30	e_3	0	0	e_0	0	$e_{0,8}$	2^{-2}
31	0	e_3	0	0	e_0	$e_{0,3}$	2^{-2}
32	0	0	e_1	0	0	$e_{1,4}$	2^{-2}
33	e_4	0	0	e_1	0	$e_{1,9}$	2^{-2}
34	0	e_4	0	0	e_1		

used in the attack, as otherwise, there is going to be a carry, and the related-key differential cannot hold. We note that the same problem exists in the first related-key differential of [7] in five other places, in rounds 0–1, 4–5, 29–30, 32–33, and rounds 26–31 (where the sign of the difference in E_{31} should be the opposite of the sign of the key difference).

The same is true for the second related-key differential used in rounds 34-69, where 10 conditions are imposed on the key. As a side observation, we note that when the keys satisfy these conditions, the probability of the transitions is increased, as we are assured that the required differences cancel. Thus, while this defines a weak key class which contains one out of 2^{16} keys (or more precisely a quartet of keys), for these weak keys, the probabilities of the differentials are actually 2^{-35} and 2^{-29} rather than 2^{-41} and 2^{-39} for the first and second differentials, respectively.

In Table 4 we summarize for the three related-key attacks the number of conditions imposed on any of the related-key differentials, derive the weak key class size, and the actual data and time complexities of the attacks in the weak key class. We ignored the impossibility issues that were mentioned earlier, but we remind the reader that these attacks still fail due to the previously mentioned reasons.

3.3 Wrong Keys That Pass the Basic Attacks

While this problem is the smallest of all, this observation can actually be used to reduce the time complexities of the attacks (usually by a negligible factor). Consider for example the last step in the attack from [7]:

"Partially decrypt all the remaining quartets (under the corresponding keys) ... For each of the remaining quartets, check whether $C'''_{a_E} \oplus C'''_{c_E} = \delta_E = e_1$ ..."

Consider for example the case where the most significant bit of the real key is flipped. As noted in [7], this has no affect on the difference of the pair. Thus, when checking the real key, and the real key with a flipped most significant bit, the same quartets are suggested. More accurately, if we consider the additive

Table 4. Conditions on the Keys in Previous Related-Key Attacks and the Effect on their Complexities

Attack	Rounds	Conditions on		Complexity		Number of
		1st Differential	2nd Differential	Data	Time	Weak Keys
[13]	57	1	0	$2^{153.8}$ RK-CP	$2^{501.4}$	2^{511}
[13]	59	0	0	$2^{149.7}$ RK-CP	$2^{498.3}$	2^{512}
[10]	70	1	0	$2^{150.8}$ RK-CP	$2^{498.1}$	2^{511}
[7]	80	6	10	$2^{143.8}$ RK-CP	$2^{388.0}$	2^{496}
[7]	80	6	8	$2^{139.8}$ RK-CP	$2^{473.1}$	2^{498}

The first three attacks fail.
The number of weak keys is the number of weak keys quartets out of all the 2^{512} possible ones which satisfy the related-key XOR differences.

differences in the last step of the attack, the additive difference depends on the additive difference of the subkey and the data, and not on the actual key bits. Thus, all bit positions which are more significant than all the bits with difference in the key, has no affect whatsoever on the difference of a pair.

Thus, in the case of the attack from [7] the number of subkeys which has more than two quartets is increased by 2^{27}. One one hand this increases the time complexity of the exhaustive key search phase by a factor of 2^{27}. On the other hand, as there is no point in guessing these key bits during the normal execution of the attack (again besides in the exhaustive key search phase), their guesses and partial decryptions during the attacks can be eliminated.

We observe that the each of these keys is suggested by the *same* quartet. Thus, increasing the data used in the attack has no effect on the correctness of the attack.

4   Fixing the Previous Attacks

We concentrate at showing how to fix the the differential attack on 55-round SHACAL-1 from [17]. We show that by using the correct modular differences we obtain a valid attack on 49-round SHACAL-1. The new modular differential uses the cases where we add two difference, either they have the opposite signs (and produce no carry) or they are in the most significant bit. We also note that when a difference in the most significant bit is introduced, its sign might change without producing a carry. This might be useful in cases where a difference is introduced, and we need to change its sign (the change of sign occurs with probability 1/2, and it may happen without carry, while for other bit positions this occurs with probability 1/2, but produces a carry).

We summarize in Table 5 the parameters of the fixed attacks: the new number of rounds, the new data and time complexity. We also list the major changes that must be done to these attacks to make them work. We note that the best attack on SHACAL-1 in the regular model (i.e., with one key) is a 51-round rectangle attack on rounds 0–50.

Table 5. The results of the fixed attacks on SHACAL-1

Attack	Rounds	Complexity		Comments
		Data	Time	
Differential [14]	28 (0–27)	2^{93} CP	2^{93}	Using the new differentials from Appendix B. Fixing 6 input bits
Differential [14]	40 (0–39)	2^{98} CP	2^{482}	As before, not using the early abort technique.
Differential [17]	49 (20–68)	2^{144} CC	2^{496}	See Section 4.1
Amplified Boomerang [14]	47 (0–46)	$2^{154.5}$ CP	$2^{502.4}$	Changing the first differential to the first 21 rounds of the differential from Appendix B.
Rectangle [2]	47 (0–46)	$2^{149.7}$ CP	$2^{478.2}$	Same change as the amplified boomerang attack. $\hat{p} = 2^{-41.42}$ rather than $2^{-43.62}$, $t_b = 12.7$ (rather than 9.9) and $r_b = 32$ rather than 25.
Rectangle [2]	48 (30–77)	$2^{149.7}$ CC	$2^{482.1}$	As before, not using the early abort technique. $t_f = 12.7$ (originally 9.9), $r_f = 32$ (origanlly 32).
Rectangle [17]	51 (0–50)	$2^{150.3}$ CP	$2^{496.9}$	Using the 24-round differential from Appendix B. Fixing 6 plaintext bits, $\hat{p} = 2^{-44}$ (rather than $2^{-47.39}$).
Rectangle [17]	50 (30–79)	2^{160} CP	$2^{505.0}$	$\hat{q} = 2^{-47.9}$ (orignally $2^{-47.8}$), $t_f = 73.7$ (originally 24.9), and $r_f = 90$ (originally 31).
Related-Key Rectangle [13]	57 (0–56)	$2^{143.6}$ RK-CP	2^{481}	Change the first related-key differential to the first one from Appendix A. $p = 2^{-35}$ after fixing 9 plaintext bits.
Related-Key Rectangle [13]	59 (0–58)	$2^{146.5}$ RK-CP	$2^{479.0}$	Replace the first differential to the 21 first rounds of the differential from Appendix B. $\hat{p} = 2^{-35.4}$ after fixing 6 plaintext bits.
Related-Key Rectangle [10]	70 (0–69)	$2^{142.7}$ RK-CP	$2^{481.9}$	As before, change the first related-key differential.

CP: Chosen Plaintexts, CC: Chosen Ciphertexts, RK-CP: Relate-Key Chosen Plaintexts.
WK: Weak Key Class (with size).

4.1 Fixing the Differential Attacks

For the differential attack in [17] we change the used differential. The basic 24-round differential is given in Table 9 in the Appendix. The basic 24-round differential from [17] (which is extended 16 more rounds) has four contradictions. Thus, we first start by fixing the first three by changing the differential conditions from XOR ones to modular ones. The fourth contradiction is solved by rotating the differential such that the problematic addition occurs with both differences in the most significant bit.

The new 24-round differential has probability of 2^{-52}, compared to the claimed probability of the flawed differential of 2^{-50}. It is possible to improve the probability of the new differential by a factor of 2^6 by fixing several plaintext bits which ensure the transitions that we seek. For example, by fixing $C_{0,22} = D_{0,22}$, we make sure that despite the difference in $B_{0,22}$, there is no difference in $IF(B_{0,22}, C_{0,22}, D_{0,22})$. We also note that by negating the signs (i.e., flipping all the signs) in the differential, we obtain a second differential with the same probability.

The extension of this differential forward and backward is a bit more complex than in [17]. This is mostly due to the fact that we have to maintain the correctness of the differential by restricting the signs of the differences. In Table 10 in the appendix we present a possible extension of the 24-round differential to the six rounds before the differential (the 24-round differential can be used also for rounds 40–63). Table 11 presents a possible extension of the 24-round differential (whether this is in rounds 24–29 or in rounds 64–68). Thus, it is possible to construct a 36-round differential for SHACAL-1 in rounds 33–68 with probability 2^{-157} (which can be improved to 2^{-144} by fixing the equivalent of 13 plain text bits).

Using this 36-round differential, we can attack rounds 18–68. This is done in a chosen ciphertext attack. The attacker has to fix 10 bits to satisfy the additive requirements of the differential, and thus, it is impossible to use the differential as-is (as its probability is 2^{-157}, i.e., 2^{157} pairs are needed). However, if we use structures of 2^{32} ciphertexts each, we eliminate the last round of the differential (round 68), and thus increase the probability of the differential by a factor of 2^{-14}, and reduce 2 conditions on the ciphertexts. In exchange for that, we cannot automatically distinguish right pairs (as each plaintext has 2^{32} candidate counterparts).

The attacker obtains 2^{144} chosen ciphertexts (in 2^{112} structures), and asks for their decryption. Then, he guesses the subkeys of rounds 68, and rounds 20–29, partially encrypts the obtained plaintexts, and then repeats the early abort technique found in [17] and in our attack described later. The resulting attack has a time complexity of about 2^{496} encryptions.

5 A New Related-Key Rectangle Attack on the Full SHACAL-1

The key schedule of SHACAL-1 is operated by a linear shift feedback register, and has slow diffusion, i.e., low difference propagations. If we fix a difference of any consecutive 16 subkeys, the differences in the remaining 64 subkeys are known. The key schedule weaknesses of SHACAL-1 allows us to obtain two consecutive good related-key differential characteristics. We can constructed a 33-round related-key differential characteristic for rounds 0–32 (E_0) without any conditions on the key. For the rounds 33–65 (E_1) we use a differential characteristic based on the the second differential used in [7] and we impose 8 conditions on the key. The characteristics are given in the Appendix. We combine the two related-key differential characteristics to obtain a 66-round related-key rectangle distinguisher for SHACAL-1.

5.1 Related-Key Differential Characteristics for SHACAL-1

We first propose a 66-round related-key rectangle distinguisher based on the differentials found in the Appendix. The input difference for the first sub-cipher

Table 6. Values for Plaintexts bits that Increase the Probability of the Differential of Table 7

A_0	B_0	C_0	D_0
$A_{0,3} = 1, A_{0,12} = B_{0,12}$	$B_{0,16} = 1, B_{0,20} = 0, B_{0,10} = C_{0,8}$	$C_{0,1} = 1$	$D_{0,3} = 1$
$A_{0,20} = 1$	$B_{0,31} = 0$		

Table 7. The First Related-Key Differential Characteristic for SHACAL-1

Round(i)	ΔA_i	ΔB_i	ΔC_i	ΔD_i	ΔE_i	ΔK_i	Probability
0	$[-8,1]$	$[3]$	$[-20,3]$	$[16,31]$	$2^{13} - 2^{10} - 2^6$	e_{31}	
1	$[-10]$	$[-8,1]$	$[1]$	$[-20,3]$	$[16,31]$	e_{31}	2^{-1}
2	$[15]$	$[-10]$	$[-6,31]$	$[1]$	$[-20,3]$	0	2^{-1}
3	$[3]$	$[15]$	$[-8]$	$[-6,31]$	$[1]$	0	2^{-4}
4	$[1]$	$[3]$	$[13]$	$[-8]$	$[-6,31]$	e_{31}	2^{-5}
5	0	$[1]$	$[1]$	$[13]$	$[-8]$	0	2^{-3}
6	$[-8]$	0	$[31]$	$[1]$	$[13]$	0	2^{-3}
7	0	$[-8]$	0	$[31]$	$[1]$	0	2^{-2}
8	$[1]$	0	$[-6]$	0	$[31]$	e_{31}	2^{-3}
9	0	$[1]$	0	$[-6]$	0	0	2^{-1}
10	$[1]$	0	$[31]$	0	$[-6]$	e_{31}	2^{-3}
11	0	$[1]$	0	$[31]$	0	0	2^{-1}
12	0	0	$[31]$	0	$[31]$	e_{31}	2^{-2}
13	0	0	0	$[31]$	0	0	2^{-1}
14	0	0	0	0	$[31]$	e_{31}	2^{-1}
15	0	0	0	0	0	0	1
...	...	...	...	...	...	...	...
30	0	0	0	0	0	e_0	1
31	e_0	0	0	0	0	0	2^{-1}
32	e_5	e_0	0	0	0	0	2^{-1}
33	$e_{0,10}$	e_5	e_{30}	0	0	e_1	2^{-2}

The key difference is $\Delta K^* = (e_{31}, e_{31}, 0, 0, e_{31}, 0, 0, 0, e_{31}, 0, e_{31}, 0, e_{31}, 0, e_{31}, 0)$.

is $\alpha = ([-8,1], [3], [3,-20], [16,31], 2^{13} - 2^{10} - 2^6)$, and the output difference is $\beta = (e_{10,0}, e_5, e_{30}, 0, 0)$ under key difference ΔK^* with probability 2^{-35}. For the second sub-cipher the input difference $\gamma = (e_1, e_1, 0, e_{30,31}, e_{31})$ becomes output difference $\delta = (0, e_3, 0, 0, e_0)$ under key difference $\Delta K'$ with probability 2^{-36}. The second differential defines a weak key class which contains one out of 2^8 keys, for these weak keys, the probability of the second differential is increased to $2^{-28} (= 2^{-36} \cdot 2^8)$. The probability of the first three rounds of the first differential can be increased by a factor of 2^9 by fixing the equivalent of 9 plaintext bits (presented in Table 6) in each of the plaintexts of the pair, and after the increase the probability of the first differential is 2^{-35}. Thus, starting with N plaintext pairs with input difference α and fixed the 9 bits in each of the plaintexts to the first sub-cipher we expect $N^2 \cdot (p^2 q^2 2^{-160}) = N^2 \cdot 2^{-286}$ right quartets. Therefore, Given 2^{144} related-key chosen plaintext pairs, we expect

$4(= (2^{144})^2 \cdot 2^{-160} \cdot (2^{-63})^2)$ right quartets, while for a random cipher only $2^{-32}(= (2^{144})^2 \cdot (2^{-160})^2)$ are expected.

The following is the derivation for the sufficient conditions in round 0 of Table 7. The input difference in round 0 is $\alpha = ([-8, 1], [3], [3, -20], [16, 31], 2^{13} - 2^{10} - 2^6)$, and the desired output difference in round 0 of $([-10], [-8, 1], [1], [3, -20], [16, 31])$.

1. According to (2) of Proposition 1, the condition $B_{0,20} = 0$ ensures that the change in the 20th bit in C_0 results in no change in A_1.
2. According to (3) of Proposition 1, the condition $B_{0,16} = 1$ ensures that the change in the 16th bit in D_0 results in no change in A_1.
3. According to (3) of Proposition 1, the condition $B_{0,31} = 0$ ensures that the change in the 31st bit in D_0 and $\Delta K_1 = 2^{31}$ result in no change in A_1.
4. From the property of the function F_0, the condition $D_{0,3} = 1$ ensures that the changes in the 2nd bits of B_0 and C_0 result in no change in A_1.
5. From $\Delta E_0 = 2^{13} - 2^{10} - 2^6$ and $\Delta A_0 = -2^8 + 2$, the condition $A_{1,10} = 1$ ensures that $A_1 = A_1[-10]$.

Therefore $\Delta A_1 = [-10]$ holds with the probability of 2^{-1} by fixing the equivalent to 4 bits in the plaintexts.

In the same way, we can prove that the conditions $C_{0,1} = 1$, $B_{0,10} = C_{0,8}$ and $A_{0,3} = A_{0,20} = 1$ ensure that $\Delta A_2 = [15]$ holds with the probability of 2^{-1}, and the condition $A_{0,12} = B_{0,12}$ ensures that $\Delta A_3 = [3]$ holds with the probability of 2^{-4}.

5.2 The Key Recovery Attack Procedure for the Full SHACAL-1 with 512-Bit Keys

Let the four different unknown keys be $K, K^* = K \oplus \Delta K^*, K' = K \oplus \Delta K', K'^* = K' \oplus \Delta K^*$, where ΔK^* is the key difference of the first related-key differential and $\Delta K'$ is the key difference for the second key differential. Assume the plaintexts P, P^*, P' and P'^* are encrypted under the keys K, K^*, K' and K'^* respectively. Denote the intermediate values encrypted under E_0 by IM, IM^*, IM' and IM'^*, respectively. (P, P^*) and (P', P'^*) are the pairs with respect to the first differential, and $(IM, IM'), (IM^*, IM'^*)$ are the pairs with respect to the second differential, i.e. $(C, C'), (C^*, C'^*)$ are the pairs with respect to the second differential.

We denote the 160-bit value X_i is by the five 32-bit words $X_{iA}, X_{iB}, X_{iC}, X_{iD}$ and X_{iE}. Also, we denote the set of all possible additive differences of ΔA_{67} by S'. The attack finds the four related-keys using 2^{146} related-key chosen plaintexts using the following algorithm:

1. Choose two pools of 2^{144} plaintext pairs (P_i, P_i^*) and (P'_j, P'^*_j) such that
   (a) $P_i^* - P_i = P'^*_j - P'_j = \alpha$;
   (b) P_i and P_j^* have the fixed bits as given in Table 6 and required by the modular differential, i.e., for P_i: $P_{iA,3} = P_{iA,8} = P_{iA,20} = P_{iB,16} = P_{iC,1} = P_{iC,20} = P_{iD,3} = 1$, $P_{iA,1} = P_{iB,3} = P_{iB,20} = P_{iB,31} = P_{iC,3} = P_{iD,16} = 0$, and $P_{iA,12} = P_{iB,12}, P_{iB,10} = P_{iC,8}$.

(c) P_i, P_i^*, P_j' and $P_j'^*$ are encrypted using the keys K, K^*, K' and K'^*, respectively, which result in the ciphertexts C_i, C_i^*, C_j', and $C_j'^*$.

2. Guess a 323-bit key quartet (k, k^*, k', k'^*) for rounds 70–79 and $K_{69,1}$, $K_{69,3}$, $K_{69,4}$. For the guessed key quartet (k, k^*, k', k'^*), and decrypt all the ciphertexts $C_i, C_i^*, C_j', C_j'^*$ from round 79 to round 70 and compute the additive difference before round 69. Denote the corresponding intermediate values by $U_i, U_i^*, U_j', U_j'^*$, respectively. Then we obtain words A, B, C, D of all words and the additive difference for all the pairs U_{iE}, U_{iE}^* and all the pairs $U_{iE}', U_{iE}'^*$. Find all quartets $(U_i, U_i^*, U_j', U_j'^*)$ satisfying $U_{iC,D,E} \oplus U_{jC,D,E}' \in S$ and $U_{iC,D,E}^* \oplus U_{jC,D,E}'^* \in S$, where $S = \{(a, b, c) : ROTR_{30}(a) \in S', b = ROTL_{30}(\Delta A_{66}) = 0, c = ROTL_{30}(\Delta B_{66}) = e_1\}$. Discard all other quartets.

3. Guess the remainder bits of K_{69} and bits 1,9 of K_{68}. For each of the guessed subkeys:

   (a) Decrypt the remaining quartets to get $U_{iE}, U_{jE}', U_{iE}^*$ and $U_{jE}'^*$. Partially decrypt all the remaining quartets $(U_i, U_i^*, U_j', U_j'^*)$ using the keys k, k^*, k' and k'^* respectively, and denote the resulting intermediate values by $(Z_i, Z_i^*, Z_j',$
   $Z_j'^*)$. We will get A, B, C, D of Z_i ($Z_i^*, Z_j', Z_j'^*$), and the additive difference between Z_{iE} and Z_{jE}' (and the additive difference between Z_{iE}^* and $Z_{jE}'^*$). Check whether $Z_{iE} \oplus Z_{jE}' = \Delta C_{66} = 0$ and discard all the quartets that do not satisfy the condition.

   (b) For each of the remaining quartets, check whether $Z_{iE}^* \oplus Z_{jE}'^* = \Delta C_{66} = 0$ and discard all the quartets that do not satisfy the condition.

4. Guess the remainder bits of K_{68} and bits 1,4 of K_{67}. For each of the guessed subkeys:

   (a) Decrypt the quartets to get $Z_{iE}, Z_{jE}', Z_{iE}^*$ and $Z_{jE}'^*$. Partially decrypt all the remaining quartets $(Z_i, Z_i^*, Z_j', Z_j'^*)$ using the keys k, k^*, k' and k'^* respectively, and denote the resulting intermediate values by $(Y_i, Y_i^*, Y_j',$
   $Y_j'^*)$. We will get A, B, C, D of Y_i ($Y_i^*, Y_j', Y_j'^*$), and the additive difference between Y_{iE} and Y_{jE}' (and the additive difference between Y_{iE}^* and $Y_{jE}'^*$). Check whether $Y_{iE} \oplus Y_{jE}' = \Delta D_{66} = 0$ and discard all the quartets that do not satisfy the condition.

   (b) For each of the remaining quartets, check whether $Y_{iE}^* \oplus Y_{jE}'^* = \Delta D_{66} = 0$ and discard all the quartets that do not satisfy the condition.

5. Guess the remainder bits of K_{67} and bits 0,3 of K_{66}. For each of the guessed subkeys:

   (a) Decrypt the quartets to get $Y_{iE}, Y_{jE}', Y_{iE}^*$ and $Y_{jE}'^*$. Partially decrypt all the remaining quartets $(Y_i, Y_i^*, Y_j', Y_j'^*)$ using the keys k, k^*, k' and k'^* respectively, and denote the resulting intermediate values by $(X_i, X_i^*,$
   $X_j', X_j'^*)$. We will get A, B, C, D of X_i ($X_i^*, X_j', X_j'^*$), and the additive difference between X_{iE} and X_{jE}' (and the additive difference between X_{iE}^* and $X_{jE}'^*$). Check whether $X_{iE} \oplus X_{jE}' = \Delta E_{66} = e_0$ and discard all the quartets that do not satisfy the condition.

   (b) For each of the remaining quartets, check whether $X_{iE}^* \oplus X_{jE}'^* = \Delta E_{66} = e_0$ and discard all the quartets that do not satisfy the condition.

6. Exhaustively search for the remaining 94 key bits by trial encryption for the suggested key k.

The first 9 fixed bits as given in Step 1(b) of P_i ensure that the probability of the first differential is increased by a factor of 2^9. According to the input difference of the plaintexts, we will know that P_i^*, P_j' and $P_j'^*$ also have the 9 fixed bits as given in Table 6, i.e. $P_{iA,3}^* = 1$, $P_{iA,3}' = 1$, $P_{iA,3}'^* = 1$, $P_{iA,12}^* = P_{iB,12}^*$, $P_{iA,12}' = P_{iB,12}'$, $P_{iA,12}'^* = P_{iB,12}'^*$, etc. Besides these bits, the nature of the modular differential, i.e., the signs, set 6 more bits to predetermined values. These 6 bits in Step 1(b) are deduced as follows: for each bit whose difference according to the differential from Table 7 is positive, we set P_i to be zero and P_i^* to be one (and of course P_j' to zero and $P_j'^*$ to one as well). If the difference is negative, we perform the same but with opposite values.

This means our related-key differential characteristic exploits plaintexts pairs for which 15 bits are effectively fixed respectively. P_i, P_i^*, P_i' and $P_i'^*$ has 15 fixed bits respectively, and we choose 2^{144} pairs (P_i, P_i^*) and $(P_j', P_j'^*)$, which can be realized while each plaintext has 160 bits.

According to the key schedule of SHACAL-1, we know that for the pairs we consider, $\Delta K_{67} = e_{1,4}$, $\Delta K_{68} = e_{1,9}$ and $\Delta K_{69} = e_{1,3,4}$. A pair which satisfies the differential has difference in bit $B_{66,3}$, i.e., the difference in B_{66} is either [3] or [−3] (or more precisely, after the XOR of the three words the difference is either [3] or [−3]), in bit $E_{66,0}$ (difference [0] or [−0]) and in bits 0, 3 of the subkey, i.e., it is either [0, 3], [0, −3], [−0, 3], or [−0, −3]. Thus, there are only 9 possible additive differences in A_{67}: 0, [1], [−1], [1, 4], [−1, −4], [4], [−4], [−1, 4] and [1, −4]. As noted earlier, that means that there is no point in guessing bits 4–31 of the subkey of round 66. Similarly, that means that in order to verify that a pair might satisfy the differential, given A_{70}, B_{70}, C_{70}, D_{70}, E_{70}, in order to achieve $\Delta E_{69} = e_1$, we can consider the modular difference of the key, and disregard the bits in positions 5–31. Thus, we only guess bits 1,3,4 of the subkey in round 69, i.e. actually only guess its key modular difference since we know whether the XOR difference between K_{69} and K_{69}' satisfy the differential.

The data complexity of this attack is 2^{146} related-key chosen plaintexts. The memory requirements are about $2^{150.33}(= 2^{146} \times 20)$ memory bytes.

In Step 1, the time complexity is 2^{146} SHACAL-1 encryptions. The time complexity of Step 2 is about $2^{465} = (2^{323} \times 2^{146} \times \frac{1}{2} \times \frac{11}{80})$ encryptions on average. The factor $\frac{1}{2}$ means the average fraction of 323-bit subkey which are used in Step 2. We guess 3 bits of K_{69} and there are 2^{32} the modular difference between E_{69} and E_{69}', so the probability of $\Delta E_{69} = e_1$ is $2^{-29} = \frac{2^3}{2^{32}}$. Also we know that there are about 9 possible ΔA_{67} values in S' and the attack starts with 2^{288} quartets, therefore we expect that $2^{288} \times (2^{-32} \times 2^{-29} \times \frac{9}{2^{32}})^2 = 2^{108}$ quartets pass Step 2.

For a given subkey guess, Step 3 consists of $2^{108} \times 2^{29} \times 2^2 = 2^{139}$ partial decryptions of one SHACAL-1 round. Therefore, the time complexity of Step 3 is about $2^{323} \times 2^{139} \times 4 \times \frac{1}{2} \times \frac{1}{80} = 2^{457}$. The time complexity of the other steps are relatively smaller. Hence, the time complexity of this attack is about 2^{465} SHACAL-1 encryptions.

A different method can be adopted in the attack. The last round of the second differential can be removed, then we will get a 66-round related-key rectangle distinguisher with probability 2^{-61}. Using the similar analysis approach, we can present a related-key rectangle attack on SHACAL-1 with data complexity of 2^{144} chosen plaintexts and time complexity of $2^{494} = (2^{354} \times 2^{144} \times \frac{1}{2} \times \frac{11}{80})$ SHACAL-1 encryptions.

6 Improving the Attack on IDEA

A careful investigation of the way XOR differences behave through addition can also be used to improve results of previous attacks. Consider for example the related-key rectangle attack on 6.5-round IDEA from [4]. The attack uses two related-key differentials, where the first related-key differential starts with an input difference $(0, 0, 0001_x, 0)$, while the key difference is in bit 40, and with probability $1/2$ the key difference cancels the input difference. While in [4], the probability of this first part of the differential was assumed to be half, it is actually 1 for plaintext pairs with the opposite sign of the key difference, and 0 for plaintext pairs with the same sign.

The above observation lead to an obvious improvement. The attacker first considers only pairs with the same sign in the differing bit, and applies the attack. If the attack fails, the attacker repeats the attack with the opposite sign.

We note that this approach indeed increases the value of $\hat{p}$ by a factor of two. Thus, for the right guess of the sign, the data complexity can be reduced by a factor of two (recall that the number of pairs is proportional to $1/\hat{p}\hat{q}$). However, the actual sign of the key difference is unknown, thus the attack has to be repeated twice — once for each guess (each time with half the data).

However, we gain a factor of two in the time complexity, as in each application we have only a quarter of the number of quartets that we expected in the original attack. As the attack is repeated twice, then the total number of analyzed quartets is reduced by a factor of two.

We note that for a differential attack a similar scenario holds (no reduction in the data complexity, but a possible reduction in the time complexity). However, for boomerang attacks, as the data complexity is proportional to $1/\hat{p}^2\hat{q}^2$, then we expect a reduction in the data complexity besides the probable reduction in time complexity.

7 Conclusion

In this paper we identified the misuse of XOR differences through addition. The observation led us to examine all the differential-based attacks on SHACAL-1, showing that these attacks fail. After pointing out the problems and by using modular differences, we fix some of the attacks, and present the best known (valid) attack on SHACAL-1 in the one key model (a rectangle attack on the first 51 rounds).

We continue to present a new related-key rectangle attack on the full SHACAL-1, which is applicable to one out of 256 keys (rather than out of 2^{14} for the previously best result). The new attack uses 2^{146} chosen plaintexts (or 2^{144} chosen plaintexts) and has a time complexity of 2^{465} SHACAL-1 encryptions (or 2^{494} SHACAL-1 encryptions, respectively).

We verified all the differentials that we used in the paper. Each differential was tested under 100 keys (or 100 key pairs), where each time we verified several rounds of the differential. The sets of rounds were chosen to be overlapping to reduce the chance that some condition from one round affects the differential's behavior in a later round.

We conclude that differential attacks should be very carefully applied when XOR differences are used in addition. We note that the related-key rectangle attack based on the modular differences can be applied to analyze other block ciphers, thus increasing the toolbox of the cryptanalyst.

References

1. Biham, E.: New Types of Cryptanalytic Attacks Using Related Keys. In: Helleseth, T. (ed.) EUROCRYPT 1993. LNCS, vol. 765, pp. 398–409. Springer, Heidelberg (1994)
2. Biham, E., Dunkelman, O., Keller, N.: Rectangle Attacks on 49-Round SHACAL-1. In: Johansson, T. (ed.) FSE 2003. LNCS, vol. 2887, pp. 22–35. Springer, Heidelberg (2003)
3. Biham, E., Dunkelman, O., Keller, N.: Related-Key Boomerang and Rectangle Attacks. In: Cramer, R.J.F. (ed.) EUROCRYPT 2005. LNCS, vol. 3494, pp. 507–525. Springer, Heidelberg (2005)
4. Biham, E., Dunkelman, O., Keller, N.: New Cryptanalytic Results on IDEA. In: Lai, X., Chen, K. (eds.) ASIACRYPT 2006. LNCS, vol. 4284, pp. 412–427. Springer, Heidelberg (2006)
5. Biham, E., Shamir, A.: Differential Cryptanalysis of DES-like Cryptosystems. In: Menezes, A.J., Vanstone, S.A. (eds.) CRYPTO 1990. LNCS, vol. 537, pp. 2–21. Springer, Heidelberg (1991)
6. Blunden, M., Escott, A.: Related Key Attacks on Reduced Round KASUMI. In: Matsui, M. (ed.) FSE 2001. LNCS, vol. 2355, pp. 277–285. Springer, Heidelberg (2002)
7. Dunkelman, O., Keller, N., Kim, J.: Related-Key Rectangle Attack on the Full SHACAL-1. In: Proceedings of SAC 2006. LNCS, Springer, Heidelberg (to appear)
8. Handschuh, H., Naccache, D.: SHACAL. In: Preproceedings of NESSIE first workshop, Leuven (2000)
9. Handschuh, H., Naccache, D.: SHACAL: A Family of Block Ciphers, the NESSIE project (submission, 2002)
10. Hong, S., Kim, J., Kim, G., Lee, S., Preneel, B.: Related-Key Rectangle Attacks on Reduced Versions of SHACAL-1 and AES-192. In: Gilbert, H., Handschuh, H. (eds.) FSE 2005. LNCS, vol. 3557, pp. 368–383. Springer, Heidelberg (2005)
11. Kelsey, J., Schneier, B., Wagner, D.: Key-Schedule Cryptoanalysis of IDEA, G-DES, GOST, SAFER, and Triple-DES. In: Koblitz, N. (ed.) CRYPTO 1996. LNCS, vol. 1109, pp. 237–251. Springer, Heidelberg (1996)

12. Kelsey, J., Schneier, B., Wagner, D.: Related-Key Cryptanalysis of 3-WAY, Biham-DES, CAST, DES-X, NewDES, RC2, and TEA. In: Han, Y., Quing, S. (eds.) ICICS 1997. LNCS, vol. 1334, pp. 233–246. Springer, Heidelberg (1997)
13. Kim, J., Kim, G., Hong, S., Lee, S., Hong, D.: The Related-Key Rectangle Attack — Application to SHACAL-1. In: Wang, H., Pieprzyk, J., Varadharajan, V. (eds.) ACISP 2004. LNCS, vol. 3108, pp. 123–136. Springer, Heidelberg (2004)
14. Kim, J., Moon, D., Lee, W., Hong, S., Lee, S., Jung, S.: Amplified Boomerang Attack against Reduced-Round SHACAL. In: Zheng, Y. (ed.) ASIACRYPT 2002. LNCS, vol. 2501, pp. 243–253. Springer, Heidelberg (2002)
15. Ko, Y., Hong, S., Lee, W., Lee, S., Kang, J.S.: Related Key Differential Attacks on 27 Rounds of XTEA and Full-Round GOST. In: Roy, B., Meier, W. (eds.) FSE 2004. LNCS, vol. 3017, pp. 299–316. Springer, Heidelberg (2004)
16. Lai, X., Massey, J.L., Murphy, S.: Markov Ciphers and Differential Cryptanalysis. In: Davies, D.W. (ed.) EUROCRYPT 1991. LNCS, vol. 547, pp. 17–38. Springer, Heidelberg (1991)
17. Lu, J., Kim, J., Keller, N., Dunkelman, O.: Differential and Rectangle Attacks on Reduced-Round SHACAL-1. In: Barua, R., Lange, T. (eds.) INDOCRYPT 2006. LNCS, vol. 4329, pp. 17–31. Springer, Heidelberg (2006)
18. Rivest, R.: The MD4 Message-Digest Algorithm. In: Menezes, A.J., Vanstone, S.A. (eds.) CRYPTO 1990. LNCS, vol. 537, pp. 303–311. Springer, Heidelberg (1991)
19. Rivest, R.: The MD5 Message-Digest Algorithm, Network Working Group Request for Comments 1321 (April 1992)
20. US National Bureau of Standards, Secure Hash Standard, Federal Information Processing Standards Publications No. 180-2 (2002)
21. Wang, X.Y., Lai, X.J., Feng, D., Chen, H., Yu, X.: Cryptanalysis of the Hash Functions MD4 and RIPEMD. In: Cramer, R.J.F. (ed.) EUROCRYPT 2005. LNCS, vol. 3494, pp. 1–18. Springer, Heidelberg (2005)
22. Wang, X.Y., Lisa, Y., Yu, H.B.: Finding collisions on the Full SHA-1. In: Shoup, V. (ed.) CRYPTO 2005. LNCS, vol. 3621, pp. 17–36. Springer, Heidelberg (2005)
23. Wang, X.Y., Yu, H.B.: How to Break MD5 and Other Hash Functions. In: Cramer, R.J.F. (ed.) EUROCRYPT 2005. LNCS, vol. 3494, pp. 19–35. Springer, Heidelberg (2005)
24. Wang, X.Y., Yu, H.B., Lisa, Y.: Efficient Collision Search Attacks on SHA-0. In: Shoup, V. (ed.) CRYPTO 2005. LNCS, vol. 3621, pp. 1–16. Springer, Heidelberg (2005)
25. Wang, X.Y.: The Collision attack on SHA-0 (in Chinese) (to appear) (1997), www.infosec.sdu.edu.cn

A   The New Related-Key Differentials of SHACAL-1

Table 8. The Second Related-Key Differential Characteristic for SHACAL-1

Round(i)	ΔA_i	ΔB_i	ΔC_i	ΔD_i	ΔE_i	ΔK_i	Probability
33	e_1	e_1	0	$e_{30,31}$	e_{31}	$e_{1,6,30}$	
34	0	e_1	e_{31}	0	$e_{30,31}$	$e_{1,30}$	2^{-3}
35	0	0	e_{31}	e_{31}	0	$[a1]$	2^{-2}
36	e_1	0	0	e_{31}	e_{31}	$[-a6]$	2^{-1}
37	0	e_1	0	0	e_{31}	$e_{1,31}$	2^{-1}
38	0	0	e_{31}	0	0	e_{31}	2^{-1}
39	0	0	0	e_{31}	0	$[s1]e_{31}$	1
40	e_1	0	0	0	e_{31}	$[-s6]e_{31}$	2^{-1}
41	0	e_1	0	0	0	0	2^{-1}
42	e_1	0	e_{31}	0	0	$[-s6]e_{31}$	2^{-2}
43	0	e_1	0	e_{31}	0	e_{31}	2^{-2}
44	e_1	0	e_{31}	0	e_{31}	$[-s6]$	2^{-3}
45	0	e_1	0	e_{31}	0	e_{31}	2^{-2}
46	e_1	0	e_{31}	0	e_{31}	$[-s6]$	2^{-3}
47	0	e_1	0	e_{31}	0	$[-s1]e_{31}$	2^{-2}
48	0	0	e_{31}	0	e_{31}	0	2^{-3}
49	0	0	0	e_{31}	0	e_{31}	2^{-1}
50	0	0	0	0	e_{31}	e_{31}	2^{-1}
51	0	0	0	0	0	0	1
...	...	...	...	...	...	...	...
60	0	0	0	0	0	0	1
61	0	0	0	0	0	$[t2]$	1
62	e_2	0	0	0	0	$[-t7]$	2^{-1}
63	0	e_2	0	0	0	e_2	2^{-1}
64	0	0	e_0	0	0	$[b3]e_0$	2^{-1}
65	e_3	0	0	e_0	0	$[-b8]e_0$	2^{-2}
66	0	e_3	0	0	e_0	$e_{0,3}$	2^{-2}

The key difference is $\Delta K' = (e_{1,6,28,29,31},\ e_{0,4,6,28,30,31},\ e_{5,28,30},\ e_{29,0},\ e_{1,4,5,29,30},\ e_{1,6,29,30,31},\ e_{1,6,29},\ e_{6,29,30,31},\ e_{29,30},\ e_{0,31},\ e_5,\ e_1,\ e_{1,4,6,30},\ e_{1,6,30,31},\ e_{4,6,29,30,31},\ e_{1,29})$. $[?i]$ denotes $[i]$ or $[-i]$. When $[?i]$ denotes $[i]$, then $[-?i]$ denotes $[-i]$, and vice versa.

Table 9. The Fixed 24-Round Differential Characteristic for SHACAL-1 for the Attack in [17]

Round (i)	ΔA_i	ΔB_i	ΔC_i	ΔD_i	ΔE_i	Probability
0	$[-0]$	$[22]$	$[-16]$	0	$[6]$	
1	$[5]$	$[-0]$	$[20]$	$[-16]$	0	2^{-3}
2	$[10]$	$[5]$	$[-30]$	$[20]$	$[-16]$	2^{-4}
3	$[-15]$	$[10]$	$[3]$	$[-30]$	$[20]$	2^{-4}
4	0	$[-15]$	$[8]$	$[3]$	$[-30]$	2^{-3}
5	$[-30]$	0	$[-13]$	$[8]$	$[3]$	2^{-4}
6	0	$[-30]$	0	$[-13]$	$[8]$	2^{-2}
7	$[8]$	0	$[-28]$	0	$[-13]$	2^{-3}
8	0	$[8]$	0	$[-28]$	0	2^{-1}
9	0	0	$[6]$	0	$[-28]$	2^{-2}
10	$[-28]$	0	0	$[6]$	0	2^{-2}
11	$[-1]$	$[-28]$	0	0	$[6]$	2^{-2}
12	0	$[-1]$	$[-26]$	0	0	2^{-1}
13	0	0	$[-31]$	$[-26]$	0	2^{-2}
14	0	0	0	$[-31]$	$[-26]$	2^{-2}
15	$[-26]$	0	0	0	$[-31]$	2^{-2}
16	0	$[-26]$	0	0	0	1
17	0	0	$[-24]$	0	0	2^{-1}
18	0	0	0	$[-24]$	0	2^{-1}
19	0	0	0	0	$[-24]$	2^{-1}
20	$[-24]$	0	0	0	0	2^{-1}
21	$[-29]$	$[-24]$	0	0	0	2^{-1}
22	$[-2, \pm 24]$	$[-29]$	$[-22]$	0	0	2^{-2}
23	$[-7, \pm 22]$	$[-2, \pm 24]$	$[-27]$	$[-22]$	0	2^{-3}
24	$[\pm\{2, 22, 24\}, -12]$	$[-7, \pm 22]$	$[-0, \pm 22]$	$[-27]$	$[-22]$	2^{-5}

B   A New Differentials of SHACAL-1

Table 10. Extension of the Fixed Differential for Rounds 33–40

Round (i)	ΔA_i	ΔB_i	ΔC_i	ΔD_i	ΔE_i	Probability
33	[±{8,10,24}]	[±{2,4,8,20,22,25,29,31},-15]	[±{0,18,22,27},2,7]	[±{6,10,13,22},-29,-30]	[±{0,4,6,10,18,22,27},-2,24]	2^{-18}
34	[-2,±20,24,25,±29]	[±{8,10,24}]	$Mask_1$	[±{0,18,22,27},2,7]	[±{6,10,13,22},-29,-30]	2^{-14}
35	[-2,±8,±20,-29]	[-2,±20,24,25,±29]	[±{6,8,22}]	$Mask_1$	$Mask_1$	2^{-9}
36	[8]	[-2,±8,±20,-29]	[-0,±18,22,23,±27]	[±{6,8,22}]	[±{6,8,22}]	2^{-8}
37	0	[8]	[-0,±6,±18,-27]	[-0,±18,22,23,±27]	[-0,±18,22,23,±27]	2^{-4}
38	[-18]	0	[6]	[-0,±6,±18,-27]	[-0,±6,±18,-27]	2^{-4}
39	[22]	[-18]	0	[6]	[6]	2^{-3}
40	[-0]	[22]	[-16]	0		

[±{$j_1, j_2, \ldots, j_n$}] stands for [±j_1, ±j_2, …, ±j_n] and $Mask_1$ = [±{0,2,6,18,20,23,27,29},-13].

Table 11. Extension of the Fixed Differential for Rounds 64–69

Round (i)	ΔA_i	ΔB_i	ΔC_i	ΔD_i	ΔE_i	Probability
64	[±{2,22,24},-12]	[-7,±22]	[-0,±22]	[-27]	[-22]	2^{-6}
65	[±0,-17,-22,±29]	[±{2,22,24},-12]	[-5,±20]	[-0,±22]	[-27]	2^{-7}
66	[±{12,20,24},-22,-28]	[±0,-17,-22,±29]	[±{0,20,22},-10]	[-5,±20]	[-0,±22]	2^{-7}
67	[0,-2,±{5,10,25},-27]	[±{12,20,24},-22,-28]	[±0,-17,-22,±29]	[±{0,20,22},-10]	[-5,±20]	2^{-11}
68	[-0,-7,±{12,17,20,22,24,28}]	[0,-2,±{5,10,25},-27]	[±{10,18,22},-20,-26]	[±0,-17,-22,±29]	[±{0,20,22},-10]	2^{-14}
69	[±0,-10,-12]	[-0,-7,±{12,17,20,22,24,28}]	[-0,-7,±{3,8,23},-25,30]	[±{10,18,22},-20,-26]	[±0,-17,-22,±29]	

[±{$j_1, j_2, \ldots, j_n$}] stands for [±j_1, ±j_2, …, ±j_n].

MRHS Equation Systems

Håvard Raddum

Selmersenteret, University of Bergen, Norway*

Abstract. We show how to represent a non-linear equation over $GF(2)$ using linear systems with multiple right hand sides. We argue that this representation is particularly useful for constructing equation systems describing ciphers using an S-box as the only means for non-linearity. Several techniques for solving systems of such equations were proposed in earlier work, and are also explained here. Results from experiments with DES are reported. Finally we use our representation to link a particular problem concerning vector spaces to the security of ciphers with S-boxes as the only non-linear operation.

Keywords: cryptanalysis, algebraic attacks, DES, non-linear equation systems.

1 Introduction

For the last years, most of the activity in cryptanalysis has been focused on algebraic attacks and solving non-linear equation systems. Several interesting properties and observations have been found and studied, and techniques for solving equation systems associated with a cipher have been proposed. So far there is no method for solving such systems which stands out as the "best" way to solve non-linear systems, the structure of the system plays a part. Moreover, it may be difficult to implement the ideas on a large system in practice, normal computers run out of memory too fast, see [1].

The traditional way of representing an equation has been by the use of a multivariate polynomial (MP) written in algebraic normal form (ANF). In [2] systems representing the block cipher DES are studied, and the authors propose to convert them to SAT-problems and use SAT-solvers. In this paper we will look at another way of representing non-linear equations, and with it follows new ways for solving systems of these equations. These methods were recently presented in [3], and earlier versions can also be found in [4] and [5].

We will use these techniques on systems representing the DES cipher for various rounds to see how they do in practice. As a side effect of our view on the equations we also discover a simply stated problem which makes a foundation of the security of a specific class of ciphers, in the same way as factoring is a fundamental problem for the security of RSA and finding discrete logarithms is a basis for the security of Diffie-Hellman key exchange.

---

* This work was done while visiting the Information Security Institute, Queensland Univeristy of Technology, Australia.

C. Adams, A. Miri, and M. Wiener (Eds.): SAC 2007, LNCS 4876, pp. 232–245, 2007.

The paper is organized as follows. In Section 2 we describe the way we represent equations, and show that systems coming from ciphers where the only non-linear part is the use of an S-box are easy to construct and are particularly suited for this representation. In Section 3 we describe some of the methods we have developed for solving our equation systems, and in Section 4 we try them on systems constructed from the DES cipher. In Section 5 we describe a problem, which must be hard to solve in order for the AES (among other ciphers) to be secure. Conclusions are made in Section 6.

2   MRHS Equation Systems

All variables in our equations will be over $GF(2)$. In most of the literature on algebraic cryptanalysis a non-linear equation over $GF(2)$ is represented as a MP $f(x_1, \ldots, x_n) = 0$. The set $V(f) = \{(x_1, \ldots, x_n) | f(x_1, \ldots, x_n) = 0\}$ is the set of satisfying assignments of f, and is what really defines the constraints the equation puts on the solution. Instead of the representation using MP, we will write a linear system with Multiple Right Hand Sides (MRHS) to describe the constraints:

$$A\mathbf{x} = [b_1, \ldots, b_s], \tag{1}$$

where A is a $(k \times n)$-matrix of full rank and the b_i's are vectors of length k over $GF(2)$. A vector $\mathbf{x}$ satisfies (1) if $A\mathbf{x} = b_i$ for some i. For shorter notation we will usually write an equation as $A\mathbf{x} = [B]$, where B is a matrix with the b_i's as columns. We keep square brackets around B to underline that the equation is not to be understood as a normal matrix/vector product where B is the product $A\mathbf{x}$, but rather that $A\mathbf{x}$ can be any column of B.

2.1   MRHS Equations vs. MP Equations

It is rather straight-forward to map between polynomial equations $f(\mathbf{x}) = 0$ and MRHS equations $A\mathbf{x} = [B]$. Given a MRHS equation E we may construct the set V of points in $GF(2)^n$ that satisfy E. This can be done by getting the solutions to the ordinary linear system $A\mathbf{x} = b_i$ and take the union of these solutions for $i = 1, \ldots, s$ as V. Then we may use a method like Lagrange interpolation to construct an f with $V(f) = V$. Both f and E will then give the same constraint on the solution space.

Conversely, given $f(\mathbf{x}) = 0$, we may compute $V(f) = \{b_1, \ldots, b_s\}$, and create the MRHS equation $I_n\mathbf{x} = [b_1, \ldots, b_s]$. As we will see, this way of creating a MRHS equation is not optimal, we should take advantage of any linearity inherent in f.

We show this with a small example. Suppose we are given the polynomial equation

$$f(x_1, x_2, x_3, x_4, x_5) = x_1x_2 + x_1x_5 + x_2x_3 + x_3x_5 + x_4 = 0. \tag{2}$$

Writing the MRHS equation as $I_5\mathbf{x} = [b_1, \ldots, b_s]$ we get $s = 16$ possible right hand sides. However, if we notice that (2) can be factored as $(x_1 + x_3)(x_2 + x_5) + x_4 = 0$ we can set up the MRHS equation

$$
\begin{bmatrix} 1\,0\,1\,0\,0 \\ 0\,1\,0\,0\,1 \\ 0\,0\,0\,1\,0 \end{bmatrix}
\begin{pmatrix} x_1 \\ x_2 \\ x_3 \\ x_4 \\ x_5 \end{pmatrix}
=
\begin{bmatrix} 0\,0\,1\,1 \\ 0\,1\,0\,1 \\ 0\,0\,0\,1 \end{bmatrix}
$$

which gives the same constraint, but only has four possible right hand sides.

2.2   MRHS Equations from Ciphers

We will now show that MRHS representation of equations is very well suited for algebraic cryptanalysis of ciphers where the only source of non-linearity is the use of S-boxes. We call this class of ciphers *S-box based ciphers*. This class contains the most important block cipher, the AES [7], as well as several other well known ciphers, like DES [8], Serpent [9], Noekeon [10], etc.

Suppose we are looking at the AES and want to construct a system of equations describing the cipher. In order to keep equations small enough to handle we need to introduce variables in each round. Let us say the bits in the cipher block right after one application of SubBytes are $x_1, \ldots, x_{128}$ and that the bits in the cipher block after the next application of SubBytes are $y_1, \ldots, y_{128}$. Look at the first of the S-boxes used between $\mathbf{x}$ and $\mathbf{y}$. The bits input to this S-box will be $l_1(\mathbf{x}) + k_1, \ldots, l_8(\mathbf{x}) + k_8$, where k_i are the first eight bits of the round key used in this round, and the l_i are linear combinations using 32 of the $\mathbf{x}$-variables coming from ShiftRows and MixColumns. The bits at the output of this S-box will be $y_1, \ldots, y_8$. We can now set up the MRHS equation for this S-box as

$$
\begin{bmatrix} l_1(\mathbf{x}) + k_1 \\ \vdots \\ l_8(\mathbf{x}) + k_8 \\ y_1 \\ \vdots \\ y_8 \end{bmatrix}
=
\begin{bmatrix} 0 & 1 & \ldots & 255 \\ S(0) & S(1) & \ldots & S(255) \end{bmatrix},
\tag{3}
$$

where both i and $S(i)$ are written as 8-bit vectors. This equation has the 256 possible input/output combinations of the S-box as right hand sides and is a compact representation of the constraints imposed by the S-box when linking the $\mathbf{x}$ and $\mathbf{y}$ variables.

To construct MRHS equations in a general S-box based cipher, we will introduce variables between applications of S-boxes, so that the input and output bits of each S-box are linear combinations of variables and constants. The matrix A will have these linear combinations as rows and the columns of B will be the possible input/output combinations for the S-box. Setting up an MRHS equation system describing a complete S-box based cipher is then easily done by constructing one equation for each S-box used in the cipher.

Note that apart from linear combinations of variables, there is no need to compute MPs. The MRHS equations are constructed directly from the cipher specifications. The size of the system depends only on the size and the number of S-boxes, and not on the degree of MPs defining the S-box or on diffusion properties of the linear operations in the cipher.

3   Techniques for Solving MRHS Equation Systems

In this section we will explain some techniques for solving an MRHS equation system. To make the presentation of this simpler, we first make a note on the number of columns in the A-matrices appearing in the MRHS equations in the system.

When setting up an MRHS equation system

$$A_1 \mathbf{x} = [B_1], \ldots, A_m \mathbf{x} = [B_m], \tag{4}$$

it is usually the case that the total number of variables in the system is quite large, but that any individual equation only involves a small subset of those variables. When writing an equation $A_i \mathbf{x} = [B_i]$, it is always assumed that $\mathbf{x} = (x_1, \ldots, x_n)^T$, where n is the **total** number of variables in the system. This is done by inserting **0**-columns in A_i for variables not occuring in the equation, such that the A_i-matrices all have exactly n columns.

A solution to (4) will be an $\mathbf{x}$-vector such that the product $A_i \mathbf{x}$ is a column found in B_i, for all $i = 1, \ldots, m$. One can say that the solution picks out the correct right hand side in each B_i, and that the other columns in B_i are wrong. The main strategy we use for trying to solve a system like (4) is to identify columns in B_i which can not be the correct right hand side for a solution, and delete them. If we are able to delete all wrong columns from each B_i we will be left with an ordinary system of linear equations (with only one right hand side), which can be easily solved.

The methods described below were all presented in [3], but we repeat them here for completeness since this work is quite recent and not well known.

3.1   Agreeing

This is the core method we use for finding right hand sides in equations that can not possibly be correct. This is done by looking for inconsistencies in a pair of equations and is done as follows. Let the equations $A_i \mathbf{x} = [B_i]$ and $A_j \mathbf{x} = [B_j]$ be given. By concatenating A_i and A_j on top of each other and expanding the columns in B_i and B_j with zeros we get the following identity:

$$\begin{bmatrix} A_i \\ A_j \end{bmatrix} \mathbf{x} = \begin{bmatrix} B_i \\ 0 \end{bmatrix} + \begin{bmatrix} 0 \\ B_j \end{bmatrix}$$

The possible right hand sides for the concatenated equation are made by picking one column from $\begin{bmatrix} B_i \\ 0 \end{bmatrix}$ and one column from $\begin{bmatrix} 0 \\ B_j \end{bmatrix}$ and adding them. Compute U such that $C = U \begin{bmatrix} A_i \\ A_j \end{bmatrix}$ is upper triangular, and let $T_i = U \begin{bmatrix} B_i \\ 0 \end{bmatrix}$ and $T_j =$

$U \begin{bmatrix} 0 \\ B_j \end{bmatrix}$. By multiplying through with U we get the equation $C\mathbf{x} = [T_i] + [T_j]$.

If $\begin{bmatrix} A_i \\ A_j \end{bmatrix}$ does not have full rank the last $r > 0$ rows of C will be all-zero. We only proceed if this is the case. Since the last r rows of C are all-zero, only columns from T_i and T_j that are equal in the last r coordinates can be added to make a possible right hand side for $C\mathbf{x}$, other choices would lead to an inconsistent system. Let Pr_i and Pr_j be the projection of T_i and T_j onto the last r coordinates, repectively. Any column in T_i whose projection is not found in Pr_j can not come from the correct column in B_i since adding it to any column of T_j will produce a right hand side inconsistent with $C\mathbf{x}$. The same applies to T_j, so all columns in T_i and T_j whose projections are not in $Pr_i \cap Pr_j$ will always create an inconsistency and the corresponding columns in B_i and B_j are wrong and can be deleted. An example of agreeing two MRHS equations can be found in the Appendix.

Agreeing pairs of equations may cause a domino effect of deletions of right hand sides. For example, say that no deletions occur when agreeing equations E_1 and E_2, but that deletions occur in E_2 when agreeing it with E_3. These deletions may cause E_1 and E_2 to disagree, so deletions will now occur in E_1 when agreeing it with E_2. These deletions may again trigger deletions in other equations, and so on. We run agreeing on every pair of equations in the system until no more deletions occur and all pairs of equations agree. We call this process the *agreeing algorithm*.

3.2   Extracting Linear Equations

The agreeing algorithm itself is normally not strong enough to solve a system of MRHS equations. When all pairs of equations agree but there still are many wrong right hand sides in the equations we may check to see if it is possible to squeeze ordinary linear equations out of them. This method is applied to equations individually and is done as follows.

Consider the equation $A\mathbf{x} = [B]$. Compute U, such that UB is upper triangular and transform the equation to $UA\mathbf{x} = [UB]$. Assume the last $r > 0$ rows of UB are all-zero, and let the r last rows of $UA\mathbf{x}$ be $l_1, \ldots, l_r$. All columns in B have 0 in the last r coordinates, so the correct column in particular have 0 in the last r coordinates. We then know the r linear equations $l_1 = 0, \ldots, l_r = 0$ must be true.

It may also be possible to make one more linear equation from the MRHS equation. We check if the all-one vector is found in the space spanned by the rows of B. This is easy to do, we may add the all-one vector to B and see if the rank of the resulting matrix increases by one, and can be done even faster when we have a basis for the row space of B in triangular form, as in UB. If we find that $\mathbf{v}B = \mathbf{1}$ for some $\mathbf{v}$, we know with certainty that the linear equation $\mathbf{v}A\mathbf{x} = 1$ is true. An example of extracting linear equations is found in the Appendix.

The linear equations produced this way can be used to eliminate variables in the system. As variables are eliminated, the rank of some of the A-matrices in the equations may not be full anymore. When this happens, we can find a vector $\mathbf{v} \neq \mathbf{0}$ such that $\mathbf{v}A = \mathbf{0}$, and we can compute $\mathbf{u} = \mathbf{v}B$. Columns in B found in positions where $\mathbf{u}$ has a 1-bit would lead to an inconsistent system, and can safely be removed as wrong columns. In this way, finding linear equations will also help to identify wrong columns and bring a solution to the system closer to the surface.

3.3 Gluing

When the agreeing algorithm works, it is because the spaces spanned by the rows of the A-matrices in some equations overlap in non-trivial common subspaces. When the agreeing algorithm stops, and no more linear equations can be extracted, we may try merging several equations into one. The spaces spanned by the A-matrices of the resulting equations will be larger, and hopefully have more overlap among them, so some new disagreements can be created. When merging two equations we say we *glue* them together.

When gluing two MRHS equations $A_i\mathbf{x} = [B_i]$ and $A_j\mathbf{x} = [B_j]$ together into a new equation $A\mathbf{x} = [B]$, much of the same steps as with agreeing are taken. The matrices A_i and A_j are concatenated, and the matrix C and the two expanded sets of right hand sides T_i and T_j are computed as explained under agreeing. Assume the last r rows of C are all-zero rows. We now create the columns in B by xoring every pair of one column from T_i and one column from T_j that are equal in the last r coordinates. The last r (all-zero) coordinates of the sum should be removed. The matrix A of the glued equation will then be C with the last r all-zero rows removed. The two equations we started with are now redundant and can be removed since all information contained in them is kept in the glued equation. Gluing reduces the number of equations in the system.

Let us say that the number of right hand sides in the equations B_i and B_j are s_i and s_j, respectively. Let $\mathbf{u} = (u_0, \ldots, u_{2^r-1})$ be a vector of integers where u_k is the number of columns in T_i that have the binary representation of k in the last r coordinates. Let $\mathbf{v} = (v_0, \ldots, v_{2^r-1})$ be the same kind of vector for T_j. The number of right hand sides in B will be the inner product $\mathbf{u} \cdot \mathbf{v} = \sum_{k=0}^{2^r-1} u_k v_k$. In general, the number of right hand sides in B will be much larger than $s_i + s_j$, and in the case $r = 0$ it will simply be $s_i s_j$.

Assume we have three MRHS equations E_1, E_2, E_3 that all pairwise agree. If we glue E_1 and E_2 into E it may be the case that E and E_3 do not agree, and that right hand sides will be removed from E_3 when agreeing it with E. What we are really doing is searching for inconsistencies across all three initial equations, and not only two as with ordinary agreeing. When gluing several equations together we will increase the probability of creating disagreements, which again will reduce the number of right hand sides.

In fact, if we could glue all equations in a system into one big MRHS equation, we would actually solve the system. What prevents us from doing that in practice is the fact that the number of right hand sides in a glued equation is (much) bigger than the number of right hand sides in the two equations we started with, assuming they agreed. In practice we have to set a limit on the number of right hand sides we are capable of storing in one MRHS equation. For the system to be solvable by gluing it is then necessary that enough disagreements occur after intermediate gluings so this threshold is never passed.

We will return to the scenario of gluing all equations in a system in Section 5.

3.4   A Complete Algorithm for Solving a System of MRHS Equations

When all pairs of equations agree, no linear equations can be extracted and we can not afford to glue any equations together, the last resort is to guess on the value of one variable, or a sum of variables. Guessing on the sum of some variables has the same effect as taking a linear equation and eliminating a variable with it. The sum of variables to be guessed could be one of the vectors occurring in the span of the rows of some A-matrices, in order to make sure some deletions of right hand sides occur. In the case for systems constructed from ciphers, it is a good idea to guess on the value of some of the user-selected key bits since these variables are special. If the value of the key bits are substituted into the system it will collapse; the rest of the system will be solved by simple agreeing alone.

We present here an algorithm where we try to find how few bits of information we need to guess in order to solve a system of MRHS equations. We call this the FewGuess algorithm, and the idea is to only guess one bit of information when all else has been tried. The maximum number of right hand sides we will handle in one equation is S. After each step in the algorithm we check if the system has been solved or become inconsistent, and exit with the number of guesses made if it has.

FewGuess

1. Run the agreeing algorithm.
2. Try to extract linear equations. If any linear equations were extracted, eliminate variables and go back to 1.
3. Glue together any pair of equations where the number of right hand sides in the glued equation is $\leq S$. If any gluings occurred go back to 1.
4. Guess on the value of a linear combination of variables, eliminate one variable and go back to 1.

This algorithm is designed to find how few bits we need to guess in order to determine whether a guess was right or wrong, and is not very efficient in terms of running time. After running this algorithm we know a set of linear combinations of variables to be guessed, and we know in which order equations were glued together. To set up a key recovery attack, we should first make all the guesses at once. Then we should glue together equations in the order given by our algorithm, and possibly run agreeing and extract linear equations first if some gluings will break the limit S.

If we need to guess b bits of information the complexity for solving a system will be of the order 2^b, multiplied with a constant that depends on S. This constant will be the complexity of running the agreeing algorithm, extracting linear equations and gluing together equations. These are not trivial operations, and implementing them in the most efficient way is a difficult task in itself. We will not investigate the complexities and the implementation issues of these operations here, but rather focus on the number of bits of information needed to guess in order to solve a system.

4   Experiments with DES

Inspired by the work in [2], we have constructed the MRHS equation system representing DES for various number of rounds, and tested the methods for solving described in the previous section. We assume the reader is familiar with the basic structure of DES, we repeat here the features that are most important for the construction of the MRHS equation system.

4.1   Constructing Equations

DES is a Feistel network, with a round function that takes a 32-bit input and a 48-bit round key to compute a 32-bit output. The bits of the round keys in DES are selected directly from the 56 user-selected key bits, so we need only 56 variables to represent the round keys. The only non-linear operation in DES is the use of the eight S-boxes in each round. We construct the equations as explained in Section 2.2, so we need that the bits at the input and output of each S-box can be written as a linear combination of variables and constants. We give variable names to the bits going into the round function in each round, except for the first and last rounds. The inputs of the first and last rounds are parts of the plaintext and ciphertext, considered constants in a cryptanalytic attack. The input and output bits of all S-boxes can then be expressed as linear combinations of variables and constants.

The number of variables in a system representing an r-round version of DES will be $56 + 32(r - 2)$. Each S-box gives one MRHS equation, so the system will consist of $8r$ equations. The S-boxes used in DES all take 6-bit inputs and produce 4-bit outputs. The A-matrix in each equation will thus consist of 10 rows, and the B-matrix will have 64 columns, one for each possible S-box input.

4.2   Results

We have tried the FewGuess algorithm on systems representing DES with a various number of rounds to see how few bits that were needed to guess in order to solve a system. The 56 key-variables are special, once these are determined the values of the other variables will be given by the system straight away. It is therefore natural to guess on the key variables when we need to guess since we know that at most 56 guesses are needed.

Table 1. Number of guesses needed to solve DES systems

# of rounds	guessing most used	guessing $k_1, k_2, \ldots$
4	3	3
5	26	17
6	34	28
7	38	38
8	38	38
10	38	38
12	38	38
16	41	38

Table 2. Number of key variables needed to guess for various limits S

S	# of guesses
2^8	48
2^{12}	45
2^{16}	41
2^{20}	36

The order of the variables to be guessed also plays a part. Since some key bits appear in round keys more often than others in DES, we tried the strategy of guessing on the most used key variables first, in the hope that eliminating these variables would create a bigger impact on the system. We also tried guessing the key bits in the order $1, 2, 3, \ldots$ to see if there was a difference. The maximum number of right hand sides we would allow in one equation was set to $S = 2^{18}$. The results were as follows.

As can be seen, the order in which the variables are guessed makes a difference, and it is not the greedy approach of guessing the most used variables first that is most efficient. A reason for this can maybe be found in the key schedule of DES. The key schedule is designed such that the key bits occuring in the inputs of the S-boxes S_1 - S_4 are all taken from $k_1, \ldots, k_{28}$. When these key bits are guessed, the inputs to S_1 - S_4 in the first and last round will be known. This will immediately give the value of 32 of the variables entering the second and the second to last rounds. When guessing on the most used key variables the guesses will be spread out over all 56 key variables and more guesses are needed before the values of all key variables entering one S-box are known.

Of course, the number of guesses increases with the number of rounds and it is necessary to guess 38 key variables to break seven rounds of DES this way. However, the number of guesses to break more rounds does not increase from 38, at least when guessing in the increasing order. It is natural to believe the number 38 is linked to the limit $S = 2^{18}$ since $18 + 38 = 56$, the number of user-selected key variables.

This suggests that 18 bits are guessed "implicitly" when storing up to 2^{18} right hand sides in the equations and that there is a number-of-guesses/memory tradeoff. The hypothesis is that setting the limit to $S = 2^l$ means we do not have to guess more than $56 - l$ key variables. We tried FewGuess on the system representing 16-round DES using other values for S and guessing the key bits in the order $1, 2, \ldots$ to check this hypothesis.

These few tests show the hypothesis is not exactly true, but almost. The order in which the variables are guessed plays a part.

5   The Security of S-Box Based Ciphers

In this section we will use the MRHS representation of equations to find an easily stated problem about vector spaces. This problem is independent of the structure of a particular S-box based cipher, and it has to be hard to solve if ciphers in this class are to remain secure.

Assume we are given an S-box based cipher and construct its MRHS equation system using a total of n variables. Let the number of input bits to the S-box(es) used be p, let the number of S-boxes used to process one encryption be q and let the number of output bits of the S-box be $k - p$. The MRHS equation system we get will be

$$A_1\mathbf{x} = [B_1], \ldots, A_q\mathbf{x} = [B_q],\tag{5}$$

where each A_i is a $k \times n$-matrix and each B_i is a $k \times 2^p$-matrix. Let us set this system up as if we are going to glue all equations into one big MRHS equation $A\mathbf{x} = [B]$ in one operation:

$$\begin{bmatrix} A_1 \\ \hline A_2 \\ \hline \vdots \\ \hline A_q \end{bmatrix} \begin{pmatrix} x_1 \\ x_2 \\ \vdots \\ x_n \end{pmatrix} = \begin{bmatrix} B_1 \\ \hline 0 \\ \hline \vdots \\ \hline 0 \end{bmatrix} + \begin{bmatrix} 0 \\ \hline B_2 \\ \hline \vdots \\ \hline 0 \end{bmatrix} + \ldots + \begin{bmatrix} 0 \\ \hline \vdots \\ \hline 0 \\ \hline B_q \end{bmatrix}\tag{6}$$

Using linear algebra we compute U such that U multiplied by the matrix on the left hand side of (6) is upper triangular. As in Section 3.3, let us call the resulting matrix C and let U multiplied with the bracket containing B_i be T_i. Multiplying through with U gives us

$$C\mathbf{x} = [T_1] + [T_2] + \ldots + [T_q],\tag{7}$$

where we are supposed to select exactly one column from each T_i and add them together to create a possible right hand side for $C\mathbf{x}$.

The matrix C has qk rows and n columns, and there are no linear relations among the variables (if there were, we would eliminate some variables first). Hence the last $qk - n$ rows of C are all-zero rows and put the constraint on the selection of the columns from the T_i's that their sum must be zero in the last $qk - n$ coordinates. If we can find such a selection of columns from the T_i's we get a consistent linear system with a unique right hand side, and solving this we get the solution to (5).

Let $Pr(\cdot)$ be the projection onto the last $qk - n$ coordinates and let $Z_i = (Pr(T_i))^T$. Concatenate the matrices Z_i like in the left hand side of (6) and call the resulting matrix Z.

$$Z = \begin{bmatrix} Z_1 \\ \dots \\ Z_q \end{bmatrix}$$

The number of rows in Z is $2^p q$ and the number of columns is $qk - n$. Our problem has been transformed to picking exactly one row from each Z_i such that they add up to $\mathbf{0}$. Similarly to the computation of U, we can compute a $(2^p q \times 2^p q)$-matrix M such that MZ is upper triangular. Let the matrix formed by the last $2^p q - qk + n$ rows of M be called M_0. Then any $\mathbf{v}$ from the row space of M_0 will give $\mathbf{v}Z = \mathbf{0}$.

Definition 1. *We say that a binary vector* $\mathbf{v} = (\mathbf{v}_1, \dots, \mathbf{v}_q)$ *where* $|\mathbf{v}_i| = 2^p$ *for some* q *and* p *has the q1-property if the Hamming weight of each* $\mathbf{v}_i$ *is one.*

We can now state the problem as follows.

A fundamental problem for S-box based ciphers. *Given a binary matrix* M_0 *with* $2^p q$ *columns for some* p *and* q. *If there are vectors in the row space of* M_0 *with the q1-property, find one.*

If we can solve this problem, the 1-bits in the found vector will indicate exactly which right hand sides that can be added together in (7) to form a consistent linear system. This would solve (5) and break any S-box based cipher, hence it must be a hard problem if these ciphers are to remain secure. On the other hand, if we can break an S-box based cipher (find its key given some plaintext/ciphertext pairs) we find the solution to the corresponding MRHS equation system and the positions of the correct right hand sides in each equation. Setting a 1-bit in these positions will give us a vector with the q1-property which is found in the rowspace of the associated M_0. This shows that solving the fundamental problem corresponding to an S-box based cipher is equivalent to breaking the cipher.

We do not propose any ideas for efficiently solving the fundamental problem here, but instead we take a look at the actual values of p, q, k and n for DES and AES to briefly see what the problem will look like in these specific instances.

For the full 16 round DES, we get $p = 6, q = 128, k = 10$ and $n = 56 + 14 \cdot 32 = 504$. The matrix M_0 will in this instance be a 7416×8192-matrix. For the full AES with 128-bit key we get $p = 8, q = 200, k = 16$ and $n = 1600$. This gives a M_0 with 49600 rows and 51200 columns. In both cases we see that the number of rows in M_0 is so much larger than the number of bits in the user-selected key that any algorithm solving the fundamental problem must be polynomial (or very close to polynomial) in the number of rows of M_0 to give an efficient attack.

6 Conclusions

The purpose of this paper is to show that the MRHS representation of non-linear equations should be taken into consideration when discussing algebraic attacks.

The representation of equations does matter. In [2] the authors do algebraic cryptanalysis of reduced-round DES, comparing their own technique to those implemented in software packages like MAGMA and Singular. The representation used for the equations is MPs, and the results are not as good as when they convert the equation system into CNF form and use a SAT-solver. There are some important differences between the MRHS representation and the MP representation.

First, the size of an MRHS equation is independent of the linear operations taking place between the use of two S-boxes. We may describe an S-box using a set of MPs in $\mathbf{x}$- (input) and $\mathbf{y}$- (output) variables. When the $\mathbf{x}$ and $\mathbf{y}$ are linear combinations of variables the size of these polynomials in ANF form will be very dependent on the number of variables in each linear combination.

Second, the degree of the MPs representing an S-box plays a crucial role for the complexity of solving a MP equation system. For MRHS equations this degree is irrelevant, the complexity of using the techniques described in this paper does not depend on it.

Third, there are fewer equations in an MRHS equation system than in a system of MP equations representing a cipher. One S-box gives rise to one MRHS equation, while there are a number of MP equations associated with one S-box. The strategies taken for solving these systems are also different in nature. When using MP representation we usually want to create *more* equations, to be able to solve by re-lienarization or find a Gröbner basis. This consumes a lot of memory in implementations. When using MRHS representation we want to *reduce* the number of equations by gluing, and to remove right hand sides.

Fourth, we are not aware of any method for finding and extracting all linear equations that might implicitly be hiding in a non-linear MP equation. The method described in Section 3.2 allows us to efficiently do this for an MRHS equation.

Using the MRHS representation also allowed us to derive a problem about finding a vector with a special property in a given vector space and show that solving this problem is equivalent to breaking any S-box based cipher. A lot of effort has been spent on the problems of factoring and discrete logarithms for assessing the security of several primitives in public key cryptography. It is reasonable to look more closely on the fundamental problem of S-box based ciphers stated in this paper, since the security of the AES depends on it.

We think that the MRHS representation of equations is better suited than MPs for systems representing an S-box based cipher. As traditional methods for solving MP equation systems tend to run out of memory, even on rather small systems, MRHS equation systems representing full ciphers can be constructed, and worked with. The MRHS representation of equations should go into the toolbox for algebraic cryptanalysis.

References

1. Cid, C., Murphy, S., Robshaw, M.: Small Scale Variants of the AES. In: Gilbert, H., Handschuh, H. (eds.) FSE 2005. LNCS, vol. 3557, pp. 145–162. Springer, Heidelberg (2005)
2. Courtois, N., Bard, G.: Algebraic Cryptanalysis of the Data Encryption Standard, Cryptology ePrint Archive, Report 2006/402 (2006), http://eprint.iacr.org/
3. Raddum, H., Semaev, I.: Solving MRHS linear equations. Extended abstract, In: International Workshop on Coding and Cryptography, April 16-20, 2007, Versailles, France (2007)
4. Raddum, H., Semaev, I.: New Technique for Solving Sparse Equation Systems, Cryptology ePrint Archive, Report 2006/475 (2006), http://eprint.iacr.org/
5. Raddum, H.: Cryptanalytic Results on Trivium (2006), available from http://www.ecrypt.eu.org/stream/triviump3.html
6. Courtois, N., Pieprzyk, J.: Cryptanalysis of Block Ciphers with Overdefined Systems of Equations, Cryptology ePrint Archive, Report 2002/044 (2002), http://eprint.iacr.org/
7. Rijmen, V., Daemen, J.: The Block Cipher Rijndael. Springer, Berlin (2002)
8. US National Bureau of Standards. Data Encryption Standard, Federal Information Processing Standards Publications No. 46 (1977)
9. Anderson, R., Biham, E., Knudsen, L.: Serpent: A Proposal for the Advanced Encryption Standard (1998), available from http://www.cl.cam.ac.uk/~rja14/serpent.html
10. Daemen, J., Peeters, M., Van Assche, G., Rijmen, V.: Nessie Proposal: Noekeon (2000), available from http://gro.noekeon.org/

A   Example of Agreeing and Extracting Linear Equations

A.1   Agreeing Example

We want to agree the following two equations:

$$\overset{A_1}{\begin{bmatrix} 1\,1\,0\,0\,0 \\ 0\,1\,0\,1\,0 \\ 0\,0\,1\,1\,0 \end{bmatrix}} \begin{pmatrix} x_1 \\ x_2 \\ x_3 \\ x_4 \\ x_5 \end{pmatrix} = \overset{B_1}{\begin{bmatrix} 0\,0\,1\,1 \\ 0\,1\,0\,1 \\ 1\,1\,1\,0 \end{bmatrix}} \qquad \overset{A_2}{\begin{bmatrix} 0\,0\,1\,0\,1 \\ 0\,1\,0\,1\,0 \\ 0\,1\,1\,0\,0 \end{bmatrix}} \begin{pmatrix} x_1 \\ x_2 \\ x_3 \\ x_4 \\ x_5 \end{pmatrix} = \overset{B_2}{\begin{bmatrix} 0\,0\,1\,1 \\ 0\,1\,0\,1 \\ 0\,0\,0\,1 \end{bmatrix}}$$

We compute U to make $\begin{bmatrix} A_1 \\ A_2 \end{bmatrix}$ triangular and find $T_1 = U \begin{bmatrix} B_1 \\ 0 \end{bmatrix}$ and $T_2 = U \begin{bmatrix} 0 \\ B_2 \end{bmatrix}$.

$$U = \begin{bmatrix} 1\,0\,0\,0\,0\,0 \\ 0\,1\,0\,0\,0\,0 \\ 0\,0\,1\,0\,0\,0 \\ 0\,0\,1\,1\,0\,0 \\ 0\,1\,0\,0\,1\,0 \\ 0\,1\,1\,0\,0\,1 \end{bmatrix} \qquad C = U \begin{bmatrix} A_1 \\ A_2 \end{bmatrix} = \begin{bmatrix} 1\,1\,0\,0\,0 \\ 0\,1\,0\,1\,0 \\ 0\,0\,1\,1\,0 \\ 0\,0\,0\,1\,1 \\ 0\,0\,0\,0\,0 \\ 0\,0\,0\,0\,0 \end{bmatrix},$$

$$T_1 = \begin{bmatrix} 0 & 0 & 1 & 1 \\ 0 & 1 & 0 & 1 \\ 1 & 1 & 1 & 0 \\ 1 & 1 & 1 & 0 \\ 0 & 1 & 0 & 1 \\ 1 & 0 & 1 & 1 \end{bmatrix} \qquad T_2 = \begin{bmatrix} 0 & 0 & 0 & 0 \\ 0 & 0 & 0 & 0 \\ 0 & 0 & 0 & 0 \\ 0 & 0 & 1 & 1 \\ 0 & 1 & 0 & 1 \\ 0 & 0 & 0 & 1 \end{bmatrix} .$$

We see that $r = 2$, and that $Pr_1 \cap Pr_2 = \{\binom{1}{0}, \binom{1}{1}\}$. The projections of the first and third columns from both T_1 and T_2 fall outside the intersection, hence the first and third columns from both B_1 and B_2 have been identified as wrong. After agreeing the equations are

$$\overset{A_1}{\begin{bmatrix} 1 & 1 & 0 & 0 & 0 \\ 0 & 1 & 0 & 1 & 0 \\ 0 & 0 & 1 & 1 & 0 \end{bmatrix}} \begin{pmatrix} x_1 \\ x_2 \\ x_3 \\ x_4 \\ x_5 \end{pmatrix} = \overset{B_1}{\begin{bmatrix} 0 & 1 \\ 1 & 1 \\ 1 & 0 \end{bmatrix}} \qquad \overset{A_2}{\begin{bmatrix} 0 & 0 & 1 & 0 & 1 \\ 0 & 1 & 0 & 1 & 0 \\ 0 & 1 & 1 & 0 & 0 \end{bmatrix}} \begin{pmatrix} x_1 \\ x_2 \\ x_3 \\ x_4 \\ x_5 \end{pmatrix} = \overset{B_2}{\begin{bmatrix} 0 & 1 \\ 1 & 1 \\ 0 & 1 \end{bmatrix}} .$$

A.2 Example of Extracting Linear Equations

We take the equation $A_1\mathbf{x} = [B_1]$, and extract linear equations from it. First we compute U to make B upper triangular, and multiply through to arrive at the following MRHS equation

$$\overset{UA_1}{\begin{bmatrix} 0 & 0 & 1 & 1 & 0 \\ 1 & 1 & 0 & 0 & 0 \\ 1 & 0 & 1 & 0 & 0 \end{bmatrix}} \begin{pmatrix} x_1 \\ x_2 \\ x_3 \\ x_4 \\ x_5 \end{pmatrix} = \overset{UB_1}{\begin{bmatrix} 1 & 0 \\ 0 & 1 \\ 0 & 0 \end{bmatrix}}$$

From the bottom row we get the linear equation $x_1 + x_3 = 0$. Adding the two top rows will create the 1-vector in UB_1, hence by adding the two top rows from UA_1 we also get the linear equation $x_1 + x_2 + x_3 + x_4 = 1$.

A Fast Stream Cipher with Huge State Space and Quasigroup Filter for Software*

Makoto Matsumoto[1], Mutsuo Saito[2], Takuji Nishimura[3],
and Mariko Hagita[4]

[1] Dept. of Math., Hiroshima University
m-mat@math.sci.hiroshima-u.ac.jp
[2] Dept. of Math., Hiroshima University
saito@math.sci.hiroshima-u.ac.jp
[3] Dept. of Math. Sci., Yamagata University
nisimura@sci.kj.yamagata-u.ac.jp
[4] Dept. of Info. Sci., Ochanomizu University
hagita@is.ocha.ac.jp

Abstract. Recent personal computers have high-spec CPUs and plenty of memory. The motivation of this study is to take these advantages in designing a tough and fast key-stream generator. Natural controversies on using a large state space for a generator are (1) effectiveness is unclear, (2) slower generation speed, (3) expensive initialization, and (4) costs in a hardware implementation.

Our proposal is to combine a linear feedback shift register (LFSR) and a uniform quasigroup filter with memory of wordsize. We prove theorems which assure the period and the distribution property of such generators, answering to (1). As for (2), the generation speed of a LFSR is independent of the state size. In addition, we propose a filter based on integer multiplication, which is rather fast in modern CPUs. We analyze the algebraic degree of such filters. We answer to (3) by a simple trick to use another small generator to initialize LFSR while outputting. We have no answer to (4), but comment that recent hardwares tend to have larger memory and sophisticated instructions.

As a concrete example, we propose CryptMT stream generator with period (no less than) $2^{19937} - 1$, 1241-dimensional equidistribution property, which is sometimes faster than SNOW2.0 in modern CPUs.

Keywords: stream cipher, combined generator, filter with memory, quasigroup filter, multiplicative filter, CryptMT, eSTREAM, period, distribution.

1 Stream Cipher

In this article, we pursue a fast stream cipher in software. We assume that the machine has plenty of memory, and a fast integer multiplication instruction.

---

* This work is supported in part by JSPS Grant-In-Aid #16204002, #18654021, #18740044, #19204002 and JSPS Core-to-Core Program No.18005.

C. Adams, A. Miri, and M. Wiener (Eds.): SAC 2007, LNCS 4876, pp. 246–263, 2007.

Let B be the set of symbols. Throughout this article, we assume B to be the set of one byte integers, which is identified with $\mathbb{F}_2{}^8$, where $\mathbb{F}_2 = \{0, 1\}$ is the two-element field. We consider a stream cipher based on a key-stream generator over B. A generator receives a key k in the set of possible keys K, then generates a sequence of elements

$$b_0(k), b_1(k), \ldots, b_n(k), \ldots, \in B.$$

A plain text (a sequence of elements of B) is encrypted by taking bitwise exor with the sequence $(b_n(k))$, and then decrypted by the same method.

1.1   Combined Generator

Such a sequence is typically generated by a finite state automaton.

Definition 1. *A finite state automaton A without input is a quadruple $A = (S, f, O, o)$, where S is a finite set (the set of states), $f : S \to S$ is a function (the state transition function), O is a set (the set of the output symbols), and $o : S \to O$ is the output function.*

For a given initial state s_0, A changes the state by the recursion $s_n := f(s_{n-1})$ $(n = 1, 2, 3, \ldots)$ and generates the sequence

$$o(s_0), o(s_1), o(s_2), \ldots \in O.$$

For a stream cipher, we prepare an *initializing* function init $: K \to S$, and take $O := B$. By setting $s_0 := \text{init}(k)$, the automaton A generates a sequence of elements in B. Its period is bounded by $\#(S)$.

To obtain a secure generator, larger $\#(S)$ and complicated f and o are desirable. However, if f is complicated, then the analysis of the sequence (such as computing the period and the distribution) often becomes difficult. A typical choice is to choose an $\mathbb{F}_2$-linear transition function. We take $S := \mathbb{F}_2{}^d$ and choose a linear transition function f. Then, the period can be computed by the linear algebra and polynomial calculus. In particular, the following linear feedback shift register generators (LFSRs) are widely used: $S := (\mathbb{F}_2{}^w)^n$ where w is the word size of the machine (e.g. $w = 32$ for 32-bit machines), and the transition is

$$f(x_1, x_2, \ldots, x_{n-1}, x_n) := (x_2, x_3, \ldots, x_n, g(x_1, \ldots, x_n)). \tag{1}$$

Here $g : (\mathbb{F}_2{}^w)^n \to \mathbb{F}_2{}^w$ is a linear function called the feedback function. This state transition is equivalent to the recursion

$$x_{i+n} := g(x_i, x_{i+1}, \ldots, x_{i+n-1}) \quad (i = 0, 1, 2, \ldots).$$

The output of LFSR is given by

$$o : S \to \mathbb{F}_2{}^w, \quad (x_1, \ldots, x_n) \mapsto x_1,$$

which is not secure as it is. A software implementation technique using a cyclic array ([9, P.28 Algorithm A]) reduces the computation of f to that of g and an index change. Consequently, the computation time is independent of the size of n, which allows a fast generator with huge state space. This type of generator is common for the pseudorandom number generation in Monte Carlo method (PRNG for MC), such as Mersenne Twister (MT19937) [10], whose period is $2^{19937} - 1$.

As a stream cipher, any linear recurring sequence is vulnerable, so we need to introduce some non-linearity. A conventional method is to choose a "highly non-linear" $o : S \to O$. In this context, o is called *a filter*.

One of the estimators of the non-linear property of a function is the *algebraic degree*.

Definition 2. *Let $h(c_1, c_2, \ldots, c_n)$ be a boolean function, i.e.,*

$$h : \mathbb{F}_2{}^n \to \mathbb{F}_2.$$

Then, the function h can be represented as a polynomial function of n variables $c_1, c_2, \ldots, c_n$ with coefficients in $\mathbb{F}_2$, namely as a function

$$h = \sum_{T \subset \{1,2,\ldots,n\}} a_T c_T$$

holds, where $a_T \in \mathbb{F}_2$ and $c_T := \prod_{t \in T} c_t$. This representation is unique, and called the algebraic normal form *of h. Its degree is called the algebraic degree of h.*

Let $h_{i,n}(s_0)$ denote the i-th bit of the n-th output $b_n(s_0)$ of the generator for the initial state s_0. This is a boolean function, when we consider $s_0 \in S = \mathbb{F}_2{}^d$ as d variables of bit. Thus, an adversary can obtain s_0 by solving the simultaneous equations $h_{i,n}(s_0) = o_{i,n}$ for unknown s_0 for various i and n, where $o_{i,n}$ are the outputs of the generator observed by the adversary. This is the *algebraic attack* (see for example [4], [3]).

A problem of a linear generator with filter is the following. Since any s_n is a linear function of the bits in $s_0 = \text{init}(k)$, the algebraic degree of $h_{i,n}(s_0)$ is bounded from the above by the algebraic degree of the i-th bit of the filter function o, namely that of the function

$$o_i : S \xrightarrow{o} \mathbb{F}_2{}^8 \xrightarrow{i\text{th}} \mathbb{F}_2.$$

To attain the high-speed generation, o_i cannot access so many bits in S, and its algebraic degree is bounded by the number of accessed bits. This decreases the merits of the large state space. A *filter with memory*, which is just a finite state automaton with input, solves this conflict (see §2.3 for its effect on the algebraic degree).

Definition 3. *A finite state automaton A with input is a five-tuple $A = (S, I, f, O, o)$. The data S, O, o are same with Definition 1. The difference is that it has another component I (the set of input symbols), and that the state transition function is of the form $f : I \times S \to S$. For an initial state s_0 and an input sequence $i_0, i_1, \ldots \in I$, A changes the state by $s_n = f(i_{n-1}, s_{n-1})$ $(n = 1, 2, 3, \ldots)$.*

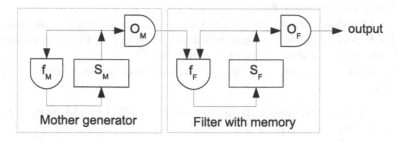

Fig. 1. Combined generator

Definition 4. *(A combined generator with filter with memory.)*
Let $A_M := (S_M, f_M, O_M, o_M)$ be an automaton without input (called the mother generator, M for mother). Let $A_F := (S_F, I_F, f_F, O_F, o_F)$ be an automaton with input (called the filter with memory, F for the filter). We assume that $O_M = I_F$. Consider a pair of initial states $s_{M,0} \in S_M$ and $s_{F,0} \in S_F$. We generate a sequence of $O_M = I_F$ by A_M with initial state $s_{M,0}$, and pass it to A_F with initial state $s_{F,0}$, to obtain a sequence of O_F as the output sequence. This amounts to considering an automaton C without input, named the combined generator: *the state space S_C of C is $S_M \times S_F$, the transition function is*

$$f_C : (s_M, s_F) \mapsto (f_M(s_M), f_F(o_M(s_M), s_F)),$$

and the output function is

$$o_C : (s_M, s_F) \mapsto o_F(s_F) \in O_F.$$

Figure 1 describes a combined generator.

Example 1. The output function o_C in the above definition depends only on S_F, but we may consider a function depending both S_M and S_F.

Such an example is famous SNOW stream cipher [5] [6]. The mother generator of SNOW2.0 is a LFSR with 512-bit state space, and its filter has 64-bit state space. Non-linearity is introduced by four copies of one same S-box of 8-bit size, based on arithmetic operations in 2^8-element filed $\mathbb{F}_{2^8}$.

SNOW has no rigorous assurance on the period and the distribution of the generated sequence. We shall introduce the notion of quasigroup filter, which allows to compute the period and distribution property.

2   Quasigroup Filter

Definition 5. *A function $f : X \times Y \to Z$ is said to be* bi-bijective *if $f(-, y) : X \to Z$, $x \mapsto f(x, y)$ is bijective for any fixed y, and so is $f(x, -) : Y \to Z$, $y \mapsto f(x, y)$ for any fixed x. If $X = Y = Z$, this coincides with the notion of a quasigroup.*

A quasigroup filter is an automaton in Definition 3 where the state transition function $f : I \times S \to S$ is bi-bijective.

Example 2. (Multiplicative filter)

Let $I = S$ be the set of odd integers in the ring $\mathbb{Z}/2^{32}$ of integers modulo 2^{32}. Let $f : I \times S \to S$ be the integer multiplication modulo 2^{32}. This is a quasigroup (actually the multiplicative group of the ring $\mathbb{Z}/2^{32}$).

We choose $o_F : S \to O_F = B$ as the function taking the 8 MSBs from the 32-bit integer.

Example 3. If we correspond a 32-bit integer x to a 33-bit odd integer $2x + 1$ modulo 2^{33}, then the multiplication formula

$$(2x + 1) \times (2y + 1) = 2(2xy + x + y) + 1$$

gives a quasigroup structure

$$\tilde{\times} : (x, y) \mapsto x \tilde{\times} y := 2xy + x + y \mod 2^{32}$$

on the set of 32-bit integers. We can consider the corresponding multiplicative filter with $I = S$ being the set of 32-bit integers.

Modern CPUs often have a fast integer multiplication for 32-bit integers. We shall discuss mathematical property of such filters in §2.3.

Example 4. (CryptMT1: MT with multiplicative filter)

We choose a LFSR described in (1) as the mother generator A_M, with $O_M = \mathbb{F}_2{}^w$. We can choose its parameters so that the period is a large Mersenne prime $Q = 2^p - 1$ (e.g. $p = 19937$ as in the case of MT19937 [10]). By identifying O_M as the set of w-bit integers, we can use the multiplicative filter A_F described in Example 3. We call this generator as *MT19937 with multiplicative filter*. The output function $o_F : S_F \to O_F = \mathbb{F}_2{}^8$ is extracting 8 MSBs. This generator is called CryptMT Version 1 (CryptMT1) [11].

2.1 k-Dimensional Distribution

Let k be an integer, and let A be an automaton without input as in Definition 1. We define its k-*tuple output function* $o^{(k)}$ by

$$o^{(k)} : S \to O^k \quad s \mapsto (o(s), o(f(s)), o(f^2(s)), \ldots, o(f^{k-1}(s))) \tag{2}$$

(i.e. $o^{(k)}$ maps the state to the next k outputs). Consider the multi-set of the possible output k-tuples for all states:

$$O^{(k)} := \{o^{(k)}(s) \mid s \in S\}.$$

This is the image of S by $o^{(k)}$ counted with multiplicities.

Definition 6. *The output of the automaton A is said to be k-dimensionally equidistributed if the multiplicity of each element in $O^{(k)}$ is same.*

This type of criteria is commonly used for PRNG for MC: MT19937 as a 32-bit integer generator has this property with $k = 623$. This criterion is equivalent to the uniformness of the function $o^{(k)}$ defined below.

Definition 7. *A mapping $g : X \to Y$ is* uniform *if the cardinality of $g^{-1}(y)$ is independent of $y \in Y$. A bijection is uniform, and the composition of uniform mappings is uniform.*

A filter with memory is uniform *if its output function is uniform.*

Example 4 is uniform. The next proposition shows that a uniform quasigroup filter increases the dimension of equidistribution by 1. A proof is in Appendix B.1.

Proposition 1. *We keep the set-up of Definition 4. Assume that A_F is a uniform quasigroup filter. Suppose that the output of A_M is k-dimensionally equidistributed. Then, the combined generator C is $(k+1)$-dimensionally equidistributed.*

Corollary 1. *CryptMT1 explained in Example 4 is 624-dimensionally equidistributed.*

We mean by a *simple distinguishing attack of order N* to choose a real function F with N variables and to detect the deviation of the distribution of the values of F applied to the consecutive N-outputs. If N does not exceed the dimension of the equidistribution, then one can observe no deviation from the true randomness, under the assumption of uniform choice of the initial state.

By this reason, it seems very difficult to apply a correlation attack or a distinguishing attack to such generators. For example, to observe some deviation of MT19937 with multiplicative filter in Example 4, one needs to observe the correlation of outputs with the lag more than 624. Because of the high nonlinearity of the multiplicative filter discussed below, we guess that this would be infeasible.

2.2 A Theorem on the Period

Theorem 1. *Consider a combined generator C as in Definition 4. Let $s_{M,0}$ be the initial state of the mother generator A_M, and assume that its state transition is purely periodic with period $P = Qq$ for a prime Q and an integer q. Let $S^o \subset S_M$ be the orbit of the state transition. Let k be an integer. Assume that the k-tuple output function of the mother generator $o_M^{(k)} : S^o \to O_M^k$ as defined in (2) is surjective when restricted to S^o. Suppose that A_F is a quasigroup filter as in Definition 1.*

Let r be the ratio of the occupation of the maximum inverse image of one element by $o_F : S_F \to O_F$ in S_F, namely

$$r = \max_{b \in O_F}\{\#(o_F^{-1}(b))\}/\#(S_F).$$

If

$$r^{-(k+1)} > q \cdot (\#(S_F))^2,$$

then the period of the output sequence of C is a nonzero multiple of Q.

A proof is given in Appendix B.2.

Example 5. For MT19937 with multiplicative filter, this theorem shows that any bit in the output sequence has a period being a multiple of the prime $2^{19937} - 1$, as follows.

We have $Q = 2^{19937} - 1$ and $q = 1$. If $o_F : S_F \to O_F = \mathbb{F}_2{}^m$ is extracting some m bits from the 32-bit integers, then $r = 2^{w-m}/2^w = 2^{-m}$. The inequality condition in the theorem is now

$$2^{m(k+1)} > 2^{2w},$$

and hence if this holds, then the m-bit output sequence has a period which is a multiple of Q.

In the case of MT19937 and the multiplicative filter, since $k = 623$ and $w = 32$, the above inequality holds for any $m \geq 1$, hence any bit of the output has a period at least $2^{19937} - 1$.

2.3   A Proposition on the Algebraic Degree of Integer Products

Definition 8. *Let us define a boolean function $m_{s,N}$ of $(s-1)N$ variables, as follows. Consider N of s-bit integer variables $x_1, \ldots, x_N$. Let*

$$c_{s-1,i} c_{s-2,i} \cdots c_{0,i}$$

be the 2-adic representation of x_i, hence $c_{j,i} = 0, 1$. We fix $c_{0,i} = 1$ for all $i = 1, \ldots, N$, i.e. assuming x_i odd. The boolean function $m_{s,N}$ has variables $c_{j,i}$ $(j = 1, 2, \ldots, s-1, i = 1, 2, \ldots, N)$, and its value is defined as the s-th digit (from the LSB) of the 2-adic expansion of the product $x_1 x_2 \cdots x_N$ as an integer.

Proposition 2. *Assume that $N, s \geq 2$. The algebraic degree of $m_{s,N}$ is bounded from below by*
$$\min\{2^{s-2}, 2^{\lfloor \log_2 N \rfloor}\}.$$

A proof is given in Appendix B.3. This proposition gives the algebraic degree of the multiplicative filter, with respect to the inputs $x_1, \ldots, x_N$.

This proposition implies that we should use MSBs of the multiplicative filter. On the other hand, using 8 MSBs among 32-bit integers as in Example 2 seems to have enough high algebraic degree. We check this using a toy model in Appendix A.

3   A Fast Initialization of a Large State Space

Consider LFSR in (1) as a mother generator. Its state space is an array of w-bit integers with size n. We need to give initial values to such a large array in the initialization. If one wants to encrypt a much shorter message than n, then this is not efficient. A possible solution is to use a PRNG with relatively small state space (called *the booter*) which can be quickly initialized, and use it to generate the initial array $x_0, x_1, \ldots, x_{n-1}$, and at the same time, its outputs are passed to the filter for key-stream generation. If the message length is smaller than n, then the mother generator is never used: the outputs of the booter are used as the output of the mother generator. If the message length exceeds n, then the first n outputs of the booter are used as the outputs of the mother generator, and at the same time for filling up the state space of the mother generator. After the state space is filled up, the mother generator starts to work. See Appendix C for more detail.

The first outputs come from the booter. One may argue why not using the booter forever, without using the mother generator. The answer is that we do not need to care about the attacks to the booter based on a long output stream.

4   A Concrete Example Using 128-Bit Instructions

Recent CPUs often have Single Instruction Multiple Data (SIMD) instructions. These instructions treat a quadruple of 32-bit integers at one time. We propose a LFSR and a uniform quasigroup filter, based on 128-bit instructions, named CryptMT Version 3 (CryptMT3) in the rest of this paper. CryptMT3 is one of the phase 3 candidates in eSTREAM stream cipher competition [13]. We shall describe the generation algorithm below.

4.1   SIMD Fast MT

In the LFSR (1), we assume that each x_i is a 128-bit integer or equivalently a vector in $\mathbb{F}_2^{128}$. We choose the following recursion: $n = 156$ and

$$
\begin{aligned}
x_{156+j} := & (x_{156+j-1} \ \& \ \texttt{ffdfafdf f5dabfff ffdbffff ef7bffff}) \oplus \\
& (x_{108+j} >>_{64} 3) \oplus x_{108+j}[2][0][3][1] \oplus (x_j[0][3][2][1]).
\end{aligned} \tag{3}
$$

Here, & denotes the bit-wise-and operation, and the hexadecimal integer is a constant 128-bit integer for the bit-mask. The notation $\oplus$ is bitwise exor. The notation

$$
(x_{108+j} >>_{64} 3)
$$

means that x_{108+j} is considered as two 64-bit integers, and each of them is shifted to the right by 3 bits. The notation $x_{108+j}[2][0][3][1]$ is a permutation of four 32-bit integers. The 128-bit integer x_{108+j} is considered as a quadruple of (0th, 1st, 2nd, 3rd) 32-bit integers, and then they are permuted by $2 \to 0, 1 \to 0, 2 \to 3, 3 \to 1$. The next notation $x_j[0][3][2][1]$ is a similar permutation. These instructions are available both in SSE2 SIMD instructions for Intel processors and in AltiVec SIMD instructions in PowerPC. We call this generator SIMD Fast MT (SFMT) (This is a variant of [14]). A description is in Figure 2. We proved its 155-dimensional equidistribution property. We proved that, if the third component $x_0[3]$ of x_0 is $\texttt{0x4d734e48}$, then the period of the generated sequence of the SFMT is a multiple of the Mersenne prime $2^{19937} - 1$. Note that since 19937 is a prime, there is no intermediate field of $\mathbb{F}_{2^{19937}}$. This is in contrast to SNOW1.0, where the existence of the intermediate field $\mathbb{F}_{2^{32}}$ introduces some weakness (see [6]).

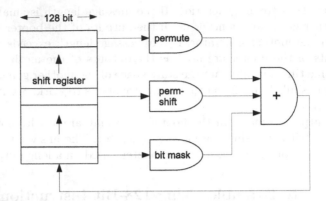

Fig. 2. The mother generator of CryptMT3: SIMD Fast Mersenne Twister
permute: $\mathbf{y} \mapsto \mathbf{y}[0][3][2][1]$.
perm-shift: $\mathbf{y} \mapsto \mathbf{y}[2][0][3][1] \oplus (\mathbf{y} >>_{64} 3)$.
bit-mask: `ffdfafdf f5dabfff ffdbffff ef7bffff`

4.2   A Modified Multiplicative Filter

Our filter A_F has $I_F = S_F$ being the set of 128-bit integers, and O_F being the set of 64-bit integers, as described below.

For given 128-bit integers $y \in I_F$ and $x \in S_F$, we define

$$f_F(y, x) := (y \oplus (y[0][3][2][1] >>_{32} 1)) \tilde{\times}_{32} x. \tag{4}$$

Here, the notation "$>>_{32} 1$" means to consider a 128-bit integer as a quadruple of 32-bit integers, and then shift each of them to the right by 1 bit. The binary operator $x \tilde{\times}_{32} y$ means that 32-bit wise binary operation $\tilde{\times}$ (see Example 3) is applied for each 32-bit components, namely, i-th 32-bit integer of $x \tilde{\times}_{32} y$ is $x[i] \tilde{\times} y[i]$ $(i = 0, 1, 2, 3)$.

The operation applied to y is an invertible linear transformation, hence is bijective. Since $\tilde{\times}$ is bi-bijective, so is f_F. The purpose to introduce the permutation-shift is to mix the information among four 32-bit memories in the filter, and to send the information of the upper bits to the lower bits. This supplements the multiplication, which lacks this direction of transfer of the information.

The output function is

$$o_F(y) := \mathrm{LSB}_{32}^{16}(y \oplus (y >>_{32} 16)). \tag{5}$$

This means that y is considered as a quadruple of 32-bit integers, and for each of them, we take the exor of the MSB 16 bits and LSB 16 bits. Thus we obtain four 16-bit integers, which is the output 64-bit integer (see Figure 3). To obtain 8-bit integers, we dissect it into 8 pieces.

CryptMT3 is the combination of the SIMD Fast MT (§4.1) and this filter. Initialization by the booter is explained in Appendix C.

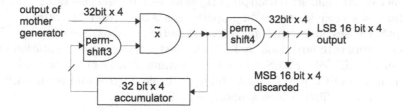

Fig. 3. Filter of CryptMT3.

perm-shift3: $\mathbf{y} \mapsto \mathbf{y} \oplus (\mathbf{y}[0][3][2][1] >>_{32} 1)$.

perm-shift4: $\mathbf{y} \mapsto \mathbf{y} \oplus (\mathbf{y} >>_{32} 16)$.

$\tilde{\times}$: multiplication of 33-bit odd integers.

Table 1. Summary from eSTREAM benchmark [2]

Primitive	Core 2 Duo			AMD Athlon 64 X2			Motorola PowerPC G4		
	Stream	Key setup	IV setup	Stream	Key	IV	Stream	Key	IV
CryptMT3	2.95	61.41	514.42	4.73	107.00	505.64	9.23	90.71	732.80
HC-256	3.42	61.31	83805.33	4.26	105.11	88726.20	6.17	87.71	71392.00
SOSEMANUK	3.67	848.51	624.99	4.41	1183.69	474.13	6.17	1797.03	590.47
SNOW-2.0	4.03	90.42	469.02	4.86	110.70	567.00	7.06	107.81	719.38
Salsa20	7.12	19.71	14.62	7.64	61.22	51.09	4.24	69.81	42.12
Dragon	7.61	121.42	1241.67	8.11	120.21	1469.43	8.39	134.60	1567.54
AES-CTR	19.08	625.44	18.90	20.42	905.65	50.00	34.81	305.81	34.11

4.3 Speed Comparison

Comparison of the speed of generation for stream ciphers is a delicate problem: it depends on the platform, compilers, and so on. Here we compare the number of cycles consumed per byte, by CryptMT3, HC256, SOSEMANUK, Salsa20, Dragon (these are the five candidates in eSTREAM software cipher phase 3 permitting 256-bit Key), SNOW2.0 and AES (counter-mode), in three different CPUs: Intel Core 2 Duo, AMD-Athlon X2, and Motorola PowerPC G4, using eSTREAM timing-tool [7]. The data are listed in Table 1. Actually, they are copied from Bernstein's page [2]. The number of cycles in Key set-up and IV set-up are also listed.

CryptMT3 is the fastest in generation in Intel Core 2 Duo CPU, reflecting the efficiency of SIMD operations in this newer CPU. CryptMT3 is slower in Motorola PowerPC. This is because AltiVec (SIMD of PowerPC) lacks 32-bit integer multiplication (so we used non-SIMD multiplication instead).

5 Conclusions

We proposed combination of a LFSR and a uniform quasigroup filter as a stream cipher in software. As a concrete example, we implemented CryptMT3 generator. CryptMT3 is as fast as SNOW2.0 and faster than AES counter-mode for recent CPUs. CryptMT3 satisfies the conditions of Theorem 1 and Proposition 1, and it can be proved to have the astronomical period $\geq 2^{19937} - 1$ and the

156-dimensional equidistribution property as a 64-bit integer generator (and hence 1241-dimensional equidistribution property as a 8-bit integer generator).

CryptMT3 uses integer multiplication instead of an S-box. This is an advantage over generators with large look-up tables for fast software implementation of the S-box, such as SNOW or AES, where cache-timing attacks might be applied [1].

A toy model of CryptMT3 shows high algebraic degrees and nonlinearity for the multiplicative filter, which supports its effectiveness.

References

1. Bernstein, D.J.: Cache-timing attack on AES
   http://cr.yp.to/antiforgery/cachetiming-20050414.pdf
2. Bernstein, D.J.: Software timings. http://cr.yp.to/streamciphers/timings.html
3. Courtois, N.: Cryptanalysis of Sfinks, http://eprint.iacr.org/2005/243
4. Courtois, N.: Fast algebraic attacks on stream ciphers with linear feedback. In: Boneh, D. (ed.) CRYPTO 2003. LNCS, vol. 2729, pp. 176–194. Springer, Heidelberg (2003)
5. Ekdahl, P., Johansson, T.: SNOW-a new stream cipher. In: Proceedings of First Open NESSIE Workshop, KU-Leuven (2000)
6. Ekdahl, P., Johansson, T.A.: A New Version of the Stream Cipher SNOW. In: Nyberg, K., Heys, H.M. (eds.) SAC 2002. LNCS, vol. 2595, pp. 47–61. Springer, Heidelberg (2003)
7. eSTREAM – The ECRYPT Stream Cipher Project – Phase 3.
   http://www.ecrypt.eu.org/stream/index.html
8. Golomb, S.: Shift Register Sequences. Aegean Park Press (1982)
9. Knuth, D.E.: The Art of Computer Programming. In: Seminumerical Algorithms, 3rd edn., vol. 2, Addison-Wesley, Reading, Mass. (1997)
10. Matsumoto, M., Nishimura, T.: Mersenne Twister: A 623-dimensionally equidistributed uniform pseudo-random number generator. ACM Transactions on Modeling and Computer Simulation 8, 3–30 (1998)
11. Matsumoto, M., Saito, M., Nishimura, T., Hagita, M.: Cryptanalysis of CryptMT: Effect of Huge Prime Period and Multiplicative Filter,
    http://www.ecrypt.eu.org/stream/cryptmtfubuki.html
12. Matsumoto, M., Saito, M., Nishimura, T., Hagita, M.: CryptMT Version 2.0: a large state generator with faster initialization,
    http://www.ecrypt.eu.org/stream/cryptmtfubuki.html
13. Matsumoto, M., Saito, M., Nishimura, T., Hagita, M.: CryptMT Stream Cipher Version 3. eSTREAM stream cipher proposals (submitted),
    http://www.ecrypt.eu.org/stream/cryptmtp3.html
14. Saito, M., Matsumoto, M.: SIMD-oriented Fast Mersenne Twister: a 128-bit Pseudorandom Number Generator. In: The proceedings of MCQMC (2006) (to appear)

Appendix

A   Simulation by Toy Models

Since the filter has a memory, it is not clear how to define the algebraic degree or non-linearity of the filter. Instead, if we consider all bits in the initial state as variables, then each bit of the outputs is a boolean function of these variables, and algebraic degree and non-linearity are defined.

However, it seems difficult to compute them explicitly for CryptMT3, because of the size. So we made a toy model and obtained experimental results. Its mother generator is a linear generator with 16-bit internal state, and generates a 16-bit integer sequence defined by

$$\mathbf{x}_{j+1} := (\mathbf{x}_j >> 1) \oplus ((\mathbf{x}_j \& 1) \cdot \mathbf{a}),$$

where $>> 1$ denotes the one-bit shift-right, $(\mathbf{x}_j \& 1)$ denotes the LSB of $\mathbf{x}_j$, $\mathbf{a} = 1010001001111000$ is a constant 16-bit integer, and $(\mathbf{x}_j \& 1) \cdot \mathbf{a}$ denotes the product of the scalar $(\mathbf{x}_j \& 1) \in \mathbb{F}_2$ and the vector $\mathbf{a}$.

Then it is filtered by

$$y_{j+1} = (\mathbf{x}_j | 1) \times y_j \mod 2^{16},$$

where $(\mathbf{x}_j | 1)$ denotes $\mathbf{x}_j$ with LSB set to 1. We put $y_0 = 1$, and compute the algebraic degree of each of the 16 bits in the outputs $y_1 \sim y_{16}$, each regarded as a polynomial function with 16 variables being the bits in $\mathbf{x}_0$. The result is listed in Table 2. The lower six bits of the table clearly show the pattern $0, 1, 1, 2, 4, 8$, which suggests that the lower bound 2^{s-2} for $s \geq 2$ given in Proposition 2 would be tight, when the iterations are many enough. On the other hand, eighth bit and higher are "saturated" to the upper bound 16, after 12 generations.

We expect that the algebraic degrees for CryptMT3 would behave even better, since its filter is modified. So, if we consider each bit of the internal state of CryptMT3 as a variable, then the algebraic degree of the bits in the outputs will be near to 19937, after some steps of generations.

Also, we computed the non-linearity of the MSB of each y_i ($i = 1, 2, \ldots, 8$) of this toy model. The result is listed in Table 3, and each value is near to 2^{16-1}. This suggests that there would be no good linear approximation of CryptMT3.

Table 2. Table of the algebraic degrees of output bits of a toy model

y_1	1	1	1	1	1	1	1	1	1	1	1	1	1	1	1	0
y_2	14	13	12	11	10	9	8	7	6	5	4	3	2	1	1	0
y_3	15	15	14	13	12	11	10	9	8	6	4	3	2	1	1	0
y_4	15	16	15	14	13	12	11	10	9	7	5	4	2	1	1	0
y_5	16	16	15	15	14	13	12	11	10	7	5	4	2	1	1	0
y_6	16	16	15	15	15	14	13	11	10	9	7	4	2	1	1	0
y_7	16	15	16	16	15	15	14	13	12	9	7	4	2	1	1	0
y_8	15	15	15	16	16	15	15	14	13	10	8	4	2	1	1	0
y_9	16	15	16	15	15	16	15	15	13	10	8	4	2	1	1	0
y_{10}	15	16	16	16	16	16	15	15	14	12	8	4	2	1	1	0
y_{11}	15	16	16	15	15	15	16	15	15	12	8	4	2	1	1	0
y_{12}	15	16	16	16	16	15	16	16	15	13	8	4	2	1	1	0
y_{13}	16	15	15	15	15	15	16	15	16	13	8	4	2	1	1	0
y_{14}	15	15	16	15	15	16	16	15	16	15	8	4	2	1	1	0
y_{15}	15	16	16	16	15	16	16	16	15	14	8	4	2	1	1	0
y_{16}	16	15	16	15	15	15	15	15	16	14	8	4	2	1	1	0

Table 3. The non-linearity of the MSB of each output of a toy model

output	y_1	y_2	y_3	y_4	y_5	y_6	y_7	y_8	y_9
nonlinearity	0	32112	32204	32238	32201	32211	32208	32170	32235

B   Proof of Theorems and Propositions

B.1   Proof of Proposition 1

Proof. Consider the k-tuple output function of the mother generator $o_M^{(k)} : S_M \to O_M^k$ as in (2). Then, the k-dimensional equidistribution property is equivalent to the uniformness of $o_M^{(k)}$. The $(k+1)$-tuple output function $o_C^{(k+1)}$ of the combined generator C is the composite

$$o_C^{(k+1)} : S_M \times S_F \xrightarrow{o_M^{(k)} \times \mathrm{id}_{S_F}} O_M^k \times S_F \xrightarrow{\mu} S_F^{k+1} \xrightarrow{o_F^{k+1}} O_F^{k+1},$$

where the second map μ is given by

$$\mu : ((x_k, x_{k-1}, \ldots, x_1), y_1) \mapsto (y_{k+1}, y_k, \ldots, y_1)$$

where y_i's are inductively defined by $y_{i+1} := f_F(x_i, y_i)$ $(i = 1, 2, \ldots, k)$. The last map o_F^{k+1} is the direct product of $k+1$ copies of o_F. The quasigroup property of f_F implies the bijectivity of μ. The last map is uniform. Since the composition of uniform mappings is uniform, we obtain the proof.

B.2   Proof of Theorem 1

Proof. We may replace S_M with the orbit starting from s_0. Then, replace S_M with its quotient set where two states are identified if the output sequences from them are identical. Thus, we may assume $\#(S_M) = P$, where P is the period of the output sequence of A_M. In this proof, we do not consider multi-sets. Consider the k-tuple output function $o_C^{(k+1)}$ as in the proof of Proposition 1. Since $o_M^{(k)}$ is surjective and μ is bijective (by the quasigroup property), the image $I \subset O_M^{n+1}$ of $S_M \times \{y_0\}$ by $\mu \circ (o_M^{(k)} \times \mathrm{id}_Y)$ has the cardinality $\#(O_M)^k$. By the assumption of the pure periodicity of x_i and the bijectivity of f_F, the output sequence $o_F(y_i)$ $(i = 0, 1, 2, \ldots)$ is purely periodic. Let p be its period. Then, $o_F^{k+1}(I) \subset O_F^{k+1}$ can have at most p elements. Thus, by the assumption on o_F and the definition of r,

$$\#(I) \leq p(r\#(S_F))^{k+1}.$$

Since $\#(O_M)^k = \#(I)$ and $\#(O_M) = \#(S_F)$, we have an inequality

$$r^{-(k+1)} \leq p\#(S_F).$$

The period P' of the state transition of C is a multiple of $P = Qq$. Since the state size of C is $P \times \#(S_F)$, $P' = Qm$ holds for some $m \leq q\#(S_F)$. Consequently, p

is a divisor of Qm. If p is not a multiple of Q, then p divides m and $p \leq q\#(S_F)$. Thus we have

$$r^{-(k+1)} \leq q\#(S_F)^2,$$

contradicting to the assumption.

B.3   Proof of Proposition 2

Let $h(c_1, c_2, \ldots, c_n)$ be a boolean function as in Definition 2, and $h = \sum_{T \subset \{1,2,\ldots,n\}} a_T c_T$ be its algebraic normal form.

The following lemma is well known.

Lemma 1. *It holds that* $a_T = \sum_{U \subset T} h(U)$, *where* $h(U) := h(c_1, \ldots, c_n)$ *with* $c_i = 0, 1$ *according to* $i \notin U$, $\in U$, *respectively.*

Proof of Proposition

Proof. For $s = 2$, the claim is easy to check. We assume $s \geq 3$.

Case 1. $s - 2 \leq \log_2 N$. In this case, it suffices to prove that the algebraic degree is at least 2^{s-2}. Take a subset T of size 2^{s-2} from $\{1, 2, \ldots, N\}$, say $T = \{1, 2, \ldots, 2^{s-2}\}$. Then, we choose $c_{1,1}, c_{1,2}, \ldots, c_{1,2^{s-2}}$ as the $\#T$ variables "activated" in Lemma 1, and consequently, the coefficient of $c_{1,1}c_{1,2} \cdots c_{1,2^{s-2}}$ in the algebraic normal form of $m_{s,N}$ is given by the sum in $\mathbb{F}_2$:

$$a_T := \sum_{U \subset T} (s\text{-th bit of } x_1 \cdots x_n, \text{ where } c_{j,i} = 1 \text{ if and only if } j = 1 \text{ and } i \in U).$$

Note that $c_{0,i} = 1$. It suffices to prove $a_T = 1$. Now, each term in the right summation is the s-th bit of the integer $3^{\#U}$, so the right hand side equals to

$$\sum_{m=0}^{2^{s-2}} \left[\binom{2^{s-2}}{m} \times \text{ the } s\text{-th bit of } 3^m \right].$$

However, the well-known formula

$$(x + y)^{2^{s-2}} \equiv x^{2^{s-2}} + y^{2^{s-2}} \quad \mathrm{mod}\, 2$$

implies that the binary coefficients are even except for the both end, so the summation is equal to the s-th bit of $3^{2^{s-2}}$.

A well-known lemma says that if $x \equiv 1 \mod 2^i$ and $x \not\equiv 1 \mod 2^{i+1}$ for $i \geq 2$, then $x^2 \equiv 1 \mod 2^{i+1}$ and $x^2 \not\equiv 1 \mod 2^{i+2}$. By applying this lemma inductively, we know that

$$3^{2^{s-2}} = (1+8)^{2^{s-3}} \equiv 1 \mod 2^s, \ \not\equiv 1 \mod 2^{s+1}.$$

This means that s-th bit of $3^{2^{s-2}}$ is 1, and the proposition is proved.

Case 2. $s - 2 > \lfloor \log_2(N) \rfloor$. In this case, we put $t := \lfloor \log_2(N) \rfloor + 2$, and hence $s > t$ and $2^{t-2} \leq N$. We apply the above arguments for $T = \{1, 2, \ldots, 2^{t-2}\}$, but this time instead of $c_{1,i}$, we activate

$$\{c_{s-t+2,i} \mid i \in T\}.$$

The same argument as above reduces the non-vanishing of the coefficient of the term $c_{s-t+2,1} \cdots c_{s-t+2,2^{t-2}}$ to the non-vanishing of

$$\sum_{m=0}^{2^{t-2}} \left[\binom{2^{t-2}}{m} \times \text{the } s\text{-th bit of } (1 + 2^{s-t+2})^m \right].$$

Again, only the both ends $m = 0$ and $m = 2^{t-2}$ can survive, and the above summation is the s-th bit of $(1 + 2^{s-t+2})^{t-2}$. Since $s - t + 2 \geq 2$, the lemma mentioned above implies that

$$(1 + 2^{s-t+2})^{2^{t-2}} \equiv 1 \bmod 2^s, \quad \not\equiv 1 \bmod 2^{s+1},$$

which implies that its s-th bit is 1.

C   The Key, IV, and the Booter

The design of the booter (see §3) goes independently of the key-stream generator. However, as the referees pointed out, we need to specify one to have a complete description of the generator. Thus, we here include the booter of CryptMT3 for self-containedness. The booter is described in Figure 4.

We choose an integer H later in §C.1. The state space of the booter is a shift register consisting of H 128-bit integers. We choose an initial state $x_0, x_1, \ldots, x_{H-1}$ and the initial value a_0 of the accumulator (a 128-bit memory) as described in the next section. Then, the state transition is given by the recursion

$$a_j := (a_{j-1} \tilde{\times}_{32} \texttt{perm-shift2}(x_{H+j-1}))$$
$$x_{H+j} := \texttt{perm-shift1}(x_j +_{32} x_{H+j-2}) -_{32} a_j,$$

where

$$\texttt{perm-shift1}(x) := (x[2][1][0][3]) \oplus (x >>_{32} 13)$$
$$\texttt{perm-shift2}(x) := (x[1][0][2][3]) \oplus (x >>_{32} 11).$$

The notation $+_{32}$ $(-_{32})$ denotes the addition (subtraction, respectively) modulo 2^{32} for each of the four 32-bit integers in the 128-bit integers. The output of the j-th step is $x_j +_{32} x_{H+j-2}$.

As described in Figure 4, the booter consists of an automaton with three inputs and two outputs of 128-bit integers, together with a shift register. In the implementation, the shift register is taken in an array of 128-bit integers with the length $2H + 2 + n$, where $n = 156$ is the size of the state array of SFMT. This redundancy of the length is for the idling, as explained below.

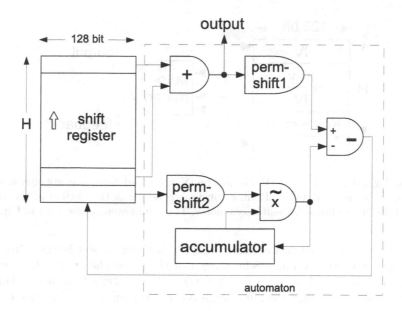

Fig. 4. Booter of CryptMT3.

perm-shift1: $\mathbf{x} \mapsto (\mathbf{x}[2][1][0][3]) \oplus (\mathbf{x} >>_{32} 13)$.

perm-shift2: $\mathbf{x} \mapsto (\mathbf{x}[1][0][2][3]) \oplus (\mathbf{x} >>_{32} 11)$.

$\widetilde{\times}$: multiplication of (a quadruple of) 33-bit odd integers.

$+, -$: addition, subtraction of four 32-bit integers modulo 2^{32}.

C.1   Key and IV Set-Up

We assume that both the IV and the Key are given as arrays of 128-bit integers. The size of each array is chosen by user, from 1 to 16. Thus, the Key-size is chosen from 128 bits to 2048 bits, as well as the IV-size. We claim the security level that is the same with the minimum of the Key-size and the IV-size.

We concatenate the IV and the Key to a single array, and then it is copied twice to an array, as described in Figure 5. To break the symmetry, we add a constant 128-bit integer $(846264, 979323, 265358, 314159)$ (denoting four 32-bit integers in a decimal notation, coming from π) to the bottom row of the second copy of the key (add means $+_{32}$). Now, the size H of the shift register in the booter is set to be $2 \times$ (IV-size + Key-size (in bits))/128, namely, the twice of the number of 128-bit integers contained in the IV and the Key. For example, if the IV-size and the Key-size are both 128 bits, then $H = 2 \times (1 + 1) = 4$. The automaton in the booter described in Figure 4 is equipped on this array, as shown in Figure 5. The accumulator of the booter-automaton is set to

$$\text{(the top row of the key array)} \mid (1, 1, 1, 1),$$

that is, the top row is copied to the accumulator and then the LSB of each of the 32-bit integers in the accumulator is set to 1.

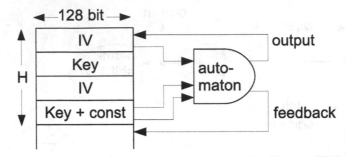

Fig. 5. Beginning of Key and IV set-up. The IV-array and Key-array are concatenated and copied to an array twice. Then, a constant is added to the bottom of the second copy of the key to break a possible symmetry. The automaton is described in Figure 4.

At the first generation, the automaton reads three 128-bit integers from the array, and write the output 128-bit integer at the top of the array. The feedback to the shift register is written into the $(H + 1)$-st entry of the array. For the next generation, we shift the automaton downwards by one, and proceed in the same way.

For idling, we iterate this for $H+2$ times. Then, the latest modified row in the array is the $(2H + 2)$-nd row, and it is copied to the 128-bit memory in the filter of CryptMT3. We discard the top $H + 2$ entries of the array. This completes the Key and IV set-up. Figure 6 shows the state after the set-up.

After the set-up, the booter produces 128-bit integer outputs, at most n times. Let L be the number of bits in the message. If $L \leq n \times 64$, then we do not need the

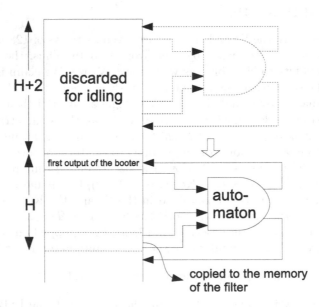

Fig. 6. After the Key and IV set-up

mother generator. We generate the necessary number of 128-bit integers by the booter, and pass them to the filter to obtain the required outputs. If $L \geq n \times 64$, then, we generate n 128-bit integers by the booter, and pass them to the filter to obtain n 64-bit integers, which are used as the first outputs. At the same time, these n 128-bit integers are recorded in the array, and they are passed to SFMT as the initial state.

To eliminate the possibility of shorter period than $2^{19937} - 1$, we set the 32 MSBs of the first row of the state array of SFMT to the magic number 0x4d734e48 in the hexadecimal representation, as explained in §4.1. That is, we start the recursion (3) of SFMT with $x_0, x_1, \ldots, x_{n-1}$ being the array of length n generated by the booter (with 32 bits replaced with a magic constant), and then SFMT produces $x_n, x_{n+1}, \ldots$. Since x_n might be easier to guess because of the constant part in the initial state, we skip x_n and pass the 128-bit integers $x_{n+1}, x_{n+2}, \ldots$ to the filter.

Cryptanalysis of White-Box DES Implementations with Arbitrary External Encodings

Brecht Wyseur[1], Wil Michiels[2], Paul Gorissen[2], and Bart Preneel[1]

[1] Katholieke Universiteit Leuven
Dept. Elect. Eng.-ESAT/SCD-COSIC,
Kasteelpark Arenberg 10, 3001 Heverlee, Belgium
{brecht.wyseur,bart.preneel}@esat.kuleuven.be
[2] Philips Research Laboratories
Prof. Holstlaan 4, 5656 AA, Eindhoven, The Netherlands
{wil.michiels,paul.gorissen}@philips.com

Abstract. At DRM 2002, Chow *et al.* [4] presented a method for implementing the DES block cipher such that it becomes hard to extract the embedded secret key in a white-box attack context. In such a context, an attacker has full access to the implementation and its execution environment. In order to provide an extra level of security, an implementation shielded with external encodings was introduced by Chow *et al.* and improved by Link and Neumann [10]. In this paper, we present an algorithm to extract the secret key from such white-box DES implementations. The cryptanalysis is a differential attack on obfuscated rounds, and works regardless of the shielding external encodings that are applied. The cryptanalysis has a average time complexity of 2^{14} and a negligible space complexity.

Keywords: White-Box Cryptography, Obfuscation, DES, Data Encryption Standard, Cryptanalysis.

1 Introduction

White-box cryptography aims to protect secret keys by embedding them into a software implementation of a block cipher. The attack model for these implementations is defined as the white-box attack model. In this model, an attacker has full control over the implementation and its execution environment. This includes static and dynamic analysis of the implementation, altering of computation, and modification of internal variables. In such a model, it is much more difficult to protect cryptographic implementations than in the classical black-box model. In the black-box model, an adversary can only use the input and output behaviour of the implementation in order to find the key. Another model is the grey-box model, where an adversary can use side-channel information such as power consumption, and timing information.

C. Adams, A. Miri, and M. Wiener (Eds.): SAC 2007, LNCS 4876, pp. 264–277, 2007.

For the black-box model, several cryptographic block ciphers have been proposed, such as DES *(Data Encryption Standard)* [13], and its successor AES *(Advanced Encryption Standard)*. Although these ciphers provide cryptographic strength in their full number of rounds, attacks have been presented on reduced round versions. Cipher designers aim to reduce the number of rounds, for which a cipher provides sufficient security, while cryptanalysists try to construct an attack on as many rounds as possible. For AES-128 and AES-192, a cryptanalysis on 7 and 8 rounds has been presented respectively (out of 10 and 12 rounds) [9]. In a white-box attack model, this game of design and cryptanalysis fails completely, since an attacker has access to the round functions, and can thus perform a cryptanalysis on a chosen part of the implementation representing a reduced number of round functions.

In 2002, Chow *et al.* [4] proposed a white-box implementation of DES. The main idea is to implement the block cipher as a network of lookup tables. All the operations of the block cipher, such as the key addition, are embedded into these lookup tables, which are then randomised to obfuscate their behaviour. This process of obfuscation intends to preclude cryptographic attacks on a reduced number of rounds, timing attacks, such as cache attacks (e.g., [11]) or implementation attacks [8]. Parallel with the white-box DES implementation proposal, Chow *et al.* [3] described a white-box AES implementation based on similar design principles. For both implementations, a variant was presented that is shielded with external encodings. Several publications describe cryptanalysis results of 'naked' white-box DES implementations, i.e., without the shielding external encodings [4,7,10]. The encoded white-box AES implementation has been cryptanalysed by Billet *et al.* [2]. They use algebraic properties of the AES to attack the implementation on the obfuscated round functions.

In this paper, we describe a cryptanalysis which applies to both naked and encoded white-box DES implementations. Independently, Goubin *et al.* [6] present similar results. Their paper describes a cryptanalysis of the improved naked white-box DES implementation proposed by Link and Neumann [10]. Based on this attack and the analysis of the typical external encodings, an attack is derived for encoded white-box DES implementations. In contrast, the attack we discuss in this paper is *independent* of the definition of the external encodings. Hence, unlike the attack of Goubin *et al.*, a white-box DES implementation cannot be protected against our attack by choosing different external encodings. The attack presented in this paper targets the internal behaviour of the implementation; it is a differential cryptanalysis [1] on the obfuscated round functions, which are accessible in a white-box environment. Because the attack is independent of the definition and implementation of the external encodings, it applies to both the (improved) naked and the encoded white-box DES implementations.

The reminder of this paper is organised as follows: in Sect. 2 we give a brief overview of the white-box DES implementation. The core of this paper, the cryptanalysis of the implementation, is described in Sect. 3. We have also implemented our attack and performed tests on white-box DES binaries. The results and considerations of the implementation are described in Sect. 4. Section 5 presents the conclusions.

2   White-Box DES Implementations

For the sake of completeness and to introduce the notation and terminology used in the description of the cryptanalysis, we briefly outline the construction of white-box DES implementations as presented by Chow *et al.* [4].

The *Data Encryption Standard* (DES) is a block cipher operating on 64-bit blocks and with a key length of 56 bits; it is a Feistel cipher with 16 rounds, embedded between an initial permutation IP before the first round, and its inverse permutation IP^{-1} after the last round. Fig. 1 (a) depicts one round of the DES. It has the following building blocks: an expansion operation E; an addition of a 48-bit round key k^r which is generated from the key schedule; 8 S-box operations S_i (each S-box is a non-linear mapping from 6 bits to 4 bits); and a bit permutation P.

A DES white-box implementation represents DES as a functional equivalent sequence of obfuscated lookup tables. In this section, we describe the transformation techniques as presented by Chow *et al.* [4]. Figure 1 (a) depicts one round of DES, and (b) a functionally equivalent representation which consist of the functions C_r and D_r. The DES permutation, XOR, and expansion operation are implemented as a 96-to-96 bit affine function D_r, which can be represented as a matrix. Using a technique referred to as *matrix decomposition* by Chow *et al.*, D_r is transformed into a sequence of lookup tables. To avoid sparse submatrices, D_r can be split into non-sparse matrices by introducing mixing bijections [4].

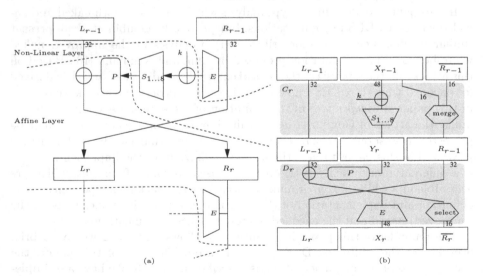

Fig. 1. (a) One round of DES (b) One round of white-box DES, before internal encodings are applied

At the heart of each round of the white-box DES implementation are 12 T-boxes that implement the C_r function. These T-boxes contain the S-boxes and the round key addition and are defined as

$$\begin{cases} T_j^r = b_0 b_1 || b_2 b_7 || S_j(b_2 b_3 b_4 b_5 b_6 b_7 \oplus k_j^r) & \forall j = 1 \dots 8 \\ T_j^r = b_0 b_1 b_2 b_3 || b_4 b_5 b_6 b_7 & \forall j = 9 \dots 12 \,, \end{cases}$$

where r denotes the round number ($1 \leq r \leq 16$), $b_{0 \dots 7}$ represent the 8 input bits to each T-box, and k_j^r represents 6 bits of the round key. The first 8 T-boxes are called *non-linear T-boxes*, as they contain the non-linear S-boxes. The other 4 are called *bypass T-boxes*. The 12 T-boxes of C_r are defined in such a way that they are functionally equivalent to the round key addition, S-box operations and the bypass of all 32 left bits (L_{r-1}) and 32 right bits (R_{r-1}). Moreover, due to the bijective relation between the inner 4 input bits and the output bits of an S-box, these T-boxes are 8-to-8 bit bijections. This 8 bit entropy property is desirable as it prevents the isolated T-boxes to leak information as described by Chow *et al.* [4]. The order of the T-boxes can be permuted. Note that in that case, the affine operations D_{r-1} and D_r must be adjusted accordingly. Denote with π the permutation operation, i.e., S_i is implemented inside $T_{\pi(i)}^r$.

The result is a network of key dependent lookup tables. To protect the key information in these tables, input and output encodings are applied to them. Let Λ be a lookup table, and f and g be random bijections. Then $g \circ \Lambda \circ f^{-1}$ is defined an encoded lookup table. We encode all the lookup tables in the network in such a way that an output encoding is canceled by the input decoding incorporated into the next lookup table. Note that these input and output encodings are not wide, because they cannot exceed the boundaries of the lookup tables they are applied to. From now on, we refer to an encoded T-box as $g_i \circ T_{\pi(i)}^r \circ f_i^{-1}$, and the internal state as the 12-byte vector $f_1 || f_2 || \dots || f_{12}(\Phi_r(L_{r-1} || X_{r-1} || R_{r-1}))$ where Φ_r is the function which arranges the bits to the inputs of the T-boxes. Remark that in Fig. 1 the internal states are depicted unencoded.

Once the full network of lookup tables has been encoded, the input encodings at the beginning and output encodings at the end of the implementation are not canceled out. Without these encodings, we call the white-box DES implementation *naked*. Attacks on a naked implementation have been presented in [4,7,10]. In order to avoid such attacks, Chow *et al.* recommend to add affine mixing bijections before and after DES. As a result, not DES, but an encoded variant $G \circ DES_k \circ F$ is implemented. F and G are called *external encodings*.

3   Cryptanalysis

Examination of the white-box DES implementation as presented by Chow *et al.* shows that plaintext input differences between the rounds do not propagate randomly. Denote the internal state before round r as the 96 bits that represent the encoded version of $L_{r-1} || X_{r-1} || \overline{R_{r-1}}$. This is a 12-byte vector $v_1^r || v_2^r || \dots v_{12}^r$, where v_j^r is the encoded input to a T-box T_j^r. In our cryptanalysis we apply changes to the internal states and analyse their propagation in the consecutive rounds to gain information about the implementation. This information is then used to recover the key. The applied technique builds on a generic strategy described for the first time by Billet *et al.* [2]. The cryptanalysis also applies to the improved implementation as presented by Link and Neumann [10], because only the inputs to the T-boxes are used. Merging C_r and D_r, or any change to $D_r \circ C_r$ (e.g., with mixing bijections) that does not change the inputs to C_r beyond the input size boundary, does not affect the attack.

Below, we present the steps to classify differences to the input of the T-boxes and show how this results in the recovery of the embedded secret key. In Sect. 3.1, we identify the set of differences which represent flips of restricted $(\overline{R_{r-1}})$ bits. This leads to the identification of flips of the two middle input bits of S-boxes in round $r + 2$, and results also in the identification of single input bit flips to S-boxes in round $r + 3$, as described in Sect. 3.2. This information is then used in Sect. 3.3 to identify the S-boxes contained inside the T-boxes, and the precise value of the input to these S-boxes. In Sect. 3.4, we explain how this leads to the recovery of the embedded key.

Initialisation Phase. At the initialisation of our cryptanalysis, we choose a random plaintext and run it through the implementation, storing all internal states. We will deduce the inputs to the S-boxes for this plaintext in Sect. 3.3. Because we are only interested in the propagation of differences applied to the internal states, the value of the plaintext is of no importance. Hence, preceding external input encodings do not affect the success of this cryptanalysis.

3.1   Finding Restricted Bit Flips

Let T_j^r be an arbitrary encoded T-box in round r, encoded with input encoding f_j^r and output encoding g_j^r. Let v_j^r denote the 8-bit input vector to the encoded T-box computed at the initialisation phase. In this section we present an algorithm to construct the set $\mathcal{S}_{\overline{R}}(T_j^r) = \{\Delta v = v_j^r \oplus v' \mid v' \in GF(2)^8; v' \neq v_j^r; f_j^r(v_j^r) \oplus f_j^r(v')$ an $\overline{R_{r-1}}$ bit flip$\}$ of all input differences to the encoded T_j^r which represent flips of *one* or *two* restricted bits ($|f_j^r(v_j^r) \oplus f_j^r(v')| = 1, 2$). Similarly, we define the sets $\mathcal{S}_R(T_j^r)$ and $\mathcal{S}_{R \setminus \overline{R}}(T_j^r)$. An input difference Δv is applied to T-box T_j^r as follows: change the jth byte of the internal state before round r from v_j^r into v', and compute the round function $D_r \circ C_r$ with this new internal state as input.

The algorithm consists of two parts: (1) constructing the set $\mathcal{S}_R(T_j^r)$ of all differences which represent *single* bit flips and some *double* bit flips of R_{r-1}, and (2) to divide this set into $\mathcal{S}_{\overline{R}}(T_j^r)$ and $\mathcal{S}_{R \setminus \overline{R}}(T_j^r)$.

Finding Single R_{r-1} Bit Flips. Let $\Delta v = v_j^r \oplus v'(= \Delta v_j^r)$ be a difference of the input of T_j^r while the inputs v_l^r to the other T-boxes T_l^r are fixed to the values from the initialisation phase ($\forall l \neq j : \Delta v_l^r = 0$). The following two properties can be proved for Δv. The proofs are given in Appendix A.

Property 1. *If Δv represents a single bit flip of R_{r-1}, then in round $r + 2$, at most 2 T-boxes are affected (i.e., their input change).*

Property 2. *If Δv represents flips of bits of L_{r-1} or Y_r, then in almost all cases more than 2 T-boxes are affected in round $r + 2$. The exceptions (false positives) can be detected by repeating this process up to α times with different fixed inputs to the other T-boxes T_l^r.*

Hence, we are able to distinguish flips Δv that represent flips of R_{r-1} bits, and build the set $\mathcal{S}_R(T_j^r)$. Algorithm 1 describes this procedure. The total number of differences representing flips of bits of R_{r-1} for all the T-boxes of one round, is exactly 40: 16 *single* flips of bits of R_{r-1} originating from X_{r-1}, 16 *single* flips of bits of $\overline{R_{r-1}}$, and 8 *double* flips of bits of $\overline{R_{r-1}}$. To agree with property 2, these double flips of restricted bits are those that affect the both middle bits of an S-box in round $r + 2$, and are bypassed together through the implementation. Therefore they cannot be distinguished from single bit flips of R_{r-1}. Because there are only 8 S-boxes, there cannot be more than 8 double bit flips. Depending on the design of Φ_r, the number of double flips can reduce, but this does not influence our cryptanalysis. To keep the discussion clear, we assume the bypass bits are ordered, and therefore we will have 8 double bit flips.

Algorithm 1. Selecting single R_{r-1} bit flips

1: Set all v_l^r
2: **for all** $\Delta v \in GF(2)^8 \backslash \{0\}$ **do**
3:     Compute 2 round functions
4:     **while** # affected T-boxes ≤ 2 and # checks $\leq \alpha$ **do**
5:         Extra check: set new v_l^r; $\forall l \neq j$
6:         Compute 2 round functions
7:     **end while**
8:     **if** # affected T-boxes ≤ 2 **then**
9:         $\Delta v \rightarrow \mathcal{S}_R(T_j^r)$
10:    **end if**
11: **end for**

Split R_{r-1} into $\overline{R_{r-1}}$ and $R_{r-1} \backslash \overline{R_{r-1}}$ Flips. Let Δv represent flips of R_{r-1} bits. The following properties can be proved for $\Delta v \in \mathcal{S}_R(T_j^r)$. The proofs are given in Appendix A.

Property 3. *If Δv represents a flip of bits of $\overline{R_{r-1}}$, there are exactly 2 propagated differences in round $r + 2$: Δm, Δn. One (say Δm, input difference to T-box T_m^{r+2}) will affect strictly more than 2 T-boxes in round $r + 4$, the other difference will affect at most 2 T-boxes in round $r + 4$. Moreover, T_m^{r+2} will be a non-linear T-box; Δm represents flips of one or both of the two middle bits of the internal S-box; and Δn represents flips of respectively one or two $\overline{R_{r+1}}$ bits.*

Property 4. *If Δv represents a flip of bits of $R_{r-1} \backslash \overline{R_{r-1}}$, there are exactly 2 propagated differences in round $r + 2$. Both affected T-boxes are non-linear T-boxes, and each of their input differences will affect strictly more than two T-boxes in round $r + 4$.*

Based on these properties, we have a tool to identify restricted bit flips, and to distinguish non-linear T-boxes. In Algorithm 2, this procedure is described. Note that during the algorithm, we also store the differences Δm representing flips of middle bits ($b_4 b_5$) to an S-box S_m in the set $\mathcal{S}_M(T_m^{r+2})$.

Algorithm 2. Split R_{r-1} into $\overline{R_{r-1}}$ and $R_{r-1} \backslash \overline{R_{r-1}}$ flips

---

1: **for all** $\Delta v \in \mathcal{S}_R(T_j^r)$ **do**
2:     Compute 2 round functions
3:     $\Delta m, \Delta n \leftarrow$ propagated differences in round $r+2$ of T_m^{r+2}, T_n^{r+2} $m \neq n$
4:     $\delta m \leftarrow$ # affected T-boxes in round $r+4$ propagated by Δm in round $r+2$.
5:     $\delta n \leftarrow$ # affected T-boxes in round $r+4$ propagated by Δn in round $r+2$.
6:     **if** $\delta m > 2$ and $\delta n = 2$ **then**
7:         $\Delta v \rightarrow \mathcal{S}_{\overline{R}}(T_j^r); \Delta m \rightarrow \mathcal{S}_M(T_m^{r+2})$
8:         Denote T_m^{r+2} as non-linear T-box
9:     **else if** $\delta m = 2$ and $\delta n > 2$ **then**
10:        $\Delta v \rightarrow \mathcal{S}_{\overline{R}}(T_j^r); \Delta n \rightarrow \mathcal{S}_M(T_n^{r+2})$
11:        Denote T_n^{r+2} as non-linear T-box
12:    **else if** $\delta m > 2$ and $\delta n > 2$ **then**
13:        $\Delta v \rightarrow \mathcal{S}_{R \backslash \overline{R}}(T_j^r)$
14:        Denote both T_m^{r+2} and T_n^{r+2} as non-linear T-box
15:    **end if**
16: **end for**

The combination of Algorithm 1 and Algorithm 2 results into the following useful information:

$$
\begin{cases}
\mathcal{S}_{\overline{R}}^r = \cup_j \mathcal{S}_{\overline{R}}(T_j^r): \text{ differences representing restricted bit flips} \\
\mathcal{S}_M^{r+2} = \cup_j \mathcal{S}_M(T_j^{r+2}): \text{ differences representing S-box middle bit flips} \\
T_{\pi(1)}^{r+2} \dots T_{\pi(8)}^{r+2}: \text{ the 8 non-linear T-boxes } (\pi \text{ unkown})
\end{cases}
$$

3.2   Finding Single Bit Flips

In Sect. 3.1, differences representing flips of the 2 middle bits ($b_4 b_5$) of the S-boxes of round $r+2$ are found. Let T_j^{r+2} be an arbitrary non-linear T-box in round $r+2$, and $\mathcal{S}_M(T_j^{r+2})$ its set of middle bit flips. We have $\mathcal{S}_M(T_j^{r+2}) = \{\Delta m_1, \Delta m_2, \Delta m_3\}$ with $\Delta m_i : v_j^{r+2} \rightarrow v_j^{r+2} \oplus \Delta m_i$ the 3 generated differences. One can verify that, except for S-box S_8, each of the four output bits of the S-box S_j^{r+2} are flipped at least once by going through one of the values $v_j^{r+2} \oplus \Delta m_1, v_j^{r+2} \oplus \Delta m_2, v_j^{r+2} \oplus \Delta m_3$. Furthermore, as the middle bits are not bypassed in the same T-box, no other output bits of the T-box are affected. Due to the diffusion property of the DES permutation P, the 4 output bits of an S-box affect a single input bit of 6 S-boxes in the next round, with two of them middle input bits (See Coppersmith [5]). Based on the previously mentioned study, the two differences representing bypass bits can be detected. Under the assumption of ordered bypass bits, we have already built this set to compare with ($\mathcal{S}_{\overline{R}}^{r+3}$). The other propagated input differences to the T-boxes in round $r+3$ represent single bit flips. Algorithm 3 describes this procedure, which constructs the set $\mathcal{S}_S(T_i^{r+3})$ of differences representing single bit flips.

As mentioned, the described property does not hold for S_8: for the input $11b_4b_501$, with arbitrary b_4 and b_5, the rightmost output bit cannot be flipped by flipping the input bits b_4 and b_5. Thus, with a probability of $1/16$, we are not able to find all single bit flips of round $r + 3$. However, it will become clear in the next section that we do not need all information to successfully apply our cryptanalysis.

Algorithm 3. Finding single bit flips

1: **for all** $\Delta v \in \mathcal{S}_M(T_{\pi(j)}^{r+2})$ $j = 1 \dots 8$ (for non-linear T-boxes) **do**
2:     Compute one round function
3:     **for all** Δw_i propagated difference to a non-linear T-box T_i^{r+3} **do**
4:        **if** $\Delta w_i \notin \mathcal{S}_S(T_i^{r+3})$ **then**
5:           $\Delta w_i \rightarrow \mathcal{S}_S(T_i^{r+3})$
6:        **end if**
7:     **end for**
8: **end for**

3.3   Obtaining the Inputs to the S-Boxes

Let T_j^{r+3} be an arbitrary non-linear T-box in round $r + 3$. Using the acquired information from the steps above, we deploy a filter algorithm to identify the S-box $(S_{\pi^{-1}(j)})$ in the T-box T_j^{r+3}, and to find the value of its 6-bit input vector $(f_j^{r+3}|_{2...7}(v_j^r) \oplus k_j^{r+3})$.

We define the set $\mathcal{P}(T_j^{r+3}) = \{(S_q, w_l) \mid 1 \leq q \leq 8, w_l \in GF(2)^6\}$ as the set of all possible pairs of S-boxes and input vectors. Our strategy is to remove all the invalid pairs from the set. We can do this by comparing the number of affected T-boxes in round $r + 4$ when a difference $\Delta v_i \in \mathcal{S}_S(T_j^{r+3}) \cup \mathcal{S}_M(T_j^{r+3})$ is applied to the input of T_j^{r+3}, with the number of affected S-boxes in a non-white-box DES simulation with a pair $(S_q, w_l) \in \mathcal{P}(T_j^{r+3})$.

We define δ_i as the number of non-linear T-boxes that are affected in round $r + 4$ when Δv_i is applied to the input of T_j^{r+3}. To verify a pair (S_q, w_l), we take part of a non-white-box DES implementation with S-box S_q and S-box input w_l, and simulate the behaviour of a flip of the i'th input bit to the S-box. Then, δ_i' is defined as the number of affected S-boxes in the next round of this simulation. Define Δw_i as the difference to the input of the internal S-box of the T-box to which Δv_i is applied ($\Delta w_i : w_l \rightarrow w_l \oplus f_j^{r+3}|_{2...7}(\Delta v_i)$).

If (S_q, w_l) is a candidate solution, it should satisfy the following conditions:

- There can only be one S_q for each round.
- $\Delta v_7 = \mathcal{S}_M(T_j^{r+3}) \backslash \mathcal{S}_S(T_j^{r+3})$ is the flip of both middle bits, represented as $\Delta w_7 = 001100$, for which δ_7' can be computed. δ_7' must be smaller or equal to δ_7.

- $\{\Delta v_3, \Delta v_4\} = \mathcal{S}_M(T_j^{r+3}) \cap \mathcal{S}_S(T_j^{r+3})$ represent the two single flips of the input bits to the S-box, but we do not know in which order. Moreover they only affect bits of Y_{r+3}, and thus we must have $\{\delta_3', \delta_4'\} \leq \{\delta_3, \delta_4\}$.
- Similarly $\{\delta_1', \delta_2', \delta_5', \delta_6'\} \leq \{\delta_1, \delta_2, \delta_5, \delta_6\}$.

Any pair (S_q, w_l) that does not fulfil these conditions is removed from the set $\mathcal{P}(T_j^{r+3})$. At the end, if only pairs with one type S_q remain, then this S_q is the internal S-box of $T_j^{r+3}(\pi(q) = j)$. As soon as S-boxes are identified, we can also make use of S-box relations between consecutive rounds. E.g., S_1 in round r does not affect S-box S_1 and S_7 in round $r + 1$. Moreover, if for example S_3 is identified in round $r + 1$, then S_1 affects its second input bit, which allows us to narrow down the conditions $(\delta_2 = \delta_2')$.

Because all 8 DES S-boxes are very different, and are highly non-linear, the filtering process will reduce most $\mathcal{P}(T_j^{r+3})$ sets to a singleton (S_q, w_l), where $S_q = S_{\pi^{-1}(j)}$ is the internal S-box and $w_l = f_j^{r+3}|_{2...7}(v_j^{r+3})$ the 6-bit input vector to this S-box.

3.4 Key Recovery

Given that we have found a sufficient number of inputs to S-boxes, we start an iterated recovery of key bits, initiated by guessing one single key bit, using the following two observations:

- The expansion operation E maps some of the input bits to 2 different S-boxes, prior to the key addition. From Sect. 3.3, we know the value of the input bits to these S-boxes, after the round key addition. Hence, if we know one of the corresponding two bits of the round key, we are able to compute the other key bit.
- The value of one single bit can be followed through several rounds. Consider an R_{r-1} bit. In round r and $r + 2$, after the expansion and the round key addition, this is the (known) input to an S-box. In round $r + 1$ it is XOR-ed with an output bit b of an S-box after the permutation P operation. Because P is known, the S-boxes in round $r + 1$ are identified and their input is known, we can compute the value of b. Hence, if one bit of the round key bit in round r or $r + 2$ is known, we can compute the other key bit.

Iterated use of these algorithms generates the DES key bits. When a new round key bit is computed, we can pull this back through the DES key schedule. This is possible, because the 48-bit round key is a fixed permutation of a subset of the 56-bit DES key. New key bits in turn result into new round key bits, to which the two described methods can be applied.

Depending on the initial key bit guess, two complementary keys k_0 and k_1 can be computed. Because of the complementation property DES exhibits, both keys are a valid result. The complementation property of DES [12] is defined as $DES_k = \bigoplus_1 \circ DES_{k \oplus 1} \circ \bigoplus_1$, where $\bigoplus_1$ represents the XOR with the all one vector. Then $G \circ DES_k \circ F = G' \circ DES_{k \oplus 1} \circ F'$, with $F' = \bigoplus_1 \circ F$ and $G' = G \circ \bigoplus_1$. Hence if k is the original DES key, and F, G the external encodings used to shield the white-box DES implementation, then the complementary key $k \oplus 1$ is also a valid DES key with external encodings F', G'.

3.5   Recovery of the External Encodings

The main goal in cryptanalysis of white-box implementations is to find the embedded secret key. However, to break specific white-boxed implementations or decode ciphertext, recovery of the external encodings can be required.

These external encoding can be recovered as follows: for every input v_{EXTin} to the encoded implementation, we are able to find the inputs to the S-boxes. For Feistel ciphers, given the input to two consecutive rounds and the secret key, the plaintext can be computed easily. Hence we are able to compute the input to the naked DES, i.e., $v_{DESin} = F(v_{EXTin})$. Moreover, we can also compute the output of the naked DES, i.e., $v_{DESout} = DES_k(v_{DESin})$. This is the input to the external output encoding for which its output v_{EXTout} is the output of the white-box implementation. Hence for any given input to the white-box implementation, we can build different input-output pairs of the external encodings. This way, with a sufficient number of chosen inputs, the external encodings can be computed. Here we assume that these encodings are not too complex, that is, rather affine or simple non-linear mapping.

Chow et al. [4] proposed a specific class of external encodings, which are block encoded affine mixing bijections. Suppose these block encodings are nibble encodings. Then, for each of the 24 nibble encodings, we run over all its possible inputs (2^4), and compute the value of the 96-bit output v_{DESin}. With the knowledge of all these mappings, we are able to recover the external input encoding. The external output encoding can be recovered similarly.

4   Implementation

We have implemented our cryptanalysis in C++, and conducted tests on a Pentium M 2GHz. On average, about $6000 \leq 2^{13}$ obfuscated round functions of the white-box DES implementation are needed to be computed to check the difference propagations. This is less than our complexity study in Appendix B indicates, due to some extra optimisations we have applied (e.g., introducing requirements regarding round $r + 1$ in Property 1 substantially improves the efficiency of the algorithm). Moreover, our tests indicate that computations with 8 consecutive obfuscated round functions is sufficient for the attack to succeed. There is no restriction on which window of 8 round functions to chose.

In the conducted tests on several white-box DES implementations, our cryptanalysis algorithm extracted the DES key in all tests in under a second. On average the cryptanalysis requires 0.64 seconds.

5   Conclusion

We have described how to extract the embedded secret key of both the naked as encoded white-box DES implementations of Chow et al. [4]. This cryptanalysis also applies to the improved implementation as presented by Link and Neumann [10], because the outputs of the T-boxes are not used, only their inputs. The attack is a differential cryptanalysis on the obfuscated rounds, and is independent of the definition of the external encodings, in contrast to the attack of Goubin *et al.* [6].

The success of this cryptanalysis originates from properties which are specific to the DES. The confusion property of the DES S-boxes, the diffusion property of the DES permutation P and the design of the expansion operation are used to extract the key. The analysis, while specific to DES, nevertheless points the way to techniques to analyse other ciphers.

Acknowledgements. This work has been developed jointly with Philips Research Laboratories and is partly funded by a Ph.D. grant of the Institute for the Promotion of Innovation through Science and Technology in Flanders (IWT-Vlaanderen); and the Concerted Research Action (GOA) Ambiorics 2005/11 of the Flemish Government, the Research Foundation - Flanders (FWO-Vlaanderen). We would also like to thank Dries Schellekens and the anonymous reviewers for their constructive comments.

References

1. Biham, E., Shamir, A.: Differential cryptanalysis of Snefru, Khafre, REDOC-II, LOKI and Lucifer (extended abstract). In: Feigenbaum, J. (ed.) CRYPTO 1991. LNCS, vol. 576, pp. 156–171. Springer, Heidelberg (1992)
2. Billet, O., Gilbert, H., Ech-Chatbi, C.: Cryptanalysis of a white box AES implementation. In: Handschuh, H., Hasan, M.A. (eds.) SAC 2004. LNCS, vol. 3357, pp. 227–240. Springer, Heidelberg (2004)
3. Chow, S., Eisen, P.A., Johnson, H., van Oorschot, P.C.: White-Box Cryptography and an AES Implementation. In: Nyberg, K., Heys, H.M. (eds.) SAC 2002. LNCS, vol. 2595, pp. 250–270. Springer, Heidelberg (2003)
4. Chow, S., Eise, P.A., Johnson, H., van Oorschot, P.C.: A white-box DES implementation for DRM applications. In: Feigenbaum, J. (ed.) DRM 2002. LNCS, vol. 2696, pp. 1–15. Springer, Heidelberg (2003)
5. Coppersmith, D.: The Data Encryption Standard (DES) and its strength against attacks. IBM J. Res. Dev. 38(3), 243–250 (1994)
6. Goubin, L., Masereel, J.-M., Quisquater, M.: Cryptanalysis of white box DES implementations. Cryptology ePrint Archive, Report 2007/035 (2007), http://eprint.iacr.org/
7. Jacob, M., Boneh, D., Felten, E.W.: Attacking an obfuscated cipher by injecting faults. In: Digital Rights Management Workshop, pp. 16–31 (2002)
8. Kerins, T., Kursawe, K.: A cautionary note on weak implementations of block ciphers. In: WISSec 2006. 1st Benelux Workshop on Information and System Security, Antwerp, BE, p. 12 (2006)
9. Kim, J., Hong, S., Preneel, B.: Related-Key Rectangle Attacks on Reduced AES-192 and AES-256. In: Fast Software Encryption (2007)
10. Link, H.E., Neumann, W.D.: Clarifying obfuscation: Improving the security of white-box DES. In: ITCC 2005. Proceedings of the International Conference on Information Technology: Coding and Computing, vol. I, pp. 679–684. IEEE Computer Society Press, Washington, DC, USA (2005)

11. Osvik, D.A., Shamir, A., Tromer, E.: Cache attacks and countermeasures: The case of AES. In: Pointcheval, D. (ed.) CT-RSA 2006. LNCS, vol. 3860, pp. 1–20. Springer, Heidelberg (2006)
12. Pfleeger, C.P.: Security in Computing. Prentice-Hall, Englewood Cliffs, New Jersey (1989)
13. Data Encryption Standard.
    http://csrc.nist.gov/publications/fips/fips46-3/fips46-3.pdf

A   Appendix: Proofs

Property 1. *If Δv represents a single bit flip of R_{r-1}, then in round $r + 2$, at most 2 T-boxes are affected (i.e., its input changes).*

Proof. When Δv represents a flip of a single bit of R_{r-1}, then in round $r + 1$ it represents a flip of single bit of L_r, as the reader can deduce from Fig. 1(b). Because of the expansion and selection operation, this will result into 2 bits flipped to round $r + 2$ (one of X_{r+1} and one of $\overline{R_{r+1}}$; or both X_{r+1} flips). Thus at most 2 T-boxes in round $r + 2$ are affected. $\square$

Property 2. *If Δv represents flips of bits of L_{r-1} or Y_r, then in almost all cases more than 2 T-boxes are affected in round $r + 2$. The exceptions (false positives) can be detected by repeating this process up to α times with different fixed inputs to the other T-boxes T_l^r.*

Proof. In round $r + 1$, besides bypass bits, these differences represent flips to the inputs of S-boxes. Therefore, the number of flips to the inputs of round $r + 2$ explodes, and strictly more than 2 T-boxes will be affected.

There are a few exceptions in which not more than 2 T-boxes are affected (*false positives*). Observe an affected S-box in round $r + 1$. (There will always be at least one affected S-box). The input to this S-box changes in at least one and at most 3 bits (one for Y_r and two for L_{r-1} bit flips). The effect on the output bits of this S-box depends on its other input bits, which depend on the inputs v_l^r set at the initialisation phase. Hence the number of affected T-boxes in round $r + 2$ will very likely change if we set other inputs to T_l^r, witch $l \neq j$. With a very high probability, 2 extra checks are sufficient to detect these false positives, if we change all the inputs to the other T-boxes ($\alpha = 2$). $\square$

Property 3. *If Δv represents a flip of single bits of $\overline{R_{r-1}}$, there are exactly 2 propagated differences in round $r + 2$: Δm, Δn. One (say Δm, input difference to T-box T_m^{r+2}) will affect strictly more than 2 T-boxes in round $r + 4$, the other difference will affect at most 2 T-boxes in round $r + 4$. Moreover, T_m^{r+2} will be a non-linear T-box; Δm represents flips of one or both of the two middle bits of the internal S-box; and Δn represents flips of respectively one or two $\overline{R_{r+1}}$ bits.*

Proof. Let $\Delta v \in \mathcal{S}_{\overline{R}}(T_j^r)$ represent a flip of single (or double) bits of $\overline{R_{r-1}}$. Then, in round $r + 2$, this will propagate to a flip of one (or both) of the two middle input bits of an S-box S_m in T-box T_m^{r+2}. Hence T_m^{r+2} is a non-linear

T-box. Denote Δm the propagated input difference to T_m^{r+2}. Furthermore, this flip will also be bypassed because of the selection operation (see Fig. 1(b)). If this would be bypassed by T_m^{r+2} as well, then this T-box has an entropy of 7, in contradiction to the T-box design. Thus a second T-box T_n^{r+2} is affected, with input difference Δn. Therefor, Δv will affect exactly 2 T-boxes T_m^{r+2}, T_n^{r+2} with input differences $\Delta m, \Delta n$.

Consider the following DES S-box design properties [5]:

$$\Delta_{in} = 0wxyz0 \Rightarrow |\Delta_{out}| \geq 2 \tag{1}$$

$$|\Delta_{in}| = 1 \Rightarrow |\Delta_{out}| \geq 2, \tag{2}$$

with Δ_{in} the input difference to an S-box, Δ_{out} its resulting output difference, and $wxyz \in GF(2)^4 \backslash \{0\}$. Because of (1), Δm represents a flip of at least two Y_{r+2} bits at the output of the S-box. Due to the DES permutation P diffusion property and (2), Δm will affect more than 2 T-boxes in round $r + 4$. Δn represents a flip of bits of R_{r+1}, and affects no more than two T-boxes in round $r + 4$ (see Property 1). □

Property 4. *If Δv represents a flip of bits of $R_{r-1} \backslash \overline{R_{r-1}}$, there are exactly 2 propagated differences in round $r + 2$. Both affected T-boxes are non-linear T-boxes, and each of their input differences will affect strictly more than two T-boxes in round $r + 4$.*

Proof. If $\Delta v \in \mathcal{S}_R(T_j^r)$ represents a flip of bits of $R_{r-1} \backslash \overline{R_{r-1}}$, then for 2 S-boxes in round $r + 2$, exactly one input bit will be affected, and thus exactly 2 non-linear T-boxes in round $r + 2$ are affected.

Because of S-box design property (2), each of these differences will represent a flip of at least two Y_{r+2} bits. As a consequence of the DES permutation P diffusion property, both these differences in round $r + 2$ will affect strictly more than two T-boxes in round $r + 4$. □

B   Complexity

We define the complexity of the cryptanalysis as the number of round functions of the white-box implementation that need to be computed. The first step described, to retrieve flips of bits of R_{r-1}, has the largest complexity. Because of the lack of any prior information on internal flips, all differences have to be computed through several rounds in order to learn this bit flip information.

In Algorithm 1, for all 12 T-boxes, and all $2^8 - 1$ possible differences, 2 rounds need to be computed to observe the difference propagation. This corresponds to a total of $12 \cdot (2^8 - 1) \cdot 2 = 6120$ round function computations. For each positive result, we perform at most 2 double checks as described in Property 2. Algorithm 2 requires 6 round computations for each difference of $\mathcal{S}_R$ (2 for Δv, 2 for Δl and 2 for Δm). Hence, 240 round functions computations are performed.

Consequently, we can retrieve all flips of bits of $\overline{R_{r-1}}$ for one round in less than 2^{13} round computations in total. As described in Property 2, from $\Delta v \in \mathcal{S}_{\overline{R}}^r$, we can efficiently compute $\Delta n \in \mathcal{S}_{\overline{R}}^{r+2}$. Because of the one-to-one relation between Δv and Δn, this is sufficient to find all the single $\mathcal{S}_{\overline{R}}^{r+2}$ bit flips. Thus, when for two consecutive rounds, $\mathcal{S}_{\overline{R}}$ is found, we can compute this set for all subsequent rounds using Property 3 only. Hence, with about 2^{14} round computations, we can compute all flips of single bits of $\overline{R_{r-1}}$ for all rounds.

The complexity of the other steps of the cryptanalysis is negligible. In Algorithm 3, for each $\Delta m \in \mathcal{S}_M^r$, one round function needs to be computed. Hence, for each round, at most 24 round computations are needed (for 16 single bit flips and at most 8 double bit flips). To compute the exact inputs to the S-boxes, a filtering process needs to be applied to each non-linear T-box. In the worst case, we need to compute the difference propagation for all 7 input differences. Thus at most 7 round computations for each of the 8 non-linear T-boxes. The simulation process for each T-box needs to be performed at most $2^6 \cdot 8 = 2^9 (= |\mathcal{P}(T_j^r)|)$ times, which is the equivalent effort of computing one white-box DES round function (which consists of $552 \sim 2^9$ lookup table computations). The total complexity to compute the inputs to all S-boxes of one round is thus $8 \cdot (7+1) = 2^6$.

The space complexity is negligible too. Most space is used in Sect. 3.3 to store the set $\mathcal{P}(T_j^r)$ of candidate pairs (S_i, w_l). We can also choose to store the simulations of these pairs. They can be pre-computed because the simulation does not require any information on the implementation or the key.

Cryptanalysis of White Box DES Implementations*

Louis Goubin, Jean-Michel Masereel, and Michaël Quisquater

Versailles St-Quentin-en-Yvelines University
45 avenue des Etats-Unis
F-78035 Versailles Cedex
{Louis.Goubin,Jean-Michel.Masereel,Michael.Quisquater}@uvsq.fr

Abstract. Obfuscation is a method consisting in hiding information of some parts of a computer program. According to the Kerckhoffs principle, a cryptographical algorithm should be kept public while the whole security should rely on the secrecy of the key. In some contexts, source codes are publicly available, while the key should be kept secret; this is the challenge of code obfuscation. This paper deals with the cryptanalysis of such methods of obfuscation applied to the DES. Such methods, called the "naked-DES" and "nonstandard-DES", were proposed by Chow *et al.* [5] in 2002. Some methods for the cryptanalysis of the "naked-DES" were proposed by Chow *et al.* [5], Jacob *et al.* [6], and Link and Neuman [7]. In their paper, Link and Neuman [7] proposed another method for the obfuscation of the DES.

In this paper, we propose a general method that applies to all schemes. Moreover, we provide a theoretical analysis. We implemented our method with a C code and applied it successfully to thousands of obfuscated implementations of DES (both "naked" and "non-standard" DES). In each case, we recovered enough information to be able to invert the function.

Keywords: Obfuscation, cryptanalysis, DES, symmetric cryptography, block cipher.

1 Introduction

In recent years, the possibility of obfuscating programs has been investigated. From a theoretical point of view, Barak *et al.* [1] have proven impossibility results for the task of obfuscating computer programs. In particular, it turns out that there exists a family of programs such that: on the one hand each program is non learnable (i.e. its execution does not give any information about its original source code), but on the other hand every obfuscator (i.e. the program producing an obfuscation) fails completely when given any program of this family as input. However it has not been proved that specific instances, particularly cryptographic primitives, are impossible to obfuscate.

* This work has been supported in part by the French ANR (Agence Nationale de la Recherche), through the CrySCoE project, and by the région Île-de-France.

C. Adams, A. Miri, and M. Wiener (Eds.): SAC 2007, LNCS 4876, pp. 278–295, 2007.

In 2002, Chow *et al.* [4,5] suggested two different obfuscations, one for the AES, the other for the DES. The AES obfuscation was cryptanalysed by Billet *et al.* [2,3] in 2004. Chow *et al.* [5] also mounted an attack on their first DES obfuscation version (called "naked-DES"). Jacob *et al.* [6] and Link and Neuman [7], proposed two other attacks on the "naked-DES". Here, breaking the "naked-DES" means recovering the secret key.

A second version of DES obfuscation, called "nonstandard-DES", was given by Chow *et al.* [5]. This "nonstandard-DES" is obtained by obfuscating the usual DES composed with initial and final secret permutations. In this context, breaking such a "nonstandard-DES" implementation means recovering the secret key and the secret initial and final permutations.

Moreover, many industrial actors have developed obfuscated implementations of cryptographic algorithms, in particular for DRM, Pay-TV, and intellectual property protection. (e.g. cloakware [12], retroguard [13], Yguard [14]).

This paper is structured as follows : In Section 2, we give an overview of the obfuscation methods given by Chow *et al.* and by Link and Neumann. Section 3 is devoted to our attack on the "naked-DES". In Section 4, we adapt our attack to the "non standard" DES. Section 5 is devoted to our implementation of this attack. In Section 6, we compare our attack to the one of Wyseur *et al.* [11]. Finally, we conclude in Section 7. All proofs are available in the appendices.

2   DES Obfuscation Methods

Chow *et al.* [5] proposed two types of DES obfuscation. The first one, called "naked-DES", produces an usual DES. The second one, called the "nonstandard-DES", is a slight modification of the standard DES algorithm. This last version is the one they recommend.

Let us describe the "naked-DES" (see Figure 7). The standard DES is implemented by means of many functions. The first one is an affine function M_1, which is the composition of the initial permutation, the expansion (slightly modified in order to duplicate all the 32 right bits), and a bit-permutation $\phi_0 : \mathbb{F}_2^{96} \to \mathbb{F}_2^{96}$. The role of ϕ_0 is to send 48 bits to the corresponding S-box entries, the 48 remaining bits being sent randomly to the T-box entries (see Figure 8). Eight of these T-boxes are derived from the eight S-boxes of the DES (see Figure 1), and the four remaining T-boxes are identities (or more generally bit permutations, see Figure 8 (T_{12})). An affine function $M_{2,1}$ follows the T-boxes. This affine function is the composition of the P and Xor operation of the standard DES, and a bit-permutation ϕ_1 (see Figure 7). Each of the 16 rounds is the composition of the T-boxes and an affine function $M_{2,i}$. The last round is followed by an affine function M_3 which is the composition of a selection function, and the final permutation. This function takes for arguments the outputs of the affine function $M_{2,16}$ of the last round and returns the ciphertext (see Figure 7).

We will denote by A_i, one of these components (T_i, M_1, $M_{2,i}$ or M_3). The obfuscator program computes numbers of random nonlinear permutations on

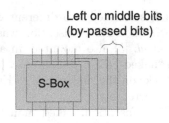

Fig. 1. T-Box

$\mathbb{F}_2^s$, $b_{k,l}$ ($s = 4$ or 8). These permutations are referred by Chow *et al.* [5] as io-block encoding bijections. Twenty-four or twelve of these io-block encoding bijections are concatenated in order to obtain nonlinear permutations on $\mathbb{F}_2^{96}$, $P_{i,j}$. Each component A_i is obfuscated between permutations $P_{i,1}$ and $P_{i,2}$. The resulting functions $P_{i,1} \circ A_i \circ P_{i,2}$ are stored in arrays in order to be used by the obfuscated program. When considering consecutive components, the final permutation of the first component, and the initial permutation of the second component, cancelled out (see Figure 7) i.e. :

$$(P_{i,1} \circ A_i \circ P_{i,2}) \circ (P_{j,1} \circ A_j \circ P_{j,2}) = P_{i,1} \circ (A_i \circ A_j) \circ P_{j,2} \ .$$

This "naked-DES" was cryptanalysed by the authors themselves [5].

In order to repair the scheme, they proposed the "nonstandard-DES". It consists in adding two affine bijections M_0 and M_4 before and after the "naked-DES", respectively (see Figure 7). It is not specified by Chow *et al.* [5] whether M_0 and M_4 are block encoded (i.e. respectively preceded and followed by nonlinear random permutations). In this paper, we consider that M_0 and M_4 are not block encoded.

Further improvement on the attack of the "naked-DES" were given by Link and Neumann [7]. They suggested another solution which consists in merging the T-boxes and the affine function $M_{2,i}$ of each round. This way, we do not have access to the T-boxes outputs. Moreover, the $M_{2,i}$ functions of the different rounds are block encoded in another way.

In this paper, we describe an attack that defeats both "nonstandard-DES" and the Link and Neumann's schemes.

3   Attack on the "Naked-DES"

As mentioned before, the "naked-DES" proposed by Chow *et al.* [5] was already cryptanalysed in the papers [5,6,7]. In this section, we show how to cryptanalyse the improved version of the "naked-DES" proposed by Link and Neumann [7]. Note that our method also works for the "naked-DES" proposed by Chow *et al.* [5]. In what follows, we will denote by "regular DES", the one described in the standard [10] (without PC1), and we will use the same notations.

Our attack is divided into two phases and is based on a truncated differential attack. Roughly speaking, the first phase consists in generating pairs of messages

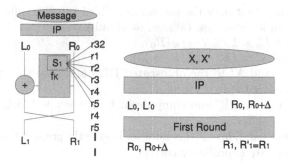

Fig. 2. One round of DES, and attack principle

(X,X') such that the right part of the images, through IP and the first round of a regular DES, are equal (for a given key K) (see Figure 2.b). The second phase consists in evaluating those pairs of messages (X, X') on the "naked-DES" and in checking a condition that we specify below. The pairs that satisfy the test provide a key candidate.

Let us go into the details. Remember that $f(., K)$ denotes the function of the regular DES, we will also denote it by $f_K(.)$ (see Figure 2.a). Let X be an initial message, (L_0, R_0) denotes its image through IP, and (L_1, R_1) is the image of (L_0, R_0) through the first round, i.e. $(L_1, R_1) = (R_0, L_0 \oplus f(R_0, K))$. Consider a function f, vectors X and Δ, the derivative $f(X) \oplus f(X \oplus \Delta)$ will be denoted by $D_\Delta f(X)$. Let us first motivate our algorithm. Let K be a fixed unknown key. Assume we want to find the first round 6-bit subkey corresponding to S_i (for the sake of clarity, we will restrain ourselves to $i = 1$). We generate candidate keys such that only the 6 key bits of S_1 of the first round are modified. For each of these keys, we compute pairs of messages (X,X') such that,

1. $\Delta = R_0 \oplus R'_0$ is zero, except for the second and third bits.
2. $L'_0 = L_0 \oplus D_\Delta f_K(R_0)$

Observe that the second and third bits of R_0 only affect the output of S_1 (see Figure 2.a) . Therefore, $f(R_0, K)$ and $f(R'_0, K)$ are identical except for the four bits corresponding to the output of S_1.

Under these conditions, in the next round we have $R_1 = R'_1$ and $L'_1(= R'_0)$ is identical to $L_1(= R_0)$ except for at most two bits. Consider now these two messages X and X' applied to the "naked-DES" with the correct key candidate. We observe that these bits (non-zero bits of $L'_1 \oplus L_1$) influence at most two io-block encoding bijections $b_{i,3}$ and $b_{j,3}$ (see Figure 8). If the key candidate is wrong, we will have $R_1 \neq R'_1$. Therefore many bits will change at the output of $M_{2,1}$, and we will be able to distinguish this situation from the correct key guess.

Here is an overview of the attack:

– Randomly choose a message X.
– Compute $(L_0, R_0) = IP(X)$ with IP public.

- Choose Δ such that only the second and third bits are different from 0.
- For any possible candidate value of 6-bit subkey:
  - Compute $L'_0 = L_0 \oplus D_\Delta f_K(R_0)$.
  - Compute $X' = IP^{-1}(L'_0, R_0 \oplus \Delta)$.
  - Apply X and X' to the obfuscated DES and save the values Y and Y' at the end of the first round.
  - Compare Y and Y' and compute in how many io-block encoding bijections they differ.
  - Reject the candidate if this number is strictly greater than 2. Otherwise, the candidate is probably correct.

This way, we can recover the 48 key bits of the first round of the DES. The 8 remaining bits are found by exhaustive search.

Remark 1. This algorithm can produce more than one candidate for the 6-bit subkey. It will provide wrong 6-bit subkeys in two situations.

1. Due to the balance property of the S-boxes and the fact they map six bits to four bits, four different inputs produce the same output. Therefore for each S-box, three wrong 6-bit subkeys will produce the same output as the correct key. To avoid this problem, we can launch this algorithm with another random initial message, or simply another Δ. In fact, we only have to change the values of the bits of R_0 and Δ corresponding to the input of S_1 (the bits 32,1,...,5). Actually, we can choose different pairs (X, X') such that the intersection of the key candidates associated to each of them is the correct key.
2. The second one is due to a propagation phenomena. Suppose we have a wrong 6-bit subkey producing a wrong S_1 output. It means that there are more than three bits of difference between (L_1, R_1) and (L'_1, R'_1). These differences could be mapped to the same io-block encoding bijection, leading to the flipping of only two io-block encoding bijections at the output of $M_{2,1}$. In this case, we launch this algorithm with several values for R_0. It leads to several lists of key candidates and the correct key belongs to the intersection. This way, wrong keys will be discarded.

4   Attack on the "Nonstandard-DES"

This section is dedicated to an attack on the "nonstandard-DES". Remind that the "nonstandard-DES" is a "naked-DES" where the affine functions M_1 and M_0 are replaced by $M_1 \circ M_0$ and $M_4 \circ M_3$ respectively (where M_0 and M_4 are mixing bijections, see Chow *et al.* [5]). As mentioned before, we assume that the inputs of $M_1 \circ M_0$ (respectively the outputs of $M_4 \circ M_3$) are not io-block encoded. Note that all the other functions are io-block encoded using bijections on $\mathbb{F}_2^4$ (the same principle applies for the obfuscation proposed by Link and Neuman [7] where the bijections are defined on $\mathbb{F}_2^8$). Moreover, we assume that the T-Boxes follow the same ordering in the different rounds. In what follows, we will not consider IP (inside M_1) w.l.o.g, for the sake of clarity.

In what follows, the term *preimage* will implicitly refer to the preimage with respect to the linear bijection M_0. Moreover, we say that a bit of a vector is *touching* an io-block encoding bijection if this bijection depends on this bit. Similarly, we will say that a vector *touches* an S-Box if non-zero bits touch it.

Our attack on the "nonstandard-DES" is based on the one on the "naked-DES". Our approach is based on a truncated differential attack. It consists in computing the images of a random vector X_0 at different levels in the obfuscated DES. We compare these values (called *initial-entries*) to the corresponding images of $X_0 \oplus \Delta$, where Δ satisfies some conditions depending on the context. This approach allows providing information about the key and the matrix M_0^{-1}, gradually. The full key and the matrix M_0^{-1} will be known at the end of the process. The way we store information about M_0^{-1} consists in considering lists of candidates for preimages of unspecified canonical vectors. Lists of candidates containing only one vector are called *distinguished* lists. This vector is then a column of M_0^{-1}. Note that these lists are actually vector spaces and can be shared by several canonical vectors. In practice, a list E will be shared by $\dim E$ canonical vectors (that are not necessary specified). Our algorithm works sequentially and consists in specifying these canonical vectors and shortening the lists. Our method can therefore be understood as a "filtering process". The different filters are described below.

Section 4.1 describes a preliminary step almost independent of the structure of the block cipher. It consists in finding vector spaces associated to a particular io-block encoding bijection at the input of the first round. This step allows getting global information about M_0^{-1}.

Section 4.2 describes a set of filters intending to refine information about M_0^{-1}. These steps are highly related to the studied block cipher. The first filter, described in Section 4.2, allows distinguishing lists that are associated to canonical vectors belonging either to right bits or left bits of the input of the first round (L_0 or R_0). The second filter, described in Section 4.2, extracts all the lists (marked as "right" in the previous filter) touching a single S-box (we will see that these lists play an important role). The third filter, described in Section 4.2, gathers the lists (marked as "left" in the previous filter) in sets associated to the output of S-boxes. Section 4.2 links T-Boxes (obfuscation of the keyed S-boxes) to S-Boxes. This information allows the last filter, presented in Section 4.2, to precisely specify the 1-to-1 link between the lists (marked as "left") and the (left) canonical vectors.

Section 4.3 explains how to extract the key and how to recover the full invertible matrices M_0^{-1} and M_4.

4.1   Block Level Analysis of $M_1 \circ M_0$

Recovering of the B_k's. Denote by K_k the space $(\{0\}^{4k-4} \times \mathbb{F}_2^4 \times \{0\}^{96-4k})$, and by $\overline{K}_k$, the space $(\mathbb{F}_2^{4k-4} \times \{0\}^4 \times \mathbb{F}_2^{96-4k})$. In what follows, the vector space spanned by a set of vectors S will be denoted $\langle S \rangle$. Also, e_i denotes the ith canonical vector (the position of the "one" is computed from the left and start from one) of the vector space $\mathbb{F}_2^{64}$. The sets $\{e_i \in \mathbb{F}_2^{64} \mid i = 1 \ldots 32\}$ and $\{e_i \in \mathbb{F}_2^{64} \mid i = 33 \ldots 64\}$ will be denoted by $\mathcal{S}_L$ and $\mathcal{S}_R$, respectively.

Ideally, we are looking for 24 vector spaces such that their vectors influence only one io-block encoding bijection at the output of $M_1 \circ M_0$. This would allow modifying only the input of one particular io-block encoding bijection. Unfortunately, due to the duplication of the bits in M_1 (because of the expansion E) this goal is impossible to reach. We will therefore try to approximate this situation and deal with the drawbacks afterwards. First we will have to give some notations, definitions and properties.

Denote by $F : \mathbb{F}_2^{64} \to \mathbb{F}_2^{96}$ the obfuscation of $M_1 \circ M_0$ (see Figure 7).

Let X be a vector in $\mathbb{F}_2^{96}$. Denote by π_k the projection $\pi_k : (\mathbb{F}_2^4)^{24} \to \mathbb{F}_2^4 :$ $X = (x_1, \ldots, x_{24}) \mapsto x_k$. Let b_k be the kth io-block encoding bijection at the output of $M_1 \circ M_0$. The function F is written as

$$F(X) = (b_1 \circ \pi_1 \circ M_1 \circ M_0(X), b_2 \circ \pi_2 \circ M_1 \circ M_0(X), \ldots, b_{24} \circ \pi_{24} \circ M_1 \circ M_0(X)) \ .$$

Definition 1. *Let k be an integer, $k \in [1, 24]$. We denote by $\mathcal{B}_k$ the vector space $\{X \in \mathbb{F}_2^{64} \mid \pi_k \circ M_1(X) = 0\}$. In other words, it is the subspace of vector X such that for any non-zero component e_i of X, $M_1(e_i)$ does not touch b_k, i.e. $\mathcal{B}_k = \langle e_j \mid \pi_k \circ M_1(e_j) = 0 \rangle$.*

Definition 2. *Let k be an integer, $k \in [1, 24]$. We denote by $\mathcal{E}_k$ the subspace of vector X such that for any non-zero component e_i of X, $M_1(e_i)$ touches b_k, i.e. $\mathcal{E}_k = \langle e_j \mid \pi_k \circ M_1(e_j) \neq 0 \rangle$.*

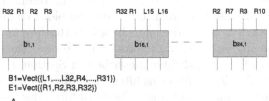

R32 R1 R2 R3   R32 R1 L15 L16   R2 R7 R3 R10

$b_{1,1}$ $b_{16,1}$ $b_{24,1}$

B1=Vect({L1,...,L32,R4,...,R31})
E1=Vect({R1,R2,R3,R32})
$\hat{E}1$=Vect({R1,R2,R3,R32,L15,L16})=B2∩B3∩...∩B15∩B17∩...∩B23

Fig. 3. Example

Remark 2. Note that $\mathbb{F}_2^{64}$ is the direct sum of $\mathcal{B}_k$ and $\mathcal{E}_k$ for any k, i.e. $\mathbb{F}_2^{64} = \mathcal{B}_k \bigoplus \mathcal{E}_k$.

We will denote by B_k the subspace $M_0^{-1}(\mathcal{B}_k)$, and by E_k the subspace $M_0^{-1}(\mathcal{E}_k)$.

Proposition 1. *For any k integer, $k \in [1, 24]$, $B_k = \{\Delta \in \mathbb{F}_2^{64} \mid D_\Delta F(\mathbb{F}_2^{64}) \subset \overline{K}_k\}$, the probability that Δ belongs to B_k, when Δ is randomly chosen, is greater or equal to $\frac{1}{2^4} = \frac{1}{16}$, and $60 \leq \dim(B_k) < 64$.*

Combining Definition 2 and Property 1, the vector space E_k can be described as the set of vectors Δ such that for any vector $X_0 \in \mathbb{F}_2^{64}$, $M_0(X_0) \oplus M_0(X_0 \oplus \Delta)$ has in total at most four non-zero components e_i, all of them touching the kth

io-block encoding bijection through M_1. Due to Property 1, it is easier to recover a basis for B_k's, than for E_k's. That is why we will first recover all the B_k's. Using Property 1, we only have to compute $D_\Delta F(X_0)$ for random $\Delta \in \mathbb{F}_2^{64}$ and determine to which space $\overline{K}_k$ it belongs. Using B_k's, we will recover E_k's, or at least, 24 vector spaces $\widehat{E}_k$ containing E_k with minimal dimension.

Recovering of the $\widehat{E}_k$'s. Let us now explain how to recover $\widehat{E}_k$. First, let us remark that for any $X \in \mathbb{F}_2^{64}$ and for any $\Delta \in \mathbb{F}_2^{64}$, we have $D_\Delta F(X) \in \overline{K}_k$ if and only if $D_\Delta \pi_k \circ M_1 \circ M_0(X) \in \overline{K}_k$. Let us introduce the following lemma.

Lemma 1. Let k be an integer belonging to $[1, 24]$. If $\mathcal{E}_j \cap \mathcal{E}_k = \{0\}$ for any integer j distinct from k belonging to $[1, 24]$, then

$$\mathcal{E}_k = \bigcap_{j \neq k} \mathcal{B}_j \ .$$

Since M_0 is a bijection, this lemma means that if $\mathcal{E}_j \cap \mathcal{E}_k = \{0\}$ for any integer $j \in [1, 24]$ different from k, then $E_k = \bigcap_{j \neq k} B_j$. Nevertheless, due to the bit-duplication, there exist indices k and j such that $\mathcal{E}_j \cap \mathcal{E}_k \neq \{0\}$ (and then $E_j \cap E_k \neq \{0\}$). Denote by J_k the set $\{j \mid \mathcal{E}_j \cap \mathcal{E}_k = \{0\}\}$, by $\widehat{\mathcal{E}}_k$ the subspace $\bigcap_{j \in J_k} \mathcal{B}_j$, and by $\widehat{E}_k$ the subspace $\bigcap_{j \in J_k} B_j$ where k is an integer belonging to $[1, 24]$.

Proposition 2. For any integer $k \in [1, 24]$, $\mathcal{E}_k \subseteq \widehat{\mathcal{E}}_k$.

Let us introduce a property that will allow us to give another characterization of J_k.

Proposition 3. For any integer $i \in [1, 24]$ and for any integer $j \in [1, 24]$

$$\dim(\mathcal{E}_i \cap \mathcal{E}_j) = 64 + \dim(B_i \cap B_j) - \dim(B_j) - \dim(B_i) \ .$$

A straightforward application of this property to the definition of J_k leads to $J_k = \{j \in [1, 24] \mid 64 = \dim(B_j) + \dim(B_k) - \dim(B_k \cap B_j)\}$. This characterization will be useful in order to compute $\widehat{E}_k$. If $\dim(\widehat{E}_k) + \dim(B_k) > 64$ then $E_k \subsetneq \widehat{E}_k$, and we have found a vector space containing strictly the one we search. Note that when $\dim(\widehat{E}_k) + \dim(B_k) = 64$, $E_k = \widehat{E}_k$. This case is particularly interesting because it reduces the complexity of the full cryptanalysis.

4.2 Bit Level Analysis of M_0^{-1}

In the previous section, we were looking for differences Δ associated to a specific io-block encoding bijection. It allowed us to get some information about M_0^{-1}. In this section, we refine our search and this will allow us to get enough information about M_0^{-1} in order to apply our method on the "naked-DES" to "nonstandard-DES". Our algorithm works sequentially and consists in a "filtering process". The different filters are described below.

Search for Candidates for Preimages of Elements Belonging to the Sets $\mathcal{S}_L$ and $\mathcal{S}_R$. Consider Δ be an element of $\mathbb{F}_2^{64}$ such that $M_0(\Delta) = e_i$ and $e_i \in \mathcal{S}_L$. The only non-zero bit of $M_1 \circ M_0(\Delta)$ touches only one io-block encoding bijection (recall that we do not consider IP). Therefore, Δ belongs to a single $\widehat{E}_k$. Assume now that $\Delta \in \mathbb{F}_2^{64}$ such that $M_0(\Delta) = e_i$ and $e_i \in \mathcal{S}_R$ then $M_1 \circ M_0(\Delta)$ has exactly two non-zero bits that may touch the same or two distinct io-block encoding bijections or equivalently Δ belongs to one or two spaces $\widehat{E}_k$. In what follows, we will call *double* an element $\Delta \in \mathbb{F}_2^{64}$ such that $M_0(\Delta) \in \mathcal{S}_R$ and the two non-zero bits of $M_1 \circ M_0(\Delta)$ touch the same io-block encoding bijection. For example, on Figure 8, the bit R_2 could be a double, since its two instances are in the input of T_1. By considering intersections between the spaces $\widehat{E}_k$, taken pairwise, we can distinguish preimages of elements of $\mathcal{S}_R$ from doubles or preimages of elements of $\mathcal{S}_L$.

Note that the intersections between spaces $\widehat{E}_k$ taken pairwise provide more information. Indeed, $\widehat{E}_i \cap \widehat{E}_j$ contains preimages of unknown canonical vectors. In particular, if $\dim(\widehat{E}_i \cap \widehat{E}_j) = 1$ then $\widehat{E}_i \cap \widehat{E}_j = \langle M_0^{-1}(e_k) \rangle$ for some k. In this case, we already know the preimage of an unknown canonical vector. When $\dim(\widehat{E}_i \cap \widehat{E}_j) > 1$ we can still take advantage of this fact even if it requires some extra searches.

Recovering Middle Bits. In order to apply our attack presented in Section 3, we need to exactly know the preimage of canonical vectors touching only a single S-Box of the first round (e.g. Right bits 2,3,6,7,10, ...). In what follows, we will refer to such a canonical vector as a *middle bit*. If a middle bit is not a double, then its two copies touch two different io-block encoding bijections. The first copy is in input of an S-box, leading to at least two bits of difference at the end of the first round of a regular DES, and 4 bits in our case, due to the expansion. The second copy is a by-passed bit (see Figure 1), leading to only one bit of difference at the end of the first round. Consider the bold path in Figure 8 starting from R_3 bit, in order to have a global view. Let us explain how we use this property.

Recall that X_0 is the initial-vector defined in Section 4. For each difference Δ belonging to the lists marked as input of the studied T-box, we apply $X_0 \oplus \Delta$ to the obfuscated DES by making an *injection fault*. This means that we set the input of this T-box to the initial-entry while we keep the input of the other T-Boxes (see Figure 4). We evaluate the number of io-block encoding bijections at

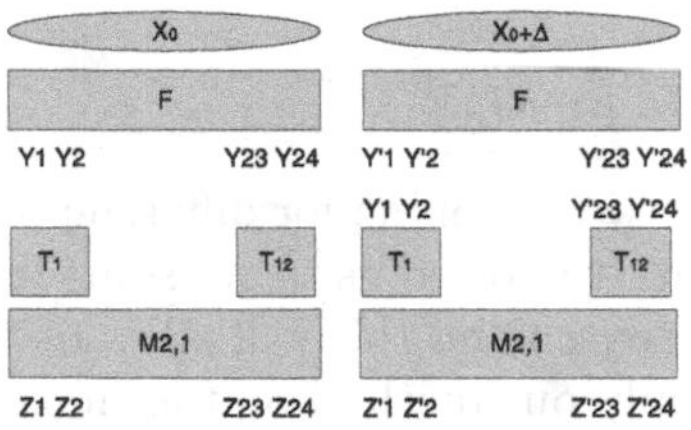

Fig. 4. Injection fault

the output of the first round that differs from the corresponding initial-entries. If only one io-block encoding bijection (at the output of the first round) differs from the corresponding initial-entry, we deduce that Δ could be the preimage of a middle bit. Therefore, a list containing preimages of several canonical vectors can be divided into two shorter lists; one list containing preimages of middle bits while the other contains preimages of non-middle bits.

Remark 3. If a T-box is touched by more than three middle bits or left bits, we deduce that this T-box does not contain any S-box. Note also that doubles can only be preimages of middle bits. Finally, a T-box touched by a double contains necessarily an S-box.

Recovering Left Bits. In order to apply our attack presented in Section 3, we need to know which group of four canonical vectors are xored with the output of each S-box of the first round. First, we determine the io-block encoding bijections that are touched by the outputs of the studied S-box and we denote by BS this set of bijections. In Figure 8, we can see that $BS = \{b_{1,3}, b_{3,3}, b_{8,3}, b_{12,3}, b_{15,3}, b_{20,3}, b_{24,3}\}$ for the S-box S_1. The elements $b_{i,3}$ of BS are characterised by $D_{\Delta_m} b_{i,3} \circ \pi_i \circ M_{2,1} \circ T \circ M_1 \circ M_0(X_0) \neq 0$, for all Δ_m belonging to a list marked as a middle bit of the studied S-box. Then, we store in an extra list $\mathcal{L}$ each Δ marked as left bits touching exactly two bijections of BS. This list contains all the preimages associated to canonical vectors that are potentially xored with the output of the S-box. Finally, we find $\Delta_l \in \langle \mathcal{L} \rangle$ such that for any bijection $b_{i,3} \in BS$ we have $D_{\Delta_m \oplus \Delta_l} b_{i,3} \circ \pi_i \circ M_{2,1} \circ T \circ M_1 \circ M_0(X_0) = 0$, where Δ_m belongs to a list marked as a middle bit of the studied S-box. This process is repeated with different Δ_m or X_0, until we find four linearly independent Δ_l or equivalently the vector space spanned by the preimages of the searched canonical vectors. We then compute the intersection between this space and all the lists. It allows us to split some of them in shorter lists (the intersection and the complementary space of the intersection). It may lead to lists containing a single vector (distinguished list).

Chaining. In this section, we will try to determine precisely the correspondence between T-boxes and S-boxes. Due to the remark in Section 4.2, we know which are the T-boxes containing an S-box. The probability that a selected T-box, denoted by T_1, contains S_1 is $1/8$. We determine the two T-Boxes that are touched by a canonical vector associated to a list marked as "right bit", "non-middle bit" and associated to T_1. Selecting one of these T-Boxes randomly, the

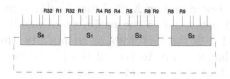

Fig. 5. Chaining

probability that it contains S_2 is $1/2$. Out of the set of unselected T-Boxes, we select the one that is touched by a canonical vector associated to a list marked as "right bit", "non-middle bit" and associated to the previous selected T-Box. We continue the process until all T-Boxes have been selected (see Figure 5). Note that the probability to determine the right correspondence is $1/8 \times 1/2 = 1/16$.

Bit Positions. At this stage, we have recovered between others, 32 preimages corresponding to unspecified left canonical vectors. In order to determine the correspondence, we use the following observation on the DES:

Out of the four left bits that are xored with the output of a specified S-Box, exactly two become (in the second round) middle bits.

Now, we just have to apply each of the preimages to the obfuscated DES and check whether the image of this vector in front of the second round is a middle bit (cf. 4.2). Assuming that the T-Boxes follow the same ordering in the different rounds, preimages corresponding to a middle bit (resp. non-middle bit) can be distinguished by observing the indices of the touched T-Boxes.

For example, for the first S-box, among the preimages of the four identified left canonical vectors,

- one of such vectors is the preimage of e_{23} (resp. e_{31}) if it is the preimage of a middle bit of S_6 (resp. S_8) in the second round.
- one of such vectors is the preimage of e_9 (resp. e_{17}) if it is not the preimage of a middle bit and it is in the input of S_2 and S_3 (resp. S_4 and S_5) of the second round.

4.3   The Attack

In Section 4.2, we have shown how to recover all the preimages of the left canonical vectors. In other words, we have recovered half of M_0^{-1} (columns and their positions). Also, some of the lists marked as middle bits contain only one vector but their corresponding canonical vector is however unknown. Therefore, some columns of M_0^{-1} are known up to their positions. Finally, the remaining lists marked as middle bits contain preimages of some canonical vectors $e_{i_1}, \ldots, e_{i_n}$ (their number is the dimension of the vector space spanned by the list). In this case, we select linearly independent vectors in the list and we associate each of them to one of the canonical vector e_{i_j}. Therefore, we are in the context of the attack of the "naked-DES" up to some adaptations. In particular, we have to choose X_0 belonging to the vector space spanned by the known columns of M_0^{-1}. The evaluation of the first round on $X_0 \oplus \Delta$ may lead to some difficulties. Indeed, we have to choose Δ belonging to the preimage of middle bits space which is not necessarily included in the vector space spanned by the known columns of M_0^{-1}. It turns out that we have to try all the candidates for this part of the matrix M_0^{-1}. For each of these candidates, we mount an attack like we did on the "naked-DES", which provides 48-bit key candidates. Note that wrong keys may be recovered. More importantly, here may be no key for this candidate for this part of the matrix M_0^{-1}. In other words, it means that we have to discard this candidate.

In order to determine the remaining part of M_0^{-1} (columns associated to non-middle bits), we apply a similar principle that we used for the "naked-DES". Indeed, we know the key and we know that for the "naked-DES" for any initial-message X_0 there always exists a difference Δ with non-zero right component such that the right part of the differential (evaluated in X_0) of the first round is zero. It means that in the context of the "nonstandard-DES", wrong candidates for M_0^{-1} can be discarded. Denote by K the space spanned by the known columns of the candidate for M_0^{-1} and by U the unknown columns of the candidate for M_0^{-1}. We have $K \oplus U = \mathbb{F}_2^{64}$. The candidate for M_0^{-1} can be discarded if there exists $X_0 \in K$ such that there does not exist Δ with a non zero-component in U such that the right part of the differential (evaluated in X_0) is zero.

At this stage, we have a 48-bit key candidate and a candidate for M_0^{-1}. We make an exhaustive search in order to determine the 8 remaining bits of the key. For each of them we try to solve a linear system in order to find the matrix M_4. If there is no solution for M_4 we deduce that the 8-bit key candidate is wrong. If all the 8-bit key candidates are wrong, we discard this particular M_0^{-1}. Note that this method also works if M_4 has io-block encoding bijections at its output.

Attack on Link and Neumann obfuscation: Our methods only use the outputs of the first and second round. In particular, we never use the outputs of the T-boxes. Therefore, our two attacks ("naked-DES", and "nonstandard-DES") can be applied on the Link and Neumann [7] obfuscation method. The only difference is that we will deal with larger lists.

5   Results

This attack was implemented with a C code. At each stage of the attack, the number of candidates decreases both for the key and for M_0^{-1}. Finally, it will lead to a unique 48-bit key candidate, a unique M_0^{-1} candidate, and a unique M_4 candidate. We have tested our attack on thousands of randomly generated

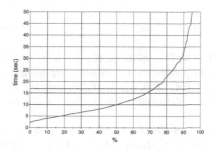

Fig. 6. Repartition of the attacks durations

obfuscated implementations of DES (both "naked" and "nonstandard" DES). Figure 6 shows the necessary time to complete the attack. We can observe that 95% of the attacks require less than 50 seconds, and 75% less than 17 seconds. The mean time is about 17 seconds. However, the attacks were executed on a standard PC. The code was not optimized and the performance can be further improved.

6   Comparison to Wyseur *et al.*'s Work

In this section, we try to clarify the differences between our paper and the one of Wyseur *et al.* [11]. The main advantage of their method is that they are able to recover the key for the "nonstandard-DES" even when the transformations M_0 and M_4 are nonlinear. They also briefly explain how to recover these transformations when they are linear, provided the key is known. Our method also allows recovering linear transformations in a short amount of time. The nonlinear case is still an open problem. Finally, Wyseur *et al.* [11] consider an obfuscation where the ϕ_i's have a restricted shape. While our model is unrestricted, they consider only ϕ_i's where all middle-bits touch only the four trivial T-boxes. It is not obvious whether their methodology can be adapted to the general case.

7   Conclusion

In this paper, we have given new techniques of cryptanalysis for the current obfuscation methods of DES. These techniques rely on a theoretical analysis and have also been implemented as a C program. We have implemented our method with a C code and have applied it successfully to more than a thousand obfuscated implementations of DES (both "naked" and "nonstandard" DES). All the studied instances have lead to a unique candidate for the DES key and for the M_0 and M_4 secret linear transformations. The key and the two linear transforms have been obtained within 17 seconds in average.

Acknowledgements. The authors would like to thank Sylvie Baudine for proofreading the text.

References

1. Barak, B., Goldreich, O., Impagliazzo, R., Rudich, S., Sahai, A., Vadhan, S.P., Yang, K.: On the (im)possibility of obfuscating programs. In: Kilian, J. (ed.) CRYPTO 2001. LNCS, vol. 2139, pp. 1–18. Springer, Heidelberg (2001)
2. Billet, O.: Cryptologie Multivariable Ph.D. thesis University of Versailles (December 2005)
3. Billet, O., Gilbert, H., Ech-Chatbi, C.: Cryptanalysis of a white box AES implementation. In: Handschuh, H., Hasan, M.A. (eds.) SAC 2004. LNCS, vol. 3357, pp. 227–240. Springer, Heidelberg (2004)

4. Chow, S., Eisen, P., Johnson, H., van Oorschot, P.: White-box cryptography and an AES implementation. In: Nyberg, K., Heys, H.M. (eds.) SAC 2002. LNCS, vol. 2595, pp. 250–270. Springer, Heidelberg (2003)
5. Chow, S., Johnson, H., van Oorschot, P., Eisen, P.: A white-box DES implementation for DRM applications. In: Feigenbaum, J. (ed.) DRM 2002. LNCS, vol. 2696, pp. 1–15. Springer, Heidelberg (2003)
6. Jacob, M., Boneh, D., Felten, E.: Attacking an obfuscated cipher by injecting faults. In: Proceedings 2002 ACM Workshop on Digital Rights Management, November 18, 2002, Washington DC, USA (2002)
7. Link, H.E., Neumann, W.D.: Clarifying obfuscation: Improving the security of white-box encoding (2004), http://eprint.iacr.org/
8. Patarin, J., Goubin, L.: Asymmetric cryptography with S-boxes. In: Proc. 1st International Information and Communications Security Conference, pp. 369–380 (1997)
9. Patarin, J., Goubin, L., Courtois, N.: Improved Algorithms for Isomorphisms of Polynomials. In: Nyberg, K. (ed.) EUROCRYPT 1998. LNCS, vol. 1403, pp. 184–200. Springer, Heidelberg (1998)
10. http://www.itl.nist.gov/fipspubs/fip46-2.htm
11. Wyseur, B., Michiels, W., Gorissen, P., Preneel, B.: Cryptanalysis of White-Box DES Implementations with Arbitrary External Encodings. Cryptology ePrint Archive, Report 2007/104 (2007), http://eprint.iacr.org/
12. http://www.cloakware.com
13. http://www.retrologic.com
14. http://www.yworks.com/en/products_yguard_about.htm

Appendix A: Proofs

Proof of Property 1: Let E be the set $\{\Delta \in \mathbb{F}_2^{64} \mid D_\Delta F(\mathbb{F}_2^{64}) \subset \overline{K}_k\}$.

- Let Δ be an element belonging to B_k. Let X be an element belonging to $\mathbb{F}_2^{64}$.

$$D_\Delta F(X) = (D_\Delta(b_1 \circ \pi_1 \circ M_1 \circ M_0(X)), \ldots, D_\Delta(b_{24} \circ \pi_{24} \circ M_1 \circ M_0(X)))$$

According to the definitions, if $\Delta \in B_k$ then $M_0(\Delta) \in \mathcal{B}_k$ or equivalently $\pi_k \circ M_1 \circ M_0(\Delta) = 0$. Writting $D_\Delta(b_k \circ \pi_k \circ M_1 \circ M_0(X))$ as (1), we have :

$$
\begin{aligned}
(1) &= b_k \circ \pi_k \circ M_1 \circ M_0(X) \oplus b_k \circ \pi_k \circ M_1 \circ M_0(X \oplus \Delta) \\
&= b_k \circ \pi_k \circ M_1 \circ M_0(X) \oplus b_k(\pi_k \circ M_1 \circ M_0(X) \oplus \pi_k \circ M_1 \circ M_0(\Delta)) \\
&= b_k \circ \pi_k \circ M_1 \circ M_0(X) \oplus b_k(\pi_k \circ M_1 \circ M_0(X) \oplus 0) \\
&= b_k \circ \pi_k \circ M_1 \circ M_0(X) \oplus b_k \circ \pi_k \circ M_1 \circ M_0(X) = 0
\end{aligned}
$$

This means that $D_\Delta F(X)$ belongs to $\overline{K}_k$ or equivalently Δ belongs to E. We conclude that $B_k \subset E$.

- Let Δ be any element of E. According to the definition of E, we have in particular $D_\Delta(0) \in \overline{K}_k$. This means that

$$b_k(0) \oplus b_k \circ \pi_k \circ M_1 \circ M_0(\Delta) = 0 \ ,$$

or equivalently

$$b_k(0) = b_k \circ \pi_k \circ M_1 \circ M_0(\Delta) \ .$$

We deduce that $\pi_k \circ M_1 \circ M_0(\Delta) = 0$ because b_k is a bijection. According to the definitions, it means that $M_0(\Delta) \in \mathcal{B}_k$ or equivalently Δ belongs to $\mathcal{B}_k$. Therefore $E \subset \mathcal{B}_k$. We conclude that $E = \mathcal{B}_k$.

– Note that in fact $\mathcal{B}_k$ is the kernel of $\pi_k \circ M_1 \circ M_0$. Since rank$(\pi_k \circ M_1 \circ M_0)$ is less or equal to 4, and greater or equal to 1, we have simultaneously $60 \leq \dim(\mathcal{B}_k) \leq 63$ and the probability that Δ belongs to $\mathcal{B}_k$ when Δ is randomly chosen, is equal to $\frac{\dim(\mathcal{B}_k)}{2^{64}}$. The results follows.   □

Proof of Lemma 1: First recall that $\mathcal{B}_k = \langle e_j \mid \pi_k \circ M_1(e_j) = 0 \rangle$ and $\mathcal{E}_k = \langle e_j \mid \pi_k \circ M_1(e_j) \neq 0 \rangle$. Let j and k be two distinct integers, then the following conditions are equivalent.

– $\mathcal{E}_j \cap \mathcal{E}_k = \{0\}$.
– $\pi_k \circ M_1(e_i) = 0$ or $\pi_j \circ M_1(e_i) = 0$ for any integer $i \in [1, 64]$.
– $\pi_k \circ M_1(X) = 0$ or $\pi_j \circ M_1(X) = 0$ for any vector $X \in \mathbb{F}_2^{64}$.

We conclude that if $X \in \mathcal{E}_j$ and $\mathcal{E}_j \cap \mathcal{E}_k = \{0\}$ then $\pi_k \circ M_1(X) = 0$ or equivalently $X \in \mathcal{B}_k$.

Consider $X \neq 0$ belonging to $\bigcap_{j \neq k} \mathcal{B}_j$. We have that $\pi_j \circ M_1(X) = 0$ for any $j \neq k$. Note that M_1 is injective. Therefore $M_1(X) \neq 0$ and $\pi_k \circ M_1(X) \neq 0$. We conclude that all the bits of $M_1(X)$ that touch b_j $(j \neq k)$ are zeros. Therefore, for any non-zero component e_i of X, $M_1(e_i)$ touches b_k or equivalently $X \in \mathcal{E}_k$, and $\bigcap_{j \neq k} \mathcal{B}_j \subset \mathcal{E}_k$.

Let us use an argument by contraposition. Consider $e_i \notin \bigcap_{j \neq k} \mathcal{B}_j$. Then, there exists $j \neq k$, such that $e_i \notin \mathcal{B}_j$, i.e. $\pi_j \circ M_1(e_i) \neq 0$ or equivalently $e_i \in \mathcal{E}_j$. Therefore, according to the previous three equivalent conditions, $e_i \notin \mathcal{E}_k$. We deduce that for any $e_i \in \mathcal{E}_k$ we have $e_i \in \bigcap_{j \neq k} \mathcal{B}_j$. It means that $\mathcal{E}_k = \langle e_i \mid e_i \in \mathcal{E}_k \rangle \subset \bigcap_{j \neq k} \mathcal{B}_j$. We conclude $\mathcal{E}_k = \bigcap_{j \neq k} \mathcal{B}_j$.   □

Proof of Property 2: Let e_i be an element of $\mathcal{E}_k$ and j be an element of J_k. We have $\pi_k \circ M_1(e_i) \neq 0$ and $\mathcal{E}_j \cap \mathcal{E}_k = \{0\}$. It implies that $\pi_j \circ M_1(e_i) = 0$, and $e_i \in \mathcal{B}_j$. Therefore, $e_i \in \bigcap_{j \in J_k} \mathcal{B}_j$, and $\langle e_i \mid e_i \in \mathcal{E}_k \rangle \subset \widehat{\mathcal{E}}_k$.   □

Proof of Property 3: We will first prove that $(\mathcal{B}_i \cap \mathcal{B}_j) \oplus \langle \mathcal{E}_i \cup \mathcal{E}_j \rangle = \mathbb{F}_2^{64}$. Consider a canonical vector $e_k \notin \mathcal{B}_i \cap \mathcal{B}_j$. This is equivalent to $\pi_i \circ M_1(e_k) \neq 0$ or $\pi_j \circ M_1(e_k) \neq 0$. In other words $e_k \in \mathcal{E}_i$ or $e_k \in \mathcal{E}_j$, or equivalently $e_k \in \langle \mathcal{E}_i \cup \mathcal{E}_j \rangle$. This means that for any canonical vectors e_k of $\mathbb{F}_2^{64}$, we have either e_k belongs to $\mathcal{B}_i \cap \mathcal{B}_j$ or e_k belongs to $\langle \mathcal{E}_i \cup \mathcal{E}_j \rangle$.

Assume that there exists a canonical vector $e_k \in (\mathcal{B}_i \cap \mathcal{B}_j) \cap \langle \mathcal{E}_i \cup \mathcal{E}_j \rangle$. We have $\pi_i \circ M_1(e_k) = \pi_j \circ M_1(e_k) = 0$, and either $\pi_i \circ M_1(e_k) \neq 0$ or $\pi_j \circ M_1(e_k) \neq 0$. It leads to a contradiction. Hence $(\mathcal{B}_i \cap \mathcal{B}_j) \cap \langle \mathcal{E}_i \cup \mathcal{E}_j \rangle$ contains no canonical vectors.

Assume now that there exists an element $\Delta \in (\mathcal{B}_i \cap \mathcal{B}_j) \cap \langle \mathcal{E}_i \cup \mathcal{E}_j \rangle$ having a non-zero component e_k. The vector Δ belongs to $(\mathcal{B}_i \cap \mathcal{B}_j)$, hence e_k belongs to $(\mathcal{B}_i \cap \mathcal{B}_j)$. Moreover Δ belongs to $\langle \mathcal{E}_i \cup \mathcal{E}_j \rangle$, hence e_k belongs to $\langle \mathcal{E}_i \cup \mathcal{E}_j \rangle$. Therefore e_k belongs to $(\mathcal{B}_i \cap \mathcal{B}_j) \cap \langle \mathcal{E}_i \cup \mathcal{E}_j \rangle$ which is impossible. We conclude that $(\mathcal{B}_i \cap \mathcal{B}_j) \cap \langle \mathcal{E}_i \cup \mathcal{E}_j \rangle = \{0\}$. Therefore $(\mathcal{B}_i \cap \mathcal{B}_j) \oplus \langle \mathcal{E}_i \cup \mathcal{E}_j \rangle = \mathbb{F}_2^{64}$.

We deduce that

$$
\begin{aligned}
64 &= \dim(\langle \mathcal{E}_i \cup \mathcal{E}_j \rangle) + \dim(\mathcal{B}_i \cap \mathcal{B}_j) \\
&= \dim(\mathcal{E}_i + \mathcal{E}_j) + \dim(\mathcal{B}_i \cap \mathcal{B}_j) \\
&= \dim(\mathcal{E}_i) + \dim(\mathcal{E}_j) - \dim(\mathcal{E}_i \cap \mathcal{E}_j) + \dim(\mathcal{B}_i \cap \mathcal{B}_j)
\end{aligned}
$$

Moreover $\mathcal{E}_i \oplus \mathcal{B}_i = \mathbb{F}_2^{64} = \mathcal{E}_j \oplus \mathcal{B}_j$. Hence $64 = 64 - dim(\mathcal{B}_i) + 64 - \dim(\mathcal{B}_j) - \dim(\mathcal{E}_i \cap \mathcal{E}_j) + \dim(\mathcal{B}_i \cap \mathcal{B}_j)$. The result follows. $\qquad \square$

Appendix B: Figures

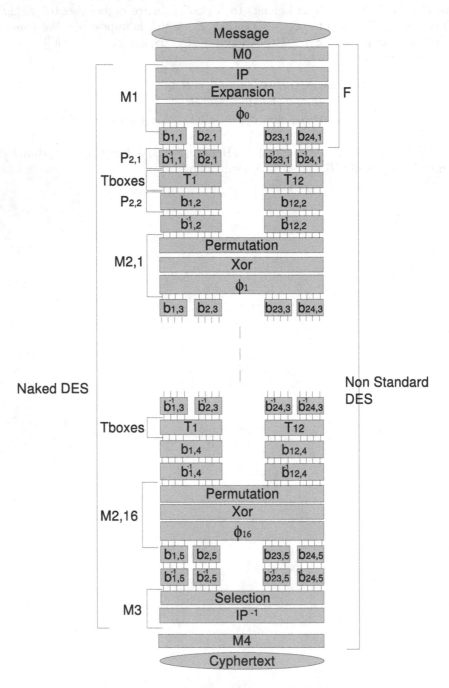

Fig. 7. "Naked-DES" and "Nonstandard-DES"

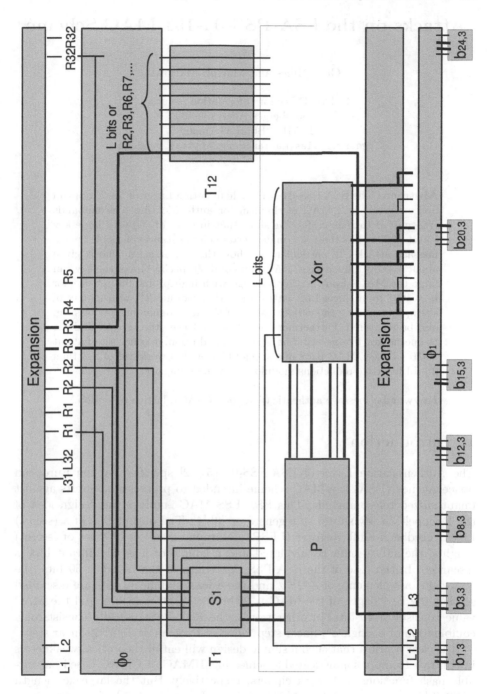

Fig. 8. General view of the attack

Attacks on the ESA-PSS-04-151 MAC Scheme

Georg Illies and Marian Margraf

Federal Office for Information Security
Godesberger Allee 185-189
D-53133 Bonn, Germany
{georg.illies,marian.margraf}@bsi.bund.de

Abstract. The ESA-PSS-04-151 Authentication Layer of the European Space Agency is a MAC mechanism for authenticating telecommands transmitted to spacecrafts. We show that in spite of the very large key length of 2940 bits there are (under certain circumstances) feasible known message attacks. In particular, we show that an attacker who is given about $n \approx$ 80-100 message/MAC pairs and 60 special bits of the key can forge the MAC of any further message with high probability ($> 5\%$ for $n = 100$) by a single LLL lattice reduction modulo 2^{48} of a matrix of size approximately $(n-60) \times n$. Most of the 2880 remaining key bits can also be recovered. Furthermore, we show that the attacker can find the 60 special key bits as well if he is given, in addition, another set of about 40-50 message/MAC pairs of a special kind with a workload of less than 2^{31} LLL lattice reductions modulo 2^{48} of the same size.

Keywords: message authentication code (MAC), lattice reduction.

1 Introduction

The Authentication Layer of ESA-PSS-04-151 [2] specified by the European Space Agency (ESA) is a MAC scheme intended to protect spacecrafts against unauthorized telecommands. This ESA-PSS MAC employs the design idea of the Rueppel-Massey subset sum generator [3],[4]: The output bits of a (secret) Linear Feedback Shift Register (LFSR) determine a subset of a set of (secret) weights, the subset sum is calculated and a couple of least significant bits is discarded. In the case of the ESA-PSS the length of the LFSR is 60 bits, the 60 weights are elements of $\mathbb{Z}/2^{48}\mathbb{Z}$ and the 8 least significant bits are discarded so that the key length of the MAC is $2940 = 60 + 60 \times 48$ bits and the MAC value consists of 40 bits. In other words, the ESA-PSS basically consists of a combination of a single $\mathbb{F}_2$-linear step followed by a single $\mathbb{Z}/2^{48}\mathbb{Z}$-linear step.

It is clear a priori that such a simple design will entail theoretical weaknesses in contrast to more sophisticated schemes like HMAC or CMAC based on suitable hash functions and block ciphers, respectively. But the large key length of 2940 bits for the ESA-PSS MAC might still ensure a level of security much more than acceptable in practice for the intended purpose: There will only be a very restricted amount of message/MAC pairs ("telecommands") given to the attacker and also the number of "on-line" tries an attacker is able to perform

C. Adams, A. Miri, and M. Wiener (Eds.): SAC 2007, LNCS 4876, pp. 296–310, 2007.

will be restricted; in particular, brute force on-line attacks are completely out of the question in spite of the relatively short MAC length of 40 bits. The attacks on the scheme described in [5] basically are *chosen message attacks*, probably a non-realistic attack scenario against spacecrafts. We are going to show that there are also feasible *known message attacks* in realistic attack scenarios abandoning to specify optimized versions of these attacks.

After describing the design of the ESA-PSS MAC in detail in Sect. 2 we first mention some preliminary observations on the scheme in Sect. 3 which explain its design idea to a certain extent. In Sect. 4 we assume that the 60 feedback coefficients of the LFSR are known to the attacker (but not the 2880 bits of the weights) and that he knows $n \approx 80\text{-}100$ message/MAC pairs. We show that by a LLL lattice reduction modulo 2^{48} of a matrix of size approximately $(n - 60) \times n$ the attacker can easily guess the MAC of any further message with high probability. Concretely, for $n = 100$ a single guess is successfull with probability $> 5\%$; further guesses with high success probability for the same message+counter can be calculated without further lattice reductions; the whole attack takes a few seconds on a PC. Also attack variants with much higher success probablility and recovering most of the bits of the weights are sketched.

In Sect. 5 we describe attack methods to find also the 60 feedback coefficients. The trivial method given in Sect. 5.1 is to use the attack of Sect. 4 as a distinguisher and apply LLL lattice reduction for each of the 2^{60} possible feedback "vectors". In fact, the matrix size for the distinguishing lattice reduction can be much smaller than in Sect. 4 ($n \approx 65$): A single one of the required lattice reductions (implemented with MAGMA) took only 0.3 seconds on a 2.2 GHz Dual Core Opteron. But even if the attack could be optimized to a certain extent the workload of 2^{60} of such lattice reductions still can hardly be regarded as feasible. In Sect. 5.2 we therefore assume that the attacker is, in addition, given a second set of about 40-50 different MACs of the same message but with different counter values which differ only in a few bit positions. Then with a workload of about 2^{30} LLL lattice reductions of even smaller size about half of the 60 bits can be determined. The remaining other half of the feedback coefficients can then be found by the method described in Sect. 5.1 but this time with only 2^{30} possible feedback vectors to check. Our (non-optimized) implementation of the attack would take about 2 months (overall) on a cluster of 100 such Opteron nodes. Knowing the feedback coefficients the attacker would then be able to effectively control the spacecraft by the method of Sect. 4. Basically the attack scenario could occur in practice as, for example, certain special telecommands could be repeated many times within a short period for test reasons.

In Sect. A.3 we explain an alternative method to find the 60 feedback coefficients, a collision attack already described in [5]. For this attack about 2^{30} message/MAC pairs are needed. Although the attack is even more efficient than that of Sect. 5.2 such a large number of messages was apparently not intended by the designers as the maximal allowed counter value for the ESA-PSS MAC is $z = 2^{30} - 1$.

Sect. 6 contains a result applicable in certain special chosen message attacks. In particular, it is shown that if the same message is sent 63 times with successive counter values $z, z + 1, z + 2, \ldots, z + 62$ an attacker monitoring the 63 message/MAC pairs can efficiently (no lattice reduction needed, just a small number of additions and subtractions) calculate the MAC of the same message with counter value $z + 63$ with a probability of about 85%. In contrast to the above known message attacks this chosen message attack appears to be a relatively harmless threat for a real spacecraft. But it in fact reveals the weakness of the scheme: The number of bits given to the attacker (2520) is much less than the key length!

It should be pointed out that our attacks do not apply to the Rueppel-Massey subset sum pseudo random generator; for partial results (no practical break) on that random generator see [1].

Notation: For simplicity we sometimes will not distinguish between an element of $\mathbb{Z}/2^{48}\mathbb{Z}$ the representing integer $x \in [0, 2^{48} - 1]$ and the bit string $(x_0, \ldots, x_{47})$ derived from its binary representation $x = \sum_{i=0}^{47} x_i 2^{47-i}$.

2 Description of the ESA-PSS Authentication Scheme

The ESA-PSS[1] Authentication Layer [2] is a MAC for the authentication of messages $m = (m_1, \ldots, m_N) \in \mathbb{F}_2^N$. In fact, a real "telecommand" m consists of bytes (octets), i.e., N is a multiple of 8.

The MAC key consists of a secret bit vector $c = (c_0, c_1, \ldots, c_{59}) \in \mathbb{F}_2^{60}$ (actually the feedback coefficients of a LFSR) and 60 "weights" $W_i \in \mathbb{Z}/2^{48}\mathbb{Z}$, $i = 0, 1, \ldots, 59$; i.e., the W_i are integers modulo 2^{48}. Thus the key length is $60 + 60 \times 48 = 2940$ bit.

The MAC of the message has a length of 40 bits. Its calculation involves four very simple steps:

Step 1. The message m is "formatted" into a $(N + 57)$-bit string $M = F_Z(m)$ by prepending a "1" bit and concatenating a certain value $Z \in \mathbb{F}_2^{56}$ specified below.

Step 2. A 60 bit value $p = L_{N,c}(M)$ is calculated with a $\mathbb{F}_2$-linear function $L_{N,c} : \mathbb{F}_2^{N+57} \to \mathbb{F}_2^{60}$ specified in A.1.

Step 3. A 48 bit value (the so-called pre-MAC) $s' = K_W(p)$ is calculated with a $\mathbb{Z}/2^{48}\mathbb{Z}$-linear form $K_W : (\mathbb{Z}/2^{48}\mathbb{Z})^{60} \to \mathbb{Z}/2^{48}\mathbb{Z}$ specified below (with the bits of p interpreted as elements of $\mathbb{Z}/2^{48}\mathbb{Z}$).

Step 4. The pre-MAC s' is truncated by deleting the 8 least significant bits which results in an integer $s = T(s')$, the MAC of m.

The MAC value is given by $\text{MAC}_{c,W,Z}(m) := s = T(K_W(L_{N,c}(F_Z(m))))$. This MAC depends on the key as the function $L_{N,c}$ (actually a 60-bit LFSR) depends on c and the function K_W (a "knapsack" function) depends on the weights W_i.

---

[1] The abbreviation PSS stands for "Procedures Standards and Specifications" (not for "Provably Secure Signature" as one might suspect).

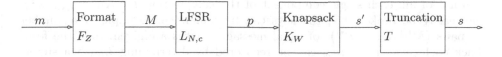

Fig. 1. MAC calculation

Here is the exact specification of the four steps:

Step 1 (Formatting): The value $Z \in \mathbb{F}_2^{56}$ is the concatenation $Z = t||z||o$, where $t \in \mathbb{F}_2^2$ is the "Logical Authentication Channel ID" (LAC ID) which can be regarded as fixed, $z = (z_0, \ldots, z_{29}) \in \mathbb{F}^{30}$ is the counter value with lsb z_{29} and $o = (0, \ldots, 0) \in \mathbb{F}_2^{24}$. (The counter z is incremented by one after the successful verification of a MAC and ensures that identical telecommands normally will not produce the same MAC unless the number of messages exceeds 2^{30}.) Thus

$$M = (M_0, \ldots, M_{N+56}) = F_Z(m) = 1||m||Z.$$

Remark 1. Actually there are three different types of messages ("Logical Authentication Channels", LACs) with respective LAC IDs $t = (t_0, t_1)$: "Principal LAC" (ID $t = (0,0)$), "Auxiliary LAC" (ID $t = (0,1)$) and "Recovery LAC" (ID $t = (1,0)$). There is a separate counter for each but apparently there is only one LFSR used for all three of them. So, for example, key bits c_i recovered from "Auxiliary" LAC telecommands can be used to attack the "Principal" LAC.

Step 2 (LFSR): The exact specification can be found in A.1; it is is needed only in A.2, A.3 and A.4.

Step 3 (Knapsack): The pre-MAC $s' \in \mathbb{Z}/2^{48}\mathbb{Z}$ is calculated via

$$s' = K_W(p) := \sum_{i=0}^{59} p_i \cdot W_i$$

with the 60 secret weights $W_0, \ldots, W_{59} \in \mathbb{Z}/2^{48}\mathbb{Z}$ and the values $p_1, \ldots, p_{59} \in \{0,1\}$ being interpreted as elements of $\mathbb{Z}/2^{48}\mathbb{Z}$.

Step 4 (Truncation): This step deletes the 8 least significant bits of the pre-MAC $s' = (s'_0, \ldots, s'_{47})$ resulting in the integer $s = T(s') = (s'_0, \ldots, s'_{39})$, i.e., $T(s') = s' \operatorname{div} 2^8$.

MAC verification: The sender transmits the string $m||t||z||s$. The receiver first checks the counter value z and then verifies the MAC value s with the knowledge of c and W, i.e., calculates $\text{MAC}_{c,W,Z}(m)$ and compares this value with s.

3   Some Preliminary Observations

In this section we are going to discuss some preliminary observations which might explain some of the design criteria of the ESA-PSS MAC.

First of all, each single component of the composition $T \circ K_W \circ L_{N,c} \circ F_Z$ can easily be broken, i.e., the keys can be found. For example, if a number of pairs $(M^{(i)}, L_{N,c}(M^{(i)}))$ of equal message lengths are given, then the feedback coefficients $c_0, \ldots, c_{59}$ can be recovered by determining $L_{N,c}$ via simple linear algebra over $\mathbb{F}_2$. Similarly, if pairs $(p^{(i)}, K_W(p^{(i)}))$ are given, the secret weights $W_0, \ldots, W_{59}$ can be recovered by solving a linear system of equations over $\mathbb{Z}/2^{48}\mathbb{Z}$.

Moreover, for the modified MAC function $T \circ K_W \circ L_{N,c}$ build by omitting the formatting step F_Z a simple chosen message attack is possible: With $H_{c,W} := K_W \circ L_{N,c}$ we have $H_{c,W}(M^1 := (1)) = W_0$ and after truncation the 40 most significant bits of W_0 are recovered. Then because of $H_{c,W}(M^{2,1} := (1,0)) = W_1 + c_0 W_0$ and $H_{c,W}(M^{2,2} := (1,0)) = W_1 + (c_0 \oplus 1)W_0$ modulo 2^{48} the bit c_0 can be determined and with this also most of the bits of W_1. Continuing in this manner $c_1, \ldots, c_{59}$ and most of the bits of the weights can be found. Prepending a "1" in the formatting step F_Z makes it impossible to forge MACs by prepending zeroes in front of a message. The 24 concatenated zeroes after the counter ensure that $F_Z(m)$ is at least 65 bits long (as the length N of a message m is at least 8) and so no bit of $L_{N,c}(F_Z(m))$ is independent of (m,t,z) or c.

Lastly, with respect to the truncation it should be remarked that for constant message length N the least significant bit of $s' = K_W(L_{N,c}(M))$ depends $\mathbb{F}_2$-linearly on the message bits, so can easily be predicted by linear algebra as soon as enough message/MAC pairs are known. More generally let $x_1, \ldots, x_n \in \{0,1\}$ and

$$f_k(x_1, \ldots, x_n) := k - \text{th least significant binary digit of } (x_1 + \cdots + x_n).$$

It is well known that

$$f_k(x_1, \ldots, x_n) = \sum_{i_1 < \cdots < i_{2^k}} x_{i_1} \cdot \ldots \cdot x_{i_{2^k}},$$

i.e., f_k is a homogeneous polynomial of degree 2^k. As a consequence the algebraic degree (in terms of the x_i) of the 6 least significant bits of the expression $\sum_{i=0}^{59} x_i W_i$ is not greater than 32. Truncating the 8 least significant bits ensures that all remaining bits have an algebraic degree of about 60 in $x_0, \ldots, x_{59}$. Similar considerations are contained in [4] where bits of expressions $\sum x_i W_i$ with outputs $x_0, x_1 \ldots$ of an LFSR are used as pseudo random generator. Apparently the design idea for the ESA-PSS scheme was taken from this Rueppel-Massey generator (see also [3]).

4   The Case of Known Feedback Coefficients c: A Known Message Attack Via Lattice Reduction

In this section we assume that the attacker knows the feedback coefficients $c = (c_0, \ldots, c_{59})$ but not the weights W_i and describe a known message attack. The attacker is given n (different) formatted message/MAC pairs

$$(M^{(0)}, s^{(0)}), \ldots, (M^{(n-1)}, s^{(n-1)})$$

(here $M^{(i)} = 1||m^{(i)}||t||z^{(i)}||o$ are the formatted messages). Now let $m^{(n)}$ be another (arbitrary) telecommand and $M^{(n)} := 1||m^{(n)}||t||z^{(n)}||o$ the corresponding formatted message. The attacker's goal is to find the corresponding MAC value $s^{(n)}$ of $M^{(n)}$.

As the coefficients of the LFSR are known to the attacker he has n valid pairs $(p^{(i)}, s^{(i)})$, $i = 0, 1, \ldots, n-1$ and, furthermore, $p^{(n)}$ with $p^{(i)} = L_{N,c}(M^{(i)}) \in \mathbb{F}_2^{60}$, $i = 0, 1, \ldots, n$. One has

$$s'^{(i)} := K_W(p^{(i)}), \quad s^{(i)} = T(s'^{(i)})$$

where the values $s'^{(0)}, \ldots, s'^{(n)}$ are unknown and $s^{(n)}$ has to be determined. In practice $n \approx 80\text{-}100$ suffices for the attack described now.

4.1   The Attack

The idea of the attack is very simple: Given $l = (l_0, \ldots, l_n) \in \mathbb{Z}^{n+1}$ such that modulo 2^{48} (in particular the $p_k^{(i)} \in \{0, 1\}$ are interpreted as values in $\mathbb{Z}/2^{48}\mathbb{Z}$)

$$\sum_{i=0}^{n} l_i p^{(i)} = 0. \tag{1}$$

Then by the linearity of the "knapsack" map K_W one has (modulo 2^{48})

$$\sum_{i=0}^{n} l_i s'^{(i)} = 0. \tag{2}$$

Now because of $s'^{(i)} = 2^8(s^{(i)} + \varepsilon^{(i)})$ with some $0 \le \varepsilon^{(i)} < 1$ equation (2) yields

$$\sum_{i=0}^{n} l_i s^{(i)} = -\underbrace{\sum_{i=0}^{n} l_i \varepsilon^{(i)}}_{=:\Delta \in \mathbb{Z}} \tag{3}$$

modulo 2^{40}. If l_n is odd, i.e., invertible modulo 2^{40} we arrive at

$$s^{(n)} = -l_n^{-1}\left(\sum_{i=0}^{n-1} l_i s^{(i)} + \Delta\right) \tag{4}$$

modulo 2^{40}. Now if *all* the l_i are small then also Δ will be small as in practice positive and negative summands of Δ will almost cancel and thus there will be a chance to guess Δ.

Such a "short" vector l satisfying (1) can be found by employing *LLL lattice reduction*, we will describe two different methods (Method 1 and Method 2) in Sect. 4.2. Explicitly the attack then runs as follows:

(1) Find a short vector l with l_n odd and satisfying (1).
(2) Choose a small integer $\tilde{\Delta}$ and calculate

$$\tilde{s}^{(n)} := -l_n^{-1} \left(\sum_{i=0}^{n-1} l_i s^{(i)} + \tilde{\Delta} \right) \quad (\mathrm{mod} \ 2^{40}).$$

(3) If $\tilde{s}^{(n)} \neq s^{(n)}$ go back to (2) and try another $\tilde{\Delta}$.

From some reasonable statistical assumptions and because of the Central Limit Theorem one would expect that the distribution of the actual values Δ is close to a normal distribution with average value 0. So one would first try such $\tilde{\Delta}$ with small absolute value and then increase the absolute value ($\tilde{\Delta} = 0, 1, -1, 2, \ldots$). Of course in practice the attacker can recognize a success of the MAC verification in step (3) (performed by the spacecraft) only indirectly by observing the reactions of the spacecraft. It appears to be realistic that the attacker can try different values of $\tilde{\Delta}$ for the same formatted message $M^{(n)} = 1||m^{(n)}||t||z^{(n)}||o$ without waiting for a reaction. Only if the counter value z was increased in the meantime (by a message of an authentic sender) the attacker needs to perform a new LLL lattice reduction.

Experimental Result: We implemented both Method 1 and Method 2 of Sect. 4.2 with MAGMA (using the `Nullspace` and LLL commands) and with $n = 100$ pairs $(p^{(i)}, s^{(i)})$; in each case the experiment was repeated 20000 times.

Method 1: Each lattice reduction took about 3 seconds on a 2.2GHz Dual-Core Opteron. The empirical mean value was $\overline{\Delta} = 0.01$ and the empirical standard deviation of Δ was $\overline{\sigma} = 6.99$. The probability that $\tilde{s}^{(n)} = s^{(n)}$ for $\tilde{\Delta} = 0$ was about 5.9% and trying all the 9 integer values in $[-4, 4]$ led to success in about 48.5% of the cases.

Method 2: The results of course depend on the constant C. With $C \approx 2^{12}$ both speed and accuracy where fine; we chose $C = 4095$. Each lattice reduction took about 0.25 seconds on a 2.2GHz Dual-Core Opteron. The empirical mean value was $\overline{\Delta} = 0.04$ and the empirical standard deviation of Δ was $\overline{\sigma} = 6.95$. The probability that $\tilde{s}^{(n)} = s^{(n)}$ for $\tilde{\Delta} = 0$ was about 5.7% and trying all the 9 integer values in $[-4, 4]$ led to success in about 49% of the cases.

Remark 2. (*i*) Observe that for $n = 100$ the number of MAC bits given to the attacker ($100 \times 40 = 4.000$) is not too much greater than the number of key bits not known to the attacker ($60 \times 48 = 2.880$). (Even for $n = 75\text{-}90$ the observed actual values of Δ turned out to be reasonably small.)

   (*ii*) By taking $p^{(n)} := (0, \ldots, 0, 1, 0, \ldots, 0)$ and applying the above attack one can also recover most of the 40 most significant bits of the weights W_i.

Remark 3. By taking into account more than just one short vector l the success probability can be increased significantly. For example, we implemented the following attack variant for $n = 100$: (1) For each of the first 30 rows of the LLL-reduced matrix check whether l_n is odd; if this is the case calculate the set of candidate $\tilde{s}^{(n)}$ with $\tilde{\Delta} \in \{-20, \ldots, 20\}$. (2) Determine the intersection of all these (not more than 30) sets of candidates. (3) If the intersection is nonemtpty choose one element at random.

In our experiments the success probability was about 20% for a single guess and about 75% for nine guesses (compared to 6% and 50%, resp., for the method described above). There is probably still much space for optimization.

4.2   LLL Lattice Reduction Methods for Attack Step (1)

Method 1: Let $l^{(0)}, \ldots, l^{(d-1)} \in \mathbb{Z}^{n+1}$ be a basis of the solution lattice of the following system of linear equations over $\mathbb{Z}$:

$$\sum_{i=0}^{n} x_i p^{(i)} = (0, \ldots, 0), \quad x_0, x_1, \ldots, x_n \in \mathbb{Z}.$$

Obviously, d (the dimension of the solution lattice) depends on the $p^{(i)}$ but $d \geq (n+1) - 60$ and typically $d \approx n - 59$. Apply LLL lattice reduction to the $\mathbb{Z}$-lattice spanned by the rows of the matrix

$$L = \begin{pmatrix} l_0^{(0)} & l_1^{(0)} & \cdots & l_n^{(0)} \\ \vdots & \vdots & \ddots & \vdots \\ l_0^{(d-1)} & l_1^{(d-1)} & \cdots & l_n^{(d-1)} \\ 2^{48} & 0 & \cdots & 0 \\ 0 & 2^{48} & \cdots & 0 \\ \vdots & \vdots & \ddots & \vdots \\ 0 & 0 & \cdots & 2^{48} \end{pmatrix}$$

to obtain short vectors of the form $(\alpha_0, \alpha_1, \ldots, \alpha_n) \in \mathbb{Z}^{n+1}$; pick out one with odd α_n and set $l_i = \alpha_i$, for $i = 0, \ldots, n$.

Method 2: Regard the $\mathbb{Z}$-lattice spanned by the rows of the matrix

$$L' = \begin{pmatrix} C \cdot p_0^{(0)} & \cdots & C \cdot p_{59}^{(0)} & 1 \, 0 \cdots 0 \\ C \cdot p_0^{(1)} & \cdots & C \cdot p_{59}^{(1)} & 0 \, 1 \cdots 0 \\ \vdots & \ddots & \vdots & \vdots \, \vdots \, \ddots \, \vdots \\ C \cdot p_0^{(n)} & \cdots & C \cdot p_{59}^{(n)} & 0 \, 0 \cdots 1 \end{pmatrix}$$

with a big constant C. Applying LLL lattice reduction results in short vectors typically of the form

$$(\underbrace{0, \ldots, 0}_{60-\text{times}}, \alpha_0, \alpha_1, \ldots, \alpha_n);$$

Pick out one with odd α_n and set $l_i = \alpha_i$, for $i = 0, \ldots, n$.

5   Known Message Attacks for Completely Unknown Key

In this section we assume that the attacker also does not know the feedback coefficient vector $c = (c_0, \ldots, c_{59})$ and we describe methods to determine c. A feasible attack is given for the case of special messages. As was seen in the previous section the knowledge of c enables an attacker to efficiently forge MACs for any message (with satisfying success probability) once about 80-100 message/MAC pairs are known. In Sect. A.3 a collision attack using an idea from [5] is described which is even more efficient but needs the unrealistic amount of about 2^{30} known message/MAC pairs.

5.1   Arbitrary Messages

Given $n + 1 \approx 80\text{-}100$ formatted message/MAC pairs $(M^{(i)}, s^{(i)})$ and a candidate c the methods described in the previous section can of course be used to check whether c is the actual feedback coefficient vector. Concretely, the attacker would calculate the values $p^{(i)} = L_{N,c}(M^{(i)})$ for each c and perform one of the lattice reduction methods of Sect. 4.2 to find two or three short vectors $(l_0, \ldots, l_n)$ satisfying (1), not necessarily with odd l_n. For each of these two or three vectors the actual value for Δ according to (3) is calculated. If c was the right guess then the values for Δ are all small; otherwise at least one of them should be large as Δ behaves like a random 40-bit value if c is a wrong guess and if the messages are "reasonably different". The reason why one has to regard more than one short vector and calculate the respective Δ is that there are 2^{60} (significantly greater than 2^{40}) candidate c. Thus with Method 1 the workload is 2^{60} LLL-lattice reductions modulo 2^{48} of a matrix of (approximate) size $(n - 59) \times (n + 1)$.

Remark 4. The lattice reduction step can be made considerably faster: Experiments indicate that $n' \approx 65$ message/MAC pairs suffice to find the correct c with Method 1 (an estimated 2^{35} of the candidate c pass the test with a single short l derived with LLL reduction). That means 6×66 lattices modulo 2^{48} instead of 40×100-lattices taking about 0.3 seconds on a 2.2GHz Dual-Core Opteron. (Method 2 with $C \approx 2^{20}$ was about as accurate and took only 0.25 seconds.) Also the experiments indicate that often a full LLL reduction will not be necessary. However, the attack still can hardly be regarded as feasible. The next subsection gives a feasible method to find c if the attacker is given, in addition, some message/MAC pairs of a special form.

5.2   A Feasible Attack for Messages of a Special Kind

We consider formatted messages $M^{(i)}$, $i = 0, 1, \ldots, n - 1$, all of equal length $N + 57$ and equal LAC ID (t_0, t_1) such that the messages differ only in the r least significant bits of the counter. In other words, there is

$$M_{\text{const}} = (1, m_0, \ldots, m_N, t_0, t_1, z_0, \ldots, z_{29}, \underbrace{0, \ldots, 0}_{24-\text{times}})$$

and with certain $\tilde{z}^{(i)}$ of the form

$$\tilde{z}^{(i)} = (\ \underbrace{0,\ldots\ldots\ldots,0}_{(N+33-r)-\text{times}}\ ,z_{29-r+1}^{(i)},\ldots,z_{29}^{(i)},\underbrace{0,\ldots,0}_{24-\text{times}}\ )$$

we have $M^{(i)} = M_{\text{const}} \oplus \tilde{z}^{(i)}$ for every $i = 0,\ldots,n-1$. The attacker is given the n message/MAC pairs $(M^{(i)}, s^{(i)})$. To perform the attack described below n should be significantly greater than $25 + r$ which, in particular, implies $r \geq 6$.

Remark 5. For "Auxiliary" telecommands $(t = (0,1))$ such a situation could really occur in practice, e.g., if for test reasons a certain command is repeated many times with different counter values.

If we define

$$p_{\text{const}} := L_{N,c}(M_{\text{const}}), \quad p_{\text{trunc}}^{(i)} := L_{N,c}(\tilde{z}^{(i)})$$

then for $p^{(i)} := L_{N,c}(M^{(i)})$ we have

$$p^{(i)} = p_{\text{const}} \oplus p_{\text{trunc}}^{(i)}.$$

Proposition 1. a) *For all $j > 23 + r$ one has $p_{\text{trunc},j}^{(i)} = 0$. The $p_{\text{trunc}}^{(i)}$ depend on $c_0,\ldots,c_{22+r}$ but not on $c_{23+r},\ldots,c_{59}$.*
b) *If*

$$\overline{p}_{\text{trunc}}^{(i)} := (p_{\text{trunc},0}^{(i)},\ldots,p_{\text{trunc},23+r}^{(i)}, 1) \in \mathbb{Z}^{25+r}$$

and $\bar{l} = (\bar{l}_0,\ldots,\bar{l}_{n-1}) \in \mathbb{Z}^n$ is such that modulo 2^{48}

$$\sum_{i=0}^{n-1} \bar{l}_i \overline{p}_{\text{trunc}}^{(i)} = 0. \tag{5}$$

then the pre-Mac values $s'^{(i)} = K_W(p^{(i)})$ modulo 2^{48} satisfy

$$\sum_{i=0}^{n-1} \bar{l}_i s'^{(i)} = 0 \tag{6}$$

c) *If the $\bar{l}$ in b) is short, i.e., its entries are small then $\sum_{i=0}^{n-1} \bar{l}_i s^{(i)}$ is small modulo 2^{40}.*

Proof. See A.2.

The attack runs as follows: For a guessed tuple $(c_0,\ldots,c_{22+r})$ of feedback coefficients the attacker searches for several short vectors $\bar{l} = (\bar{l}_0,\ldots,\bar{l}_{n-1}) \in \mathbb{Z}^n$ satisfying (5). One of the two methods of Sect. 4.2 can be applied if n is significantly larger than $25 + r$ (the length of $\overline{p}_{\text{trunc}}^{(i)}$), e.g., $n \approx 40\text{-}50$ for $r = 7$. If the guessed tuple was the right one then

$$\sum_{i=0}^{n-1} \bar{l}_i s^{(i)} \approx 0 \tag{7}$$

modulo 2^{40} is satisfied according to Prop. 1, otherwise the approximation will be violated for some of the $\bar{l}$. (It is necessary to test more than one of the $\bar{l}$ as for some wrong guesses with small Hamming distance to the correct one also the Hamming distance of the resulting $p^{(i)}$ are small.) So the workload is 2^{23+r} LLL lattice reductions modulo 2^{48} of a matrix of a size of about $(n - 25 - r) \times n$. After that only about 2^{37-r} candidate vectors $(c_0, \ldots, c_{59})$ remain as the first $23 + r$ bits have just been determined. With another set of about $n_g = 80\text{-}100$ message/MAC pairs of general kind (reasonably different and independent of the set of n pairs of the special kind) the attack of Sect. 5.1 can be performed with only about 2^{37-r} LLL lattice reductions to find the remaining bits $c_{23+r}, \ldots, c_{59}$. For $r = 7$ the overall workload is about 2^{30} modulo 2^{48} lattice reductions of size $(n - 25 - r) \times n$ plus 2^{30} modulo 2^{48} lattice reductions of size $(n_g - 60) \times n_g$. Once again, both groups of lattice reductions can be made faster by the observations described in Remark 4, in particular $n_g \approx 65$ suffices. Experiments with $n = 45$ indicate that if the $n = 45$ counter values where randomly picked out of 2^7 successing counter values then in the typical case the bits $c_0, \ldots, c_{29}$ can in fact be determined as described with workload of 2^{30} times about 0.2 seconds on a 2.2. GHz Dual-Core Opteron for the LLL reductions. (In some cases when the 45 counter values follow certain patterns also some wrong guesses can pass the test, increasing the workload for the remaining bits; here effects described in Sect. 6 come into play.) Then with $n_g \approx 65$ the overall workload would sum up to about 2 months on a 100 node cluster of 2.2Ghz Dual-Core Opterons. There is probably still much space for improvement.

Remark 6. If the formatted messages $M^{(i)}$ do not only differ in the counter values but there are only, e.g., 2 or 3 different occurring pairs (m, t) then the above attack can easily be adapted in the obvious way by adding a further bit or two, respectively, to the vectors $\overline{p}^{(i)}_{\text{trunc}}$.

6   A Chosen Message Attack

In this section we describe a special but very efficient chosen message attack not requiring any lattice reductions. We consider $n = 2^r$ (different) formatted messages $M^{(\mu)}$, $\mu = (\mu_1, \ldots, \mu_r) \in \mathbb{Z}_2^r$, all of equal length $N + 57$ differing only at r fixed bit positions (counter bits in practice). In other words, there are pairwise distinct bit positions $j_1, \ldots, j_r \in \{1, \ldots, N + 30\}$ and $M_{\text{const}} \in \mathbb{Z}^{N+57}$ such that

$$M^{(\mu)} := M_{\text{const}} \oplus \sum_{i=1}^{r} \mu_i e_{j_i}$$

with $e_j \in \mathbb{Z}_2^{N+57}$ having only one non-vanishing component, namely, at bit position j. We have the following observation:

Proposition 2. *In the situation above let $\Lambda \in \text{Mat}(\mathbb{Z}_2, 60 \times r)$ be the matrix such that*

$$L_{N,c} \left(\sum_{i=1}^{r} \mu_i e_{j_i} \right) = \Lambda \mu$$

and let $\lambda_0, \lambda_1, \ldots, \lambda_{59} \in \mathbb{Z}_2^r$ be the rows of Λ. Then for the values $s'^{(\mu)} :=$ $K_W(L_{N,c}(M^{(\mu)}))$ the following equation is valid modulo 2^{48} for all $\nu \in \mathbb{Z}_2^r \backslash \{0\}$ such that $\nu \oplus \lambda_i \neq 0$ for all rows λ_i:

$$\sum_{\mu \in \mathbb{Z}_2^r} (-1)^{\langle \mu, \nu \rangle} s'^{(\mu)} = 0. \tag{8}$$

Hence, the MAC values $s^{(\mu)} := T(s'^{(\mu)})$ satisfy the (modulo 2^{40}) inequality

$$\left| \sum_{\mu \in \mathbb{Z}_2^r} (-1)^{\langle \mu, \nu \rangle} s^{(\mu)} \right| < 2^r. \tag{9}$$

Proof. See A.4.

Remark 7. Actually (9) is a very coarse estimate: If the $\varepsilon^{(i)}$ (comp. the derivation of (3)) were independent and equally distributed on $[0, 1]$ then the standard deviation of the alternating sum on the left hand side of (9) (whose average will be 0) would be about $2^{\frac{r}{2}}/3$. In practice it is even significantly lower.

If an attacker is in the described situation the approximation (9) can deliver much information about the unknown feedback coefficients: A ν will usually satisfy (9) if and only if it does not occur as a row of the matrix Λ. This could improve the efficiency of the attack in Sect. 5.2 but we will not describe the details. Instead we give a very simple and efficient example chosen message attack exploiting the above proposition.

Example 1 (r = 6). An attacker observed that for 63 successive times the same pair m, t was transmitted (perhaps an "Auxiliary" command) and only the counter bits $z_{24}, \ldots, z_{29}$ were different, actually assuming all 63 binary strings from 000000 to 111110. The attacker can then derive the MAC value $s^{(111111)}$ from the previous 63 MAC values by the following method: Because of (9) for every $\nu \in \mathbb{Z}_2^6 \backslash \{0\}$ he calculates the candidate value

$$s_{(\nu)}^{(111111)} := -(-1)^{\langle (1,1,1,1,1,1), \nu \rangle} \sum_{\mu \neq (111111)} (-1)^{\langle \mu, \nu \rangle} s^{(\mu)}.$$

modulo 2^{40}. Of these 63 values there will be at least about 20 which are almost equal, the others will be random integers in $[0, 2^{40}[$. (This can easily be seen: The probability that a certain ν does not occur among 60 independent random row vectors λ_i is $(63/64)^{60}$, so the expectation value of the number of non-occurring ν is $63 \times (63/64)^{60} \approx 24.5$.) Now the arithmetic mean of these more than 20 almost equal values will with high probability be equal to the MAC value $s^{(111111)}$ the attacker is searching for. In our experiments this attack lead to the correct MAC value in about 85% of the cases.

Remark 8. Observe that in the above example the information given to the attacker ($2520 = 63 \times 40$ bit) is much less than the information of the key (2940 bit)!

7 Conclusion

We described several attacks on the ESA-PSS-04-151 Authentication Layer. It was shown that also from a practical point of view the scheme can be broken under certain circumstances. The scheme thus is not sufficiently secure for the intended use. A practical implication of this paper is that for implementations already or still in use transmitting the same message several times with different counter values should be avoided (compare Sect. 5.2 for details).

Acknowledgment. We thank Andreas Wiemers for interesting remarks.

References

1. von zur Gathen, J., Shparlinski, I.E.: Predicting Subset Sum Pseudorandom Generators. In: Handschuh, H., Hasan, M.A. (eds.) SAC 2004. LNCS, vol. 3357, pp. 241–251. Springer, Heidelberg (2004)
2. Telecommand Decoder Specification, ESA PSS-04-151, Issue 1. ESA, Paris (September 1993)
3. Rueppel, R.A., Massey, J.L.: Knapsack as a nonlinear function. In: IEEE Intern. Symp. of Inform. Theory, p. 46. IEEE Press, Los Alamitos (1985)
4. Rueppel, R.A.: Analysis and design of stream ciphers. Springer, New York (1986)
5. Spinsante, S., Chiaraluce, F., Gambi, E.: Numerical verification of the historicity of the ESA telecommand authentication approach, talk given at Spaceops 2006, Rome (2006), on-line: http://www.aiaa.org/spaceops2006/presentations/55955.ppt

A   Appendix

A.1   The LFSR

In this section the exact specification of Step 2 in Sect. 2 is given. The 60-bit LFSR in Fig. 2 is initialized with all bits 0. Then the bits $M_0, M_1, \ldots, M_{N+56}$ of M are fed in one by one.

More formally (recall length$(M) = N + 57$) let $p(0), p(1), \ldots, p(N+57) \in \mathbb{F}_2^{60}$ recursively be defined by $p(0) = (0, \ldots, 0)$ and

$$p_0(k+1) := M_k \oplus \bigoplus_{i=0}^{59} c_i p_i(k)$$

$$p_{i+1}(k+1) := p_i(k), \quad i = 1, \ldots, 58$$

for $k = 0, \ldots, N + 56$. Then

$$p = L_{N,c}(M) := p(N+57)$$

and the map $L_{N,c}$ obviously is $\mathbb{F}_2$-linear in M (but not in the secret vector c).

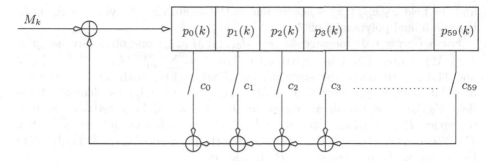

Fig. 2. The 60−bit LFSR

A.2   Proof of Proposition 1

a) Clear from the description in A.1.

b)

$$\sum_{i=0}^{n-1} \bar{l}_i s'^{(i)} = \sum_{i=0}^{n-1} \bar{l}_i \left(\sum_{j=0}^{59} p_j^{(i)} W_j \right)$$

$$= \sum_{j=0}^{23+r} \left(\sum_{i=0}^{n-1} \bar{l}_i (p_{\mathrm{trunc},j}^{(i)} \oplus p_{\mathrm{const},j}) \right) W_j + \sum_{j=24+r}^{59} \left(\sum_{i=0}^{n-1} \bar{l}_i \right) p_{\mathrm{const},j} W_j$$

$$= 0$$

modulo 2^{48} because of

$$\sum_{i=0}^{n-1} \bar{l}_i (p_{\mathrm{trunc},j}^{(i)} \oplus p_{\mathrm{const},j}) = \begin{cases} \displaystyle\sum_{i=0}^{n-1} \bar{l}_i \bar{p}_{\mathrm{trunc},j}^{(i)} & \text{for } \bar{p}_{\mathrm{const},j}^{(i)} = 0 \\ \displaystyle\sum_{i=0}^{n-1} \bar{l}_i (1 - \bar{p}_{\mathrm{trunc},j}^{(i)}) & \text{for } \bar{p}_{\mathrm{const},j}^{(i)} = 1 \end{cases}$$

and because of (5) which also implies $\sum_{i=0}^{n-1} \bar{l}_i = 0$ (observe that the last component of $\bar{p}_{\mathrm{trunc}}^{(i)}$ is 1).

c) This approximation follows from (6) in the same way as (3) follows from (2).   □

A.3   A Collision Attack for Finding c

The vector c can be found even more efficiently than by the attack of Sect. 5.2 using a collision method which can already be found in [5]. We will briefly describe the attack here restricting ourselves to the case of an irreducible feedback polynomial $P_c(x) := x^{60} + c_0 x^{59} + \ldots + c_{59} \in \mathbb{F}_2[x]$. (Allthough not specified in [2] this will probably be the case in actual implementations.) Let $A_c : \mathbb{F}_2^{60} \to \mathbb{F}_2^{60}$ be the step function of the LFSR, i.e., if $a \in \mathbb{F}_2^{60}$ is a state then $A_c(a)$ is the state after one clocking (without exterior bits being fed in). A_c is an $\mathbb{F}_2$-endomorphism and the field $\mathbb{F}_2[x]/P_c(x)$ is isomorphic to the algebra $\mathbb{F}_2[A_c]$ via $x \mapsto A_c$ as P_c is the minimal polynomial of A_c.

For a (formatted) message $M = (M_0, \ldots, M_{N+56})$ one obviously has $p = L_{N,c}(M) = Q_M(A_c)((1,0,\ldots,0))$ with $Q_M(x) := \sum_{i=0}^{N+56} M_i x^{N+56-i} \in \mathbb{F}_2[x]$ and $(1,0,\ldots,0)$ being the state of the LFSR register with all bits zero except bit position p_0. Now if $p = (0,\ldots,0)$ then $Q_M(A_c)$ as element of the field $\mathbb{F}_2[A_c]$ must vanish as otherwise $Q_M(A_c)$ would be invertible. So $p = 0$ implies $P_c(x)|Q_M(x)$. Thus if $M^{(1)}, M^{(2)}$ are such that $p^{(1)} = p^{(2)}$ then $P_c(x)|(Q_{M^{(1)}}(x)+Q_{M^{(2)}}(x))$. So by factoring the polynomial $Q_{M^{(1)}}(x)+Q_{M^{(2)}}(x)$ just a few candidates remain for P_c, i.e., for c.

Now if the attacker is given about $\sqrt{2} \cdot 2^{30}$ message/MAC pairs (M,s) there will on average be one pair of these pairs with equal $p \in \{0,1\}^{60}$ (birthday paradox). Then by the method above some candidate c are given which can be tested as described in Sect. 5.1.

Unfortunately for the attacker there will on average be 2^{20} pairs of the messages $(M^{(1)}, M^{(2)})$ with the same MAC value s and as he does not "see" the p-value it is not clear which of these pairs is "the one" with equal p. So he must factorize $Q_{M^{(1)}}(x) + Q_{M^{(2)}}(x)$ for all of these 2^{20} pairs and then perform the LLL reduction method of Sect. 5.1. This method is still faster than the one described in Sect. 5.2 (about 2^{20} instead of about 2^{31} lattice reductions). However, in practice it is hardly imaginable that such a huge number of telecommands is transmitted during the lifetime of a spacecraft; this is reflected by the design of the ESA-PSS as there are only 2^{30} different possible counter values anyway.

A.4   Proof of Proposition 2

Let

$$p^{(\mu)} := L_{N,c}(M^{(\mu)}) = p_{\text{const}} \oplus \Lambda\mu$$

with $p_{\text{const}} := L_{N,c}(M_{\text{const}})$. Then

$$p_i^{(\mu)} = \frac{1}{2}\left(1 - (-1)^{\langle \mu, \lambda_i\rangle \oplus p_{\text{const},i}}\right). \tag{10}$$

With $s'^{(\mu)} = \sum_{i=0}^{59} p_i^{(\mu)} W_i$ we obtain

$$\sum_{\mu \in \mathbb{Z}_2^r} (-1)^{\langle \mu, \nu\rangle} s'^{(\mu)} = \sum_{i=0}^{59}\left(\sum_{\mu \in \mathbb{Z}_2^r} (-1)^{\langle \mu, \nu\rangle} p_i^{(\mu)}\right) W_i$$

modulo 2^{48}. Because of (10) and applying $\sum_{\mu \in \mathbb{Z}_2^r}(-1)^{\langle \mu, \nu\rangle} = 0$ for all $\nu \neq 0$ as well as $(-1)^{p_{\text{const},i}} \sum_{\mu \in \mathbb{Z}_2^r}(-1)^{\langle \mu, \lambda_i \oplus \nu\rangle} = 0$ (remember $\nu \oplus \lambda_i \neq 0$) equation (8) is an immediate consequence (treat the inner sum as an expression in rational numbers) from which also (9) follows at once. $\square$

The Security of the Extended Codebook (XCB) Mode of Operation

David A. McGrew and Scott R. Fluhrer

Cisco Systems, Inc.
170 West Tasman Drive, San Jose, CA 95134
{mcgrew,sfluhrer}@cisco.com

Abstract. The XCB mode of operation was outlined in 2004 as a contribution to the IEEE Security in Storage effort, but no security analysis was provided. In this paper, we provide a proof of security for XCB, and show that it is a secure tweakable (super) pseudorandom permutation. Our analysis makes several new contributions: it uses an algebraic property of XCB's internal universal hash function to simplify the proof, and it defines a *nonce mode* in which XCB can be securely used even when the plaintext is shorter than twice the width of the underlying block cipher. We also show minor modifications that improve the performance of XCB and make it easier to analyze. XCB is interesting because it is highly efficient in both hardware and software, it has no alignment restrictions on input lengths, it can be used in nonce mode, and it uses the internal functions of the Galois/Counter Mode (GCM) of operation, which facilitates design re-use and admits multi-purpose implementations.

1   Introduction

There are several scenarios in which *length-preserving, deterministic encryption* is useful. An encryption method is length-preserving if the ciphertext has exactly the same number of bits as does the plaintext. Such a method must be deterministic, since it is impossible to accommodate random data (such as an initialization vector) within the ciphertext. In some cases, deterministic length-preserving encryption exactly matches the requirements. For example, in some encrypted database applications, determinism is essential in order to ensure a direct correspondence between plaintext values being looked up and previously stored ciphertext values.

In some other cases, there is a length-preservation requirement that makes it impossible to provide all of the security services that are desired. Length-preserving algorithms cannot provide message authentication, since there is no room for a message authentication code, and they cannot meet some strong definitions of confidentiality [1]. Essentially, these algorithms implement a codebook; repeated encryptions of the same plaintext value with the same key result it identical ciphertext values. An adversary gains knowledge about the plaintext by seeing which ciphertext values match, and which do not match. Despite these

C. Adams, A. Miri, and M. Wiener (Eds.): SAC 2007, LNCS 4876, pp. 311–327, 2007.

limitations, in many scenarios it may be desirable to use length-preserving encryption because other methods are unworkable. Length-preservation may allow encryption to be introduced into data processing systems that have already been implemented and deployed. Many network protocols have fixed-width fields, and many network systems have hard limits on the amount of data expansion that is possible. One important example is that of disk-block encryption, which is currently being addressed in the IEEE Security in Storage Working Group [2].

Our goal is to provide the best security possible, given the length-preservation limitation. We require our cipher to be a *pseudorandom permutation*; it is indistinguishable from a uniformly chosen random permutation on the set of messages to a computationally bounded adversary. Because we want our cipher to handle plaintexts whose size may vary, we require the cipher to be a pseudorandom *arbitrary length* permutation: for each of the possible plaintext lengths, the cipher acts as a pseudorandom permutation. To provide as much flexibility as possible, we allow the plaintext lengths to vary even for a single fixed key.

In some cases, some additional data can be associated with the plaintext. By using this data as an input, we can provide better security, by letting each distinct associated data value act as an index into a set of pseudorandom permutations. That is, we require the cipher to be a *pseudorandom arbitrary-length permutation with associated data*: for each plaintext length and each value of the associated data, the cipher acts as a pseudorandom permutation. For maximum flexibility, we allow the length of the associated data field to vary even for a single fixed key. In the disk block example, we can use the block number as the associated data value. This will prevent some attacks which rely on the codebook property, since identical plaintext values encrypted with distinct associated data values give unrelated ciphertext values.

The use of an associated data input to a pseudorandom permutation first appeared in the innovative Hasty Pudding Cipher of Schroeppel [3], where it was called a 'spice', and was given a rigorous mathematical treatment by Liskov, Rivest, and Wagner [4], who called it a 'tweak'. Our security goal follows that of the latter work, with the distinction that we allow the associated data to have an arbitrary length.

1.1   Comparison to Existing Work

Naor and Reingold [5] outlined an mode of operation implementing arbitrary length permutation which used a hash-ECB-hash method in which the hash stages are invertible. Other work used a Feistel approach [6]. These early designs do not include a provision for associated data. More recently, block cipher modes of operation that implement pseudorandom arbitrary-length permutations with associated data have been defined. The first such algorithms to be proven secure were the CMC [7] and EME [8] modes of Halevi and Rogaway. CMC cannot be efficiently pipelined; EME can be pipelined, but lacks flexibility. EME* [9] was designed to address that issue. All of those algorithms use an encrypt-mix-encrypt approach, and do not use universal hashing. ABL4 [10] uses a four-round unbalanced Feistel network. The original XCB version [11], HCTR [12], and

HCH [13], use a hash-CTR-hash approach. PEP [14] and TET [15] make use of the hash-ECB-hash approach. Some of the modes have restrictions on the lengths of their inputs (CMC, EME, PEP), or require length-specific precomputation (TET). A detailed comparison of these modes is beyond the scope of this paper, but we highlight some differences below.

XCB encrypts nw bits of data with only $n + 1$ block cipher invocations and $2n + 6$ multiplications in $GF(2^w)$, where w is the number of bits in the block cipher inputs and outputs. The relative efficiency of these modes of operation depends on the relative efficiency of a block cipher invocation and a multiplication in $GF(2^w)$. In software, XCB is faster than EME* if the time taken by that multiply is less than half of the time taken by the block cipher; otherwise, EME* is faster. Multiplication can be done efficiently using precomputed tables, so that XCB outperforms EME*, but in practice the size of such tables could be undesirable, and the performance of the two modes should be considered roughly equivalent. HCTR is faster than XCB by a single block cipher invocation. ABL4 and PEP are considerably less efficient. XCB uses only a single hash key, which is a significant advantage for software implementations, because it reduces the amount of memory needed to store and encryption or decryption context.

In hardware, XCB has the lowest latency of any of these modes; in this context, latency measures the time between when encryption starts and when the first bit of the ciphertext leaves the circuit. XCB also has the merit that a single circuit can implement both encryption and decryption; the algorithms are equivalent up to a reversal of their subkeys.

XCB is unique in that it has been shown to be secure in nonce mode, and can securely accept plaintexts with lengths between w and $2w$ bits when the associated data contains a nonce. This property allows XCB to protect short plaintexts. An example of an application where that feature is useful is the use of Secure RTP [16] to protect voice over IP with the widely used G.729 voice codec, in which case the plaintext is 20 octets long.

The basic components of XCB are identical to those of the Galois/Counter Mode (GCM) of operation [17], making XCB easy to implement given an implementation of GCM, and making compact GCM/XCB implementations possible.

2   XCB Definition

This section contains the specification for XCB for use with w-bit block ciphers. A typical value is $w = 128$, as with the Advanced Encryption Standard (AES) [21].

2.1   Interface

The encryption operation takes as input a secret key K, a plaintext P, and associated data Z, and outputs a ciphertext C. This operation is denoted as $C = E(K, Z, P)$. The values K, P, Z, and C are bit strings. The length of C is identical to that of P.

The decryption operation takes as input a secret key K, a ciphertext C, and associated data Z, and outputs a plaintext P. This operation is denoted as $P = D(K, Z, C)$. The identity $D(K, Z, E(K, Z, P)) = P$ holds for all values of K and Z.

There are two distinct ways in which XCB can be used. For any fixed value of the key, if all of the values of the associated data Z in all of the encryption operations are distinct, then the plaintext can have a length between w and 2^{39} bits, inclusive. We call this *nonce mode*. Otherwise, if the associated data values are *not* distinct, then the plaintext must have a length between $2w$ and 2^{39} bits, inclusive. We call this *normal mode*.

2.2 Notation

The two primitive functions used in XCB are block cipher encryption and multiplication over the field $GF(2^w)$. The block cipher encryption of the value X with the key K is denoted as $\mathbf{e}(K, X)$, and the block cipher decryption is denoted as $\mathbf{d}(K, X)$. (Note that we reserve the symbols E and D to denote XCB encryption and decryption, respectively.) The number of bits in the inputs and outputs of the block cipher is denoted as w. The multiplication of two elements $X, Y \in GF(2^w)$ is denoted as $X \cdot Y$, and the addition of X and Y is denoted as $X \oplus Y$. Addition in this field is equivalent to the bitwise exclusive-or operation, and the multiplication operation is as defined in GCM [17]. We denote the number of bits in a bit string X as $\#X$.

The function $\text{len}(S)$ returns a $w/2$-bit string containing the nonnegative integer describing the number of bits in its argument S, with the least significant bit on the right. The expression 0^l denotes a string of l zero bits, and $A\|B$ denotes the concatenation of two bit strings A and B. The function $\mathbf{msb}_t(S)$ returns the initial t bits of the string S. We consider bit strings to be indexed starting on the left, so that bit zero of S is the leftmost bit. When S is a bit string and $0 \le a < b < \#S$, we denote as $S[a; b]$ the length $b - a$ subtring of S consisting of bits a through b of S. The symbol $\{\}$ denotes the bit string with zero length.

2.3 Definition

The XCB encryption operation is defined in Algorithms 1; the decryption operation is similar and is left implicit. The values K_e, K_d, and K_c can be stored between evaluations of these algorithms, in order to trade off some storage for a decreased computational load.

The function $\mathbf{c} : \{0, 1\}^k \times \{0, 1\}^w \to \{0, 1\}^l$, where the output length l is is bounded by $0 \le l \le 2^{39}$, generates an arbitrary-length output by running the block cipher $\mathbf{e}$ in counter mode, using its w-bit input as the initial counter value. Its definition is

$$\mathbf{c}(K, W, l) = \mathbf{e}(K, W)\|\mathbf{e}(K, \text{incr}(W))\| \ldots \|\mathbf{msb}_t(\mathbf{e}(K, \text{incr}^{s-1}(W)), \quad (1)$$

where we make the number of bits l in the output an explicit parameter for clarity; $s = \lceil l/w \rceil$ is the number of w-bit blocks in the output and $t = l \bmod w$

Algorithm 1. The XCB encryption operation. Given a key $K \in \{0,1\}^k$, a plaintext $\mathbf{P} \in \{0,1\}^m$ where $m \in [w, 2^{39}]$, and associated data $Z \in \{0,1\}^n$ where $n \in [0, 2^{39}]$, this operation returns a ciphertext $\mathbf{C} \in \{0,1\}^m$.

$$H \leftarrow \mathbf{e}(K, 0^w)$$
$$K_e \leftarrow \mathbf{msb}_k(\mathbf{e}(K, 0^{w-3}\|001)\|\mathbf{e}(K, 0^{w-3}\|010))$$
$$K_d \leftarrow \mathbf{msb}_k(\mathbf{e}(K, 0^{w-3}\|011)\|\mathbf{e}(K, 0^{w-3}\|100))$$
$$K_c \leftarrow \mathbf{msb}_k(\mathbf{e}(K, 0^{w-3}\|101)\|\mathbf{e}(K, 0^{w-3}\|110))$$
$$A \leftarrow \mathbf{P}[\#\mathbf{P} - w; \#\mathbf{P} - 1]$$
$$B \leftarrow \mathbf{P}[0; \#\mathbf{P} - w - 1]$$
$$C \leftarrow \mathbf{e}(K_e, A)$$
$$D \leftarrow C \oplus \mathbf{h}_1(H, Z, B)$$
$$E \leftarrow B \oplus \mathbf{c}(K_c, D, \#B)$$
$$F \leftarrow D \oplus \mathbf{h}_2(H, Z, E)$$
$$G \leftarrow \mathbf{d}(K_d, F)$$
$$\mathbf{return}\ E\|G$$

is number of bits in the trailing block. Here the function $\mathrm{incr} : \{0,1\}^w \to \{0,1\}^w$ is the increment operation that is used to generate successive counter values. This function treats the rightmost 32 bits of its argument as a nonnegative integer with the least significant bit on the right, increments this value modulo 2^{32}. More formally,

$$\mathrm{incr}(X) = X[0; w - 33]\ \|\ (X[w - 32; w - 1] + 1 \bmod 2^{32}), \tag{2}$$

where we rely on the implicit conversion of bit strings to integers.

The functions $\mathbf{h}_1$ and $\mathbf{h}_2$ are defined in terms of the underlying hash function $\mathbf{h}$ as

$$\mathbf{h}_1(H, Z, B) = \mathbf{h}(H, 0^w\|Z, B\|0^{\#B \bmod w + w})$$
$$\mathbf{h}_2(H, Z, B) = \mathbf{h}(H, Z\|0^w, E\|0^{\#B \bmod w}\|\mathrm{len}(Z\|L)\|\mathrm{len}(B)). \tag{3}$$

The function $\mathbf{h} : \{0,1\}^w \times \{0,1\}^a \times \{0,1\}^c \to \{0,1\}^w, a \in [w, 2^{39}], c \in [0, 2^{39}]$ is defined by $\mathbf{h}(H, A, C) = X_{m+n+1}$, where the variables $X_i \in \{0,1\}^w$ for $i = 0, \dots, m + n + 1$ are defined as

$$X_i = \begin{cases} 0 & \text{for } i = 0 \\ (X_{i-1} \oplus A_i) \cdot H & \text{for } i = 1, \dots, m-1 \\ (X_{m-1} \oplus (A_m^*\|0^{w-v})) \cdot H & \text{for } i = m \\ (X_{i-1} \oplus C_{i-m}) \cdot H & \text{for } i = m+1, \dots, m+n-1 \\ (X_{m+n-1} \oplus (C_n^*\|0^{w-u})) \cdot H & \text{for } i = m+n \\ (X_{m+n} \oplus (\mathrm{len}(A)\|\mathrm{len}(C))) \cdot H & \text{for } i = m+n+1. \end{cases} \tag{4}$$

Here we let A_i denote the w-bit substring $A[(i-1)w; iw - 1]$, and let C_i denote $C[(i-1)w; iw - i]$. In other words, A_i and C_i are the ith blocks of A and C, respectively, if those bit strings are decomposed into w-bit blocks. Here u and v

denote the number of bits in the trailing blocks of A and C, respectively. This function is identical to GHASH, the universal hash that is used as a component of the AES Galois/Counter Mode (GCM) of Operation [17] when $w = 128$.

2.4   Improvements in Our Version

The initial version of XCB appeared on the IACR eprint website in 2004 [11]. Our new definition of XCB incorporates changes that make its security properties easier to analyze. First, only a single hash key is used, which enables algebraic relations about the hash function to be brought to bear during the analysis. This change also benefits software implementations by relieving them of the need to store precomputed tables for an additional hash key. Second, the inputs to the hash functions are slightly rearranged, in order to make use of the properties of the hash function; this strategy is explained through the lemmas and theorems of Section 3.1. Additionally, the new design reorders the operations in a way that makes XCB more amenable to pipelined implementation, by changing the way that plaintexts are mapped to internal variables.

3   Security Analysis

In this section, we analyze the security of XCB in the concrete security model introduced by Bellare et. al. [18], and show that XCB is a secure pseudorandom arbitrary-length permutation with associated data (ALPA), using only the assumption that $\mathbf{e}$ is a secure w-bit pseudorandom permutation, as follows. We review the properties of $\mathbf{h}$ and how they are used in XCB (Section 3.1), then define our security model and analyze security under the assumption that $\mathbf{e}$ is a random permutation (Section 3.2), then bound the security when $\mathbf{e}$ is a pseudorandom permutation (Section 3.3).

3.1   Properties of h and XCB

In this section we describe several properties of the hash function $\mathbf{h}$, and some properties of XCB that follow from them. Foremost, $\mathbf{h}$ is an ϵ-almost xor universal function; loosely speaking, this means that the exclusive-or of any two hash values has a low probability to take on any particular value. We provide a precise definition below.

Definition 1. *A function* $f : \{0,1\}^k \times \{0,1\}^m \to \{0,1\}^t$ *is ϵ-almost xor universal if*

$$\mathbf{P}[f(K,M) \oplus f(K,M') = a \mid K \xleftarrow{R} \{0,1\}^k] \leq \epsilon \tag{5}$$

for all $M \neq M' \in \{0,1\}^m$ *and all* $a \in \{0,1\}^t$

Here the expression $\mathbf{P}[\mathbb{E} \mid \mathbb{F}]$ denotes the probability of the event $\mathbb{E}$ given that the event $\mathbb{F}$ has occurred, and the expression $K \xleftarrow{R} \{0,1\}^k$ means that K is chosen uniformly at random from the set $\{0,1\}^k$. We diverge slightly from the usual definition for explicitness[1]. This definition extends naturally to the case in which f has multiple arguments, as is the case below.

Lemma 1 (h is ϵ-AXU). *The function* $\mathbf{h}$ *defined by Equation 4 is* $\epsilon_h(l)$-*almost xor universal where* $\epsilon_h(l) = \lceil l/w + 2 \rceil 2^{-w}$ *whenever the inputs* A *and* C *are restricted to so that the sum of their lengths is* l *or fewer bits.*

The proof of this lemma appears in Appendix A.

Because the increment function incr() defined in Equation 2 that is used to generate successive counters does not commute with addition in $GF(2^w)$, we need to establish another property of $\mathbf{h}$, which is related to but slightly different from the ϵ-almost xor universal property.

Theorem 1 (h is unlikely to collide with $\mathrm{incr}^s(\mathbf{h})$). *For any* $A, A', C, C', E,$ E' *where either* $A' \neq A$ *or* $C' \neq C$ *or both inequalities hold, and any index* s,

$$\mathbf{P}[\mathbf{h}(H, A, C) \oplus E = \mathrm{incr}^s(\mathbf{h}(H, A', C') \oplus E') \mid H \xleftarrow{R} GF(2^w)] \leq \epsilon_h(l), \quad (6)$$

whenever the inputs A *and* C *are restricted to so that the sum of their lengths is* l *or fewer bits.*

This theorem is proved in Appendix A.

The function $\mathbf{h}(H, A, C)$ has the property that it is linear in terms of its arguments A and C, and this fact is used in the XCB design. We next establish the linear property in Theorem 2, then we use it to show a useful expression for the XCB variables F and C in Theorem 3.

Theorem 2 (h is linear). *For any* $H \in V^w$ *and any* A, A', C *and* C' *such that* $\#A = \#A'$ *and* $\#C = \#C'$,

$$\mathbf{h}(H, A, C) \oplus \mathbf{h}(H, A', C') = \mathbf{h}(H, A \oplus A', C \oplus C') \oplus (len(A) \| len(C)) \cdot H.$$

The proof appears in Appendix A.

A simple relationship between F and C follows from this theorem, which is captured in the next lemma. The proof is simple, so we include it in this section.

Theorem 3 (F **and** C **have a simple relation**)

$$F = C \oplus \mathbf{g}(H, V(Z), \mathbf{c}(K_c, D, \#B)), \quad (7)$$

where $\mathbf{g}(H, A, C) = \mathbf{h}(H, A, C) \cdot H$ *and* $V(Z) = (Z \| 0^w) \oplus (0^w \| Z)$.

Proof

$$F = C \oplus \mathbf{h}(H, Z \| 0^w, E \| 0^{\#B \bmod w} \| (len(Z \| 0^w) \| len(B)))$$
$$\oplus \mathbf{h}(H, 0^w \| Z, B \| 0^{\#B \bmod w+w}) \quad (8)$$
$$= C \oplus \mathbf{h}(H, (Z \| 0^w) \oplus (0^w \| Z), \mathbf{c}(K_c, D, len(D))) \cdot H.$$

---

[1] In the standard definition, g would define a hash function family, and the selection of a key K would choose a particular hash function from that family of functions.

Figure 1 illustrates these identities. The lowest term of the function $\mathbf{h}$, considered as a polynomial in H, cancels with the term $(\text{len}(A)\|\text{len}(C))) \cdot H$. The presence of $\text{len}(Z\|0^w)\|\text{len}(B)$ as the last block of the last argument to $\mathbf{h}$ makes the coefficient of H^2 in that polynomial match that of the usual coefficient of H in $\mathbf{h}$, and the other coefficients are similarly shifted by one. The presence of the term $0^{\#B \bmod w}$ ensures the alignment of the final w bits.   □

During the evaluation of an XCB encryption or decryption operation, the first argument of $\mathbf{h}$, during both of its evaluations, has the value 0^w prepended or appended to it. If these 0^w terms had not been incorporated into the design, then the second argument to $\mathbf{g}$ in Theorem 3 would have been $0^{\#Z}$, and the variable F would have no dependancy on Z during an encryption operation. This aspect of the XCB design utilizes the property captured in the following simple lemma.

Lemma 2. *The function $V(Z)$ defined in Theorem 3 has the property that, for any two distinct values Z and Z', the values $V(Z)$ and $V(Z')$ are distinct.*

The validity of this lemma follows from the fact that $V(Z)$ is an invertible transformation of Z; it is easy to compute Z given $V(Z)$ by considering successive w-bit blocks of V.

evaluation	H^7	H^6	H^5	H^4	H^3	H^2	H
first	0^w	Z_1	Z_2	E_1	$E_2^*\|0^{\#B \bmod w}$	0^w	$\text{len}(Z\|0^w)\|\text{len}(B)$
second	Z_1	Z_2	0^w	E_1	$E_2^*\|0^{\#B \bmod w}$	$\text{len}(Z\|0^w)\|\text{len}(B)$	$\text{len}(Z\|0^w)\|\text{len}(B)$
equivalent	Z_1	$Z_1 \oplus Z_2$	Z_2	S_1	$S_2^*\|0^{\#B \bmod w}$	$\text{len}(Z\|0^w)\|\text{len}(B)$	0^w

Fig. 1. An example of the evaluation of $\mathbf{h}$ during an XCB encryption operation; the table entries are the coefficients of the terms of H in the column headings. The third row shows the equivalent hash operation as in Equation 8. Z_i and E_i denote the ith blocks of Z and E, respectively, and S_i denotes the ith block of $\mathbf{c}(K_c, D, \#B)$.

Lastly, the function $\mathbf{g}$ as defined in Theorem 3 is almost xor universal as well, as shown by the following lemma; the proof is in Appendix A.

Lemma 3 (g is almost xor universal). *The function $\mathbf{g}$ is $(\epsilon_h(l) + 2^{-w})$-almost xor universal when its second and third inputs are restricted so that their lengths sum to l or fewer bits.*

3.2   Security in the Ideal Model

In this section, we show that XCB is secure against adaptive chosen plaintext/ciphertext attacks, by showing that it is a secure ALFA under the 'ideal' assumption that $\mathbf{e}$ is a random permutation. More specifically, we model $\mathbf{e}(K_e, X)$, $\mathbf{e}(K_d, X)$, and $\mathbf{e}(K_c, X)$ as independent random permutations. We first establish our security model.

We denote the set of all functions that map $\{0,1\}^m$ to $\{0,1\}^n$ as $\mathbf{F}_{m,n}$. A *random function* is a function chosen uniformly at random from $\mathbf{F}_{m,n}$. We denote as $\mathbf{I}_n$ the set of all uniquely invertible functions in $\mathbf{F}_{n,n}$, and a *random permutation* is a function chosen uniformly at random from $\mathbf{I}_n$.

A keyed pseudorandom function (PRF) is a subset $\mathbf{PRF}_{m,n} \subseteq \mathbf{F}_{m,n}$ in which the key selects a particular function from $\mathbf{PRF}_{m,n}$. Similarly, a keyed pseudo-random permutation (PRP) is a subset $\mathbf{PRP}_n \subseteq \mathbf{I}_n$ in which the key selects a particular function from $\mathbf{PRP}_n$. In the following, we assume that a key chosen uniformly at random will choose a function from $\mathbf{PRF}_{m,n}$ or $\mathbf{PRP}_n$ uniformly at random.

To measure the 'pseudorandomness' of a particular keyed pseudorandom function $F \subseteq \mathbf{F}_{m,n}$, we use the conventional indistinguishability experiment in which an adversary is challenged to distinguish the PRF from a random function. The adversary is given access to an oracle that provides an interface to a function $f \in \mathbf{F}_{m,n}$. When the adversary provides an input $x \in \{0,1\}^m$ to the oracle, the oracle returns $f(x)$. The adversary is free to choose the inputs adaptively. At the outset of the experiment, the oracle makes a choice to either select f from F or from $\mathbf{F}_{m,n}$. This choice is made uniformly at random and kept hidden from the adversary. At the conclusion of the experiment, the adversary guesses from which set the function has been chosen. We view the adversary as a probabilistic algorithm and consider the probability that it will correctly distinguish a PRF from a random function. We let C_F denote the event that the function f was chosen from the PRF F at the outset of the experiment, and let G_F denote the event that the adversary guesses that the function f was chosen from that PRF at the conclusion of the experiment. An adversary's effectiveness at distinguishing F from a random function is measured by the advantage A_F^{PRF} defined as

$$A_F^{\mathrm{PRF}} = \mathbf{P}[G_F \mid C_F] - \mathbf{P}[G_F \mid C_F^c]. \tag{9}$$

Here $\mathbb{E}^c$ denotes the complement of the event $\mathbb{E}$, that is, the event that $\mathbb{E}$ does not occur. An adversary's advantage in distinguishing a PRP P from a random permutation is defined similarly as

$$A_P^{\mathrm{PRP}} = \mathbf{P}[G_P \mid C_P] - \mathbf{P}[G_P \mid C_P^c] \tag{10}$$

where the events C_P and G_P are the analogues of C_F and G_F. In the PRP experiment, we give the attacker access to two oracles, one for P, and one for the inverse function P^{-1}. In this case, q counts the total number of queries. Definition 2 encapsulates these ideas.

Definition 2. *A PRF F is (q, a)-secure if any adversary making at most q oracle queries has advantage A_F^{PRF} that is less than or equal to a. Similarly, a PRP P is (q, a)-secure if any adversary making at most q oracle queries is has advantage A_P^{PRP} that is less than or equal to a.*

The definition of a secure ALPA is identical, taking into account the fact that the adversary is presented with an ALPA oracle instead of a PRP oracle.

We label the XCB internal variables as $\{A_i, B_i, C_i, D_i, E_i, F_i, G_i\}$ for the ith invocation. If the the ith query is to the XCB encryption oracle, then the adversary determines the values of A_i and B_i, and is given E_i and G_i in return.

If the ith query is to the XCB decryption oracle, then the adversary determines the values of E_i and G_i and is given A_i and B_i in return. We assume without loss of generality that the adversary never repeats a query, and never asks for the decryption of a ciphertext value returned by a previous encryption query, and never asks for the encryption of a plaintext value returned by a previous decryption query.

The basic idea behind our proof is that the each of the ciphertext values $B \oplus \mathbf{c}(K_c, D, \#B))\|\mathbf{d}(K_d, F)$ returned from an encryption query are indistinguishable from random as long as the values D and F do not repeat across different invocations of that function, and the functions $\mathbf{c}$ and $\mathbf{e}$ are indistinguishable from random. Similarly, the plaintext values $E \oplus \mathbf{c}(K_c, D, \#B))\|\mathbf{e}(K_e, C)$ returned from a decryption query are indistinguishable from random as long as the values of D and C do not repeat. We handle our use of the PRP $\mathbf{e}$ as a PRF in the standard way, using the PRP-PRF switching lemma [18].

Lemma 4 (e is a good PRF). *If a function f is a (q, a)-secure w-bit PRP, then it is a $(q, a + q(q-1)2^{-w-1})$-secure PRF.*

We also make use of the fact that the outputs of a PRP are unpredictable to an adversary, as given by the following lemma.

Lemma 5 (e is unpredictable). *If $\mathbf{e}$ is a random permutation, an adversary with oracle access to $\mathbf{e}$ can cause the output $\mathbf{e}(X)$ of the ith query to be equal to a particular value Y with probability no greater than $(2^w - i)^{-1}$, for any fixed value of Y.*

We next define an event Ω whose occurrence ensures the security of XCB in the ideal model, as long as $\mathbf{c}$ and $\mathbf{e}$ are secure PRFs. The event Ω is the conjunction of the events $\Omega_1 \cap \Omega_2 \cap \cdots \cap \Omega_i$, where Ω_i is the event that the following conditions hold during the ith query to the ALPA oracle:

1. $D_i \neq \mathrm{incr}^s(D_j)$ for each integer s such that $-\lceil \#P_i/w \rceil + 1 \leq s \leq \lceil \#P_j/w \rceil - 1$, for all $j < i$, and
2. If the ith query is an encryption query, then $F_i \neq F_j$; if it is a decryption query, then $C_i \neq C_j$, for all $j < i$.

The first condition ensures that, during the invocation of the function $\mathbf{c}$, all of the inputs to $\mathbf{e}$ using the key K_c are distinct from all of the inputs that have previously been made with that key.

We next assume that $\Omega_1, \Omega_2, \ldots, \Omega_{i-1}$ have occurred and show that Ω_i will occur with probability close to one. We bound the total length of the data processed during each query as $l > \#P_i + \#Z_i$.

Lemma 6. *For any of the previous queries $j < i$, and for any single value of s such that $-2^w < s < 2^w$,*

$$\mathbf{P}[D_i = \mathrm{incr}^s(D_j)] \leq (2^w - i)^{-1} + \epsilon_h(l), \text{ and}$$
$$\mathbf{P}[D_i = D_j] \leq \epsilon_h(l),$$

given that the events $\Omega_1, \Omega_2, \ldots, \Omega_{i-1}$ have occured. Here j is either an encryption or decryption query.

Proof. We first assume that the ith query is an encryption query, in which case the condition that $D_i = \text{incr}^s(D_j)$ can be expressed as

$$\mathbf{e}(K_e, A_i) \oplus \mathbf{h}_1(H, Z_i, B_i) = \text{incr}^s(\mathbf{e}(K_e, A_j) \oplus \mathbf{h}_1(H, Z_j, B_j)). \qquad (11)$$

We first consider the case that the inputs to the first invocation of $\mathbf{h}_1$ are identical during queries i and j; that is, $Z_i = Z_j$ and $B_i = B_j$. In this case $A_i \neq A_j$ because the queries are required to be distinct. In this case, $D_i \neq D_j$ follows from the invertibility of $\mathbf{e}$. From Lemma 5, the probability that $D_i = \text{incr}^s(D_j)$ will occur for some value $s \neq 0$ is at most $(2^w - i)^{-1}$, for any particular values of j and s. Otherwise, if $A_i = A_j$, then the inputs to $\mathbf{h}$ must be distinct, and $\mathbf{P}[D_i = \text{incr}^s(D_j)] \leq \epsilon_h$ follows from Theorem 1; this bound holds for $0 \leq j < i$.

When the ith query is a decryption query, then similar arguments hold by considering the functions $\mathbf{h}_2$ and $\mathbf{d}$ and the variable G instead of the functions $\mathbf{h}_1$ and $\mathbf{e}$ and the variable A. Thus the probability that $D_i = \text{incr}^s(D_j)$ is no more than $(2^w - i)^{-1} + \epsilon_h(l)$, for any values of j and s. $\qquad \square$

Lemma 7. $\mathbf{P}[\Omega_i \mid \Omega_1 \cap \Omega_2 \cap \cdots \cap \Omega_{i-1}] \geq 1 - (i-1)\lceil l/w + 2 \rceil 2^{1-w}.$

Proof. Since Lemma 6 holds for any value of s, the probability that it holds for *any* value of s in the range under consideration is no more than $((2^w - i)^{-1} + \epsilon_h(l))\lceil (2l)/w - 2 \rceil$.

We now assume that $D_i \neq D_j$ and consider the probability that $F_i = F_j$ when the ith query is an encryption query. From Theorem 3, that event is equivalent to the condition that

$$\mathbf{g}(H, V(Z_i), \mathbf{c}(K_c, D_i, \#B_i)) \oplus \mathbf{g}(H, V(Z_j), \mathbf{c}(K_c, D_j, \#B_j)) = C_i \oplus C_j. \qquad (12)$$

If XCB is being used in normal mode (as defined in Section 2.1), then $\#B_i, \#B_j \geq w$, and the initial w bits of $\mathbf{c}(K_c, D_i, \#B_i)$ and $\mathbf{c}(K_c, D_j, \#B_j)$ must be distinct, because D_i and D_j are distinct and $\mathbf{e}$ is an invertible function. If XCB is being used in nonce mode (as defined in Section 2.1), then $Z_i \neq Z_j$, in which case $V(Z_i) \neq V(Z_j)$. In either mode, the inputs to the invocations of $\mathbf{g}$ are distinct, and $\mathbf{P}[F_i = F_j \mid D_i \neq D_j] \leq \epsilon_h(l) + 2^{-w}$ from Lemma 3. Thus, when the ith query is an encryption query, and the events $\Omega_1, \Omega_2, \ldots, \Omega_{i-1}$ have occurred, then

$$\mathbf{P}[F_i \neq F_j \mid D_i \neq D_j]\mathbf{P}[D_i \neq D_j] \geq (1 - \epsilon_h(l) - 2^{-w})(1 - \epsilon_h(l)$$
$$\geq 1 - 2(\epsilon_h(l) + 2^{-w}). \qquad (13)$$

When the ith query is a decryption query, then similar arguments show that $\mathbf{P}[C_i \neq C_j \mid D_i \neq D_j]\mathbf{P}[D_i \neq D_j]$ is bounded by the same value.

Equation 13 holds for each value of j between 1 and $i - 1$, inclusive. Thus $\mathbf{P}[\Omega_i \mid \Omega_1 \cap \Omega_2 \ldots \cap \Omega_{i-1}]$ is at least

$$1 - \sum_{j=1,i-1} 2(\epsilon_h(l) + 2^{-w}) + ((2^w - i)^{-1} + \epsilon_h(l))\lceil (2l)/w - 2 \rceil$$
$$\geq 1 - (i-1)\epsilon_\Omega. \qquad (14)$$

where $\epsilon_\Omega = \lceil l/w + 2 \rceil^2 2^{2-w}$. $\qquad \square$

We can now bound the probability of the event Ω.

Lemma 8 (Ω is likely). *The probability* $\mathbf{P}[\Omega]$ *is at least* $1 - i^2\lceil l/w + 2\rceil^2 2^{2-w}$.

Proof. For any set of events $A_1, A_2, \ldots, A_n$ such that $\mathbf{P}[A_1 \cap A_2 \cap \ldots \cap A_n] > 0$,

$$\mathbf{P}[A_1 \cap A_2 \cap \ldots \cap A_n] = \mathbf{P}[A_n \mid A_1 \cap A_2 \cap \ldots \cap A_{n-1}] \times$$
$$\mathbf{P}[A_{n-1} \mid A_1 \cap \ldots \cap A_{n-2}] \times \mathbf{P}[A_{n-2} \mid A_1 \cap \ldots \cap A_{n-3}] \times \cdots \times \mathbf{P}[A_1].$$

The probability $\mathbf{P}[\Omega_1 \cap \Omega_2 \ldots \cap \Omega_i]$ is thus no less than

$$\prod_{j=1,}^{i} (1 - (j-1)\epsilon_\Omega) \geq (1 - i\epsilon_\Omega)^i \geq 1 - 2i^2\epsilon_\Omega. \tag{15}$$

Theorem 4 (XCB is secure in the ideal model). *If* $e(K_c, *), e(K_d, *),$
$e(K_e, *)$ *are independent random permutations and* H *is chosen uniformly at random, then XCB is a* $(q, q^2\lceil l/w + 2\rceil^2 2^{3-w})$-*secure arbitrary length PRP with associated data with input length between* w *and* l *bits in nonce mode, and with input length between* $2w$ *and* l *bits otherwise.*

Proof. If the event Ω occurs, then the adversaries advantage is no greater than that due to our use of the PRP e as a PRF. No more than $q\lceil l/w\rceil)$ queries are made to e in which it needs to be considered as a PRF. The result follows directly from Lemmas 4 and 8.

3.3   Security as a Block Cipher Mode

Up to this point, we have assumed that the function e is a random permutation, while in fact it is a block cipher. Our next step is to assume that the advantage with which any adversary can distinguish that function from a random permutation is low, and then show that this assumption implies that XCB is an ALPA.

Theorem 5. *If* e *is a* (q, a)-*secure* w-*bit PRP, then XCB is a* $(q, a + q^2\lceil l/w + 2\rceil^2 2^{3-w} + 22 \cdot 2^{-w})$-*secure* l-*bit arbitrary length PRP with associated data.*

The proof is in the Appendix.

4   Conclusions

We have shown that our version of XCB is secure in the concrete reduction-based security model, whenever it is used with a block cipher that can be regarded as a secure PRP in that model. We also introduced the definition of nonce mode for a pseudorandom permutation, and showed that XCB is secure when used in this mode.

Acknowledgments

We thank the anonymous referees, whose careful reading and constructive comments substantially improved this paper.

References

1. Bellare, M., Desai, A., Jokipii, E., Rogaway, P.: A concrete security treatment of symmetric encryption. In: Proceedings of the 38th FOCS, IEEE Computer Society Press, Los Alamitos (1997)
2. IEEE Security in Storage Working Group. Web page, http://siswg.org
3. Schroeppel, R.: Hasty Pudding Cipher Specification. In: First AES Candidate Workshop (August 1998), available online at
   http://www.cs.arizona.edu/people/rcs/hpc/hpc-spec
4. Liskov, M., Rivest, R., Wagner, D.: Tweakable Block Ciphers. In: Yung, M. (ed.) CRYPTO 2002. LNCS, vol. 2442, Springer, Heidelberg (2002)
5. Naor, M., Reingold, O.: A pseudo-random encryption mode. Manuscript (1997), available from http://www.wisdom.weizmann.ac.il/naor
6. Anderson, R., Biham, E.: Two Practical and Provably Secure Block Ciphers: BEAR and LION. In: Proceedings of the Third International Workshop on Fast Software Encryption, Cambridge, UK, pp. 113–120 (1996)
7. Halevi, S., Rogaway, P.: A tweakable enciphering mode. In: Boneh, D. (ed.) CRYPTO 2003. LNCS, vol. 2729, pp. 482–499. Springer, Heidelberg (2003)
8. Halevi, S., Rogaway, P.: A Parallelizable Enciphering Mode. In: 2004 RSA Conference Cryptography Track. LNCS, Springer, Heidelberg (2004)
9. Halevi, S.: EME*: extending EME to handle arbitrary-length messages with associated data. In: Canteaut, A., Viswanathan, K. (eds.) INDOCRYPT 2004. LNCS, vol. 3348, pp. 315–327. Springer, Heidelberg (2004)
10. McGrew, D., Viega, J.: Arbitrary block length mode. Standards contribution (2004), available on-line from
    http://grouper.ieee.org/groups/1619/email/pdf00005.pdf
11. McGrew, D., Fluhrer, S.: The Extended Codebook (XCB) Mode of Operation, Cryptology ePrint Archive: Report 2004/278 (October 25, 2004)
    http://eprint.iacr.org/2004/278
12. Wang, P., Feng, D., Wu, W.: HCTR: A variable-input-length enciphering mode. In: Feng, D., Lin, D., Yung, M. (eds.) CISC 2005. LNCS, vol. 3822, pp. 175–188. Springer, Heidelberg (2005)
13. Chakraborty, D., Sarkar, P.: HCH: A new tweakable enciphering scheme using the hash-encrypt-hash approach. In: Barua, R., Lange, T. (eds.) INDOCRYPT 2006. LNCS, vol. 4329, pp. 287–302. Springer, Heidelberg (2006)
14. Chakraborty, D., Sarkar, P.: A new mode of encryption providing a tweakable strong pseudo-random permutation. In: Robshaw, M. (ed.) FSE 2006. LNCS, vol. 4047. pp. 293–309. Springer, Heidelberg (2006)
15. Halevi, S.: Invertible Universal Hashing and the TET Encryption Mode. In: Menezes, A. (ed.) CRYPTO 2007. LNCS, vol. 4622. Springer, Heidelberg (2007)
16. Baugher, M., McGrew, D., Naslund, M., Carrara, E., Norrman, K.: The Secure Real-time Transport Protocol. IETF RFC 3711 (March 2004)
17. McGrew, D., Viega, J.: The Galois/Counter Mode of Operation (GCM). NIST Modes of Operation Process (submission) (January 2004), available online at
    http://csrc.nist.gov/CryptoToolkit/modes/proposedmodes/

18. Bellare, M., Kilian, J., Rogaway, P.: The Security of the Cipher Block Chaining Message Authentication Code. J. Comput. Syst. Sci. 61(3), 362–399 (2000)
19. McGrew, D., Fluhrer, S.: The Extended Codebook (XCB) Mode of Operation, Version 2, IEEE P1619 (submission)
    grouper.ieee.org/groups/1619/email/pdf00019.pdf
20. Krawczyk, H.: LFSR-based hashing and authentication. In: Franklin, M. (ed.) CRYPTO 2004. LNCS, vol. 3152, Springer, Heidelberg (2004)
21. U.S. National Institute of Standards and Technology. The Advanced Encryption Standard. Federal Information Processing Standard (FIPS) 197, (2002)
22. Biggs, N.: Discrete Mathematics. Oxford University Press, Oxford (1993) (Revised Edition)

A   Proofs

In this appendix we provide proofs for some of the Lemmas and Theorems.

Proof (Lemma 1). We consider two distinct inputs (A, C) and (A', C'), then analyze the probability of the event that

$$\mathbf{h}(H, A, C) \oplus \mathbf{h}(H, A', C') = a, \tag{16}$$

for some fixed value $a \in \{0, 1\}^w$. We assume that these inputs are formatted as described in Section 2, in which A, C, A', and C' consist of m, n, m', and n' w-bit blocks, respectively, the final blocks of which have lengths v, u, v', and u', respectively. We assume without essential loss of generality that $m + n \geq m' + n'$, and we define $f = m + n - m' - n'$.

We define the blocks $D_i \in \{0, 1\}^w$ for $1 \leq i \leq m + n + 1$ as

$$
D_i = \begin{cases}
A_i & \text{for } i = 1, \ldots, m-1 \\
A_m^* \| 0^{w-v} & \text{for } i = m \\
C_{i-m} & \text{for } i = m+1, \ldots, m+n-1 \\
C_n^* \| 0^{w-u} & \text{for } i = m+n \\
\text{len}(A) \| \text{len}(C) & \text{for } i = m+n+1
\end{cases} \tag{17}
$$

$$
D_i' = \begin{cases}
0^w & \text{for } i = 1, \ldots, f \\
A_{i-f} & \text{for } i = f, \ldots, f+m'-1 \\
A_{m'}^* \| 0^{w-v} & \text{for } i = f+m' \\
C_{i-f+m'} & \text{for } i = f+m+1, \ldots, f+m'+n'-1 \\
C_{n'}^* \| 0^{w-u} & \text{for } i = f+m'+n' \\
\text{len}(A) \| \text{len}(C) & \text{for } i = f+m'+n'+1
\end{cases} \tag{18}
$$

The condition that Equation 16 holds can be expressed as $R(H) = 0$, where the polynomial R of degree at most $m + n + 1$ over $GF(2^w)$ is defined by

$$R(H) = a \oplus \bigoplus_{i=1,}^{m+n+1} (D_i \oplus D_i') \cdot H^{m+n-i+2}. \tag{19}$$

The polynomial R must be nonzero, that is, at least one of its coefficients must be nonzero, because the pairs (A, C) and (A', C') are distinct. There are at most $m+n+1$ values of $H \in GF(2^w)$ for which $R(H) = 0$ holds. This follows from the fact that an dth degree polynomial over $GF(2^w)$ has at most d distinct roots (this is the fundamental theorem of algebra over a finite field; see, for example, [22, Theorem 15.8.2]), and the fact that R is nonzero. The probability that $R(H) = 0$ holds, given that H is chosen at random from $GF(2^w)$, is $(m + n + 1)/2^w \leq \lceil l/w + 2 \rceil 2^{-w}$, when the cumulative length of the inputs is restricted to l bits.

For each vector D, there is a unique pair (A, C) where both A and C are bit strings as described in Section 1, and vice-versa. This is because the last element of D unambiguously encodes the lengths of both A and C. Thus, the probability that $R(H) = 0$ holds for any two given messages (A, C) and (A', C'), and a given vector a, is equal to the probability that $\mathbf{h}(H, A, C) \oplus \mathbf{h}(H, A', C') = a$. Equation 16 holds with probability $\lceil l/w + 2 \rceil 2^{-w}$ for any given values of $(A, C), (A', C')$, and a. □

Proof (Theorem 1). We let D_i and D'_i be the coefficients defined as in Equation 17, then we define the polynomials R_1 and R_2 as

$$R_1(H) = E \oplus \bigoplus_{i=1,}^{m+n+1} D_i \cdot H^{m+n-i+2} \tag{20}$$

and

$$R_2(H) = E' \oplus \bigoplus_{i=1,}^{m+n+1} D'_i \cdot H^{m+n-i+2}. \tag{21}$$

The condition $\mathbf{h}(H, A, C) \oplus E = \mathrm{incr}^s(\mathbf{h}(H, A', C') \oplus E')$ can be expressed as

$$R_1(H) = \mathrm{incr}^s(R_2(H)) = T \tag{22}$$

for some value of $T \in \{0, 1\}^w$. For any fixed value of T, there are at most $m+n+1$ values of H such that $R_1(H) = T$, and at most $m+n+1$ values of H such that $R_2(H) = \mathrm{incr}^{-s}(T)$. Thus the number of values of H that satisfy both equations is at most $m + n + 1$. When H is drawn uniformly at random, the chance of choosing one of these values is at most $(m + n + 1)2^{-w} = \epsilon_h(l)$, where l is an upper bound on the total number of bits in A and C. □

Proof (Theorem 2). We consider the evaluation of $\mathbf{h}(H, A, C)$ and $\mathbf{h}(H, A', C')$, and let X_i be as defined in equation 4, and let X'_i be defined similarly, but with $X'_i, A'_i,$ and C'_i replacing $X_i, A_i,$ and C_i, respectively. We define δX_i to be $X_i \oplus X'_i$, δA_i to be $A_i \oplus A'_i$, and δC_i to be $C_i \oplus C'_i$. Then we note that

$$\delta X_i = \begin{cases} 0 & \text{for } i = 0 \\ (\delta X_{i-1} \oplus \delta A_i) \cdot H & \text{for } i = 1, \ldots, m-1 \\ (\delta X_{m-1} \oplus (\delta A_m^* \| 0^{w-v})) \cdot H & \text{for } i = m \\ (\delta X_{i-1} \oplus \delta C_{i-m}) \cdot H & \text{for } i = m+1, \ldots, m+n-1 \\ (\delta X_{m+n-1} \oplus (\delta C_n^* \| 0^{w-u})) \cdot H & \text{for } i = m+n \\ \delta X_{m+n} \cdot H & \text{for } i = m+n+1. \end{cases} \tag{23}$$

In the case $i^{i=m+n+1}$ of the previous equation, the term $(\text{len}(A)\|\text{len}(C)))$ does not appear due to cancelation. Thus $\mathbf{h}(H, A, C) \oplus \mathbf{h}(H, A', C') = \delta X_{m+n+1} = \mathbf{h}(H, A \oplus A', C \oplus C') \oplus (\text{len}(A)\|\text{len}(C))) \cdot H$. □

Proof (Lemma 3). The condition that $\mathbf{g}(H, A, C) \oplus \mathbf{g}(H, A', C') = a$ holds can be expressed as $S(H) = 0$, where the polynomial S of degree at most $m + n + 2$ over $GF(2^w)$ is defined by

$$S(H) = a \oplus \bigoplus_{i=1,}^{m+n+1} (D_i \oplus D'_i) \cdot H^{m+n-i+3}. \tag{24}$$

Here D_i and D'_i are as defined in Equation 17. The result follows from arguments similar to those made for Lemma 1. □

Proof (Theorem 5). We build an **e**-distinguisher out of an XCB distinguisher by implementing XCB by replacing each invocation of **e** and its inverse by a call to the block cipher oracle, running the XCB distinguisher against that XCB implementation. We denote as C_{XCB} the event that the ALPA oracle is chosen to be XCB. If the XCB-distinguisher indicates that it believes that the inputs were created by XCB (that is, the event G_{XCB} occurs), then our E-distinguisher indicates that the block cipher oracle is E (that is, the event G_e occurs).

We proceed by first considering the case that K_c, K_d, K_e, and H are chosen uniformly at random. We call this algorithm RXCB, and we define the events C_{RXCB} and G_{RXCB} analogous to C_{XCB} and G_{XCB}, respectively. Our analysis uses the following facts.

Fact 1. $\mathbf{P}[G_{\mathbf{e}} \mid C_{\mathbf{e}}] = \mathbf{P}[G_{RXCB} \mid C_{RXCB}]$, *because the events $C_{\mathbf{e}}$ and C_{RXCB} both provide equivalent inputs to the distinguisher, and the distinguishers are identical.*

Fact 2. *For any three events A, B and C (with $\mathbf{P}[B] \neq 0$),*

$$\mathbf{P}[A \mid B] = \mathbf{P}[A \mid B \cap C]\mathbf{P}[C \mid B] + \mathbf{P}[A \mid B \cap C^c]\mathbf{P}[C^c \mid B].$$

Fact 3. *The events $B_{\mathbf{e}}^c \cap \Omega$ and B_{RXCB}^c provide equivalent inputs to the distinguishers.*

The advantage with which our distinguisher works against **e** is

$$\begin{aligned}
A_{\mathbf{e}} &= \mathbf{P}[G_{\mathbf{e}} \mid C_{\mathbf{e}}] - \mathbf{P}[G_{\mathbf{e}} \mid B_{\mathbf{e}}^c] \\
&= \mathbf{P}[G_{\text{RXCB}} \mid C_{\text{RXCB}}] - \mathbf{P}[G_{\mathbf{e}} \mid B_{\mathbf{e}}^c] \\
&= \mathbf{P}[G_{\text{RXCB}} \mid C_{\text{RXCB}}] - \mathbf{P}[G_{\mathbf{e}} \mid B_{\mathbf{e}}^c \cap \Omega]\mathbf{P}[\Omega \mid B_{\mathbf{e}}^c] - \mathbf{P}[G_{\mathbf{e}} \mid B_{\mathbf{e}}^c \cap \Omega^c]\mathbf{P}[\Omega^c \mid B_{\mathbf{e}}^c] \\
&\geq \mathbf{P}[G_{\text{RXCB}} \mid C_{\text{RXCB}}] - \mathbf{P}[G_{\text{RXCB}} \mid B_{\text{RXCB}}^c] - \mathbf{P}[G_{\mathbf{e}} \mid B_{\mathbf{e}}^c \cap \Omega^c]\mathbf{P}[\Omega^c \mid B_{\mathbf{e}}^c] \\
&= A_{\text{RXCB}} - \mathbf{P}[G_{\mathbf{e}} \mid B_{\mathbf{e}}^c \cap \Omega^c]\mathbf{P}[\Omega^c \mid B_{\mathbf{e}}^c] \\
&\geq A_{\text{RXCB}} - \mathbf{P}[\Omega^c \mid B_{\mathbf{e}}^c], \tag{25}
\end{aligned}$$

using the facts outlined above. Here A_{RXCB} denotes the adversary's advantage at distinguishing RXCB from a randomly chosen ALPA.

We next consider the case in which XCB is used exactly as defined in Algorithm 1, with K_c, K_d, K_e, and H being derived via seven invocations of $\mathbf{e}$, instead of being set to uniformly random values. Consider the experiment of distinguishing XCB from RXCB; from Lemma 4, we know that

$$A_{\mathrm{XCB}} - A_{\mathrm{RXCB}} = 43 \cdot 2^{-w-1}.$$

Combining this result with Equation 25 gives the theorem.   □

A Generic Method to Design Modes of Operation Beyond the Birthday Bound[*]

David Lefranc[1], Philippe Painchault[1], Valérie Rouat[2], and Emmanuel Mayer[2]

[1] Cryptology Laboratory
Thales
160 Boulevard de Valmy – BP 82
92704 Colombes Cedex – France
firstname.lastname@fr.thalesgroup.com
[2] DGA / CELAR
BP 57419
35174 Bruz Cedex – France
firstname.lastname@dga.defense.gouv.fr

Abstract. Given a PRP defined over $\{0,1\}^n$, we describe a new generic and efficient method to obtain modes of operation with a security level beyond the birthday bound $2^{n/2}$. These new modes, named NEMO (for New Encryption Modes of Operation), are based on a new contribution to the problem of transforming a PRP into a PRF. According to our approach, any generator matrix of a linear code of minimal distance d, $d \geq 1$, can be used to design a PRF with a security of order $2^{dn/(d+1)}$. Such PRFs can be used to obtain NEMO, the security level of which is of the same order $(2^{dn/(d+1)})$. In particular, the well-known counter mode becomes a particular case when considering the identity linear code (of minimal distance $d = 1$) and the mode of operation CENC [7] corresponds to the case of the the the parity check linear code of minimal distance $d = 2$. Any other generator matrix leads to a new PRF and a new mode of operation. We give an illustrative example using $d = 4$ which reaches the security level $2^{4n/5}$ with a computation overhead less than 4% in comparison to the counter mode.

Keywords: symmetric encryption, modes of operation, PRP, PRF, birthday bound, counter mode, CENC.

1 Introduction

An encryption mode of operation is an algorithm which uses a pseudo-random permutation (PRP) defined over $\{0,1\}^n$ to encrypt a message of size tn bits into a string of size tn bits. Several modes of operation exist such as electronic code book (ECB), chaining block cipher (CBC), counter (CTR). The latter is one of the most interesting since it presents both efficiency and security.

Using the framework of [4] for concrete security, Bellare *et al.* [2] proved the two following properties.

---

[*] Patent pending.

C. Adams, A. Miri, and M. Wiener (Eds.): SAC 2007, LNCS 4876, pp. 328–343, 2007.
© Springer-Verlag Berlin Heidelberg 2007

- The CTR mode used with a PRP defined over $\{0, 1\}^n$ cannot be used to encrypt more than $2^{n/2}$ blocks; this bound is generally called the *birthday bound*.
- The CTR mode used with a PRF is as secure as the PRF itself.

The birthday bound concerns almost all modes of operation when using a PRP as primitive. But, reaching a security level beyond such a bound can be easily obtained using a pseudo-random function (PRF) instead of a PRP. However, such an approach is not widespread. Some reasons can explain this fact: on one hand, block ciphers (PRP) have been studied and cryptanalyzed for several years so that they are implemented everywhere; on the other hand, designing a secure and efficient PRF from scratch is not so easy.

An alternative to this lack of consideration for PRFs consists in constructing a PRF from a given PRP. Such a problem has already been extensively analyzed. For example, in 1998, Bellare *et al.* [5] suggested the *re-keying construction* an illustrative special case of which the PRF F is defined from the PRP E by $F(K, x) = E\big(E(K, x), x\big)$. But, this solution significantly increases the number of calls to the PRP.

In 1998, Hall *et al.* [6] suggested the *truncate construction*. It truncates the output of the given PRP, but it does not preserve the security of the latter.

In 2000, Lucks [9] suggested the construction

$$Twin^d(K, x) = E(K, dx) \oplus E(K, dx + 1) \ldots \oplus E(K, dx + d - 1)$$

for all $d \geq 1$ (the case $d = 2$ has also been independently analyzed in [3]). The security of $Twin^d$ depends on d: the larger d, the more secure the PRF. According to a targeted level of security, an adequate value d can be chosen. However, the computation overhead is also highly dependant on d.

Finally, in 2006, Iwata suggested the mode of operation CENC [7]. To our knowledge, it is the only mode (with a full[1] security proof) that is beyond the birthday bound. CENC is also based on a PRF built from a PRP. The main advantage of this PRF is that it outputs a string of several blocks of n bits (not only one n-bit block as $Twin^d$). However, the level of security can not be adjusted.

In this paper, we add a new contribution to the problem of constructing a PRF from a PRP. Our solution is the convergence of $Twin^d$ and CENC without their drawbacks. We propose a generic method to construct efficient PRFs with several n-bit output blocks (as the one involved in CENC) and with an adjustable security level (as $Twin^d$) of order $2^{dn/(d+1)}$ depending on a parameter d. Our approach is based on linear code theory. More precisely, it relies on the generator matrix associated to a linear code of minimal distance d. Our solution is both a theoretical generalisation and a practical method to obtain secure and efficient PRFs from PRPs.

---

[1] Two modes of operation beyond the birthday bound have been suggested, but one of them was proved in a weak security model [1] and the other one has no security proof [8].

With such a generalization, the PRF involved in CENC becomes a particular case of our method when used with the parity check code ($d = 2$). And, considering any linear code of minimal distance $d \geq 3$ leads to a new PRF with a level of security of order (at least) $2^{3n/4}$ which is beyond the security of Iwata's PRF.

The organisation of this paper is the following. In section 2, we recall security notions and we describe more precisely $Twin^d$ and the PRF of CENC. In section 3, we describe our generic method to obtain new PRFs with a security level of order $2^{dn/(d+1)}$. In particular, we show that the PRF of CENC becomes a particular case of our construction, when considering the parity check code (of minimal distance $d = 2$). In section 4, we describe NEMO, our New Encryption Modes of Operation which preserve the security of our PRFs. Finally, in section 5, we present a direct application of our method to obtain a PRF with a security level of order $2^{4n/5}$. This PRF can be used to obtain a mode of operation with a security level of order $2^{4n/5}$ with a computation overhead around 4% (in comparison to the CTR mode).

2   Preliminaries

2.1   PRFs and PRPs Security

We denote by $Rand(m, n)$ the set of all functions $F : \{0, 1\}^m \rightarrow \{0, 1\}^n$ and we denote by $Perm(n)$ the set of all permutations defined over $\{0, 1\}^n$.

Let $E : \{0, 1\}^k \times \{0, 1\}^n \rightarrow \{0, 1\}^n$ be a block cipher. For each key $K \in \{0, 1\}^k$, we denote by E_K the bijection defined by $E_K(x) = E(K, x)$. A block cipher E determines the family

$$\mathcal{F}(E) = \left\{ E_K, K \in \{0, 1\}^k \right\}.$$

Let $\mathcal{D}$ be an algorithm, called a distinguisher, having access to an oracle parametrized by a bit b. According to b, the oracle simulates a function randomly chosen in $\mathcal{F}(E)$ or in $Rand(n, n)$. We denote by $\mathcal{D}(t, q)$ an algorithm $\mathcal{D}$ making q queries to the oracle and with a running time bounded by t.

The adversarial (distinguisher) advantage $\mathrm{Adv}_E^{\mathrm{prf}}(t, q)$ in distinguishing the block cipher from a truly random function is a good estimate for the quality of a block cipher. It is defined by

$$\mathrm{Adv}_E^{\mathrm{prf}}(t, q) = \max_{\mathcal{D}(t, q)} \left\{ \Pr[\mathcal{D} = 1 \mid b = 1] - \Pr[\mathcal{D} = 1 \mid b = 0] \right\}.$$

In the same way, we now assume that the oracle simulates a function randomly chosen in $\mathcal{F}(E)$ or in $Perm(n)$. The adversarial (distinguisher) advantage $\mathrm{Adv}_E^{\mathrm{prp}}(t, q)$ in distinguishing the block cipher from a truly random permutation is a good estimate for the quality of a block cipher. It is defined by

$$\mathrm{Adv}_E^{\mathrm{prp}}(t, q) = \max_{\mathcal{D}(t, q)} \left\{ \Pr[\mathcal{D} = 1 \mid b = 1] - \Pr[\mathcal{D} = 1 \mid b = 0] \right\}.$$

2.2 Security Analysis of Modes of Operation

To analyze the security of a mode of operation used with a block cipher E, we consider the real or random indistinguishably notion [2] against a chosen plaintext attack (cpa). More precisely, let $\mathcal{A}$ be an adversary having access to an oracle parametrized by a bit b. According to b, the oracle encrypts the requested plaintext or a random string of the same size. We denote by $\mathcal{A}(t, q)$ an adversary making q requests to the oracle and $\mathcal{A}$ with a running time bounded by t.

The security of the mode of operation $mode[E]$ in the real or random model against a chosen plaintext attack is denoted by $\mathrm{Adv}^{\mathrm{ror\text{-}cpa}}_{mode[E]}(t, q)$ and is defined by

$$\mathrm{Adv}^{\mathrm{ror\text{-}cpa}}_{mode[E]}(t, q) = \max_{\mathcal{A}(t,q)} \left\{ \Pr[\mathcal{A} = 1 \mid b = 1] - \Pr[\mathcal{A} = 1 \mid b = 0] \right\}.$$

2.3 The $Twin^d$ Construction

In [9], Lucks analyzes the security of the PRF $Twin^d$. Let $P \in Perm(n)$, $Twin^d$ is defined by

$$Twin^d : \{0, 1\}^{n - \lceil \log_2 d \rceil} \longrightarrow \{0, 1\}^n$$
$$x \longmapsto P(dx) \oplus P(dx + 1) \oplus \cdots \oplus P(dx + d - 1).$$

The security of $Twin^d$ is given by $\mathrm{Adv}^{\mathrm{prf}}_{Twin^d}(t, q) \leq \frac{qd^2}{2^n} + \frac{d^d}{2^{dn-1}} \sum_{0 \leq i < q} i^d$, for any q, $q \leq 2^{n-1}/d^2$.

2.4 The CENC Construction

CENC is a mode of operation presented by Iwata [7]. It is based on a PRF, denoted by F^+ which has two parameters: a permutation P of $Perm(n)$ and an integer u. The PRF F^+ is defined by

$$F^+ : \{0, 1\}^n \longrightarrow \left(\{0, 1\}^n\right)^u$$
$$x \longmapsto \left(P(x) \oplus P(x+1), P(x) \oplus P(x+2), \ldots, P(x) \oplus P(x+u)\right).$$

The security of F^+ is given by $\mathrm{Adv}^{\mathrm{prf}}_{F^+}(t, q) \leq \frac{(u+1)^4 q^3}{2^{2n+1}} + \frac{u(u+1)q}{2^{n+1}}$ assuming all the q requests x_i, are such that for all i, j, $1 \leq i < j \leq q$, the sets $\{x_i, x_i + 1, \ldots, x_i + u\}$ and $\{x_j, x_j + 1, \ldots, x_j + u\}$ are disjoint. Such a constraint does not matter since it exactly reflects the different calls to F^+ in CENC. Indeed, given a message of size kun bits, the algorithm CENC uses k calls to the PRF F^+. The first nu bits are encrypted using the output of $F^+(x)$, the nu following bits are encrypted using the output of $F^+(x + u + 1)$ and so on until the nu last bits encrypted using the output of $F^+\left(x + (k - 1)(u + 1)\right)$.

3   New PRFs Based on Linear Code

3.1   Description

Let P be a permutation in $Perm(n)$. Our new PRFs are parametrized by a generator matrix $G = (g_{i,j}) \in \mathcal{M}_{u \times \ell}(GF(2))$, associated to a linear code defined over $GF(2)$ of length ℓ, of dimension u and of minimal distance d so that G is of size $u \times \ell$. Define $\omega = 1 + \lfloor \log_2 \ell \rfloor$. For any given generator matrix G and any permutation P, we construct a new PRF $F : \{0,1\}^{n-\omega} \to (\{0,1\}^n)^u$, defined by

$$F(x) = \Big(\bigoplus_{\substack{1 \le j \le \ell \\ g_{1,j} \ne 0}} P(\ell x + j - 1), \bigoplus_{\substack{1 \le j \le \ell \\ g_{2,j} \ne 0}} P(\ell x + j - 1), \ldots, \bigoplus_{\substack{1 \le j \le \ell \\ g_{u,j} \ne 0}} P(\ell x + j - 1) \Big).$$

As for $Twin^d$ and the underlying PRF of CENC, when using this PRF for encryption, we will rather use a modification of this PRF to be able to use n-bit input strings instead of $(n - \omega)$-bit input strings. Thus, in the following we will consider and prove the security of the PRF $F^+ : \{0,1\}^n \to (\{0,1\}^n)^u$ defined by

$$F^+(x) = \Big(\bigoplus_{\substack{1 \le j \le \ell \\ g_{1,j} \ne 0}} P(x + j - 1), \bigoplus_{\substack{1 \le j \le \ell \\ g_{2,j} \ne 0}} P(x + j - 1), \ldots, \bigoplus_{\substack{1 \le j \le \ell \\ g_{u,j} \ne 0}} P(x + j - 1) \Big).$$

The security analysis will be the same as for F, since during the proof we assume that the q requests x_i, $1 \le i \le q$, are such that for all i, j, $1 \le i < j \le q$, the sets $\{x_i, x_i + 1, \ldots, x_i + \ell - 1\}$ and $\{x_j, x_j + 1, \ldots, x_j + \ell - 1\}$ are disjoint.

3.2   Example

Let us consider the matrix G of size $u \times \ell$ with $\ell = u + 1$ associated to the parity check code of minimal distance $d = 2$. The canonical form of G corresponds to the identity matrix $u \times u$ with a last additional column filled with "1". An equivalent form of the matrix G is

$$G' = \begin{bmatrix} 1 & 1 & 0 & 0 & \ldots & 0 & 0 & 0 \\ 1 & 0 & 1 & 0 & \ldots & 0 & 0 & 0 \\ & & & & \vdots & & & \\ 1 & 0 & 0 & 0 & \ldots & 0 & 1 & 0 \\ 1 & 0 & 0 & 0 & \ldots & 0 & 0 & 1 \end{bmatrix}.$$

According to our method, this matrix defines a PRF $F^+ : \{0,1\}^n \to (\{0,1\}^n)^u$ such that

$$F^+(x) = \big(P(x) \oplus P(x + 1), P(x) \oplus P(x + 2), \ldots, P(x) \oplus P(x + u) \big).$$

Thus, to encrypt u blocks, it requires $u + 1$ calls to the permutation P.

This PRF is exactly the same as the one from CENC (see section 2.4). The security bound given by Iwata is

$$\mathrm{Adv}_{F+}^{\mathrm{prf}}(t, q) \leq \frac{(u+1)^4 q^3}{2^{2n+1}} + \frac{u(u+1)q}{2^{n+1}}$$

in comparison with our bound (given in theorem 1) equal to

$$\mathrm{Adv}_{F+}^{\mathrm{prf}}(t, q) \leq \frac{(u+1)^4 q^3}{2^{2n}} + \frac{(u+1)^2 q}{2^n}.$$

A second example consists in considering the generator matrix $u \times u$ of the identity code (of minimal distance $d = 1$). Our PRF F^+ just corresponds to the PRP, and has the same security (*i.e.* $\frac{q u^2}{2^n} + \frac{u^2 q^2}{2^n}$). Indeed, we obtain $F^+(x) = (P(x), P(x+1), \ldots, P(x + u - 1))$. Our security bound is of same order as the birthday bound (security of any permutation). Our bound is not optimal because of the method used in the security proof (however, the significant terms are almost the same).

3.3   Security Theorem

The security of our new PRFs is given in the following theorem.

Theorem 1. *Let* $G = (g_{i,j}) \in \mathcal{M}_{u \times \ell}(GF(2))$ *a generator matrix associated to a linear code defined over* $GF(2)$, *of length* ℓ, *of dimension* u *and of minimal distance* d. *Let* P *be a random permutation with an* n-*bit output. Let* F^+ *be our PRF parametrized with* G *and* P. *Let* q *be the number of requests* x_i *(*$1 \leq i \leq q$*) sent to the oracle. If* $q \leq 2^{n-1}/\ell^2$, *and if for all* i, j, $1 \leq i < j \leq q$, $\{x_i, x_i + 1, \ldots, x_i + \ell - 1\} \cap \{x_j, x_j + 1, \ldots, x_j + \ell - 1\} = \emptyset$, *then*

$$Adv_{F+}^{prf}(t, q) \leq \frac{q\,\ell^2}{2^n} + \frac{N\,\ell^d\,q^{d+1}}{2^{dn}}$$

with $N = \sum_{k=0}^{u-1} \binom{d+k-1}{d-1}$.

Remark 1. The binomial coefficient $\binom{d+k-1}{d-1}$ involved in N can be bounded by $(d + k - 1)^{d-1}$ so that

$$N = \sum_{k=0}^{u-1} \binom{d+k-1}{d-1} \leq \sum_{k=0}^{u-1}(d+k-1)^{d-1} \leq u(d+u-2)^{d-1} \leq \ell^d.$$

The last inequality relies on the Singleton bound recalled in definition 3. As a consequence,

$$\mathrm{Adv}_{F+}^{\mathrm{prf}}(t, q) \leq \frac{q\,\ell^2}{2^n} + \frac{\ell^{2d}\,q^{d+1}}{2^{dn}}.$$

The proof of the theorem is given in appendix A.

4 NEMO: New Encryption Modes of Operation Beyond the Birthday Bound

4.1 Description

We describe how to use our new PRFs to obtain NEMO. The approach is the same as the one used in CENC and is a generalisation of the counter mode.

Let P be a n-bit permutation, G be a generator matrix of size $u \times \ell$ of a binary linear code (of minimal distance d), $F^+ : \{0,1\}^n \to \left(\{0,1\}^n\right)^u$ be our new PRF constructed from P and G, and M be a message of size m n-bit blocks denoted by $M_1, \ldots, M_m$ ($m \geq 1$). Let α and r be such that $0 \leq \alpha$, $0 \leq r < u$ and $m = \alpha \times u + r$. To encrypt M, F^+ can be used to obtain a mode denoted NEMO[F^+], as described in algorithm 1.

Algorithm 1. NEMO[F^+] : a mode of operation using our PRF F^+

Input: a message M of $\alpha \times u + r$ n-bit blocks denoted by M_j, $1 \leq j \leq \alpha \times u + r$.
Output: the encrypted message C of $\alpha \times u + r$ n-bit blocks associated to M.

Let x be an initial value.
for i **from** 0 **to** $\alpha - 1$ **do**
    Compute $F^+(x + i \times \ell) = (S_1, \ldots, S_u) \in \left(\{0,1\}^n\right)^u$
    for j **from** 1 **to** u **do**
        $C_{i \times u + j} = M_{i \times u + j} \oplus S_j$
    Compute $F^+(x + \alpha \times \ell) = (S_1, \ldots, S_u) \in \left(\{0,1\}^n\right)^u$
    for j **from** 1 **to** r **do**
        $C_{\alpha \times u + j} = M_{\alpha \times u + j} \oplus S_j$
    Store $x + (\alpha + 1) \times \ell$ in place of x
    Return $C_1, \ldots, C_{\alpha \times u + r}$

4.2 Security of NEMO

We give the security level of NEMO using the framework recalled in section 2.2.

Theorem 2. *Let P be a n-bit random permutation. Let $G = (g_{i,j}) \in \mathcal{M}_{u \times \ell}$ $(GF(2))$ a generator matrix associated to a linear code defined over $GF(2)$, of length ℓ, of dimension u and of minimal distance d. Let F^+ be the PRF parametrized with G. Let NEMO[F^+] be the mode of operation described in algorithm 1. Then, we have*

$$Adv_{\text{NEMO}[F^+]}^{ror\text{-}cpa}(t,q) \leq \frac{(L/u + q)\ell^2}{2^n} + \frac{N\,\ell^d\,(L/u + q)^{d+1}}{2^{dn}}$$

with $N = \sum_{k=0}^{u-1} \binom{d+k-1}{d-1}$ and L is the overall number of n-bit blocks requested to the oracle.

Remark 2. The security level of the mode of operation relies on the term $\frac{N\,\ell^d\,(L/u+q)^{d+1}}{2^{dn}}$ which is of order $\mathcal{O}\left(\frac{q^{d+1}}{2^{dn}}\right)$. The security of NEMO is beyond the birthday bound for any $d \geq 2$.

Proof. The proof of this theorem is quite simple. It relies on a contradiction argument. Let $\mathcal{A}(t, q)$ be an adversary with a running time bounded by t and making q requests to an oracle parametrized by a bit b. According to b, the oracle encrypts the requested plaintext or a random string of the same size. We denote by M_i, $1 \le i \le q$, the q messages requested to the oracle. For all i, $1 \le i \le q$, we denote by L_i the n-bit block size of M_i and we define $L = L_1 + \cdots + L_q$.

The q requests M_i leads to $\lceil L_1/u \rceil + \lceil L_2/u \rceil + \cdots + \lceil L_q/u \rceil \le L/u + q = \tilde{q}$ calls to the PRF F^+. Thus if the advantage of the adversary is greater than

$$\frac{\tilde{q}\,\ell^2}{2^n} + \frac{N\,\ell^d\,\tilde{q}^{d+1}}{2^{dn}}$$

with $N = \sum_{k=0}^{u-1} \binom{d+k-1}{d-1}$, this adversary can be used to obtain the same advantage against our new PRF, which is in contradiction with the security of the PRF given in theorem 1.

5 Applications

In this section we present a direct application of our method to construct a PRF with a high level of security. The security level of the CTR mode and of the CENC mode are respectively of order $2^{n/2}$ and of order $2^{2n/3}$. Using a linear code, the minimal distance of which is $d = 4$, we build a PRF with a level of security of order $2^{dn/(d+1)} = 2^{4n/5}$.

Let C be a linear code of length 256 and of dimension 247. Its minimal distance is 4. The generator matrix of C may be viewed as the join of two matrices $C = (M|I)$ where M is a matrix with 247 rows and 9 columns, and where I is the identity matrix of dimension 247. The transpose of M is equal to

$$
\left(
\begin{smallmatrix}
1111111111111111111111111111111111111111111111111 \\
1111111111111111111111111111111111111111111111111 \\
1111111111111111111111111110000000000000000000000 \\
1111111111111110000000000000111111100000000000000 \\
1111110000011111110000000011111110000000111111000 \\
1100110001110011000011110001110011000111001110011 \\
1010101010101010101010101010101010101010101010101 \\
1001011001101001011010010110100110010110100101101 \\
1001011001101001011010010110100110010110100101101 \\
\end{smallmatrix}
\cdots
\right.
$$

$$
\cdots
\begin{smallmatrix}
1111111111111111110000000000000000000000000000000 \\
0000000000001111111111111111111111111111100000000 \\
0000000000001111111111111111111111111111100000000 \\
1111100000001111111000000000111111100000001111111 \\
1100001111000111000011100001110000111000011100001 \\
1010101010101010101010101010101010101010101010101 \\
0101100110100101100101101001011010010110100101100 \\
\end{smallmatrix}
\cdots
$$

$$
\cdots
\begin{smallmatrix}
1111111111111111111111110000000000000000000000000 \\
0000000000000000000000011111111111111111111111111 \\
0000000000000000000000011111111111111111111111111 \\
1111111111110000000000011111111111111111111000000 \\
0000111100001111000011100001110001111000011100001 \\
1010101010101010101010101010101010101010101010101 \\
0110011010010110100101100101101001011010010110101 \\
\end{smallmatrix}
\cdots
$$

$$
\cdots
\begin{smallmatrix}
0000000000000000000000000000000000000000000000000 \\
1111111111111111111111111111111111110000000000000 \\
1111111111100000000000000000000000000000001111111 \\
0000000011111111111111111000000000011111111000000 \\
1001100011100110001110011000111001100011100111000 \\
0101010101010101010101010101010101010101010101010 \\
0011010010110010110100110100101101001011100101101 \\
\end{smallmatrix}
\right)
$$

$$
\left(
\begin{smallmatrix}
0000000000000000000000000000000000000000000000000 \\
0000000000000000000000000000000000000000000000000 \\
1111111111111111111111110000000000000000000000000 \\
1111110000000000000011111111111111111111000000000 \\
0000011111100000000111111100000000011111110000000 \\
1100000111110001100011000111001110010011001110011 \\
1010101010101010101010101010101010101010101010101 \\
1010010110100110010110100110100101101001011010111 \\
\end{smallmatrix}
\right)
.
$$

The information rate of C is $247/256 \approx 0.965$. This means that the computation overhead in comparison to the counter mode is between 3% and 4%. In this construction, we need to compute and store 9 cipher blocks. The 247 next outputs will be the combination of one new cipher block with some of the first 9 cipher blocks.

6   Conclusion

In this paper we present a new contribution to the problem of transforming a PRP into a PRF. Our new construction allow to reach a security level beyond the birthday bound $(2^{n/2})$. It is based on a linear code with a minimal distance d, and its security level is of order $2^{dn/(d+1)}$. This work leads to New Encryption Modes of Operation, named NEMO, which generalize the CTR mode, and the CENC mode. Actually, the CTR mode can be built from a linear code, the minimal distance of which is 1, and the CENC mode can be seen as a special case of our model with a linear code, the minimal distance of which is 2. From a practical point of view, the computation overhead is very small and tends to zero.

References

1. Belal, A.A., Abdel-Gawad, M.A.: 2D-Encryption Mode. In: Schmalz, M.S. (ed.) SPIE 2003, vol. 4793, pp. 64–75 (2003)
2. Bellare, M., Desai, A., Jokipii, E., Rogaway, P.: A Concrete Security Treatment of Symmetric Encryption. In: FOCS 1997 (1997)
3. Bellare, M., Impagliazzo, R.: A tool for obtaining tighter security analyses of pseudorandom function based constructions, with applications to PRP to PRF conversion (1999)
4. Bellare, M., Kilian, J., Rogaway, P.: The Security of Cipher Block Chaining. In: Desmedt, Y.G. (ed.) CRYPTO 1994. LNCS, vol. 839, pp. 341–358. Springer, Heidelberg (1994)
5. Bellare, M., Krovetz, T., Rogaway, P.: Luby-Rackoff Backwards: increasing Security by Making Block Ciphers Non-invertible. In: Nyberg, K. (ed.) EUROCRYPT 1998. LNCS, vol. 1403, pp. 266–280. Springer, Heidelberg (1998)
6. Hall, C., Wagner, D., Kelsey, J., Schneier, B.: Building PRFs from PRPs. In: Krawczyk, H. (ed.) CRYPTO 1998. LNCS, vol. 1462, pp. 370–389. Springer, Heidelberg (1998)
7. Iwata, T.: New Blockcipher Modes of Operation with Beyond the Birthday Bound Security. In: Robshaw, M. (ed.) FSE 2006. LNCS, vol. 4047, pp. 310–327. Springer, Heidelberg (2006)
8. Knudsen, L.R.: Block Chaining Modes of Operation. NIST call for new modes of operation (2000)
9. Lucks, S.: The Sum of PRPs Is a Secure PRF. In: Preneel, B. (ed.) EUROCRYPT 2000. LNCS, vol. 1807, pp. 470–484. Springer, Heidelberg (2000)
10. MacWilliams, F.J., Sloane, N.J.A.: The theory of error-correcting codes. North-Holland, Amsterdam (1977)

A Security Proof of Theorem 1

A.1 Notations and Definitions

To make easier the understanding of the proof, we introduce the following notations. From an n-bit input x, the computation of $F^+(x)$ can be decomposed in the two following steps:

- compute the ℓ-tuple $\big(P(x), P(x+1), \ldots, P(x+\ell-1)\big)$,
- apply to the above ℓ-tuple an application denoted $\tilde{F}^+ : \big(\{0,1\}^n\big)^\ell \rightarrow \big(\{0,1\}^n\big)^u$ such that $\tilde{F}^+\big(P(x), \ldots, P(x+\ell-1)\big)$ is equal to

$$\Big(\bigoplus_{\substack{1 \le j \le \ell \\ g_{1,j} \ne 0}} P(x+j-1), \bigoplus_{\substack{1 \le j \le \ell \\ g_{2,j} \ne 0}} P(x+j-1), \ldots, \bigoplus_{\substack{1 \le j \le \ell \\ g_{u,j} \ne 0}} P(x+j-1) \Big).$$

The function $\tilde{F}^+$ is defined by the matrix G.

Lucks has introduced properties to prove the security of $Twin^d$ [9]. He only considers the case of an image set included in $\{0,1\}^n$. Here we extend his definitions to fit with image sets included in $\big(\{0,1\}^n\big)^u$.

Definition 1. *Let ℓ and u be two integers and $f : \big(\{0,1\}^n\big)^\ell \rightarrow \big(\{0,1\}^n\big)^u$. The set $T \subseteq \big(\{0,1\}^n\big)^\ell$ is* fair *for f, if for every $y \in \big(\{0,1\}^n\big)^u$*

$$\Big|\big\{(t_1, \ldots, t_\ell) \in T \mid f(t_1, t_2, \ldots, t_\ell) = y\big\}\Big| = \frac{|T|}{2^{un}}.$$

If $T \subseteq \big(\{0,1\}^n\big)^\ell$ is fair for $f : \big(\{0,1\}^n\big)^\ell \rightarrow \big(\{0,1\}^n\big)^u$, there is a uniform distribution over the output of f when applied to an element randomly picked in T. However, we will consider sets that are not fair, but almost fair. Such a property is defined as follows.

Definition 2. *Let ℓ and u be two integers and $f : \big(\{0,1\}^n\big)^\ell \rightarrow \big(\{0,1\}^n\big)^u$. The set $T \subseteq \big(\{0,1\}^n\big)^\ell$ is* z-fair *for f, if:*

- *a set $V \subseteq \big(\{0,1\}^n\big)^\ell$ exists with $|V| = z$ and $V \cap T = \emptyset$, such that $V \cup T$ is fair for f. The set V is called a "completion set" for T;*
- *or if a set $U \subseteq T$ with $|U| = z$ exists such that $T \setminus U$ is fair for f. The set U is is called an "overhanging set" for T.*

During the proof, we will also require some linear code theory results. In particular, we recall the Singleton bound (see [10] for example).

Definition 3 (Singleton bound). *Any linear code of length ℓ, of dimension u and of minimal distance d verifies $\ell - u \ge d - 1$.*

An other important result is that any generator matrix of size $u \times \ell$ associated to a linear code defined over $GF(2)$, of length ℓ and of dimension u has some equivalent forms in which the identity matrix of $u \times u$ appears.

A.2   Overview of the Proof

As recalled in section 2.1, to analyse the security of our PRF, we consider a distinguisher making q requests x_i, $1 \leq i \leq q$, to an oracle. The latter simulates the PRF or a random function of $Rand(n, nu)$, depending on the value of a bit parameter b.

The general idea of the proof is the same as the one for $Twin^d$ [9]. For a given request x_i, $1 \leq i \leq q$, we denote T_i the set of all possible instantiations of the ℓ-tuple $\big(P(x_i), P(x_i + 1), \ldots, P(x_i + \ell - 1)\big)$. To simulate our PRF, the oracle randomly picks an element in T_i and apply $\tilde{F}^+$ on it. For each request, if the set T_i is fair (see definition 1 on the previous page), there is a uniform distribution over the output of $\tilde{F}^+$ so that the distinguisher has no advantage (to determine the value of the bit b).

However, the set T_i is not fair. The goal of the proof is to show that T_i is almost fair, i.e. T_i is z_i-fair, for a given z_i to determine. Let us denote T_i^* the fair set obtained from T_i. We analyse the oracle simulation assuming it randomly picks an ℓ-tuple in T_i^* instead of T_i. In a second step of the simulation, the oracle will verify that the selected element can actually be used as an instantiation, i.e. it is also in T_i (so that the simulation is not altered).

As it will be proved, T_i^* and T_i will only differ from few elements; i.e. T_i is z_i-fair with a small z_i. Thus, if the selected ℓ-tuple is in $T_i^* \cap T_i$ (most of the time as proved later), the distinguisher has no advantage over the bit b. And, if the picked element is not in $T_i^* \cap T_i$, the probability of such an event (equals to $z_i/|T_i|$) bounds the advantage of the distinguisher for the request. By summing this advantage among the q different requests, we obtain the advantage of the distinguisher.

The main goal of the proof is to bound the value z_i, for each request x_i, $1 \leq i \leq q$.

A.3   Security Analysis of F^+ (and F)

In theorem 1, the hypothesis $\forall (i, j) \in \mathbb{N}^2$, $1 \leq i < j \leq q$, $\{x_i, x_i + 1, \ldots, x_i + \ell - 1\} \cap \{x_j, x_j + 1, \ldots, x_j + \ell - 1\} = \emptyset$ ensures that among the q requests x_i, we will exactly have to instantiate $q \times \ell$ outputs of the permutation P since there will not exist collision over the input of the permutation P. For each request x_i, $1 \leq i \leq q$, we denote

- T_i the set of all possible instantiations of $\big(P(x_i), P(x_i+1), \ldots, P(x_i+\ell-1)\big)$;
- T_i^* the fair set constructed from T_i;
- $(\pi_{i,1}, \ldots, \pi_{i,\ell})$ the ℓ-tuple used to instantiate $\big(P(x_i), \ldots, P(x_i + \ell - 1)\big)$;
- L_i, the set of all the values $\pi_{k,j}$, $1 \leq k < i$, $1 \leq j \leq \ell$ appearing in the chosen instantiations of previous requests x_k, $1 \leq k < i$.

Remark 3. For all i, $2 \leq i \leq q - 1$, $|L_i| = \ell(i - 1)$.

Simulation Description. The oracle simulation can be summed up by algorithm 2 on page 340. In a first step of the simulation, for each request x_i,

$1 \leq i \leq q$, we first accept to instantiate $(P(x_i), P(x_i + 1), \ldots, P(x_i + \ell - 1))$ with ℓ-tuples containing eventually two equal components (which cannot exist since P is a permutation). Thus, we consider T_i defined by

$$T_i = \Big\{ (t_1, \ldots, t_\ell), \quad \forall j, \quad 1 \leq j \leq \ell, \quad t_j \in \{0,1\}^n \setminus L_i \Big\}.$$

Note that the cardinality of T_i verifies

$$
\begin{aligned}
|T_i| &= \big(2^n - \ell(i-1)\big)^\ell \\
&\geq 2^{\ell n} - \ell\big(\ell\,(i-1)\,2^{\ell(n-1)}\big) = 2^{\ell n} - \ell^2\,(i-1)\,2^{\ell(n-1)}.
\end{aligned}
\tag{1}
$$

The fair set T_i^* also contains ℓ-tuples with eventually two equal components. As said in the overview of the proof, the oracle first randomly picks $(\pi_{i,1}, \pi_{i,2}, \ldots, \pi_{i,\ell})$ in the fair set T_i^*. In a second step, the oracle checks if $(\pi_{i,1}, \pi_{i,2}, \ldots, \pi_{i,\ell})$ is also in $T_i^* \cap T_i$. If not, (step denoted "Bad case 1" in algorithm 2 on the next page), the oracle then randomly picks a new ℓ-tuple in T_i.

Finally, let C^* be the subset of $\big(\{0,1\}^n\big)^\ell$ containing ℓ-tuples with at least 2 equal components. The cardinality of C^* is bounded by

$$(2^n - |L_i|)^{\ell-1} \binom{\ell}{2} \leq (2^n)^{\ell-1}\ell^2/2.$$

The oracle checks if $(\pi_{i,1}, \pi_{i,2}, \ldots, \pi_{i,\ell})$ is in C^*. In such a case (denoted "Bad case 2" in algorithm 2) a new ℓ-tuple with ℓ different components is randomly picked in $T_i \cap \overline{C^*}$. (Thus, for each request x_i, $1 \leq i \leq q$, the set L_i always contains exactly $\ell(i-1)$ elements).

These two steps "Bad case 1" and "Bad case 2" ensure a valid oracle simulation and if no such "bad case" appends, the distinguisher has no advantage since the ℓ-tuple has been randomly picked in a fair set. The advantage of the distinguisher is bounded by the probability of the event "Bad case 1" or "Bad case 2". The main technical point of the proof is to bound the value z_i such that the T_i, $1 \leq i \leq q$, is z_i-fair.

Fairness of T_i. We first give a useful lemma. Without loss of generality, we assume that the u columns of identity matrix $u \times u$ are already in G.

Lemma 1. *Let G be the generator matrix (of size $u \times \ell$) associated to a linear code defined over $GF(2)$, of length ℓ, of dimension u and of minimal distance d such that the u columns of the identity matrix are the u columns $i_1, \ldots, i_u$ of G. Let $\tilde{F}^+$ be the function defined on page 337 and let $T \subseteq \big(\{0,1\}^n\big)^\ell$. If the components $i_1, \ldots, i_u$ of T are defined over $\{0,1\}^n$, then the set T is fair for $\tilde{F}^+$.*

Proof. The components $i_1, \ldots, i_u$ of T are associated to the columns of the identity matrix appearing in G. Thus, these components correspond to the terms $P(x - 1 + j)$, for all $j \in \{i_1, \ldots, i_u\}$ and are used only once and each for only one of the u components of the output of $\tilde{F}^+$. Thus, for any instantiation of the $\ell - u$

Algorithm 2. Oracle simulation

$bad \leftarrow 0$
for i **from** 1 **to** q **do**
    Determine the fair set T_i^* from T_i
    Randomly pick an element $(\pi_{i,1}, \ldots \pi_{i,\ell})$ in T_i^*
    {Bad case 1}
    if $(\pi_{i,1}, \ldots \pi_{i,\ell}) \notin T_i^* \cap T_i$ **then**
        $bad \leftarrow 1$
        Randomly pick a new element $(\pi_{i,1}, \ldots \pi_{i,\ell})$ in T_i
    {Bad case 2}
    if $(\pi_{i,1}, \ldots \pi_{i,\ell}) \in C^*$ **then**
        $bad \leftarrow 1$
        Randomly pick a new element $(\pi_{i,1}, \ldots \pi_{i,\ell})$ in $T_i \cap \overline{C^*}$
    Output $\tilde{F}^+(\pi_{i,1}, \ldots \pi_{i,\ell})$

other components of T, there is a bijection between the image set $\left(\{0,1\}^n\right)^u$ and the u components $P(x - 1 + j)$, for all $j \in \{i_1, \ldots, i_u\}$. As a consequence, T is fair and each image element $y \in \left(\{0,1\}^n\right)^u$ is reached as often as the number of possible instantiations of the $\ell - u$ other components.

The core of the proof consists in decomposing the set T_i into a union and/or difference of subsets of $\left(\{0,1\}^n\right)^\ell$, $1 \leq j$, each verifying only one of the two following properties:

Property 1: u components $i_1, i_2, \ldots, i_u$ are defined over $\{0,1\}^n$ and there exists a generator matrix G', equivalent to G, which contains the identity matrix $u \times u$ in columns $i_1, i_2, \ldots, i_u$. Lemma 1 can be applied to conclude that the set is fair for $\tilde{F}^+$;
Property 2: d components are defined over L_i. These sets will be of negligible cardinality in comparison with the cardinality of T_i, and will correspond to completion or overhanging sets for T_i.

For the proof, we consider the list of images $\mathcal{L}(T_i)$ obtained by applying $\tilde{F}^+$ to T_i. In this list, an element of $\left(\{0,1\}^n\right)^u$ appears as often as its number of pre-images in T_i.

    The method to obtain an adequate decomposition consists in the recursive algorithm named $Decomposition(\text{MAT}, T)$ and described in algorithm 3. It takes as input a generator matrix MAT and a subset T of $\left(\{0,1\}^n\right)^\ell$. The algorithm is initialized with G and T_i.

    Let us consider the tree of the recursive execution of the algorithm $Decomposition(G, T_i)$. The root corresponds to the set T_i. At each generation of the tree, the definition set of one of the ℓ components of a given node is modified into $\{0,1\}^n$ or L_i which leads to two child nodes. Thus, after $u + d - 1$ generations in the tree, each leaf verifies property 1 or 2 (the sets involved in the $(u+d-1)^{\text{th}}$ generation of the tree contain $d - 1$ components defined over L_i and u components defined over $\{0,1\}^n$). Using the Singleton bound ($\ell \geq u + d - 1$), and since

---

Algorithm 3. *Decomposition*(MAT, T)

Let k, $1 \leq k \leq u$ be the least integer such that the kth row of MAT contains no "1" with a corresponding component in T defined over $\{0,1\}^n$. {We select the first row involving no component of T defined over $\{0,1\}^n$}

Let j, $1 \leq j \leq \ell$ be the least integer such that $\text{MAT}_{k,j} = 1$ and the jth component of T is defined over $\{0,1\}^n \setminus L_i$.

Decompose T into the form $A \setminus B$ according to the jth component such that the jth component of A and B are now defined respectively over $\{0,1\}^n$ and L_i {We obtain $\mathcal{L}(T) = \mathcal{L}(A) - \mathcal{L}(B)$}

Compute the generator matrix MAT′, equivalent to MAT, such that the kth row of MAT′ is the only row with a "1" in column j {We obtain the kth column of the identity matrix $u \times u$}

if A verifies property 1 then
  return A and execute *Decomposition*(MAT, B)
else
  if B verifies property 2 then
    return B and execute *Decomposition*(MAT′, A)
  else
    execute *Decomposition*(MAT′, A) and *Decomposition*(MAT, B)

---

the algorithm *Decomposition* is applied to G and T_i, it is always possible to obtain $u + d - 1$ generations in the tree, i.e. *Decomposition*(G, T_i) always ends with sets verifying property 1 or 2.

Let us evaluate the number denoted N of sets verifying property 2. These sets have k, $0 \leq k \leq u - 1$, components defined over $\{0,1\}^n$ among the first $k + d - 1$ generations in the tree. Thus, the number of sets verifying property 2 is given by

$$N = \sum_{k=0}^{u-1} \binom{d+k-1}{d-1}.$$

The cardinality of such a set with exactly k, $0 \leq k \leq u - 1$, components defined over $\{0,1\}^n$ is $|L_i|^d \times 2^{nk} \times (2^n - |L_i|)^{\ell - d - k}$.

When the algorithm ends, we obtain one of the two following equalities, depending of the parity of d.

$$\mathcal{L}(T_i) = \sum_j \mathcal{L}(A_j^i) - \sum_j \mathcal{L}(B_j^i) - \sum_{j=1}^{N} \mathcal{L}(C_j^i) \qquad \text{if } d \text{ is odd,} \qquad (2)$$

$$\mathcal{L}(T_i) = \sum_j \mathcal{L}(A_j^i) - \sum_j \mathcal{L}(B_j^i) + \sum_{j=1}^{N} \mathcal{L}(C_j^i) \qquad \text{if } d \text{ is even.} \qquad (3)$$

In both equalities, the sets C_j^i verify property 2 and the sets A_j^i and B_j^i verify property 1: lemma 1 can be applied, i.e. the sets A_j^i and B_j^i are fair.

After a first step of the decomposition algorithm, we obtain $\mathcal{L}(T) = \mathcal{L}(A) - \mathcal{L}(B)$ where A has no component defined over L_i and B has one component defined over L_i. When applying the algorithm to A and B, we obtain $\mathcal{L}(A) = \mathcal{L}(A_1) - \mathcal{L}(A_2)$ and $\mathcal{L}(B) = \mathcal{L}(B_1) - \mathcal{L}(B_2)$ so that we obtain $\mathcal{L}(T) = \mathcal{L}(A_1) - \mathcal{L}(A_2) - \mathcal{L}(B_1) + \mathcal{L}(B_2)$. The set A_1 has no component defined over L_i, A_2 and B_1 have one component defined over L_i and B_2 has two such components. It is quite easy to see by induction that the sign of a term $\mathcal{L}(D)$ is directly linked to the parity of the number of components of D defined over L_i. Thus, in equalities (2) and (3), the sets A^i_j (resp. B^i_j) have an even (resp. odd) number of components defined over L_i. Since the sets C^i_j have exactly d components defined over L_i, the sign of $\mathcal{L}(C^i_j)$ depends on the parity of d. This justifies the distinction over the parity of d in equalities (2) and (3).

Let us first consider equality (2). The sets C^i_j, $1 \leq j \leq N$ are not necessarily disjoint. However, if $|T_i| + \sum_{j=1}^{N} |C^i_j| \leq 2^{n\ell}$, there are enough ℓ-tuples in $\left(\{0,1\}^n\right)^\ell \setminus T_i$ to construct a set C such $\mathcal{L}(C) = \sum_{j=1}^{N} \mathcal{L}(C^i_j)$. In the same way for equality (3), if $0 \leq |T_i| - \sum_{j=1}^{N} |C^i_j|$ there is enough ℓ-tuples in T_i to construct a set $C \subseteq T_i$ such $\mathcal{L}(C) = \sum_{j=1}^{N} \mathcal{L}(C^i_j)$. Thus, we can rewrite equalities (2) and (3) as

$$\mathcal{L}(T_i \cup C) = \sum_j \mathcal{L}(A^i_j) - \sum_j \mathcal{L}(B^i_j) \qquad \text{if } d \text{ is odd,}$$

$$\mathcal{L}(T_i \setminus C) = \sum_j \mathcal{L}(A^i_j) - \sum_j \mathcal{L}(B^i_j) \qquad \text{if } d \text{ is even.}$$

Since the sets A^i_j and B^i_j are fair, the set C is a completion set for T_i if d is odd or an overhanging set for T_i if d is even. Thus, T_i is z_i-fair, with

$$z_i = |C| = \sum_{k=0}^{u-1} \binom{d+k-1}{d-1} |L_i|^d \times 2^{nk} \times (2^n - |L_i|)^{\ell-d-k}$$

$$\leq \ell^d \times |L_i|^d \times 2^{n(\ell-d)} \leq \ell^{2d}(i-1)^d \, 2^{n(\ell-d)}$$

(the first inequality uses the remark 1).

The inequalities $|T_i| + \sum_{j=1}^{N} |C^i_j| \leq 2^{n\ell}$ and $0 \leq |T_i| - \sum_{j=1}^{N} |C^i_j|$ are verified if

$$1 \leq i \leq q \leq 2^{n-1}/\ell^2. \tag{4}$$

For a given request x_i, an ℓ-tuple randomly picked in T^*_i may not be in $T^*_i \cap T_i$ with a probability $p_{1,i}$ verifying

$$p_{1,i} = \frac{z_i}{|T_i|} \leq \frac{\ell^{2d}(i-1)^d \, 2^{n(\ell-d)}}{|T_i|}.$$

Using inequality (1) and inequality (4), we obtain $|T_i| \geq 2^{n\ell-1}$ so that

$$p_{1,i} \leq \frac{\ell^{2d}}{2^{dn-1}}(i-1)^d.$$

As explained previously, an ℓ-tuple randomly picked in T_i may also be in $T_i \cap C^* \neq \emptyset$. This is a problematic case and a new ℓ-tuple must be chosen to leave the simulation correct. As seen previously, $|T_i| \geq 2^{n\ell-1}$, so the probability $p_{2,i}$ of this event verifies

$$p_{2,i} = \frac{|C^*|}{|T_i|} \leq \frac{(2^n)^{\ell-1}\ell^2/2}{2^{n\ell-1}} \leq \frac{\ell^2}{2^n}.$$

Thus, at each request x_i, $1 \leq i \leq q$, the advantage of the distinguisher is bounded by $p_{1,i} + p_{2,i}$. The overall advantage of the distinguisher is given by

$$\sum_{i=1}^{q} \left(\frac{\ell^{2d}}{2^{dn-1}}(i-1)^d + \frac{\ell^2}{2^n} \right) \leq \frac{q^{d+1}\ell^{2d}}{2^{dn}} + \frac{q\ell^2}{2^n}.$$

The security level is determined by the term $\frac{q^{d+1}\ell^{2d}}{2^{dn}}$ which is beyond the birthday bound for any $d \geq 2$.

Passive–Only Key Recovery Attacks on RC4

Serge Vaudenay and Martin Vuagnoux

EPFL
CH–1015 Lausanne, Switzerland
http://lasecwww.epfl.ch

Abstract. We present several weaknesses in the key scheduling algorithm of RC4 when the secret key contains an initialization vector – a cryptographic scheme typically used by the WEP and WPA protocols to protect IEEE 802.11 wireless communications. First, we show how the previously discovered key recovery attacks can be improved by reducing the dependency between the secret key bytes. Then, we describe two new weaknesses related to the modulo operation of the key scheduling algorithm. Finally, we describe a passive-only attack able to significantly improve the key recovery process on WEP with a data complexity of 2^{15} eavesdropped packets.

Keywords: RC4, stream cipher, cryptanalysis, key related attack, WEP.

1 Introduction

RC4 is a stream cipher designed by Ronald Rivest in 1987. It had been initially a trade secret until the algorithm was anonymously posted to the Cypherpunks mailing list in September 1994. Nowadays, RC4 is still widely used: it is the default cipher of the SSL/TLS protocol and a cryptographic primitive of the WPA protocol. Its popularity probably comes from its simplicity and the cheap computational cost of the encryption and decryption. Due to its straightforwardness, RC4 has initiated extensive research, revealing weaknesses in case of misuse. The most famous example is the attack on the WEP (*Wired Equivalent Privacy*) protocol.

WEP is a part of the IEEE 802.11 wireless standard ratified in 1999 [1]. It was designed to provide confidentiality on wireless communications by using RC4. In order to simplify the key set up, WEP uses preinstalled fixed keys. However, RC4 is a stream cipher: the same secret key must never be used twice. To prevent any repetition, WEP concatenates to the key an initialization vector (IV), where the IV is a 24-bit value which is publicly disclosed in the header of the protocol.

The first analysis of the WEP standard has been done in 2001 by Borisov, Goldberg and Wagner in [2]. They demonstrated major security flaws revealing that WEP does not provide confidentiality, integrity and authentication. The same year, Fluhrer, Mantin and Shamir in [3] showed a noteworthy ciphertext-only attack on WEP based on the concatenated IV scheme on RC4. They proved that the secret part of the key can be recovered if a large amount of encrypted

C. Adams, A. Miri, and M. Wiener (Eds.): SAC 2007, LNCS 4876, pp. 344–359, 2007.

packets with some specific IV values are passively eavesdropped. In fact, these so called *weak keys* or *weak IV classes* were previously discovered by Andrew Roos [4] and David Wagner [5] four years before the publication of the IEEE 802.11b standard.

A practical issue of the key recovery process is to passively obtain a large amount of encrypted packets (about 4 millions of encrypted packets to recover the secret key with a success probability of 50%). To reduce this constraint, David Hulton [6] in 2002, Andrea Bittau [7] in 2003 and a hacker nicknamed Korek [8,9] in 2004 highlighted more weak IV classes. Thus, the amount of encrypted packets needed to recover the secret key with the same probability of success has been divided by four.

On the active side, WEP is not protected against active replay attacks: it is possible to replay some specific eavesdropped packets to generate wireless network traffic. Thus, the amount of encrypted packets with different IVs may be obtained faster. In 2004, tools merging all these attacks were publicly disclosed [10,11].

In 2005, Mantin presented additional attacks on truncated RC4 in [12], based on the Jenkins correlations [13]. In 2006, Klein applied the same correlations to WEP [14] to provide a remarkable known-plaintext attack which does not need weak IVs to recover the secret key. The same year, Bittau, Handley and Lackey presented in [15] new active attacks able to inject and decrypt data without recovering the secret key (these attacks are based on the fragmentation feature provided by the IEEE 802.11 standard). Finally, in 2007, a correlation related to the first three bytes of the secret key and the first byte of the keystream has been presented in [16].

In order to correct the weaknesses discovered before 2004, the Wi-Fi Alliance proposed in [17] a WEP improved protocol called WPA (*Wi-Fi Protected Access*). It has been established that WPA must be hardware compatible with existing WEP capable devices to be deployed as a software patch. Basically, WPA is a WEP wrapper which contains anti-replay protections and a key management scheme to avoid key reuse. However, the correlations discovered in this paper are still almost theoretically applicable to WPA despite that the RC4 secret key is completely different for each encrypted packet. In 2004, the Wi-Fi Alliance finally proposed a new standard called IEEE 802.11i or WPA2 [18], where RC4 can be replaced by AES.

Limitation of the Existing Attacks. Almost all key recovery attacks are related to the value of the IV: each recovered secret key byte is provided by a specific weak IV class. However, an attacker does not control the value of the IV. It means that the attacker cannot recover the secret byte $K[i]$ if he was not able to eavesdrop encrypted packets from its weak IV class.

In parallel, Klein's key recovery attack is related to the knowledge of the plaintext, which cannot be completely determined with passive-only attacks. Indeed, the secret key byte $K[i]$ cannot be recovered if the ith byte of the plaintext is unknown.

Moreover, all existing key recovery attacks suffer from a relation between the secret key bytes. To recover the byte $K[i]$ of the secret key, we need to successfully rederive the previous bytes $K[0], K[1], \ldots, K[i-1]$. In practice, this constraint is a significant limitation because if the key recovery process does not work for only one key byte (because not enough encrypted packets were captured by the attacker from the concerning weak IV class or because a byte of the plaintext is unknown), all the following key bytes will be probably mis-recovered. Furthermore, WPA and some implementations of WEP filter the weak IV classes discovered by Fluhrer, Mantin and Shamir in [3].

Our Contribution. In this paper, we propose an improvement, applicable to all the key recovery attacks to significantly reduce the key dependency. Therefore, it becomes possible to independently recover some parts of the secret key. It means that even if an attacker has passively eavesdropped a very limited number of encrypted packets, he is now able to recover a part of the secret key[1]. The missing key bytes may be recovered by an exhaustive search. Because we can do the assumption that the secret key byte $K[i]$ can be recovered even if the preceding key bytes are unknown, new weak IV classes have been discovered. These new attacks improve the global key recovery process.

By significantly reducing the secret key byte dependency, we have highlighted additional weaknesses. In RC4, the key is used modulo its size. It means that the secret key byte $K[i]$ is equal to $K[i + k\ell]$ (where ℓ is the size of the key, $k = 1, 2, \ldots$ and $i = 0, 1, 2, \ldots, \ell - 1$). This property was irrelevant for the existing key recovery attacks because the whole secret key had to be recovered to attack the repetition. Without the secret key byte dependency, we are able to provide new weak IV classes attacking $K[i + k\ell]$, where $k = 1, 2, \ldots, m$. A practical analysis of this improvement is given in order to prove the efficiency of these new key recovery attacks on WEP.

Structure of the Paper. Section 2 describes the foundation of the key recovery attacks on WEP, in particular the attack discovered by Fluhrer, Mantin and Shamir in [3] and the Klein attack, described in [14]. In Section 3, we study how to reduce the key bytes dependency. In section 4, we explain how to exploit the modulo operation in the KSA and how the repetition of the secret key provides new weak IV classes. Section 5 describes our practical attack. Finally we conclude with further improvements.

2   Foundation of the Key Recovery Attacks

2.1   Description of RC4

The stream cipher RC4 is divided into two parts: the Key Scheduling Algorithm (KSA) and the Pseudo Random Generator Algorithm (PRGA). The KSA

---

[1] This attack has been independently rediscovered later in April 2007 by Tews, Weinmann, and Pyshkin in [19]. It is based on [14] but applies to active attacks. In this paper, we decided to focus on passive ones since it is the gateway for the WPA analysis.

generates an initial state from a random key K of ℓ words of n bits as described in Algorithm 1. It starts with an array $\{0, 1, \ldots, N-1\}$, where $N = 2^n$ and swaps N pairs. At the end, we obtain the initial state S_{N-1}.

Algorithm 1. RC4 Key Scheduling Algorithm (KSA)

1: **for** $i = 0$ to $N-1$ **do**
2:     $S[i] \leftarrow i$
3: **end for**
4: $j \leftarrow 0$
5: **for** $i = 0$ to $N-1$ **do**
6:     $j \leftarrow j + S[i] + K[i \bmod \ell]$
7:     swap($S[i], S[j]$)
8: **end for**

Once the initial state S_{N-1} created, it will be used by the second part of RC4, the PRGA. Its role is to generate a keystream of bytes which will be XORed with the plaintext to obtain the ciphertext. Thus, RC4 computes the loop of the PRGA each time a new keystream byte z_i is needed, according to Algorithm 2.

Algorithm 2. RC4 Pseudo Random Generator Algorithm (PRGA)

1: $i \leftarrow 0$
2: $j \leftarrow 0$
3: **loop**
4:     $i \leftarrow i + 1$
5:     $j \leftarrow j + S[i]$
6:     swap($S[i], S[j]$)
7:     keystream byte $z_i = S[S[i] + S[j]]$
8: **end loop**

Let $S_i[k]$ denotes the value of the array S at the index k, after the round i in the KSA. Let $S_i^{-1}[p]$ be the index of the value p in the array S after the round i in the KSA. For example $S_i^{-1}[S_i[k]] = k$ and $S_i[S_i^{-1}[p]] = p$. Let j_i be the value of j during the round i where the rounds are indexed in accordance with i. Thus, the KSA has rounds $0, 1, \ldots, N-1$ and the PRGA has rounds $1, 2, \ldots$ Let S_1' denotes the array S after the first round of the PRGA (i.e. S_1' is equal to S_{N-1} with $S_{N-1}[1]$ and $S_{N-1}[S_{N-1}[1]]$ swapped). We define z_1, the first byte of the keystream as:

$$z_1 = S_1'[S_1'[1] + S_1'[S_{N-1}[1]]] = S_1'[S_{N-1}[S_{N-1}[1]] + S_{N-1}[1]] \qquad (1)$$

2.2 KSA Evolution

Definition 1 (p–protected). *During the KSA process, if $S_p^{-1}[m] \leq p$, we say that the value m is p-protected.*

To illustrate this definition, we present an example with the first three rounds of some KSA process. The values in bold are i–protected. We remark that if $m = S_i[k]$ is i–protected, then $m = S_{i+1}[k]$ if and only if $j_{i+1} \neq k$. In the KSA, this happens with probability of about $1 - 1/N$.

S_i							i	j_i	i–protected values
0	1	2	3	4	...	255	Init	Init	
3	1	2	0	4	...	255	0	3	$\{3\}$
1	3	2	0	4	...	255	1	0	$\{1, 3\}$
1	3	42	0	4	...	255	2	42	$\{1, 3, 42\}$

During the KSA, a permutation is done between two values at the end of each round. The indices of the two swapped values are given by i and j_i. Although the value of i is predictable, the evolution of j_i depends on the secret key and may be considered as random. To facilitate the analysis of the KSA we will approximate some rounds of the KSA by an idealized version in which step 6 assigns a random byte in register j.[2] However, even if j_i is considered as random, it is possible to guarantee with a relatively high probability that some values will not be modified during the process of the KSA. We propose to redefine the Evolution lemma given by Mantin in [12]:

Lemma 2 (Evolution Lemma). *Consider an idealized KSA where j is picked randomly for the last $(N - p)$ rounds. Let $\mathcal{I}$ be a set of p–protected values of cardinality x. The probability that no element of $\mathcal{I}$ is swapped during the last $(N - p)$ rounds of the KSA is*

$$P(x, p) = \left(\frac{N - x}{N} \right)^{N-p}$$

Furthermore, if $\mathcal{I}$ is a set of $(p-1)$–protected values and $\mathcal{J}$ is a non-intersecting set of p–protected values, the probability that no element of $\mathcal{I}$ is swapped during round p and no element of $\mathcal{I} \cup \mathcal{J}$ is swapped during the last rounds is

$$P(\#\mathcal{I}, \#\mathcal{J}, p) = \frac{N - \#\mathcal{I}}{N} \left(\frac{N - \#\mathcal{I} - \#\mathcal{J}}{N} \right)^{N-p}$$

2.3   Description of WEP

According to [1], WEP uses RC4 with $N = 256$ and $n = 8$ to provide confidentiality. The key contains a 24-bit long IV concatenated to a secret key of 40 or 104 bits. Thus, the complete key size is either 64 or 128 bits. Consider a 64-bit (8 bytes) key size:

$$K = K[0]||K[1]||K[2]||K[3]||\ldots||K[7] = IV_0||IV_1||IV_2||K[3]||\ldots||K[7]$$

---

[2] This approximation was also used by Mironov in [20].

where IV_i represents the ith byte of the IV and $K[3]||\ldots||K[7]$ the secret part of the key. In theory, the value of the IV should be random but in practice, it is a counter mostly in *little-endian* and incremented by one each time a new 802.11b frame is encrypted. Thus, each packet uses a slightly different key. The key K is used by RC4 and the resulting keystream is XORed with the plaintext to obtain the ciphertext. Unfortunately, a portion of the plaintext is practically constant [21] and some of the following bytes can be derived. They correspond to the LLC header and the SNAP header and some bytes of the TCP/IP encapsulated frame. For example, by XORing the first byte of the ciphertext with the constant value 0xAA, we obtain the first byte of the keystream.

2.4   Description of WPA

WPA has been designed for use with an IEEE 802.1X authentication server with the aim to distribute different keys to each user. However, it can also be used in a lightweighted mode called "pre-shared key" (WPA-PSK), where every user is given the same key. According to [17], each user must enter a pass-phrase to access the network. The pass-phrase may be from 8 to 63 printable ASCII characters or 64 hexadecimal digits. The major improvement in WPA over WEP is the Temporal Key Integrity Protocol (TKIP), a key management scheme to avoid key reuse. TKIP is a key scheduling in two phases used to generate a completely different RC4 key for each transmitted packet (called *Per Packet Key*). Thus, even if the attacks based on weak IVs and the Klein attack still exist, an attacker will have only one trial to recover a specific RC4 secret key. Moreover, a filter avoids the use of some weak IV classes (but only the weak IV class discovered by Fluhrer Mantin and Shamir in [3]). In addition, WPA also provides packet integrity which prevents replay attacks being executed. Thus, only passive key recovery attacks are theoretically applicable to WPA.

2.5   The Fluhrer Mantin and Shamir (FMS) Attack

To understand how key recovery attacks work, we briefly present the FMS attack. According to [3], this attack uses the property of some specific IV values called *weak keys*. Let $IV_0 = 3, IV_1 = 255$ and IV_2 equals some arbitrary value $x \notin \{251, 252\}$. We assume that j_3 is different from $\{0, 1\}$. Our goal is to obtain the value of the first secret byte of the key $K[3]$. Due to the assumption on x, $x + 5$ is different from $\{0, 1\}$. Together with the assumptions on j_3, we obtain that the first four rounds of the KSA are given by:

S_i							i	j
0	1	2	3	4	$\cdots$	255		
3	1	2	0	4	$\cdots$	255	0	$0 + 0 + IV_0 = 3$
3	0	2	1	4	$\cdots$	255	1	$3 + S_0[1] + IV_1 = 3$
3	0	$x+5$	1	4	$\cdots$	255	2	$3 + S_1[2] + IV_2 = x + 5$
3	0	$\cdot$	$S_2[j_3]$	$\cdot$	$\cdots$	255	3	$x + 5 + S_2[3] + K[3] = j_3$

Because $K[3]$ is unknown, we cannot predict the values of $S[i]$, $i \in \{3, \ldots, 255\}$ after the round 2, however they will eventually change, according to the KSA. Now we suppose that $S_2[0] = S_3[0] = S_{255}[0] = 3$, $S_2[1] = S_3[1] = S_{255}[1] = 0$ and $S_3[3] = S_{255}[3] = S_2[j_3]$. Following the Evolution lemma with $\mathcal{I} = \{0, 3\}$, $\mathcal{J} = \{S_2[3]\}$ and $p = 3$, the probability that $j_3 \neq \{0, 1\}$ and $S_2[j_3]$ remains at the same place is $P(2, 1, 3) \approx 5\%$. According to our assumptions and (1), the first byte of the keystream generated by the PRGA is:

S						i	j
3	0	·	$S_2[j_3]$	·	$\cdots$ 255		
0	3	·	$S_2[j_3]$	·	$\cdots$ 255	1	$j + S_{255}[i] = 0 + 0 = 0$

$$z_1 = S_1'[S_1'[1] + S_1'[S_{255}[1]]] = S_1'[S_{255}[0] + S_{255}[1]] \overset{5\%}{=} S_p[S_{p-1}[0] + S_{p-1}[1]] = S_2[j_3]$$

Note that $z_1 \neq \{0, 3\}$ when this holds. We can now easily recover the secret key byte $K[3]$ because the first byte of the keystream can be recovered: $z_1 = S_2[j_3] = c_0 \oplus \mathtt{0xAA}$ where c_0 is the first byte of the ciphertext and $\mathtt{0xAA}$ the first constant byte of the plaintext, the LLC header. Thus, $K[3] = S_2^{-1}[z_1] - S_2[3] - j_2 = S_2^{-1}[z_1] - x - 6$. We notice that the weak IV class given by $IV_0 = 3$, $IV_1 = 255$ and $IV_2 = x$ can be described as a specific S_2 table state class where $S_2[1] = 0$ and $S_2[0] = 3$.

We can generalize the FMS attack: we need a large amount of encrypted packets where the value of the IV gives the state S_{p-1} such that $S_{p-1}[1] = 0$, $S_{p-1}[0] = p$ and $z_1 \neq \{0, p\}$. This defines the weak IV class which recovers the secret key byte $K[p]$. The secret key byte is rederived with a probability of success $P_{\mathsf{FMS}}(p) = P(2, 1, p)$ according to the Evolution lemma.

$$K[p] \overset{P_{\mathsf{FMS}}(p)}{=} S_{p-1}^{-1}[z_1] - S_{p-1}[p] - j_{p-1}$$
$$= S_{p-1}^{-1}[z_1] - \sum_{j=1}^{p} S_{j-1}[j] - \sum_{i=0}^{p-1} K[i] \qquad (2)$$

The attacker will then collect the probed values for $K[p]$, according to (2) and finally select the one with the highest vote. Note that to rederive the secret key byte $K[p]$, the attack must successfully recover the previous bytes $K[p-1], \ldots, K[3]$ in order to compute $S_{p-1}[p]$ and j_{p-1}.

Nowadays, there are dozens of known key recovery attacks similar to the FMS attack. In order to have a relevant list of the known attacks, one has to read [22] or the source code of the tool Aircrack [11] or Weplab [10]. These attacks are divided into three categories. The first kind of attack uses only z_1 and the state of the array S_{p-1} of the KSA to recover the secret key (typically the FMS attack). The second one uses z_1 and z_2. Note that they can easily be extended to the combination of every known z_i to provide more weak IV classes. The last one highlights the unprobable secret key bytes, they are called *negative attacks*.

2.6   The Klein Attack

In 2006, Andreas Klein presented in [14] a practical application of the Jenkins correlation [13] to WEP.

Theorem 3. *Let S'_i be the ith step of the PRGA where the internal state is a random permutation, and a random value j,*

$$\Pr\left(z_i + S'_i[j] \bmod N = c\right) = \begin{cases} \frac{2}{N} & if\ c = i \\ \frac{N-2}{N(N-1)} & if\ c \neq i \end{cases}$$

Klein demonstrated a strong correlation in the 7th step of the PRGA which is not related to a specific weak IV class. It means that each eavesdropped packet may rederive the secret key.

$$S'_i[j] \overset{P_j}{=} i - z_i \qquad \text{(From Theorem 3 with } P_j = 2/N) \qquad (3)$$

$$S'_{i-1}[i] \overset{P'}{=} S_i[i] \qquad\qquad P' = ((N-1)/N)^{N-2} \qquad (4)$$

$$S'_i[j] = S'_{i-1}[i] \qquad\qquad \text{(step 6 of the PRGA)} \qquad (5)$$

$$S_i[i] = S_{i-1}[j_i] \qquad\qquad \text{(KSA)} \qquad (6)$$

$$j_i = S_{i-1}[i] + j_{i-1} + K[i] \qquad \text{(step 6 of the KSA)} \qquad (7)$$

From (3) with respectively (4), (5), (6) and (7) we have

$$K[p] \overset{P_{\text{Klein}}}{=} S_{p-1}^{-1}[p - z_p \bmod N] - S_{p-1}[p] - j_{p-1} \bmod N \qquad (8)$$

which hold with a probability

$$P_{\text{Klein}} = \frac{2}{N} \cdot \left(\frac{N-1}{N}\right)^{N-2} + \frac{N-2}{N(N-1)} \cdot \left(1 - \left(\frac{N-1}{N}\right)^{N-2}\right) \approx \frac{1.36}{N} \qquad (9)$$

A significant limitation of the Klein key recovery attack is that to recover the secret key byte $K[i]$, the ith byte of the keystream has to be known.

3   The VX Attack: How to Reduce the Secret Key Bytes Dependency

A major issue related to all key recovery attacks is that if a secret key byte has not been correctly recovered, the whole key will be probably mis-recovered due to the key byte dependency (to rederive $K[i]$, the previous secret key bytes $K[i-1], K[i-2], \ldots, K[3]$ must be successfully recovered). In this section we present a new attack, called VX, able to recover more efficiently the secret key by significantly reducing the key bytes dependency.

3.1   The FMS Key Recovery Attack

The paradigm of this attack is to recover independently the sum of the secret key bytes by computing some predictable parts of the equation (2). Consider the FMS attack described above. According to (2), we obtain

$$\sum_{i=0}^{p} K[i] \overset{P_{\text{FMS}}(p)}{=} S_{p-1}^{-1}[z_1] - \sum_{j=1}^{p} S_{j-1}[j] \tag{10}$$

Consider that we only know the state S_2 specified by the IV. We define $P_1(p)$, the probability that $S_{p-1}^{-1}[z_1] = S_2^{-1}[z_1]$ in the idealized version of the KSA by

$$P_1(p) = \Pr\left(S_{p-1}^{-1}[z_1] = S_2^{-1}[z_1]\right) = \left(\frac{N-1}{N}\right)^{p-2}, p \geq 2 \tag{11}$$

The array S_j with $j = 0, 1, \ldots, p-1$ is partially known if p is small, because it is close to the initialization state of S at the beginning of the KSA where $S[i] = i$. Thus the sum $\sum_{j=1}^{p} S_{j-1}[j]$ is equivalent to $S_0[1] + S_1[2] + \sum_{j=3}^{p} S_2[j]$ with a probability $P_2(p)$.[3]

$$P_2(p) = \Pr\left(\sum_{j=1}^{p} S_{j-1}[j] = S_0[1] + S_1[2] + \sum_{j=3}^{p} S_2[j]\right)$$

$$\approx \prod_{m=3}^{p} \left(\frac{N-p+m}{N}\right), p \geq 3 \tag{12}$$

Thus, we can recover independently each sum of the key bytes $K[0\ldots p]$, where $K[i\ldots j] = K[i] + K[i+1] + \ldots + K[j], j \geq i$ with a probability of success $P_{\text{VX}_F}(p) = P_{\text{FMS}}(3) \cdot P_1(p) \cdot P_2(p)$ and $p = 3, 4, \ldots, \ell-1$. Indeed, using (11) and (12) in (10), we have

$$K[3\ldots p] \overset{P_{\text{VX}_F}(p)}{=} S_2^{-1}[z_1] - S_0[1] - S_1[2] - \sum_{j=3}^{p} S_2[j] - \sum_{v=0}^{2} IV_v \tag{13}$$

since the key bytes $K[0], K[1]$ and $K[2]$ are known and different for each packet because they correspond to the IV, we store the votes for the secret and fixed part of the key, the sum $K[3\ldots p]$. Equation (13) is a correlation between a byte depending on the secret key only and a byte which can be computed from the 802.11b frame only. Finally, each secret key byte $K[i]$ can be recovered with

$$K[p] = K[3\ldots p] - K[3\ldots(p-1)]$$

3.2   The Klein Key Recovery Attack

The same technique can be applied to the Klein key recovery attack. Indeed, the dependency is based on the same values, only the probability P_{FMS} is different. According to (8) we have,

---

[3] This is an improvement of the correlation discovered by Roos in [4].

$$\sum_{i=0}^{p} K[i] \stackrel{P_{\mathsf{Klein}}(p)}{=} S_{p-1}^{-1}[p - z_p \bmod N] - \sum_{j=1}^{p} S_{j-1}[j]$$

Thus, we can apply the same technique described above and we obtain that

$$K[3 \ldots p] \stackrel{P_{\mathsf{VX}_K}(p)}{=} S_2^{-1}[p - z_p \bmod N] \tag{14}$$

$$-S_0[1] - S_1[2] - \sum_{j=3}^{p} S_2[j] - \sum_{v=0}^{2} IV_v$$

where

$$P_{\mathsf{KleinTot}} = P_1(p) \cdot P_2(p) \cdot \left(\frac{N-1}{N}\right)^{N-2}$$

$$P_{\mathsf{VX}_K}(p) = \frac{2}{N} \cdot P_{\mathsf{KleinTot}} + \frac{N-2}{N(N-1)} \cdot (1 - P_{\mathsf{KleinTot}})$$

Note that for some values of the key bytes, the Klein attack may not work.

4   Weaknesses in the Modulo Operation of the KSA

During the KSA of RC4, the key is used modulo its size. It means that the secret key byte $K[i] = K[i + k\ell]$, where ℓ is the size of the key, $k = 1, 2, \ldots, m$ and $i = 3, \ldots, \ell - 1$. We remark that if an attacker is unable to recover the secret key byte $K[i]$ (because not enough frames were captured from its weak IV class or because the keystream byte needed to recover the secret key byte is unknown), he could be interested to recover the key byte $K[i + \ell]$ (through another weak IV class or another keystream byte) instead of $K[i]$. Due to the key bytes dependency, this property was irrelevant for the existing key recovery attacks. Indeed, the whole secret key had to be recovered to attack the modulo repetition.

4.1   Weakness in the Repetition of the Secret Key

According to the VX attack, it is possible to recover *independently* the value of the secret key bytes sum $K[3 \ldots p]$ where $p = i + k\ell, k = 0, 1, \ldots m$ and $i = 3, \ldots \ell - 1$. Consider the FMS attack described above and the equation (13). We define,

$$\overline{K}[p] \triangleq K[3 \ldots i] + k \cdot K[3 \ldots (\ell - 1)]$$

$$\stackrel{P_{\mathsf{VX}_F}(p)}{=} S_2^{-1}[z_1] - S_0[1] - S_1[2] - \sum_{j=3}^{p} S_2[j] - (k+1) \cdot \sum_{v=0}^{2} IV_v \tag{15}$$

If an attacker has not enough weak IV to recover the sum $K[3 \ldots i]$ but he is able to rederive correctly $K[3 \ldots (\ell - 1)]$, the targeted sum can be recovered when a vote for $\overline{K}[p]$ is collected, according to (15) with $k \geq 1$. The same technique can be used with the Klein attack when the keystream byte needed to recover the secret key byte is unknown.

4.2 Weakness in the Repetition of the IV

In the previous section, we have seen that the key repetition can be used to recover a part of the secret key if the sum $K[3\ldots(\ell-1)]$ has been correctly rederived. An interesting feature of WEP is that the three first repeated bytes of the key are publicly disclosed, they correspond to the IV. Because these values are known, they can be used to recover more efficiently the critical secret key bytes sum $K[3\ldots(\ell-1)]$. For $p = i + k\ell$ with $i = \{0,1,2\}$ we define $\overline{K}[p] = k \cdot K[3\ldots(\ell-1)]$. Thus,

$$\overline{K}[p] \triangleq k \cdot K[3\ldots(\ell-1)]$$

$$P_{VK_F}(p) \over = S_2^{-1}[z_1] - S_0[1] - S_1[2] - \sum_{j=3}^{p} S_2[j] - k \cdot \sum_{j=0}^{2} IV_j - \sum_{j=0}^{i} IV_j \quad (16)$$

Thus, four weak IV classes, instead of only one are dedicated to the recovery of the critical sum above. The same technique can be used with the Klein attack: four different keystream bytes may rederive the secret key sum. This finally leads us to many attack on byte $\overline{K}[p]$ where all bytes are linked by,

$$\overline{K}[p] = \begin{cases} k \cdot K[3\ldots(\ell-1)] + K[3\ldots(p \bmod \ell)] & \text{for } p \bmod \ell = 3\ldots\ell-1 \\ k \cdot K[3\ldots\ell-1] & \text{for } p \bmod \ell = 0,1,2 \end{cases} \quad (17)$$

5 Attack Principle

The principle of the attack is composed of three parts. The first one collects the IVs and the known keystream bytes of the passively eavesdropped 802.11 packets. Note that some keystream bytes are unknown (the Appendix A gives the probable plaintext bytes, for TCP and ARP packets, needed to recover the keystream bytes). For each known keystream byte z_p, the extended Klein attack described above will return a probed byte n for the sum of secret key bytes $\overline{K}[p]$ weighted by P_v the success probability of the vote. The key recovery attacks based on the IV are similarly used, by using the IV and the two first bytes of the keystream z_1 and z_2.

Once the vote process is accomplished, we use two techniques to rederive more efficiently the secret key sum $\overline{K}[\ell-1]$. Firstly we take profit of the modulo repetition of the IV according to (16). Secondly, we do an autocorrelation on the r discrete signals $\overline{K}[3] + k \cdot \overline{K}[\ell-1] || \overline{K}[4] + k \cdot \overline{K}[\ell-1] || \ldots || \overline{K}[\ell-2] + k \cdot \overline{K}[\ell-1]$ $k = 0, 1, \ldots, r$ where the time shifting value corresponds to $\overline{K}[\ell-1]$. When the autocorrelation is maximized for a given $\overline{K}[\ell-1]$, it is considered as the most probable value. We merge the results given by the autocorrelation for each potential value of $\overline{K}[\ell-1]$ with the votes given by (16) and we sort them according to their votes. Once $\overline{K}[\ell-1]$ is fixed we compute the votes for the repeated secret keys and we merge all the votes.

Finally, we successively test the first M secret keys, according to their distance to the most probable value (with the highest amount of vote). Note that each time a new value for $\overline{K}[\ell-1]$ is selected, we have to recompute the votes for all the repetition of the secret key bytes. See Algorithm 3 for more details.

Algorithm 3. VX Key Recovery Attack

$VX(IV, Z)$: IV, the set of known keystream bytes Z where z_i is the ith byte of the keystream.

Data: V is a $(N \times (\ell \cdot m - 3))$ matrix
Data: V' is a $(N \times (\ell - 1))$ matrix
Output: The secret key K

1: **for** each passively eavesdropped packet $\{IV, Z\}$ **do**
2:     $(n, p, P_v) \leftarrow$ WeakAttack(IV, z_1, z_2)
3:     $V_{n,p} \leftarrow V_{n,p} + P_v$
4:     $(n, p, P_v) \leftarrow$ KleinAttack(IV, Z)
5:     $V_{n,p} \leftarrow V_{n,p} + P_v$
6: **end for**
7: **for** each r repetition of the secret key **do**
8:     **for** $n = 0$ to $N - 1$ **do**
9:         $V_{n,r \cdot \ell - 1} \leftarrow V_{n,r \cdot \ell - 1} + V_{n,r \cdot \ell} + V_{n,r \cdot \ell + 1} + V_{n,r \cdot \ell + 2}$
10:    **end for**
11: **end for**
12: $V \leftarrow$ Autocorrelation(V)
13: $V' \leftarrow$ MergeVotes(V)
14: **for** $i = 0$ to M **do**
15:    pick K the next most probable secret key in V'
16:    **if** K uses another value for $\overline{K}[\ell - 1]$ **then**
17:        $V \leftarrow$ Autocorrelation(V)
18:        $V' \leftarrow$ MergeVotes(V)
19:    **end if**
20:    **if** K is correct **return** K
21: **end for**

5.1   Practical Results on WEP

To demonstrate the improvement of the VX attack, we tried to recover randomly generated WEP 104-bit secret keys with a limited number of frames and randomly chosen IVs.

A first issue concerning the Klein attack, which is more efficient than the key recovery attacks based on weak IVs, is the ability to obtain the plaintext. Thus, we firstly concentrated our analysis on passively eavesdropped ARP frames because the plaintext of an ARP frame can be practically guessed until the 32nd byte (see Appendix A). Then, we chose a more realistic scenario where the eavesdropped traffic is mainly based on TCP frames (we used real network traffic dumps for this scenario). According to Appendix A, when a TCP frame is passively eavesdropped, the first and the second byte of the keystream, used by the key recovery attacks based on weak IVs are practically always known. However, the following keystream bytes needed for the Klein attack cannot be completely recovered. By significantly reducing the key bytes dependency and according to the modulo repetition, the VX attack is able to recover the secret key, even if some keystream bytes are still unknown.

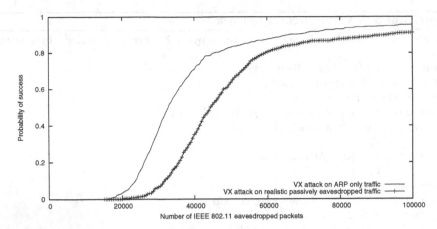

Fig. 1. The probability to recover the correct key after an exhaustive search of 2^{20} trials, according to the number of passively eavesdropped packets

The table (Figure 1) gives the average number of ARP frames needed to recover the complete secret key with an exhaustive search on a keyspace subset of $M = 2^{20}$ entries (with the highest probability of success, according to our votes). We notice that the average amount of ARP packets needed to recover the secret key with a probability $> 1/2$ is 32,700. The same table gives, according to the second scenario, the average number of frames needed to recover the complete secret key with an exhaustive search on a subset keyspace of $M = 2^{20}$ entries (with the highest probability of success, according to our votes). We notice that the average amount of packets needed to recover the secret key for the same probability is 44,500.

If we compare the VX attack with the previously published passive-only key recovery attacks on WEP [10,11], we reduce the data complexity from 2^{20} to 2^{15} for the same success probability to recover the secret key. We significantly reduce the computational complexity as well because the recomputation of the votes is not needed for each key trial.

Moreover, the VX attack can be transformed to an active one and needs about 25% less eavesdropped packets than the attack described in [19] thanks to the weaknesses in the modulo repetition and the use of the enhanced key recovery attacks based on weak IVs.

6   Conclusion

In this paper, we have seen that all the previously discovered key recovery attacks (the Klein attack as well as the key recovery attacks based on weak IVs) suffer from a relation between the secret key bytes. To rederive the ith byte of the secret key, we have to successfully recover the $(i - 1)$ previous key bytes. In practice, this constraint is a significant limitation because if the key recovery process does not work for only one byte of the key, the complete key will be probably mis-recovered.

According to the VX attack presented in this paper, we are now able to significantly reduce the key bytes dependency and thus, to recover correctly each key byte with a stronger probability, even if some preceding secret key bytes are still unknown.

Because the ith byte of the secret key can be recovered even if some previous bytes are missing, new weak IV classes appear.

Moreover, it becomes possible to take profit of the modulo repetition weaknesses of the secret key in the KSA of RC4 described in this paper, to improve the global key recovery process.

We showed that the Klein attack needs to know the $(i-1)^{th}$ byte of the keystream to recover the ith byte of the secret key. However, this information cannot always be obtained with passive-only key recovery attacks. Associated to the enhanced attacks based on weak IVs and the modulo repetition weaknesses of the secret key (both presented in this paper), a part of the missing secret key bytes can be passively recovered.

Consequently, the VX attack is to the best of our knowledge, the most efficient passive-only key recovery attack on WEP. The previous ones needed about one million of passively eavesdropped packets to recover the secret key with a probability bigger than one half. The VX attack needs about 44,500 packets for the same success probability.

A question raised in this paper is the motivation to find new key recovery attacks on WEP: a still widely used protocol, but already broken since 2001. The weaknesses highlighted in this paper concern theoretically WPA as well. Indeed, only passive attacks are applicable on WPA because of anti-replay protections.In spite of the fact that the VX attack cannot be practically exploited on WPA, it represents a relevant first step for its analysis.

References

1. IEEE: ANSI/IEEE standard 802.11b: Wireless LAN Medium Access Control (MAC) and Physical Layer (phy) Specifications (1999)
2. Borisov, N., Goldberg, I., Wagner, D.: Intercepting mobile communications: the insecurity of 802.11. In: MOBICOM, pp. 180–189 (2001)
3. Fluhrer, S., Mantin, I., Shamir, A.: Weaknesses in the key scheduling algorithm of RC4. In: Vaudenay, S., Youssef, A.M. (eds.) SAC 2001. LNCS, vol. 2259, pp. 1–24. Springer, Heidelberg (2001)
4. Roos, A.: A class of weak keys in RC4 stream cipher (sci.crypt) (1995)
5. Wagner, D.: Weak keys in RC4 (sci.crypt) (1995),
   http://www.cs.berkeley.edu/~daw/my-posts/my-rc4-weak-keys
6. Hulton, D.: Practical exploitation of RC4 weaknesses in WEP environments (2001),
   http://www.dachb0den.com/projects/bsd-airtools/wepexp.txt
7. Bittau, A.: Additional weak IV classes for the FMS attack (2003),
   http://www.cs.ucl.ac.uk/staff/a.bittau/sorwep.txt
8. Korek: Need security pointers (2004),
   http://www.netstumbler.org/showthread.php?postid=89036#post89036

9. Korek: Next generation of WEP attacks? (2004),
   http://www.netstumbler.org/showpost.php?p=93942&postcount=35
10. Martin, J.I.S.: Weplab, http://weplab.sourceforge.net/
11. Devine, C., Otreppe, T.: Aircrack, http://www.aircrack-ng.org/
12. Mantin, I.: A practical attack on the fixed RC4 in the WEP mode. In: Roy, B. (ed.)
    ASIACRYPT 2005. LNCS, vol. 3788, pp. 395–411. Springer, Heidelberg (2005)
13. Jenkins, R.: Isaac and RC4, http://burtleburtle.net/bob/rand/isaac.html
14. Klein, A.: Attacks on the RC4 stream cipher. Personal Andreas Klein website
    (2006), http://cage.ugent.be/~klein/RC4/RC4-en.ps
15. Bittau, A., Handley, M., Lackey, J.: The final nail in WEP's coffin. In: S&P, pp.
    386–400. IEEE Computer Society Press, Los Alamitos (2006)
16. Paul, G., Rathi, S., Maitra, S.: On non-negligible bias of the first output bytes of
    RC4 towards the first three bytes of the secret key. In: WCC 2007. International
    Workshop on Coding and Cryptography, pp. 285–294 (2007)
17. IEEE: ANSI/IEEE standard 802.11i: Amendment 6 Wireless LAN Medium Access
    Control (MAC) and Physical Layer (phy) Specifications, Draft 3 (2003)
18. IEEE: ANSI/IEEE standard 802.11i: Amendment 6: Wireless LAN Medium Access
    Control (MAC) and Physical Layer (phy) Specifications (2004)
19. Tews, E., Weinmann, R.P., Pyshkin, A.: Breaking 104 bit WEP in less than 60
    seconds. Cryptology ePrint Archive, Report 2007/120 (2007),
    http://eprint.iacr.org/
20. Mironov, I.: (Not so) random shuffles of RC4. In: Yung, M. (ed.) CRYPTO 2002.
    LNCS, vol. 2442, pp. 304–319. Springer, Heidelberg (2002)
21. Postel, R.: Rfc1042 (1988) http://rfc.net/rfc1042.html
22. Chaabouni, R.: Breaking WEP Faster with Statistical Analysis. Ecole Polytech-
    nique Fédérale de Lausanne, LASEC, Semester Project (2006)

A   Appendix

ARP Packet	
0xAA	DSAP
0xAA	SSAP
0x03	CTRL
0x00	
0x00	ORG Code
0x00	
0x08	ARP
0x06	
0x00	Ethernet
0x01	
0x08	IP
0x00	
0x06	Hardware size
0x04	Protocol
0x00	Opcode Request/Reply
0x??	
0x??	MAC addr src
0x??	
0x??	
0x??	
0x??	
0x??	
0x??	IP src
0x??	
0x??	
0x??	
0x??	MAC addr dst
0x??	
0x??	
0x??	
0x??	
0x??	
0x??	IP dst
0x??	
0x??	
0x??	

TCP Packet	
0xAA	DSAP
0xAA	SSAP
0x03	CTRL
0x00	
0x00	ORG Code
0x00	
0x08	IP
0x00	
0x45	IP Version + Header length
0x??	Packet length
0x??	
0x??	IP ID RFC815
0x??	
0x??	Fragment type and offset
0x??	TTL
0x06	TCP type
0x??	Header checksum
0x??	
0x??	IP src
0x??	
0x??	
0x??	
0x??	IP dst
0x??	
0x??	
0x??	
0x??	Port src
0x??	
0x??	Port dst
0x??	

Fig. 2. The tables above represent the plaintext bytes of 802.11 data frames encapsulating resp. ARP and TCP protocols. The value in white are almost fixed or can be computed dynamically. The values in light grey can be guessed. The values in dark grey are not predictable.

Permutation After RC4 Key Scheduling Reveals the Secret Key

Goutam Paul[1] and Subhamoy Maitra[2]

[1] Department of Computer Science and Engineering,
Jadavpur University, Kolkata 700 032, India
goutam_paul@cse.jdvu.ac.in
[2] Applied Statistics Unit, Indian Statistical Institute,
203, B T Road, Kolkata 700 108, India
subho@isical.ac.in

Abstract. A theoretical analysis of the RC4 Key Scheduling Algorithm (KSA) is presented in this paper, where the nonlinear operation is swapping among the permutation bytes. Explicit formulae are provided for the probabilities with which the permutation bytes after the KSA are biased to the secret key. Theoretical proofs of these formulae have been left open since Roos's work (1995). Based on this analysis, an algorithm is devised to recover the l bytes (i.e., $8l$ bits, typically $5 \leq l \leq 16$) secret key from the final permutation after the KSA with constant probability of success. The search requires $O(2^{4l})$ many operations which is the square root of the exhaustive key search complexity 2^{8l}. Further, a generalization of the RC4 KSA is analyzed corresponding to a class of update functions of the indices involved in the swaps. This reveals an inherent weakness of shuffle-exchange kind of key scheduling.

Keywords: Bias, Cryptanalysis, Key Scheduling, Permutation, RC4, Stream Cipher.

1 Introduction

Two decades have passed since the inception of RC4. Though a variety of other stream ciphers have been discovered after RC4, it is still the most popular and most frequently used stream cipher algorithm due to its simplicity, ease of implementation, speed and efficiency. RC4 is widely used in the Secure Sockets Layer (SSL) and similar protocols to protect the internet traffic, and was integrated into Microsoft Windows, Lotus Notes, Apple AOCE, Oracle Secure SQL, etc. Though the algorithm can be stated in less than ten lines, even after many years of analysis its strengths and weaknesses are of great interest to the community. In this paper, we study the Key Scheduling Algorithm of RC4 in detail and find out results that have implications towards the security of RC4. Before getting into the contribution in this paper, we first revisit the basics of RC4.

C. Adams, A. Miri, and M. Wiener (Eds.): SAC 2007, LNCS 4876, pp. 360–377, 2007.

The RC4 stream cipher has been designed by Ron Rivest for RSA Data Security in 1987, and was a propriety algorithm until 1994. It uses an S-Box $S = (S[0], \ldots, S[N-1])$ of length N, each location being of 8 bits. Typically, $N = 256$. S is initialized as the identity permutation, i.e., $S[i] = i$ for $0 \leq i \leq N-1$. A secret key of size l bytes (typically, $5 \leq l \leq 16$) is used to scramble this permutation. An array $K = (K[0], \ldots, K[N-1])$ is used to hold the secret key, where each location is of 8 bits. The key is repeated in the array K at key length boundaries. For example, if the key size is 40 bits, then $K[0], \ldots, K[4]$ are filled by the key and then this pattern is repeated to fill up the entire array K.

The RC4 cipher has two components, namely, the Key Scheduling Algorithm (KSA) and the Pseudo-Random Generation Algorithm (PRGA). The KSA turns the random key K into a permutation S of $0, 1, \ldots, N-1$ and PRGA uses this permutation to generate pseudo-random keystream bytes. The keystream output byte z is XOR-ed with the message byte to generate the ciphertext byte at the sender end. Again, z is XOR-ed with the ciphertext byte to get back the message byte at the receiver end.

Any addition used related to the RC4 description is in general addition modulo N unless specified otherwise.

Algorithm KSA	Algorithm PRGA
Initialization:	*Initialization:*
For $i = 0, \ldots, N-1$	$i = j = 0$;
$S[i] = i$;	*Output Keystream Generation Loop:*
$j = 0$;	$i = i + 1$;
Scrambling:	$j = j + S[i]$;
For $i = 0, \ldots, N-1$	Swap($S[i], S[j]$);
$j = (j + S[i] + K[i])$;	$t = S[i] + S[j]$;
Swap($S[i], S[j]$);	Output $z = S[t]$;

Note that defining the array K to be of size N enables us to write $K[i]$ instead of the typical $K[i \bmod l]$ in the description of the algorithm. This is done for the sake of simplification in the subsequent analysis of the algorithm.

1.1 Outline of the Contribution

In this paper, the update of the permutation S in different rounds of the KSA is analyzed and it is theoretically proved that after the completion of the KSA, the initial bytes of the permutation will be significantly biased towards some combination of the secret key bytes. Such biases were observed by Roos in [15] for the first time. It has been noted in [15] that after the completion of the KSA, the most likely value of the i-th element of the permutation for the first few values of i is given by $S[i] = \frac{i(i+1)}{2} + \sum_{x=0}^{i} K[x]$. However, the probability

$P(S[i] = \frac{i(i+1)}{2} + \sum_{x=0}^{i} K[x])$ could not be theoretically arrived in [15] and experi-

mental values have been provided as in Table 1 below.

Table 1. The probabilities experimentally observed by Roos [15]

i	$P(S[i] = \frac{i(i+1)}{2} + \sum_{x=0}^{i} K[x])$														
0-15	.370	.368	.362	.358	.349	.340	.330	.322	.309	.298	.285	.275	.260	.245	.229	.216
16-31	.203	.189	.173	.161	.147	.135	.124	.112	.101	.090	.082	.074	.064	.057	.051	.044
32-47	.039	.035	.030	.026	.023	.020	.017	.014	.013	.012	.010	.009	.008	.007	.006	.006

We theoretically prove for the first time with what probabilities the final permutation bytes after the KSA are correlated with the secret key bytes. Roos [15] commented that "Swapping is a nasty nonlinear process which is hard to analyze." That process is analyzed in a disciplined manner in this paper that unfolds the effect of swapping in the KSA of RC4 (see Lemma 1, Lemma 2 and Theorem 1 in Section 2).

In Section 3, we use these biases to show that if the permutation after the KSA is available, then one can retrieve the key bytes in time much less than the exhaustive key search. For a secret key of size $8l$ bits ($40 \leq 8l \leq 128$), the key can be recovered in $O(2^{\frac{8l}{2}})$ effort with a constant probability of success. In a shuffle-exchange kind of stream cipher, for proper cryptographic security, one may expect that after the key scheduling algorithm one should not be able to get any information regarding the secret key bytes from the random permutation in time complexity less than the exhaustive key search. We show that the KSA of RC4 is weak in this aspect.

Further, we consider the generalization of the RC4 KSA where the index j can be updated in different manners. In RC4 KSA, the update rule is $j = (j + S[i] + K[i])$. We show that for any arbitrary secret key and for a certain class of update functions (see Section 4) which compute the new value of the index j in the current round as a function of "the permutation S and j in the previous round" and "the secret key K", it is always possible to construct explicit functions of the key bytes which the final permutation will be biased to. This shows that the RC4 KSA cannot be made more secure by replacing the update rule $j = j + S[i] + K[i]$ with any rule from a large class that we present. Such bias is intrinsic to shuffle-exchange kind of paradigm, where one index (i) is updated linearly and another index (j) is modified pseudo-randomly.

1.2   Background

There are two broad approaches in the study of cryptanalysis of RC4: attacks based on the weaknesses of the KSA and those based on the weaknesses of the PRGA. Distinguishing attacks are the main motivation for PRGA-based approach [1,3,6,7,8,13,14]. Important results in this approach include bias in the keystream output bytes. For example, a bias in the second output byte being zero has been proved in [6] and a bias in the equality of the first two output bytes has been shown in [14]. In [10], RC4 has been analyzed using the theory of random shuffles and it has been recommended that initial 512 bytes of the keystream output should be discarded in order to be safe.

Initial empirical works based on the weaknesses of the RC4 KSA were done in [15,17] and several classes of weak keys had been identified. Recently, a more general theoretical study has been performed in [11] which includes the observations of [15]. The work [11] shows how the bias of the "third permutation byte" (after the KSA) towards the "first three secret key bytes" propagates to the first keystream output byte (in the PRGA). Thus, it renews the interest to study how the permutation after the KSA (which acts as a bridge between the KSA and the PRGA) is biased towards the secret key, which is theoretically solved in this paper.

Some weaknesses of the KSA have been addressed in great detail in [2] and practical attacks have been mounted on RC4 in the IV mode (e.g. WEP [4]). Further, the propagation of weak key patterns to the output keystream bytes has also been discussed in [2]. Subsequently, the work [5] improved [2]. In [9, Chapter 6], correlation between the permutations that are a few rounds apart have been discussed.

2   Theoretical Analysis of the Key Scheduling

Let S_0 be the initial permutation and $j_0 = 0$ be the initial value of the index j before the KSA begins. Note that in the original RC4, S_0 is the identity permutation. Let j_{i+1} be the updated value of j and S_{i+1} be the new permutation obtained after the completion of the round with i as the deterministic index (we call it round $i + 1$), $0 \leq i \leq N - 1$. Then S_N would be the final permutation after the complete KSA.

We now prove a general formula (Theorem 1) that estimates the probabilities with which the permutation bytes after the RC4 KSA are related to certain combinations of the secret key bytes. The result we present has two-fold significance. It gives for the first time a theoretical proof explicitly showing how these probabilities change as functions of i. Further, it does not assume that the initial permutation is an identity permutation. The result holds for any arbitrary initial permutation. Note that though j is updated using a deterministic formula, it is a linear function of the pseudo-random secret key bytes, and is therefore itself pseudo-random. If the secret key generator produces the secret keys uniformly at random, which is a reasonable assumption, then the distribution of j will also be uniform.

The proof of Theorem 1 depends on Lemma 1 and Lemma 2 which we prove below first.

Lemma 1. *Assume that during the KSA rounds, the index j takes its values from $\{0, 1, \ldots, N-1\}$ uniformly at random. Then, $P(j_{i+1} = \sum_{x=0}^{i} S_0[x] + \sum_{x=0}^{i} K[x]) \approx (\frac{N-1}{N})^{1+\frac{i(i+1)}{2}} + \frac{1}{N}, 0 \leq i \leq N-1$.*

Proof. One contribution towards the event $E : (j_{i+1} = \sum_{x=0}^{i} S_0[x] + \sum_{x=0}^{i} K[x])$ is approximately $(\frac{N-1}{N})^{\frac{i(i+1)}{2}}$. This part is due to the association based on the recursive updates of j and can be proved by induction on i.

- *Base Case*: Before the beginning of the KSA, $j_0 = 0$. Now, in the first round with $i = 0$, we have $j_1 = j_0 + S_0[0] + K[0] = 0 + S_0[0] + K[0] = \sum_{x=0}^{0} S_0[x] + \sum_{x=0}^{0} K[x]$ with probability $1 = (\frac{N-1}{N})^{\frac{0(0+1)}{2}}$. Hence, the result holds for the base case.
- *Inductive Case*: Suppose, that the result holds for the first i rounds, when the deterministic index takes its values from 0 to $i-1$, $i \geq 1$. Now, for the $(i+1)$-th round, we would have $j_{i+1} = j_i + S_i[i] + K[i]$. Thus, j_{i+1} can equal $\sum_{x=0}^{i} S_0[x] + \sum_{x=0}^{i} K[x]$, if $j_i = \sum_{x=0}^{i-1} S_0[x] + \sum_{x=0}^{i-1} K[x]$ and $S_i[i] = S_0[i]$.

By *inductive hypothesis*, we get $P(j_i = \sum_{x=0}^{i-1} S_0[x] + \sum_{x=0}^{i-1} K[x]) \approx (\frac{N-1}{N})^{\frac{i(i-1)}{2}}$.
Further, $S_i[i]$ remains the same as $S_0[i]$, if it has not been involved in any swap during the previous rounds, i.e., if any of the values $j_1, j_2, \ldots, j_i$ has not hit the index i, the probability of which is $(\frac{N-1}{N})^i$. Thus, the probability that the event E occurs along the above recursive path is $\approx (\frac{N-1}{N})^{\frac{i(i-1)}{2}} \cdot (\frac{N-1}{N})^i = (\frac{N-1}{N})^{\frac{i(i+1)}{2}}$.
A second contribution towards the event E is due to random association when the above recursive path is not followed. This probability is approximately $\left(1 - (\frac{N-1}{N})^{\frac{i(i+1)}{2}}\right) \cdot \frac{1}{N}$. Adding these two contributions, we get the total probability $\approx (\frac{N-1}{N})^{\frac{i(i+1)}{2}} + \left(1 - (\frac{N-1}{N})^{\frac{i(i+1)}{2}}\right) \cdot \frac{1}{N} = (1 - \frac{1}{N}) \cdot (\frac{N-1}{N})^{\frac{i(i+1)}{2}} + \frac{1}{N} = (\frac{N-1}{N})^{1+\frac{i(i+1)}{2}} + \frac{1}{N}$.   □

Corollary 1. *If the initial permutation is the identity permutation, i.e., $S_0[i] = i$ for $0 \leq i \leq N-1$, then $P(j_{i+1} = \frac{i(i+1)}{2} + \sum_{x=0}^{i} K[x]) \approx (\frac{N-1}{N})^{1+\frac{i(i+1)}{2}} + \frac{1}{N}$ for $0 \leq i \leq N-1$.*

Lemma 2. *Assume that during the KSA rounds, the index j takes its values from $\{0, 1, \ldots, N-1\}$ uniformly at random. Then, $P(S_N[i] = S_0[j_{i+1}]) \approx (\frac{N-i}{N}) \cdot (\frac{N-1}{N})^{N-1}$, $0 \leq i \leq N-1$.*

Proof. During the swap in round $i+1$, $S_{i+1}[i]$ is assigned the value of $S_i[j_{i+1}]$. Now, the index j_{i+1} is not involved in any swap during the previous i many rounds, if it is not touched by the indices $\{0, 1, \ldots, i-1\}$, the probability of which is $(\frac{N-i}{N})$, as well as if it is not touched by the indices $\{j_1, j_2, \ldots, j_i\}$, the probability of which is $(\frac{N-1}{N})^i$. Hence, $P(S_{i+1}[i] = S_0[j_{i+1}]) \approx (\frac{N-i}{N}) \cdot (\frac{N-1}{N})^i$. After round $i+1$, index i is not touched by any of the subsequent $N-1-i$ many j values with probability $(\frac{N-1}{N})^{N-1-i}$. Hence, $P(S_N[i] = S_0[j_{i+1}]) \approx (\frac{N-i}{N}) \cdot (\frac{N-1}{N})^i \cdot (\frac{N-1}{N})^{N-1-i} = (\frac{N-i}{N}) \cdot (\frac{N-1}{N})^{N-1}$. $\qquad\square$

Theorem 1. *Assume that during the KSA rounds, the index j takes its values from $\{0, 1, \ldots, N-1\}$ uniformly at random. Then, $P\Big(S_N[i] = S_0\Big[\sum_{x=0}^{i} S_0[x] + \sum_{x=0}^{i} K[x]\Big]\Big) \approx (\frac{N-i}{N}) \cdot (\frac{N-1}{N})^{[\frac{i(i+1)}{2}+N]} + \frac{1}{N}$, $0 \leq i \leq N-1$.*

Proof. $S_N[i]$ can equal $S_0\Big[\sum_{x=0}^{i} S_0[x] + \sum_{x=0}^{i} K[x]\Big]$ in two ways. One way is that $j_{i+1} = \sum_{x=0}^{i} S_0[x] + \sum_{x=0}^{i} K[x]$ following the recursive path as in the proof of Lemma 1, and $S_N[i] = S_0[j_{i+1}]$. Combining the results of Lemma 1 and Lemma 2, we get the contribution of this part $\approx (\frac{N-1}{N})^{\frac{i(i+1)}{2}} \cdot (\frac{N-i}{N}) \cdot (\frac{N-1}{N})^{N-1} = (\frac{N-i}{N}) \cdot (\frac{N-1}{N})^{[\frac{i(i+1)}{2}+(N-1)]}$. Another way is that neither of the above events happen and still $S_N[i]$ equals $S_0\Big[\sum_{x=0}^{i} S_0[x] + \sum_{x=0}^{i} K[x]\Big]$ due to random association. The contribution of this second part is approximately $\Big(1 - (\frac{N-i}{N}) \cdot (\frac{N-1}{N})^{[\frac{i(i+1)}{2}+(N-1)]}\Big) \cdot \frac{1}{N}$. Adding these two contributions, we get the total probability $\approx (\frac{N-i}{N}) \cdot (\frac{N-1}{N})^{[\frac{i(i+1)}{2}+(N-1)]} + \Big(1 - (\frac{N-i}{N}) \cdot (\frac{N-1}{N})^{[\frac{i(i+1)}{2}+(N-1)]}\Big) \cdot \frac{1}{N} = (1 - \frac{1}{N}) \cdot (\frac{N-i}{N}) \cdot (\frac{N-1}{N})^{[\frac{i(i+1)}{2}+(N-1)]} + \frac{1}{N} = (\frac{N-i}{N}) \cdot (\frac{N-1}{N})^{[\frac{i(i+1)}{2}+N]} + \frac{1}{N}$. $\qquad\square$

Corollary 2. *If the initial permutation is the identity permutation, i.e., $S_0[i] = i$ for $0 \leq i \leq N-1$, then $P(S_N[i] = \frac{i(i+1)}{2} + \sum_{x=0}^{i} K[x]) \approx (\frac{N-i}{N}) \cdot (\frac{N-1}{N})^{[\frac{i(i+1)}{2}+N]} + \frac{1}{N}$ for $0 \leq i \leq N-1$.*

Table 2. The probabilities following Corollary 2

i	$P(S[i] = \frac{i(i+1)}{2} + \sum_{x=0}^{i} K[x])$
0-15	.371 .368 .364 .358 .351 .343 .334 .324 .313 .301 .288 .275 .262 .248 .234 .220
16-31	.206 .192 .179 .165 .153 .140 .129 .117 .107 .097 .087 .079 .071 .063 .056 .050
32-47	.045 .039 .035 .031 .027 .024 .021 .019 .016 .015 .013 .011 .010 .009 .008 .008

In the following table (Table 2) we list the theoretical values of the probabilities to compare with the experimental values provided in [15] and summarized in our Table 1.

After the index 48 and onwards, both the theoretical as well as the experimental values tend to $\frac{1}{N}$ (= 0.0039 for $N = 256$) as is expected when we consider the equality between two randomly chosen values from a set of N elements.

3   Recovering the Secret Key from the Permutation After the KSA

In this section, we discuss how to get the secret key bytes from the random-looking permutation after the KSA using the equations of Corollary 2.

We explain the scenario with an example first.

Example 1. Consider a 5 byte secret key with $K[0] = 106, K[1] = 59, K[2] = 220, K[3] = 65$, and $K[4] = 34$. We denote $f_i = \frac{i(i+1)}{2} + \sum_{x=0}^{i} K[x]$. If one runs the KSA, then the first 16 bytes of the final permutation will be as follows.

i	0	1	2	3	4	5	6	7	8	9	10	11	12	13	14	15
f_i	106	166	132	200	238	93	158	129	202	245	105	175	151	229	21	142
$S_{256}[i]$	230	166	87	48	238	93	68	239	202	83	105	147	151	229	35	142

The strategy of key recovery would be to consider all possible sets of 5 equations chosen from the 16 equations $S_N[i] = f_i$, $0 \leq i \leq 15$, and then try to solve them. Whether the solution is correct or not can be checked by running the KSA and comparing the permutation obtained with the permutation in hand. Some of the choices may not be solvable at all. The case of correct solution for this example correspond to the choices $i = 1, 4, 5, 8$ and 12, and the corresponding equations are:

$$K[0] + K[1] + (1 \cdot 2)/2 = 166 \tag{1}$$
$$K[0] + K[1] + K[2] + K[3] + K[4] + (4 \cdot 5)/2 = 238 \tag{2}$$
$$K[0] + \ldots + K[5] + (5 \cdot 6)/2 = 93 \tag{3}$$
$$K[0] + \ldots + K[8] + (8 \cdot 9)/2 = 202 \tag{4}$$
$$K[0] + \ldots + K[12] + (12 \cdot 13)/2 = 151 \tag{5}$$

In general, the correctness of the solution depends on the correctness of the selected equations. The probability that we will indeed get correct solutions is related to the joint probability of $S_N[i] = f_i$ for the set of chosen i-values. Note that we do not need the assumption that the majority of the equations are correct. Whether indeed the equations selected are correct or not can be cross-checked by running the KSA again. Moreover, empirical results show that in a significant proportion of the cases we get enough correct equations to solve for the key.

For a 5 byte key, if we go for an exhaustive search for the key, then the complexity would be 2^{40}. Whereas in our approach, we need to consider at the most $\binom{16}{5} = 4368 < 2^{13}$ sets of 5 equations. Since the equations are triangular in form, solving each set of 5 equations would take approximately $5^2 = 25$ (times a small constant) $< 2^5$ many additions/subtractions. Hence the improvement over exhaustive search is almost by a factor of $\frac{2^{40}}{2^{13} \cdot 2^5} = 2^{22}$.

From Corollary 2, we get how $S_N[i]$ is biased to different combinations of the key bytes. Let us denote $f_i = \frac{i(i+1)}{2} + \sum_{x=0}^{i} K[x]$ and $P(S_N[i] = f_i) = p_i$ for $0 \le i \le N - 1$. We initiate the discussion for RC4 with secret key of size l bytes. Suppose we want to recover exactly m out of the l secret key bytes by solving equations and the other $l - m$ bytes by exhaustive key search. For this, we consider n $(m \le n \le N)$ many equations $S_N[i] = f_i$, $i = 0, 1, \ldots, n - 1$, in l variables (the key bytes). Let EI_t denote the set of all independent systems of t equations, or, equivalently, the collection of the indices $\{i_1, i_2, \ldots, i_t\} \subseteq \{0, 1, \ldots, n - 1\}$, corresponding to all sets of t independent equations (selected from the above system of n equations).

If we want to recover m key bytes by solving m equations out of the first n equations of the form $S_N[i] = f_i$, in general, we need to check whether each of the $\binom{n}{m}$ systems of m equations is independent or not. In the next Theorem, we present the criteria for checking the independence of such a set of equations and also the total number of such sets.

Theorem 2. *Let $l \ge 2$ be the RC4 key length in bytes. Suppose we want to select systems of m independent equations, $2 \le m \le l$, from the following n equations, $m \le n \le N$, of the form $S_N[i] = f_i$ involving the final permutation bytes, where*

$$f_i = \frac{i(i+1)}{2} + \sum_{x=0}^{i} K[x], \ 0 \le i \le n - 1.$$

1. *The system $S_N[i_q] = f_{i_q}$, $1 \le q \le m$, of m equations selected from $S_N[i] = f_i$, $0 \le i \le n - 1$, corresponding to $i = i_1, i_2, \ldots, i_m$, is independent if and only if any one of the following two conditions hold: either (i) $i_q \bmod l$, $1 \le q \le m$, yields m distinct values, or (ii) $i_q \bmod l \ne (l-1)$, $1 \le q \le m$, and there is exactly one pair $i_x, i_y \in \{i_1, i_2, \ldots, i_m\}$ such that $i_x = i_y \pmod{l}$, and all other $i_q \bmod l, q \ne x, q \ne y$ yields $m - 2$ distinct values different from $i_x, i_y \pmod{l}$.*

2. *The total number of independent systems of* m (≥ 2) *equations is given by*

$$|EI_m| = \sum_{r=0}^{m} \binom{n \bmod l}{r}\binom{l-n \bmod l}{m-r}(\lfloor \tfrac{n}{l}\rfloor + 1)^r(\lfloor \tfrac{n}{l}\rfloor)^{m-r}$$

$$+ \binom{n \bmod l}{1}\binom{\lfloor \frac{n}{l}\rfloor + 1}{2}\sum_{r=0}^{m-2}\binom{n \bmod l-1}{r}\binom{l-n \bmod l-1}{m-2-r}(\lfloor \tfrac{n}{l}\rfloor + 1)^r(\lfloor \tfrac{n}{l}\rfloor)^{m-2-r}$$

$$+ \binom{l-n \bmod l-1}{1}\binom{\lfloor \frac{n}{l}\rfloor}{2}\sum_{r=0}^{m-2}\binom{n \bmod l}{r}\binom{l-n \bmod l-2}{m-2-r}(\lfloor \tfrac{n}{l}\rfloor + 1)^r(\lfloor \tfrac{n}{l}\rfloor)^{m-2-r},$$

where the binomial coefficient $\binom{u}{v}$ *has the value* 0, *if* $u < v$.

Proof. (*Part 1*) First, we will show that any one of the conditions (i) and (ii) is sufficient. Suppose that the condition (i) holds, i.e., $i_q \bmod l$ $(1 \leq q \leq m)$ yields m distinct values. Then each equation involves a different key byte as a variable, and hence the system is independent. Now, suppose that the condition (ii) holds. Then there exists exactly one pair $x, y \in \{1, \ldots, m\}$, $x \neq y$, where $i_x = i_y \bmod l$. Without loss of generality, suppose $i_x < i_y$. Then we can subtract $S_N[i_x] = f_{i_x}$ from $S_N[i_y] = f_{i_y}$ to get one equation involving some multiple of the sum $s = \sum_{x=0}^{l-1} K[x]$ of the key bytes. So we can replace exactly one equation involving either i_x or i_y by the new equation involving s, which will become a different equation with a new variable $K[l-1]$, since $l-1 \notin \{i_1 \bmod l, i_2 \bmod l, \ldots, i_m \bmod l\}$. Thus, the resulting system is independent.

Next, we are going to show that the conditions are necessary. Suppose that neither condition (i) nor condition (ii) holds. Then either we will have a triplet x, y, z such that $i_x = i_y = i_z = \bmod\ l$, or we will have a pair x, y with $i_x = i_y \bmod l$ and $l-1 \in \{i_1 \bmod l, i_2 \bmod l, \ldots, i_m \bmod l\}$. In the first case, subtracting two of the equations from the third one would result in two equations involving s and the same key bytes as variables. Thus the resulting system will not be independent. In the second case, subtracting one equation from the other will result in an equation which is dependent on the equation involving the key byte $K[l-1]$.

(*Part 2*) We know that $n = (\lfloor \tfrac{n}{l}\rfloor)l + (n \bmod l)$. If we compute $i \bmod l$, for $i = 0, 1, \ldots n-1$, then we will have the following residue classes:

$$[0] \qquad = \{0, l, 2l, \ldots, (\lfloor \tfrac{n}{l}\rfloor)l\}$$
$$[1] \qquad = \{1, l+1, 2l+1, \ldots, (\lfloor \tfrac{n}{l}\rfloor)l + 1\}$$
$$\vdots \qquad\qquad \vdots \; \vdots$$
$$[n \bmod l-1] = \{n \bmod l-1, l+(n \bmod l-1), 2l+(n \bmod l-1), \ldots,$$
$$(\lfloor \tfrac{n}{l}\rfloor)l + (n \bmod l-1)\}$$
$$[n \bmod l] \qquad = \{n \bmod l, l+(n \bmod l), 2l+(n \bmod l), \ldots, (\lfloor \tfrac{n}{l}\rfloor - 1)l$$
$$+(n \bmod l)\}$$
$$\vdots \qquad\qquad \vdots \; \vdots$$
$$[l-1] \qquad = \{l-1, l+(l-1), 2l+(l-1), \ldots, (\lfloor \tfrac{n}{l}\rfloor - 1)l + (l-1)\}$$

The set of these l many residue classes can be classified into two mutually exclusive subsets, namely $A = \{[0], \ldots, [n \bmod l-1]\}$ and $B = \{[n \bmod l], \ldots, [l-1]\}$, such that each residue class $a \in A$ has $\lfloor \frac{n}{l} \rfloor + 1$ members and each residue class $b \in B$ has $\lfloor \frac{n}{l} \rfloor$ members. Note that $|A| = n \bmod l$ and $|B| = l - (n \bmod l)$.

Now, the independent systems of m equations can be selected in three mutually exclusive and exhaustive ways. Case I corresponds to the condition (i) and Cases II & III correspond to the condition (ii) stated in the theorem.

<u>Case I</u>: *Select m different residue classes from $A \cup B$ and choose one i-value (the equation number) from each of these m residue classes.* Now, r of the m residue classes can be selected from the set A in $\binom{n \bmod l}{r}$ ways and the remaining $m - r$ can be selected from the set B in $\binom{l-n \bmod l}{m-r}$ ways. Again, corresponding to each such choice, the first r residue classes would give $\lfloor \frac{n}{l} \rfloor + 1$ choices for i (the equation number) and each of the remaining $m - r$ residue classes would give $\lfloor \frac{n}{l} \rfloor$ choices for i. Thus, the total number of independent equations in this case is given by $\sum_{r=0}^{m} \binom{n \bmod l}{r} \binom{l-n \bmod l}{m-r} (\lfloor \frac{n}{l} \rfloor + 1)^r (\lfloor \frac{n}{l} \rfloor)^{m-r}$.

<u>Case II</u>: *Select two i-values from any residue class in A. Then select $m - 2$ other residue classes except $[l-1]$ and select one i-value from each of those $m-2$ residue classes.* We can pick one residue class $a \in A$ in $\binom{n \bmod l}{1}$ ways and subsequently two i-values from a in $\binom{\lfloor \frac{n}{l} \rfloor + 1}{2}$ ways. Of the remaining $m - 2$ residue classes, r can be selected from $A \setminus \{a\}$ in $\binom{n \bmod l-1}{r}$ ways and the remaining $m - 2 - r$ can be selected from $B \setminus \{[l-1]\}$ in $\binom{l-n \bmod l-1}{m-2-r}$ ways. Again, corresponding to each such choice, the first r residue classes would give $\lfloor \frac{n}{l} \rfloor + 1$ choices for i (the equation number) and each of the remaining $m-2-r$ residue classes would give $\lfloor \frac{n}{l} \rfloor$ choices for i. Thus, the total number of independent equations in this case is given by $\binom{n \bmod l}{1} \binom{\lfloor \frac{n}{l} \rfloor + 1}{2} \sum_{r=0}^{m-2} \binom{n \bmod l-1}{r} \binom{l-n \bmod l-1}{m-2-r} (\lfloor \frac{n}{l} \rfloor + 1)^r (\lfloor \frac{n}{l} \rfloor)^{m-2-r}$.

<u>Case III</u>: *Select two i-values from any residue class in $B \setminus \{[l-1]\}$. Then select $m-2$ other residue classes and select one i-value from each of those $m-2$ residue classes.* This case is similar to case II, and the total number of independent equations in this case is given by $\binom{l-n \bmod l-1}{1} \binom{\lfloor \frac{n}{l} \rfloor}{2} \sum_{r=0}^{m-2} \binom{n \bmod l}{r} \binom{l-n \bmod l-2}{m-2-r} (\lfloor \frac{n}{l} \rfloor + 1)^r (\lfloor \frac{n}{l} \rfloor)^{m-2-r}$.

Adding the counts for the above three cases, we get the result.   □

Proposition 1. *Given n and m, it takes $O(m^2 \cdot \binom{n}{m})$ time to generate the set EI_m using Theorem 2.*

Proof. We need to check a total of $\binom{n}{m}$ many m tuples $\{i_1, i_2, \ldots, i_m\}$, and using the independence criteria of Theorem 2, it takes $O(m^2)$ amount of time to determine if each tuple belongs to EI_m or not.   □

Proposition 2. *Suppose we have an independent system of equations of the form $S_N[i_q] = f_{i_q}$ involving the l key bytes as variables corresponding to the tuple $\{i_1, i_2, \ldots, i_m\}$, $0 \le i_q \le n-1$, $1 \le q \le m$, where $f_i = \frac{i(i+1)}{2} + \sum_{x=0}^{i} K[x]$. If* there is one equation in the system involving $s = \sum_{x=0}^{l-1} K[x]$, then we would have at most $\lfloor \frac{n}{l} \rfloor$ many solutions for the key.

Proof. If the coefficient of s is a, then by Linear Congruence Theorem [16], we would have at most $gcd(a, N)$ many solutions for s, each of which would give a different solution for the key. To find the maximum possible number of solutions, we need to find an upper bound of $gcd(a, N)$.

Since the key is of length l, the coefficient a of s would be $\lfloor \frac{i_s}{l} \rfloor$, where i_s is the i-value $\in \{i_1, i_2, \ldots, i_m\}$ corresponding to the equation involving s. Thus, $gcd(a, N) \leq a = \lfloor \frac{i_s}{l} \rfloor \leq \lfloor \frac{n}{l} \rfloor$.   □

Let us consider an example to demonstrate the case when we have two i-values (equation numbers) from the same residue class in the selected system of m equations, but still the system is independent and hence solvable.

Example 2. Assume that the secret key is of length 5 bytes. Let us consider 16 equations of the form $S_N[i] = f_i$, $0 \leq i \leq 15$. We would consider all possible sets of 5 equations chosen from the above 16 equations and then try to solve them. One such set would correspond to $i = 0, 1, 2, 3$ and 13. Let the corresponding $S_N[i]$ values be 246, 250, 47, 204 and 185 respectively. Then we can form the following equations:

$$K[0] = 246 \tag{6}$$
$$K[0] + K[1] + (1 \cdot 2)/2 = 250 \tag{7}$$
$$K[0] + K[1] + K[2] + (2 \cdot 3)/2 = 47 \tag{8}$$
$$K[0] + K[1] + K[2] + K[3] + (3 \cdot 4)/2 = 204 \tag{9}$$
$$K[0] + \ldots + K[13] + (13 \cdot 14)/2 = 185 \tag{10}$$

From the first four equations, we readily get $K[0] = 246, K[1] = 3, K[2] = 51$ and $K[3] = 154$. Since the key is 5 bytes long, $K[5] = K[0], \ldots, K[9] = K[4], K[10] = K[0], \ldots, K[13] = K[3]$. Denoting the sum of the key bytes $K[0] + \ldots + K[4]$ by s, we can rewrite equation (10) as:

$$2s + K[0] + K[1] + K[2] + K[3] + 91 = 185 \tag{11}$$

Subtracting (9) from (11), and solving for s, we get $s = 76$ or 204. Taking the value 76, we get

$$K[0] + K[1] + K[2] + K[3] + K[4] = 76 \tag{12}$$

Subtracting (9) from (12), we get $K[4] = 134$. $s = 204$ does not give the correct key, as can be verified by running the KSA and observing the permutation obtained.

We now present the general algorithm for recovering the secret key bytes from the final permutation obtained after the completion of the KSA.

Algorithm RecoverKey
Inputs:
1. The final permutation bytes: $S_N[i]$, $0 \leq i \leq N - 1$.
2. Number of key bytes: l.
3. Number of key bytes to be solved from equations: m $(\leq l)$.
4. Number of equations to be tried: n $(\geq m)$.
Output:
The recovered key bytes $K[0], K[1], \ldots, K[l-1]$, if they are found.
Otherwise, the algorithm halts after trying all the $|EI_m|$ systems of
m independent equations.
Steps:
1. For each distinct tuple $\{i_1, i_2, \ldots, i_m\}$, $0 \leq i_q \leq n - 1$, $1 \leq q \leq m$ do
1.1. If the tuple belongs to EI_m then do
1.1.1 Arbitrarily select any m variables present in the system;
1.1.2 For each possible assignment of the remaining $l - m$ variables do
1.1.2.1 Solve for the m variables;
1.1.2.2 Run the KSA with the solved key;
1.1.2.3 If the permutation obtained after the KSA is the same as
the given S_N, then the recovered key is the correct one.

If one does not use the independence criteria (Theorem 2), all $\binom{n}{m}$ sets of equations need to be checked. However, the number of independent systems is $|EI_m|$, which is much smaller than $\binom{n}{m}$. Table 3 shows that $|EI_m| < \frac{1}{2}\binom{n}{m}$ for most values of l, n, and m. Thus, the independence criteria in step 1.1 reduces the number of iterations in step 1.1.2 by a substantial factor.

The following Theorem quantifies the amount of time required to recover the key due to our algorithm.

Theorem 3. *The time complexity of the RecoverKey algorithm is given by*

$$O\left(m^2 \cdot \binom{n}{m} + m^2 \cdot |EI_m| \cdot \lfloor \tfrac{n}{l} \rfloor \cdot 2^{8(l-m)}\right),$$

where $|EI_m|$ is given by Theorem 2.

Proof. According to Proposition 1, for a complete run of the algorithm, checking the condition at step 1.1 consumes a total of $O(m^2 \cdot \binom{n}{m})$ amount of time.

Further, the loop in step 1.1.2 undergoes $|EI_m|$ many iterations, each of which exhaustively searches $l - m$ many key bytes and solves a system of m equations. By Proposition 2, each system can yield at the most $O(\lfloor \frac{n}{l} \rfloor)$ many solutions for the key. Also, finding each solution involves $O(m^2)$ many addition/subtraction operations (the equations being traingular in form). Thus, the total time consumed by step 1.1.2 for a complete run would be $O(m^2 \cdot |EI_m| \cdot \lfloor \frac{n}{l} \rfloor \cdot 2^{8(l-m)})$.

Hence, the time complexity is given by $O\left(m^2 \cdot \binom{n}{m} + m^2 \cdot |EI_m| \cdot \lfloor \frac{n}{l} \rfloor \cdot 2^{8(l-m)}\right)$. $\square$

Next, we estimate what is the probability of getting a set of independent correct equations when we run the above algorithm.

Proposition 3. *Suppose that we are given the system of equations $S_N[i] = f_i$, $i = 0, 1, \ldots, n - 1$. Let c be the number of independent correct equations. Then*

$$P(c \geq m) = \sum_{t=m}^{n} \sum_{\{i_1, i_2, \ldots, i_t\} \in EI_t} p(i_1, i_2, \ldots, i_t),$$

where EI_t is the collection of the indices $\{i_1, i_2, \ldots, i_t\}$ corresponding to all sets of t independent equations, and $p(i_1, i_2, \ldots, i_t)$ is the joint probability that the t equations corresponding to the indices $\{i_1, i_2, \ldots, i_t\}$ are correct and the other $n - t$ equations corresponding to the indices $\{0, 1, \ldots, n - 1\} \setminus \{i_1, i_2, \ldots, i_t\}$ are incorrect.

Proof. We need to sum $|EI_t|$ number of terms of the form $p(i_1, i_2, \ldots, i_t)$ to get the probability that exactly t equations are correct, i.e.,

$$P(c = t) = \sum_{\{i_1, i_2, \ldots, i_t\} \in EI_t} p(i_1, i_2, \ldots, i_t).$$

Hence, $P(c \geq m) = \sum_{t=m}^{n} P(c = t) = \sum_{t=m}^{n} \sum_{\{i_1, i_2, \ldots, i_t\} \in EI_t} p(i_1, i_2, \ldots, i_t).$ □

Note that $P(c \geq m)$ gives the success probability with which one can recover the secret key from the permutation after the KSA.

As the events $(S_N[i] = f_i)$ are not independent for different i's, theoretically presenting the formulae for the joint probability $p(i_1, i_2, \ldots, i_t)$ seems to be extremely tedious. In the following table, we provide experimental results on the probability of having at least m independent correct equations, when the first n equations $S_N[i] = f_i, 0 \leq i \leq n - 1$ are considered for the RecoverKey algorithm for different values of n, m, and the key length l, satisfying $m \leq l \leq n$. For each probability calculation, the complete KSA was repeated a million times, each time with a randomly chosen key. We also compare the values of the exhaustive search complexity and the reduction due to our algorithm. Let $e = \lceil \log_2(m^2 \cdot \binom{n}{m} + m^2 \cdot |EI_m| \cdot \lfloor \frac{n}{l} \rfloor \cdot 2^{8(l-m)}) \rceil$. The time complexity of exhaustive search is $O(2^{8l})$ and that of the RecoverKey algorithm, according to Theorem 3, is given by $O(2^e)$. Thus, the reduction in search complexity due to our algorithm is by a factor $O(2^{8l-e})$. One may note from Table 3 that by suitably choosing the parameters one can achieve the search complexity $O(2^{\frac{8l}{2}}) = O(2^{4l})$, which is the square root of the exhaustive key search complexity. The results in Table 3 clearly show that the probabilities (i.e., the empirical value of $P(c \geq m)$) in most of the cases are greater than 10%. However, the algorithm does not use the probabilities to recover the key. For certain keys the algorithm will be able to recover the keys and for certain other keys the algorithm will not be able to recover the keys by solving the equations. The success probability can be interpreted as the proportion of keys for which the algorithm will be able to successfully recover the key. The keys, that can be recovered from the permutation after the KSA using the RecoverKey algorithm, may be considered as weak keys in RC4.

It is important to note that the permutation is biased towards the secret key not only after the completion of the KSA, rather the bias persists in every round

Table 3. Running the RecoverKey algorithm with different parameters

l	n	m	$\binom{n}{m}$	$|EI_m|$	$8l$	e	$8l-e$	$P(c \geq m)$
5	16	5	4368	810	40	18	22	0.250
5	24	5	42504	7500	40	21	19	0.385
8	16	6	8008	3472	64	34	30	0.273
8	20	7	77520	13068	64	29	35	0.158
8	40	8	76904685	1484375	64	33	31	0.092
10	16	7	11440	5840	80	43	37	0.166
10	24	8	735471	130248	80	40	40	0.162
10	48	9	1677106640	58125000	80	43	37	0.107
12	24	8	735471	274560	96	58	38	0.241
12	24	9	1307504	281600	96	50	46	0.116
16	24	9	1307504	721800	128	60	68	0.185
16	32	10	64512240	19731712	128	63	65	0.160
16	32	11	129024480	24321024	128	64	64	0.086
16	40	12	5586853480	367105284	128	64	64	0.050

of the KSA. If we know the permutation at any stage of the KSA, we can use our key recovery technique to get back the secret key [12]. Moreover, the PRGA is exactly the same as the KSA with the starting value of i as 1 (instead of 0) and with $K[i]$ set to 0 for all i. Thus, if we know the RC4 state information at any round of PRGA, we can deterministically get back the permutation after the KSA [12] and thereby recover the secret key.

4 Intrinsic Weakness of Shuffle-Exchange Type KSA

In the KSA of RC4, i is incremented by one and j is updated pseudo-randomly by the rule $j = j + S[i] + K[i]$. Here, the increment of j is a function of the permutation and the secret key. One may expect that the correlation between the secret key and the final permutation can be removed by modifying the update rule for j. Here we show that for a certain class of rules of this type, where j across different rounds is uniformly randomly distributed, there will always exist significant bias of the final permutation after the KSA towards some combination of the secret key bytes with significant probability. Though the proof technique is similar to that in Section 2, it may be noted that the analysis in the proofs here focus on the weakness of the particular "form" of RC4 KSA, and not on the exact quantity of the bias.

Using the notation of Section 2, we can model the update of j in the KSA as an arbitrary function u of (a) the current values of i, j, (b) the i-th and j-th permutation bytes from the previous round, and (c) the i-th and j-th key bytes, i.e.,

$$j_{i+1} = u(i, j_i, S_i[i], S_i[j_i], K[i], K[j_i]).$$

For subsequent reference, let us call the KSA with this generalized update rule as GKSA.

Lemma 3. *Assume that during the GKSA rounds, the index j takes its values from $\{0, 1, \ldots, N-1\}$ uniformly at random. Then, one can always construct functions $h_i(S_0, K)$, which depends only on i, the secret key bytes and the initial permutation, and probabilities π_i, which depends only on i and N, such that $P(j_{i+1} = h_i(S_0, K)) = (\frac{N-1}{N})\pi_i + \frac{1}{N}$, $0 \le i \le N-1$.*

Proof. By induction on i, we will show (i) how to construct the recursive functions $h_i(S_0, K)$ and probabilities π_i and (ii) that one contribution towards the event $(j_{i+1} = h_i(S_0, K))$ is π_i.

- *Base Case*: Initially, before the beginning of round 1, $j_0 = 0$. In round 1, we have $i = 0$ and hence $j_1 = u(0, 0, S_0[0], S_0[0], K[0], K[0]) = h_0(S_0, K)$ (say), with probability $\pi_0 = 1$.
- *Inductive Case*: Suppose, $P(j_i = h_{i-1}(S_0, K)) = \pi_{i-1}$, $i \ge 1$ (*inductive hypothesis*). We know that $j_{i+1} = u(i, j_i, S_i[i], S_i[j_i], K[i], K[j_i])$. In the right hand side of this equality, all occurrences of $S_i[i]$ can be replaced by $S_0[i]$ with probability $(\frac{N-1}{N})^i$, which is the probability of index i not being involved in any swap in the previous i many rounds. Also, due to the swap in round i, we have $S_i[j_i] = S_{i-1}[i-1]$, which again can be replaced by $S_0[i-1]$ with probability $(\frac{N-1}{N})^{i-1}$. Finally, all occurrences of j_i can be replaced by $h_{i-1}(S_0, K)$ with probability π_{i-1} (using the inductive hypothesis). Thus, j_{i+1} equals $u(i, h_{i-1}(S_0, K), S_0[i], S_0[i-1], K[i], K[h_{i-1}(S_0, K)])$ with some probability π_i which can be computed as a function of i, N, and π_{i-1}, depending on the occurrence or non-occurrence of various terms in u. If we denote $h_i(S_0, K) = u(i, h_{i-1}(S_0, K), S_0[i], S_0[i-1], K[i], K[h_{i-1}(S_0, K)])$, then (i) and (ii) follow by induction.
  When the recursive path does not occur, then the event

$$(j_{i+1} = u(i, h_{i-1}(S_0, K), S_0[i], S_0[i-1], K[i], K[h_{i-1}(S_0, K)]))$$

  occurs due to random association with probability $(1 - \pi_i) \cdot \frac{1}{N}$. Adding the above two contributions, we get $P(j_{i+1} = h_i(S_0, K)) = \pi_i + (1 - \pi_i) \cdot \frac{1}{N} = (\frac{N-1}{N})\pi_i + \frac{1}{N}$. $\qquad\square$

Theorem 4. *Assume that during the GKSA rounds, the index j takes its values from $\{0, 1, \ldots, N-1\}$ uniformly at random. Then, one can always construct functions $f_i(S_0, K)$, which depends only on i, the secret key bytes and the initial permutation, such that $P(S_N[i] = f_i(S_0, K)) \approx (\frac{N-i}{N}) \cdot (\frac{N-1}{N})^N \cdot \pi_i + \frac{1}{N}$, $0 \le i \le N-1$.*

Proof. We will show that $f_i(S_0, K) = S_0[h_i(S_0, K)]$ where the function h_is are given by Lemma 3.

Now, $S_N[i]$ can equal $S_0[h_i(S_0, K)]$ in two ways. One way is that $j_{i+1} = h_i(S_0, K)$ following the recursive path as in Lemma 3 and $S_N[i] = S_0[j_{i+1}]$.

Combining Lemma 3 and Lemma 2, we find the probability of this event to be approximately $(\frac{N-i}{N}) \cdot (\frac{N-1}{N})^{N-1} \cdot \pi_i$. Another way is that the above path is not followed and still $S_N[i] = S_0[h_i(S_0, K)]$ due to random association. The contribution of this part is approximately $\left(1 - (\frac{N-i}{N}) \cdot (\frac{N-1}{N})^{N-1} \cdot \pi_i\right) \cdot \frac{1}{N}$. Adding the above two contributions, we get the total probability $\approx (\frac{N-i}{N}) \cdot (\frac{N-1}{N})^{N-1} \cdot$

$\pi_i + \left(1 - (\frac{N-i}{N}) \cdot (\frac{N-1}{N})^{N-1} \cdot \pi_i\right) \cdot \frac{1}{N} = (1 - \frac{1}{N}) \cdot (\frac{N-i}{N}) \cdot (\frac{N-1}{N})^{N-1} \cdot \pi_i + \frac{1}{N} = (\frac{N-i}{N}) \cdot (\frac{N-1}{N})^{N} \cdot \pi_i + \frac{1}{N}$. □

Next, we discuss some special cases of the update rule u as illustrative examples of how to construct the functions f_is and the probabilities π_is using Lemma 3. In all the following cases, we assume S_0 to be an identity permutation and hence $f_i(S_0, K)$ is the same as $h_i(S_0, K)$.

Example 3. Consider the KSA of RC4, where

$$u(i, j_i, S_i[i], S_i[j_i], K[i], K[j_i]) = j_i + S_i[i] + K[i].$$

We have $h_0(S_0, K) = u(0, 0, S_0[0], S_0[0], K[0], K[0]) = 0 + 0 + K[0] = K[0]$. Moreover, $\pi_0 = P(j_1 = h_0(S_0, K)) = 1$. For $i \geq 1$,
$h_i(S_0, K) = u(i, h_{i-1}(S_0, K), S_0[i], S_0[i-1], K[i], K[h_{i-1}(S_0, K)])$
$\quad = h_{i-1}(S_0, K) + S_0[i] + K[i]$
$\quad = h_{i-1}(S_0, K) + i + K[i]$.

Solving the recurrence, we get $h_i(S_0, K) = \frac{i(i+1)}{2} + \sum_{x=0}^{i} K[x]$. From the analysis in the proof of Lemma 3, we see that in the recurrence of h_i, $S_i[i]$ has been replaced by $S_0[i]$ and j_i has been replaced by $h_{i-1}(S_0, K)$. Hence, we would have $\pi_i = P(S_i[i] = S_0[i]) \cdot P(j_i = h_{i-1}(S_0, K)) = (\frac{N-1}{N})^i \cdot \pi_{i-1}$. Solving this recurrence, we get $\pi_i = \prod_{x=0}^{i} (\frac{N-1}{N})^x = (\frac{N-1}{N})^{\frac{i(i+1)}{2}}$. These expressions coincide with those in Corollary 1.

Example 4. Consider the update rule

$$u(i, j_i, S_i[i], S_i[j_i], K[i], K[j_i]) = j_i + S_i[j_i] + K[j_i].$$

Here, $h_0(S_0, K) = u(0, 0, S_0[0], S_0[0], K[0], K[0]) = 0 + 0 + K[0] = K[0]$ and $\pi_0 = P(j_1 = h_0(S_0, K)) = 1$. For $i \geq 1$,
$h_i(S_0, K) = u(i, h_{i-1}(S_0, K), S_0[i], S_0[i-1], K[i], K[h_{i-1}(S_0, K)])$
$\quad = h_{i-1}(S_0, K) + S_0[i-1] + K[h_{i-1}(S_0, K)]$
$\quad = h_{i-1}(S_0, K) + (i-1) + K[h_{i-1}(S_0, K)]$.
From the analysis in the proof of Lemma 3, we see that in the recurrence of h_i, $S_{i-1}[i-1]$ and j_i are respectively replaced by $S_0[i-1]$ and $h_{i-1}(S_0, K)$. Thus, we would have $\pi_i = (\frac{N-1}{N})^{i-1} \cdot \pi_{i-1}$. Solving this recurrence, we get

$$\pi_i = \prod_{x=1}^{i} (\frac{N-1}{N})^{x-1} = (\frac{N-1}{N})^{\frac{i(i-1)}{2}}.$$

Example 5. As another example, suppose

$$u(i, j_i, S_i[i], S_i[j_i], K[i], K[j_i]) = j_i + i \cdot S_i[j_i] + K[j_i].$$

As before, $h_0(S_0, K) = u(0, 0, S_0[0], S_0[0], K[0], K[0]) = 0 + 0 \cdot S[0] + K[0] = 0 + 0 + K[0] = K[0]$ and $\pi_0 = P(j_1 = h_0(S_0, K)) = 1$. For $i \geq 1$,

$$\begin{aligned} h_i(S_0, K) &= u(i, h_{i-1}(S_0, K), S_0[i], S_0[i-1], K[i], K[h_{i-1}(S_0, K)]) \\ &= h_{i-1}(S_0, K)]) + i \cdot S_0[i-1] + K[h_{i-1}(S_0, K)] \\ &= h_{i-1}(S_0, K)]) + i \cdot (i-1) + K[h_{i-1}(S_0, K)]. \end{aligned}$$

As in the previous example, here also the recurrence relation for the probabilities is $\pi_i = (\frac{N-1}{N})^{i-1} \cdot \pi_{i-1}$, whose solution is $\pi_i = \prod_{x=1}^{i}(\frac{N-1}{N})^{x-1} = (\frac{N-1}{N})^{\frac{i(i-1)}{2}}$.

Our results show that the design of RC4 KSA cannot achieve further security by changing the update rule $j = j + S[i] + K[i]$ by any rule from a large class that we present.

5   Conclusion

We theoretically prove Roos's [15] observation about the correlation between the secret key bytes and the final permutation bytes after the KSA. In addition, we show how to use this result to recover the secret key bytes from the final permutation bytes with constant probability of success in less than the square root of the time required for exhaustive key search. Since the final permutation is in general not observable, this does not immediately pose an additional threat to the security of RC4. However, for a perfect key scheduling, any information about the secret key from the final permutation should not be revealed, as the final permutation may in turn leak information in the PRGA. Our work clearly points out an intrinsic structural weaknesses of RC4 KSA and its certain generalizations.

References

1. Fluhrer, S.R., McGrew, D.A.: Statistical Analysis of the Alleged RC4 Keystream Generator. In: Schneier, B. (ed.) FSE 2000. LNCS, vol. 1978, pp. 19–30. Springer, Heidelberg (2001)
2. Fluhrer, S.R., Mantin, I., Shamir, A.: Weaknesses in the Key Scheduling Algorithm of RC4. In: Vaudenay, S., Youssef, A.M. (eds.) SAC 2001. LNCS, vol. 2259, pp. 1–24. Springer, Heidelberg (2001)
3. Golic, J.: Linear statistical weakness of alleged RC4 keystream generator. In: Fumy, W. (ed.) EUROCRYPT 1997. LNCS, vol. 1233, pp. 226–238. Springer, Heidelberg (1997)
4. LAN/MAN Standard Committee. Wireless LAN medium access control (MAC) and physical layer (PHY) specifications, 1999 edn., IEEE standard 802.11 (1999)
5. Klein, A.: Attacks on the RC4 stream cipher (February 27, 2006) (last accessed on June 27, 2007), available at http://cage.ugent.be/~klein/RC4/

6. Mantin, I., Shamir, A.: A Practical Attack on Broadcast RC4. In: Matsui, M. (ed.) FSE 2001. LNCS, vol. 2355, pp. 152–164. Springer, Heidelberg (2002)
7. Mantin, I.: A Practical Attack on the Fixed RC4 in the WEP Mode. In: Roy, B. (ed.) ASIACRYPT 2005. LNCS, vol. 3788, pp. 395–411. Springer, Heidelberg (2005)
8. Mantin, I.: Predicting and Distinguishing Attacks on RC4 Keystream Generator. In: Cramer, R.J.F. (ed.) EUROCRYPT 2005. LNCS, vol. 3494, pp. 491–506. Springer, Heidelberg (2005)
9. Mantin, I.: Analysis of the stream cipher RC4. Master's Thesis, The Weizmann Institute of Science, Israel (2001)
10. Mironov, I.: (Not So) Random Shuffles of RC4. In: Yung, M. (ed.) CRYPTO 2002. LNCS, vol. 2442, pp. 304–319. Springer, Heidelberg (2002)
11. Paul, G., Rathi, S., Maitra, S.: On Non-negligible Bias of the First Output Byte of RC4 towards the First Three Bytes of the Secret Key. In: Proceedings of the International Workshop on Coding and Cryptography, pp. 285–294 (2007)
12. Paul, G., Maitra, S.: RC4 State Information at Any Stage Reveals the Secret Key. IACR Eprint Server, eprint.iacr.org, number 2007/208 (June 1, 2007)
13. Paul, S., Preneel, B.: Analysis of Non-fortuitous Predictive States of the RC4 Keystream Generator. In: Johansson, T., Maitra, S. (eds.) INDOCRYPT 2003. LNCS, vol. 2904, pp. 52–67. Springer, Heidelberg (2003)
14. Paul, S., Preneel, B.: A New Weakness in the RC4 Keystream Generator and an Approach to Improve the Security of the Cipher. In: Roy, B., Meier, W. (eds.) FSE 2004. LNCS, vol. 3017, pp. 245–259. Springer, Heidelberg (2004)
15. Roos, A.: A class of weak keys in the RC4 stream cipher. Two posts in sci.crypt, message-id 43u1eh$1j3@hermes.is.co.za and 44ebge$llf@hermes.is.co.za (1995), available at http://marcel.wanda.ch/Archive/WeakKeys
16. Silverman., J., Friendly, A.: Introduction to Number Theory, 2nd edn., p. 56. Prentice Hall, Englewood Cliffs (2001)
17. Wagner, D.: My RC4 weak keys. Post in sci.crypt, message-id 447o1l$cbj@cnn. Princeton.EDU (September 26, 1995), available at http://www.cs.berkeley.edu/~daw/my-posts/my-rc4-weak-keys

Revisiting Correlation-Immunity in Filter Generators

Aline Gouget[1] and Hervé Sibert[2]

[1] Gemalto, 6 rue de la Verrerie, F-92190 Meudon, France
`aline.gouget@gemalto.com`
[2] NXP Semiconductors, 9 rue Maurice Trintignant, F-72081 Le Mans Cedex 9, France
`herve.sibert@nxp.com`

Abstract. Correlation-immunity is a cryptographic criterion on Boolean functions arising from correlation attacks on combining functions. When it comes to filtering functions, the status of correlation-immunity lacks study in itself and, if it is commonly accepted as a requirement for nonlinear filter generators, this is for other concerns. We revisit the concept of correlation-immunity and clear up its meaning for filtering functions. We summarize existing criteria similar to correlation-immunity and attacks in two different models, showing that such criteria are not relevant in both models. We also derive a precise property to avoid correlations due to the filter function only, which appears to be a bit looser than correlation-immunity. We then propose new attacks based on whether this property is verified.

Keywords: Nonlinear filter generator, Boolean function, correlation-immunity, distinguishing attacks.

1 Introduction

Most stream ciphers proposed in the literature are built upon Linear Feedback Shift Registers (LFSR). One well-known proposal for destroying the linearity inherent to LFSRs is to use a nonlinear function to filter the contents of a single LFSR. All the components of a filter generator (i.e. the LFSR, the filtering function and the taps) must be chosen carefully to ensure the cryptographic security of the keystream generated by the generator. As often in symmetric cryptography, criteria on the filter generator components are mostly derived from known attacks.

The correlation-immunity property is a well-known cryptographic criterion for Boolean functions. Correlation-immunity is sometimes stated as a criterion dedicated to combining functions only, and sometimes as a requirement that also applies to filtering functions. In order to clear up the role of correlation-immunity for filtering functions, we investigate known distinguishing attacks on filter generators that consist in finding correlation relations between the keystream bits by using properties of the filter function only.

C. Adams, A. Miri, and M. Wiener (Eds.): SAC 2007, LNCS 4876, pp. 378–395, 2007.
© Springer-Verlag Berlin Heidelberg 2007

1.1   Related Work

The *nonlinear filter model* is a classical model of synchronous stream ciphers that involves a nonlinear Boolean function to filter the contents of a single shift register.

The *correlation-immunity* criterion has been introduced by Siegenthaler [15] for combining functions, in order to protect them from a "divide and conquer" attack well-known under the name *(fast) correlation attack* [17,11,4,5]. These attacks also apply to nonlinear filter generators [16,7]. Notice that such attacks require that the internal state memory of the generator is updated in a deterministic way. The only criterion on the filtering function involved in this attack is the nonlinearity of the Boolean function, not the correlation-immunity. Canteaut and Filiol [3] studied the fast correlation attack given in [5] for filter generators and they showed that the keystream length which guarantees a successful attack does not depend on the filtering function, except for functions which are very close to affine functions. Then, they suggest that the choice of the Boolean function in the design of a filter generator should be mostly conditioned by other types of attacks. Thus, fast correlations attacks are out of the scope of this paper.

Anderson [1] found other correlations in nonlinear filter generators and proposed an *optimum correlation attack*. This attack is based on the (un)balancedness of the *augmented filter function*. The update of the internal state memory of the generator is assumed to be probabilistic. Hence, this attack does not take advantage of a deterministic update, and it targets correlation relations between the keystream bits that arise from properties of the filter function only. Golic [8] studied a different definition of the augmented filter function and derived a construction of Boolean functions that resist the optimum correlation attack. Still in [8], Golic recommended to use in practice only filtering functions coming from his construction (with additional criteria on the filtering function including correlation-immunity). However, it is unclear to what extent this construction captures all the filtering functions that are immune to this attack, as Dichtl [6] showed by exhibiting such a filtering function that does not follow Golic's construction.

The relevance of the correlation-immunity criterion for filtering functions has been partially studied by Ding *et al.* [7]. Many Boolean functions which are not correlation-immune can be transformed into correlation-immune functions by performing a linear transform on the input variables and adding a linear function. Indeed, Ding *et al.* gave a general method to construct, from a correlation immune function f that filters an LFSR, an equivalent filter generator which differs from the original one only by its initial state vector and by its filter function g, which is not correlation immune. Even if there is no efficient method known to construct such an equivalent generator, stream ciphers with correlation immune filter functions are theoretically vulnerable provided that those with non-correlation-immune functions are. In [7], the authors concluded that using correlation-immune filter functions may not get any advantage in the case when the filter function and the feedback polynomial of the LFSR are known.

Thus, from the state of the art on the application of the correlation-immunity criterion to filtering functions, it is still unclear to what extent one must or not choose a correlation-immune function when designing a filter generator.

1.2   Our Contribution

In this paper, we give in-depth analysis of correlation-related criteria in filter generators. We investigate known distinguishing attacks on filter generators that take advantage of correlation relations between the keystream bits that arise from properties of the filter function only. So as to better understand the attacks, we introduce two security models for filter generators depending on the memory update procedure: the *probabilistic* nonlinear filter model and the *deterministic* nonlinear filter model. We show that considering separately these two models helps to shed light on the design criterion for filtering function, while there is no interest to do the same for combining generators.

We revisit the *optimal correlation attack* [1,8] that targets correlation due to the filtering function. We precisely study the criteria to resist this attack depending on whether it is performed in the probabilistic or in the deterministic model. We show that the relevance of this criterion in the deterministic model is questionable, and that it does not target the initial attack in this model.

Next, we reconsider the original observation of Anderson and give a practical criterion on the filter to avoid the optimal correlation attack in both models. This criterion also thwarts a recent distinguishing attack focusing on a filtering function [19]. We call this new criterion *quasi-immunity*, since it appears to be a bit looser than correlation-immunity. This criterion embeds previous criteria, and it turns out to be the criterion most directly related to correlations of the filtering function.

We then provide the complexity of different types of attack against filtering function that do or do not meet the quasi-immunity requirement. We show that if the filtering function f does not fulfil the quasi-immunity criterion (of order 1), then there always exists a distinguisher between random sequences and keystream outputted by the filter generator even when considering the probabilistic filter generator model. We next evaluate the cost of state recovery attack depending on whether the filtering function fulfils the quasi-immunity criterion. Finally, we discuss the construction of equivalent filter generators that are potentially weaker against such attacks.

1.3   Organization of the Paper

In Section 2, we give the main cryptographic properties of Boolean functions, we briefly describe the components of filter generators and update procedure, and we summarize well-known criteria on the filter generator components. In Section 3, we study correlation attacks targeted at the filtering function in filter generators, and next we derive a new criterion called "quasi-immunity" criterion. In Section 4, we study the complexity of general attacks for filters that do or do not meet the new criterion. At last, we give directions for future work and we conclude.

2 Preliminaries

In this section, we briefly recall the main properties of Boolean functions. Next, we describe the components of a filter generator and give the main known design criteria.

2.1 Boolean Functions

Every n-variable Boolean function f can be uniquely represented by its *algebraic normal form*, $f(x_1, \ldots, x_n) = \sum_{I \subseteq \{1, \ldots, n\}} a_I \prod_{i \in I} x_i$, where the a_I's are in $\mathbb{F}_2$. The terms $\prod_{i \in I} x_i$ are called *monomials*. For any Boolean function f of n variables, we denote by $\mathcal{F}(f)$ the quantity $\mathcal{F}(f) = \sum_{x \in GF(2)^n} (-1)^{f(x)} = 2^n - 2w_H(f)$, where $w_H(f)$ is the Hamming weight of f, related to the Fourier transform of f. In the following, we denote by $e_1, \ldots, e_n$, the n coordinate vectors of the vector space $GF(2)^n$ with Hamming weight 1. For $u \in GF(2)^n$, we denote by φ_u the linear Boolean function $x \mapsto x \cdot u$ where $\cdot$ denotes the inner product.

A Boolean function f is called *balanced* if 0 and 1 have the same number of pre-images by f. The *nonlinear order* of a Boolean function f equals the maximum degree of those monomials whose coefficients are nonzero in its algebraic normal form. The nonlinearity of an n-variable Boolean function f is the minimum Hamming distance between f and the set of affine functions.

An n-variable Boolean function f is *correlation-immune of order m* with $1 \leq m \leq n$ if the output of f and any m input variables are statistically independent. The correlation-immunity criterion can be characterized by means of Walsh coefficients:

Proposition 1. *[20] A Boolean function $f : GF(2)^n \to GF(2)$ is correlation-immune of order m if, and only if, $\mathcal{F}(f + \varphi_u) = \sum_{x \in GF(2)^n} (-1)^{f(x)+u \cdot x} = 0$ for all u with $1 \leq w_H(u) \leq m$.*

The nonlinear order and the nonlinearity of a Boolean function are both affine invariant whereas the correlation-immunity is not [12].

2.2 Nonlinear Filter Generators

A nonlinear filter generator is defined by a finite memory, a filtering function, a tapping sequence defining the input stages to the filter function and a procedure to update the memory.

Finite memory. We assume that every nonlinear filter has a finite input memory of r bits. The value of the initial state of the memory is assumed to be random. At each time t, the $r - 1$ first bits of the memory are shifted right by one position and the leftmost bit is a new bit, that is either random, or determined by the current bits in the register. The indexes in the register are numbered from right to left, starting at 1. We denote by $s = (s_t)_{t=-r}^{\infty}$ the binary sequence of the state memory. Then, the finite sequence $(s_t)_{t=-r}^{-1}$ is the initial state of the memory.

It is recommended to choose $r \geq 2L$ where 2^L is the target security level to avoid time-memory tradeoff attacks [2,9]. More precisely, the number of possible initial states before keystream generation should be at least 2^{2L}.

Filtering function. Let f be a Boolean function of n non-degenerate input variables with $1 \leq n \leq r$. The inputs of the filtering function f are some values $s_{t-\gamma_1}, s_{t-\gamma_2}, \ldots, s_{t-\gamma_n}$ of the finite memory, where $\gamma = (\gamma_i)_{i=1}^n$ is an increasing sequence of positive integers such that $\gamma_1 = 1$, and $\gamma_n \leq r$. The output sequence $z = (z_t)_{t=0}^{\infty}$ of f is called the keystream sequence.

The function f must be balanced since the output sequence is expected to be balanced. The nonlinear order of f must be high enough and f should include many terms of each order up to the nonlinear order of f [13]. Indeed, filter generators can be vulnerable to the Berlekamp-Massey algorithm if the linear complexity of the output sequence is too small. Also, the Boolean function f must not be close to affine functions in order to avoid fast correlation attacks [3].

Taps. The sequence $\gamma = (\gamma_i)_{i=1}^n$ defining the indexes of the input to the filtering function is called the *tapping sequence*, and the corresponding output sequence $z = (z_t)_{t=0}^{\infty}$ is defined by $z_t = f(s_{t-\gamma_1}, \ldots, s_{t-\gamma_n}), \quad t \geq 0$. The choice of the tapping sequence defining the input stages to the filter function f must be done as indicated in [8]: the input memory size should be close to its maximum value $r - 1$, and the set of the tap positions should be a full positive difference set.

Update of the leftmost bit. In the literature, depending on the context, authors either consider that the leftmost bit is a random bit, or that it is determined by the current bits in the register. Nevertheless, these two points of view and their impact in terms of security model have not been studied or even underlined. We call these two models respectively the *probabilistic* nonlinear filter model and the *deterministic* nonlinear filter model.

Probabilistic nonlinear filter model. At each time t, the leftmost bit b is the output of an unbiased random bit source. In this case, the input sequence is perfectly random and then $s = (s_t)_{t=-r}^{\infty}$ is a random sequence. In this model, the aim of an attack is not to recover the key since the knowledge of $(s_t)_{t=-r}^{i-1}$ does not reveal anything about s_i. Here, the aim is to distinguish the keystream sequence z from a random sequence. Thus, an attack on the nonlinear filter generator in the probabilistic model reveals weaknesses of the filter.

Deterministic nonlinear filter model. At each time t, the leftmost bit b is computed from the current memory state, e.g. by using a linear feedback of the register. The best-known criterion on the feedback polynomial is that it should be a primitive polynomial of degree r to ensure that the LFSR sequence $s = (s_t)_{t=-r}^{\infty}$ is a binary maximum-length sequence of period $2^r - 1$ [14]. In this model, the aim of an attack can be either to recover the initial state or to distinguish the keystream from a random sequence.

A successful attack in the probabilistic nonlinear filter model can be adapted to the deterministic model, whereas the converse is not true. However, a criterion to prevent an attack in the probabilistic model does not always translate to the deterministic model.

3   Correlation Attacks on the Filtering Function

In this section, we first review the *optimal correlation attack* presented by Anderson [1] that targets correlations due to the filtering function, before studying criteria to resist this attack in the probabilistic and deterministic models. Next, we consider a distinguishing attack on a filter generator that targets exactly the *optimal correlation* of Anderson. At last, we deduce the *quasi-immunity* criterion for filtering functions.

In the sequel, we assume the filtering function f to be balanced.

3.1   The Optimal Correlation Attack

The *optimal correlation attack* proposed by Anderson [1] is the first attack on filter generators that exploits correlations due to the filtering function only. This attack relies on the fact that each bit going along the register is input to the filtering function at each one of its taps. This results in correlations between the internal register state and the keystream produced. These correlations are avoided if an *augmented filter function* defined accordingly is balanced.

This *augmented filter function* is constructed as follows: consider a single bit b moving along the register. Each time this bit is at a tap location, the filter combines it with other register bits to form a keystream bit. The augmented function is the vectorial function that maps all these (independent) register bits to the n-bit-vector consisting of the n values that involve bit b. One can then distinguish the generator from a random sequence by studying the distribution of the n-tuples in the output sequence that correspond to the output of the augmented filter function.

Anderson provides an example of a filter whose taps are consecutive entries of the register:

$$f(x_1, x_2, x_3, x_4, x_5) = x_1 + x_2 + (x_1 + x_3)(x_2 + x_4 + x_5) + (x_1 + x_4)(x_2 + x_3)x_5.$$

This Boolean function is balanced, correlation-immune of order 2 and of non-linear order 3. However, the augmented function that maps 9-tuples of the shift register sequence to 5-tuples of the keystream output is not balanced, which yields an attack. Notice that here, as the attacks takes place in the probabilistic model, we assume that all 9-tuples are equiprobable.

3.2 Analysis of the Optimal Correlation Attack - Probabilistic Model

Both in [1] and in [8], the authors consider a probabilistic model in which the input sequence $s = (s_t)_{t=-r}^{\infty}$ is regarded as a sequence of balanced and independent bits. The output sequence $z = (z_t)_{t=0}^{\infty}$ is a sequence of balanced bits if and only if the filter function f is balanced. The aim of the attacker is to distinguish the keystream outputted by the filter from a random sequence.

Augmented filter function. The augmented filter function $\bar{h}$ constructed by Anderson in [1] makes it possible to find an *optimal correlation* between the output keystream bits and the internal state of the register. The keystream bit produced at time t is equal to

$$z_t = f(s_{t-\gamma_1}, \ldots, s_{t-\gamma_n}) \ .$$

The function $\bar{h}$ is defined as follows. Consider the n^2 (not necessarily distinct) variables involved in the n values of the filter function at time $t + \gamma_1, \ldots, t + \gamma_n$, which all involve the bit s_t, and denote by G the set of all independent variables among those n^2 variables. The function $\bar{h}$ maps every element of G to the corresponding n-tuple of keystream bits $(z_{t+\gamma_i})_{i=1\ldots n}$.

In [8], Golic studied the randomness of the keystream in the probabilistic model. Assuming that the input sequence $s = (s_t)_{t=-r}^{\infty}$ is a sequence of balanced and independent bits, the output sequence $z = (z_t)_{t=0}^{\infty}$ is a sequence of balanced bits if and only if the filter function f is balanced. The output sequence z is *purely random* if and only if for each $t \geq 0$, the output bit z_t is balanced for any fixed value of the previous output bits $(z_i)_{i=0}^{t-1}$.

For a finite nonlinear filter generator with input memory size r, z_t depends only on the current input bit s_t and on the r preceding input bits $(s_i)_{i=t-r}^{t-1}$. Golic showed that the output sequence is purely random given that the input sequence is such if and only if the vectorial Boolean function F_{M+1} that maps $2M + 1$ consecutive input bits to the $M + 1$ corresponding consecutive output bits is balanced, where $M = \gamma_n - \gamma_1$.

It appears that Golic's construction generalizes the augmented filter function $\bar{h}$ and the corresponding attack to an arbitrary choice of taps for the filter. The criterion for the keystream to be *purely random* and thus to resist the optimum correlation attack in the probabilistic model is the balancedness of this *new* augmented filter function.

We now precisely establish the link between the augmented functions of Anderson and Golic.

Proposition 2. *If the augmented function of Golic F_{M+1} is balanced, then the augmented function of Anderson $\bar{h}$ is balanced.*

Proof. The functional graph in Figure 1 links $\bar{h}$ and F_{M+1} augmented functions, with P and Q being projections respectively from the $2M + 1$ bit variables onto those involved in $\bar{h}$, and from the $M + 1$ consecutive output bits to the subset

$$\begin{array}{ccc} \mathbb{F}_2^{2M+1} & \xrightarrow{\ F_{M+1}\ } & \mathbb{F}_2^{M+1} \\ {\scriptstyle P}\downarrow & & \downarrow{\scriptstyle Q} \\ G & \xrightarrow{\ \ \bar{h}\ \ } & \mathbb{F}_2^n \end{array}$$

Fig. 1. Commutative diagram of augmented functions of Anderson and Golic

of n output bits observed at $t + \gamma_n, \ldots, t + \gamma_1$. Using the commutative diagram in Figure 1, the proof is straightforward. $\qquad\square$

Remark 1. The augmented function $\bar{h}$ is a restriction of the augmented function F_{M+1}, and both functions $\bar{h}$ and F_{M+1} coincide if all the filter taps are consecutive. Thus, $\bar{h}$ being balanced does not imply that F_{M+1} also is. Indeed, for the register with output $z_t = s_{t-3} + s_{t-6} \cdot s_{t-1}$, the function $\bar{h}$ is balanced, whereas F_{M+1} is not.

Golic's formulation in the same framework as Anderson is thus a generalization that enables finding optimal so-called correlations, as it involves the whole memory of the generator. Thus, a nonlinear filter generator is immune to the optimum correlation attack in the probabilistic model if, and only if, Golic's augmented filter function is balanced.

Unfortunately, straightforward study of the balancedness of F_{M+1} is too complex when the taps of the function are located at both ends of the register as recommended in [8].

Criterion on the filter function. We now study the criterion on the filter function for the augmented filter function F_{M+1} to be balanced, which is equivalent to the output being purely random. Golic in [8] gave a characterization in terms of the filter function f and the tapping sequence γ in the following theorem, for which only the sufficiency of the conditions was proven:

Theorem 1. [8] *For a nonlinear filter generator with the filter function f and independent of the tapping sequence γ, the output sequence is purely random given that the input sequence is such if (and only if) $f(x_1, \ldots, x_n)$ is balanced for each value of $(x_2, \ldots, x_n)$, that is, if*

$$f(x_1, \ldots, x_n) = x_1 + g(x_2, \ldots, x_n), \tag{1}$$

or if $f(x_1, \ldots, x_n)$ is balanced for each value of $(x_1, \ldots, x_{n-1})$, that is, if

$$f(x_1, \ldots, x_n) = x_n + g(x_1, \ldots, x_{n-1}), \tag{2}$$

Function F_{M+1} depends on the choice of the taps, while Theorem 1 gives a characterization independent from the tap sequence. However, filtering functions that yield a purely random output for a specific choice of the taps exist, thus contradicting Theorem 1. Indeed, Sumarokov in [18] had already defined perfectly balanced Boolean functions as those functions whose augmented function is balanced when the taps are consecutive, and had given an example that is not of the form (1) or (2). Dichtl [6] also found a similar filtering function. More recently, Logachev [10] gave a general construction to obtain new such functions.

Then, it appears that perfect balancedness of filter functions was not properly defined by Golic, and the definition should enclose the choice of the taps. The filter function to consider is thus the $M+1$-variable Boolean function constructed from f and $\gamma = (\gamma_i)_{i=1}^n$ by adding $M + 1 - n$ mute variables. However, filtering functions of the form (1) or (2) have the particularity that the associated augmented functions are balanced regardless of the choice of the taps.

To summarize, the set of filters that thwart the optimum correlation attack in the probabilistic model includes not only the functions from [8], but also functions whose suitability may depend on the choice of the taps.

3.3 Analysis of the Optimal Correlation Attack - Deterministic Model

We now consider a deterministic model such that the memory is updated using a deterministic linear relation. At each clock, the new leftmost bit is a linear combination of the memory state bits. Then, the input sequence $s = (s_t)_{t=-r}^{\infty}$ is regarded as a sequence of balanced bits which are dependent. The output sequence $z = (z_t)_{t=0}^{\infty}$ is a sequence of balanced bits if and only if the filter function f is balanced. The aim of the attacker is to distinguish the keystream, *i.e.* the output of the filtering function, from a random sequence.

In this case, the approach of [1] and [8] is not valid anymore. Indeed, a very simple counterexample shows that correlation may appear even in the case of functions of the form (1) or (2).

Proposition 3. *Consider the filter generator consisting of a 4-bit register with:*

$$\begin{cases} z_t = s_{t-2} + s_{t-4} \cdot s_{t-3} \\ s_t = s_{t-4} + s_{t-3} \end{cases}$$

The deterministic counterparts of the augmented functions of Anderson and Golic are unbalanced.

Proof. Anderson's augmented function $\bar{h}$ is defined as follows:

$$\bar{h}: \qquad \mathbb{F}_2^4 \qquad \rightarrow \qquad \mathbb{F}_2^3$$
$$s_{t-4}, s_{t-3}, s_{t-2}, s_{t-1} \mapsto (s_{t-2} + s_{t-4} \cdot s_{t-3}, s_{t-1} + s_{t-3} \cdot s_{t-2}, s_t + s_{t-2} \cdot s_{t-1})$$

Taking the correlation into account yields $s_t + s_{t-2} \cdot s_{t-1} = s_{t-4} + s_{t-3} + s_{t-2} \cdot s_{t-1}$. Thus, the edge random variable x_4 (in the random input model) which had a balancing role disappears, and, whenever pattern 101 appears in the keystream, the register content is 0101, hence the result. □

The reason for this observation is that, as feedback bits are produced by bits that have already passed through the register and mixed in previous values of the filter function, the criterion in Theorem 1 is less relevant. Indeed, there is no reason to consider the edge bits as being "more random" than the others, and to consider filtering functions of the form (1) or (2) only.

We now study the augmented function of Golic with respect to the deterministic model in general. Remember that the augmented function F_{M+1} maps $2M + 1$ consecutive input bits to the $M + 1$ corresponding consecutive output bits. A proper choice of the taps implies maximizing the size of the range of the inputs to the filter [8], so that the length of the register is equal to $M + 1$. Therefore, among the $2M + 1$ input bits of F_{M+1}, the last M bits are uniquely determined by the first $M + 1$ input bits. Therefore, we have

Proposition 4. *Consider a register with length $M + 1$, filtered by a Boolean function f whose distance between the extremity taps is M. In the deterministic model, the augmented function F_{M+1} maps the internal state of size $M + 1$ to the first $M + 1$ output bits.*

In the deterministic model, the balancedness of the original augmented filter function is not relevant, as not all inputs of the function are possible. Therefore, instead of studying the augmented function F_{M+1} itself, it is necessary to study its restriction to its possible inputs. This amounts to study the balancedness of the first $M + 1$ output bits of the nonlinear filter, which is related to well-known distinguishing attacks consisting in studying the distribution of the first output bits, and also to algebraic attacks.

3.4 A Practical Criterion to Avoid Optimal Correlations

As we have seen, in the deterministic model, not only cannot we assume that the leftmost bit is perfectly random, but also the definition of the augmented filter function is no longer sound. Instead of studying the augmented function, it is necessary to take the feedback function into account and to study the output sequence itself.

Therefore, in this section, we refer to the probabilistic model, and we consider a distinguishing attack on a filter generator that attempts to exploit a weakness of the filtering function only to distinguish the output of the filtering function from a random sequence.

The study of the balancedness of Golic's augmented filter function F_{M+1} captures related biases, but the complexity is too high when the length between extreme taps is maximal: in this case, F_{M+1} maps $2r - 1$-bit-vectors to r-bit-vectors, which makes finding a bias as hard as an exhaustive search.

We thus come back to the original idea of Anderson in [1] to derive a criterion that prevents optimal correlations from appearing in the output, by considering only the n output bits that share an equal bit in the input to the filter.

The aim of the attack is to correlate n keystream bits that are output within intervals equal to each difference between two consecutive tap positions having at least one bit in common.

We denote by $x(t)$ the input of the filtering function at time t, i.e. , $x(t) = [s_{t-\gamma_1}, \ldots, s_{t-\gamma_n}]$. At time t, the value of the i-th variable x_i which is $s_{t-\gamma_i}$ is denoted by $x_i(t)$.

Proposition 5. *Consider a nonlinear filter generator with filter f, where f is an n-variable Boolean function. Assume that the input sequence $s = (s_t)_{t=-r}^{\infty}$ is purely random, and that the tapping sequence γ is a full positive difference set. For $1 \leq i \leq n$, let $\delta_i = \gamma_i - \gamma_1$.*

Then, for every $t > 0$, the n-tuple $(z_{t+\delta_i})_{1 \leq i \leq n}$ is unbiased, if and only if,

$$\mathcal{F}(f + \varphi_{e_i}) = \sum_{x \in GF(2)^n} (-1)^{f(x)+x_i} = 0 \tag{3}$$

for at least $n-1$ integers i, $1 \leq i \leq n$.

Proof. First, notice that the bit $s_{t-\gamma_1}$ is at tap x_i at time $t + \delta_i$ for each i, $1 \leq i \leq n$. For $1 \leq i \leq n$, let p_i be the probability defined by

$$p_i = \text{Prob}\left(f(x(t + \delta_i)) = 0 \mid x_i(t + \delta_i) = 1\right).$$

The LFSR sequence being balanced, we have

$$\text{Prob}(f(x(t)) = 0) = \frac{1}{2} = \frac{1}{2}(\text{Prob}(f(x(t)) = 0 \mid x_i(t) = 1)$$
$$+ \text{Prob}(f(x(t)) = 0 \mid x_i(t) = 0)).$$

We deduce

$$\begin{aligned} p_i &= \text{Prob}\left(f(x(t + \delta_i)) = 0 \mid x_i(t + \delta_i) = 1\right) \\ &= \text{Prob}\left(f(x(t + \delta_i)) = 1 \mid x_i(t + \delta_i) = 0\right) \end{aligned}$$

$$\begin{aligned} 1 - p_i &= \text{Prob}\left(f(x(t + \delta_i)) = 0 \mid x_i(t + \delta_i) = 0\right) \\ &= \text{Prob}\left(f(x(t + \delta_i)) = 1 \mid x_i(t + \delta_i) = 1\right). \end{aligned}$$

Thus, the probability that $f(x(t+\delta_i))$ is equal to a given bit b_i given $x_i(t+\delta_i) = s_{t-\gamma_1} = 0$ is equal to $(1-b_i)(1-p_i)+b_i p_i$, and it is equal to $(1-b_i)p_i+b_i(1-p_i)$ given $x_i(t + \delta_i) = s_{t-\gamma_1} = 1$.

As the choice of the taps is a full positive difference set, two n-tuples of bits input to the filter share at most one bit in common, and their other bits are supposed to be independent. Therefore, the n-tuple $(z_t, z_{t+\delta_2}, \ldots, z_{t+\delta_n})$ is equal to a given n-tuple $(b_1, \ldots, b_n)$ of bits with probability $\frac{1}{2}\prod_{i=1}^{n}((1 - b_i)(1 - p_i) + b_i p_i) + \frac{1}{2}\prod_{i=1}^{n}(b_i(1 - p_i) + p_i(1 - b_i))$. In order to have no bias in $(z_t, z_{t+\delta_2}, \ldots, z_{t+\delta_n})$, it is thus necessary and sufficient that the equality $\frac{1}{2}\prod_{i=1}^{n}((1 - b_i)(1 - p_i) + b_i p_i) + \frac{1}{2}\prod_{i=1}^{n}(b_i(1 - p_i) + p_i(1 - b_i)) = \frac{1}{2^n}$ holds for all choices of b_i's. This is equivalent to all the p_i's being equal to $\frac{1}{2}$, apart from at most one p_i. This is true if and only if Equation 3 holds for at least $n-1$ integers i, $1 \leq i \leq n$. $\square$

The attack we considered also generalizes the attack against the stream cipher Decim presented by Wu and Preneel in [19] where a bias in the probability that two output bits with a common input bit were equal was taken advantage of. Therefore, the criterion in Proposition 5 thwarts this attack, as it encompasses all the biases arising from the fact that several outputs of the function can share a common input bit.

Remark 2. Notice that the condition stated in Proposition 5 is close to the correlation-immunity of order 1, as introduced in Proposition 1. Indeed, this new criterion allows for at most one unbalanced 1-variable restriction, instead of none.

Definition 1. *We say that a Boolean function satisfying the property in Proposition 5 is* quasi-immune to correlations of order 1.

Quasi-immunity of order 1 is not only close to correlation-immunity of order 1, but it is also close to the perfect balancedness definition from Golic. Indeed, it is also a criterion on the filter function only, and a function that is not quasi-immune has a bias, as shown in the proof of Proposition 5, so its output for a random input cannot be random. Moreover, functions satisfying the criterion given by Golic in Theorem 1 are quasi-immune of order 1.

   More precisely, quasi-immunity of order 1 is exactly equivalent to the balancedness of the augmented filter function $\bar{h}$ of Anderson in the setting of Proposition 5. Unlike the balancedness of F_{M+1}, the balancedness of $\bar{h}$ is thus easy to check, which makes quasi-immunity a practical criterion to avoid optimal correlation attacks. However, this criterion should be completed to avoid key recovery attack based on a weakness of the filtering function. We will see in the next section that this amounts to bound the bias of the only possible unbalanced 1-variable restriction of a quasi-immune function.

4   Attack Complexity and Quasi-immunity

In this section, we compare different types of attacks targeting filtering functions that are quasi-immune to correlations of order 1, and functions that are not.

4.1   Distinguishing Attack

The scope of this attack is to distinguish the output sequence from a random sequence.

Case of a quasi-immune filtering function. In the probabilistic model, the input sequence is assumed to be random. In this case, if f is perfectly balanced, then the output is also random. Therefore, the output cannot be distinguished from a random sequence.

   However, as we have shown, this is not always the case in the deterministic model. On the contrary, in this model, some quasi-immune functions which are not perfectly balanced, might result in balanced augmented functions with a properly chosen feedback polynomial. Recall that a function f that is quasi-immune to correlations of order 1 has at most one restriction e_i, $1 \le i \le n$, such that $x_1, \ldots, x_n \mapsto f(x_1, \ldots, x_n) \oplus \varphi_{e_i}(x_1, \ldots, x_n) = f(x_1, \ldots, x_n) \oplus x_i$ is unbalanced.

Case of a non quasi-immune filtering function. When a function is not quasi-immune to correlations of order 1, then there exist two unbalanced restrictions e_i and e_j, with two associated probabilities both distinct from $\frac{1}{2}$:

$$p = \text{Prob}\,(f(x(t)) = b_1 \mid x_i(t) = 1) \text{ and}$$

$$q = \text{Prob}\,(f(x(t+\gamma)) = b_2 \mid x_j(t+\gamma) = 1)$$

Without loss of generality (by exchanging b_i and $\bar{b}_i$ if necessary), we assume $p < \frac{1}{2}$ and $q < \frac{1}{2}$. Then, the output bits pair $(z_t, z_{t+\gamma})$ related to the two inputs $x(t)$ and $x(t+\gamma)$ is equal to (b_1, b_2) or $(\bar{b}_1, \bar{b}_2)$ with probability $pq + (1-p)(1-q) > \frac{1}{2}$. Therefore, in order to distinguish between the output and a random sequence, it is sufficient to consider pairs of output bits distant from one another by γ, and to check that pairs (b_1, b_2) and $(\bar{b}_1, \bar{b}_2)$ appear with probability $pq + (1-p)(1-q)$. Thus, if the filtering function f is not quasi-immune to correlations of order 1, then there always exists a distinguisher between random sequences and keystream output by the filter generator (even when considering the probabilistic filter generator model).

4.2   State Recovery Attack

A standard aim of an attack against an LFSR-based cipher is to retrieve the internal content of the register. This attack takes place necessarily in the deterministic model.

Case of a quasi-immune filtering function. In the case of a quasi-immune function f, if there is one unbalanced restriction e_i, it is possible to guess the internal state of the cipher as the output bit is correlated to the bit with unbalanced restriction. For instance, suppose

$$p = \text{Prob}\,(f(x(t)) = b \mid x_i(t) = 1) \neq \tfrac{1}{2},$$

with $p < \frac{1}{2}$ for instance (otherwise exchange b and $\bar{b}$). Then, for each bit in the output, we guess the input bit with probability $1 - p$. The complexity of the related attack is $\left(\frac{1}{1-p}\right)^r$.

Remark 3. Even if f is perfectly balanced, it can have unbalanced restrictions, so perfect balancedness is not sufficient to avoid such correlation attacks. Here, we need to choose f and r such that $(\frac{1}{1-p})^r \geq 2^k$ where k is the security parameter.

Case of a non quasi-immune filtering function. Suppose now that the function is not quasi-immune to correlations of order 1. Then, we have:

Proposition 6. *Let (x_i, x_j) be a pair of variables whose relative restrictions are unbalanced, and let*

$$p = Prob\,(f(x(t)) = b_1 \mid x_i(t) = 1),$$

$$q = Prob\,(f(x(t+\gamma)) = b_2 \mid x_j(t) = 1),$$

with b_1 and b_2 such that $p < \frac{1}{2}$ and $q < \frac{1}{2}$. Then, the nonlinear filter generator with filter f and internal state of length r is vulnerable to a state recovery attack of complexity $\mathcal{O}\left(P(r)\left(1 + \frac{pq}{(1-p)(1-q)}\right)^r\right)$, with P a polynomial corresponding to the resolution of a linear system.

The proof is given in Appendix A.

4.3   Building of a Weaker Equivalent Filter Generator

From the attacker side, the first step to attack a filter generator by focusing on the filtering function is to look for an equivalent filter generator with a weaker filtering function. Indeed, correlation-immunity is not an affine invariant, and neither is quasi-immunity. Indeed, the quasi-immunity of the filtering function of a given filter generator does not guarantee the quasi-immunity of the filtering functions of equivalent generators.

We consider an LFSR of length r with feedback polynomial $C(x) = 1 + c_1 x + c_2 x^2 + \cdots + c_{r-1} x^{r-1} + x^r$. The sequence generated by the LFSR with feedback polynomial C and initial value $[s_{-r}, \ldots, s_{-1}]$ is denoted by $s = (s_t)_{t=-r}^{\infty}$. The filtering function f_0 is an n-variable Boolean function where $0 < n \le r$. Let $\gamma = (\gamma_i)_{i=1}^n$ be an increasing sequence of positive integers such that $\gamma_1 = 1$, and $\gamma_n \le r$.

We denote by $\widetilde{f_0}$ the r-variable Boolean function constructed from f_0 and $\gamma = (\gamma_i)_{i=1}^n$ by adding $r - n$ mute variables. The function $\widetilde{f_0}$ is defined by $\widetilde{f_0}(x_1, \ldots, x_r) = f_0(x_{\gamma_1}, x_{\gamma_2}, \ldots, x_{\gamma_n})$. The keystream sequence $z = (z_t)_{t=0}^{\infty}$ is the output sequence of $\widetilde{f_0}$, i.e. $z_t = \widetilde{f_0}(s_{t-1}, \ldots, s_{t-r})$, $t \ge 0$. We consider in the following the filter generator $\mathcal{FG}_0 = \left(C, \widetilde{f_0}, [s_{-r}, \ldots, s_{-1}]; z = (z_t)_{t=0}^{\infty}\right)$.

For every $i > 0$, it is possible to construct an equivalent generator $\mathcal{FG}_i$ with the same feedback polynomial and output sequence, but with different initial state and filtering function: $\mathcal{FG}_i = \left(C, \widetilde{f_i}, [s_{-r+i}, \ldots, s_{-1+i}]; z = (z_t)_{t=0}^{\infty}\right)$.

We now show how to construct $\widetilde{f_i}$. Given an LFSR state $[x_1, \ldots, x_r]$, the previous state is computed using the transformation

$$A: \quad \{0,1\}^r \quad \rightarrow \quad \{0,1\}^r$$
$$x_1, \ldots, x_r \mapsto (x_r + c_{r-1}x_1 + c_{r-2}x_2 + \cdots + c_1 x_{r-1}, x_1, \ldots, x_{r-1}),$$

For every $i \ge 1$, we have: $\widetilde{f_i}(x_1, \ldots, x_r) = \widetilde{f_{i-1}} \circ A(x_1, \ldots, x_r)$. We deduce that $\widetilde{f_i}(x_1, \ldots, x_r) = \widetilde{f_0} \circ A^i(x_1, \ldots, x_r)$, where $A^i(x_1, \ldots, x_r)$ denotes the iteration of i times the transformation A.

Proposition 7. *Consider a filter generator with a balanced and quasi-immune of order 1 filtering function f_0. All the functions $\widetilde{f_i}$ are quasi-immune of order 1 for every $i \ge 0$ if, and only if, for every $i > 0$, one of the following properties is satisfied:*

1. *the function* $x_1, \ldots, x_r \mapsto \tilde{f}_i \circ A(x_1, \ldots, x_r) \oplus x_r$ *is balanced,*
2. *the restrictions of* $\tilde{f}_i$ *following* x_j, *for all* $2 \le j \le r$, *are all balanced.*

The proof is given in Appendix B.

Remark 4. Balancedness is invariant under linear transformations. Hence, Condition 1 of Proposition 7 is fulfilled if and only if the function $x_1, \ldots, x_r \mapsto (\tilde{f}_i \circ A + \varphi_{e_r}) \circ A^{-1}(x_1, \ldots, x_r)$ is balanced, *i.e.* , if and only if $x_1, \ldots, x_r \mapsto \tilde{f}_i(x_1, \ldots, x_r) \oplus x_1 \oplus c_{r-1}x_2 \oplus \cdots \oplus c_2x_{r-1} \oplus c_1x_r$ is balanced.

As we have seen, the quasi-immunity criterion is not affine-invariant, so it should be satisfied not only by the filtering function of a given filter generator, but also by the filtering functions of equivalent generators. Thus, the filtering function f_0 should be chosen such that $\tilde{f}_i$ is quasi-immune of order 1 for every $i \ge 0$. Note that this requirement is clearly a consequence of taking the linear feedback into consideration, and it is therefore related to the notion of an extended augmented function as mentioned in Section 3.3.

4.4   Summary of Our Results on Attacks Complexity

Recall that if the filtering function of a filter generator is balanced then all the filtering functions $\tilde{f}_i$, $i \ge 0$, of equivalent generators are balanced since the balancedness is an affine invariant. We summarize our complexity attack results by taking into account, given a filter generator, all the filtering functions of equivalent generators.

Proposition 8. *Let f be the filtering function of a filter generator, and let $\tilde{f}_i$, $i \ge 0$, be the filtering functions of the equivalent generators. Assuming that f is balanced, we have:*

1. *if $\tilde{f}_i$ is quasi-immune and has a unique unbalanced restriction x_j, then the filter generator is vulnerable to a state recovery attack that exploits this restriction, with time and space complexity $\mathcal{O}\left(\left(\frac{1}{\max(p,1-p)}\right)^r\right)$, where p is the probability that the value of the restriction of $\tilde{f}_i$ in x_j is equal to 0 (c.f. subsection 4.2);*
2. *if f_i is not quasi-immune, then the filter generator is vulnerable to a straightforward distinguishing attack based on a bias of $pq + (1-p)(1-q) - \frac{1}{2}$, with p and q being the probabilities relative to two distinct unbalanced restrictions of $\tilde{f}_i$ (c.f. subsection 4.1);*
3. *if f_i is not quasi-immune, then the filter generator is vulnerable to a state recovery attack of time and space complexity $\mathcal{O}\left(\left(1 + \frac{pq}{(1-p)(1-q)}\right)^r\right)$ (c.f. subsection 4.2).*

Thus, when designing a filter generator, the filtering function must be chosen quasi-immune of order 1 to avoid distinguishing attacks focusing on the filtering function. Furthermore, the at most unbalanced 1-variable restriction must be chosen such that $\mathcal{O}\left(\left(\frac{1}{\max(p,1-p)}\right)^r\right) \ge 2^k$ where k is the security parameter to avoid key reconstruction attack focusing on the filtering function.

5 Conclusion

In the case of nonlinear filter generators, correlation-based attacks and the criteria to avoid them depend heavily on the considered security model. We have shown that perfect balancedness prevents the optimal correlation attack in the probabilistic model, but that it does not apply to the deterministic model. In the deterministic model, perfect balancedness is equivalent to the absence of bias in the output of the system.

We also extracted a precise criterion on filtering Boolean functions, related to correlation between the output bits as in the optimal correlation attack, based on the fact that input bits at different stages may be correlated in case of nonlinear filter generators. This is a major difference with combiners, and pointing this out clears up the status of correlation-based attacks against nonlinear filter generators. We also provided the complexity of different types of attacks against filtering function that do or do not satisfy this new criterion.

Still, several criteria related to correlation exist, but their relevance is now clear. This should provide a convenient basis for designers. Moreover, we believe that the distinction between two security models is also promising, and new attacks should refer to one model or the other in order to precise their relevance.

References

1. Anderson, R.J.: Searching for the Optimum Correlation Attack. In: Preneel, B. (ed.) Fast Software Encryption. LNCS, vol. 1008, pp. 137–143. Springer, Heidelberg (1995)
2. Biryukov, A., Shamir, A.: Cryptanalytic Time/Memory/Data Tradeoffs for Stream Ciphers. In: Okamoto, T. (ed.) ASIACRYPT 2000. LNCS, vol. 1976, pp. 1–13. Springer, Heidelberg (2000)
3. Canteaut, A., Filiol, E.: On the influence of the filtering function on the performance of fast correlation attacks on filter generators. In: Proceedings of 23rd Symposium on Information Theory in the Benelux, Louvain-la-Neuve, Belgique, pp. 299–306 (2002)
4. Canteaut, A., Trabbia, M.: Improved Fast Correlation Attacks Using Parity-Check Equations of Weight 4 and 5. In: Preneel, B. (ed.) EUROCRYPT 2000. LNCS, vol. 1807, pp. 573–588. Springer, Heidelberg (2000)
5. Chepyzhov, V., Johansson, T., Smeets, B.J.M.: A Simple Algorithm for Fast Correlation Attacks on Stream Ciphers. In: Schneier, B. (ed.) FSE 2000. LNCS, vol. 1978, pp. 181–195. Springer, Heidelberg (2001)
6. Dichtl, M.: On Nonlinear Filter Generators. In: Biham, E. (ed.) FSE 1997. LNCS, vol. 1267, pp. 103–106. Springer, Heidelberg (1997)
7. Ding, C., Xiao, G., Shan, W.: The Stability Theory of Stream Ciphers, vol. 561. Springer, Berlin (1991)
8. Dj.Golic, J.: On the Security of Nonlinear Filter Generators. In: Gollmann, D. (ed.) Proceedings of Fast Software Encryption 1996. LNCS, vol. 1039, pp. 173–188. Springer, Heidelberg (1996)
9. Hong, J., Sarkar, P.: New Applications of Time Memory Data Tradeoffs. In: Roy, B. (ed.) ASIACRYPT 2005. LNCS, vol. 3788, pp. 353–372. Springer, Heidelberg (2005)

10. Logachev, O.A.: On Perfectly Balanced Boolean Functions. Cryptology ePrint Archive, Report 2007/022 (2007), http://eprint.iacr.org/
11. Meier, W., Staffelbach, O.: Fast Correlation Attacks on Certain Stream Ciphers. Journal of Cryptology 1(3), 159–176 (1989)
12. Meier, W., Staffelbach, O.: Nonlinearity Criteria for Cryptographic Functions. In: Quisquater, J.-J., Vandewalle, J. (eds.) EUROCRYPT 1989. LNCS, vol. 434, pp. 549–562. Springer, Heidelberg (1990)
13. Menezes, A.J., Vanstone, S.A., Van Oorschot, P.C.: Handbook of Applied Cryptography. CRC Press, Inc., Boca Raton, FL, USA (1996)
14. Rueppel, R.A.: Analysis and design of stream ciphers. Springer, New York (1986)
15. Siegenthaler, T.: Correlation-immunity of nonlinear combining functions for cryptographic applications. IEEE Transactions on Information Theory 30(5), 776–780 (1984)
16. Siegenthaler, T.: Cryptanalysts Representation of Nonlinearly Filtered ML-Sequences. In: Pichler, F. (ed.) EUROCRYPT 1985. LNCS, vol. 219, pp. 103–110. Springer, Heidelberg (1986)
17. Siegenthaler, T.: Decrypting a Class of Stream Ciphers Using Ciphertext Only. IEEE Trans. Computers 34(1), 81–85 (1985)
18. Sumarokov, S.N.: Zaprety dvoichnyx funkcii i obratimost' dlya odnogo klassa kodiruyushchix ustrojstv (Defects of Boolean functions and invertibility of a class of coding circuits, in Russian). Obozrenie prikladnoj i promyshlennoj matematiki 1(1), 33–55 (1994)
19. Wu, H., Preneel, B.: Cryptanalysis of the Stream Cipher DECIM. In: Robshaw, M. (ed.) FSE 2006. LNCS, vol. 4047, pp. 30–40. Springer, Heidelberg (2006)
20. Xiao, G., Massey, J.L.: A spectral characterization of correlation immune combining functions. IEEE Transactions on Information Theory IT-34(3), 569–571 (1988)

A   Proof of Proposition 6

Proof. Every bit in the input sequence $(s_t)_{t=0}^{\infty}$ is a linear combination of the initial state bits of the register, that is, in the variables $(s_t)_{t=-r}^{-1}$. Therefore, in order to reconstruct the initial state, one can proceed as follows: first, guess $R \geq r$ bits of the input sequence, write the R equations in the r initial state bits, solve the system to find the initial state, and at last check that the guess is correct by comparing the keystream it generates with the actual keystream. In practice, R is chosen to be equal to r, and, if the system solving leads to multiple solutions, there are two solutions: either we add one (or more) equation(s) by guessing some more input bits, or we drop this system and construct another from r new input bits.

In order to guess R bits of the input sequence, we parse the keystream into pairs of bits distant from one another by γ, and guess the value of the corresponding input bit $x_k(t) = x_j(t+\gamma)$. When the pair belongs to $B = \{(b_1, b_2), (\bar{b}_1, \bar{b}_2)\}$, then we guess the input bit - 0 when (b_1, b_2) is observed, 1 for $(\bar{b}_1, \bar{b}_2)$ - with probability $\frac{(1-p)(1-q)}{pq+(1-p)(1-q)}$.

If the pair belongs to $B' = \{(b_1, \bar{b}_2), (\bar{b}_1, b_2)\}$, then we guess it with probability $\frac{\max(p(1-q), q(1-p))}{p+q-2pq}$. However, it is easy to show that $\frac{\max(p(1-q), q(1-p))}{p+q-2pq} < \frac{(1-p)(1-q)}{pq+(1-p)(1-q)}$, so the R bits we guess are those producing pairs of B.

We notice that knowing the output pair $(z_t, z_{t+\gamma})$ does not impact the probability that the pair $(z_{t+\gamma}, z_{t+2\gamma})$ belongs to B or not, as the bit $z(t+\gamma)$ is the first bit of exactly one pair of bits in B and in B'. Therefore, the probability that a pair of bits is or is not in B does not depend on previous output, and it is equal to $pq + (1-p)(1-q)$. This value being greater than $\frac{1}{2}$, finding such pairs of bits is easy.

Let us now assume that we know R pairs of output bits distant from one another by γ, and that all these pairs belong to B. Then, the success probability of reconstruction is

$$\left(\frac{(1-p)(1-q)}{pq + (1-p)(1-q)} \right)^R.$$

In practice, we have $R = r$, and the reconstruction complexity (both in time and space) is thus $\mathcal{O}(P(r)\left(1 + \frac{pq}{(1-p)(1-q)}\right)^r)$, with P the polynomial corresponding to solving the system to retrieve the r bits of the initial state. $\square$

B   Proof of Proposition 7

Proof. For $\widetilde{f_0}$, if the filtering function f_0 fulfils the quasi-immunity criterion, then so does the entire function $\widetilde{f_0}$. Indeed, f_0 is balanced and thus $x_1, \ldots, x_r \mapsto \widetilde{f_0}(x_1, \ldots, x_r) \oplus \varphi_{e_j}(x_1, \ldots, x_r)$ is balanced for every mute variable x_k. Therefore, $\widetilde{f_0}$ is quasi-immune.

Suppose now that $\widetilde{f_i}$ is a r-variable quasi-immune function such that $x_1, \ldots, x_r \mapsto \widetilde{f_i}(x_1, \ldots, x_r) + \varphi_{e_j}(x_1, \ldots, x_r)$ is unbalanced for every j such that $1 \leq j \leq r$, apart for at most one value j_0 of j.

Due to the special form of A, we have:

$$\begin{cases} (\widetilde{f_i} + \varphi_{e_j}) \circ A(x) = \widetilde{f_{i+1}}(x) \oplus x_{j-1} \\ (\widetilde{f_i} + \varphi_{e_1}) \circ A(x) = \widetilde{f_{i+1}}(x) \oplus x_r \oplus c_{r-1}x_1 \oplus c_{r-2}x_2 \oplus \cdots \oplus c_1 x_{r-1} \end{cases}$$

If $j_0 > 1$, then $x_1, \ldots, x_r \mapsto \widetilde{f_{i+1}}(x_1, \ldots, x_r) \oplus x_j$ is balanced for every $1 \leq j \leq r-1$, apart from $j = j_0 - 1$. As $\widetilde{f_{i+1}}$ is quasi-immune if, and only if, it is unbalanced for at most one 1-variable restriction, then it is quasi-immune if, and only if, $x_1, \ldots, x_r \mapsto \widetilde{f_{i+1}}(x_1, \ldots, x_r) \oplus x_r$ is also balanced, which is equivalent to $x_1, \ldots, x_r \mapsto \widetilde{f_i} \circ A(x_1, \ldots, x_r) \oplus x_r$ being balanced.

If $j_0 = 1$, then $x_1, \ldots, x_r \mapsto \widetilde{f_{i+1}}(x_1, \ldots, x_r) \oplus x_j$ is balanced for every $1 \leq j \leq r-1$, so $\widetilde{f_{i+1}}$ is quasi-immune. $\square$

Distinguishing Attack Against TPypy

Yukiyasu Tsunoo[1], Teruo Saito[2], Takeshi Kawabata[2], and Hiroki Nakashima[2]

[1] NEC Corporation
1753 Shimonumabe, Nakahara-Ku, Kawasaki, Kanagawa 211-8666, Japan
tsunoo@BL.jp.nec.com
[2] NEC Software Hokuriku, Ltd.
1 Anyoji, Hakusan, Ishikawa 920-2141, Japan
{t-saito@qh,t-kawabata@pb,h-nakashima@vt}.jp.nec.com

Abstract. TPypy is a tweaked version of the Py stream cipher algorithm submitted to eSTREAM. Py uses a kind of processing referred to as a 'rolling array', the mixing of two types of array and one variable, to generate the keystream. TPypy is proposed as a highly secure stream cipher that fixes all of the previously identified weaknesses of Py.

This paper reports a significant bias in the pseudo-random generation algorithm of TPypy that can be exploited to distinguish the keystream obtained from multiple arbitrary secret key and initial vector pairs from a truly random number sequence using about 2^{199} words.

Keywords: distinguishing attack, ECRYPT, eSTREAM, Py family of stream ciphers, TPypy.

1 Introduction

Many stream ciphers have been proposed over the past 20 years. Most of them are constructed using a linear feedback shift register (LFSR), which is easily implemented in hardware, but the software implementations are mostly slow. In 1987, Rivest designed the RC4 stream cipher, which is suited to software implementation [11]. RC4 has been implemented for many applications, including the Secure Socket Layer (SSL) and Wired Equivalent Privacy (WEP), and is one stream cipher that is widely used around the world.

In the past few years, several modified RC4 algorithms have been proposed. One of them is the Py stream cipher proposed by Biham and Seberry for eSTREAM in 2005 [1,3]. The secret key is up to 32 bytes long and the initial vector (IV) is up to 16 bytes long. Both are selectable in multiples of one byte. An 8-byte keystream is generated at each time. However, from a security standpoint, the designers limited the keystream that can be generated for one secret key and IV pair to 2^{64} bytes. Py employs processing called a 'rolling array' to generate a keystream while mixing two arrays and one variable.

For the analysis of Py, a number of distinguishing attacks that focus on weaknesses in the pseudo-random generation algorithm (PRGA) have been proposed [6,9,10]. None of those methods, however, threaten the security of Py because of

C. Adams, A. Miri, and M. Wiener (Eds.): SAC 2007, LNCS 4876, pp. 396–407, 2007.

the limit on the length of the keystream. Nevertheless, the designers have further proposed Pypy, a model in which security can be guaranteed without a limit on the length of the keystream [4]. Pypy includes the modification that a 4-byte keystream is generated at each time.

Since 2006, however, a number of key recovery attacks that exploit weakness in the IV schedule have been reported [7,13,14,15]. Those methods pose a security problem for Py, Py6, and Pypy. Accepting those reports, Biham and Seberry tweaked the IV schedule and proposed a secure model as TPy, TPy6, and TPypy [5]. On the basis of various analyses [7,9,14], however, the Py family of stream ciphers was not selected as a phase 3 candidate by eSTREAM.

Here, we report a significant bias in the output sequence of the newly proposed TPypy PRGA based on a detailed analysis. Exploiting that bias allows the keystream that can be obtained with mulitple arbitrary secret key and IV pairs to be distinguished from a truly random number sequence with about 2^{199} words. Furthermore, our method succeeds with a greatly smaller amount of data than results that have been reported previously [8,12].

The Py family of stream ciphers is explained in Section 2. Section 3 explains the distinguishing attack on TPypy and Section 4 is the conclusion.

2   Py Family of Stream Ciphers

In this section, we explain the Py family of stream ciphers. For a more detailed description refer to the proposal papers [3,4,5].

2.1   Proposals and Analyses of the Py Family of Stream Ciphers

In this section, we summarize the flow of the Py family of stream cipher proposals as well as analyses of them.

In 2005, Biham and Seberry proposed Py [3] to improve implementability and security. Py has an 8-bit index array P and a 32-bit array Y for mixing data as an internal state. It changes these arrays by a process known as 'rolling array'. An evaluation of the implementability of Py by Biham et alia showed Py to be about 2.5 times as fast as RC4 on a 32-bit processor. Py6 was also proposed at the same time as a model that has fast initialization. For security reasons, however, Biham et alia limited the keystreams that can be generated by one secret key and IV pair to 2^{64} bytes in Py and 2^{40} bytes in Py6.

Nevertheless, in 2006 Paul et alia proposed a distinguishing attack against Py [9]. By their method, Py output can be distinguished from a truly random number sequence using a keystream of about $2^{89.2}$ bytes. In the same year, Crowley increased the efficiency of the method of Paul et alia with respect to amount of data by applying a hidden Markov model [6]. By Crowley's method, Py can be distinguished from a truly random number sequence with a keystream of about 2^{72} bytes. In the same year, Paul et alia also showed that the same method could be applied to Py6 [10]. With the method of Paul et alia, Py6 can be distinguished from a truly random number sequence with a keystream of about $2^{68.61}$ words (64 bits/word).

The security standard of Py and Py6 are that attack is not possible with a keystream of less than 2^{64} bytes for Py and of less than 2^{40} bytes for Py6, so the method of [6,9,10] does not go as far as to threaten the security Py or Py6. Nevertheless, Biham et alia proposed at the FSE 2006 rump session a further modified algorithm as Pypy, to which the method of [6,9,10] cannot be applied, even with keystreams larger than 2^{64} bytes [4]. Although Pypy is basically the same algorithm as Py, only 32 bits of data are output as the keystream, which is half that of Py.

After that, Wu and Preneel proposed a key recovery attack that exploits the weakness in the IV schedule of Py and Pypy that equivalent keystreams can be output from different IV [13,14]. By that method, the Py and Pypy with a 16-byte secret key and a 16-byte IV can be broken by using 2^{24} chosen IV and assuming 72-bit keys. After that, Isobe et alia showed that an improvement in the efficiency of the Wu et alia method allows 16-byte secret key and 16-byte IV Py and Pypy to be broken by using 2^{24} chosen IV and a 48 bit key [7]. In 2007, Wu et alia further improved the efficiency of their attack and reported that 16-byte secret key and 16-byte IV Py and Pypy can be broken by using 2^{23} chosen IV and a 24-bit key [15].

To prevent attacks that exploit the weakness of the IV schedule, Biham et alia improved the IV schedule and proposed TPy, TPy6, and TPypy [5]. TPy, TPy6, and TPypy inherit the respective security standards of Py, Py6, and Pypy, so TPypy can be considered the model that has the highest security of the Py family of stream ciphers.

Recently, Kogiso and Shimoyama proposed a distinguishing attack against Pypy [8]. By their method, Pypy can be distinguished from a truly random number sequence with a keystream of about 2^{220} words. Because Pypy and TPypy have the same PRGA structure, this attack can also be applied to TPypy. Sekar et alia also proposed a distinguishing attack against TPypy and TPy [12] that can distinguish TPypy from a truly random number sequence with a keystream of about 2^{281} words.

2.2 Description of TPypy

TPypy has arrays P and Y, and 32-bit variable s. P is an array of 256 bytes that contains a permutation of all values from 0 to 255, and Y is an array of 260 32-bit words indexed from -3 to 256. TPypy uses a process called a 'rolling array' to mix the data of arrays P and Y and variable s to generate the keystream. The keystream is output 32 bits at a time. The encryption generates a keystream whose length is the number of bytes of the input plaintext, with the ciphertext generated by a taking the bit-wise exclusive-OR of the plaintext.

TPypy consists of roughly three phases: the key schedule, which performs initialization with the secret key; the IV schedule, which performs initialization with the IV; and the keystream generating PRGA. In the analysis we report here, we are concerned only with the structure of the PRGA, so we omit explanation

Input: $Y[-3,...,256]$, $P[0,...,255]$, **a 32-bit variable** s
Output: **32-bit random output**

/* update and rotate P */
1. swap($P[0]$, $P[Y[185]$ & 0xFF]);
2. rotate(P);

/* Update s */
3. s += $Y[P[72]] - Y[P[239]]$;
4. s = ROTL32(s, (($P[116] + 18$) & 31));

/* Update 4 bytes (least significant byte first) */
5. output(($s \oplus Y[-1]$) + $Y[P[208]]$);

/* Update and rotate Y */
6. $Y[-3]$ = (ROTL32(s, 14) $\oplus Y[-3]$) + $Y[P[153]]$;
7. rotate(Y);

Fig. 1. PRGA of TPypy

related to the key schedule and the IV schedule. The TPypy PRGA is shown in Fig. 1. TPypy is a modification of the initialization of Pypy, so it has the same PRGA structure as Pypy.

In Fig. 1, the $\oplus$ symbol refers to a bit-wise exclusive-OR operation. The bit-wise AND operation is denoted as &. Addition and subtraction with modulus 2^{32} are denoted as + and −. ROTL32(X, i) denotes i-bit rotation of word X to the left. The exchange of entry 0 and entry j of array P is denoted as swap($P[0]$, $P[j]$). The notation rotate(P) means a cyclic rotation of the elements of array P by one position.

In this paper, the keystream at time t is defined as O_t. In the same way, the arrays P and Y, and the internal variable s at time t are denoted as P_t, Y_t, s_t. After completion of the IV schedule, it becomes P_0, Y_1, s_0, and the output at time $t = 1$ is as follows.

$$O_1 = (s_1 \oplus Y_1[-1]) + Y_1[P_1[208]]$$

Bit n of word X is defined as $X_{(n)}$. Here, $n = 0$ means the least significant bit.

3   Distinguishing Attack

In this section, we explain a bias that exists in the TPypy output sequence and show that the bias can be exploited to distinguish the output from a truly random number sequence.

3.1 Bias in Output Sequence

In this section, we show that Theorem 1 holds for the TPypy output sequence.

Theorem 1. *When the following conditions hold,*
$O_{1(0)} \oplus O_{3(0)} \oplus O_{6(0)} \oplus O_{7(0)} = 0$ *necessarily holds.*

C1. $P_6[208] = 254$
C2. $P_7[208] = 255$
C3. $P_2[116] \equiv -18 \ (mod \ 32)$
C4. $P_2[72] = P_3[239] + 1$
C5. $P_2[239] = P_3[72] + 1$
C6. $P_4[116] \equiv -18 \ (mod \ 32)$
C7. $P_4[72] = P_5[239] + 1$
C8. $P_4[239] = P_5[72] + 1$
C9. $P_3[116] \equiv P_5[116] \equiv -18 \ (mod \ 32)$ or $P_3[116] \equiv P_5[116] \equiv 0 \ (mod \ 32)$
C10. $P_7[116] \equiv -18 \ (mod \ 32)$
C11. $P_1[208] = 4$
C12. $P_3[208] = 3$
C13. $P_3[153] = P_7[72] + 4$
C14. $P_5[153] = P_7[239] + 2$

Proof. First, from the TPypy output generation equation, we derive the following.

$$O_1 = (s_1 \oplus Y_1[-1]) + Y_1[P_1[208]]$$
$$O_3 = (s_3 \oplus Y_3[-1]) + Y_3[P_3[208]]$$
$$O_6 = (s_6 \oplus Y_6[-1]) + Y_6[P_6[208]]$$
$$O_7 = (s_7 \oplus Y_7[-1]) + Y_7[P_7[208]]$$

Thus, if $Z_{(0)} = O_{1(0)} \oplus O_{3(0)} \oplus O_{6(0)} \oplus O_{7(0)}$, we have

$$
\begin{aligned}
Z_{(0)} = {} & s_{1(0)} \oplus Y_1[-1]_{(0)} \oplus Y_1[P_1[208]]_{(0)} \\
& \oplus s_{3(0)} \oplus Y_3[-1]_{(0)} \oplus Y_3[P_3[208]]_{(0)} \\
& \oplus s_{6(0)} \oplus Y_6[-1]_{(0)} \oplus Y_6[P_6[208]]_{(0)} \\
& \oplus s_{7(0)} \oplus Y_7[-1]_{(0)} \oplus Y_7[P_7[208]]_{(0)}
\end{aligned} \tag{1}
$$

Here, when conditions C1 and C2 hold, the following relations are derived from the values of A' and B' for the state transitions of array Y in Fig. 2.

$$A' = Y_6[P_6[208]] = Y_6[254] = (ROTL32(s_3, 14) \oplus Y_1[-1]) + Y_3[P_3[153]] \tag{2}$$
$$B' = Y_7[P_7[208]] = Y_7[255] = (ROTL32(s_5, 14) \oplus Y_3[-1]) + Y_5[P_5[153]] \tag{3}$$

From the relation of Eq. (2) and Eq. (3), Eq. (1) is as follows.

$$
\begin{aligned}
Z_{(0)} = {} & s_{1(0)} \oplus s_{3(18)} \oplus Y_3[P_3[153]]_{(0)} \oplus Y_1[P_1[208]]_{(0)} \\
& \oplus s_{3(0)} \oplus s_{5(18)} \oplus Y_5[P_5[153]]_{(0)} \oplus Y_3[P_3[208]]_{(0)} \\
& \oplus s_{6(0)} \oplus s_{7(0)} \oplus Y_6[-1]_{(0)} \oplus Y_7[-1]_{(0)}
\end{aligned} \tag{4}
$$

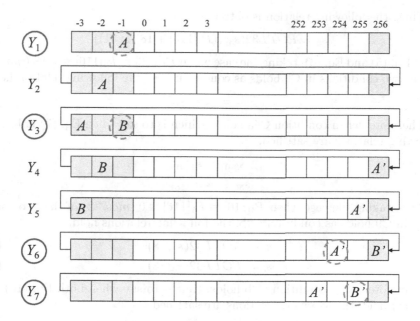

Fig. 2. State transitions of array Y

Next, from the update equation for variable s of TPypy, we derive the following.

$$s_3 = ROTL32(s_2 + Y_3[P_3[72]] - Y_3[P_3[239]], ((P_3[116] + 18) \,\&\, 31))$$
$$s_2 = ROTL32(s_1 + Y_2[P_2[72]] - Y_2[P_2[239]], ((P_2[116] + 18) \,\&\, 31))$$

Thus, when conditions C3 through C5 hold,

$$P_2[116] + 18 \equiv -18 + 18 \equiv 0 \ (mod \ 32)$$
$$Y_2[P_2[72]] = Y_2[P_3[239] + 1] = Y_3[P_3[239]]$$
$$Y_2[P_2[239]] = Y_2[P_3[72] + 1] = Y_3[P_3[72]]$$

also hold, so the following relation is obtained.

$$s_3 = ROTL32(s_1, ((P_3[116] + 18) \,\&\, 31)) \tag{5}$$

In the same way, we derive the following from the update equation of variable s of TPypy.

$$s_5 = ROTL32(s_4 + Y_5[P_5[72]] - Y_5[P_5[239]], ((P_5[116] + 18) \,\&\, 31))$$
$$s_4 = ROTL32(s_3 + Y_4[P_4[72]] - Y_4[P_4[239]], ((P_4[116] + 18) \,\&\, 31))$$

Thus, when conditions C6 to C8 hold, the following also hold.

$$P_4[116] + 18 \equiv -18 + 18 \equiv 0 \ (mod \ 32)$$
$$Y_4[P_4[72]] = Y_4[P_5[239] + 1] = Y_5[P_5[239]]$$
$$Y_4[P_4[239]] = Y_4[P_5[72] + 1] = Y_5[P_5[72]]$$

Thus, the following relation is obtained.

$$s_5 = ROTL32(s_3, ((P_5[116] + 18) \& 31)) \tag{6}$$

In Eq. (5) and Eq. (6), taking the case when $P_3[116] \equiv P_5[116] \equiv -18 \ (mod \ 32)$ of the two conditions in C9 holds as condition C9a, the following relation holds.

$$s_5 = s_3 = s_1 \tag{7}$$

Therefore, when condition C9a holds, which is to say when Eq. (7) holds, the following relations are satisfied.

$$s_{3(0)} = s_{1(0)} \tag{8}$$

$$s_{5(18)} = s_{3(18)} \tag{9}$$

Also, taking the case when $P_3[116] \equiv P_5[116] \equiv 0 \ (mod \ 32)$ of the two conditions in C9 holds as condition C9b, the following relations hold.

$$s_3 = ROTL32(s_1, 18) \tag{10}$$

$$s_5 = ROTL32(s_3, 18) \tag{11}$$

Therefore, when condition C9b holds, that is to say when both Eq. (10) and Eq. (11) hold, the following relations are satisfied.

$$s_{3(18)} = s_{1(0)} \tag{12}$$

$$s_{5(18)} = s_{3(0)} \tag{13}$$

In other words, when condition C9 holds, either both Eq. (8) and Eq. (9) hold, or both Eq. (12) and Eq. (13) hold, so Eq. (4) becomes as follows in either case.

$$Z_{(0)} = Y_3[P_3[153]]_{(0)} \oplus Y_1[P_1[208]]_{(0)} \oplus Y_5[P_5[153]]_{(0)} \oplus Y_3[P_3[208]]_{(0)}$$
$$\oplus s_{6(0)} \oplus s_{7(0)} \oplus Y_6[-1]_{(0)} \oplus Y_7[-1]_{(0)} \tag{14}$$

Also, when condition C10 holds, the following relation is satisfied.

$$s_7 = s_6 + Y_7[P_7[72]] - Y_7[P_7[239]]$$

Thus, Eq. (14) becomes as follows.

$$Z_{(0)} = Y_3[P_3[153]]_{(0)} \oplus Y_1[P_1[208]]_{(0)} \oplus Y_5[P_5[153]]_{(0)} \oplus Y_3[P_3[208]]_{(0)}$$
$$\oplus Y_6[-1]_{(0)} \oplus Y_7[-1]_{(0)} \oplus Y_7[P_7[72]]_{(0)} \oplus Y_7[P_7[239]]_{(0)} \tag{15}$$

Finally, when conditions C11 through C14 hold, the following hold.

$$Y_1[P_1[208]] = Y_1[4] = Y_6[-1]$$
$$Y_3[P_3[208]] = Y_3[3] = Y_7[-1]$$
$$Y_3[P_3[153]] = Y_3[P_7[72] + 4] = Y_7[P_7[72]]$$
$$Y_5[P_5[153]] = Y_3[P_7[239] + 2] = Y_7[P_7[239]]$$

Thus, from Eq. (15), the following relation necessarily holds.

$$Z_{(0)} = O_{1(0)} \oplus O_{3(0)} \oplus O_{6(0)} \oplus O_{7(0)} = 0 \tag{16}$$

This completes the proof.   □

3.2 Probability of Distinguisher Existing and Amount of Data Required

In this section, we consider the probability that Eq. (16), which is used as the distinguisher, holds. If the TPypy output sequence is a truly random number sequence, the probability that the Eq. (16) distinguisher holds is 2^{-1}. The probability that Eq. (16) holds depends on the structure of the TPypy PRGA and does not depend on the key schedule or the IV schedule. Therefore, in the following estimation, we take it that variable s and arrays P and Y are independent and follow a uniform distribution after completion of the IV schedule.

First, we consider conditions C3, C6, C9, C10, which concern the number of rotations for updating variable s. When condition C3 holds, the relation $P_2[116] \equiv -18 \ (mod\ 32)$ holds, which is to say $P_2[116] \in \{14, 46, 78, 110, 142, 174, 206, 238\}$. Therefore, we take the probability that condition C3 holds to be $Pr[C3]$ and get the following.

$$Pr[C3] = \frac{8}{256}$$

In the same way, when the relation $P_3[116] \equiv -18 \ (mod\ 32)$ or $P_3[116] \equiv 0 \ (mod\ 32)$ holds, $P_3[116] \in \{14, 46, 78, 110, 142, 174, 206, 238\}$ or $P_3[116] \in \{0, 32, 64, 96, 128, 160, 192, 224\}$. However, it is clear from the TPypy updating equation for array P that the value of $P_2[116]$ can transition only to $P_3[115]$ or $P_3[255]$ as a result of the restriction imposed by condition C3. Considering this restriction condition, the probability that conditions C3, C6, C9, and C10 hold simultaneously can be estimated in the following way according to Bayes' theorem.

$$\begin{aligned} Pr[C3 \cap C6 \cap C9 \cap C10] &= Pr[C3 \cap C6 \cap C9a \cap C10] \\ &+ Pr[C3 \cap C6 \cap C9b \cap C10] \\ &= \frac{8}{256} \cdot \frac{7}{255} \cdot \frac{6}{254} \cdot \frac{5}{253} \cdot \frac{4}{252} \\ &+ \frac{8}{256} \cdot \frac{8}{255} \cdot \frac{7}{254} \cdot \frac{7}{253} \cdot \frac{6}{252} \end{aligned}$$

Next, consider that an entry of array P has a particular value, and that there is a relationship between the entries of array P. We assumed that these conditions occur independently with probability of approximately 2^{-8}.[1] Also, if for each condition there are multiple patterns for the combinations for which terms cancel in the $Z_{(0)}$ relationship, the number of combinations is also taken into account. Taking conditions C11 and C12 for example, in Eq. (15), $Y_1[P_1[208]]$ and $Y_6[-1]$, and $Y_3[P_3[208]]$ and $Y_7[-1]$ cancel out, but $Y_3[P_3[208]]$ and $Y_6[-1]$, $Y_1[P_1[208]]$ and $Y_7[-1]$ canceling out is another possibility. However, when considering the number of combinations for which the various terms can cancel in the $Z_{(0)}$ relationship equation, the following constraints apply.

---

[1] Actually, the constraint condition of the previous time applies, but it is difficult to accurately evaluate all of the conditions, so in this work we performed an approximate evaluation.

- For the combinations of $Y_6[-1]$ and $(Y_7[-1], Y_7[P_7[72]], Y_7[P_7[239]])$, the terms cannot cancel.
- For variable pairs at the same time t, the terms cannot cancel.

Also, because conditions C4 and C5, and conditions C7 and C8 are subject to the constraint that Eq. (7) must be satisfied in units of the word because Eq. (9) holds when condition C9a holds, their respective combinations are limited to one case. Taking these constraint conditions into consideration, the numbers of combinations that are possible for the various conditions are listed in Table 1. Specific examples of all of the conditions are given in the appendix A.

Table 1. Numbers of combinations of the conditions

Conditions	Combinations
$C1 \cap C2$	1
$C4 \cap C5 \cap C9a$	1
$C4 \cap C5 \cap C9b$	2
$C7 \cap C8 \cap C9a$	1
$C7 \cap C8 \cap C9b$	2
$C11 \cap C12 \cap C13 \cap C14$	24

Therefore, defining event E for which all of the conditions C1 through C14 hold, the probability that event E holds, $Pr[E]$, is as follows.

$$
\begin{aligned}
Pr\,[E] &= Pr\left[\bigcap_{i=1}^{14} Ci\right] \\
&= Pr\left[\bigcap_{i=1}^{2} Ci\right] \times \left\{ \begin{array}{l} Pr\left[\left(\bigcap_{i=3}^{8} Ci\right) \cap C9a \cap C10\right] \\ +Pr\left[\left(\bigcap_{i=3}^{8} Ci\right) \cap C9b \cap C10\right] \end{array} \right\} \times Pr\left[\bigcap_{i=11}^{14} Ci\right] \\
&= 1 \cdot \left(\frac{1}{256}\right)^2 \times \left\{ \begin{array}{l} 1 \cdot \left(\frac{1}{256}\right)^2 \times 1 \cdot \left(\frac{1}{256}\right)^2 \times \frac{8}{256} \cdot \frac{7}{255} \cdot \frac{6}{254} \cdot \frac{5}{253} \cdot \frac{4}{252} \\ +2 \cdot \left(\frac{1}{256}\right)^2 \times 2 \cdot \left(\frac{1}{256}\right)^2 \times \frac{8}{256} \cdot \frac{8}{255} \cdot \frac{7}{254} \cdot \frac{7}{253} \cdot \frac{6}{252} \end{array} \right\} \\
&\quad \times 24 \cdot \left(\frac{1}{256}\right)^4 \\
&\approx 2^{-99.04}
\end{aligned}
$$

Here, when any of the conditions C1 through C14 are not satisfied, assuming that the probability that Eq. (16) holds is ideally 2^{-1}, the probability that Eq. (16) holds for the TPypy output sequence, $Pr[Z_{(0)} = 0]$, is as follows.

$$
Pr\,[Z_{(0)} = 0] = Pr\,[Z_{(0)} = 0 \mid E] \cdot Pr\,[E] + Pr\,[Z_{(0)} = 0 \mid E^c] \cdot Pr\,[E^c]
$$

$$= 1 \cdot 2^{-99.04} + \frac{1}{2} \cdot (1 - 2^{-99.04})$$

$$= \frac{1}{2} \cdot (1 + 2^{-99.04})$$

This is large compared to the 2^{-1} probability for a truly random number sequence.

Here, we regard N samples as independent binary sequences that follow the biased distribution D_{BIAS}. In addition, denoting a uniform distribution as D_{UNI}, the amount of data N required for constructing the optimal distinguisher can be obtained from the following Theorem 2 [2].

Theorem 2. *Taking the input to an optimal distinguisher to be a binary random variable z_i $(0 \leq i \leq N - 1)$ that follows D_{BIAS}, to achieve an advantage greater than 0.5 requires at least the number of samples from the optimal distinguisher derived by the following equation.*

$$N = 0.4624 \times M^2 \quad where$$

$$P_{D_{BIAS}}[z_i = 0] - P_{D_{UNI}}[z_i = 0] = \frac{1}{M}$$

Thus, from Theorem 2, the amount of data N that is required to distinguish the TPypy output sequence from a uniform distribution can theoretically be estimated as $2^{198.96}$. Here, Theorem 1 constructs a distinguisher for $Z_{(0)} = O_{1(0)} \oplus O_{3(0)} \oplus O_{6(0)} \oplus O_{7(0)} = 0$, but it is clear that the same relation holds for any time t $(t \geq 1)$.

$$O_{t(0)} \oplus O_{t+2(0)} \oplus O_{t+5(0)} \oplus O_{t+6(0)} = 0$$

Therefore, when about 2^{199} words of the keystream obtained with multiple arbitrary secret key and IV pairs are collected, it is possible to distinguish the TPypy output sequence from a truly random number sequence. Therefore, the countermeasure of discarding the first few words of the keystream is ineffective against the method described in this paper.

4   Conclusion

We have reported a bias in the output sequence of TPypy, which has the highest security of the Py family of stream ciphers. That bias can be exploited to distinguish the keystream obtained with multiple arbitrary secret key and IV pairs from a truly random number sequence by using about 2^{199} words. This method can also be applied to Pypy in exactly the same way. Furthermore, our method is powerful in that it succeeds with a greatly smaller amount of data that results that have been reported previously.

Acknowledgements. The authors would like to thank the anonymous referees of SAC 2007 whose helpful remarks that improved the paper.

References

1. eSTREAM, the ECRYPT Stream Cipher Project, available at
   http://www.ecrypt.eu.org/stream/
2. Baignères, T., Junod, P., Vaudenay, S.: How Far Can We Go Beyond Linear Crypt-analysis? In: Lee, P.J. (ed.) ASIACRYPT 2004. LNCS, vol. 3329, pp. 432–450. Springer, Heidelberg (2004)
3. Biham, E., Seberry, J.: Py (Roo): A Fast and Secure Stream Cipher Using Rolling Arrays. eSTREAM, the ECRYPT Stream Cipher Project, Report 2005/023 (2005)
4. Biham, E., Seberry, J.: Pypy: Another Version of Py. eSTREAM, the ECRYPT Stream Cipher Project, Report 2006/038 (2006)
5. Biham, E., Seberry, J.: Tweaking the IV Setup of the Py Family of Stream Ciphers – The Ciphers TPy, TPypy, and TPy6. eSTREAM, the ECRYPT Stream Cipher Project, Report 2007/038 (2007)
6. Crowley, P.: Improved Cryptanalysis of Py. In: SASC 2006 - Stream Ciphers Re-visited, Workshop Record, pp. 52–60 (2006)
7. Isobe, T., Ohigashi, T., Kuwakado, H., Morii, M.: How to Break Py and Pypy by a Chosen-IV Attack. In: SASC 2007 - The State of the Art of Stream Ciphers, Workshop Record, pp. 340–352 (2007)
8. Kogiso, M., Shimoyama, T.: A Distinguishing Attack on the Stream Cipher Pypy. In: Symposium on Cryptography and Information Security - SCIS, IEICE Technical Report, 2A2-2 (2007) (in Japanese)
9. Paul, S., Preneel, B., Sekar, G.: Distinguishing Attacks on the Stream Cipher Py. In: Robshaw, M. (ed.) FSE 2006. LNCS, vol. 4047, pp. 405–421. Springer, Heidelberg (2006)
10. Paul, S., Preneel, B.: On the (In)security of Stream Ciphers Based on Arrays and Modular Addition. In: Lai, X., Chen, K. (eds.) ASIACRYPT 2006. LNCS, vol. 4284, pp. 69–83. Springer, Heidelberg (2006)
11. Schneier, B.: Applied Cryptography, 2nd edn. John Wiley & Sons, Chichester (1996)
12. Sekar, G., Paul, S., Preneel, B.: Weaknesses in the Pseudorandom Bit Generation Algorithms of the Stream Ciphers TPypy and TPy. eSTREAM, the ECRYPT Stream Cipher Project, Report 2007/037 (2007)
13. Wu, H., Preneel, B.: Attacking the IV Setup of Py and Pypy. eSTREAM, the ECRYPT Stream Cipher Project, Report 2006/050 (2006)
14. Wu, H., Preneel, B.: Key Recovery Attack on Py and Pypy with Chosen IVs. eSTREAM, the ECRYPT Stream Cipher Project, Report 2006/052 (2006)
15. Wu, H., Preneel, B.: Differential Cryptanalysis of the Stream Ciphers Py, Py6 and Pypy. In: Naor, M. (ed.) EUROCRYPT 2007. LNCS, vol. 4515, pp. 276–290. Springer, Heidelberg (2007)

A   Specific Examples of Conditions

Specific examples of the combinations that are possible for the conditions listed in Table 1 are shown in Table 2, Table 3, and Table 4. For conditions C1 and C2, the single conditions shown by Theorem 1 are omitted.

Table 2. Specific examples of conditions $C4 \cap C5 \cap C9$

C4	C5	C9
$P_2[72] = P_3[239] + 1$	$P_2[239] = P_3[72] + 1$	$P_3[116] \equiv P_5[116] \equiv -18 \ (mod\ 32)$
$P_2[72] = P_3[239] + 1$	$P_2[239] = P_3[72] + 1$	$P_3[116] \equiv P_5[116] \equiv 0 \ (mod\ 32)$
$P_2[72] = P_3[72] + 1$	$P_2[239] = P_3[239] + 1$	$P_3[116] \equiv P_5[116] \equiv 0 \ (mod\ 32)$

Table 3. Specific examples of conditions $C7 \cap C8 \cap C9$

C7	C8	C9
$P_4[72] = P_5[239] + 1$	$P_4[239] = P_5[72] + 1$	$P_3[116] \equiv P_5[116] \equiv -18 \ (mod\ 32)$
$P_4[72] = P_5[239] + 1$	$P_4[239] = P_5[72] + 1$	$P_3[116] \equiv P_5[116] \equiv 0 \ (mod\ 32)$
$P_4[72] = P_5[72] + 1$	$P_4[239] = P_5[239] + 1$	$P_3[116] \equiv P_5[116] \equiv 0 \ (mod\ 32)$

Table 4. Specific examples of conditions $C11 \cap C12 \cap C13 \cap C14$

C11	C12	C13	C14
$P_1[208] = 4$	$P_3[208] = 3$	$P_3[153] = P_7[72] + 4$	$P_5[153] = P_7[239] + 2$
$P_1[208] = 4$	$P_3[208] = 3$	$P_3[153] = P_7[239] + 4$	$P_5[153] = P_7[72] + 2$
$P_1[208] = 4$	$P_3[153] = 3$	$P_3[208] = P_7[72] + 4$	$P_5[153] = P_7[239] + 2$
$P_1[208] = 4$	$P_3[153] = 3$	$P_3[208] = P_7[239] + 4$	$P_5[153] = P_7[72] + 2$
$P_1[208] = 4$	$P_5[153] = 1$	$P_3[208] = P_7[72] + 4$	$P_3[153] = P_7[239] + 4$
$P_1[208] = 4$	$P_5[153] = 1$	$P_3[208] = P_7[239] + 4$	$P_3[153] = P_7[72] + 4$
$P_3[208] = 2$	$P_1[208] = 6$	$P_3[153] = P_7[72] + 4$	$P_5[153] = P_7[239] + 2$
$P_3[208] = 2$	$P_1[208] = 6$	$P_3[153] = P_7[239] + 4$	$P_5[153] = P_7[72] + 2$
$P_3[208] = 2$	$P_3[153] = 3$	$P_1[208] = P_7[72] + 6$	$P_5[153] = P_7[239] + 2$
$P_3[208] = 2$	$P_3[153] = 3$	$P_1[208] = P_7[239] + 6$	$P_5[153] = P_7[72] + 2$
$P_3[208] = 2$	$P_5[153] = 1$	$P_1[208] = P_7[72] + 6$	$P_3[153] = P_7[239] + 4$
$P_3[208] = 2$	$P_5[153] = 1$	$P_1[208] = P_7[239] + 6$	$P_3[153] = P_7[72] + 4$
$P_3[153] = 2$	$P_1[208] = 6$	$P_3[208] = P_7[72] + 4$	$P_5[153] = P_7[239] + 2$
$P_3[153] = 2$	$P_1[208] = 6$	$P_3[208] = P_7[239] + 4$	$P_5[153] = P_7[72] + 2$
$P_3[153] = 2$	$P_3[208] = 3$	$P_1[208] = P_7[72] + 6$	$P_5[153] = P_7[239] + 2$
$P_3[153] = 2$	$P_3[208] = 3$	$P_1[208] = P_7[239] + 6$	$P_5[153] = P_7[72] + 2$
$P_3[153] = 2$	$P_5[153] = 1$	$P_1[208] = P_7[72] + 6$	$P_3[208] = P_7[239] + 4$
$P_3[153] = 2$	$P_5[153] = 1$	$P_1[208] = P_7[239] + 6$	$P_3[208] = P_7[72] + 4$
$P_5[153] = 0$	$P_1[208] = 6$	$P_3[208] = P_7[72] + 4$	$P_3[153] = P_7[239] + 4$
$P_5[153] = 0$	$P_1[208] = 6$	$P_3[208] = P_7[239] + 4$	$P_3[153] = P_7[72] + 4$
$P_5[153] = 0$	$P_3[208] = 3$	$P_1[208] = P_7[72] + 6$	$P_3[153] = P_7[239] + 4$
$P_5[153] = 0$	$P_3[208] = 3$	$P_1[208] = P_7[239] + 6$	$P_3[153] = P_7[72] + 4$
$P_5[153] = 0$	$P_3[153] = 3$	$P_1[208] = P_7[72] + 6$	$P_3[208] = P_7[239] + 4$
$P_5[153] = 0$	$P_3[153] = 3$	$P_1[208] = P_7[239] + 6$	$P_3[208] = P_7[72] + 4$

Author Index

Lecture Notes in Computer Science

Sublibrary 4: Security and Cryptology

Vol. 4298: J.K. Lee, O. Yi, M. Yung (Eds.), Information Security Applications. XIV, 406 pages. 2007.

Vol. 4296: M.S. Rhee, B. Lee (Eds.), Information Security and Cryptology – ICISC 2006. XIII, 358 pages. 2006.

Vol. 4284: X. Lai, K. Chen (Eds.), Advances in Cryptology – ASIACRYPT 2006. XIV, 468 pages. 2006.

Vol. 4283: Y.Q. Shi, B. Jeon (Eds.), Digital Watermarking. XII, 474 pages. 2006.

Vol. 4266: H. Yoshiura, K. Sakurai, K. Rannenberg, Y. Murayama, S.-i. Kawamura (Eds.), Advances in Information and Computer Security. XIII, 438 pages. 2006.

Vol. 4258: G. Danezis, P. Golle (Eds.), Privacy Enhancing Technologies. VIII, 431 pages. 2006.

Vol. 4249: L. Goubin, M. Matsui (Eds.), Cryptographic Hardware and Embedded Systems - CHES 2006. XII, 462 pages. 2006.

Vol. 4237: H. Leitold, E.P. Markatos (Eds.), Communications and Multimedia Security. XII, 253 pages. 2006.

Vol. 4236: L. Breveglieri, I. Koren, D. Naccache, J.-P. Seifert (Eds.), Fault Diagnosis and Tolerance in Cryptography. XIII, 253 pages. 2006.

Vol. 4219: D. Zamboni, C. Krügel (Eds.), Recent Advances in Intrusion Detection. XII, 331 pages. 2006.

Vol. 4189: D. Gollmann, J. Meier, A. Sabelfeld (Eds.), Computer Security – ESORICS 2006. XI, 548 pages. 2006.

Vol. 4176: S.K. Katsikas, J. López, M. Backes, S. Gritzalis, B. Preneel (Eds.), Information Security. XIV, 548 pages. 2006.

Vol. 4117: C. Dwork (Ed.), Advances in Cryptology - CRYPTO 2006. XIII, 621 pages. 2006.

Vol. 4116: R. De Prisco, M. Yung (Eds.), Security and Cryptography for Networks. XI, 366 pages. 2006.

Vol. 4107: G. Di Crescenzo, A. Rubin (Eds.), Financial Cryptography and Data Security. XI, 327 pages. 2006.

Vol. 4083: S. Fischer-Hübner, S. Furnell, C. Lambrinoudakis (Eds.), Trust and Privacy in Digital Business. XIII, 243 pages. 2006.

Vol. 4064: R. Büschkes, P. Laskov (Eds.), Detection of Intrusions and Malware & Vulnerability Assessment. X, 195 pages. 2006.

Vol. 4058: L.M. Batten, R. Safavi-Naini (Eds.), Information Security and Privacy. XII, 446 pages. 2006.

Vol. 4047: M.J.B. Robshaw (Ed.), Fast Software Encryption. XI, 434 pages. 2006.

Vol. 4043: A.S. Atzeni, A. Lioy (Eds.), Public Key Infrastructure. XI, 261 pages. 2006.

Vol. 4004: S. Vaudenay (Ed.), Advances in Cryptology - EUROCRYPT 2006. XIV, 613 pages. 2006.

Vol. 3995: G. Müller (Ed.), Emerging Trends in Information and Communication Security. XX, 524 pages. 2006.

Vol. 3989: J. Zhou, M. Yung, F. Bao (Eds.), Applied Cryptography and Network Security. XIV, 488 pages. 2006.

Vol. 3969: Ø. Ytrehus (Ed.), Coding and Cryptography. XI, 443 pages. 2006.

Vol. 3958: M. Yung, Y. Dodis, A. Kiayias, T.G. Malkin (Eds.), Public Key Cryptography - PKC 2006. XIV, 543 pages. 2006.

Vol. 3957: B. Christianson, B. Crispo, J.A. Malcolm, M. Roe (Eds.), Security Protocols. IX, 325 pages. 2006.

Vol. 3956: G. Barthe, B. Grégoire, M. Huisman, J.-L. Lanet (Eds.), Construction and Analysis of Safe, Secure, and Interoperable Smart Devices. IX, 175 pages. 2006.

Vol. 3935: D.H. Won, S. Kim (Eds.), Information Security and Cryptology - ICISC 2005. XIV, 458 pages. 2006.

Vol. 3934: J.A. Clark, R.F. Paige, F.A.C. Polack, P.J. Brooke (Eds.), Security in Pervasive Computing. X, 243 pages. 2006.

Vol. 3928: J. Domingo-Ferrer, J. Posegga, D. Schreckling (Eds.), Smart Card Research and Advanced Applications. XI, 359 pages. 2006.

Vol. 3919: R. Safavi-Naini, M. Yung (Eds.), Digital Rights Management. XI, 357 pages. 2006.

Vol. 3903: K. Chen, R. Deng, X. Lai, J. Zhou (Eds.), Information Security Practice and Experience. XIV, 392 pages. 2006.

Vol. 3897: B. Preneel, S. Tavares (Eds.), Selected Areas in Cryptography. XI, 371 pages. 2006.

Vol. 3876: S. Halevi, T. Rabin (Eds.), Theory of Cryptography. XI, 617 pages. 2006.

Vol. 3866: T. Dimitrakos, F. Martinelli, P.Y.A. Ryan, S. Schneider (Eds.), Formal Aspects in Security and Trust. X, 259 pages. 2006.

Vol. 3860: D. Pointcheval (Ed.), Topics in Cryptology – CT-RSA 2006. XI, 365 pages. 2006.

Vol. 3858: A. Valdes, D. Zamboni (Eds.), Recent Advances in Intrusion Detection. X, 351 pages. 2006.

Vol. 3856: G. Danezis, D. Martin (Eds.), Privacy Enhancing Technologies. VIII, 273 pages. 2006.

Vol. 3786: J.-S. Song, T. Kwon, M. Yung (Eds.), Information Security Applications. XI, 378 pages. 2006.

Vol. 3108: H. Wang, J. Pieprzyk, V. Varadharajan (Eds.), Information Security and Privacy. XII, 494 pages. 2004.

Vol. 2951: M. Naor (Ed.), Theory of Cryptography. XI, 523 pages. 2004.

Vol. 2742: R.N. Wright (Ed.), Financial Cryptography. VIII, 321 pages. 2003.